DATE DUE

The Christian Socialist Revival
1877-1914

THE CHRISTIAN

SOCIALIST REVIVAL

1877-1914

Religion, Class, and Social Conscience
in Late-Victorian England

PETER d'A. JONES

PRINCETON UNIVERSITY PRESS

PRINCETON, NEW JERSEY

1968

For Edie

Edith Adeline Rutter, 1880-1959
Grandmother, teacher, friend

FOREWORD

I AM VERY GRATEFUL to many libraries and their staffs for help in the writing of this study. The work was principally carried out in the following centers:

London—British Library of Political and Economic Science; The British Museum Reading Room; Dr. Williams' Library; Friends' House Library; Methodist Archives and Research Centre; Sion College (Anglican Library) ; Swedenborg Society Library (and New-Church Archives) ; University of London Library, Senate House.

Provincial Libraries—MUNICIPAL LIBRARIES: Bradford Public Library; Bristol Public Library; Dover Public Library; Leeds Central Reference Library; Leicester City Library; Liverpool Public Library; Manchester Central Reference Library; Sheffield Public Library; Wakefield Central Library.

OTHERS: The Bodleian Library, Oxford; The Community of the Resurrection, Mirfield, Yorkshire; The John Rylands Library, Manchester; Manchester University Arts Library; Nottingham University Library.

American Libraries—Berkeley Public Library, Berkeley, California; Boston Public Library; Lynn Public Library, Lynn, Massachusetts; New York Public Library; Ohio Historical Society, Columbus; Widener Library, Harvard University; The William Allan Neilson Library, Smith College, Northampton, Massachusetts; Wisconsin State Historical Society, Madison.

In particular I would like to thank the staff of the Neilson Library, Smith College, and of the British Library of Political and Economic Science, and of Dr. Williams' Library; Father Arkell, CR; Mr. E. H. Milligan of Friends' House; Rev. J. C. Bowmer of the Methodist Archives; Rev. C. H. Presland and Mr. A. A. Drummond of the Swedenborg Society; Mr. W. S. Haugh of Bristol; Mr. B. Corrall and Rev. R. E. Roberts of Dover; Mr. A. B. Gaver of Leeds; Mr. W.R.M. McClelland of Leicester; Mr. N. Carrick of the Liverpool Record Office; Mr. N. Willox of Wakefield;

vii

Mr. R. S. Smith of Nottingham University; and for other inquiries, Rev. A. M. Allchin of Pusey House and Rev. E. A. Payne, General Secretary of the Baptist Union.

This book is based on a doctoral dissertation of London University (London School of Economics and Political Science), the research for which was first undertaken in 1953-1955 but delayed by many exigencies until its completion in 1963. Originally the thesis was supervised by Mr. H. L. Beales, and the author benefited from his proverbial knowledge, insight, and understanding. In later years Mr. Ralph Miliband and Mr. William Pickles kindly agreed to take over the supervision, and I am especially grateful to them both for constructive criticism and consideration at all times. Dr. Ann Bohm, the secretary of the Graduate School at the London School of Economics, also deserves my thanks, together with her thoughtful staff.

The final leg of the research and writing of the original dissertation was made possible by a grant from the Danforth Foundation, St. Louis, Missouri and by a year's leave of absence from the Smith College History Department in 1963. As a research student in earlier years (1954-1955) the author was sustained in part by a David Holt Scholarship from his city of birth (Hull, Yorkshire) and by a London School of Economics Bursary. To all these my happy thanks are due.

The conversion of the dissertation into a book was made possible by two awards from the American Council of Learned Societies and the Social Science Research Council in 1965. (Naturally, these bodies are not responsible in any way for the opinions or statements expressed in the book.)

I want especially to thank Fenner Brockway, MP, and Mr. Stephen James Thorne for their direct help in this study. Despite the responsibilities of a very heavy parliamentary session in 1963, Lord Brockway was extremely kind and enormously informative in the chats we had about socialist history. Mr. Thorne, last secretary of the Socialist Quaker Society and at present recording clerk to the Society of Friends, also went out of his way in that same year to spare me time for a thoroughly enjoyable conversation at Friends' House, from which I gained insights not available through books and documents alone. In its final form the manuscript was read by my friend and colleague Professor Herman Ausubel of Columbia University, and I am indebted to his good judgment. The faults which remain are my own.

CONTENTS

x i

x i i i

Part One

The Setting

LIST OF SOCIETIES WITH
KEY TO ABBREVIATIONS

ANGLICAN SOCIETIES
Guild of St. Matthew—GSM
Christian Social Union—CSU
Church Socialist League

NONCONFORMISTS
Christian Socialist Society
Christian Socialist League
Christian Social Brotherhood
Christian Socialist Fellowship
Free Church Socialist League
New-Church Socialist Society (Swedenborgian)—NCSS
Socialist Quaker Society—SQS

SECULAR GROUPS
Independent Labour Party—ILP
Trade Union Congress—TUC
Fabian Society
Social Democratic Federation (Marxist)—SDF
Socialist League

CHAPTER I

Introduction: Socialism and Religion

AT THE VERY HEIGHT of the British socialist revival of the 1880's a leading English Marxist, Ernest Belfort Bax, announced with obvious satisfaction that the Christian religion was a total failure. As a moral force, he wrote, Christianity had achieved success only in the case of certain "isolated individuals"; "societies at large" had remained untouched by its message. Socialism, with its true "concern for the social whole," stood in sharp contrast to individualistic and outmoded Christianity. Belfort Bax exemplifies one sort of relationship between religion and socialism. His acid exposé is a reliable guide to some of the standard antireligious arguments of his age. For Bax "the old theological questions," immortality and so on, had had "no more ethical or religious importance than . . . the origin of the irregular Greek verbs." The worship of "a semi-mythical Syrian of the first century"—Jesus Christ—had produced nothing but a "morbid, eternally-revolving-in-upon-itself transcendent morality." Bax castigated the "Oriental" and "subjective" Christian ethic that tried to force upon men "an impossible standard of 'personal holiness' which, when realized, has seldom resulted in anything but (1) an apotheosized priggism (e.g., the Puritan type), or (2) an epileptic hysteria (e.g., the Catholic saint type) ."[1]

Socialism and religion have not always appeared in such antithetical terms. Few of Bax's fellow socialists in fact were as hostile to Christianity, and aggressive secularism waned very rapidly in England after the death in 1893 of the champion of agnosticism, Charles Bradlaugh. Belfort Bax was perhaps the most extreme example of a small group of late-Victorian socialists who did choose to be actively antireligious. On the whole British socialism (and still more the

[1] E. Belfort Bax, *The Religion of Socialism*, 3rd ed. (London, 1891), pp. xi, 96-98.

3

British labor movement) bore a distinct coloration of "religion," however ill-defined and untheological that religion might be—a patina impermeable enough to resist the vitriol of Bax. Not that a great deal of resistance to secularism was called for: the mass of the urban working-class population, alienated as they were from organized religion or "churchianity," were equally unlikely to be attracted to organized antireligion.

The enigma of Christian socialism

Although a noticeable characteristic of the socialist and labor movement was its "religiosity" (the use of Christian rhetoric became especially marked after the formation of the Independent Labour Party in 1893), the relationship between socialism and Christianity in Britain in the eighties and nineties was nevertheless ambiguous. Some of its ambiguity was age-old, historical, and inescapable, inherent in the very nature and function of religion and its enigmatic role as a force in human society. The rest of the uncertainty derived from "local" sources—the alienation of the urban masses, the establishment of a minority church, the injection of social "class" into all aspects of Victorian life, the unsettling background provided by uneven economic expansion, continued population growth and the accompanying structural changes, and so on. This ambiguity is nowhere more apparent than among those groups of men and women who, going beyond mere religiosity and the socialist-trade union ethic, felt able to describe themselves as "Christian Socialists."

Many of these, but not all, were Anglicans and derived part of their inspiration from the earlier Christian socialist movement within the Church of England, led by the pioneers J. M. Ludlow, F. D. Maurice, and Charles Kingsley. Christian socialists of all denominations faced, as Christians, the same major dilemma of an industrialized society: the alienation of the masses from organized religion. All over the nation urban congregations were declining in size. Young men of genuine talent could not be easily tempted into a career in the Christian ministry. The churches lacked a common tongue with the bulk of the working people in the cities, many of whom had been given the right to vote in 1867 and had by 1880 already experienced a decade of state-provided nonsectarian elementary education under the controversial Forster Act. The masses were becoming subject to an emerging popular culture which was itself as much a rival to the churches and chapels in the struggle to capture the attention of the British public as were socialism and the labor movement.

Victorian religion had also failed on another count: its extreme denominationalism. But here the Christian socialists of the 1880's and 1890's were to make very little effort at all. Their activities, even as socialists, were far from ecumenical in spirit.

The host of politically and socially active Christian reformers who worked in organized propaganda groups or simply as individuals in these decades certainly made enough stir to justify use of the phrase "Christian Socialist Revival" to describe the period. Their societies were small in size but numerous. Research reveals the existence of a Swedenborgian Socialist Society in London in the late nineties, a Socialist Quaker Society (begun in 1898), and (Roman) Catholic Socialist Societies in Glasgow and Leeds, although the records of many such groups have been lost. The Clifton and Bristol Christian Socialists and the Leicester Christian Socialist Society, for example, though mentioned frequently enough in the socialist and reform journals of the period, seem to have left little or no physical trace in the archives of their respective cities. However, the variety and extension of the traceable groups is such that one may risk the generalization, on evidence to be reviewed shortly, that no major religious denomination and few large cities were without a Christian socialist organization of some kind at one time during the period of the revival.

Furthermore, although no self-styled "Christian Socialist" society ever gained a very wide membership within any single denomination, as radical nuclei (or "ginger groups"),

5

they did manage to attract to their membership some of the best Christian talent available. This was particularly true of the Anglican reformers, many of whom (if not deliberately passed over by church authorities for their radical activities) became leading dignitaries of the Church. When even the Baptists (who proved to be very conservative politically) produced a socialist, he was also one of their greatest religious leaders—Rev. John Clifford. The liveliest Quakers, such as J. T. Harris, were socialists, as were the most interesting and influential Swedenborgians, the Rev. S.J.C. Goldsack and George Trobridge (the Royal Academician and biographer of Swedenborg).

On the other hand, despite their unusual variety and fascinating qualities as individuals, and despite the moral courage they revealed in opposing the conventional wisdom and morality of their epoch, many Christian socialists were curiously naive in matters of theory. Certainly no startling advances or breakthrough in the evolution of socialist thought came as a result of their work. They did give a fillip to Guild Socialism in the 1900's and revived the old Christian socialist tradition of producers' cooperatives in so doing. If indeed the label "Christian socialist" has had any distinctive connotation at all in the history of modern socialist thought since Buchez, that connotation has been (with some exceptions) *personalist* rather than individualist, *voluntarist* rather than statist, and *associationist* rather than collectivist. The one reform proposal that has recurred is the adoption of producers' cooperatives of one sort or another. Among the late Victorians the idea reappeared embodied in communitarianism and later in pluralism. But many people called themselves Christian socialists who did not share this root-concept in any shape, and at first glance the political ideas they held can be seen to range from the Single Tax to syndicalism.

The High Church and Broad Church Anglicans (designated "sacramental socialists" in this book, for reasons to be explained), the Quakers, and the Swedenborgians came the nearest to developing a coherent body of socialist doctrine fitting their own creeds. Sacramental socialism, Quaker socialism, and Swedenborgian socialism provoked the strongest criticisms from the orthodox religionists of their respective churches on the grounds of theology. Nevertheless, many of their adherents felt, as did Christian socialists in other denominations, that it was impossible to be what they deemed "Christian" without being simultaneously what they deemed "socialist." For such men and women Christian socialism was not conceived as merely one particular reading of the Christian message, but as its only possible ultimate meaning.

The widely accepted "Social Gospel" of the twentieth century has long since abandoned the theological individualism, social complacency, and automatic political conservatism which characterized Victorian religious orthodoxy. Some sections of Christianity in Britain, as in the United States and elsewhere, began to move to the "left" in the decades after about 1880. This shift in social attitude and doctrinal interpretation came about through a variety of pressures, not least of which was the vital necessity for the churches, if they were to survive, to come to terms with the *de facto* emergence and existence of the welfare state, the labor movement, socialism, and changing social and economic conditions. But it is also true that a major *internal* pressure, pushing acceptance of the Social Gospel, was the dissatisfaction felt within the denominations and expressed by courageous and dissident souls like the Christian socialists. Their own religious faith very often was deeply shaken by the discoveries of science, Biblical criticism, and comparative religion, and by key reinterpretive books such as *Lux Mundi* (1889) and *The New Theology* (1907). Their social consciences were aroused by experiences in settlement houses and missions, and by countless government reports and frank "Blue Books," private investigations, such as those of Charles Booth, into the conditions of poverty, and the short but highly effective Congregationalist pamphlet, *The Bitter*

Cry of Outcast London (1883). They became, in consequence, the advance guard of the twentieth-century Social Gospel.

The Christian socialists could not convert their churches *en masse* even to their own brands of "socialism"; but among their ranks certain individuals did make significant contributions to the history of the labor movement, the Independent Labour Party, the Fabian Society, and other bodies. In London and the provinces Christian socialists played important roles in the newly evolving local governments; and by acting as radical pressure groups within the denominations and helping to accelerate acceptance of the Social Gospel, they may even have prevented organized religion from suffering a still greater decline in the twentieth than in the late nineteenth century.

Christians, radicals, and socialists

The intellectual fuzziness which characterized much of Christian socialist writing and expression makes it very difficult to provide a foolproof political terminology to differentiate between the socialists themselves and to analyze their ideas. When Christian socialists spoke or wrote of "socialism" they could mean anything from outright nationalization of all resources by the State, to a mild measure of church disestablishment or municipal control of the milk trade. Generally, in the pages that follow, those Christian socialists who favored economic measures are described as more radical; those who were shy of public control or ownership of the economic machinery are considered less radical in their socialism.[2] This distinction breaks down with the Guild Socialist ideas of the Church Socialist League

[2] The Christian socialists are not alone to be blamed for fuzziness. Fabian socialists deliberately blurred the distinction between "radical" and "socialist" political action in order to present their collectivist brand of socialism as the inevitable historical outgrowth of the British radical tradition. It was favorable to Fabian permeation policy for the public to be unsure of where radicalism ended and collectivism began. See A. M. McBriar, *Fabian Socialism and English Politics, 1884-1918* (London, 1962), pp. 242-243.

after 1906, since Guild Socialists fervently *rejected* state ownership or control from the center (collectivism) in favor of worker control and functional democracy. Yet it is clear that Guild Socialists were more radical than collectivists if by radical action we mean literally an *uprooting* of existing institutions—in the case of guildsmen the abolition of the wage system. The medievalist wing of the guildsmen would have uprooted industrialism altogether, abolished advanced division of labor, ignored technological innovation, and deliberately reverted to a handicraft–peasant-proprietorship–rural economy: a very "radical" proposal indeed, but in the opposite direction to collectivism and to increasing trust in the democratic central state.

In practice only a small number of Christian socialists came to favor either large-scale state socialism and thorough nationalization of the means of production, distribution, and exchange on the one hand, or the producer-controlled guild economy on the other. Most Christian socialists stopped short, on the collectivist track, at municipal "gas-and-water" socialism coupled with various types of welfare and factory-control legislation or consumer action of a respectable variety. One area of public policy—imperialism and war—did arouse deep and widespread radicalism (strong dissent with official British policy, merging into pacifism) among Christian socialists. Most of them bitterly opposed the Boer War at a time when it took great moral fortitude to do so; and this was true not only of the Quaker socialists. In fact, Christian socialists preserved more of a united front against colonial war than did British socialists in general.

The leaven of Frederick Denison Maurice

Why the Christian dissidents of the 1880's and 1890's chose for themselves the title "Christian Socialist" rather than some other description is in itself an instructive question. The answer is at least twofold. First, the socialist revival proper of those decades made the idea of socialism and the vocabulary and rhetoric of socialism more fashionable—and even, with the adhesion of the Fabians, ultimately more respectable. No doubt also, some Christians imagined, rightly or wrongly, that adopting the name "socialist" would help to attract workingmen to the religious fold. Second, some (though by no means all) of the Christian socialists looked back to the example of the midcentury pioneers, Maurice, Ludlow, and Kingsley, men who had deliberately chosen the title "Christian Socialist." They did not look back to, or even seem aware of, the Christian Owenites and the Chartist churches.[3] The Anglicans in particular, members of the Guild of St. Matthew, the Christian Social Union, and the Church Socialist League, all came strongly under the influence of Maurician theology. One leading Anglo-Catholic socialist, Rev. Conrad Noel, called Maurice and Kingsley "the Catholic Fathers of the nineteenth century," and in June 1883 an anonymous London parson declared: ". . . but for the *Christian Socialist* of 1850, the *Christian Socialist* of 1883 would never have seen the light."[4]

When they made open avowal of debt to the men of the 1850's, the later Christian socialists paid greatest respects not to the economic ideas of the founder of the earlier movement, J. M. Ludlow, but to the religious thinking of Maurice. This is not to say that they were not influenced by or did not favor the schemes of producers' cooperatives advanced by Ludlow. But surprisingly few if any references to Ludlow's work by name are to be found in their writings. The cooperative associations of the 1850's and even the support given by the pioneer Christian socialists to the new-model trade union, the Amalgamated Society of Engineers, in 1852 are seldom referred to in their journals. On the other hand, considerable coverage is given to the theological innovations of Maurice, and several leaders of the revival movement had been personally trained by Maurice in their youth, including Stewart Headlam, founder of the Guild of St. Matthew, and B. F. Westcott, later president of the Christian Social Union.

[3] See Harold U. Faulkner, *Chartism and the Churches* (New York, 1916).
[4] *Christian Socialist*, No. 1 (June 1883), p. 8.

What was the "leaven" of F. D. Maurice?[5] The keynote
of his theology was a very English concept of reason (confused no doubt in a very English way with reasonableness),
and a rejection of supernaturalism. He wanted to make
Anglicanism a "rational faith." For this reason he became
the adopted leader of the Broad Church school, which later
was to take as its manifesto one of the two most influential
books of the century in Anglican history, Essays and Reviews
(1860).[6] Broad Churchmen tried to account for the latest
historical criticisms and scientific discoveries in their faith.
They liked Maurice's relaxed, philosophical approach to
theology, his insistence that dogma is comparatively unimportant except pragmatically—insofar as it influences character. Among Nonconformist theological liberals this pragmatism would go still further; Maurice's orthodox enemies
rightly saw in his preference for philosophy and reason the
thin end of the wedge that would ultimately dislodge supernaturalism. By the time of his death (1872) their outlook
was already becoming intellectually unrespectable, and
Maurice's long struggle was beginning to show results. In
each of his battles with Anglican conservatives over such
matters as biblical criticism, the nature of revelation, the
universality of Christ's kingdom, the future treatment of
sinners, and so on a fundamental disagreement was illustrated, deeply separating Maurice from his orthodox opponents: his broader, more generous conception of the realm

5 The word "leaven" is taken from a reminiscent article by Ludlow,
"The Christian Socialist Movement of the Middle of the Century,"
Atlantic Monthly, LXXVII (January 1896), 109-118 (p. 117). Weekly
Bible meetings at Maurice's home were, said Ludlow, "the very heart
of the movement" (p. 112).

6 The second book was Lux Mundi (1889), the inspiration of the
Christian Social Union. Essays and Reviews brought disturbances far
afield—in the Quaker world, for example, where David Duncan, angry
young man of the Manchester Society of Friends, defended the book
in a famous lecture of 1861. (See R. C. Scott, "Authority or Experience: J. W. Rowntree and the Dilemma of 19th Century British
Quakerism," Journal of Friends' Historical Society, Vol. 49, No. 2
[Spring 1960], p. 78.) For comment on the Broad Church school see
Charles Booth, Life and Labour of the People in London, 3rd Ser., Vol.
16: Religious Influence (London, 1902), p. 53.

of the Kingdom of God. Maurice was repelled (as the atheist Ernest Belfort Bax was fifty years later) by Victorian attempts to restrict religion to a narrow moralism, to a mere anxiety for personal moral behavior and personal salvation. In Maurice's view the Kingdom must encompass nothing less than the whole of God's creation, and religion cannot stand aloof; it must therefore concern itself intimately with the fate of all mankind and with the condition of the secular world in which men are forced to live.[7] A distinction must be made between "God's order" and "man's system."[8]

The refusal to admit any moral connection between Christian faith and political and social life went back at least to the eighteenth century, when it had become firmly established among Nonconformists and Anglicans alike. On into the Victorian age Nonconformist individualism penetrated deeply into the evangelical wing of the Established Church so that it became difficult to distinguish between the social ideas of most middle-class Protestant sects and evangelical Anglicanism—soaked as they all were in the morbid fear of personal sin. The search for individual salvation was all the more frantic and urgent because mid-Victorian religion promised everlasting torment for the sinner and a comfortable middle-class heaven for the good. The poor, they all agreed, should perfect themselves spiritually through the divine gift of their poverty, the rich through personal asceticism and the exercise of Christian charity. "The poor ye always have with ye . . ." they reiterated constantly—reduce poverty and you merely reduce the area for the proper exercise of Christian charity, and then how will the rich be saved?[9]

[7] E. R. Wickham, *Church and People in an Industrial City* (London, 1957), pp. 193-194. In Bishop Wickham's excellent phrase, Maurice "earthed" the Gospel.

[8] J. Lewis, K. Polanyi, and D. K. Kitchin (eds.), *Christianity and the Social Revolution* (London, 1935), pp. 188-189.

[9] Among other critics, Charles Booth condemned the "general failure" of evangelicalism, which he attributed to its "blindly self-satisfied piety." Eventually becoming unpopular at home, the evangelicals, he said, had to spend their energies on foreign missions. See C. Booth, *Life and Labour*, 3rd Ser., Vol. 16, p. 52.

Maurice rejected forthrightly these relentless interpretations of the divine message. He found the notion of everlasting torment barbaric (and unreasonable). As Stewart Headlam, the Anglo-Catholic socialist, told his colleagues in the Fabian Society many years later: "You, ladies and gentlemen, probably do not know what it is to have been delivered . . . from the belief that a large proportion of the human race are doomed to endless misery. You are free-born mainly through Maurice's work and courage."[10] The sense of "release" of Stewart Headlam was shared by reformers of a quite different religious temper. John Trevor, ex-Unitarian minister and founder of the barely-Christian Labour Church, wrote: "I was brought up with a vivid sense of the reality of Heaven and Hell—especially of Hell." Trevor's childhood, by no means atypical of the period, was in some ways a nightmare of fear and guilt. "How to escape Hell," he said, "was the absorbing problem of my early years."[11] This problem Maurice attacked head-on in his controversial *Theological Essays* of 1853, redefining the word "eternal" in a nontemporal way. For Maurice "eternal life," for instance, meant life *of a certain quality*, not life unending. "Eternal life" was to know God, to seek the truth, and to practice righteousness.[12] Again this pragmatism went much too far for some of the orthodox, and Maurice was subsequently forced out of his chair at King's College, London.[13]

[10] F. G. Bettany, *Stewart Headlam: A Biography* (London, 1926), p. 20.

[11] John Trevor, *Theology of the Slums* (Manchester, n.d. [1895?]), p. 1; *My Quest For God* (London, 1897), pp. 4-5.

[12] James Dombrowski, *Early Days of Christian Socialism in America* (New York, 1936), pp. 15-16.

[13] He had been made Professor of English and History (1840) and then of Moral Philosophy (1846) at KCL, after graduating from both Cambridge (1826) and Oxford (1834) and working for several years as a Warwickshire curate. Maurice was born in 1805, the son of a Unitarian minister; but he became a strenuous defender of the Established Church and a pamphleteer for university religious tests. Apart from various church posts, he was later Knightsbridge Professor of Moral Philosophy at Cambridge (from 1866). See *The Life of F. D. Maurice, Chiefly Told in His Own Letters*, edited by his son, F. Maurice, 2 vols. (London, 1884); A. M. Ramsey, *F. D. Maurice and the Conflict of Modern Theology* (London, 1951).

The French associationists: Buchez and Lamennais

If the theology of Christian socialism was Maurician and peculiarly English, its economics was French, and derived mainly from certain French socialist theorists of the 1830's and 1840's, Buchez, Blanc, and Lamennais. This influence came directly and personally through J. M. Ludlow, the real founder of the Christian socialist movement of the fifties, who had lived in Paris and had seen for himself French experimentation with cooperative associations.[14] Ludlow was attracted most by the theories of Buchez, while his colleague the novelist Charles Kingsley owed much to Lamennais.

Between the revolutions of 1789 and 1848 France produced some of the most creative minds in the history of socialist thought. In this respect neither Buchez nor Lamennais is normally ranked with Saint-Simon, Fourier, Proudhon, or even with Blanc. Perhaps an antireligious bias among historians accounts to some degree for this. Certainly the judgments of history and the judgments of historians are not always one and the same. Buchez in particular has been underestimated; he owed much to Saint-Simonianism but broke clearly away from that movement and took an independent path, which Louis Blanc later followed.

Buchez,[15] a doctor of medicine who underwent religious conversion and became the real founding father of the French cooperative movement, experimented with various

[14] J. M. Ludlow, 1821-1911. Educated in France, moved to London in 1838, called to the bar in 1843. Largely responsible for promoting the Industrial and Provident Societies Act of 1852. See N. C. Masterman, *J. M. Ludlow: Builder of Christian Socialism* (Cambridge, 1963).

[15] P.-J.-B. Buchez (1796-1865). Prof. Cuvillier provides us with a masterly one-paragraph biography of Buchez: "Cet ancien Carbonaro devenu Saint-Simonien, puis chef d'une école catholique sociale qui eut son heure d'influence, historien de la Révolution française, fondateur des premières associations ouvrières de production, soudain passé, en Février, au tout premier rang, puisqu'il fut le premier président de l'Assemblé Nationale de 1848, mais bientôt dépassé par les événements, suspect lors du coup d'Etat, confiné enfin dans une digne retraite sous le second Empire." See Armand Cuvillier, *P.-J.-B. Buchez et les Origines du Socialisme Chrétien* (Paris, 1948), p. 5.

radical ideas before settling down to develop his theory of producers' cooperatives. For a time he joined the short-lived (1816-1820) French branch of that secret Italian revolutionary movement known as the Carbonari ("charcoal-burners"), which struggled against the tide of postwar political reaction after 1815 and brought about several unsuccessful uprisings in Naples and Piedmont in the early 1820's and in 1831. The Carbonari borrowed the ritual of Freemasonry and leaned heavily on Christian humanitarianism. They were assimilated into Mazzini's republican "Young Italy" movement in the 1830's; but Buchez had already left them long before and had been in and out of Saint-Simonianism. At first a fervent materialist and Saint-Simon disciple, Buchez broke away in 1829 because as a newly converted Catholic he could not stomach the unorthodox religious ideas which had become associated with the cult since Saint-Simon's publication of *The New Christianity* in the last year of his life (1825). It is interesting for a study of the differing Protestant and High Church or Catholic responses to nineteenth-century industrialism and socialism that Buchez himself wavered between Protestantism and Romanism. He finally chose the Catholic faith for its more *social* character and theology.[16]

Saint-Simon was not so much a fully fledged socialist as a herald of industrial society, a hater of residual feudalism and of his own class, the old landed aristocracy. He proposed that the world be ruled by a scientific elite. The Saint-Simonians who followed him never lost this elitist strain. They recognized that competitive capitalism should be replaced by some condition of cooperation or association; but their associationist utopia was to be structured in a clear hierarchy, a base of industrial workers and an apex of entrepreneurs. Very paternalistic about workingmen, Saint-Simon envisioned his "captains of industry" as a "natural aristocracy" without which society could not function.[17] The work-

16 See J.-B. Duroselle, *Les Débuts du Catholicisme Social en France, 1822-1870* (Paris, 1951), p. 82.

17 ". . . les protecteurs nés et les chefs naturels de la classe ouvrière" (Cuvillier, pp. 38-39).

ers were incapable of self-leadership. Buchez began with a Saint-Simonian base but evolved beyond this to the more democratic vision of a society in which, eventually and gradually, the employers would be permanently replaced by workers. True worker-managed productive associations would take over the entrepreneurial function. Unlike Fourier, whose *phalanxes* would unite all classes and allow for cooperation between workers and capitalists, Buchez aimed at eliminating the capitalist elite altogether.[18]

Two characteristics above all distinguish Buchez from the Saint-Simonians: his more advanced class consciousness and his optimistic perception of the future social role of historic Christianity. Both characteristics help to explain his egalitarian outlook and his greater faith in the abilities of the common people. Saint-Simon spoke of two great social classes: the workers (*les travailleurs*) and the idlers (*les oisifs*). The idlers, chiefly landed gentry and civil or ecclesiastical dignitaries, performed no useful social function. The workers, including capital-owners along with factory hands and peasants, produced the nation's wealth. Buchez, however, like Marx a few years later, placed the capitalists squarely in the idler category. His own bipartite division of society was simply between a nonfunctional minority, who owned all the means of production, and a functional majority, who worked for the owners. The capitalists were equally as parasitic as the landed aristocracy, and, furthermore, they exercised tyrannical authority over the workers.[19]

[18] Barbara P. Petri, *The Historical Thought of P.-J.-B. Buchez* (Washington, D.C., 1958), p. 118. In view of Buchez's independent development of these ideas, the judgment of Prof. Duroselle about the *Buchéziens* ("ils ont tout puisé, directement ou indirectement, dans l'oeuvre des grands initiateurs du socialisme, Saint-Simon et Fourier") seems unjust (Duroselle, p. 80).

[19] "Aujourd'hui, la société européenne est, sous le rapport des intérêts matériels, partagée en deux classes. De ces deux classes, l'une est en possession de tous les instruments de travail, terres, usines, maisons, capitaux; l'autre n'a rien: elle travaille pour la première" (*Introduction à la Science de l'Histoire*, 1833); "Ces entrepreneurs sont de purs parasites, dout l'intervention sans utilité est cependant si chèrement payée que rarement ils manquent de faire une fortune

The disagreement between Buchez and Saint-Simon is not unlike the later debate between the American reformer Henry George and the English socialists (Fabians and Marxists) : George saw land ownership as the root of all social evil and wished to destroy it (peacefully, by rent appropriation through a Single Tax on the increment of land values) ; but the socialists of the 1880's could not understand why George stopped short at land rents—why not go on to tax the unearned interest on capital too? Henry George thought that capitalists performed an important and productive economic function; the socialists either denied this function (as Buchez did) or, recognizing the *function* itself, demanded that the State should perform it.[20] Insofar as some British Christian socialists of the 1880's and 1890's followed George rather than the Fabians or Marx, they failed to catch up with Buchez, their spiritual founder.

Buchez's egalitarianism and identification with the worker was strengthened by his historical image of the Christian religion. The world, he believed, had passed through four great stages, the last of which was brought on by Christianity, with its essential principles: equality, fraternity, and charity. The Roman Church had failed so far to apply Christianity to the social order. But application *was* possible, because God had guaranteed social progress by directly endowing each individual with a sense of social morality. In other words, the social optimism of Buchez was founded on his belief in an essentially benevolent God—a God very different from the vengeful, punishing deity of British evangelicalism and orthodox Nonconformity. Where Saint-Simon abandoned Christianity, believing its day was over, and tried to create a new religion, Buchez sought a reconciliation between Catholicism and the onrushing forces of democracy. To achieve this, he hoped for an awakened, socially educated clergy, a trained band of Christian revolutionaries.[21]

grande ou médiocre" (article by Buchez in the journal *L'Européen*, 17 December 1831). Both are quoted in Cuvillier, *loc.cit.*

[20] Peter d'A. Jones, "Henry George and British Socialism, 1879-1931," unpublished thesis (Manchester University, 1953), passim (hereafter cited as Jones, Manchester thesis).

[21] Petri, p. 119.

The radical forces set in motion by the French Revolution would be Christianized—as Maurice and Kingsley wanted to Christianize Chartism.

How was God's benevolent purpose to be fulfilled? Through the medium of *voluntarism,* the voluntary establishment of workers' cooperative associations *apart from* the State. For a decade (1840-1850) Buchez's disciples managed a journal, *L'Atelier,* to extol the virtues of producers' cooperatives and of independent association. Buchez was not a rigid opponent of state action or intervention, however; in fact, he lent his support to the schemes of Louis Blanc. *L'Organisation du Travail* (September 1840), Blanc's rhetorical and popular book, which advocated state ownership of major industries and equal wages and established the famous socialist principle "From each according to his capacities, to each according to his need," borrowed, unasked, as its main reform proposal Buchez's original idea of producers' cooperatives. (Blanc even echoed the title of the *Buchézien* journal in his phrase *ateliers sociaux*).[22] Unfortunately, the attempt to make a reality of Blanc's "national workshops" scheme during the 1848 Revolution collapsed miserably. The Paris *ateliers,* from February 1848, began to offer work on every fourth day for the unemployed, with pay for the whole week. A massive immigration of the jobless to the French capital swamped the administrators. Harsh control measures had to be introduced; the *ateliers* failed, and with the June insurrection Blanc fled to England. Buchez was himself President of the National Assembly at the time (May-June 1848).

Louis Blanc was not an *étatiste* of the Saint-Simonian type; his paternal, welfare-minded democratic central state was not to be all-powerful. Its function was to safeguard liberty, to ensure just distribution (equality of wages), and to own but *not to manage* public industries. The last would be left in the hands of the workers and administered by

[22] Cuvillier, pp. 45-52; Maxime LeRoy (ed.), *Les Précurseurs Français du Socialisme, de Condorcet à Proudhon* (Paris, 1948), p. 326.

self-governing agencies.[23] The plan was not dissimilar to that of some English Guild Socialists in the years around World War I, in which the guilds were chartered or legally created by the State but not directed by it. As we shall see, this kind of guild plan excited Christian socialists in the 1900's (especially the Quakers and some Anglicans) because they were disenchanted with Fabian collectivism and the Labour Party's "truckling" to the Liberals and here was a noncollectivist scheme of worker emancipation which promised to remove the threat of the all-powerful bureaucratic State. For the very same reason, because it seemed to obviate the necessity for authoritarian or bureaucratic centralism, J. M. Ludlow was attracted to Louis Blanc's plan. Moreover, Blanc, though not an overt "Christian" socialist, shared Buchez's faith in a benevolent Deity, ruling the world in the common interest of mankind.

Ludlow imbibed this teaching directly, in Paris. For him, as for Buchez, socialism was not a mere technique of social reorganization but a divine religious ideal, a challenge to the Church and to the individual believer and not to the State alone.[24] F. D. Maurice would surely have been an "optimist" in any case (his was what is today called a "gut reaction") ; but the French teachings of Buchez and Blanc buttressed his faith and smoothed the way for his conversion to socialism by the more radical and economically informed Ludlow.[25] Maurice constantly insisted that the Kingdom of God was *already in existence* on earth; despite its manifold man-made sins, the world was still the direct manifestation of God's order. Though man had deviated from Divine Principles, the world was still God's creation, and was therefore always capable of a return to righteousness.[26]

[23] L. A. Loubere, *Louis Blanc* (Chicago, 1961), pp. 31ff.; Elie Halévy, *Histoire du Socialisme Européen* (Paris, 1948), p. 63. Halévy calls Blanc, inexactly, a State Socialist. See also G.D.H. Cole, *History of Socialist Thought*, Vol. I: *The Forerunners* (London, 1954), pp. 168ff.

[24] Masterman, p. 2.

[25] C. E. Raven, *Christian Socialism, 1848-1854* (London, 1920) , p. 55; Maurice B. Reckitt, *Maurice to Temple* (London, 1947), p. 19; Masterman, passim.

[26] F. Maurice, *Life of F. D. Maurice*, II, 44.

Maurice and Ludlow had more powerful intellects than had their colleague Charles Kingsley.[27] But in some ways Kingsley had wider influence, especially through his popular novels. He was also an effective pamphleteer. He wrote, among other things, the group's most sensational polemic (on the horrors of sweated labor in the clothing trade), *Cheap Clothes and Nasty* (1850). The tone, characteristic of the man and of the English movement, was highly ethical: the capitalist system, he said, was morally destroying both the worker and the employer: "The continual struggle of competition . . . will weaken and undermine more and more the masters, who are already many of them speculating on borrowed capital, while it will depress the workmen to a point at which life will become utterly intolerable. . . ." Heavily reminiscent of Marx's "increasing immiserization" theme, *Cheap Clothes and Nasty* goes on to show that palliatives such as improved public education will only increase the bitterness and self-consciousness of the worker; ". . . the boiler will be strained to bursting pitch. . . . What then? Look at France and see."[28]

Kingsley himself had looked at France, and what he saw was Lamennais. A man very different in temperament and style from Buchez (and totally different from Kingsley), Lamennais (1782-1854) was a born extremist. Never a real Christian socialist, he stood for a very radical brand of egalitarian, papist theocracy, that is, until he broke with the Pope and became an equally extreme anticlerical. A colleague of Chateaubriand and Montalembert, he fought bitterly against Gallicanism and in favor of greater papal authority in France. Fiery in language, intemperate in spirit, and a rigid zealot in everything he undertook, Lamennais began a journal, *L'Avenir*, in October 1830, bearing the masthead "God and Liberty" and dedicated to "liberate"

---

[27] Kingsley (1819-1875), novelist, divine, public-health reformer. Educated at King's College, London and Cambridge; Vicar of Eversley, Hants., from 1844 and Professor of History at Cambridge, 1860-1869. Later Canon of Chester (1869-1873) and of Westminster (1873-1875).

[28] *Works of Charles Kingsley* (London, 1887), Vol. III: *Cheap Clothes and Nasty*, esp. p. lxxxvii.

the French Catholic Church from monarchical authority. Only complete separation of Church and State, he believed, would guarantee true religious liberty in France. Lamennais was at first welcomed by Rome as a useful ultramontane ally. Popes Leo XII (1823-1829) and Pius VIII (1829-1830) encouraged him;[29] but a successor, the archconservative Gregory XVI (1831-1846), refused to support Lamennais in his disputes with the royalist-minded French clergy and issued an encyclical against political liberalism, *Mirari Vos* (1832). The encyclical did not mention Lamennais by name, but *L'Avenir* had advocated a decentralized society made up of workers' cooperatives formed under the wing of a powerful Roman Church and managed by it; an alliance of Church and people against King and aristocracy; universal suffrage, public education, and all the standard liberal freedoms of press, assembly, speech, and so on; and self-government for "oppressed peoples"—the Irish, Poles, Belgians, and Italians.[30] What irritated Gregory was not Lamennais's ultramontane rhetoric so much as what has been called his *plebéianisme exacerbé*.[31] Immediately after *Mirari Vos*, Lamennais seemed prepared to submit to the Pope's authority; but he wavered, finally revolted altogether, and wrote *Les Paroles d'un Croyant* (April 1834), announcing his conversion to liberal humanitarianism *outside* the Faith. Gregory responded instantly with a second encyclical, *Singulari Nos* (June 1834), repudiating Lamennais directly for his "wild license of opinions and speech," and the reformer spent the last twenty years of his life in relative obscurity.[32]

The radicalism of Lamennais was conceived within a theocratic framework. This longing for churchly govern-

[29] J. N. Moody (ed.), *Church and Society: Catholic Social and Political Thought and Movements, 1783-1950* (New York, 1953), pp. 121ff.

[30] E. L. Woodward, *Three Studies in European Conservatism* (London, 1962), pp. 262-264.

[31] LeRoy, p. 269.

[32] Anne Fremantle (ed.), *The Papal Encyclicals in Their Historical Context* (New York, 1956), p. 128; Jean-René Dorré, *Lamennais* (Paris, 1962), pp. 456-459; P. H. Spencer, *Politics and Belief in Nineteenth-Century France* (London, 1954), pp. 46-49.

ment distinguishes his thought fairly sharply from that of most of the British Christian socialists of both the 1850's and 1880's. Not even the ritualists or Anglo-Catholics would have gone so far as to demand a church-dominated social organization, though the medievalist wing of the Guild Socialists came near to Lamennais in this ideal and F. D. Maurice pinned high hopes on the moral leadership of a reformed national church. The pluralist philosopher J. N. Figgis, who was a major inspiration to the Guild Socialists, argued in scholarly fashion for greater church autonomy. But on the whole Anglican Christian socialists of the more churchly sort limited themselves to advocating independent monasteries—like the Community of the Resurrection in Yorkshire. The Nonconformist socialists, of course, were farthest from Lamennais. One Christian Fabian, Stewart Headlam, in his plea for disestablishment of the Church of England (an unusual proposal for a High Churchman) adopted arguments similar to those of Lamennais for separation of Church and State. There were, however, significant differences between the types of state from which Headlam and Lamennais respectively wanted the Church to be separated, differences between the churches concerned, and still greater differences between the two men in the ultimate goals of this separation. Lamennais foresaw the Catholic Church as a real and powerful political force; in Nonconformist England, Headlam wished chiefly to make the Anglican minority church more honest by disestablishing it.

On the other hand, Lamennais shared certain characteristics with the later Christian socialists of Britain. Like them, he had a bark worse than his bite; he used scalding language to expound a social philosophy which, ultimately, was quite gradualist. Like them, he emphasized the twin themes of the Fatherhood of God and its necessary corollary, the brotherhood of man. With J. M. Ludlow, F. D. Maurice, and Charles Kingsley, he found human progress to be assured and guaranteed because God was benevolent and had implanted within man a social morality, which must finally triumph. Through education and association, through mutual improvement and a heightened sense of Christian duty, man could conquer the forces of Satan: political tyranny, economic selfishness, inequality, and poverty. God's plan would then be fully realized on earth in a society based on equality, brotherhood, Christian rights supported by Christian duties, political democracy, and—above all—free association. Since Lamennais objected to all the existing socialist schools of his day (especially that of Louis Blanc) and gave little indication in his own writings of the form his new society would take or how it would be constructed from the old, we are left unenlightened on these matters. Everything will work out, he seemed to say, if only the people achieve solidarity and association.[33]

The Mauricians and the middle-class Establishment

The English Christian socialists of the 1850's through Ludlow and to a lesser extent through Kingsley swallowed whole the French doctrines of association. Though each had side interests (Kingsley's sanitation crusade was one), all were united for a time in their campaign to establish producers' cooperatives. But, unlike Lamennais, they were not by any means political democrats. Even J. M. Ludlow stood by Maurice in opposing the demand for closer links with trade-union and labor organizations when that demand came from E. V. Neale and Thomas Hughes. They did support the engineers' union in 1852, but Maurice in particular felt that the British worker was unfit for political democracy; he still needed years of education and spiritual uplift—a virtual moral revolution, in fact. "So help me God," Maurice exclaimed a year before the great Reform Bill of 1867 gave the urban worker the vote, "I do not mean to follow the will of a majority."[34] Hughes and Neale, in contrast, wanted to accept the worker as he was and side

[33] "Rien ne résiste à l'union du droit et du devoir," he proclaimed in ch. xv of his *Livre du Peuple* ("La Délivrance par l'Association"). "Comment sortirez-vous de cette funeste dépendance?" he asked the workers. "En vous unissant, en vous associant" (LeRoy, pp. 297-298).

[34] H. G. Wood, *F. D. Maurice* (Cambridge, 1950), p. 161 (statement of 1886).

with him in his battles. Maurice's concept of a reformed national church, standing above all classes as an ideal reconciliator and arbiter, made it impossible for him to take part in, or even admit the existence of, the class struggle. He openly favored social leadership by the upper-middle-class elite of which he was a member.

The paternalism of the leading Christian socialists is nowhere better (or worse) exemplified than in their earliest action—a pious criticism of the Chartists for being too narrowly political and for failing to appeal to the higher creative and spiritual faculties of the nation. Immediately after the Chartist debacle of 1848 they prepared placard homilies addressed to the workers, informing them they were not yet ready for self-government. How galling these must have been to the Chartists one can only imagine.[35] A little more of Buchez and a little less of the Establishment in the Christian socialist message to the workers might have considerably widened its appeal.[36]

Maurice, Kingsley, and Ludlow honestly detested the "caste morality" of Victorian England; but their own group self-image (they saw themselves as "mediators . . . between young England of the middle and upper classes and the working-people"[37]), was soaked through with middle-class self-consciousness and irrepressible condescension. Charles Kingsley's famous novel of 1851, *Yeast,* which hides what is essentially an attack on agricultural laborers' housing conditions in the middle of an aristocratic love and friendship story, was courageous enough for its day; but the novel is extremely pious, and the ultimate hope it offers to the worker is that some day soon a new generation of "young

[35] For a sample of the homiletic cadence see the *Appeal to the Chartists* of April 1848: H. U. Faulkner, *Chartism and the Churches,* pp. 133-134 (Appendix VI).

[36] In face of the evidence, it is difficult to accept Prof. Christensen's claim that the Christian socialists effectively broke through the class barrier and won over the workers. See T. Christensen, *Origins and History of Christian Socialism, 1848-1854* (Aarhus, 1962), p. 238.

[37] Maurice, quoted in K. S. Inglis, *Churches and the Working-Classes in Victorian England* (London, 1963), p. 19.

gentlemen" will emerge as "the guides and the guardians of the labouring men."[38] The more radical J. M. Ludlow could denounce the Chartist cry for the primacy of working-class grievances as "the very quintessence of competitive selfishness," and the group generally took a high moral tone with trade unions—even in their weak condition of the 1850's—as "selfish embodiments of class interest."[39] All in all, the Marxist claim that the chief function of Christian socialism was to hush up the class struggle is not entirely without foundation. A British socialist leader of later years not unsympathetic toward Christianity, Ramsay MacDonald, observed of the Mauricians: "They can never be dissociated from a pose of snobbishness and from an antiquated and fanciful view of the superiority and inferiority of classes."[40]

The "Christian Socialism" of the 1850's thus stood for cooperation rather than collectivism or state intervention, for profit-sharing and copartnership rather than for public ownership. The movement expressed a Broad Church theology which emphasized rationality and tolerance, and it introduced to Britain the socialist ideas of the French writers of the 1830's and 1840's, which its members had imbibed in varying degrees. From among these ideas the Christian socialists did not take up the public ownership side of Blanc's work, but were attracted by the producers' cooperative asso-

[38] The preface to the fourth edition (1859) writes with satisfaction of the great improvements in the countryside since the novel was first conceived, the "altered temper of the young gentlemen," the diminution of "swearing" and "foul songs" on the hunting field and in the officers' barracks. This "growing moral earnestness" is due to the Oxford Movement, Kingsley claims, which has sown good seed "in the hearts of young gentlemen and young ladies." He hopes that the virtues of the rural worker will not be destroyed by "the boundless and indiscriminate almsgiving which has become the fashion of the day." This is a far cry from Buchez and Lamennais. See Charles Kingsley, *Yeast*, 4th ed. (London, 1859) pp. vii-xiii: also see Kingsley's *Works*, DeLuxe ed. (Philadelphia, 1899), IV.

[39] *Christian Socialist*, 14 June 1851 and 7 December 1850; quoted in C. K. Gloyn, *The Church in the Social Order* (Forest Grove, Oregon, 1942), p. 135.

[40] J. Ramsay MacDonald, *The Socialist Movement* (London, 1911), p. 79.

ciations originally conceived by Buchez. Like Buchez, Blanc, and Lamennais, the English group rejected the idea of violent revolutionary change and class war. Although quite conservative politically, and middle-class-conscious socially, its members were courageous in positively identifying "socialism" as a "Christian" ideal for the first time in England since the Industrial Revolution. Without the breakthrough of the 1850's the struggles of the 1880's would have been incomparably harder.

Maurician socialists fought a losing battle against the placid indifference of the main body of the Established Church, against public absorption in the Crimean War, and against the unresponsiveness of British workers to their calls. The Church of England remained an upper-class social organization—"the Tory party at prayer," in the words of one wag. Christian socialists in the late-Victorian period were less inhibited about attacking the Establishment itself than the Mauricians were. Men like Stewart Headlam, C. L. Marson, and Thomas Hancock were more alive to the need for eradicating class consciousness, snobbery, and elitism, and for smashing the upper-class Tory image of Anglicanism. The Church Socialist League (founded in 1906), with its taproots in Yorkshire radicalism, came much nearer to economic socialism (in the doctrines of Conrad Noel, for instance) or to Guild Socialism (reviving some of the aims of Buchez) than did the men of midcentury. They demanded immediate economic and social change and were not content to wait for Maurice's spiritual revolution to take place in the breasts of workingmen. In fact, a chief bugbear of the League was the widespread notion, created by the attitudes of the Mauricians, that "Christian" socialism was a milk-and-water affair. As Conrad Noel wrote in 1910, Maurice "would have drawn back from the development of economic socialism as expressed by churchmen today."[41]

However, not all the men of the Christian socialist revival

[41] *Socialism in Church History* (London, 1910), p. 250.

were more radical than Maurice or Ludlow—except perhaps in language. Some were less so. Those who criticized Maurice for his timidity were still happy to take over his title for the movement, "Christian Socialism." It is interesting that Maurice gave careful thought to this title; the reasons he offered for deliberately adopting it (according to a letter to Ludlow, apparently as late as 1852) were: *"Tracts on Christian Socialism* is, it seems to me, the only title which will define our object, and will commit us at once to the conflict we must engage in sooner or later with the unsocial Christians and the unChristian socialists."[42] In other words, Maurice was clearly as keen (perhaps keener) to fight the "unChristian socialists" as he was to reform British capitalist society. He was in constant fear that the cooperative associations were absorbing too much time and energy and diverting his little band away from what he thought to be its main work—the proclamation of the already existing "Divine order." Maurice's theology was thus never fully consonant with the associationist-socialist work of Christian socialism, and he began to focus efforts on adult education instead. J. M. Ludlow's movement was virtually dissolved by Maurice in 1855 (when the Society for Promoting Working-Men's Associations was suspended); but Ludlow lacked the courage and the will to take over the leadership. It was the tragedy of his life that, in the words of his own autobiography: "Mr. Maurice had his way and the comparatively broad stream of Christian socialism was turned into the narrow channel of a Working-Men's College."[43]

Christian socialists reorganize: the late Victorians

The oldest socialist body in Britain in the 1880's was Stewart Headlam's Anglo-Catholic Guild of St. Matthew of 1877.[44] The Guild stood for what is characterized in this

---

[42] F. Maurice, *Life of F. D. Maurice*, II, 34-35.

[43] Christensen, pp. 361-366.

[44] "Anglo-Catholic" implies Anglicans who reject the title "Protestant" and regard the Church of England as the true Catholic Church and Rome as the aberration. Some went over to Rome; but a large number felt too strongly about the *English* church to do so.

study as "sacramental socialism," a phrase which stands for the belief that the best proof and witness of the socialism of Christ is in the Holy Sacraments of the Church—especially Baptism and the Mass (or, as some Anglicans preferred to call it, the Lord's Supper). This sacramental or High Church Anglican socialism is illustrated best by Headlam's Guild and by the later Church Socialist League (1906), its more radical successor. The Christian Social Union (CSU) was "sacramental" but much less "socialist" in outlook, though it had the support of many economic radicals when the Union was begun by Scott Holland, Gore, and Westcott in 1889. The Community of the Resurrection, a religious order founded by Charles Gore in 1892, also contained several brother monks of "advanced" political opinions, among them Father Paul Bull, who gave valuable moral support to various North of England socialist movements from their Community House at Mirfield in Yorkshire, known affectionately as "the Quarry." The Church Socialist League, for instance, a heavily Northern body dominated by Anglo-Catholics, was linked by two of its active members, Father Bull and Father S. Healy, to this Anglican monastery at Mirfield. The GSM, the CSU, and the Church Socialist League were strictly Anglican societies, to which only baptized members of the Church of England could belong.[45] A broader group known as the Christian Socialist Society was established in London in 1886. Even this Society failed to attract enough Anglicans to become a truly interdenominational organization. Despite the membership and journalistic aid of Rev. C. L. Marson, the brilliant High Church writer who edited its organ, *The Christian Socialist,* for three years while concurrently a prominent member of Headlam's GSM, the Christian Socialist Society remained largely Nonconformist, nondoctrinal, and "ethical." Rev. John Clifford's Christian Socialist League, founded in 1894,

[45] The short forms GSM and CSU have been used here because they were used by contemporaries. It is less convenient to use the short form CSL because of the existence of the (Nonconformist) Christian Socialist League; curiously, *Church* Socialist League members do not seem to have used the short form themselves.

which transformed itself into the Christian Social Brotherhood in 1898, was even more clearly Nonconformist and won the support of only one major Anglican—another GSM member, Canon H. C. Shuttleworth.

The ephemeral Free Church Socialist League begun by Rev. Herbert Dunnico at Swansea in 1909 had a built-in denominational bias in its title, as did the New-Church Socialist Society (Swedenborgian), established in 1896, and the more important Socialist Quaker Society of 1898. (The last, however, formed at its demise in 1924 the basis for a wider fellowship, the Society of Socialist Christians.) An American group, the Christian Socialist (or Social) Fellowship, established a British section in 1909, chiefly supported by Congregationalists.

On the two theological wings were the Roman Catholic Church and the unsectarian Labour Church. The Catholics had a large working-class population to deal with, many of them immigrants, concentrated in urban areas. The Faith responded to this challenge to some degree with the formation of the Catholic Social Guild, a kind of Catholic CSU, in the 1900's; there were also one or two more adventurous Catholic Socialist Societies to be found, such as the one in Leeds and the one founded in Glasgow in 1906.[46] From 1891 the Labour Church exerted considerable local influence in the North of England, but since it was not a Christian movement and since it deserves to be studied separately, it is not treated at length (except insofar as Christian socialists were associated with it) in this book.

The Labour Church was a serious attempt to create or synthesize a true working-class religion; thus, its history falls under that of popular religion or of British working-class culture. The doctrines of its founder, John Trevor, were closer to the Ethical Culture movement than to Christianity. "The attempt to bring the thought of Jesus into the

[46] The Roman Church is not covered by this book for a number of reasons, not the least of which is the previous existence of a good study by A. P. McEntee, *The Social Catholic Movement in Great Britain* (New York, 1927).

life of today as a guide and standard is an anachronism," said Trevor, addressing the International Socialist Congress of 1906 in London; ". . . the Labour Church is not a Christian Socialist Church, but is based simply on the conception of the Labour Movement as being itself a religious movement."[47] Trevor wished to found a new religion, not to refurbish an old one.

The history of these formal organizations does not take up the whole story of Christian socialism by any means. For instance, Congregationalism supplied countless individual Christian socialists, perhaps more than any other single sect, but in the list of Christian socialist societies it hardly figures. The Rev. R. J. Campbell's League of Progressive Thought and Social Service of 1908 came the nearest to a socialist society established within Congregationalism. Yet numerous Christian reformers, many of whom would have described themselves as "Christian Socialists" were brought up in the Congregational fold—including Campbell himself, Andrew Mearns, W. C. Preston, J. Bruce Glasier, Will Reason, Percy Alden, and J. Bruce Wallace. For this reason, the final section of this study will evaluate the part played by each of the major Protestant denominations in the Christian socialist revival in late-Victorian Britain.

[47] *Labour Prophet*, v, No. 56, pp. 123-127.

CHAPTER II

The Socialist Revival

The late-Victorian economy: erratic growth and structural change

IT IS NOT POSSIBLE to make easy causal connections between the "Socialist Revival" of the eighties and nineties and the "Great Depression" of the same years. In the first place, what was actually happening to the British economy at that time is by no means certain. Revisionist economic historians have maintained a complex debate for some years on the true nature of the so-called Great Depression.[1] Second, we have as yet no workable, settled theory about the relationship between economic change and social movements. There are many unanswered questions. Is a "socialist revival" more likely to occur during economic depression than during years of growth? Do trade unions grow more powerful in "hard times" when workers are feeling the pinch of unem-

[1] The first basic "revision" was H. L. Beales's article of 1934, "The Great Depression in Industry and Trade," *Economic History Review*, v (October 1934), 65-75. He placed the alleged depression between 1873 and 1896, with crisis years in 1879, 1886, and 1893, and slightly better years in 1882, 1889-1890, and 1899. More recent scholars seem to be returning to Beales's view that the "Great Depression" is an inappropriate title for these years, of which "the outstanding fact was the rapid industrialization of other countries and the continued industrialization of this." For samples of recent revisionist articles, see A. E. Musson, "British Industrial Growth during the 'Great Depression' (1873-96): Some Comments," *Economic History Review*, 2nd Ser., xv, No. 3 (April 1963), pp. 529-533 and "British Industrial Growth, 1873-96: A Balanced View," *Economic History Review*, 2nd Ser., xvii, No. 2 (December 1964), pp. 397-403; D. J. Coppock: "British Industrial Growth during the 'Great Depression' (1873-96): A Pessimist's View," *Economic History Review*, 2nd Ser., xvii, No. 2 (December 1964), pp. 389-396; D. H. Aldcroft, "The Entrepreneur and the British Economy, 1870-1914," *Economic History Review*, 2nd Ser., xvii, No. 1 (August 1964), pp. 113-134; Charles Wilson, "Economy and Society in Late Victorian Britain," *Economic History Review*, 2nd Ser., xviii, No. 1 (August 1965), pp. 183-198; John Saville (ed.), "Studies in the British Economy, 1870-1914," *Yorkshire Bulletin of Economic and Social Research*, Special Number, Vol. 17, No. 1 (May 1965).

ployment, wage cuts, and shutouts; or conversely, do hard times wipe out union treasuries and cut back membership?[2] Is the demand for independent labor representation—for a working-class political party, staffed by workingmen—more likely to arise under conditions of economic expansion or not? Expansion brings rising employment, higher wages, more leisure time, and educational opportunities, the effect of which could be to produce a less deferential working class, tough-minded about political action. Alternatively, improved material comforts could dull the workers' wits and pacify the potential radical leaders among them. *Embourgeoisement* can mean liberation or sedation.

Lack of theoretical tools and uncertainty about economic facts undermine the historian's confidence in the viability of generalizations. But there is no way out, for instance into merely intellectual history. *Some* complex relationship between structural economic change and social thought and movements does exist at any given moment. It is not feasible to ignore the economic setting until our knowledge and theory improve; we must therefore do our best with the material at hand.

The late Victorians themselves believed there was a "Great Depression." Their anxiety about the economy was expressed in the establishment of at least five Royal Commissions (two on agriculture, two on trade and industry, and one on the monetary system), and in countless speeches, meetings, pamphlets, and books. What disturbed them most was falling prices—a worldwide phenomenon, but one which affected Britain differentially, because the momentum of her first wave of industrialization seemed to have passed. The Board of Trade wholesale-price index (1900 = 100) reveals a steady yearly drop from 129 in 1880 to 98.8 in 1887, rising slightly to the low 100's until 1893, and then falling once more to 88.2 by 1896 (the nadir). The index fluctuated thereafter in the 90's and did not reach the 100's again until

[2] For an American hypothesis on trade-union growth cycles, see the article by Irving Bernstein reprinted in W. Galenson and S. M. Lipset, *Labor and Trade Unionism* (London and New York, 1960), pp. 73ff.

1906 (100.8), except for the single index-year of 1900 itself.[3] With the price fall came a squeeze on profits. Falling prices proved favorable to those on fixed or guaranteed incomes, but they exerted downward pressure on profits and changed to some degree the overall structure of income distribution, reducing, for instance, the number of people with incomes of over £5,000. At the other end of the social scale, the *real* income of employed workers rose, partly through falling prices for the staples of life. Over the period of the alleged depression, according to one reliable estimate, real wages (1850 = 100, not allowing for unemployment) rose from an index of 128 in 1873 to 176 in 1896 (the low point of the price decline) and continued moving upward, to a high of 183 (1900).[4]

The statistics of rising real wages and falling commodity prices do not of course present a true picture of British working-class living conditions in the late-Victorian era, because many people were out of work for long stretches of time. The evidence indicates growing (and more erratic) rates of unemployment during the Great Depression, especially among the masses of the unskilled.[5] If we are seeking an economic explanation for the socialist revival, it does seem likely that high and erratic unemployment under conditions of general economic expansion and rising living standards is likely to cause great discontent. Poverty in the midst of progress, particularly the general progress of one's own social class, is likely to hurt deeply.[6]

[3] Other indices more or less support the Board of Trade figures. The year 1896 is also the low point on the Sauerbeck-*Statist* index; 1895 and 1896 on the Rousseau index. See B. R. Mitchell and Phyllis Deane, *Abstract of British Historical Statistics* (Cambridge, 1962), pp. 471-476.

[4] *Ibid.*, pp. 343-344.

[5] For unemployment percentages among members of certain trade unions, see Mitchell and Deane, pp. 64-65. The percentage for all the unions in this table rose from 1.2 percent unemployed (1873) to a high of 11.4 percent (1879), fell to 2.3 percent (1882), and then rose very sharply once more to 10.2 percent (1886). It is significant that the last year, 1886, was one of great labor unrest and socialist activity.

[6] The problem of "felt" poverty in industrial society is considered in an American historical context in *Robert Hunter's "Poverty": So-*

In some significant economic sectors, such as heavy industries and the export trades, unemployment was especially high in certain years (1879, 1885, and 1886, for example). Though absolute output in these sectors (and for the economy as a whole) was of course still increasing, the *rate* of expansion was falling off; there was a *deceleration* of growth, and Britain, the world's workshop of the mid-Victorian era, was now being outpaced by Germany and the United States. A panic-stricken book by E. E. Williams, *Made in Germany,* published in 1896, expressed British anxieties about this falling back. Various explanations were offered, ranging from a loss of competitive nerve among British entrepreneurs to technical illiteracy among the workers. (As early as 1868 a Royal Commission on Scientific Institutions had lamented the absence of technical schools in Britain.) Various solutions were suggested, ranging from deliberate economic and military imperialism (which seemed to some observers to help extend the life of British capitalism up to World War I) to tariff reform. But particular explanations and particular solutions usually failed to grapple with the roots of Britain's problem, which were twofold and lay in historical timing and in ongoing structural change.

Britain had experienced the world's first Industrial Revolution, and the outstanding characteristic of such a breakthrough (apart from its irreversibility) is that it inevitably affects the pattern, timing, and character of all subsequent industrial revolutions elsewhere. It is not only that lessons are learned, but the whole world is now different: the *idea* of industrialization is now realized and made manifest for the first time and forever. No nation, not even the British Empire, which once extended to perhaps one-quarter of the world, could have maintained its primacy indefinitely. By migration and cultural diffusion the revolution spread eastward across the face of Europe and westward over the At-

cial Conscience in the Progressive Era, ed. Peter d'A. Jones (New York, 1965), pp. vi-xxiv (Editor's Introduction).

lantic. Some nations, for a complex of cultural and sociological, geographic, political, and economic reasons, were more receptive to industrialization than others; but few nations escaped its appeal and none the reverberations of its impact. The latest nations to industrialize had the newest equipment, the most economical technology, the most receptive public and private attitudes. Even within national boundaries the latest *areas* to industrialize had the most modern and efficient capital plant (so, for instance, New England's steam-powered cotton mills were to be challenged by the electrically powered mills of the southern states) . Late-Victorian Britain suffered various competitive impediments: capital tied up in obsolescent plant and equipment that had been established in the early and middle nineteenth century; major industries encumbered with heavy fixed charges (royalties, rents, interest rates, relatively expensive freight costs) ; prodigal wastage of fuel resources; and failure to develop human capital. Germany and the United States came later, and while they did not both possess *everything* that Britain lacked, their advantages as newcomers proved to be more than adequate.

Meanwhile the British economy of the eighties and nineties was experiencing internal structural changes that were sure to cause social dislocations. By the 1870's the economy was "mature" in the sense that its basic productive framework was already mapped out. The intensive capital-goods, heavy-industry phase of its history was coming to an end. Railway construction, for example, was of necessity slowing down. The economy could absorb only so many miles of track; as a growth industry, railway construction could no longer maintain itself. Foreign construction demand was also slackening, with considerable impact on the iron and steel industry. Shipbuilding, too, was passing through an "over-production" phase, with difficult adjustments to make. Technology (from sail, to steam, to diesel; from timber, to iron, to steel) had lengthened the life span of vessels, increased their carrying capacity and speed, and created highly competitive conditions both for shipbuilding and for the carrying trade to which British shipyards and shippers did not always adjust very smoothly.

Railways and ships had provided a large part of the demand for the basic industries, coal and iron and steel. The original Industrial Revolution, the breakthrough to an exponential growth curve, had been based on coal, iron, and steam power. By the late-Victorian period what has been called a "second wave" of the revolution was taking place, and Britain was not its main focus. The second wave was based on steel, oil, electric power (and later the internal-combustion engine), rubber and the "new" chemical industries. In steel Britain still produced talented entrepreneurs, though the industry as a whole took too little notice of the native genius of the Gilchrist-Thomas process of 1879 (which would revolutionize the Lorraine ore field now held by Germany) and continued to use native and imported phosphoric iron ores. In the United States uniform and rapidly growing demand facilitated large economies of scale in steel production, while the British industry remained subservient to a multitude of many specialized, small markets.[7] By 1900 Britain was surpassed by both Germany and the United States in steel production, and other competitors were also emerging. Coal output, too, lagged behind the American total, and unlike her geographically more fortunate Atlantic cousin, Britain lacked a native oil supply. Among the newer industries of the "second wave," electrical power and products were developed particularly slowly in Britain.

Painful adjustments in the basic industries and lack of initiative in the new did not mean a diminution of general living standards; but where in the economy was future growth to be generated? The Empire provided outlets for restive capital, and there was a renewal of British investments in the New World—in the mines and the range-cattle

[7] W.H.B. Court, *A Concise Economic History of Britain, from 1750 to Recent Times* (Cambridge, England, 1964), p. 221.

industry of the American West, for example.[8] At home new growth sectors were arising, though their development has been obscured by the statistical investment aggregates of some economic investigators. Growth came from new and miscellaneous industries, particularly in the production of *consumer* goods: soap, bicycles, household goods of all kinds, patent medicines, domestic fuel oil, jams, cheap clothing, and so on. A real revolution took place in the structure and size of the distributive trades, reflected, for example, in an eightfold expansion of the number of multiple stores between 1880 and 1900.[9] Falling commodity prices, especially of raw materials, did not depress but actually stimulated the consumer-goods boom; purchasing power of retail customers rose.[10] The consumer industries suffered less unemployment, they created the fortunes of a new group of entrepreneurs, and they were supported by a new, urban mass market (lacking in Germany, whose economic development had not yet reached that stage), sustained by the

[8] For brief reference see Peter d'A. Jones, *The Consumer Society: A History of American Capitalism* (London and Baltimore, 1965), pp. 169ff. For details see, for example, C. C. Spence, *British Investments and the American Mining Frontier, 1860-1901* (Ithaca, 1958), and R. A. Billington, *Westward Expansion*, 2nd ed. (New York, 1960), pp. 685ff. and Bibliography, p. 844.

[9] See the article by Charles Wilson (*Economic History Review*, 2nd Ser., XVIII, No. 1 [August 1965], pp. 183-198), to which I owe a good deal for this section. The idea of a structural change from capital-goods to consumer-goods growth sectors in US history was adapted in my own *America's Wealth* (New York, 1963); the revised and more explicit paperback version of that book is *The Consumer Society*, cited in note 8 above. Professor Wilson's article helps to remove a difficulty in W. W. Rostow's stage theory when applied to late-Victorian Britain: Rostow's alleged "gap" between Britain's economic "maturity" and the onset of "high-mass consumption" (which Rostow does not recognize until the 1920's). See C. Wilson, p. 186.

[10] "Economically as well as socially, this is the heart of the matter: that the Armstrongs, Whitworths and Brasseys were giving way to (or being joined by) the Levers, the Boots, the Harrods, Whiteleys and Lewises. . . . It was precisely in the years of the 'Great Depression' that the distributive trades were revolutionized. . ." (C. Wilson, pp. 189-190). See also, for greater detail on the "retail revolution," J. B. Jefferys, *Retail Trading in Britain, 1850-1950* (London, 1954).

advertising techniques of the new popular press. The expansion of the consumer industries and service trades, with continued technical improvement in other sectors, in turn produced an enlargement of the middle classes, especially the lower-middle class of "white collar" workers: retail assistants, clerks, accountants, and so on—a growing group portrayed brilliantly in the novels of H. G. Wells toward the end of the period.

What of agriculture, the traditionally depressed heart of the Great Depression? Historical revision has altered our view of this sector too. The notion of a *general* agricultural depression, due mainly to the competition of American wheat, was based on the evidence of price and acreage changes of native wheat. But that crop made up only 22 percent of gross farm output (England only, at current prices), 1867-1876, and had fallen to a mere 7 percent by the period 1894-1903. The idea of the Great Depression, in farming as in the industrial sector, owed much to an ignorance of or failure to take account of *structural* change. All farmers did *not* grow corn. The livestock interest was strong and growing. Gross output of *all* arable crops (including wheat, barley, the lesser cereals, potatoes, hay and straw, fruit and vegetables, etc.) fell from a value of £65 million (England, 1867-1871) to £41 million. In contrast, gross livestock output rose from £64 million to £71 million. The point was that, in addition to enjoying favorable prices, dairy and livestock farmers in the North and West profited by every price fall suffered by cereal producers of the South and East: cheaper grain meant cheaper feed for livestock and cheaper bread for the consuming masses (which in turn, *ceteris paribus,* meant higher consumption of dairy products).[11] In sum, there simply was no monolithic "agricultural depression" any more than there was a monolithic "industrial retardation" in the late-Vic-

[11] For this particular historical revision we are indebted to a seminal article by T. W. Fletcher, "The Great Depression of English Agriculture, 1873-96," *Economic History Review*, 2nd Ser., XIII, No. 3 (April 1961), pp. 417-432 (figures rounded), 423-424.

torian era. It was a time of great technical innovation in many fields, a "second wave" of the Industrial Revolution, and the rise to competitive economic power of new nations with very modern capital plant. The British economy experienced erratic but continued expansion, sufficient to support continued improvements in mass living standards. The expansion, however, was accompanied by complex and painful changes in the economic structure, shifts of emphasis and investment in agriculture and industry alike, and the rise to prominence and to purchasing power of the greatly expanded middle and lower-middle classes, which were to give a different direction and character to the consumer market as well as to British society itself.

Economic change and social class

The socialist revival, it thus appears, did not come at a time of increasing Marxist "immiserization" and widening class polarity between, on the one hand, a capitalist bourgeoisie, diminishing in numbers and growing in power, and, on the other, a subject proletariat pressed ever closer to subsistence and helplessness, their ranks continually increased in number through constant downward pressure on the lower-middle class. On the contrary, the revival came at a time when the middle segment (or at least the lower-middle segment) of society was expanding rapidly, a profit squeeze in some industries seemed to be cutting down the proportion of higher incomes, and the gulf between the classes, which had been almost unbridgeable in the late eighteenth century and early-Victorian period (because there was little or nothing in between) , was narrowing. This did *not* necessarily mean a softening of class hostilities—far from it. One could argue that alienation between the social classes is *fostered* by the expansion of the middle ranks of society. The rural dichotomy between peasant and landlord is so total that any class consciousness on the part of the laborer, directed toward improving his social status, is almost entirely unthinkable. It is no accident that the language of "class" is a post-Industrial Revolution creation.

With the coming of industry, Disraeli's "Young England" movement even hoped to unite worker and landlord against upstart industrialist. Disraeli's hope came to nothing, but was not entirely without foundation; perhaps classes so far apart can exhibit such loyalties. In times of social change and upheaval, when social status is less permanently fixed by birth and custom, when strange new vistas open up and new classes arise, performing new social and economic functions, the whole nourished by an economy undergoing great technical and structural change, one can perhaps logically expect a battle royal between the classes—even a socialist revival.

If this theory is already presuming too much, given the present state of our knowledge of what was happening in the late-Victorian economy, one can fall back on simpler and more obvious explanations for growing class consciousness in the eighties and nineties. The working class was by then more homogeneous and concentrated. The Victorian urban revolution, with its system of class ghettoes, "East Ends" and "West Ends," had wrought its deep effects in British society for some time. The second wave of industrialization, too, more factory-centered than the first, demanded large numbers of semiskilled and unskilled workers rather than skilled artisans. So differentials among workers based on skills tended to decrease. There was a growing conformity: urban living, with improved public transportation (the lack of which had helped to defeat the Chartists in earlier years because they could not coordinate easily), public elementary education (offered on a large scale for the first time in 1870 and free after 1891), and the "new unionism" of the semiskilled and unskilled that emerged in the 1890's. All these developments tended to give the British worker a common background of experiences and training, and to nurture class consciousness.[12] Insofar as the upper-middle class did *not* share this common background (which became a virtual subculture), growing alienation between the classes

[12] H. M. Pelling, *A History of British Trade Unionism* (London, 1963), pp. 85-86.

was a result of the great distance between them, although it was not as great as between preindustrial classes. On the other hand, insofar as the expanding lower segment of the middle class *did* share this common heritage with the workers (for instance, the state school system), the earlier theory is not weakened.

The socialist revival: political and intellectual origins

Between the late 1850's and the early 1880's there was no socialist movement as such in Britain. The decay of Chartism and the winding up of the Christian socialist Society for Promoting Working Men's Associations by Maurice in 1855 left a vacuum, filled only by the cooperative movement (which followed the *consumer*-controlled model of the Rochdale Pioneers rather than the *producers'* associations model of Buchez and Ludlow) and by the relatively mild, job-conscious "new-model" unionism of the skilled artisans. Karl Marx, who had lived in London for over thirty years, died there in perfect obscurity in 1883. These were, of course, the great plateau years of the Pax Britannica, free trade, the world hegemony of British capitalism, and the ascendancy at home of the middle class: a thirty-year stretch of relative social quiescence and steady economic expansion (ironically coincident with the years of Marx's residence), which lay at the very heart of the era we call "Victorian."

The absence of a socialist movement did not mean, however, the absence of social reform, which became more noticeable toward the end of the period. A. V. Dicey's classic study of 1905, *Law and Public Opinion in England during the Nineteenth Century,* dated the end of the "individualist" era and the opening of "collectivism" from 1870, the year, among other things, of the Forster Education Act, the declared aim of which was to cover the country with good elementary schools. A crucial enfranchisement act (1867), giving the vote to urban workers, had preceded this measure. Disraeli's great six-year Tory social-reform ministry was to open in 1874 and produce a mass of legislation: the first major working-class-housing act of the century (1875), factory measures (including the important codification of 1878), a public health act (1878), the Plimsoll Act protecting sailors by introducing a compulsory load-line on the sides of vessels (1876), and labor reforms, including two acts of 1875 legalizing peaceful picketing, abolishing imprisonment for "breach of contract" (e.g., strikes), and making employer and worker equal legal partners to a civil contract. (Significantly, the "Master and Servant Act" was retitled the "Employers and Workmen Act.")

The two major political parties in the years after 1870 both developed more radical wings in response to changing political and economic conditions. Randolph Churchill (1849-1894) provided for the Conservatives a short-lived revival of "Tory Democracy" (the "Fourth Party"), which tried to capture the working-class vote by advocating the extension of Disraeli's social reform policies; but his hasty and ill-judged resignation from the Cabinet in 1886 suddenly terminated his political career. For the Liberals, a great Unitarian manufacturer, Joseph Chamberlain (1836-1914), provided a longer progressive contribution. As a radical (and Republican) Lord Mayor, Chamberlain had already achieved fame by introducing "gas-and-water" socialism to Birmingham in the early 1870's: municipal ownership of public utilities, coupled with aggressive slum clearance, park development, and building of municipal libraries— even a municipal bank. Elected to Parliament in 1876, he began to build up constituency organization through the "National Liberal Federation," which was really designed to win the local Radical and Liberal clubs over to the Chamberlain view of where the party was going, in opposition to the old Whig stalwarts. Chamberlain's Federation helped to win the election of 1880 for the Liberal Party and took him into the Cabinet, where (with Sir Charles Dilke) he pushed for the parliamentary reform and redistribution acts of 1884 and 1885. These extended the vote to the rural laborer and reapportioned seats to give fairer weight to industrial cities and mining districts. The election of 1885 was again won by the Liberals with Chamberlain's help. This time it was his radical *Unauthorized Programme,* written with Dilke, that did the trick. It offered radical reform at home, to attract the now extended electorate, and imperialism abroad.

The *Unauthorized Programme* of 1885 represents a marked shift to the left by one of the two major political parties of late-Victorian Britain. Chamberlain's scheme contained many "socialistic" ideas and rhetoric. The rich were to be "ransomed" by high taxation; the masses were to have free education, better social services, and decent housing; farmers would receive the protection of fair-rent tribunals, security of tenure, and proper compensation for unexhausted improvements; farm laborers would be offered the chance of a small holding; compulsory land-purchase powers would be instituted to meet public needs; the Anglican Church would be disestablished; MP's would be paid; and plural voting would be eliminated.

Chamberlain had stolen some of the thunder of socialism at the very moment of its rebirth. Though no socialist himself, he was quick to demand that socialism should not be regarded as a "stigma" but as a "modern tendency pressing for recognition." Just as the Fabians were soon to do, Chamberlain claimed that "the path of legislative progress in England has been for years, and must continue to be, distinctly socialistic."[13] It was a clever maneuver to claim socialist ideals for liberal radicalism, as the Fabians maneuvered later to claim radicalism (indeed, the whole of previous Victorian legislative history) for their brand of collectivist socialism.

While the Liberal Party was being weaned from *laissez-faire* individualism to some degree of state interventionism, liberal intellectual orthodoxy—the conventional wisdom of

[13] G.D.H. Cole, *History of Socialist Thought,* Vol. II: *Marxism and Anarchism, 1850-1890* (London, 1957), 388-389.

the day derived from the Smith-Bentham-Ricardo-John Stuart Mill school—was coming under strong pressure not only from outside forces (such as German idealism, French positivism), but from internal disquiet and ferment. Mill himself, as is well known, died a socialist of sorts, having found the liberal panacea of political democracy inadequate to the needs of the day. The very extension of political democracy, he discovered, itself dictated the subsequent extension of economic and social privileges.[14]

Intellectual inroads on liberal orthodoxy came from many directions at once. Three inroads—in philosophy, law, and economics—might adequately illustrate the many-sided nature of the problem. In philosophy, the English (chiefly Oxford) idealist school of F. H. Bradley and Bernard Bosanquet, led primarily by T. H. Green, drew deep drafts of Hegel, passed beyond the old liberal dichotomy between the individual and the State, and developed a deeper understanding of man-in-the-social-system. Community life alone gives significance to the individual, creates the means for his moral and personal development, invests him with liberties, rights, and duties. The future of the individual therefore lies in the betterment of the community. Thus T. H. Green and his colleagues paved the way in philosophy for collectivism and in politics for broadening of state power. Green we shall soon consider at greater length because he was such a direct and personal influence on so many Christian socialists of the eighties and nineties; an excellent (if intellectually lesser) exemplar of the British Hegelian school was the lawyer and philosopher R. B. Haldane (1856-1928), a prominent "Limp" (Liberal Imperialist), deep personal friend of the Webbs, and reformer of education and the army, who gradually deserted the Liberal camp for Labour and became Lord Chancellor in England's first Labour government in 1924.

The liberal conventional wisdom was opposed by Hegel-

14 John Stuart Mill, *Autobiography*, Dolphin ed. (New York, n.d. [1960?]), pp. 174-175; and *Socialism*, ed. Helen Taylor (Chicago, 1879; reprinted from the *Fortnightly Review*), passim.

ian idealism in philosophy; in law it was opposed by many influences, including Comte and Gierke. The positivism of August Comte[15] was "popularized" (if that is the correct word for what always remained a small cult in Britain) by two men in particular, Professor Edward Beesly and Frederic Harrison. Positivism—the rejection of metaphysics and the reliance on the offerings of the "positive" empirical sciences only—has some obvious, if not necessary, affinities with socialism, at least with socialism of the secular kind, and Beesly was very sympathetic to English working-class movements.[16] Applied to historical jurisprudence, as it was (along with social Darwinism) in *Ancient Law* (1861) by Sir Henry Maine (1822-1888), positivism encouraged a less deductive approach, the rejection of "natural law" and "natural rights," and a more "positive" historical study of the facts of each stage of legal evolution, giving weight to relativity and to the pressures of environment on legal systems. Maine's "Historical Method" was essentially comparative: to analyze societies in terms of their legal structures and to compare societies at the same stage of evolution. With Maine this method produced a conservative political outlook, and his *Popular Government* (1885) was an attack on democratic progress; but his scientific method could also be turned to other uses. For example, F. W. Maitland (1850-1906), excited by the speculations of the great German jurist Gierke, adopted the concept of the "real personality" and spontaneous origin of the *group*.[17] Supporting his claims by historical and comparative studies, he maintained that groups—churches and trade unions, for instance—have inherent rights, which they do not owe to the State. Out of Maitland's work came the more developed pluralist theories of the Anglo-Catholic monk J. N. Figgis, whose impact on Christian socialist thought in the 1900's was crucial, leading many into Guild Socialism after 1906.

---

[15] Like Buchez, Comte (1798-1857) was an ex-Saint-Simonian.

[16] For E. S. Beesly (1831-1915), history professor at University College, London, see G.D.H. Cole, *History of Socialist Thought*, II, 385ff.

[17] A useful guide is R. L. Schuyler (ed.), *Frederic William Maitland: Historian* (Berkeley and Los Angeles, 1960).

Theories of a "collective," "community," or "group" nature had thus deeply permeated English philosophy and jurisprudence by the 1880's. In economics the old simplistic and abused concept of "individualism" received even harder knocks. As the economic and social conditions that had supported *laissez-faire* orthodoxy crumbled away, Liberal political economy, its position long invalidated by the external realities of cyclical and structural change, popular distress, and the rise of "felt" poverty, also came under strong pressure from within. If "the failure of Liberal governance, the exhaustion and impotence of Liberal thought"[18] were not enough, from the late 1870's onward, and markedly in the 1890's, the new "marginal utility" analysis began to displace the naive abstract deductions of classical theory, and brought into question the very core of accepted economic dogma. Fighting a classical overinsistence on costs and supply, the marginalists developed a subjective theory of economic value, built around the demand factor. This quite naturally led to a new intellectual interest in the theoretical problem of distribution, which, not by accident, was a major problem of late-Victorian economic life.[19] Apart from this more sophisticated and realistic body of economic theory, a new school applied the *historical* method to economics (as in law), and this proved of even greater value in encouraging men of intelligence to turn their attention to the need for economic and social reform. The marginalists, led by W. S. Jevons (1835-1882), owed a great deal to the Austrians Karl Menger and Eugen Böhm-Bawerk; the new historical school, led by such men as Arnold Toynbee, owed a great deal to the rival German school of William Roscher and Gustav Schmoller. Unlike the Austrians, the German historicists displayed an impatience with theory altogether and emphasized the detailed study of actual institutions and economic policies. Economic history emerged as a respectable academic discipline, and its earliest

[18] Max Beer, *A History of British Socialism* (London, 1929), II, 226-227.
[19] Jones, *The Consumer Society*, p. 247.

practitioners in Britain tended to be reformers—mostly Christian socialists of one sort or another. Meanwhile, as W. Cunningham, Arnold Toynbee, W. J. Ashley, and the other economic historians provided material and historical arguments useful for the development of British socialist theory, the marginal school of economic theory produced Britain's leading Unitarian socialist, the great Dante scholar and author of *The Commonsense of Political Economy* (the bible of marginalism), Rev. Prof. P. H. Wicksteed, whose work will be considered in some detail later. It was Wicksteed who convinced George Bernard Shaw, and through him the Fabian Society, that the classical Labor Theory of Value taken by Marx from Ricardo and others, was theoretically untenable and useless to socialism. Hence Fabian economics became Jevonian.

Theories of philosophy, jurisprudence, and economics were somewhat remote from the mass of the British public, and one should not be too confident in tracing the intellectual lineage of the socialist revival. Many of the socialists of the eighties, and many more people in the labor movement, had never heard of Green, Maitland, or Wicksteed. Maitland was probably the most obscure of the three; Wicksteed had success on the so-called popular platform, and the ideas of T. H. Green received unusually wide dissemination (considering their philosophical character) in a best-selling novel, Mrs. Humphrey Ward's *Robert Elsmere* (1888). The book was dedicated to Green, who also featured in it as "Professor Grey."[20]

[20] See Melvin Richter, *The Politics of Conscience: T. H. Green and His Age* (Cambridge, Mass., 1964), pp. 27-30, and Mrs. Humphrey Ward's *Robert Elsmere*. The latter and other British novels like it were very similar to American popular novels of the same period. William Dean Howells' *Annie Kilburn* (1888), A. W. Tourgee's *Murvale Eastman, Christian Socialist* (1890), and Charles M. Sheldon's *In His Steps* (1898) all dealt with the question of religious faith and social responsibility (as did Mrs. Ward's best seller). *Robert Elsmere* sold half a million copies in the United States during its first year of American sales, and another million or so in the decade that followed. (The historical field of popular culture is wide open for study by comparative historians.) See Wallace Evan Davies, "Religious Issues in Late

Nevertheless, the "trickle-down" of idealism, positivism, pluralism, and marginalism was relatively small. There was an older and more established English tradition, critical of industrial society and all its ways, and one which did secure considerable publicity in the popular press and elsewhere; this we may call the "aesthetic reaction" to industrialism— the tradition that links Coleridge and the Lake Poets, Carlyle, Ruskin, and William Morris. This was the true lineage of countless British late-Victorian reformers and socialists, and John Ruskin in particular was one of the writers most widely quoted in the literature, newspapers, and journals of the working-class movement. Ruskin's doctrines of *meaningful* labor, his hatred of orthodox *laissez-faire* liberalism, his cutting distinction between "wealth" and "illth," his experimentation with a cooperative community in Sheffield,[21] all made him very attractive to the moral and utopian type of socialist and, understandably, to Christian socialists generally.[22] William Morris was, of course, the leading socialist exponent of Ruskinian ideals during the revival years; but he died in 1896, at a point in time when British socialism, under the aegis of the Fabians and the new Independent Labour Party, was becoming increasingly dominated by collectivist and state socialist notions. The aesthetic tradition was henceforward virtually ignored, at least until the emergence of Guild Socialism, which had a medievalist and "arts-and-crafts" aspect (largely Christian).

The catalyst: Henry George and the Single Tax

One could dramatize for popular consumption the conflict between religious faith and social conscience; but it was hardly possible to do the same for the economics of Jevonian

---

Nineteenth-Century American Novels," *Bulletin of the John Rylands Library*, Vol. 41, No. 2 (March 1959), pp. 328-359.

21 Ruskin's Guild of St. George had the cooperation of a group of Sheffield socialists on this project at Totley from 1876. For an account see W.H.G. Armytage, *Heavens Below: Utopian Experiments in England, 1560-1960* (London, 1961), pp. 292ff.

22 The "aesthetic reaction" is handled ably in Raymond Williams, *Culture and Society, 1780-1950* (New York, 1960).

marginal utility. Before Henry George one would have thought it an impossible task for any kind of economics. But the American George did the impossible: he wrote a world's best seller in economics. His *Progress and Poverty,* published in the United States in 1879 and in England the following year, sold up to seven million copies in ten languages. Unexpectedly, since George had intended it as a polemical attack on what he took to be orthodox economics, and as a logically reasoned, step-by-step analysis of the need for one great Single Tax on the economic rent of land, *Progress and Poverty* became in fact the first real working-class textbook or primer in the principles of economics. In Britain its publication came when the Forster Education Act of 1870 was reaching fruition.

The basic argument of *Progress and Poverty* is perfectly clear. George began with a wholehearted acceptance of the classical approach of Smith, Ricardo, and Mill. He declared economics to be a deductive, not an inductive, science. Its main postulates, George claimed, stemmed from the "laws of nature." Its infallible logical analysis traced the working out of axiomatic principles of common sense.[23]

First, two "false ideas" were swept away: the Wages Fund Theory[24] and Malthusianism. Neither the notion that wages form a fixed and limited fund derived from capital, nor the belief that a divine miscalculation could cause the creation of more souls than food to sustain them, was acceptable to Henry George's optimistic, perfectibilist frame of mind. Despite his religiosity of expression George sought an earthly solution to an economic problem. He could not "reconcile the idea of human immortality with the idea that nature wastes men by constantly bringing them into being where there is no room for them." George knew nothing of Maurice and the Christian socialists of the 1850's, but his attitude at this point is thoroughly Maurician. How

[23] J. Dorfman, *The Economic Mind in American Civilization* (New York, 1949), III, 143-144.
[24] George did not seem to realize that J. S. Mill had already abandoned this theory in 1869 (Jones, Manchester thesis, p. 30).

could "an intelligent and beneficent Creator" be responsible for the "wretchedness and degradation which are the lot of such a large proportion of human kind"?[25] Obviously, the Malthusian theory must be wrong.

The argument now moves to the field of distribution and takes up Ricardo's law of economic rent ("God's Law of Rent") .[26] Land is nonreproducible; its value varies with demand. Those who own land have the power to appropriate "so much of the wealth produced by the exertion of labor and capital upon it as exceeds the return which the same application of labor and capital could secure in the least productive occupation in which they freely engage."[27] In their capacity of rent-receivers, landlords perform no useful function (if they also add capital and labor to the soil, this is a separate consideration and a different social role) . Rent is simply a toll levied by monopoly; it charges producers for the right to produce. In the words of the Georgeist anthem, "God gave the land to the people."

For George, labor and capital are in the same camp; the enemy is the landowner. The laws of wages and interest are mere corollaries of the law of rent, and marginal land fixes wages and interest, which vary inversely with rent. If rent increases proportionately with productive power, then neither wages nor interest can profit, for:

$$\text{As Produce} = \text{Rent} + \text{Wages} + \text{Interest},$$
$$\text{Therefore, Produce} - \text{Rent} = \text{Wages} + \text{Interest}.$$

Thus George was no anticapitalist, but in some ways a *laissez-faire* free trader.[28] He defended interest ("the return

[25] Henry George, *Progress and Poverty*, 2nd ed. (London, 1919), pp. 395-396.

[26] Henry George, *The Condition of Labour: An Open Letter to Pope Leo XIII*, new ed. (London, 1934, p. 73).

[27] George, *Progress and Poverty*, p. 119.

[28] George did distinguish between the legitimate earnings of capital and unjust monopoly profits. He spent much of his life fighting monopolies of various kinds (e.g., news syndicates). His doctrine is very American: an acceptance of capitalism, with reservations regarding imperfect competition. Yet he conceived the achievement of *Progress and Poverty* to be "to unite the truth perceived by the school of Smith and

to Capital") with a theory of "organic productivity": Interest is inherent in "the power of increase which the reproductive force of nature, and the in effect analogous capacity for exchange, give to capital." The Labor Theory of Value justifies wages; the organic productivity theory justifies interest. There is no justification for rent.[29] George's findings on the theory of distribution are tabulated thus:

The Current Statement	*The True Statement*
RENT depends on the margin of cultivation, rising as it falls and falling as it rises.	ditto.
WAGES depend upon the ratio between the number of laborers and the amount of capital devoted to their employment.	WAGES depend on the margin of cultivation, falling as it falls and rising as it rises.
INTEREST depends upon the equation between the supply of and the demand for capital; or upon Wages (or the cost of labor) rising as wages fall and falling as wages rise.	INTEREST (its ratio with Wages being fixed by the net power of increase which attaches to capital) depends on the margin of cultivation, falling as it falls and rising as it rises.[30]

Why does rent increase with every material advance of society? Population and technology are the key, said George, to material expansion. Increase of population tends constantly to reduce the margin of cultivation and thus to increase the proportion of aggregate produce taken by rent. Technology ("improvements in the industrial arts") tends in the same direction, and if population were stationary and land were privately held, the technical advance would itself produce "all the effects attributed by the Malthusian doctrine to pressure of population." This is not the complete story, however, for in a progressive society (like the California that George knew), expectation of future progress causes speculation in land values, and the "constant tendency of rent to overpass the limit where production would

Ricardo to the truth perceived by the school of Proudhon and Lassalle; to show that '*laissez-faire*' (in its true full meaning) opens the way to a realization of the noble dreams of socialism" (*ibid.*, p. viii).

[29] *Progress and Poverty*, pp. 121 and 133.
[30] *Ibid.*, pp. 155-156.

cease" causes industrial depressions. The withholding of land for abnormally high speculative prices forces the margin of cultivation further down than is necessary for production. This extension of the margin beyond the normal limit impels labor and capital to cease producing in self-defense, for it implies the reduction of their normal returns. The slowing of production at any single point in the interdependent economic fabric is reflected elsewhere in a cessation of demand, and depression ensues until either the speculative advance in rent is lost or there is an increase in labor efficiency or in the advance of the industrial arts, which enables the normal rent-line to overtake the speculative rent-line. Otherwise, both labor and capital must agree to accept smaller returns.[31]

In sum, in an expanding society, rising urban and rural land values give to owners of land a large unearned increment in rents. This increment is created by society, and it should go to society. What is the answer? For the State to *buy* all the land would be unjust (the rent-receivers do not deserve any compensation, except for capital improvements); neither is it necessary for the State to *nationalize* the land:

> Let the individuals who now hold it still retain, if they want to, possession of what they are pleased to call "their" land. . . . Let them buy and sell, bequeath and devise it. We may safely leave them the shell, if we take the kernel. It is not necessary to confiscate land; it is only necessary to confiscate rent.[32]

Simply *tax* away the unearned increment. The technique is nonrevolutionary and gradual; it is just; and existing democratic legislatures can perform it easily. Moreover, the revenue from this Single Tax would support the government and relieve taxation of capital and of individual initiative.

The beneficial effects of a single tax on the increment of land values knew no bounds whatsoever in George's imagi-

31 *Ibid.*, Bk. v, passim.
32 *Ibid.*, p. 288.

nation. Book x of *Progress and Poverty* builds up his taxing technique into an entire philosophy of universal history. But more important from the point of view of stirring up the social conscience of the British public in the 1880's was the force of his moral indictment of existing society and of private property in land:

> From this fundamental injustice flow all the injustices which distort and endanger modern development, which condemn the producer of wealth to poverty, and pamper the non-producer in luxury, which rear the tenement house with the palace, plant the brothel behind the church, and compel us to build prisons as we open new schools.[33]

George was not a land nationalizer; his concrete suggestions were not very socialistic: he merely treated land exceptionally, which the classical economists had done for decades. His aim—the gradual increase of taxation of land values until finally the state appropriation of the full value of the economic rent was being achieved—was merely socialization not of land but of rent (the "kernel," as George explained, but not the "shell"). Nevertheless, George was often called a land nationalizer and a socialist. The confusion over his real political position illustrates several things: the general confusion and lack of differentiation among reformers in the early eighties; George's own uncertainty (at least up to 1887) as to whether he should support collectivist proposals beyond the Single Tax or not; and the radical flavor of George's fiery language. He championed trade unions (he was a Knight of Labor) and came out openly for various measures of municipal socialism. If he had become Mayor of New York in 1886 (before his disagreement with the socialists), it would have been interesting to see what reforms George would have introduced in that city. Fate never gave this charismatic personality the opportunity to grow and flourish in public office. George's position as godfather of the British socialist revival thus remains paradoxical.

[33] *Ibid.*, pp. 240-241.

The powerful messianic appeal that Henry George made for social action centered on a problem of age-old significance in Britain (land and land ownership), and his agitation was part of the greatest single political issue faced by nineteenth-century parliaments (Ireland). But his great success in the eighties was the product not only of good timing and brilliantly popular expository writing. It was also a measure of George's skill and amazing energy as an orator in the six visits he paid to the British Isles between 1881 and 1890. In Ireland he was twice arrested, became a subject of a parliamentary question, and took a decisive role in the split in the Irish party between the Parnell parliamentary-action group and the Michael Davitt land-reform group, which determined in large measure the future course of Irish political history. George held public debates in speech and print with the Duke of Argyll, Herbert Spencer, H. M. Hyndman, R. B. Cunninghame Graham, and the Pope himself, adapting his style to Welsh miners, English intellectuals, Scots crofters. Three of his visits took the form of highly organized and very extensive lecture tours, and covered Ireland, England, Scotland, and Wales. Between his visits, George's British campaign for the Single Tax was carried on by a well-planned organization led by able men. His converts were legion; from H. M. Hyndman and William Morris to Webb, Shaw, and Hardie, all the prominent socialists of the period acknowledged the early influence of Henry George and revealed him as the greatest single educational force molding the British working class. George's impact was felt on the Marxist and revolutionary socialists, on the Fabian collectivists and Christian socialists, the trade unionists and radical socialists (municipal socialists and the like), and on the ILP and Labour Party membership.[34] Many of the Christian socialists were disciples of the Single Tax, especially Stewart Headlam's group in the Guild of St. Matthew; but, as we shall see, others repudiated George and went beyond land-value taxation in their demands.

[34] For a full account of this see Jones, Manchester thesis, passim.

Like secular socialists, they supported the idea of George's tax so long as it was not single.

In the late 1870's and early 1880's the social question had become centered in the public mind, rightly or wrongly, on the land question. A number of explanations can be found for this. Historical revision has revealed no general agricultural depression; wheat farmers suffered, as we have seen, while thousands of "small, hard-working family farmers" grew livestock profitably with the help of cheap imported cereals. The Georgeists and other antilandlord radicals, adherents of peasant proprietorship, and so on, were guilty of "confused idealism" no doubt.[35] Yet these structural changes in British agriculture did produce distress and dislocation and a public outcry about the state of farming which did not die down until the early twentieth century. One point was that during the 1880's and 1890's Britain finally revoked her agrarian past; agriculture was firmly established as nothing more than the handmaiden of industry; in this period was consummated the nation's urbanization.[36] Another point was that the fate of the British landowning class now seemed sealed, after centuries of economic, social, and political hegemony. The political decline of the landed interest was to be nowhere better illustrated than in Lloyd George's budget of 1909, its rejection by the Lords, and the consequent Parliament Act of 1911, which permanently reduced the power of the once-proud upper house to a mere suspensory veto. (The Single Taxers were not satisfied with Lloyd George's budget despite its land-value duties; but they had little hope of further advances in a Single Tax direction until Philip Snowden's Labour Party budget of 1931, the land-tax clauses of which were repealed by the Tories in 1934.) It was obviously no accident that the land question was a major issue in the domestic politics of the late Victorians and that land nationalization or Georgeist taxation of land values featured as the chief plank of

[35] Fletcher, p. 431.
[36] R.C.K. Ensor, *England, 1870-1914* (London, 1949), pp. 118ff.

all the initial socialist platforms of the 1880's, whether drawn up by the Guild of St. Matthew or by the Democratic Federation.

These organizations were also initially concerned about the Irish question. C. S. Parnell had emerged as the political leader of the Irish Home Rule movement in 1878, and the following year Michael Davitt, through the Irish National Land League, came to dominate the economic side of the nationalist movement. Among the earliest English socialist groups, Hyndman's Democratic Federation (established in June 1881), which was to be built up on the support of the London Radical workingmen's clubs, took land reform as its major plank, and as its first concerted action sent a commission to Ireland to study Davitt's land-reform proposals. Hyndman, who was a land nationalizer long before he became a Marxist (he took up with the idea in Australia during his travels of 1869-1871), served in Davitt's Land League.[37] It seems quite possible that he met Henry George for the first time in Ireland in the fall of 1881. Such links help to account for George's early influence on various members of the Democratic Federation. His close friendship with, and strong influence over, Michael Davitt, his own deep personal involvement in the politics of the Irish land movement, and his book *Progress and Poverty* enabled Henry George to combine in one forceful, magnetic, Christian appeal the two great issues of the day, land and Ireland. For both these problems he offered a single answer.

George's economics theory was of course non-Jevonian. He could never have made any great theoretical contribution to marginal analysis. His economic importance to the British socialist revival is as one who narrowed the gap between the orthodox view of a " 'closed,' unself-conscious, spontaneously functioning society of tradition and inheritance" and the new " 'open,' self-conscious society of choice, plan and design"[38] which the welfare state and socialism

---

[37] Jones, Manchester thesis, pp. 146ff. For Henry George's role in Ireland see pp. 81ff.

[38] The phrases come from T. W. Hutchison's *Review of Economic*

would make possible. George vindicated the open society in which human action could and should rationally be taken in the cause of social justice. In language which the newly literate working classes, or the leaders among them, could grasp, he abolished two theoretical pillars of economic orthodoxy. His economic propaganda was all the more successful because he was ignorant of Jevons and criticized classical theory entirely on its own grounds, the only grounds he knew. His "clearing up" of various fallacies of classical economics, though belated compared with the work of advanced thinkers such as Jevons,[39] was certainly not without point for the majority, and in fact the Ricardian theory of rent, on which George depended so much, was left standing in only superficially altered form—"like some Anglo-Saxon masonry left in a Norman cathedral"[40]—as part of the new production and distribution theory put together in the 1890's.

It was in his Labor Theory of Value that George was as scholastic and obsolete as Marx; but he did not alienate the British workingman with a doctrine of positivism or atheism, nor stifle him with a rigid dialectical philosophy, as did E. Belfort Bax and Hyndman. Henry George's approach was entirely consonant with the existing political prejudices and the Victorian religiosity of the majority of his listeners, of both middle and working classes.

Doctrines, 1870-1929 (London, 1953), p. 7 (though they are not applied there to Henry George).

[39] The truth is that Henry George made a great personal impact on Britain's leading disseminator of *Jevonian* economics—P. H. Wicksteed —as a later chapter will show.

[40] Hutchison, p. 14.

CHAPTER III

Church and Society in the 1880's

STRUCTURAL economic change, political and intellectual ferment, the Georgeist campaign, and the eventual reemergence of socialism on the British scene affected the churches very deeply. Even the most obscure and isolated sects could not remain uninfluenced. They all faced the same fundamental problem in the late-Victorian era: the alienation of the urban mass of the people from organized religion.

Social class and religious behavior

We have but poor means of measuring the depth of religious feeling in any given society, even in the present day, let alone past historical periods. One cannot help agreeing with the twentieth-century urbanite who stubbornly refuses to consider himself a non-Christian even though he attends church only once or twice in a lifetime; for church attendance is certainly an unreliable guide in itself to the potency of religious faith. Perhaps if historical statistics for late-Victorian churchgoing could be accurately ascertained, they would at least be an objective guide to one aspect of religious *behavior*. And the late Victorians themselves were very much concerned, publicly and privately, with the decline in congregations.

Unfortunately, of all historical statistics the religious are probably the most misleading, the hardest to collect and to verify, and the least informative when all the work is done. Denominational self-estimates of the numbers of the faithful can be accepted only after vigorous investigation to learn how the figures were compiled and at what age young people are considered full members of the Church. A group practicing adult baptism would naturally have smaller numbers than one which claimed all children for the Church the minute they were born (or even earlier). Moreover, denominational officials seem by nature unscientific and shy of facts and figures even today; how much more so in the eighties and nineties, when the controversy over church attendance was at its height. The modern student of church statistics in the late nineteenth century faces a mass of conflicting contemporary opinions. While the general consensus seemed to be that attendance was down and that the largest absences were of male urban workers, individual opinions of quite a different character also abound.

In London, R. Mudie-Smith, the editor of an important religious census (by the *Daily News*) of 1902-1903, took for granted that there was in fact a decline in attendance, that this decline reflected an alienation of the working classes, and that only a social gospel could save the situation. Mudie-Smith reported in his matter-of-fact way:

> Nothing has so alienated the people . . . as the age-long opposition of the churches to their most elementary rights as human beings. . . . If we cannot make our politics part of our religion we have no right to cast even a vote. If we cannot take our Christianity into a borough council, we ourselves ought to remain outside.[1]

This was trenchant criticism. Thirty years earlier in his biting satirical novel, *Erewhon* (1872), Samuel Butler had suggested a more complacent attitude on the part of his fellow Victorians. In the utopia of Erewhon the "Musical Banks" (churches) were also unattended; but Mrs. Nosnibor told the visiting hero not to impute from this observation "any want of confidence in the bank," for "the heart of the country was thoroughly devoted to these establishments."[2] The "heart of the country" may or may not have remained "devoted," but—as the shrewd student Charles Booth understood—churchgoing is a habit, a social usage. It is a habit a nation can fall out of; Britain did.

[1] R. Mudie-Smith (ed.), *The Religious Life of London*, Daily News Census (London, 1904), p. 13.
[2] Samuel Butler, *Erewhon*, New American Library paperback ed. (New York, 1961), p. 117.

The facts of church attendance have a bearing on our understanding of why Christian socialism came back to life in the 1880's. If congregations were declining, what kind of people were affected? What was the differential impact on the denominations? Is it likely that Christian social radicalism was a ruse to woo the workers, an attempt to fill halls rather than to "Christianize" capitalist society or to produce a Kingdom of God on earth? Richard Hofstadter has written of a "status revolution" in the United States during the same period, in which professional people, intellectuals, clerics, and others became "progressive" in defiant response to their loss of social status and their displacement in the social hierarchy by industrialists and salesmen with "new" wealth and "new" talents.[3] Was this also true of British middle-class reformers? It is surely the case that social dissidence on the part of church folk was often as much a reflection of a class or prestige struggle *inside* a particular denomination as it was a rejection of the external capitalist society. Angry young Friends, up against the wealthy elder statesmen and great business families of the Society of Friends, helped to establish the Socialist Quaker Society in 1898. Without some kind of statistical knowledge it is difficult to judge such hypotheses; we must examine the known figures, however poor they may be.

The two chief sources for facts about church attendance and strength in Britain were the census of 1886 and that of 1902-1903. An official census of 1851 directed by Horace Mann was considered by Mudie-Smith as "of little value" because the churches had furnished their own returns.[4] Dr. W. R. Nicoll's census of 1886 for the *British Weekly* took place all on one day—a cold but bright Sunday in October—and covered 1,500 places of worship. (A later survey of mission halls was carried out in November 1887.[5]) Based

---

[3] *The Age of Reform* (New York, 1955).

[4] For an analysis of how the census of 1851 was taken and a judgment of its findings, see K. S. Inglis, "Patterns of Religious Worship in 1851," *Journal of Ecclesiastical History*, XI, No. 1 (April 1960), pp. 74-86.

[5] Jane T. Stoddart, in Mudie-Smith (ch. IX), pp. 280-293.

on returns from independent reporters, the 1886 census was of incomparably greater validity than that of 1851; but the results did not differentiate between sexes and ages, no services were counted before 11 A.M., and any generalizations had to be based on that one Sunday, 24 October 1886. The later *Daily News* census of 1902-1903, claimed by Mudie-Smith for the above reasons as "the first scientific attempt in the history of this country to discover the number of those who attend places of worship in the Metropolis," took place over a complete year, from November to November, including every Sunday in a winter noted for its severity. The editor, however, discounted the effects of bad weather on church attendance except in certain famous meeting places, such as St. Paul's, and in Sunday afternoon services.[6] The census applied only to London, and we have no figures of comparable detail for the provinces.[7]

The census of 1902-1903 dealt with London suburbia (outer London) as well as with inner London, while that of 1886 was concerned only with inner London. Taking first the gross comparison between 1886 and 1902-1903 for inner London we see:

British Weekly Census
1. London population (1881) : 3,816,483
2. Church attenders (1886, and,
   including mission halls, 1887) : 1,167,312

Daily News Census
1. London population (1902) : 4,536,541
2. Church attendance (1902-1903, including
   "twicers") : 1,003,361[8]

Estimating a London population for 1886 of 3,971,000 (since it was increasing at about 31,000 p. a.) , this gives us:

[6] Mudie-Smith, pp. 1, 16-17.
[7] For Sheffield, as well as for general estimates, see E. R. Wickham, *Church and People in an Industrial City*, pp. 165ff.
[8] My calculations, based on data in Mudie-Smith, p. 281.

1886–1903: London population *increased* by about 565,000

1886–1903: Gross church attendance *fell* by 164,000

The 1902-1903 figures will bear closer examination. In inner London, 2,688 places of worship were visited (including 62 synagogues), and a total attendance of 1,003,361 counted (including "twicers"). Mudie-Smith estimated that 39 percent were "twicers," giving 832,051 as the number of total *worshipers*. For the 29 boroughs of inner London he calculated a population of 4,536,541, of which 66,237 were institutionalized people and should be deducted, giving a lesser total of 4,470,304. Considering the number of children, the sick, the aged, and those forced to work on Sunday, Mudie-Smith generously estimated that 50 percent of that total could have gone to church if they had so wished. Since out of the 2,235,152 who could possibly attend only 1,003,361 did so, 58 percent failed to attend church (1,401,-101). Put another way, one in 2.68, or roughly *one-third,* were moved to attend a place of religious worship in inner London in 1902-1903.

In the suburbs, 1,358 places of worship were investigated within a 12-mile radius of Charing Cross, with a total population (excluding the institutionalized) of 1,770,032 and a total number of actual worshipers (excluding "twicers") of 420,382. Taking the number of *possible* worshipers again at a generous 50 percent discount—885,016—we see that a few more people went to church in outer London than in inner London. About 53 percent stayed at home; one in 2.10 attended church, chapel, or synagogue.

Mudie-Smith's general conclusion for the whole of the London area was that four people out of every five were "either careless or hostile as regards public worship."[9]

Denominational differences

These were all gross figures. The most startling fact that emerges from a denominational breakdown is that the

[9] My calculations, on basis of Mudie-Smith data; *ibid.,* pp. 16-18.

church which, as we shall see, led the Christian socialist revival, was at this same time suffering the heaviest losses. The *Church of England* lost about 140,000 members between the two censuses of 1886 and 1902-1903—140,000 out of the total loss for all churches of 164,000. Gross Anglican attendances in 1886 (inner London, excluding missions) had amounted to 535,715; the same gross total for 1902-1903 was 396,196, representing a clear loss of 139,519.[10]

The gross total attendance figures for all Nonconformist Protestant churches fell by only five or six thousand from 1886 to 1903, and the Anglican lead in attendances over the Nonconformist total was thereby considerably narrowed from 165,000 (1886) to only 32,000 (1903). (Actual Nonconformist totals, exclusive of missions, were: 1886—369,349; 1902-1903—363,882.) Jane Stoddart concluded that "in the Church of England there are only three worshippers in 1902-3 for every four who were found there in 1886."[11]

Anglican losses occurred in all areas of London and in all classes of people, rich, middle, and poor, but naturally enough they were heaviest in the poorest districts except where the church was fortunate enough to have a popular or radical preacher—usually a High Churchman—like Rev. J. E. Watts-Ditchfield at St. James-the-Less, Bethnal Green. In Southwark some congregations were halved between the two censuses; in Hackney the Anglicans lost over 5,000 while the Nonconformists gained about 1,000—not even counting the Salvation Army. Perhaps the most spectacular loss for the Church of England was at St. Paul's Cathedral itself, which in 1886 had a combined morning and evening congregation of 4,705, reduced in 1903 to 2,337. Anglicans might complain that the census was taken on a particularly wet Sunday in May 1903; but only a few streets away at the City Temple the Rev. R. J. Campbell, the renegade Congre-

10 *Ibid.*, p. 281; my calculation. From the figures given on pp. 17-18 we can estimate that at this time, taking inner and outer London together, Anglicans made up 43.1 percent of all worshipers, Nonconformists 43.6 percent, Roman Catholics 7.6 percent, and remainder 5.7 percent.
11 *Ibid.*, pp. 281-282.

gationalist (soon to be converted to socialism), held a crowd of 7,008 on the very same day at the opening of his city pastorate.[12]

Meanwhile, the *Baptists,* perhaps of all sects the most conservative and the least concerned about social reform, were expanding throughout London. They suffered no decline at all in overall numbers in the metropolis. In the wealthy borough of Paddington the Fabian socialist, Rev. John Clifford, preached to a crowd of 2,213 in 1903 (1886: 2,479) at his famous Westbourne Park Chapel, while the chief Wesleyan Methodist church in the district (Sutherland Avenue) suffered a fall from 1,403 (1886) to 540, and the Anglicans saw some of their West London congregations dwindle to one-half or one-third as the new "weekend" habit spread among the well-to-do. The tremendous importance of individual preachers in London was emphasized by the shrinking of the Baptist audience at Spurgeon's Tabernacle, Southwark, from a remarkable 10,589 (1886) to 3,625 (1903) as a result of the death of that terrifying preacher in 1892.[13] In contrast, numbers doubled at Woolwich Baptist Tabernacle (1886: 1,124 to 1903: 2,244) under the pastorate of Rev. J. Wilson.

Congregationalists were at their strongest in middle-class Northwest and Central London, and the biggest congregation of any church in the whole metropolis was the City Temple, where R. J. Campbell's crowd amounted to one-third of all church attendance for the City of London area (7,008 out of 22,597). Congregationalism seemed to be waning in the poorer East End—Poplar, Spitalfields, for example—though in Hackney the church remained very strong, with 29,492 Congregational worshipers as against 18,609 Anglicans. Farther east, slum residents were not to be "drawn into the ordinary middle-class chapel." The contemporary

12 *Ibid.,* pp. 287-288; p. 126 (table).

13 My comparisons: for data see *ibid.,* pp. 288-290, 101, and 283. C. H. Spurgeon (1834-1892) was one of the three greatest Baptists of the century (with Alexander Maclaren and John Clifford) and a hell-fire preacher whose death produced press adulations that sickened Stewart Headlam. See *Church Reformer,* XI, No. 3 (March 1892), p. 52.

comment was that in place of Congregational respectability "They prefer the bright, homely services at the halls, the lively singing, the picturesque gospel address, the kindly handgrasps when they come and leave, and the certainty that shabby clothes will not be noticed."[14]

Wesleyan Methodism, the third largest Nonconformist denomination, did not lend itself to easy comparison between the censuses of 1886 and 1903 because the church had been revolutionized by the "Forward Movement" led by its leader, Rev. Hugh Price Hughes. During this transformation there were some gains and some losses, and while we know the Wesleyans were better off than the Anglicans, other generalizations are not possible. Certainly one can see the justification of the census writer's conclusion that "the Forward Movement saved London Methodism";[15] but we shall see more of this under a later chapter.

In Tables 1 to 4, which follow, all percentages are rounded and do not necessarily add up to 100 percent; only major denominations mentioned in this study are included. (For the data on which Tables 1 to 4 are based see Mudie-Smith, pp. 271, 447-448.)

TABLE 1

Some Denominational Percentages (London, Census of 1902-1903)

| | PERCENTAGE OF WORSHIPERS | |
	Inner London	Outer London
Anglican	42.8	46.2
Nonconformist	41.2	44.6
(including, *among others,* the following):		
Baptist	10.8	10.7
Congregationalist	10.5	10.5
All Methodists	10.7	13.1
(Wesleyan alone)	7.8	8.7
Salvation Army	2.2	3.2
Unitarian	0.4	0.1
Quaker	0.3	0.3
Swedenborgian	0.1	0.1
Roman Catholic	9.3	6.2

[14] Mudie-Smith, pp. 290-291. [15] *Ibid.,* pp. 293, 266.

TABLE 2

PERCENTAGES OF TOTAL POPULATION ATTENDING
CHURCH IN LONDON, 1902-1903

INNER LONDON

About 22.5 percent of the *total* population
attended *all* places of worship in 1902-1903*

Anglican	10
Nonconformist	9
Roman Catholic	2
Others	1.5

22.5

OUTER LONDON

About 28 percent of the *total* population
attended *all* places of worship in 1902-1903†

Anglican	13	(slightly over)
Nonconformist	13	(slightly under)
Roman Catholic	1.5	
Others	0.5	

28.0

* Inner London, 1886, approx. 30.6 percent.
† No comparison available for Outer London, 1886.

TABLE 3

RATIO OF ALL WORSHIPERS TO TOTAL POPULATION BY
SELECTED DISTRICTS, 1902-1903 (INNER LONDON)*

Middle-Class Districts		Poor Districts	
Marylebone	1 in 5	Bethnal Green	1 in 17
Lewisham	1 in 5	Deptford	1 in 13
Kensington	1 in 6	Fulham	1 in 13
Westminster	1 in 6	Shoreditch	1 in 16

*Morning services only.

Some lessons of the census of 1902-1903

Apart from the interesting apparent correlation between
large congregations and conservatism (as among the Baptists, although Clifford was a great exception), and between
dwindling congregations and radicalism (as in some sections

TABLE 4

DENOMINATIONAL TOTALS (INNER LONDON) 1902-1903,
INCLUDING MISSIONS

Anglican		429,822
Nonconformist:		
Baptist	108,455	
Methodist	106,201	
Congregationalist	105,535	
Presbyterian	24,778	
Salvation Army	22,402	
Unitarian	3,599	
Quaker	2,987	
Swedenborgian	852	
Total		374,809
Roman Catholic		93,572

of the Church of England), what general lessons were taught by the census of 1902-1903? Mudie-Smith, in his cool and dispassionate way, indicated at least four: the importance of the individual popular preacher; the importance of suitably attractive church buildings; the need for the churches to go out to the people directly with open-air meetings in the style of Wesley; and above all, and less superficially, the pressing lack of a true social gospel. In Mudie-Smith's view, "The outstanding lesson of the census is that the power of preaching is undiminished. Wherever there is the right man in the pulpit there are few if any empty pews."[16]

Since many churches did have empty pews, the implication was that good preachers were few in number; but the census editor did not try to explain the inability of religion to attract better-qualified exponents. Instead, he was content to lay down the rule that a good preacher should have "a large heart, and if he is to be believed by the people, a small salary." (Mudie-Smith thought that "the masses subconsciously believe that a large stipend is not in harmony with the teaching and example of Jesus Christ.")

[16] *Ibid.*, p. 7.

The Church of England, he averred, gave too much attention to the service and not enough to the sermon; "in consequence the preaching standard is not high. I don't think it can be denied that the average sermon in the Established Church is below the average Free Church sermon." Other explanations of the greater loss in attendance borne by the Church of England must include organizational failures (the Nonconformist churches, or the least "established" of them, showed greater flexibility in administration and structure and a greater awareness of the need for efficiency in reaching the public) ; the continuing *momentum* of the Nonconformist movement among the lower-middle and middle classes; and the differential effects of the growing "weekend" habit, which, it has been argued, made more serious inroads in churches that did not emphasize so much the "Nonconformist conscience."[17]

An interesting distinction is often made between the religious behavior of men and that of women. Mudie-Smith believed firmly that *sermons* attracted men, *services* women; hence the larger proportion of men in Nonconformist chapels than in Anglican churches. Some evidence supports his view: Stewart Headlam's High Church goings-on in the Guild of St. Matthew attracted far more women than men; but this is a loaded example, since Headlam befriended the London chorus girls with his Church and Stage Guild. At the other end of the theological spectrum, John Trevor's Labour Church was always begging for more women members.[18] But on the whole, Mudie-Smith's theory is not especially useful. *All* religious bodies attracted more women than they did men, and the explanations which have so far

[17] Wickham, pp. 168ff. Bishop Wickham seems to imply that the religious habit is lost sooner in suburbia than elsewhere; he contrasts the higher degree of social stability of the industrial North with the "Greater London hinterland."

[18] The Labour Church plea was apparently unanswered. A Labour Church Conference on the subject "How Can We Reach the Women?" was held in March 1892. See *Labour Prophet*, I, No. 3 (March 1892), p. 24. (The *Labour Prophet* itself, however, always managed to attract plenty of lively women writers.)

been given to account for this are legion—ranging from the "hat-spoiling" theory (men had to doff their hats and got them sat on) to the more serious "opportunity-cost" theory in which the church or chapel functioned as a "pub" for wives, getting them out of the house and away from the family. What else was there for women to do? Men had their voting and their electoral meetings, their trade unions, and so on; British women had few civil rights before the First World War.

The late-Victorian emphasis on church building was more than a superficial consideration, for one of the most bitter and telling attacks made upon orthodoxy by Christian socialists was directed against the system of pew rents and segregated seating predominant in all middle-class churches, whether Congregational or Anglican. Mudie-Smith and, more comprehensively, Percy Alden demanded radical changes in the internal physical organization of churches to defeat the insidious rise of class barriers inside the house of God. Future buildings "must be the antithesis of those now in existence." Those churches,

> with cold, repellent stone walls, furnished with forbidding, divisive pews (some cushioned and carpeted and others bare and uncomfortable) . . . must give place to large, handsome central halls, well lit and well ventilated, furnished throughout with seats of one pattern, which permit of no arbitrary divisions based on class distinction.

> In a word, the churches, instead of being built in a style which fosters the spirit of caste, must symbolize . . . the universal Fatherhood of God, the Universal Brotherhood of Man.[19]

The church should become an aggressive center of social work, open seven days a week. Busy Wesleyan mission halls stood in sharp contrast to empty Wesleyan Gothic churches; Baptist tabernacles were crowded. The lesson was obvious.

What was being advocated here was the "institutional

[19] Mudie-Smith, pp. 8-10.

church," that phenomenon which spread so rapidly in the USA and did much to differentiate American and European religions of similar denominations. The most thoroughgoing British exponent of the social club-church was Percy Alden (1863-1944), whom we shall deal with later as a member of the Christian Socialist League, the Christian Social Brotherhood, the Socialist Quaker Society, and the Fabian Society. Alden established the Mansfield House (Congregational) Settlement in 1890 and served as Radical-Liberal MP for Tottenham from 1906. He outlined "The Ideal Church for East London" in 1904; what he wanted was space to seat one thousand, a good organ, a platform instead of a pulpit, chairs instead of pews, classrooms, games rooms, with a workingmen's club attached, free medical benefits, free legal aid, a maternity club, lads' and girls' clubs, a band, a glee club, a "coffee palace," adult extension classes. . . . In fact, a recent satire by the American novelist Peter de Vries on the present-day institutional churches of the United States reads quite reasonably when set against Percy Alden's vast scheme of half a century ago.[20] But as early as 1872 the too-eager clergyman, anxious to "accommodate" his congregation, had come to the keen attention of Samuel Butler; Erewhon's Musical Banks ran the gamut from architectural gimmickry to baby care.[21]

Despite Samuel Butler's well-justified satire, the institutional church, combined with a good campaign of open-air preaching by Britain's leading (rather than by her inferior) men, such as Mudie-Smith demanded, may have done much

[20] *The Mackerel Plaza* (London, 1963): De Vries' chief character, the "Peoples' Liberal" clergyman, explains, "Our church is, I believe, the first split-level church in America. It has 5 rooms, and 2 baths downstairs—dining area, kitchen and 3 parlours. . . . There is a small worship-area at one end" (p. 10).

[21] *Erewhon*, p. 119. A Musical Bank manager explains to the hero of the novel: ". . . now they had put fresh stained glass windows into all the banks in the country, and repaired the buildings, and enlarged the organs; the presidents, moreover, had taken to riding in omnibuses and talking nicely to people in the streets, and to remembering the ages of their children, and giving them things when they were naughty, so that all would henceforth go smoothly."

to delay the decay of Victorian religion. Mudie-Smith wrote: "Let the Bishop of London, Dr. Clifford, the Dean of Westminster, Dr. Horton, the Rev. R. J. Campbell and the Rev. F. B. Meyer, to name but a few, preach in the various parks, and the movement would spread." But without a *permanent* change of attitude on the part of the churches toward labor and social reform, without that apparently permanent shift to the "left" which has in fact taken place in twentieth-century Anglo-American religion, it is a moot point how long the churches could have held out. Today the gospel is almost everywhere a "social gospel." Few, if any, men of any denomination preach hell-fire and freedom of contract, blind obedience to authority, and a divinely ordained class system. Mudie-Smith, therefore, was on strong grounds in his call for a social gospel:

> We owe the revival of the eighteenth century to the rediscovery of personal responsibility. The revival of the twentieth century we shall owe to the discovery of the *worth of the entire man and the responsibility of the community*. Our forefathers were content with a Heaven after death; we demand a Heaven here.[22]

For each particular denomination there were more specific lessons to be derived from the census of 1902-1903, but the problems were extremely complex. In East London the Nonconformists were stronger than expected, and the Anglicans, despite years of arduous work by ritualists and High Churchmen in the slums, could hardly hold their own. In West London, where attendance at an Anglican church still conferred social status and prestige, much less labor was necessary by parsons. In South London, according to C.F.G. Masterman's report, the richer sections were not Anglican (like the West End) but Baptist, and the care of the poor was thus left to the Church of England and the Roman Catholics. Masterman claimed to have seen "the poor in bulk" at only two places of religious worship in

[22] Mudie-Smith, pp. 12, 13-14 (italics mine).

South London—"Mr. Meakin's great hall in Bermondsey and St. George's Roman Catholic Cathedral at Southwark." In South London as in the rest of the capital the middle classes attended church and chapel, the workers and the poor stayed away.[23]

Working-class alienation: its content

Statistics can tell us little about the social content of alienation—*why* the masses stayed away from churches and chapels. A study of the social literature of the day, labor biographies, and the memoirs of slum clergymen reveals several "grievances" held consistently by labor representatives against organized religion. Most of them are obvious and could be easily deduced: that institutionalized religion ("churchianity") was conservative and a buttress of the established order; that it taught submission instead of critical analysis and revolt against oppression; that it (or some of its many rival branches) offered rewards in the next world to compensate for humility and degradation in this world; that its "brotherhood" was hypocrisy because it offered mere charity instead of justice and equality; that its organization was financially and administratively dependent on the wealthy and well-placed, even among those churches that began life as popular democratic sects, like the Congregationalists and Baptists, the well-to-do Unitarians and industrial-empire-building Quakers; that its very structure, its buildings, its language, its whole style perpetuated class distinctions and restricted social mobility.[24] All this could be

[23] Masterman, in Mudie-Smith, p. 196.

[24] In his *Christianity and the Working Classes* (London, 1906), George Haw, a shrewd observer of the religious scene, painted a telling picture of class alienation: "Imagine the bewilderment of a working-man without previous training entering a strange place of worship, no matter of what denomination. The formalism, the social caste, the archaic language, and in some cases the medieval ceremony, leave his mind a blank and his heart unsatisfied. He could not find his place in the Service Book, even supposing that one were handed to him. He could make nothing of the mumbling of the congregation and next to nothing of the prayers and lessons, certainly not if he were in an Established Church. The sermon in nine cases out of ten would be on a

claimed, and fairly, in the late nineteenth century without any mention of dogma or articles of belief. Few churches, whatever their theology, could easily escape these charges. The snobbery and exclusiveness of church leaders knew no bounds. As early as 1856 Bishop Tait of London had tried to "democratize" the Anglicans and go out to the people. He led open-air meetings and talked to porters, transport workers, and postmen; he opened St. Paul's on Sunday nights, and for one winter the cathedral thronged with people— but the Chapter refused to continue the practice throughout the year! All the new district churches erected to meet expanding population needs during the great building program of the midcentury had pew rents. They remained half-empty.[25]

Victorian religion—according to an established historical pattern for faiths which lose contact with the poor and the disinherited—had become (in the phrase of Richard Niebuhr about other sects) "bound in the forms of middle-class culture." It seemed inevitable that Niebuhr's next stage should then be applicable to Britain: "the secularisation of the masses, and the transfer of their religious fervour to secular movements, which hold some promise of salvation from the evils that afflict them."[26] The British labor movement, with its heavy ethical overtones, was perfectly suited to act as a vehicle for this transfer of piety. *Par excellence* the Methodist-infiltrated trade-union movement, the Independent Labour Party, and the Labour Church met this need.

---

lower intellectual level than a labour address, and not spoken with anything like the same clearness and conviction. Were it the church of the popular Nonconformist preacher he would be received coldly, made to stand about until the seat-holders had arrived, and then probably hustled into a back or an uncomfortable seat, and at the collection he would feel he was being called upon to pay for an unprofitable experience, an unintelligible service and an uninspiring address" (pp. 23-24).

[25] See Randall Davidson, *Life of Archbishop Tait* (London, 1891), I, 264, quoted also in Wickham, p. 113. For the working-class attitude to the new district churches see Wickham, pp. 115-116.

[26] H. Richard Niebuhr, *The Social Sources of Denominationalism* (New York, 1957), p. 32.

In a word, socialism itself filled the vacuum left in some lives by the decline of traditional religious belief.

It is not surprising that many members of the better-off skilled workers had little interest in "churchianity," and if pushed to explain their religious position would often reveal the vaguest, untheological notions of God, notions proudly and independently held without reference to any priest or parson. As Charles Booth perceived: "Among working men a kind of *sublimated trade unionism* is the most prevalent gospel; a vague bias towards that which is believed to be good for one's fellow men."[27] At bottom, this is what many Labour Church supporters meant by John Trevor's phrase, "the religion of the labour movement"; and as S. G. Hobson, the ex-Quaker Fabian who became a leading Guild Socialist, has pointed out, the "ILP creed" was for most men much more than a political doctrine. It appeared at a time when Yorkshire Nonconformity was in process of disruption, and it filled a definite spiritual gap.[28]

With the "submerged" class, however, the unskilled and frequently unemployed, those thousands of poverty-stricken families whose lot was championed by the Congregationalist pamphlet *The Bitter Cry of Outcast London* in 1883, no arguments against or about institutionalized religion were either possible or necessary. For "the poor" there was no upward mobility, nor were there avenues of opportunity to be closed by Christian snobbery and prejudice, nor any trade-union organization to be attacked from the pulpit. For them there was simply the fact of their abject poverty. Here, more than anywhere, Percy Alden's words were true, that gardens became streets, men became "hands," and the public house replaced the church and supplied "the only social link" in the urban jungle. Said Alden, ". . . all ties with the past have been broken, especially the bond of religion; disintegration has set in." *Apathy* rules, and therefore "the strong arm of the church and the still stronger

[27] Charles Booth, *Life and Labour*, 3rd Ser., Vol. 16, p. 37 (italics mine).

[28] S. G. Hobson, *Pilgrim to the Left* (London, 1938), pp. 38-39.

arm of the municipality must give that opportunity for physical and mental development without which . . . spiritual life becomes an impossibility."[29] In such battle areas the churches should have recognized the call for aid totally without regard to the lack of church attendance and even the irreligion and depravity of the flock.[30]

One observer, C.F.G. Masterman, did manage to grasp the truth of the situation. As far as proselytizing among the "submerged" is concerned, "We come *from outside* with our gospel," he wrote, "aliens with alien ideas." It was a clash of alien subcultures:

> The Anglican church represents the ideas of the upper classes, of the universities, of a vigorous life in which bodily strength, an appearance of knowledge, a sense of humour, occupy prominent places. The large Nonconformist bodies represent the ideas of the middle classes, the strenuous self-help and energy which have stamped their ideas upon the whole of imperial Britain. . . . Each totally fails to apprehend a vision of life as reared in a mean street, and now confronting existence on a hazardous weekly wage, from a block dwelling. . . . Our movements and inexplicable energies are received with a mixture of tolerance and perplexity.[31]

Such cool realism and empathy were rare indeed in Victorian Britain. Too often the "industrial missioners" sent to

[29] In Mudie-Smith, pp. 21, 29.

[30] The ILP leader, Keir Hardie, when MP, wrote an "open letter to the clergy" in his *Labour Leader* (23 June 1905): "The Archbishop of Canterbury . . . said he had to devote 17 hours a day to his work and had no time left in which to form opinions on how to solve the unemployed question. The religion which demands 17 hours a day for organisation and leaves no time for a single thought about starving and despairing men, women and children has no message for this age" (quoted in Haw, *Christianity*, pp. 4-5).

[31] Masterman, in Mudie-Smith, p. 196 (italics mine). Compare H. F. May's comment on the American clergy: "Little in their experience fitted them to understand the motives of non-Protestant, slum-dwelling wage-earners" (*Protestant Churches and Industrial America* [New York, 1949], p. 91).

slum areas by the churches were third-rate men who had failed elsewhere and regarded their slum appointments as the outward manifestation of this failure.[32] Masterman, despite the patronizing touches of the last sentence of his statement, comes closer here perhaps to understanding the problem of the poor in relation to the churches and to organized religion than did many self-styled "Christian socialists."

C.F.G. Masterman, Percy Alden, George Haw, and some other commentators caught glimpses into the true nature of working-class alienation. For instance, they correctly perceived that it was essentially a *class* phenomenon.[33] But were they asking the right questions? The late Victorians usually assumed a falling-off from righteousness, a *decline* of churchgoing among the urban workers. But had the urban proletariat of post-Industrial Revolution days ever gone to church in large numbers at all?

The answer was No. There was no falling off from previously higher levels of church attendance by the workers. The so-called boom attendances of the midcentury and the large church-building programs resulted chiefly from the increase in middle- and lower-middle-class churchgoing, as a natural consequence of general population increase; in fact, all that church and chapel attendances did was to keep up with population growth. There was an absolute but no relative increase in churchgoing; and the increase did not affect the working class.[34] In the succinct statement of one contemporary, "It is not that the Church of God has lost the great towns; it has never had them."[35]

[32] Alden, in Mudie-Smith, p. 37.

[33] *Vide* Wickham, p. 176, quoting Charles Booth: "Wherever the regular working-class is found, and in whatever proportion to the rest of the inhabitants, it seems equally impervious to the claims of religion. . . . While those who do join any church become almost indistinguishable from the *class* with which they then mix, the change that has really come about is not so much *of* as *out of* the class to which they have belonged."

[34] Wickham, ch. IV.

[35] A. F. Winnington-Ingram, *Work in Great Cities* (London, 1896), p. 22 (quoted in Wickham, p. 3).

Migration from the countryside and accommodation to the new urban life sapped religious faith. The city environment did not encourage the maintenance of old social usages and habits like churchgoing. Apart from the absence of adequate physical facilities, the remoteness of clergymen, and the deep-dyed snobbery and class consciousness of the various denominations, the urban worker had little *time* for churchgoing. Factory hours were long and extended over Sundays; all the family could work (when factories were not idle); and with continued economic growth and the emergence of a large consumer market in the late-Victorian period, the range of urban distractions was greatly extended. The newest generations, born and bred in industrial towns, had never gone regularly to church or chapel to begin with. Moreover, the physical setting of working-class life was not conducive to that "solitude and reflection" which enabled the better-off middle classes to remain overtly religious.[36] As early as 1854 the organizer of the religious census of 1851, Horace Mann, had suggested most of these explanations. (For Mann, however, the ultimate cause of absence from church and chapel was a deep "unconscious secularism," a "genuine repugnance to religion itself" felt by the working class.[37])

Britain was not the only nation to experience these social changes. Churchgoing by workers was also low, for example, in Catholic France and in Belgium, Italy, Spain, and even in Latin America.[38] In the United States, too, the urban

---

[36] Wickham, pp. 14, 110-111, 176-178.

[37] *Ibid.*, pp. 110-111.

[38] See François-André Isambert, *Christianisme et Classe Ouvrière* (Paris, 1961), pp. 43-53. The study of the sociology of religion remained undeveloped for decades, until the pioneer work of French scholars, particularly Prof. Gabriel Le Bras, the expert in canon law, who led the way with a key article in 1931. Antireligious and positivist prejudice were a formidable stumbling block to the scientific understanding of religion in society. Great expansion has taken place in the discipline since World War II. An excellent survey of the literature in the field is given in ch. 1 of C. K. Ward's *Priests and People: A Study in the Sociology of Religion* (Liverpool, 1961). For a general American introduction see Milton Yinger, *Sociology Looks at Religion* (New York, 1963) and *Religion, Society and the Individual* (New York,

workers were alienated from institutionalized religion: but it is harder to distinguish a historic "working class" in that heterogeneous nation of immigrants; the "primitive" revivalist tradition was deeply entrenched at grass-roots level; and, for a complex of reasons, at least one large underprivileged group, Negro Americans, have to this day remained fundamentally religious. In the United States perhaps more than elsewhere urban workers occasionally evolved their own religious organizations—sects of various types. But the sects were not necessarily "liberal" or "radical" in economic and political doctrines. Excluded from middle-class society and scorned by the middle-class churches, the sects provided their own standards of value. Emphasizing varying degrees of *Grace,* they substituted religious status for the social status denied to their underprivileged members.[39] Thus, in the United States at least, such sects tended to be deliberately separatist; they stood aloof from the "sinful" outside society which excluded them; they became highly moralistic and fundamentalist. They were essentially *apolitical.*

British experience was different. Greater working-class homogeneity, concentration, and self-identification made it more difficult for religious sects like the Primitive Methodists to resist the magnetic pull of the more-developed British labor movement. However, recent scholarship has questioned some previous assumptions about the political character of English Methodism, and there is no doubt that Methodists were more prone to support movements for *political* rights in the early and mid-nineteenth century (for instance, Chartism) than they were to encourage the radicals of later years to fight for *economic* reforms or socialism.[40] The La-

---

1957). Also useful is Louis Schneider, *Religion, Culture and Society: A Reader in the Sociology of Religion* (New York, 1964).

[39] See, for instance, the famous study by Liston Pope, *Millhands and Preachers: A Study of Gastonia* (New Haven, 1945), pp. 137ff.

[40] The standard view (of heavy Methodist sympathetic participation in working-class politics) is given in the many works by R. F. Wearmouth. For a "revisionist" outlook see K. S. Inglis, *Churches and the Working-Classes*; and for an earlier hint see H. M. Pelling, *Origins of the Labour Party, 1880-1900* (London, 1954), p. 132.

bour Church, of course, was not to be compared with other primitive sects, since it was an attempt to create a working-class religion founded on and expressing the brotherhood ideals and solidarity of the labor movement itself. Quite unlike Primitive Methodism or the Salvation Army (which only offered workers a vulgarized version of middle-class Protestantism embodied in a new institutional format), the Labour Church rejected the hidden attempts at bourgeoisi-fication so often found in other religious appeals to the working class.

The revival of the Christian social conscience

To the average Victorian priest or parson "the poor"— and even the mass of the working classes—were little less foreign than the Andaman Islanders. This was the ultimate moral failure of Victorian religion and the problem faced by the new generation of Christian reformers that arose in the 1880's and 1890's. Within their own churches many of their very leaders cared less about the material and spiritual welfare of the working classes than the workers were alleged to care about religion.[41] Alienation was a two-way relationship.

The great change of heart which came about in the last twenty years of the nineteenth century was produced by the work of a relatively small number of activists within the various denominations, and for many years the majority of priests, parsons, ministers, and lay preachers did not share it. The same was true of socialism in the society at large—a minority movement, emerging in the eighties and only gradually broadening into a more general welfare-state movement (akin to the Social Gospel) in the twentieth century. Obviously, the revival of the Christian social conscience was part of the general socialist and reform revival

41 Inglis, *Churches and the Working-Classes*, p. 21. Dr. Inglis also quotes (p. 14) from a Congregational statement of 1854, which chastizes the workers for neglecting religion and suggests that the poor would be more welcome in chapel if they washed more often (*British Quarterly Review*, XIX [1854], 444-450).

already described. It shared similar political and intellectual roots and was stimulated by the same crises and circumstances—such as the labor unrest of the eighties, the emergence of the "New Unionism" of the unskilled, with Annie Besant's London matchgirls' strike of 1888 and the great Dock Strike of 1889.[42] The Christian Socialist Society was founded in 1886, a year of crisis and street demonstrations, and the Christian Social Union in 1889, the year of the dockers' triumph.

But the Guild of St. Matthew was established in 1877, the *Christian Socialist* journal in 1883, the Labour Church in 1891, the Christian Socialist League in 1894, and so on, without any clear impetus from a strike situation or economic crisis, and even 1889 was the year not only of the dockers' revolt but also of the publication of *Lux Mundi* and *Fabian Essays*—a fruitful year for the creation of the Christian Social Union with its message of Christian Fabianism. The year 1906 was also a turning point in the history of Christian socialism, the chief single influence being political, a crucial general election.

In truth nothing less than the whole complex of urban problems can be taken as the specifically nonreligious source of the Christian socialist revival in Britain. A still broader interpretation of the movement sees Christian socialism as one phase of a recurring cyclical intervention by religion in politics, which rises and falls according to national economic prosperity, rising when the economy declines (allegedly in the 1840's and 1850's, the 1880's and 1890's, and the years between world wars), and falling when it recovers.[43] As for the industrial cities, the great forcing grounds of new social thought, their condition was a standing moral indictment of a Christian society. Into their

[42] The contrast, established by the Webbs, between the "Old" and the "New" Unionism has been questioned by recent work, as has the role of the Dock Strike of 1889 in transforming the unions. See A.E.P. Duffy, "New Unionism in Britain, 1889-1890: A Reappraisal," *Economic History Review*, 2nd Ser., XIV, No. 2 (December 1961), pp. 306-319.

[43] See, for instance, W. James, *The Christian in Politics* (London, 1962), pp. 108-109.

hearts crowded the poor and the submerged; out of their souls came the bitter cry which shook orthodox religion to its depths. In the eighties and nineties more and more church folk, aroused by the revelations of the city missions and settlement houses and by the countless governmental and private investigations, turned their attention to a study of this apparently irreducible problem.

The earliest and perhaps the most effective of all religious pamphlets attacking the slums was the Congregationalist tract with the stunning title *The Bitter Cry of Outcast London* (1883). We shall discuss this brilliant example of the literature of exposure in a later chapter. William Booth's plan for salvation, *In Darkest England— and the Way Out* (1890), was followed a few years later by Charles Booth's massive studies of the London poor, which were to become a quarry of information for many years for social reformers and students of all varieties. In the eighties the churches began to supplement published information of the above sort with a much closer and more intimate acquaintanceship with city life, gained from the new settlement houses and slum missions.

As early as the 1860's the social historian J. R. Green (1837-1883) had chosen to live for nine years in East London as the Vicar of Stepney, and though his plans (with Ruskin and Edward Denison) to build a settlement there came to nothing, one of his young associates, Edmund Hollond, founded in 1869 the Charity Organisation Society.[44] This society was heavily criticized in later years for dispensing a degrading form of charity rather than social justice; but it nevertheless provided a training ground for several

[44] D. O. Wagner, *The Church of England and Social Reform since 1854* (New York, 1930), p. 176. The Charity Organisation Society was much hated by men like Stewart Headlam and the group who managed the *Christian Socialist*. A favorable view is given in Helen Bosanquet's *Social Work in London, 1869-1912: A History of the Charity Organisation Society* (London, 1914). A balanced recent treatment is ch. VI of A. F. Young and E. T. Ashton, *British Social Work in the Nineteenth Century* (London, 1956).

brilliant young men from the universities—such as Charles Marson (GSM), Scott Holland (CSU), and Sidney Ball (Fabian Society). Arnold Toynbee himself visited the East End in 1879 under the Society's auspices. Toynbee's tragic death in 1883 precipitated the settlement movement: at a meeting held in the rooms of a future Primate (Cosmo Gordon Lang), participants, including Samuel Barnett, J. A. Spender, and F. S. Marvin, established Toynbee Hall. Barnett (1844-1913) became its first warden, and widened his group of associates to include men of the caliber of W. J. Ashley, James Bryce, Canon Fremantle, J. R. Seeley, and Alfred Marshall.[45]

Toynbee Hall was a resounding success, and other denominations and colleges followed suit, establishing settlement houses in the slums of most great cities. Oxford House was led for its first and most radical two years (1885-1887) by the Christian socialist novelist and agitator Father J. G. Adderley. Mansfield House was led for the Congregationalists by Percy Alden; Rev. F. H. Stead took over the Robert Browning Settlement at Walworth, which rapidly became a trade-union and labor headquarters. Whether or not the settlement movement was effective in spreading the gospel in the cities or in improving living conditions there, its impact on the younger clergy was enormous. To read about working-class life was one thing; to live it was another.[46] Many clergymen lived insulated lives and were apparently totally unaffected by great social changes. But in the industrial cities the younger activists rediscovered the social conscience of Christianity.

[45] Mrs. H. O. Barnett, *Life of Samuel Barnett* (London, 1914), II, 308ff.

[46] Almost without exception the clerical socialists received their indoctrination in the city. Rev. C. L. Marson, a mordant critic of capitalism, adored Soho and pined for the city streets: "How I love it—the smell of garlic and cooked stuffs, and petrol, and the rush of life; there is no place in the world like Soho!" (*Church Socialist*, III, No. 29 [May 1914], pp. 85-88).

Part Two

Sacramental Socialism

CHAPTER IV

The Oxford Movement and the Established Church

Theology of Christian socialism: an introduction

No DOUBT as a result of their real experience of city life, Christians, like agnostics, could become "socialists" for other than religious reasons. But such conversions would merely make them Christians who happened to be socialists, or socialists who happened to be Christians. True "Christian socialists" however, men and women who were socialists *because* they were Christians, developed in the last decades of the nineteenth century a series of purely religious grounds for their socialist beliefs. Naturally, they owed a debt to F. D. Maurice, though perhaps not as heavy a debt as one might have supposed. Also, they could not help but be influenced by nonreligious intellectual currents of the day: the historical school of economics, which obviously preferred the ethics of medievalism to those of industrialism; the philosophical idealism of T. H. Green, who, as we have already observed, tutored several leading CSU men;[1] the more general "consciousness of sin among men of intellect and property," of which Beatrice Webb has written;[2] and

---

[1] "It was Green who charged us with the ardour which made him always the active champion of the poor. . . ," wrote Scott Holland. Green and Toynbee together built at Oxford a "social philosophy to represent the Hegelian idea of the world as the manifestation of Divine Will." In place of Green's social-service state, the Christians could simply put the concept of a national church. See H. Scott Holland, *Bundle of Memories* (London, 19—?), pp. 89, 145; and A. V. Woodworth, *Christian Socialism in England* (London, 1903), pp. 92-93.

[2] Beatrice Webb, *My Apprenticeship* (London, 1926), pp. 179-180: "The origin of the [reform] ferment is to be discovered in a new consciousness of sin among men of intellect and men of property. . . . The consciousness of sin was a collective or class consciousness. . . ." See also Arnold Toynbee's poignant lecture on Henry George, given just before his own death, deeply confessing his middle-class guilt about the workers: "We—the middle classes I mean, not merely the very

ironically, even the positivist Comte's *religion of humanity,* to which the CSU's first president, Westcott, admitted his debt.[3]

Such nonreligious, intellectual stimuli were especially important for the brilliant young circle of Oxford and Cambridge men who organized and led the Christian Social Union in the 1890's. However, the ultimate ground for any genuine Christian socialism for the truly pious Christian had to be found in theology. If one is a socialist *because* one is a Christian, clearly there must be some theological foundation. Can we discern a general *theology* of Christian socialism that would apply to most, if not to all, denominations? After studying statements from all over the field of religion in the late nineteenth century, it seems safe to make the generalization that Christian socialists stood usually for one or more of the following theological arguments, or slight variations upon them:

1. *From patristics:* that many of the church fathers were socialists and communists.

2. *From the New Testament and the ethics of the Sermon on the Mount:* that Jesus Christ was a socialist.

3. *From the sacraments and the Book of Common Prayer:* that the modern church in its worship, symbol, and ritual exhibits a socialist faith.

4. *From the doctrine of Divine Immanence:* that God's presence everywhere, in nature and in man, destroys the artificial distinction between the "sacred" and the "secu-

---

rich—we have neglected you; instead of justice we have offered you charity, and instead of sympathy we have offered you hard and unreal advice. . . . You have to forgive us, for we have wronged you, we have sinned against you grievously—not knowingly always, but still we have sinned, and let us confess it; but if you will forgive us,—nay, whether you will forgive us or not—we will serve you, we will devote our lives to your service, and we cannot do more. . . . We are willing to give up the life we care for, the life with books and with those we love. We will do this and only ask you to remember one thing in return . . . if you get a better life, you will really lead a better life" ("Mr. George in England," lecture of 18 June 1883, London; quoted in B. Webb, *My Apprenticeship*, pp. 182-183) .

[3] B. F. Westcott, *Social Aspects of Christianity* (London, 1887), p. xii.

lar" worlds, sanctifies the material life, and supports the socialist call for a Kingdom of God *on earth.*

While the sacramental ground was most useful to Anglicans and the argument from Divine Immanence was chiefly adopted and developed by liberal Nonconformists,[4] no single theme became the intellectual property of any one denomination. "Immanentalism"—if one may coin this word for want of a better—was to be found in the thought of the Anglican Christian Social Union, and was not confined to the disciples of the renegade Congregationalist R. J. Campbell, although it was indeed the keystone of Campbell's "New Theology" movement of 1906-1907.[5] Similarly, the sacraments were rejected by very few Nonconformists; only the Quakers and the Salvation Army among the significant Protestant sects dispensed with them entirely. One can, therefore, find traces of "sacramental socialism" in Nonconformist thought. And the "historical" arguments from patristics never became the monopoly of High Churchmen and Roman Catholics alone, though of course such arguments were nearer to hand in those churches than in Dissenting chapels and meetinghouses. Rev. C. L. Marson and Rev. T. Hancock of the Guild of St. Matthew and Father Paul Bull, a monk of the Community of the Resurrection, were perhaps the principal writers to develop the historical argument to its fullest extent within the Church of England; but the new school of economic history provided ammunition for all reformers.

The one religious argument for socialism which united all radical Christians and cut across denominational lines was that from the New Testament. Within this argument all Christian socialists emphasized the *personality* of Jesus Christ. It was, after all, an age of great religious controversy.

---

[4] See, for instance, the socialist evangelist Rev. J. Stitt Wilson's article, "Social Evolution in the Light of the Divine Immanence," *Brotherhood*, xxist year, AU (Alpha Union) Ser., No. 4 (15 October 1907), pp. 147-152.

[5] Rev. J. R. Illingworth, one of the Christian Social Union leaders, host for many years to the "Holy Party," and *Lux Mundi* essayist, himself wrote an important treatise, *Divine Immanence*, in 1898.

Apart from Darwinian skepticism and the antireligious propaganda of the secularists, the very scholars of the Faith seemed to cast doubt on the validity of the miracles, to question the historical record afforded by scripture, and to reveal inconsistencies and inadequacies in the Gospels. The natural reply of Christian men to this flood of "higher criticism" was to base their faith not on documentation and Holy Writ, but upon the unmistakable message and example of the personal character of Jesus. Again, as with the sacraments and patristics, this was an easier excuse for Roman and Anglo-Catholics—since they never had based their Christianity on the Bible alone—than for Protestants. Nevertheless, belief in the personality of the incarnate Christ throughout his short life and the glorious nature of his death for mankind is to be discovered at the core of *all* Christian socialist thought. In Christian socialist doctrine the Incarnation and the Crucifixion bind God to man and men to each other through Jesus Christ: "Fatherhood of God, Brotherhood of Man." In this respect Christian socialism was a "Christ-centered" faith.

The proof of these general statements about Christian socialist theology will be seen throughout this book as we go deeper into the history of this complex movement. Theological problems will be analyzed as they come up with each particular group in turn. Ultimately, a clear distinction between the "theology" and the "social philosophy" of Christian socialism cannot be profitably maintained.

Sacramental socialism and the Oxford Movement

The type of Christian socialism that we may call "sacramental" was represented by three societies between the 1880's and the First World War: the Guild of St. Matthew, the Christian Social Union, and the Church Socialist League. Each of these groups had distinctive characteristics. Headlam's Guild largely embodied the idiosyncrasies of its founder, a Single-Taxer, London County Councillor, self-appointed spokesman for secular education, anti-Puritan, and balletomane. The Christian Social Union reflected exactly the scholarly, deprecatory, disarmingly unpious but not unself-satisfied character of its upper-class members, Gore, Scott Holland, Westcott, and their friends of the clerical, public school, and Oxford elite. The latter-day radicalism of the Church Socialist League captured the spirit of the North of England, in revolt at last against the intellectual dominance of the Home Counties and London, genuinely more at one with the labor movement and the working class than any of its predecessors.

On the other hand, despite these differences, the same personnel may be found in two—sometimes, as in the case of that unregenerate aristocratic radical, Rev. Conrad Noel, in all three—of the groups. Noel's milder friend Rev. Percy Dearmer served in both GSM and CSU; Revs. G. Algernon West, W. E. Moll, C. L. Marson, and P.E.T. Widdrington, in the GSM and the League; Rev. F. L. Donaldson, leader of the Leicester unemployed, in all three societies.[6] The bohemianism of the Guild, the academicism of the Union, the radical idealism of the League, seemed occasionally even to express different *phases* in the lives of the same men. But through all their thoughts ran the connecting link of Maurician theology and the zeal of the Oxford Movement.

Sacramental socialism in general was "staffed" by young High Churchmen. Its roots thus go back beyond Maurice to the original Oxford Movement. It is true that the Christian Social Union included some older men who, like Bishop Westcott, would have more readily described themselves as Broad Churchmen and would certainly have dissociated themselves from the activities of the ritualists in the 1870's and 1880's. But even these men were deeply imbued with

[6] Conrad Noel, *An Autobiography* (London, 1945), pp. viii-ix and passim, and *Church Socialist*, I, No. 2 (February 1912), pp. 3-5. Also see Nan Dearmer, *Life of Percy Dearmer* (London, 1940), passim; *Church Socialist Quarterly*, IV, No. 3 (July 1909), pp. 187-188, and *Reformers' Yearbook* (formerly *Labour Annual*), 1909, p. 152 (for W. E. Moll); *Labour Annual*, 1895, p. 179, and *Church Socialist*, III, No. 29 (May 1914), pp. 85-88 (for C. L. Marson); *Church Socialist*, I, No. 3 (March 1912), pp. 3-5 (for F. L. Donaldson); and M. B. Reckitt, *P.E.T. Widdrington, A Study in Vocation and Versatility* (London, 1961), pp. 4, 34, 44. (Details on these men follow later.)

the spirit and fervor of the Oxford revival and with its crusade to revitalize the Church of England.

The first phase of the Oxford Movement (1833-1845), led by its three Oriel Fellows, Keble, Newman, and Pusey, was chiefly theological and liturgical. It was in the second phase, especially in the 1870's and 1880's, that the social aspects of the revival became fully developed. "Tractarianism" (as the movement was known in its early stages) was a positive reaction against an alleged decline of church life and the spread of "liberalism" in theology; and its proponents dreamed of restoring the High Church ideals of the seventeenth century. Undoubtedly, the romantic movement in literature and the new interest in things medieval helped to stimulate the revival,[7] as did fear that the Catholic Emancipation Act of 1829 would encourage many Anglicans to enter the Roman fold. The Tractarians regarded the Protestant Reformation as a calamity, and linked to it the rise of *laissez-faire* utilitarianism, a connection which the new school of economic history would make in greater detail before long. On the other hand, they did not favor Rome, despite the fact that Newman, Faber, and other illustrious members did finally join that church. Their *Tracts for the Times* were intended to defend the historic Church of England against "Popery and Dissent," and Newman's Tract No. 1 (1833) was a defense of the true apostolic succession of the Anglican Church against the claims of the aberrant Rome.

J. H. Newman (1801-1890) viewed the Church of England at this time as a great Via Media or middle way between Nonconformity and popery. His Tract No. 90, *Remarks on a Certain Passage in the Thirty-Nine Articles* (1841), however, caused such a great crisis that no further tracts were issued at all, and only four years later, after great spiritual conflict, Newman was accepted into the Roman Church, becoming a cardinal in 1879. J. Keble (1792-1866), whose

7 "The Oxford Movement began as a chapel in the great unfinished cathedral of the Romantic Revival" (L. E. Elliott-Binns, *Religion in the Victorian Era* [London, 1946], p. 226).

sermon of 14 July 1833 at Oxford on "National Apostasy" (about an alleged plan to suppress ten Irish bishoprics) is taken as the opening date of the Oxford Movement, proved more stable in his defense of the Church of England as a divine institution. His colleague, E. B. Pusey (1800-1882), remained a staunch Anglican and a staunch believer at the same time in the Real Presence (of the Body and Blood of Christ at the Sacrament of the Lord's Supper) —a model for later Anglo-Catholics.

The Book of Common Prayer may contain, as Stewart Headlam or Father Paul Bull would maintain, a social policy for Britain, but the Oxford Movement did not go much beyond defending the Book itself as a rule of faith for the Church of England. Indeed, there was in Tractarianism no *necessary* social message, except insofar as its adherents revivified medieval organicism in their reclamation of the corporate life of the Church, an exalted ideal of the priesthood, and a genuine religious faith for weekdays as well as Sundays. Newman was aristocratic and antiliberal, Keble an unbending High Tory who "never appreciated the this-worldly meaning of the Faith." Of the trio, Pusey alone showed any concern for social reform. What Pusey achieved was to establish some of the first ritualist slum parishes, such as St. Saviour's, Leeds, in the 1840's. "We need missionaries among the poor of our towns; organized bodies of clergy living among them," he wrote, "licensed preachers in the streets and lanes of our cities; brotherhoods or guilds, which should replace socialism. . . ." Church industrial missionaries should "grapple with our manufacturing system as the Apostles did with the slave-system of the ancient world."[8] In practice the social work of the original Oxford Movement went no further than the encouragement of settlement houses.[9]

---

[8] E. Pusey, *The Councils of the Church* (1957), quoted by Ruth Kenyon in N. P. Williams and C. Harris, *Northern Catholicism* (London, 1933), pp. 384-385, 391.

[9] W. G. Peck, a Christian socialist of the 1920's, fails to make a real case for an implicit social reform message in Tractarianism in his *Social Implications of the Oxford Movement* (London and New York, 1933).

F. D. Maurice, who was enthusiastic about Tractarianism at its inception but later broke with Pusey over the doctrine of baptism,[10] acknowledged nevertheless his debt to the Tractarians for "the great principle of a *social faith, the principle that we exist in a permanent communion which was not created by human hands and cannot be destroyed by them*" (italics mine). A later and much more radical Christian socialist, Conrad Noel, claimed that Tractarian theology laid "the foundations of Catholicism in religion and Socialism in practice" because it stood for "the outward and visible Church and the ministry of men, the Incarnation of God and the Communion of the Saints, sensuous worship and the need of man's forgiveness."[11] If the social message of the earlier Oxford Movement was minimal, its theology was obviously crucial to the development of sacramental socialism.

The central doctrine of sacramental socialists of the eighties was a reemphasis or rediscovery of the Incarnation —Christ's whole life on earth as a man—and its significance for all men. In the words of a later Anglo-Catholic, "the essential truth about mankind is that it is the family and mystical Body of God. The Church is the Sacrament of that universal and essential fact—its outward sign and witness." Or as Charles Booth summarized the High Church position as he found it in 1902: "Christ the Son of God—Himself being God, having died on the Cross . . . made provision of the means of grace for all mankind through His Church and its Sacraments, . . . to reject these means is to reject Salvation." According to Aquinas, a sacrament is "the sign of a sacred thing, insofar as it sanctifies men" (*signum rei*

---

[10] Maurice was the Tractarian nominee for an academic post in political economy, which he accepted in 1836 (F. Maurice, *Life of F. D. Maurice*, I, 213ff.). He thought Pusey conceived of God only in transcendental, supernatural terms, and that his doctrine of baptism denied the immanental God-in-nature. Pusey's God was too remote for Maurice's taste and purpose (Williams and Harris, p. 391).

[11] F. D. Maurice, *On The Right and Wrong Methods of Supporting Protestantism* (London, 1843), p. 10; also quoted in K. S. Inglis, *Churches and the Working-Classes*, pp. 263-264; Conrad Noel, *Socialism in Church History* (London, 1910), pp. 253-254.

sacrae in quantum est sanctificans homines), and according to the Anglican Book of Common Prayer, it is "an outward and visible sign of an inward and spiritual grace." In the two sacraments which the Anglican catechism alone recognizes as "generally necessary to salvation" and ordained by Christ himself, the "outward and visible signs" are water (Baptism) and bread and wine (the Eucharist or Lord's Supper), while the "inward and spiritual graces" relating to them are "a death unto sin and a rebirth unto righteousness" and "the Body and Blood of Christ, which are verily and indeed taken and received by the faithful in the Lord's Supper."[12]

The sacraments are thus "an ever-fresh offering and acceptance of the Body and Blood of Christ on the altar of God."[13] They continually reaffirm the worth of every man to God in a *communal* act of worship:

> . . . the declared Real Presence of the Eternal Christ beneath the bread and wine of the Mass is the focused manifestation of the essential fact that "in Him all things consist". . . . So will (like the bread and wine) the whole world and its products manifest Him in whom they consist *when they are used and shared by all mankind in the Holy Communion for which the race is created.*[14]

So it appeared to an ardent ritualist and economic socialist of the Catholic Crusade in the 1920's. As "ordinances mediated throughout the Church" the sacraments have an essentially social structure; they express also the objectivity of God's action on the human soul (for "the reception of God's gifts is normally dependent not on changing subjec-

---

[12] D. D. Egbert and S. Persons, *Socialism in American Life* (Princeton, 1952), I, 226-227; G. C. Binyon, *The Christian Socialist Movement in England* (London, 1931), pp. 202-203 (quotation from R. Woodfield); Charles Booth, *Life and Labour*, 3rd Ser., Vol. 16, pp. 49-50; *Book of Common Prayer*, 19: "The Catechism." The Council of Trent, the Roman Church's 19th ecumenical council (1545-1563), had claimed that *seven* sacraments were ordained by Christ: Baptism, Confirmation, the Eucharist, Presence, Extreme Unction, Order, and Matrimony.

[13] Charles Booth, *loc.cit.*

[14] G. C. Binyon, *loc.cit.* (italics mine).

tive feelings but on obedience to the Divine Will"); and they continually exhibit the principle of Christ's Incarnation. In sum, the sacraments, since they form "the means whereby the union of God and Man consequent on the Incarnation is perpetuated in Christ's mystical Body of His Church,"[15] symbolize God's Fatherhood and man's brotherhood and unity. How far the Church of England as an institution perpetuated "the union of God and Man" in practice, and symbolized man's brotherhood and unity, is another matter.

A troubled Establishment

Tom Mann, the ardent strike leader and SDF member (who ended up in the British Communist Party after the First World War), had once considered taking Anglican orders. "What attracted me to the Established Church," he explained, "was the fact that it was about the most perfectly organized body in this country. I love organization. I thought that instead of attacking the Church from outside, it might be possible to direct it from within."[16] But from the inside the late-Victorian Church did not appear so "perfectly organized." In truth, the Establishment was deeply troubled, and, in the light of the statistical evidence we have already examined, its anxiety was fully justified.

The troubles of the Established Church arose directly out of the fact of its establishment. On the one hand, it was losing relative strength to the Nonconformists, and on the other, its close identification through its establishment with the "ruling-classes" ruined its image with the very people it was losing—the urban masses. Moreover, the "organization" admired by Tom Mann was top-heavy, inflexible, and unwieldy. How could it compete successfully with the direct tactics of the Salvation Army, for instance, or the self-governing congregations of the urban sects? The training in public speaking and social organization that so many Brit-

15 *Oxford Dictionary of the Christian Church* (London, 1962), p. 1198.
16 *Memoirs* (London, 1923), pp. 119-120.

ish trade unionists and socialists acquired in Methodist halls and chapels could never have been received within the walls of an Anglican church. It would have taken a deep revolution, an uprooting of the Established Church's whole social structure for a manual worker to become a parson. Indeed, no genuine attempt of any sort was made to provide facilities to train working boys for the Anglican ministry until Gore's Community of the Resurrection created its college in Yorkshire. The Church of England was ineradicably associated in the public mind, and to a large extent in practice, with the Tory squire and the urban moneyed elite. If any one institution helped to perpetuate residual feudalism in British social life, that institution was the Anglican Establishment.

The Church suffered from structural defects. Its parish system, modeled on a preindustrial social structure, was fitted to the needs of small, rural, socially homogeneous communities and was incapable of coping with the dense urban populations of the late nineteenth century, crowded into class-segregated ghettoes in which "those who made jam" had virtually no social contact with "those who ate jam." Fearful of becoming indistinguishable from congregational churches, and anxious to maintain the fiction of being a "national church," Anglicans refused to consider radical rethinking of the parish structure.[17] Instead, they tried to patch it up, to make do by splitting some large parishes, by "experimenting" with interparish organizations and diocesan conferences (to bring rich and poor parishes into cooperation and to plan evangelism at the bishopric level), and by appointing special missionary clergymen for problem areas. Too often the missioners hated and resented their job or, if they were popular (like Father Robert Dolling in Portsmouth, a ritualist and political radical),[18] found themselves hamstrung through lack of adequate funds (having no regular parish), discouraged by old-fashioned superiors, and even dismissed for unorthodoxy. Meanwhile, clergy

---

[17] See Inglis, *Churches and the Working-Classes*, pp. 23ff.
[18] See R. Dolling, *Ten Years in a Portsmouth Slum* (London, 1896).

were increasingly hard to recruit; their numbers did not expand in ratio with population growth, and, in fact, the number of ordinations began an *absolute* decline in the 1890's. Salaries for junior clergy were low, structural changes in the economy were creating a bigger demand for professional services of all kinds (e.g., accounting, teaching, managing) , and the established sources of recruitment for parsons were not widened. The English Church Union (dominated by the High Church element) established the Church of England Working Men's Society in 1876 to recruit lay evangelists and help the Church with its enormous staffing problem; also the Church Army was created by Rev. Wilson Carlile in 1882 to meet the competition in industrial areas of the (Nonconformist) Salvation Army (William Booth, 1878) . But the impact of Anglican efforts was muted. The Church of England mastered the art of doing too little too late. Pew rents, for example, were not finally abolished until the twentieth century.[19]

In the competitive struggle for adherents, whatever special advantages the Church derived from its establishment seemed to be dissipated. Nonconformist ministers, for example, could theoretically afford to take less of a chance in the pulpit as far as radical or unorthodox opinions were concerned (Christian socialism, perhaps) because they were ultimately under the legal thumb of the chapel trustees, whereas the beneficed Anglican parson was free from such localized pressures. In practice, however, over half of all Anglican livings in England were controlled by *individual* patrons, and, as we shall see, the hierarchy was not slow to "purge" political or theological heresy in the late nineteenth century. The Fabian socialist Stewart Headlam was constantly being dismissed and never rose above the status of curate; he finally gave up all hope of ever being beneficed and was able to hold services only when friendly clergy invited him. Headlam's case was unusual, perhaps, and more than his socialism was involved in it; the hierarchy

[19] Inglis, *Churches and the Working-Classes*, p. 55.

did become more enlightened in later years, particularly after the influence of the Christian Social Union began to be felt.

The contrast between the high spiritual hopes and ideals of the Oxford revival and the sterner realities of the problems and frailties of the Church of England as an institution needs no further emphasis. Karl Marx derided the Establishment in 1855 as the "twin sister" of the "English oligarchy," and dismissed the Church's "countless attempts at reorganization."[20] The criticism was only too just. Thirty-five years later Sidney Webb had much the same judgment to make: "The prevailing evil of the English Church is the aristocratic taint of the majority of its beneficed clergy. As Ruskin put it, they dine with the rich and preach to the poor. Until they are more willing to dine with the poor and preach to the rich, its popular influence will be limited." Still, Webb could say that the Established Church was "obviously a Socialist institution *in form*"[21]—part of the idea, perhaps, that Tom Mann also tried to express.

For the activist minority of sacramental socialists this idea was something on which to build a new Church of England. Where the Oxford revival of the 1870's had hit the headlines only with the persecution of certain luckless ritualist priests, the movement of the eighties and nineties took on much greater social significance. The sacramental socialists offered more far-reaching solutions to the Church's predicament than their Tractarian predecessors could ever have imagined. Some of them even went so far as to suggest disestablishment as the only hope for a true rebirth of Anglicanism. Above all, with their socialist proposals for society at large, they struggled to reintegrate the spiritual experiences of the Church's sacraments, especially the Eucharist, with the daily economic life of the people. It was therefore

[20] See his article on the demonstrations in Hyde Park (*Neue Oder-Zeitung*, 28 June 1855) in Marx and Engels, *On Religion* (New York, 1964), pp. 127-134.

[21] *Socialism in England* (London, 1890), p. 69.

doubly ironical that in order to achieve this reintegration many of them felt the necessity to exclude the unbaptized from the ranks of their own Christian socialist organizations. This was the ultimate ambiguity of the alliance between the Oxford Movement and socialism.

CHAPTER V

Stewart Headlam and the Guild of St. Matthew, 1877-1909

THE ORGANIZATION that Rev. Stewart Headlam created and dominated was never very large. Enrollment in the Guild of St. Matthew never rose beyond about four hundred, and in its peak years of growth, 1894 and 1895, Anglican parsons made up almost 25 percent of the membership. It was a tiny, clerical-minded, and exclusive pressure group. And despite its in-group consciousness and exclusive character, the Guild was torn apart by dissensions; not even the authority of Headlam could keep it together. Yet the GSM was the pioneer Christian socialist society of the revival period in Britain, and performed the essential ground-breaking tasks which made it possible for larger and more effective organizations, such as the Christian Social Union, to follow.

The man and his circle

"Religion was alive again," wrote Bernard Shaw of the early 1890's, "coming back upon men, even upon clergymen, with such power that not the Church of England itself could keep it out."[1] No more ardent exponent of this new religious spirit could be found than Stewart Duckworth Headlam, Shaw's close colleague for years on the Fabian socialist executive. And "the Church of England itself" could not silence him, though it often tried.

Headlam was a stubbornly independent man, an eccentric even, but of great moral courage and tenacity. He was always an outsider. As a boy he broke with the opinions of his family. Within his chosen church (to which he remained devoted all his life) he became an implacable rebel and openly spurned his bishop. He rejected "Protestantism," and plumped for an uncompromising form of Anglo-

[1] *Plays Pleasant*, Penguin ed. (London, 1946), Preface.

99

Catholic ritualism—though in outside life, when leading socialist marches of the unemployed, for instance, he was equally uncompromising in refusing to wear priestly garb. Constantly in trouble with the Anglican authorities over his "High Churchliness," he never considered leaving that faith for Rome, and he firmly repudiated papal authority. In an age of gentility and convention, Headlam campaigned on behalf of chorus girls, the popular theater, freedom of opinion for atheists, and drink. He stood staunchly for anti-Sabbatarianism, anti-Puritanism, antitemperance, and gaily went to the local pub for a drink with his pupil-teacher disciples. His fight for secular education deeply upset some of his own clerical supporters, and his bohemianism irritated many of his severe Fabian socialist colleagues (not Shaw, of course). Scarcely having met the man, Headlam went bail for Oscar Wilde when all of self-righteous middle-class England was against him; and as London County Councillor, he fought the London County Council.

Headlam was born on 12 January 1847 at Wavertree, near Liverpool, and lived to the age of seventy-seven. His father and grandfather were both underwriters in the city of Liverpool, and fortunately—since he could never keep a job—Headlam had private means.[2] Home life was hectic. His parents were devout and fiercely disputatious, his father evangelical and his uncle an ex-High Church curate. Stewart reacted violently against his father's "Bible religion," condemnation of the theater and cards, and strict Sabbatarianism. Eton, which he attended between 1860 and 1865, proved to be a "liberating influence" for the boy, and he remained all his life an enthusiastic Old Etonian.[3] Though the school was all sport in those days, Headlam's housemaster was the Rev. J. L. Joynes, father of the socialist James Leigh Joynes, who had traveled with Henry George

[2] He left £3,743 on his death in 1924, despite the huge expenses of a long life in radical movements with little or no income. See F. G. Bettany, *Stewart Headlam*, p. 243.

[3] *Ibid.*, pp. 1-12. At Cambridge, however, Headlam had to drop his Eton friends because he could not afford to hunt with them, and they never visited him later in his slum parish of Bethnal Green (Bettany, p. 14).

in Ireland and with whom Stewart became deeply involved in the Single Tax organizations of the 1880's. A greater influence still was his tutor, William Johnson, Fellow of King's, Cambridge, and a friend of F. D. Maurice and Charles Kingsley. Johnson (who also taught the young Henry Scott Holland during these years), naturally led Headlam to Maurice. The boy went to Cambridge in 1865, had his fear of hell-fire removed by Maurice, as we have seen, and received a very low Third in 1868.

After a year of baiting a luckless evangelical parson to whom his father had sent him in order to eradicate the influence of Maurice, Stewart moved to the Temple in London and under the tutelage of Dean Vaughan made parish visits in the working-class Strand area. It was Headlam's first taste of cockney life, and from that time forward he devoted himself to the service of the common people of London. For three years from the autumn of 1870 Headlam was curate of St. John's, Drury Lane, and lived in humble rooms over a stationer's shop in Broad Court among his poor parishioners. He began a heavy program of parish visiting, refused to limit his ministrations to Anglican churchgoers, and gave straight-from-the-shoulder Maurician sermons on the eternal life, which upset the conventional Victorian views of some parishioners, who still believed or hoped that 50 percent would go to Hell and 50 percent to Heaven. One particularly nervous local schoolmistress wrote to the new curate: "It is nowhere stated that all men shall be saved. Neither is it anywhere said that the punishment of the wicked shall not be everlasting."[4]

Clearly, Headlam was not destined to last at Drury Lane; but it was here that he met a sturdy old aristocratic Christian socialist, Rev. Thomas Wodehouse, a "real saint," whose well-known little book *The Grammar of Socialism* influenced Headlam's evolving radical thought.[5] Wode-

[4] *Ibid.*, pp. 22-26, 32; also see *Crockford's Clerical Directory*, 1886, p. 542.

[5] The first edition that I have so far been able to trace, however, seems to date from 1878—five years *after* Headlam left Drury Lane. The GSM published a second edition in 1884.

house, a Balliol graduate of 1840, was curate and subsequently chaplain of the Savoy from 1864 to his retirement in 1890. His *Grammar* was a catechism of thirty-eight questions and answers with notes, a forceful identification of socialist principles with Christian teaching. "If Christians would only act up to the ideas embodied in this little *Grammar*," wrote one critic, "all the attacks upon Christianity by its enemies would at once be deprived of their *raison d'être*."[6] Wodehouse's message was simple: "Sirs, ye are brethren; why do ye wrong one to another?" Full of the Wodehouse spirit, Headlam took up at Drury Lane his controversial defense of the popular theater, especially the ballet, by forming the Church and Stage Guild (May 1879).[7] The Anglican authorities were outraged at the thought of a "dancing priest," and a daring lecture given by Headlam on "Theatres and Music-Halls" cost him his second job. He had already lost the first after his sermons came into the hands of an anxious bishop.[8]

While the Church and Stage Guild was socially disturbing and a genuinely democratic challenge to middle-class cant and snobbery, Headlam's second guild, the GSM, went still further by advocating radical economic reform. The Guild of St. Matthew was founded on St. Peter's Day, 1877 as a parish organization. Gradually, closely following its warden's personal evolution, the GSM became increasingly economic and radical in its demands. Visiting the poor, examining schools, heckling at secularist meetings, taking slum children swimming, addressing crowds of workers, Headlam soon gained immense knowledge of urban social conditions. From Bethnal Green, the slum he dearly loved, Headlam wrote to a friend in horror: "For making 12 dozen doll's frocks a woman gets 4d., working hard and

---

[6] *Crockford's Clerical Directory*, 1886, p. 1311, and 1894, p. 1472; *Christian Socialist*, II, No. 16 (September 1884), p. 52.

[7] The history of this organization can be traced through the annual reports in the *Church Reformer*, 1885-1895. The Church and Stage Guild faded after about 1900.

[8] The sparse details of Headlam's clerical career are to be found in *Crockford's Clerical Directory*, 1886, p. 542.

with the help of her little girl, she can earn about 8d. a day. . . ."[9] Such conditions needed explaining.

To the early influence of Thomas Wodehouse was now added that of the American Henry George. We have seen that *Progress and Poverty* was published in England in 1880 and that George became a personal friend of Headlam's during the six hectic visits to Britain in the 1880's. Headlam remained faithful to George's Single Tax on land values; it remained his main economic goal at all times.[10] Yet he allowed himself a wide margin of politically useful ambiguity, since most of his socialist colleagues had passed beyond the Single Tax and on to other things. Stewart Headlam became a leading member of the Georgeist Land Reform Union at its inception in 1883, but was also a leading Fabian socialist for thirty-eight years (from December 1886 until his death). He served on the Committee of Fifteen which drew up the "Basis" of the Fabian Society in 1887, wrote an important Fabian Tract, served on the Fabian executive in 1890-1891 and for the ten years from 1901 to 1911, and frequently presided and lectured at Fabian debates. Moreover, he had even for a time in 1884 expressed interest in Hyndman's Democratic Federation.[11] Perhaps in later years Headlam tended to vote Liberal and identify with that party (he was inimical to the Independent Labour Party), but during the 1880's, on the admission of Sidney Webb himself, Headlam was on the "left wing" of the Fabian Society.[12]

A further influence in Headlam's radicalism came from a group of three young curates, George Sarson, John Elliotson Symes, and Thomas Hancock. Headlam's life in the tiny Drury Lane parish had been lonely; at Bethnal Green

[9] Bettany, p. 84.

[10] Jones, Manchester thesis, pp. 86ff.; Bettany, pp. 233-234; E. R. Pease, *History of the Fabian Society* (London, 1916), pp. 75-76, 251.

[11] *Justice*, 19 January 1884; H. M. Hyndman, *Further Reminiscences* (London, 1912), p. 212.

[12] E.g., Bettany, p. 136. Webb said of Headlam: "It was his persistence . . . that secured . . . the declarations that were afterwards considered most extreme [in the Basis]."

he branched out and joined the new Junior Clergy Society (established in December 1873), a young group which often met in the vestry of St. Martin-in-the-Fields, and of which the radical three were all active members. Hancock said to Headlam at their opening session at King's College, "We'll take our places on the extreme left!"[13] George Sarson, perhaps Headlam's most intimate personal friend, graduated from Cambridge a year after he did, with a similar lack of brilliance, and was ordained at about the same time (1873). Sarson was a Maurician and a sacramentalist, a church reformer who demanded the election of priests by parishioners. The abolition of patronage, he declared, would produce not only a better clergy but better laymen: "We talk glibly of the Established Church. The beneficed clergy and patrons are very strongly established. The church itself has yet to be established."[14] With Headlam he wrote a paper to startle the Church Congress of 1877 on "The Church's Mission to the Upper Classes" and later produced his own *The Holy Eucharist and Common Life* (London, 1884) on the social significance of the Lord's Supper. George Sarson knew Henry George well, and was an ardent Single-Taxer;[15] but his work in the London slums was cut short by ill health, and he was forced to take up a country benefice. Dover, however, felt the impact of his radical sacramentalism, and he maintained a long and important correspond-

---

[13] *Ibid.*, p. 38.

[14] *Crockford's Clerical Directory*, 1886, p. 1043. Sarson was curate of Holy Trinity, Westminster, 1871-1874, and of St. Martin-in-the-Fields, 1874-1878; Rector of Orlestone, Kent, 1878-1885 and finally Vicar of Holy Trinity, Dover, from 1886 until his death in 1902. See *Church Reformer*, v, No. 8 (August 1886), pp. 180-183 for his radical paper on church appointments, presented at the Canterbury Diocesan Conference of July 1886.

[15] *Church Reformer*, III, No. 8 (15 August 1886), p. 192; and G. C. Binyon, *The Christian Socialist Movement in England*, p. 113. Sarson reviewed *Progress and Poverty* in the *Modern Review* (January 1883), after discussing fine points with George directly, and he published a review pamphlet on the book for the Land Reform Union. See Sarson to George, 16 September 1882, Henry George Collection (henceforward cited as HGC), New York Public Library; *Christian Socialist*, No. 4 (September 1883), p. 55; and H. George, Jr., *Life of Henry George* (New York, 1900), p. 404.

ence with Headlam, used by the latter's unscientific biographer and unfortunately now lost.[16] In the view of his old friend, who outlived him by twenty-two years, Sarson was "a loyal churchman of no party who saw the good and evil in all parties, a faithful parish priest, a fine friend in times of need and a candid critic"—an opinion which smacks more of loyalty than candor, for the man was obviously a devoted High Church protagonist, and split with Headlam himself over the educational policy of the GSM in 1891, siding with Symes and Shuttleworth in a move which threatened the very existence of the Guild.[17]

Sarson's brother-in-law, the economist Rev. John Elliotson Symes, made more of a mark in the world, ending up as Principal of University College, Nottingham. The two men were very different in type. Educated, like Headlam and Sarson, at Cambridge, Symes graduated more brilliantly than either of them (1871), being President of the Union.

[16] Research in Dover reveals that Sarson's church was destroyed by German bombing in World War II. Through the kind help of Rev. E. Roberts of St. Mary's, Dover (with which the old parish is now amalgamated), we have a good picture of what Holy Trinity, Dover, was like when a sacramental socialist took over a formerly evangelical parish in the mid-1880's: "Till 1885 in Holy Trinity there had been no surplice choir, a plain communion table, no cross or candles, Holy Communion had only been celebrated about twice a month. . . . But in 1885 came a vicar with an outlook no doubt then considered new and possibly dangerous . . . the Rev. G. Sarson. For 17 years he laboured, facing inevitably much opposition, to deepen the devotion of his people and train them to a more sacramental view. . . . All the changes mentioned above were gradually introduced in his time. . . . The young were carefully trained and communicant guilds set up. . . . He took a prominent stand too, in social questions, earning thereby the enmity of some. It may have been for this, or for his church politics, that his effigy in canonicles was once carried round and burned and thrown in the sea" (*Holy Trinity Centenary Book*). I would also like to thank Mr. Bernard Corrall, Borough Librarian of Dover.

[17] Sarson and Headlam did not always see eye to eye on the *Church Reformer*'s policy either, and when Sarson unguardedly dismissed some of Headlam's associates as "ungentlemanly" he was not allowed to forget it—"I have a good many ungentlemanly meetings on during the next 10 days," wrote Headlam on a postcard, and later, "You see, our Lord and Isaiah were so ungentlemanly that I prefer to be so also." See Bettany, pp. 89, 117; for Headlam's later uncritical eulogy of Sarson see Binyon, p. 113.

When Headlam was at Bethnal Green and Sarson at St. Martin's, Symes served as curate at St. Phillip's, Stepney. Like his brother-in-law he soon left London (1880) and entered academic life in the North of England. Symes was a member of the GSM and the Church and Stage Guild, as was his wife, Sarson's sister (they were married by Headlam), but he was much more of a moderate than his companions. Even theologically Symes was Broad Church rather than High Church and more concerned with the higher criticism and with developing a rationally acceptable Anglican faith than with ritual or the sacraments. Economically, Symes defended the principle of private property in capital, and was prepared to attack monopoly only in land. He was a Henry Georgeist who simply never got beyond the stage of land-value taxation. Having met George in 1882, Symes subsequently joined the Land Reform Union and was elected to its General Committee.[18] He heard in advance of George's second visit to Britain, and wrote in 1883 inviting him to speak at Nottingham: "Things have been moving since then [1882]. Your book more than any other has made the cry of the poor heard. The more strictly economic parts have made hundreds of converts and yet have not made anything like the mark they should with scientific economists or with amateurs."[19]

To remedy this failing, Symes's own economics textbook when it appeared was heavily loaded in favor of the Single Tax. In January 1884 he spoke at a Georgeist "clerical conference" at the Charing Cross Hotel (with Headlam in the chair), warning "socialists who speak as if capital was of no assistance to labour" that they would end up by "driving capital abroad." The *Christian Socialist* vigorously repudiated this standard conservative argument as an "old bugbear,"[20] and four years later Headlam found it necessary to

18 Symes was, in fact, a founder-member of the Georgeist Land Reform Union and had seceded from A. R. Wallace's Land Nationalization Society. See *Christian Socialist*, No. 5 (October 1883), p. 72, and Jones, Manchester thesis, pp. 21 and 120.

19 Symes to George, 22 November 1883, HGC.

20 By 1890 Symes's text was in its third edition, and a year later he

censure his former ally for publishing an "obselete" economics textbook "on the old pre-Ruskinian lines, . . . which
ignores the existence of 'illth' side by side with wealth."
Symes's *Political Economy,* he said with disgust, "is hardly
worthy of the clergyman who so boldly advocated socialism
by taxation some years ago in London. . . . We shall be
glad to see what our scientific socialist friends have to say
. . . especially on Mr. Symes's extraordinary admiration for
employers." This particular criticism is curious, coming
from an ardent Georgeist like Headlam, and perfectly illustrates the basic ambiguity of Headlam's position in the
Single Tax movement; his own interests were much wider
than any single tax or measure. Most amusing, he said, was
Symes's "useful admission" that "the idle rich and the idle
poor, clergymen, schoolmasters, actors, musicians, thieves,
domestic servants, and others have to live on what the directly productive classes produce."[21] Not surprisingly, J. E.
Symes retired from the Council of the GSM in the year of
Headlam's review.[22]

The third young curate of the Junior Clergy Society, Rev.
Thomas Hancock, was of much greater and more lasting significance for the Anglican socialist movement. In fact, his
theological work surpassed by far that of Headlam. Hancock died in 1903, a year after George Sarson's death. This
very brilliant man was educated at Merchant Taylor's

---

became Principal of Nottingham. His book *Newcastle Sermons* was published in 1883 (*Crockford's Clerical Directory,* 1886, p. 1147, and 1894,
p. 1290). There is surprisingly very little material on Symes at the
University of Nottingham. For the review of his textbook see *Christian
Socialist,* No. 9 (February 1884), p. 131.

21 *Church Reformer,* VII, No. 6 (June 1888), pp. 131-132; for a
favorable review see *Christian Socialist,* VIII, No. 71 (April 1889), pp.
60-61. Because Symes (like Henry George) defended capital, Bernard
Shaw once called him to his face "*a chaplain on a pirate ship*" (Bettany,
p. 54).

22 He continued to argue with socialists about the taxation of capital
—for instance with Sidney Webb in 1889. See *Church Reformer,* VIII,
No. 2 (February 1889), pp. 40 and 46; and VIII, No. 3 (March 1889), pp.
60-61. His *Companion to a School History of England* (London, 1889)
received sarcastic treatment in Headlam's *Church Reformer,* VIII, No.
12 (December 1889), pp. 280-281, as "an entirely 'safe' book."

School but never attended college.[23] He won an essay prize judged by F. D. Maurice, and on Maurice's direct recommendation, he was ordained in 1863. Systematically and cruelly overlooked by the church authorities all his life, Hancock lived from hand to mouth for years until H. C. Shuttleworth became rector of St. Nicholas Cole Abbey in the City (London's business section) and immediately made him a lecturer there (1884-1903).[24] He had been virtually unemployed for ten years. No one could argue that the Victorian Church of England was a "meritocracy"; Hancock was one of its most unusual and learned sons. He was, said Headlam, "a teacher of teachers": "If every preacher in London could have been compelled to hold his tongue and come and learn from Hancock, say once a month, it would have been well for them and for the church. . . . The Bishops—what might they not have done!"[25]

Thomas Hancock was a brilliant, complex writer and a church historian and theologian of the first rank. His greatest delight was to show historically that Archbishop Laud was a democrat who had resisted enclosures, and that famous Anglican clerics of that day—Hooper, Latimer, Bancroft, Adams—had attacked "landlordism and robbery."[26] Immensely prolific (he wrote over seventy pieces for the *Church Reformer* alone and reviewed for the *Church Quarterly*, the *Saturday Review*, and other journals), Hancock was most devastating when he directed his brilliance against capitalist society. His social sermons, among them "The Social Carcase and the Antisocial Vultures" (on the labor dis-

[23] Hancock's father and uncles were successful businessmen and tried to force him into commerce. He was apprenticed at the Gutta-Percha Works, and then to a woodcarver, subsequently migrating to a sculptor's studio, where he fell in with the Rossetti circle. He attended the Workingmen's College, came under Maurice's spell, and gave himself a rigorous course of reading in the British Museum (*Commonwealth*, VIII, No. 11 [November 1903], pp. 338-340).

[24] Hancock had held various curacies in England from 1861 to 1875, and had been a chaplain in Germany in 1875 and in 1880 (*Crockford's Clerical Directory*, 1886, p. 514, and 1894, p. 578).

[25] *Commonwealth, loc.cit.*

[26] S. C. Carpenter, *Church and People, 1789-1889*, 3 vols. (London, 1959), II, 327-328.

tress of 1886), "The Magnificat as the Hymn of the Universal Social Revolution," "Jesus Christ, the Supreme Ritualist," and "The Banner of Christ in the Hands of Socialists," might be delivered to tiny audiences at Cole Abbey, but reprinted in papers like the *Church Reformer* or *Commonwealth*, and gathered together in volumes for general publication, they achieved a wider notice. Hancock was in truth *the* theologian of Anglo-Catholic socialism.[27]

Because the Church of England faced so many problems as an institution, Headlam and Sarson favored its total disestablishment, and many Christian socialists supported their position. Only disestablishment, they argued, could democratize the Church, destroy patronage, give the lay body genuine rights and responsibilities, and free the clergy from arbitrary episcopal power. Hancock did not agree. He was "a stout Church and State man."[28] That is why his colleague Rev. J. G. Adderley called Hancock, despite his "radical" language, a conservative. Like Maurice, Hancock thought there was no need to reconstruct society; we are already within God's order. All we need is to realize the one society that really exists, inwardly and outwardly, having faith in God, the Church and its sacraments, and in the inevitable vindication of democracy as the principle which underlies the Gospel of Christ.[29]

Hancock was an uncompromising High Churchman who never lost an opportunity to excoriate the Nonconformists and what he called their "Capitalist-Liberationist Press." "They know at heart," he wrote, "that the Church [of England] is much more liberal, radical and socialist than any of the sects is capable of becoming. Their anxiety now is

[27] Binyon, pp. 113-115; Bettany, pp. 115-116; *Church Reformer*, v, No. 2 (March 1886), and IX, No. 2 (February 1890), pp. 31-33; T. Hancock, *Christ and the People* (London, 1875) and *The Pulpit and the Press* (London, 1884).

[28] "No law which the State could pass," said Headlam, "would more tend to bring about a better social state, than the disestablishment of the present beneficed clergy, patrons and bishops, and the self-establishment of the Church, strong, democratic and free" (Binyon, p. 143; Bettany, p. 115).

[29] *Commonwealth*, VIII, No. 11 (November 1903), p. 331.

that this truth should not be discovered by the new voters."[30] A Nonconformist summer conference in 1885 debated the question of disestablishment, and Hancock fumed:

> Imagine a rich man like Mr. Spurgeon [Baptist leader] daring to call himself "poor" in contrast with "the State-paid clergy." . . . There are "Established" priests working for the objects of the GSM who get exactly nothing a year from the Church for their services to the Church and Nation. There are many priests who would gladly work for sums which Mr. Spurgeon's pew-openers may get.

As for the "unblushing," rich Congregationalists with their astonishing claim "that Independency aims at procuring 'the world for the many,' " their whole history belies any pretensions to such democracy: "Their writings everywhere charge the Catholic, Historic, National Church with being too wide, too broad, too liberal, too humane. . . . They first separated from the Church in every parish on the very ground that the parish church . . . was not sufficiently exclusive and narrow." Congregationalist notions of "the elect," said Hancock, are "aristocratic, Calvinist, antinational and antihuman," and assume that "humanity as an entirety is damned and reprobate." Methodists, too, were only "a little less illiberal"; but at least in Methodist doctrine people could be "converted" and so could enter the ranks of the "saved." (Every man was capable of "conversion.") Worst of all, the sects were decaying in any case, being consumed at both ends by reversions to the Church of England (!) and lapses into Unitarianism or skepticism. Nonconformity was *propped up by Capitalism.*[31]

[30] *Church Reformer*, IV, No. 6 (15 June 1885), pp. 125-126.

[31] Hancock was harsher still with the Salvation Army. "The unthinking madness and fashion of the world or age, which some days ago followed Mr. Barnum, yesterday followed Mr. Stanley, today follows Mr. Booth. One day we run to Olympia to see the biggest show ever puffed together; another day we hope that a new continent is opened for our Babylonish competition and robbery; another we are fascinated by a huge scheme for feeding and employing the victims whom our Babylonish competition and robbery have driven to starvation, forced

Hancock was a "left-wing" Christian socialist. He regarded the more moderate and respectable Christian Social Union with some contempt. Its Object No. 2 was, he complained, an "enfeebled" version of the GSM's third Object, an "exceeding watery paraphrase" because it replaced the clear phrase "the Incarnation" with the word "Christianity."[32] The Incarnation, said Hancock, symbolizes clearly "the universal relation of man *as man* to God." It was dangerous for the CSU to replace "Incarnation" with the word "Christianity," which could open the floodgates to "superior-caste" Christianity (Unitarianism), "elect- or self-separating-caste" Christianity (Puritanism), "converted-caste" Christianity (Methodism), or "illuminated-caste" Christianity (mysticism). In contrast, use of the word "Incarnation" asserts "the direct relationship of the vulgar, everyday carpenter, fisherman, publican, . . . tailor and docker to God in Christ Jesus."

At Cole Abbey, Hancock preached that the *pulpit* was the only hope for social salvation because the "free Press" was controlled by the forces of Mammon and dare not handle explosive economic and social material honestly. It was the duty of priests to preach *socialism*.[33] An apocalyptic note entered his famous sermon on "The Social Carcase": "Unless England repents and rises out of her moral and social death, the Son of Man must appear and let loose 'the vultures' by whose dreadful ministry He will destroy the carcase of a corrupt and putrid civilisation."[34] Struck by the use of *religious* banners by the workers in the socialist parades of 1886, Hancock predicted a great "invasion of the

---

idleness, prostitution and vagabondage." The Salvation Army offered the rich charity *by proxy* for the relief of guilt. "It is a separatist, not a common army . . . the latest English evolution of the Moravian Methodist conception that the life of religion begins in an emotion towards God, and is marked by the instantaneous flight from the terror of Hell to the assurance of Heaven." For all of the above quotations from Hancock, see *Church Reformer*, IX, No. 21 (December 1889), pp. 278-281.

[32] *Church Reformer*, VIII, No. 12 (December 1889), pp. 273-274.

[33] *Church Reformer*, III, No. 8 (15 August 1884), pp. 174-176.

[34] Binyon, pp. 131-132.

churches by the poor socialists"—the exact opposite of the hope and demand of the German-American anarchist Johann Most for a mass *exodus* of the working classes from the Church.

Yet for all his fire, brilliance, and learning, how *right* was Hancock? His extreme denominationalism, which was indeed the source of his own radicalism, blinded him to many social realities. The Church of England—as revealed by all the historical evidence we have reviewed—was in decline; and the Nonconformist bodies were, in fact, slowly adopting a social gospel despite Hancock's heavy sarcasm. Thomas Hancock's personal tragedy was that, even within the very narrow circle of his own Anglo-Catholic friends, few could understand his complex sermons.[35]

The three angry young curates, Sarson, Symes, and Hancock, together with Stewart Headlam, began in the late seventies a concerted program: agitation at Church Congresses, heckling visits to secularist meetings, and public demonstrations in favor of Christian social action, church reform, the Single Tax, the unemployed, trade unions, and the "Continental" Sunday, and in opposition to slums, poverty, illiteracy, secularism, Puritanism, bishops, snobbery, and cant. At Croydon in 1877 they were content to distribute pamphlets. Three years later at the Leicester Church Congress they were emboldened openly to debate "Existing Forms of Unbelief" and to admit personal acquaintance with the secularist leaders Charles Bradlaugh and Annie Besant. "It is because the Christian church has not got itself recognized as a society for the promotion of righteousness in this world," Headlam told the Congress, "that the secular society is so strong." He was tired of the Church's bleating about empty churches while it closed its eyes to social evils. Rashly he went on to address the astonished members on "Church Patronage and the Position and Claims of Curates," and demanded an *elected* Diocesan Council for each bishopric, to select all candidates for clerical posts. He must have enjoyed announcing:

[35] See Headlam's evidence in *Commonwealth*, VIII, No. 11 (November 1903), pp. 338-340.

At present the Bishop, by a stroke of his pen, without giving any reason, may deprive a curate of his position in the Church and it may be, all his means of getting his bread and butter. . . . It is monstrous that we should be in the absolute arbitrary power of a few Bishops. . . . It is absurd to say Convocation is the voice of the Church, it is hardly the squeak of the Church.

Perhaps the whole thing was, as Symes suggested, "half a mission, half a lark," but the group rounded off their Leicester propaganda by standing in the doorways and handing out to all the delegates who passed by leaflets on Poverty, the Moral Dangers of Workshop Life, Preferment, and the need to have trade-union leaders at Church Congresses. At the Reading Congress of 1883 Headlam gave a rabidly anti-Sabbatarian speech aimed at the evangelicals and set up a Guild of St. Matthew bookstall, run by his able lieutenant, Frederick Verinder, to sell George's *Progress and Poverty*.[36]

Headlam's Guild: the Single Tax and socialism

Meanwhile the Guild of St. Matthew had moved toward economic reform. Organized in 1877 by the parishioners of St. Matthew's, Bethnal Green, as an expression of regard for their popular curate, its original aim was to fight Bradlaugh and secularism and to interest people in the sacraments. With Headlam's (fortunate) dismissal from Bethnal Green in 1878, the Guild soon lost its purely local character and became a nationally organized propagandist society. The Guild declared itself—in that year of socialist declarations, 1884—for Headlam's "Priest's Political Programme," and adopted the resolution:

Whereas the present contrast between the great body of the workers who produce much and consume little, and of those classes which produce little and consume much is contrary to the Christian doctrines of brotherhood and justice, this meeting urges on all Churchmen *the duty of supporting such measures as will tend—*

[36] Bettany, pp. 84-87.

   (a) to restore to the people the value which they give to the land;

   (b) to bring about a better distribution of the wealth created by labour;

   (c) to give the whole body of the people a voice in their own government;

   (d) to abolish false standards of worth and dignity.[37]

Plank (a) represented the Georgeist basis which remained the keystone of GSM policy throughout its existence—land-value taxation; (b) and (c) were standard socialist-radical demands of the day; (d) has never yet been successfully accomplished in Britain (one could argue this), and many of the Christian socialists of the eighties and nineties—who were Republicans—would blame this failure (the persistence of "class" snobberies and deference) on the surviving institutions of "residual feudalism," i.e., the aristocracy, the monarchy, the debutante season, the House of Lords, the Establishment of the Church of England, and all that these imply. Plank (d) was unusual for a British socialist platform; Keir Hardie would have appreciated its significance perhaps more than the middle-class Fabians did. Its adoption by Headlam was ambiguous. He lectured the Fabians on the dangers of bureaucratic elitism,[38] and claimed to be a democrat first and a collectivist second. But he never went enough beyond Henry George to embrace Guild Socialism, and he was condescending to the working-class ILP.

The GSM possessed three "Objects" and three "Rules." The Objects, as they finally took shape, were:

   1. To get rid, by every possible means, of the existing prejudices, especially on the part of secularists, against the Church, her Sacraments and doctrines, and to endeavour to justify God to the people.

---

[37] *Church Reformer*, III, No. 10 (October 1884) (italics mine). The resolution was adopted at an open-air meeting in Trafalgar Square. See also Binyon, p. 143.

[38] Most of all, said Sidney Webb, Headlam distrusted "the Puritanism of the Progressive Party in the L.C.C. [London County Council], which he detected or suspected in many socialists and other reformers" (Bettany, p. 138).

2. To promote frequent and reverent worship in the Holy Communion and a better observance of the teaching of the Church of England, as set forth in the Book of Common Prayer.

3. To promote the study of social and political questions in the light of the Incarnation.

The first Object, in Headlam's own words, deliberately "borrows a phrase of Kingsley's ['to justify God to the people'] and sums up what was to be our work." The last six words of Object 3, "in the light of the Incarnation," formed "the *raison d'être* of all our Christian socialism."[39] To carry out the Objects, the Rules committed members: first, to propagandize Object 1 both collectively and by personal influence; second, to communicate with each other on all great festivals and to celebrate Holy Communion regularly on Sundays and Saints' Days; and third, to meet annually in united worship and for business on the Feast of St. Matthew (21 September).[40]

Down to 1884 a good deal of the energy of Guild members such as Sarson, Symes, Hancock, and Headlam, as we have seen, was expended in fighting *secularism,* not capitalism or landlordism. The annual meeting of September 1883 was chiefly concerned with the exclusion of the freethinker Charles Bradlaugh from the House of Commons for refusal to take the required oath. Headlam, Rev. C. E. Escreet, and other GSM members fought *against* Bradlaugh's exclusion and demanded the right of simple affirmation for nonbelievers. These High Church radicals fought against the legal persecution of secularists by the government. The Guild wanted to give atheism a free hand and to fight it fairly and squarely on religious grounds by open, public debate—an idea which shocked many timid church folk.[41]

The year 1884 brought a change to a more radical eco-

[39] Binyon, pp. 119f.; A. V. Woodworth, *Christian Socialism*, pp. 104-105; Bettany, pp. 79-81.
[40] Bettany, p. 80; Woodworth, *loc.cit.* The reports of these annual September meetings (published in Headlam's *Church Reformer* and elsewhere) are a good general guide to the history of the GSM.
[41] *Christian Socialist*, No. 5 (October 1883), p. 67.

nomic and political outlook. In Newcastle a budding GSM branch died out because its local warden accused Headlam of stirring up class violence in a speech he gave there on "The Sins That Cause Poverty."[42] But a new branch was organized at Oxford the following year by F. L. Donaldson of Merton, a future leader in all three Anglican Socialist organizations, the GSM, the CSU, and the Church Socialist League. In April 1884 at a farewell banquet for Henry George, Headlam declared private property in land to be in ethical opposition both to the Ten Commandments and to the teaching and life of Jesus Christ. Also in October the Guild held the open-air demonstration in Trafalgar Square at which Headlam's resolution was affirmed. The warden himself said in later life that 1884 was the high-water mark of Guild history.[43] The GSM had distinguished itself, so Headlam firmly believed, from the mild cooperative reformism of the Mauricians of the 1850's. He boasted:

> While showing all respect for cooperative shirtmakers and cooperative decorators, and for the many little communistic societies of monks and nuns, and for all other little private experiments, we at the same time call upon churchmen to take a wider view, and advocate and support such legislation as will help to remedy private evils.[44]

The legislation he actually proposed, however, went little further than Henry Georgeism. To the Single Tax demand

[42] Bettany, pp. 82-83. Headlam at this time did not hesitate (in his own peculiar way) to criticize the workers. "Every one of you who takes more beer than he needs is guilty of a sin," he preached, "because he is wasting a good thing—wasting good liquor!" This was too much for the local clergy, and the Bishop of Newcastle sent for Headlam in London (at the Athenaeum!) to reprimand him for his antiteetotalism. The same lecture was also given to the Batterson Liberal Association in 1884. Headlam condemned class distinction as the prime curse of England (*Christian Socialist*, No. 10 [March 1884], p. 149).

[43] London *Times* (7 April 1884), p. 6; Bettany, *loc.cit.* It is hard, in face of the evidence, to agree with Headlam's judgment; the peak of Guild activity was reached in the later 1880's and 1890's. Perhaps Headlam was sensitive to the opposition to his leadership *within* the Guild, which became evident after 1884.

[44] Bettany, pp. 143-144.

for "land restoration" (which was not even land nationalization, as we have seen, but the confiscatory taxation of the increment of land values), Headlam added the progressive income tax, and a vague plea for the eradication of "wage-slavery" which did not specify the method to be used. On the other hand, we must remember that at this time (1884) "socialism," even of the Fabian variety, was not sharply defined, and that for some years London Fabians (especially Headlam himself) were closely allied with London Liberals as a matter of deliberate Fabian policy and shared Liberal-Radical aims for the future of London government itself. Moreover, the Guild distinguished itself from the Mauricians in its educational work and in its much more sweeping proposals for church reform. Quite naturally Guild members were deeply involved with the problems faced by the Establishment. Thirty years after Maurice, Kingsley, and Ludlow, they could no longer afford the somewhat pious attitude toward the Church that their predecessors had adopted; the situation had deteriorated still further. The three major issues to be associated with the GSM were thus the reform and extension of public secular education, church reform, and the Single Tax.

Two prototypes: Shuttleworth and Moll

The impact of the Guild of St. Matthew on Anglicans, Nonconformists, socialists, labor leaders, and British public opinion in general is not to be measured mainly by its campaign on these three issues. The Guild's membership included many talented men with varying ideas and policies, and within its confines was to be found a fairly wide range of Christian and socialist opinion. (The political spread was wider, given the Anglican emphasis of the Guild's Christianity.) Some of the future founders of Guild Socialism, for instance, were trained in Headlam's group. In large part the Guild of St. Matthew owed such public recognition as its work achieved to the unusual personalities of certain members. The theologian Thomas Hancock was outstanding in the dissident trio already described; Symes and Sarson remain essentially minor figures in Christian socialist history. Of greater interest and importance were H. C. Shuttleworth and W. E. Moll; each in some ways typified a different kind of GSM adherent.

Rev. Henry Carey Shuttleworth (1850-1900) vies with Stewart Headlam as the model for Bernard Shaw's Christian socialist character, Morell, in *Candida*.[45] He was the ideal type, the perfect exemplar, of the jolly, back-slapping, high-living, broad-minded, liberal athletic Anglican parson so often caricatured in fiction and film, of which Charles Kingsley was the early mode. Perhaps he sometimes forgot, as Headlam suggested caustically, that "the priest's main work is to say the Mass and not to shake hands."[46] He came of a North of England family, but was born in Cornwall (where his father was a local vicar) and was something of a professional "Cornishman." Shuttleworth was not especially gifted academically; he got a Second in Theology at Oxford in 1873. Yet he was a considerable musician, not perhaps as talented as his distinguished musical and Christian socialist colleague Percy Dearmer; but he wrote with some authority on liturgical music and was an active member of Headlam's Church and Stage Guild. (His wife was treasurer and a member of Headlam's famous deputation to the Bishop of London in 1887 on behalf of chorus girls.) Shuttleworth's career was a smooth success; he had already been a minor canon at St. Paul's Cathedral for four years (since the age of twenty-six) when he joined the Guild of St. Matthew in 1880. At St. Paul's he managed to scandalize the orthodox with his genial, relaxed sacramental radicalism. "If insurrection should break out in England," screamed an evangelical organ, "it will be due, and largely indeed, to the clerical and other firebrands, Mr. Shuttleworth and his

45 In G. Bernard Shaw, *Plays Pleasant*. See M. B. Reckitt, *Maurice to Temple*, p. 123.

46 *Commonwealth*, VIII, No. 6 (June 1903), pp. 165-167. Shuttleworth was "the first to combine chasubles before the Altar with flannels before the stumps." See G.W.E. Russell, *H. C. Shuttleworth: A Memoir* (London, 1903), pp. 1-19; *Labour Annual*, 1895, p. 186; *Crockford's Clerical Directory*, 1886, p. 1075; and Reckitt, *Maurice to Temple*, p. 122.

friends, who are seeking to propagate what they call Christian Socialism."[47] The orthodox evangelicals were baffled by this "alliance utterly inexplicable between the Ritualists and the Revolutionaries."[48]

Shuttleworth was no revolutionary, though he must have seemed a firebrand to his superiors in the church and to many of his parishioners. He led a charmed life, though it was short; he died at fifty. Shuttleworth's secret weapon was *popularity*. He was one of the church's most successful preachers, a "big draw." Anyone who met him, liked him— or almost anyone, for this can be in itself an irritating characteristic.

In 1883, at a period when other bright young radicals and High Churchmen were being deliberately overlooked or sent into the rural depths of the country, Shuttleworth was made Rector of St. Nicholas Cole Abbey in the heart of the City. (Perhaps, for once, dissidence paid: it has been suggested that the promotion to Cole Abbey was a "kick upstairs" to get the young rebel out of the hair of the Dean and Chapter of St. Paul's; they controlled the living.) The overnight result was that Cole Abbey became a "useful centre of socialist lectures" and propaganda, and the fiery Thomas Hancock was immediately given a job as Lecturer. Shuttleworth turned "a museum-piece of 17th Century architecture" into a "packed and pulsating church." A unique club, with a *bar,* let men and women mix on an equal footing and discuss whatever they wished: a great liberty, no doubt.[49]

Dame Fortune smiled a second time on young Shuttleworth in 1883; he was appointed Lecturer in Pastoral and Liturgical Theology at F. D. Maurice's old college, King's, London (and seven years later he took the Chair).[50] Shuttle-

[47] It is inaccurate to call Shuttleworth, as Binyon (p. 150) does, "a red hot Ritualist." His theological and social views were milder than Headlam's, and the latter despaired of his friend's growing "conservatism" in older life. Furthermore, Shuttleworth was not a strict ritualist.

[48] Russell, *Shuttleworth*, pp. 19-20; Reckitt, *Maurice to Temple*, p. 123; *Labour Annual*, 1895, *loc.cit.*

[49] *Church Reformer*, IX, No. 9 (September 1890), p. 213.

[50] *Loc.cit.*

worth's influence was therefore very much wider than that of most GSM members. He spoke at many Church Congresses, published Congress papers, created the Oxford branch of the GSM in 1885 (with his former choirboy, the leader of the Leicester march of the unemployed, F. L. Donaldson), and lectured heavily for the Guild; he was also a prolific and successful writer.[51]

George Bernard Shaw's Morell in *Candida* bears more resemblance to Shuttleworth than to Stewart Headlam. "Reverend James Mavor Morell" is also terribly charming and popular, a little too good to be true (or too good for his own good), artistic and vain ("a great baby") . . . and Shaw pits against him (as a possible rival for his wife's affections) the self-seeking poet Eugene Marchbanks, in Shaw's own words "a dramatic antagonist for the clear, bold, sure, sensible, benevolent, salutarily short-sighted Christian Socialist idealism" of Morell.[52] In one of his brilliant and characteristically detailed stage directions Shaw sets the Headlam-Shuttleworth scene: "An adept eye can measure the parson's casuistry and divinity by Maurice's *Theological Essays* and a complete set of Browning's poems, and the reformer's politics by a yellow-backed *Progress and Poverty, Fabian Essays, A Dream of John Ball,* Marx's *Capital. . . .*" On stage Morell "glances through Mr. Stewart Headlam's leader and the Guild of St. Matthew news" in the *Church Reformer* between planning talks to anarchists and countless other self-imposed social duties. The characterization in *Candida* is so shrewd, it seems superfluous to attempt a portrait of the Shuttleworth type here.

As a Christian socialist Shuttleworth was milder but more tolerant than Hancock. He encouraged the largely Nonconformist Christian Socialist Society (as did his GSM colleague C. L. Marson), and was himself a member of the Christian

---

[51] Among Shuttleworth's works were: *Last Words of the Saviour* (3rd ed., 1879) ; *St. Barnabas Stories* (4th ed., 1880) ; *The Church and Popular Amusements* (1880); *Sunday Observance* (1884); *The English Church and the New Democracy* (1885); *Songs* (1885); and *The Place of Music in Public Worship* (1892).

[52] Shaw's Preface to *Plays Pleasant.*

Socialist League established by the Baptist Fabian John Clifford in 1894. Like Stewart Headlam, he refused to make personal enemies out of nonreligious or antireligious leaders, and enjoyed, among others, the friendship of Annie Besant.[53] He was also popular among trade-union men, and encouraging to John Trevor's non-Christian Labour Church movement.[54] Like most of his comembers, Shuttleworth was an admirer of Henry George and was elected to the Committee of the English Land Restoration League (ELRL) in May 1884, with Headlam and W. E. Moll, when that society was formed out of the previous Land Reform Union.[55] He knew George personally, but did not limit his own political aims to the Single Tax. No one scheme, he felt, could save England. The problem with Booth's Salvation Army, for example, was the impermanency of its soup-and-shelter proposals. Socialists, in contrast, as Shuttleworth told his students, attacked the real *causes* of poverty. History revealed that emotional revivalist waves were always followed by troughs of materialism; press adulation of William Booth was a useful antisocialist dodge.[56]

[53] *Christian Socialist*, v, No. 45 (February 1887), p. 29; *Labour Annual*, 1895, p. 111; *Church Reformer*, v, No. 8 (August 1886), p. 175. Shuttleworth had to defend the Anglican Church against Annie Besant's attacks by *admitting* that it had been served by unworthy men and "exploited by unscrupulous and powerful persons for their own ends."

[54] Trevor approached his invited lecture to Shuttleworth's High Church curate's club with some suspicion, but was rapidly charmed by his host and touched by the experience (*Labour Prophet*, vi, No. 78 [June 1898], p. 187). A secularist worker said: "Such men as Mr. Shuttleworth blunt the swords of our scabbards"—which was, of course, the intention and the *raison d'être* of the GSM (Binyon, p. 151).

[55] *Christian Socialist*, ii, No. 13 (June 1884), p. 13.

[56] Address to King's College Union, 16 December 1890. The chairman (Dean T. Collings, GSM) called Shuttleworth "the most popular young men's parson in London, a good radical, a better Socialist, and the best guide, philosopher and friend of every King's [College] man" (*Church Reformer*, ix, No. 12 [December 1890], p. 286). Shuttleworth lectured on Christian socialism to many groups, including the conservative English Church Union and the radical Junior Clergy Society. See *Christian Socialist*, No. 1 (June 1883), p. 3, and No. 6 (November 1883), p. 81.

So Shuttleworth spread himself widely—and perhaps eventually too thinly—becoming among other things president of the anti-Sabbatarian National Sunday League, which fought for "the opening of museums, art galleries and libraries on Sundays; maintaining the 'Sunday Evenings for the People,' and Sunday Excursions, Sunday bands in the parks and [the general promotion of] intellectual and elevating recreation on that day." He "shepherded the young men of the shops and warehouses around St. Paul's Cathedral and preached against social apathy, sweating and slum ownership," exuding Maurician confidence, enormous faith in the future, and conviction society would improve. "Poverty," he said, "is not a mysterious dispensation of Providence, which for some inscrutable reason, is the stern lot of the majority of our race; but an evil, brought about by causes which can be remedied."[57]

Shuttleworth's popularity and charm wore thin for Stewart Headlam. The two men clashed more than once in the Guild's history. Headlam said he preferred the younger Shuttleworth, the radical minor canon, to the successful professor and rector, surrounded by his worshiping disciples; but his "earlier and more valuable work" did exhibit "two great qualities of courage and chivalry."[58] Headlam was a touchy leader and got on best with minor characters, like Rev. Thomas Hill, for example, a straightforward and loyal Single Taxer who as late as 1905 was still agitating for the unadulterated taxation of land values and writing pamphlets for the Georgeist-Headlamite English Land Restoration League.[59]

With another major figure in the Guild of St. Matthew, W. E. Moll, Headlam remained friendly all his life; but the two men were geographically separated for much of the

[57] *Church Reformer*, III, No. 8 (15 August 1884), p. 192 (advertisement); S. C. Carpenter, *Church and People*, II, 327; A. Reid (ed.), *Vox Clamantium: The Voice of the People* (London, 1894), p. 39.

[58] *Commonwealth*, VIII, No. 6 (June 1903), pp. 165-167.

[59] Hill was a GSM executive member in 1884 and Vicar of North Somercotes, Lincs. from 1894. See *Commonwealth*, X, No. 7 (July 1905), pp. 215-216. Also see Hill's book *The Church, Capital, Labour and Land* (Louth, 1908).

time. Rev. W. E. Moll (?1857-1932) was, like Shuttleworth, an ideal type of one sort of sacramental socialist, but it was a very different type. Moll was no charmer, no habitué of cultured metropolitan circles, no fashionable professor adored by his students. He was an Independent Labour Party stalwart, a tough champion of Tyneside labor organizers in the 1890's, and quite naturally he became a leading light of the North of England dissident High Church group, the militant Church Socialist League of the later 1900's. Moll was a close friend of Stewart Headlam's from 1879 until the latter's death in 1924: an acquaintanceship of forty-five years' duration. He came to Christian socialism through Henry George, served as a committee member of the ELRL, and joined the GSM immediately upon graduating from Oxford in 1878. Moll worked as a socialist curate in various parts of London from 1879 to 1893, especially in Soho, where his most important social work was begun. There he trained C. L. Marson, and gave the "unchurched" Stewart Headlam a chance to hold Masses. But Moll passed beyond the Single Tax stage of reform thinking and left the Guild of St. Matthew behind. Quite unlike Headlam, a middle-class elitist who scorned the idea of working-class MP's, Moll went heart and soul for the Independent Labour Party after 1893. Perhaps the Moll-Headlam friendship was a sympathy of unlikes, and the Shuttleworth-Headlam disagreement an antipathy of likes. At any rate, Moll, having come to Soho in a crucial year, 1884, left it for the North of England in another important year, 1893, when the ILP was first created at Bradford; and from then on he is identified with Northern radicalism, trade unionism, and a deeper socialism than the GSM embodied. He remained a High Church sacramentalist.

Moll joined the National Administrative Council of the ILP, and though an ardent Christian socialist, he turned down the post of chairman of the Church Socialist League to devote himself more fully to Labour affairs.[60] At St. Phil-

[60] *Reformers' Yearbook*, 1909, p. 152; *Church Socialist Quarterly*, iv, No. 3 (July 1909), pp. 187-188; *Christian Socialist*, ii, No. 13 (June

lip's, Newcastle-on-Tyne, Moll employed as curates the brothers-in-law Rev. P.E.T. Widdrington and Rev. Paul Stacy, and also Rev. Conrad Noel. Marson, Widdrington, Stacy, and Noel make up a formidable list of Christian socialist curates for one priest to have trained, as we shall see. Marson became the *méchant garçon* of the Guild of St. Matthew, and the other three helped to lead the Christian socialist revival through its Guild Socialist-dominated phase of the 1900's. All four were opinionated, assertive, and ebullient young men. It is no wonder that at least two of them ended up at odds with their incumbent, and Headlam's personal intervention was called for.

W. E. Moll's political and theological position can be readily inferred from the jobs he chose and the men he employed. He was a sacramental socialist of the sturdier sort —less cranky than some, more practical and down to earth about the realities of poverty, unemployment, and working-class alienation. "As a Catholic, I boldly avow myself a Christian socialist," he announced to the English Church Union in 1885:

> As a Catholic I believe that the Church is the Body of Christ, filled with His Spirit, bound to do the works which He did on earth. . . . As a Catholic I believe that the Church is the Kingdom of Heaven on earth—an organised society for the promotion of righteousness and freedom and truth among nations.[61]

His labors among the Tyneside workers in support of their strikes and union activities arose directly from his sacramental faith: "In politics, so far from having nothing to do with them, it always has been and always must be the mission of the Church to realise the unity of mankind revealed by the Incarnation." The "great enigma of our times," said Moll, quoting Henry George, was *"the association of poverty*

1884), p. 13; *Crockford's Clerical Directory*, 1886, p. 825, and 1894, p. 926.
[61] *Church Reformer*, IV, No. 6 (15 June 1885), pp. 121-122.

with progress." He claimed to "look back upon almost 14 years' daily life with the very poor,"[62] and asked, "Are men to look in vain to the Church of Christ for guidance as they set themselves the solution of this problem?" For Moll it was *blasphemous* to blame "the Divine Will" for human poverty and to rip from its context the statement "The poor ye always have with ye" as an argument for economic and political stagnation. "Surely the poverty is bad enough: but to fix it upon the Father of us all is possible only to men whose god is gold." The true cause of human poverty, he said, was economic maldistribution and "wage-slavery" (the favorite phrase of the later Guild Socialists). "There can be no remedy while a political economy prevails which teaches Christian men to say that there are those for whom God has placed no plate at the banquet of life."

Moll agreed with Headlam and others that the only hope for the Anglican church was disestablishment. The only hope for society at large was socialism—the socialism of the sacraments:

> I take it that as Catholics we really believe in the Sacraments. What is the message of Baptism to you and me as we face this great social problem? Is it not that all the baptized are equally children of God? . . . that the sacred society of the Church is a Brotherhood?

Why need Christians be suspicious of politics? Echoing the idealist philosopher T. H. Green, Moll defended the positive state: "We Christian socialists, *regarding the State as a sacred organism,* feel it our duty to get such laws made as will help the workers to get a fair share." The Church has failed the people. In Ireland ("the Established Church there never took the side of the people"), in Scotland (the helpless and ignored crofters), and among the English trade unionists, what has the Church ever done? Nothing much. The "gospel of tea meetings and mission halls," the gospel of "a

[62] It is difficult to place these "14 years" before 1885 on the available evidence, since Moll was still a student in the late 1870's, and two of his only curacies (Clapham and Regent Street) were in well-to-do areas of London.

beautiful Heaven hereafter and a dreary Hell here," what use were these? The workers demanded a new gospel—"a gospel that is honest work for all and honest pay."[63] We can see that long before he went North to live with the Newcastle workers, Moll was already leaning toward the labor movement; he was an egalitarian socialist rather than a "middle-class" socialist.

Moll and Shuttleworth were two usefully contrasting types of Anglican socialists in the Guild of St. Matthew. Other members, of later significance in socialist history, included Conrad Noel, F. L. Donaldson, P.E.T. Widdrington, G. A. West, C. L. Marson, N. E. Egerton Swann, and Percy Dearmer. All but Dearmer (Christian Social Union) were active members of the Church Socialist League after 1906 and will be discussed later. Marson was also conspicuous as editor of the *Christian Socialist,* as we have seen, and played a large role in the growing opposition to Headlam inside the GSM.

Early activities of the Guild

Throughout 1884 the GSM, inspired by its new radical policy statement, spread the gospel of sacramental socialism and the Single Tax in places as far apart as Folkestone, Liverpool, London, Preston, Northampton, Plymouth, Wellingborough, and Oldham.[64] The year 1885 opened with another open-air demonstration—of the unemployed—held outside the Royal Exchange in January.[65]

In May the Oxford branch was founded with Shuttleworth as president and John Carter as secretary.[66] Carter afterward became chief organizer of the Oxford Christian Social Union and go-between of its American branch. An at-

[63] *Church Reformer,* IV, No. 6 (15 June 1885), pp. 122-125. In the opinion of Rev. G. A. West (Church Socialist League), "No parson in England has done as much for the cause of socialism as the Rev. W. E. Moll" (*Church Socialist Quarterly,* IV, No. 3 [July 1909], p. 187).

[64] Jones, Manchester thesis, p. 238.

[65] *Justice,* 24 January 1885, pp. 1, 6.

[66] Not in 1884 as Bettany suggests, p. 83. See *Church Reformer,* IV, No. 6 (15 June 1885), p. 139.

tempt was made to establish an American GSM too, through the American Churchmen's Society; but it came to nothing.[67] Unlike the later and more successful CSU, the Guild's executive was wary of extending too many branches—perhaps, as internal critics suggested, because Headlam was jealous of his own personal control—and preferred its "country members" to be affiliated directly with the London headquarters. The pressure for local organization could not be altogether resisted, however. Four groups emerged in the capital, and one or two of the provincial branches, particularly the one at Bristol (a center of Christian socialism throughout these years), were very successful. Much depended on the local warden or president whether a branch would survive or not. On the other hand, Headlam and his able lieutenant, Frederick Verinder, had a genius for publicity and brought attention to the Guild at every opportunity, constantly writing letters to the press, publishing leaflets and broadsheets, and inviting distinguished men to their meetings. Bernard Shaw, claimed Headlam, used GSM meetings as his "training ground for public speaking and debate." Shaw himself said that Headlam's *Church Reformer* was "one of the best socialist journals of that day." John Morley thought the paper contained "enough matter in it to stock five ordinary newspapers," and John Ruskin affirmed this view: "I have never yet looked through a paper I thought so right or likely to be so useful."[68]

Stewart Headlam worked very hard proselytizing with the GSM gospel; but much of the real administrative work, especially of the Georgeist Single Tax campaigns, fell on the shoulders of Frederick Verinder. In the post of executive secretary of the GSM,[69] Verinder bore the weight of imple-

---

[67] *Church Reformer*, III, No. 8 (15 August 1884), p. 188.

[68] Bettany, pp. 87, 104, 109. Certainly Headlam's *Church Reformer* is a mine of material for the social historian of today.

[69] Other executive members of the GSM in 1884 were: Hon. Treasurer, J. F. Harries; Council: J. E. Symes, T. Hill, H. C. Shuttleworth, W. E. Moll, Mrs. Clymer (Ella Dietz, the actress from the Church and Stage Guild), and three laymen—J. T. Sharp, A. W. Crickmay, and J. C. Wheeler (*Church Reformer*, III, No. 8 [15 August 1884], p. 188).

menting policy decisions and putting campaigns on the road. In 1884 he was also made General Secretary of the English Land Restoration League and thus became the virtual leader of the British Single Tax movement. Verinder was a layman, a devoted personal disciple and ex-student of Headlam, "discovered" by Headlam doing "pupil-teaching" in a national school in Bethnal Green. A man of great organizational ability and stamina, the GSM's most frequent speaker next to Headlam, he also subedited the *Church Reformer.* Verinder was well liked throughout the labor movement; but he had little originality. He was a bureaucrat of social reform, a campaign planner, an editor of other men's ideas. Principally, Verinder functioned as Headlam's mouthpiece, defender, and aide.[70]

The organization that Verinder administered was never very large. The Guild in 1884 numbered about 100 members, one-third of them Anglican priests. After that year, membership rose but never exceeded 400. By 1890 the Guild had about 200 members. Its curve of growth and decline is shown in Table 5.

The years of greatest growth were 1884 to 1895. The sharp decline after 1895 is attributed by Bettany to Headlam's daring and controversial aid to Oscar Wilde, which brought several immediate resignations; but many other factors were also involved.

[70] "I was by his side at every election from 1888 to 1922," said Verinder (Binyon, p. 151). He defended Headlam against C. L. Marson's attacks in 1895 (*Church Reformer,* XIV, No. 10 [October 1895], pp. 219ff.). Born in Bethnal Green, 1858, Verinder was the son of a Wiltshire farm laborer, and became a pupil-teacher, joining Headlam's special evening group to study Shakespeare, Tennyson, history, and the Bible. Prepared by Headlam for confirmation and completing his term at the school (1872-1877), Verinder became Assistant Master at Tottenham Grammar School (1878-1883). He studied science at London University but was prevented from completing his degree by outside political activities. Besides his work on the *Church Reformer,* the GSM, and the ELRL, Verinder edited the *Democrat* for two years until it amalgamated with Davitt's *Labour World* and organized the Single Taxers' Red Van campaign, later copied by the Land Nationalisation Society and by Blatchford's Clarion movement (*Labour Annual,* 1895, p. 191; Bettany, pp. 36ff.; Jones, Manchester thesis, pp. 234-235; *Labour Prophet,* VI, No. 74 [February 1898], p. 159).

TABLE 5[71]

GROWTH AND DECLINE OF THE GSM

YEAR	TOTAL MEMBERSHIP	HOLY ORDERS
1877	40	—
1884	100*	35*
1885	126	40
1887	172	—
1888	185	52
1890	201	70*
1891	228	73
1893	285	77
1894	333	93
1895	364	99
1906	200*	—

*Approximate.

The distinguishing policy note of 1885 was Headlam's list of questions to candidates for election, suggested to the Fabians and also to Christian socialists in the *Church Reformer*. He told his colleagues to ask their political candidates to support:

1. Free education
2. The rating of unoccupied land in towns
3. An increase in the land tax
4. The conferring on municipalities of the power to rate the dwellings of the poor
5. An eight-hours bill
6. A bill shortening the hours in shops
7. Increased power for municipalities to undertake industrial work for the purpose of relieving distress[72]

These demands were very specific and concrete, if somewhat

[71] Table 5 is pieced together from scattered information in *Church Reformer*, VII, No. 10 (October 1888), p. 233; X, No. 10 (October 1891), pp. 233-236; XIII, No. 10 (October 1894), p. 231; XIV, No. 4 (April 1895), pp. 93-94 and No. 10 (October 1895), p. 229; Bettany, p. 81; and D. O. Wagner, *The Church of England and Social Reform*, p. 191.

[72] Wagner, pp. 191ff.; H. M. Lynd, *England in the Eighteen-Eighties* (London, 1945), pp. 319-320.

limited, and not at all like the vague, idealistic generalities associated with Christian socialism in the minds of secular reformers of the day. In 1886 the Guild organized a series of public meetings on Christian socialism, and its members took part in the major street demonstrations of that year in London. Many a priestly garb was seen in unemployment marches, and Headlam put himself at the head of more than one.[73] Thomas Hill put the motion of 1884 ("Whereas the present contrast between the condition of the great body of the workers, who produce much and consume little . . .") once more to a public meeting and was supported by C. E. Escreet, F. L. Donaldson, and Shuttleworth. More socialist and labor protests came in 1887, and the motion was passed for yet a third time, unanimously, by a crowd in Trafalgar Square. When the Home Secretary refused to see a GSM deputation and banned all meetings in Trafalgar Square, Stewart Headlam openly defied him (November). Though prevented by strong police threats from putting further resolutions to the crowd, he did address them.

A series of GSM memorials, manifestos, and petitions ensued in the late eighties and nineties. At the Lambeth Pan-Anglican Conference of 1888 the Guild Council submitted a memorial on socialism; in 1889 it petitioned the Commons in support of the Oaths Bill. Statements were issued on a broad range of topics: Labour Day, Clerical Appointments and Tenure, the Parish Councils Bill, education, and so on. Meetings were held at Essex Hall in the early nineties about the sacraments and socialism, with Bernard Shaw good-naturedly heckling Percy Dearmer on the subject of baptism as the "sacrament of equality."[74]

The figures of Guild membership continued to creep up gradually to their peak of 1895, but at the height of its greatest success appeared the flaws which would eventually

---

[73] In 1886 he officiated at the funeral of the first socialist martyr, Linnell, leading the long procession through London. Cunninghame-Graham, William Morris, and W. T. Stead accompanied the coffin (Bettany, p. 136).

[74] *Christian Socialist*, III, No. 43 (December 1886), p. 85; Bettany, pp. 84, 87-89.

disable the society. There were four crisis years in the GSM's history: 1889, 1891, 1895, and 1906. In the first and the last of these years, rival organizations were founded (the CSU and the Church Socialist League), and in the middle two the Guild was split by inner discord. The inner storm of 1891 arose over education policy and was caused by Headlam's rather high-handed manifesto, *The Duty of the Clergy towards Board Schools and Elementary Education*. It was a London School Board election year, and Headlam was a candidate.[75]

Two controversial issues: state education and the ILP

Standing himself for a universal system of *secular* education, Headlam was unusual for a High Churchman, and his views were at variance with those of most of his Anglican socialist colleagues. He demanded that the Church of England scrap its voluntary (religious) schools, at least in areas already served by adequate state schools. The latter, Board Schools, had been created by the Forster Act of 1870, under the Cowper-Temple clause, which provided that no "catechisms or religious formularies distinctive of any particular denomination" were allowed to be taught in any tax-aided school. School Boards were not compelled to teach any religion at all; they were *permitted* to teach nondenominational religion. In practice, of course, "nondenominational" meant Nonconformist, if only vaguely so, because it necessarily threw all the pedagogical emphasis on the Bible itself. Also, Anglican and other private religious schools which received state aid were made, by the "timetable clause," to schedule religious teaching conveniently (usually at the beginning of the day) so that pupils could legally absent themselves for that hour on grounds of conscience. The 1870 Act had thus created a dual system rather than a monolithic state system—mainly out of practical necessity: the churches had built so many schools in the first half of the

[75] Headlam served on the Board from 1888-1904, was not given a place on the new LCC (London County Council) Education Committee immediately, but finally won a seat in 1907 (Bettany, pp. 145ff.).

nineteenth century that it was impracticable to scrap them (6,000 National Society, Anglican, state-aided schools and 1,500 British Society, Wesleyan, state-aided schools were operating by 1870).[76] Headlam came to be a staunch defender of the Board Schools under the Forster Act, though many Anglicans regarded that measure as a defeat for the Church. Ever since 1839, when the pro-Nonconformist Whig reform ministry had created a Privy Council Committee to administer increasing state grants to existing church schools, the High Church wing had bitterly *opposed* the principle of state inspection. One High Church parson said he "would never permit an emissary of Lord John Russell, or any other Turkish Bashaw, to enter his school."[77] Headlam's contrary view was logically derived from his basic premise, that the Church of England should in any case be disestablished.

Right or wrong, it seems evident that Headlam imposed his manifesto on the Guild without any adequate preparatory discussion or exploration of other members' views. Shuttleworth, in some ways usually more tolerant than the warden himself, found himself unable to countenance the abolition of voluntary schools. He opposed the manifesto and won the support of Sarson, Symes, Escreet, and Hill. The London press immediately publicized the division and talked of the Guild's dissolution, which idea Shuttleworth's opposition group firmly repudiated.[78] The annual meeting at Sion College in September 1891 was "the largest and most animated gathering ever held by the Guild during the

[76] Marjorie Cruickshank, *Church and State in English Education, 1870 to the Present Day* (London, 1963), pp. 1-4.

[77] *Ibid.*, p. 5.

[78] The *Daily Chronicle* (22 October 1891) claimed that the GSM was falling apart. Shuttleworth, Escreet, and Hill each wrote a letter to that paper making clear their determination *not* to resign from the Guild. Hill admitted that "before the vote on the school question was actually taken some of us did consider that possible necessity; but wiser counsels prevailed." Escreet stated, "we were obliged to express our dissent but we by no means cease to value the plucky and faithful leadership of our Warden" (*Church Reformer*, x, No. 11 [November 1891], pp. 259-260). The writing was on the wall, nevertheless.

14 years of its existence." The meeting did not close until 11:10 P.M., and a large number of nonmembers were present.

Headlam moved the adoption of his manifesto, seconded of course by Verinder. Shuttleworth demanded an amendment to eliminate the voluntary schools clause, but was defeated, 25 to 8. Headlam's manifesto was then adopted, 26 to 9. Several "sleeping" members and others came in from the suburbs especially to support the warden out of loyalty to the past; he still had sufficient personal following at that time to control the situation. Thomas Hancock supported Headlam (against his own rector) for reasons absolutely characteristic: narrowly Anglican, he wished to get rid of "the Pope's schools" and what he regarded as papist intrigue in Britain. There should be no schism in the national educational system, which should teach a common national history.[79] Shuttleworth protested against the vote, composed almost solely of London members, and published a formal declaration signed by almost half of all clerical members and a quarter of all lay members of the Guild in England. There were three Council members' signatures (Shuttleworth, Escreet, and Hill), 29 Anglican parsons (including such leading figures as Sarson, Symes, Carter, Rev. C. W. Stubbs, Rev. W.H.C. Malton, and Rev. Philip Peach), and 36 lay members (of whom Dean T. C. Collings of King's College, London, was one). It was a serious moment in Guild history.[80]

Torn by the educational controversy, the GSM also suffered a certain loss of impetus elsewhere. The death of Charles Bradlaugh in 1891 and Annie Besant's conversion

---

[79] *Church Reformer*, x, No. 10 (October 1891), pp. 233-236.

[80] Percy Dearmer, who favored Headlam, wrote to his future bride: "I was full of a great sick feeling about the clergy after the GSM debate—just the arguments one has heard against the suffrage and every other reform. So that an 'hour of darkness' came over me, and I asked myself whether the clergy could ever come to Christian views, since even out of that small, disreputable GSM there arose ten Tories! . . . I thought at first that Headlam's education move was very bad policy: but since Shuttleworth's speech and Hill's, I am very glad that we had that little sifting" (1 October 1891). See Nan Dearmer, *Life of Percy Dearmer*, pp. 70-74.

to theosophy two years earlier removed the two top leaders of the secularist movement from the field and brought that agitation to an end. Ironically, this took the wind out of the sails of the Guild, partly built as it was on a campaign to combat atheist prejudice and the organized secularist movement. Headlam confessed freely in 1892 that "the decay of the narrow Protestant and Calvinist individualism which once dominated English theology, has robbed the secularist controversy of much of the importance which it had in the early days of the Guild." In some degree, he implied, the Guild was facing the cost of its own success. The world was changing:

> The failure of repeated attempts to get up a "heresy hunt" in connection with the publication of *Lux Mundi*; the recent utterances of the Archbishop of Canterbury in his *Living Theology*; . . . the Primate's action in opening Mr. Barrett's picture gallery while the East End dissenters were protesting because it was not closed against the people on Sundays, are small but significant straws; and the writings of such men as Mr. Clifford and Rev. R. F. Horton . . . show that the liberal teachings of a revived Catholicism are finding an echo even among dissenters.[81]

There was no fall in GSM membership as a result of the crisis of 1891, but instead a continuation of the process of slow growth. The London branch gained eight new members in 1893, including two of importance (G. A. West and

[81] *Church Reformer*, XI, No. 10 (October 1892), p. 235. Some of the secularists, moreover, had been sympathetic to labor. Charles Bradlaugh himself was not radical in economics; but Annie Besant (1847-1933), with her advanced social ideas and one-time Fabian membership, was a more formidable opponent for the GSM. Headlam's journal lamented her leadership of the London Matchgirls' strike in July 1888: "It was indeed the sword of the Lord which Mrs. Besant so effectively wielded; it was indeed the spirit of Jesus Christ which she exhibited; but it is a crying scandal that the Bishop of the great church in this diocese [London] should have left it to an atheist. . . . The spirit of the Lord Jesus, it would seem, prefers the strong, tender, poor atheist to the rich, hard, narrow Bishop and chooses her nowadays to work out His emancipating will" (*Church Reformer*, VII, No. 8 [August 1888], p. 171).

Thomas Hancock's son, Rev. Aidan Hancock of Hammersmith, who later joined the Church Socialist League). The later philosopher of "Christian sociology," P.E.T. Widdrington, became secretary of the Oxford GSM branch, and a new Bristol branch was opened in February 1894 with the sardonic and brilliant Rev. C. L. Marson as president. Forty-eight new members joined in 1894; one of the Guild veterans—C. W. Stubbs—became Dean of Ely.

Stubbs's preferment was a landmark for the Guild of St. Matthew, whose members were rarely promoted by the hierarchy. He was an uncompromising Broad Church Christian socialist, and had even tried to manage his own communitarian "Home Colony" on glebe lands while Vicar of Stokenham (South Devon, 1884-1888).[82] The author of seven or eight well-circulated books on socialism and reform, Dean Stubbs was also a prolific lecturer and Georgeist, pushing *Progress and Poverty* in Oxford, and speaking for the Glasgow branch of the Christian Socialist Society (1887), the GSM, Cambridge University (Select Preacher, 1881), and other bodies. He was even booked to address the World's Labour Congress of the Chicago World's Fair in 1893, but at the last minute could not attend.[83] In Stubbs's view, "the Christian Church, in the idea of its Founder, had for its object the reorganization and restitution of *society*, no less than the salvation and deliverance of the individual." From this he moved on to a kind of Christian socialist inevita-

[82] *Church Reformer*, XIII, No. 1 (January 1894), pp. 18f.; XIII, No. 2 (February 1894), pp. 42-43; XIII, No. 3 (March 1894), p. 64. Vice-president of the Bristol branch was Rev. A. H. Easton; its secretary was a very active lay Christian socialist and Bristol councillor, H. H. Gore (*Christian Socialist*, VII, No. 78 [November 1889], p. 164).

[83] Charles William Stubbs (not to be confused with W. Stubbs, Bishop of Oxford). Educated at Cambridge (B.A., 1868) and ordained priest in 1869. Pastorates in Sheffield and elsewhere; Vicar of Wavertree, Liverpool, 1888-1894; Dean of Ely, 1894, and later Bishop of Truro. See *Crockford's Clerical Directory*, 1885, p. 1136, and 1894, p. 1277; *Christian Socialist*, No. 1 (June 1883), p. 12; V, No. 55 (December 1887), p. 189; Henry Demarest Lloyd to Prof. J. H. Gray, 25 March 1893, Gray to Lloyd, 20 June 1893, Stubbs to Lloyd, 7 August 1893, Henry Demarest Lloyd Papers, Wisconsin State Historical Society, Madison (hereafter cited as WSHS). Stubbs had planned to speak in Chicago on "The Economics of Christ."

bility argument: "We believe, therefore, that there is an order of society which is the best, that towards this order the
world is gradually moving *according to a definite Divine
plan.*" Socialism was merely a stage in a divine social evolution, and "an educational revelation is ceaselessly descend-
ing from God to Man." Stubbs owed much to Mazzini, and
wrote a poem in his honor ("Christ's creed, in sooth, was
thine . . ."). Dean Stubbs was naturally unpopular with the
Anti-Socialist Union, the Middle-Classes Defence League,
and other right-wing pressure groups. One Scots conservative, J. M. McCandlish, damned "our socialist Dean" out
of hand, and went on to condemn universal suffrage and
democracy for good measure. Vituperation had little effect
on Stubbs, however, and none on his career, since he ended
up a bishop.[84]

Meanwhile Headlam had not been idle. His Fabian Tract
No. 42, *Christian Socialism,* was read to the Society on 8
January 1892 and published in that year. In this tract he
treated Christ's miracles as "secular, socialistic works" and
his parables, comparing the real world with the Kingdom
of Heaven, as an ethical blueprint for the future socialist
earthly society. Christ's teaching was never "other-worldly,"
argued Headlam, and try how they may to distort his sayings ("Blessed are ye poor," and "The poor ye always have
with you"), the antisocialists cannot convince, for their fallacious interpretation would contradict the whole tenor of his
life and work. Christ intended the Church to extend all
over the globe the merciful work he began in Palestine;
hence its early leaders, like St. Paul and St. James, were de-
fenders of the poor and of labor, the Church's chief sacra-

[84] Sermon at St. Clement's, Notting Hill, 21 December 1886, for the
GSM: *Church Reformer,* VI, No. 2 (February 1887), p. 35; *Christian
Socialist,* No. 4 (September 1883), p. 61; J. M. McCandlish, *A Study
of Christian Socialism* (Edinburgh and London, 1898). Stubbs's writings
include: *Village Politics* (1878), a well-known work which went through
several editions; *Christ and Democracy* (1883)—also popular, e.g., 3rd
ed., 1894—collected sermons and addresses, four for the GSM; *Christian
Secularism,* two lectures, published by GSM as a pamphlet (1883);
Christ and Economics (1893); and *Charles Kingsley and the Christian
Social Movement* (1899).

ments (Baptism and Holy Communion) are sacraments of brotherhood, and the Catechism is directly aimed at the evil of one man living on his brother's labor. Today, Headlam said, the Church is "gagged and fettered." Churchmen should therefore unite with socialists and fight for better education, an eight-hour day, and land restoration.[85]

The argument throughout was crystal clear and a good summary of the sacramental socialist position; but the policy directive—the Single Tax—must have disappointed the Fabians of 1892. It was misleading that Headlam claimed to speak for *all* Christian socialists, because the majority of them were not in fact satisfied with Henry George's theory.[86] Nonetheless, Headlam alleged in his Tract of 1892 that "The main plank in the platform of the Christian socialist, the chief political reform at which he aims, . . . is summed up in the resolution moved by the English Land Restoration League in Trafalgar Square . . ." and followed this with a full exposition of Henry George's Single Tax: "We Christian socialists then, maintain that this is the most far-reaching reform . . . [and] that morality is impossible without it."[87] There were in existence at this time the Christian Social Union, the Labour Church, and the Christian Socialist Society, none of which accepted the Single Tax, besides countless individual, unorganized Christian socialists. Headlam's assurance, his willful insularity as regards other groups (especially those outside the Anglican fold—the unbaptized), is but one example of a sin which beset most sacramental, or, more justly, most Christian socialists.[88]

[85] *Christian Socialism*, Fabian Tract No. 42 (London, 1892), passim.

[86] See, for instance, *Christian Socialist*, No. 8 (January 1884), pp. 114-115; No. 12 (May 1884), pp. 184-186; v, No. 52 (September 1887), p. 135; v, No. 53 (October 1887), pp. 147-148; and v, No. 55 (December 1887), p. 182.

[87] Headlam, *Christian Socialism*, pp. 11, 13.

[88] In justice it must be said that except for occasions like this, Headlam was a remarkably tolerant and broad-minded man: witness his friendship with and defense of atheists and non-Christians, and his insistence, no doubt irritating to secularists, that Bradlaugh was in truth "a man of God." Yet Headlam preferred atheists to Nonconformists and often claimed, as in 1883, that it was "better to be an atheist than a Calvinist"—better to have no opinion of God than to

The Guild of St. Matthew displayed provincialism of a dangerous sort in 1893. Along with some other socialists and reform groups, but more positively, the *Church Reformer* spurned the idea of independent labor representation. Stewart Headlam had no time for the idea of a working-class political party. In this he shared the prejudices of his former teacher F. D. Maurice. The *Church Reformer* was a personal vehicle for Headlam but was at the same time supposed to be the GSM's unofficial organ, carrying full reports of Guild meetings and decisions. Too close identification of the GSM with the *Church Reformer* was a bone of contention with dissident Guild members. Though the *Reformer* was stridently anti-Establishment and pro-Labour, it was also hostile to Nonconformity (especially in Thomas Hancock's articles) and milder in its republicanism than other Christian socialist papers.[89] Toward the High Church Gladstone it showed a tempered respect, supporting his treatment of the Irish Home Rule question of 1886 and bemoaning his political defeat, which it blamed, characteristically and unfairly, not on Anglicans but on "the dissenters [who are] . . . more Protestant than Christian, more in sympathy with the comfortable classes than with the oppressed masses."[90]

On several occasions in the early 1890's the *Church Reformer* expressed disapproval of the independent labor party idea. Finally, in 1893, the year of the historic Bradford Conference, which established the ILP, Headlam published a blast—"Feeble Fabians"—against the demand by a member of the Fabian Society (in the *Fortnightly Review*) for fifty

---

have an unworthy one, i.e., that God is avenging and cruel (*Christian Socialist*, No. 7 [December 1883], p. 101).

89 Compare almost any edition of the *Church Reformer* with the *Christian Socialist* or *Brotherhood*, for example. For a specific case, the *Reformer* was much less critical of the Jubilee proceedings (v, No. 7 [July 1886], p. 146) than the *Christian Socialist*, and was fairly complimentary to Victoria herself. In contrast, the *Christian Socialist* was antimonarchical and recommended "Her Most Gracious Majesty to put her heavy foot down" (iii, No. 37 [June 1886], p. 195).

90 *Church Reformer*, v, No. 8 (August 1886), pp. 169-170.

independent Labour MP's.[91] In truth, the Fabian Society was not at all in the lead as regards independent labor representation, and did anything but actively discourage the ILP in its infant stage. The idea of a worker's political party lay vaguely behind the socialism of the eighties and began to become an articulate aim in about 1887-1888. Friedrich Engels wrote in 1887 that the immediate question before British socialism was the foundation of a Labour Party with a clear class program. H. H. Champion, onetime editor of the *Christian Socialist*, took up the cry for an independent party in 1887, and in 1888, with his help, the penniless miner's leader Keir Hardie contested an election in mid-Lanark. The later foundation of Hardie's Scottish Labour Party, the growth of regional labor electoral groups (London, Bradford, Salford, and elsewhere), and the establishment of two labor newspapers, Joseph Burgess's *Workman's Times* (1890) and Robert Blatchford's *Clarion* (1891), all advanced the movement. At a meeting in the Manchester *Clarion* offices in the spring of 1892, seven men tentatively created an ILP; but Blatchford turned down its presidency because he feared the party would become known merely as "Blatchford's Party." Stimulated by the electoral successes of 1892 (three Independents and twelve "Lib-Labs" elected), the Bradford Conference of January 1893 firmly established the new political party.[92]

The Fabian reaction to this new development was mixed. A strong minority, committed to their policy of "permeation," thought it was too early to play labor politics. They were already too deeply involved with Liberal-Radicals in London government. Headlam, who was in some ways the most deeply involved Fabian, reacted the most violently against the ILP. After 1887, when Bernard Shaw's Fabian Tract, *The True Radical Programme,* had successfully capitalized on Joseph Chamberlain's earlier and milder *Unauthorized Programme* of 1885, the Fabian Society deliberately

---

[91] *Church Reformer*, XII, No. 11 (November 1893), pp. 244-245.

[92] See May Morris, *William Morris, Artist, Writer, Socialist,* 2 vols. (Oxford, 1936), II, 336; and H. M. Pelling, *Origins of the Labour Party,* the best secondary source.

chose to become a "ginger group" among the London Radicals. Webb joined the Holborn Liberal and Radical Association. Headlam accompanied him, but also served on the executive of the Strand Association, along with his Christian socialist GSM and Fabian clerical colleagues, W. E. Moll and W. A. Oxford.[93] At this stage the Fabians had gone too far to pull out and encourage independent party action. Vehement debates rocked the Society in the early 1890's—Headlam, Shaw, Webb, Pease, and William Clarke standing for continued permeation and the London Liberal alliance, and Hubert Bland, Joseph Burgess, and S. G. Hobson (whom we shall meet as an active Socialist Quaker Society member and Guild Socialist in later chapters) demanding full support for Keir Hardie. Yet the *Fortnightly Review* manifesto of 1893, *To Your Tents, O Israel!* which Headlam so strongly resisted, was in fact drafted by Sidney Webb and Bernard Shaw. Their manifesto can be explained as a diversionary tactic, a flanking movement; but it did point the way nevertheless to a future solution, namely *trade-union subsidy* of an independent labor party. The Fabians held Keir Hardie's little group in contempt; Shaw likened the ILP of 1893 to the Democratic Federation of 1883, as a tiny, misdirected effort. Hence the demand he made for a "trade union party. . . , to raise £30,000 and finance fifty candidates for Parliament."[94]

Stewart Headlam felt unable to go along with this policy directive and condemned it outright: "The Fabians now are only stepping haltingly several years behind Messrs. Champion and Maltman Barry, who were not a conspicuous success." It was a defection, an aberration from true Fabianism, he thought, and such a policy could result only in split Liberal-Radical votes and consequent Tory victories. It was "absurd to think that because a man is paid wages by the hour he will on that account be a better M.P." Headlam

---

[93] A. M. McBriar, *Fabian Socialism and English Politics*, pp. 234-237; see also pp. 22-24.

[94] Pelling, *Origins of the Labour Party*, pp. 119-120; Anne Fremantle, *This Little Band of Prophets* (London, 1959), p. 99.

refused "to vote for a man simply because he is a carpenter and will try to improve the carpenters' wages"; yet he did not seem to notice any class bias of his own in this view. He was blind to the possible nest-feathering attitudes of existing middle-class MP's. Unlike the Maurice-Kingsley group, Headlam was not by nature an elitist; he was less so, in fact, than most of his Fabian colleagues. But he was driven to declare: "To advocate the introduction of workingmen, as such, into Parliament, as the Fabians now seem to be doing, is *utterly absurd*."[95]

What Webb, Shaw and Headlam alike underestimated was the viability of Hardie's ILP, with its roots in provincial radicalism. Engels, with customary insight, saw this. Writing in January 1893, he explained:

> The Fabians here in London are a band of careerists who have understanding enough to realize the inevitability of the social revolution, but who could not possibly entrust this tremendous job to the crude proletariat alone, and are therefore kind enough to set themselves at the head.

True dynamism, said Engels, would come from "the rush towards socialism in the provinces," not from London, "the home of cliques." If only "the petty private ambitions and intrigues of the London would-be great men are now held in check somewhat, and the tactics do not turn out too wrong-headed, the Independent Labour Party may succeed in detaching the masses from the Social Democratic Federation, and in the provinces from the Fabians too, and then force unity." A few weeks later Engels added:

> Lancashire and Yorkshire are again taking the lead in this movement too, as in the chartist movement. People like Sidney Webb, Bernard Shaw and the like, who wanted to permeate the Liberals with socialism, must now allow themselves to be permeated by the spirit of the workingmen members of their own society. . . . Either

[95] *Church Reformer*, XII, No. 11 (November 1893), pp. 244-245 (italics mine).

they remain alone, officers without soldiers, or they must go along.[96]

Engels' analysis was remarkably accurate, except that the workingmen by whom the Fabians finally allowed themselves to be won over were not in their own Society but in the Labour Party and trade-union movement. Also, though the Fabians were undoubtedly middle class themselves and given to elitist views of political *methods,* their *aims* were always egalitarian. "Most of the members of the Fabian Society are educated, middle-class people," William Clarke explained to an American audience in 1893, ". . . What is to be the relation of these educated middle-class people to the swarming multitudes of workers? This is a vital social question, the most vital we have immediately before us." Clarke himself envisaged leadership of the working "multitudes" by an educated elite, a happy "union of culture and labour." But Shaw and the Webbs wanted to go beyond this, beyond mere equality of opportunity as worshiped in the United States to a true, classless society. Shaw believed that *equal incomes* alone could never produce true equality; he once suggested "the intermarriageability test" as the only true index of classlessness.[97]

The ILP, under Keir Hardie's undogmatic, opportunist leadership, based on hard experience and deep sentiment, signified, in Hardie's own words, "a revolt against the assumption that working people are in any sense inferior, either mentally or morally, to any other section of the community."[98] The future, as Engels discerned (though he mis-

[96] Engels to Sorge, 18 January 1893; Engels to Sorge, 18 March 1893 (K. Marx and F. Engels, *Letters to Americans, 1848-1895* [New York, 1953], pp. 246-247, 249).

[97] William Clarke, "The Fabian Society and its Work" (a lecture delivered in Boston in the winter of 1893-1894, and first published in the *New England Magazine*), in the US edition of *Fabian Essays,* Introduction by Edward Bellamy (Boston, 1894), p. xxxvii; George Bernard Shaw, *Intelligent Woman's Guide to Socialism* (London, 1928), I, 68-69, and II, 442; McBriar, p. 156.

[98] J. K. Hardie, *After Twenty Years: All About the ILP* (London, 1913), p. 11. "To dogmatise about the form which the Socialist State

understood its true nature), lay with the idea of independent labor representation and with the movement begun at the Bradford Labour Institute in 1893. The ILP was a profoundly *Northern* product; of its 300 or more branches in 1895, 100 were to be found in Yorkshire, 70 in Lancashire and Cheshire, 40 in Scotland, 18 in the Northeast, and 23 in the Midlands. London claimed 29 branches. As Keir Hardie suggested to a visiting American Progressive in 1899, ". . . everyone who breathes the air of London loses hope. If you want to see the socialist movement, spend more time in the provinces and you will see that everywhere socialism is making headway."[99] The rivalry between the capital and the provinces runs throughout the socialist history of these years and is reflected in Christian socialism by the creation in 1906 of the Church Socialist League in the North of England. Understandably, given Stewart Headlam's refusal to recognize the potentiality of the ILP (he despised Keir Hardie), it was the League which became the Guild's chief rival after 1906 and syphoned off many of Headlam's members. Ironically, the *Church Reformer* at the beginning of 1893 complained that as a journal it had "entirely failed" to capture working-class readers. The paper considered dissolving because, it lamented, "They do not read what we write."[100] Perhaps "they," the workers, were too busy reading Robert Blatchford's *Clarion* and listening to Keir Hardie!

The *Church Reformer*'s anti-ILP policy continued into 1895:

> The ILP is a logical impossibility. . . . To form a little party (and to give it a big name) pledged only to vote

shall take, is to play the fool," wrote Hardie (*From Serfdom to Socialism* [London, 1907], p. 96).

[99] Donald Read, *The English Provinces, c. 1760-1960: A Study in Influence* (New York, 1964), pp. 194-198; Robert Hunter, *Socialists at Work* (New York, 1908), p. 101. For more on Hunter see the editorial introduction to my edition of his important study of 1904, *Poverty: Social Conscience in the Progressive Era* (New York, 1965).

[100] *Church Reformer*, XII, No. 1 (January 1893), pp. 3-4.

straightaway for the realisation of your ideal, and to keep out all others who would help towards realising it, is political suicide, immoral as all suicide is.[101]

ILP men, Headlam claimed, were less pro-Labour than anti-Liberal. The notion of party discipline in voting offended him. The title "Labour Party" was objectionable, for the great mass of the nation were workers and had very different and divided interests; and the Liberals had done such good work (Parish Councils, a more just taxation, Factory Acts, reform of the Welsh Church, trade-union conditions guaranteed in state employment, an attempt at Irish Home Rule . . .) that it was foolish for socialists to "play with the ILP." Rev. Percy Dearmer, however, came out in bitter opposition to the warden's stand and castigated the Liberal Party. The Liberals had done nothing toward the Old Age Pension scheme he said, except to "smother it in a Commission." Their party was "a sectional Party. . .; it reviled and attacked the Church and bowed before the Nonconformist Conscience in all things." The Liberal defeat in the 1895 election, helped by the ILP splitting the vote, was all for the best, Dearmer argued, because Liberals had always "looked at the working-classes through bourgeois spectacles." Headlam countered this by condemning the ILP for its lack of a foreign policy, its unconcern over disestablishment, its failure "to see that land monopoly is the main cause and root of poverty," and its silence on the question of secular education.[102] It was scarcely a reply calculated to increase the circulation of the *Church Reformer,* which finally collapsed three months later.

Dissension and decay

Sidney Webb wrote in 1890 that the Guild of St. Matthew had "become an essentially Socialistic body," and Headlam's *Church Reformer* "a frankly Socialist medium of great ability." The Anglo-Catholic socialist Conrad Noel,

[101] *Church Reformer*, xiv, No. 5 (May 1895), pp. 99-100.
[102] *Loc.cit.; Church Reformer,* xiv, No. 9 (September 1895), pp. 198-202 and 201-202.

looking back from the vantage point of the 1940's, however, said: "The weakness of the Guild was that beyond a general support of the working-class movement it confined itself to land reform, and was dominated by the teaching of Henry George."[103] In 1890 Webb could not see the future of the Guild; in 1942 Noel had apparently forgotten much of its past. The GSM declined for a number of reasons.

The death of his journal in December 1895 was but the last blow in a year of calamities for Headlam. That year the tide turned against the Guild of St. Matthew, despite its remaining fifteen years of official life. Neither the suggested dissolution of 1903 nor even the creation of the Church Socialist League in 1906 had such a bad effect on the Guild as did three other events: the loss of its paper, the Oscar Wilde affair, and the deep rift between C. L. Marson and the warden.

There is a temptation to dismiss Headlam's aid to Wilde as a quixotic moment in Headlam's life. It was a large-hearted and impulsive gesture; yet it was not unusual: the action was expressive of his whole way of life. Headlam was not an intimate of the *Yellow Book* crowd; but for an Anglican priest his life was rather bohemian. He lived *among* "the people," but never believed it necessary to live *like* them. Independent means gave him the chance to furnish his rooms (especially in the house at 31, Upper Bedford Place, in which he lived from 1886) in an individual style. The decor was by A. H. Mackmurdo, a famous architect; the house contained "exquisite mahogany furniture" with William Morris cretonne upholstery, much admired by aesthetes like Percy Dearmer and Bernard Shaw. The paintings proved something of a shock for many visitors.[104] Perhaps an odd room would be occupied by a destitute balle-

---

[103] Sidney Webb, *Socialism in England*, p. 64; Conrad Noel, *Autobiography*, p. 60. (Noel died in 1942; his autobiography was edited by the High Church Fabian, Sidney Dark.)

[104] According to Rev. F. L. Donaldson, who adds, "but as you came to know Headlam you soon understood that the only reason for their presence was the appeal they made to the artist that was in him. He was an artist and at the same time a gentleman" (Bettany, p. 94).

rina, another by her brother. "As a Scotsman and a Nonconformist, I well remember the shock it gave me," said the eminently respectable Keir Hardie, "that the leading member of the Guild divided his attention fairly evenly between socialism and the ballet." But Headlam in the flesh, "a dapper little gentleman puffing contentedly on a big cigar," was reassuring. He must have made a personal contrast at Fabian meetings with the Baptist Rev. John Clifford or with Sidney Webb. Headlam's bohemianism was not bizarre or offensive, however. He was socially polished at all levels of society.[105]

It was through an artist friend in the Anti-Puritan League that Headlam entered the Oscar Wilde case.[106] Justifying his action at the time, he said:

> I became bail for Mr. Oscar Wilde on public grounds: I felt that the action of a large section of the Press, of the theatrical managers, . . . and of his publishers, was calculated to prejudice his case before his trial had even begun.

[105] Wagner, p. 218; *Church Socialist Quarterly*, IV, No. 3 (July 1909), p. 194. Headlam's dress was plain: he habitually wore "a low collar and white tie . . . suggesting an old style Low Church clergyman of the Whateley type," reported G. K. Chesterton (Bettany, p. 129). Percy Dearmer describes him at a Board School soirée: "Headlam was delightful, and to see him waltzing with the little girls and leading them to their places would have done anyone good. . . . I wish I had his lovely manners. He came in afterwards and had a beer" (Dearmer to Lord Beauchamp, 10 October 1891, in Nan Dearmer, p. 80).

[106] Selwyn Image (Slade Professor of Fine Art at Oxford). Image was approached, but had no money to spare for Wilde's bail and passed the case on to Headlam. The Anti-Puritan League was apparently founded at Headlam's Upper Bedford Place home; its members also included G. K. Chesterton, Cecil Chesterton, and Edgar Jephson. Issuing a few pamphlets, it caused a brief flutter among the Nonconformists and quietly died. See Bettany, pp. 128-129. Headlam's attitude is reflected in the *Church Reformer*: "Our foods are to be prescribed for us by the vegetarian (unless the newer sect of fruit-and-nut men get the upper hand first); we are to drink nothing of which teetotallers do not approve; and our dresses are to be regulated by people who think it an outrage on decency to have any ankles" (XIV, No. 6 [June 1895], p. 126). Besides the Church and Stage Guild, Headlam also helped to found, and became president (1914-1924), of the London Shakespeare League.

In other words, Headlam sprang to Wilde's aid in the same way he had earlier defended Charles Bradlaugh:

> I was a surety, not for his character, but for his appearance in court to stand his trial. I had very little personal knowledge of him at the time; I think I had only met him twice.[107]

Headlam, certainly, was a confirmed libertarian; but his own unfortunate wife had turned out to be a homosexual, which must undoubtedly have given him a deeper understanding of Oscar Wilde's sorry plight.

The Wilde trial revealed late-Victorian England at its very worst. Wilde was arrested on a morals charge in April 1895 and released a month later on the very high bail of £5,000. Persecuted by the press, the courts (his bail was not only exorbitant but difficult to obtain), and by former friends and actor-colleagues, Wilde's very name was pasted over on the billboards advertising his play *The Importance of Being Earnest,* which had been a great success two weeks before. Headlam paid half of his bail, Lord Douglas of Hawick the other half. "I knew quite well," wrote Headlam in a projected autobiography, which he never finished, "that this action of mine would with many people damage my already damaged reputation and that it would sadly try some of my best friends whom I had already tried a great deal."[108] Out on bail for a ghastly two weeks before his trial, Wilde could not get a hotel anywhere in London. The manager of the St. Pancras Station Midland Hotel actually ordered him out into the street when he found the playwright eating dinner there with Lord Douglas. Wilde eventually stayed with some liberal-minded Jewish business friends of his mother. Despite all this persecution, Headlam called for Wilde every morning of the trial, took him to the Old Bailey, and escorted him away again each evening through the jeering mobs. Headlam's own house was threatened with

[107] *Church Reformer,* xiv, No. 6 (June 1895), p. 124.
[108] Sir Compton Mackenzie, *Certain Aspects of Moral Courage* (New York, 1962), pp. 61-66.

violence. Wilde received the savage sentence of two years' hard labor; no remission of any kind was given him during the sentence; his health was permanently undermined, and he died at the age of forty-six. Stewart Headlam's actions were the only break in the solid barrage of cowardice and hypocrisy over the Wilde affair; he showed moral courage of a high order. Two years later Headlam was at Pentonville Jail to meet Wilde, as he had promised—at six o'clock on a May morning in 1897. "Of all the public difficulties I have been in this was the most painful," he confessed.[109]

Headlam knew full well when he decided to help Wilde that the Guild of St. Matthew and his own life's work would suffer badly. To meet Wilde two years later, having experienced the full impact of the reactions, was an added stroke of real courage and grit. The effect on his friends was only too evident. Intellectuals, such as the Liberal journalists H. W. Massingham and Sir Henry Norman, broke off their friendships with Headlam. Rev. J. G. Adderley, an otherwise courageous and hard-working Christian socialist, left the Guild of St. Matthew immediately, succumbing to what Sir Compton Mackenzie has described as "the prevailing hysteria."[110] There were twelve resignations from the GSM, and Shuttleworth gave up the presidency of the Oxford branch (though there may have been no connection here with the Wilde business).[111] Most important, C. L. Marson, "a man of culture, wit and charm," allowed himself to "behave with mobster vulgarity." Marson turned his merciless invective against the warden, and tried to raise a mu-

---

109 Bettany, p. 130. Of Wilde, Headlam said, "I like to think of him as I knew him for those six hours on that spring morning [of his release] and to hope that somewhere and somehow the beauty of his character may be garnered and the follies and weaknesses burnt up" (Bettany, pp. 131-132). Bettany claims that Wilde wanted a Roman Catholic priest on that morning but "they would have nothing to do with him" at Farm Street (I have been unable to check this statement).

110 Mackenzie, pp. 61-62. Adderley, however, later changed his mind.

111 *Church Reformer*, XIV, No. 5 (May 1895), p. 102; XIV, No. 7 (July 1895), pp. 162, 166. "I lost a housemaid," Headlam reported, "who fled at once" (Bettany, *loc.cit.*).

tiny inside the Guild as well as at a London School Board meeting.[112] He was all for building a New Jerusalem, he averred, but not for "wading through a Gomorrah first." The public identified Headlam with the Guild, even when he was "chivalrously rushing into police court to bail out Jane Cakebread or some other notorious criminal."[113]

The words could not have been more tart. But Marson had been building up resentment against Headlam's leadership for some months. In February 1894 he had accused the warden of injustice in a criticism of Bishop Westcott—a man who "was called a Chartist when still an undergraduate," and who was "so far the only Bishop" to show much interest in social reform. "You are very bitter against one who is on our side," complained Marson. Headlam refused to take the charge seriously, and certainly it was most uncharacteristic of Marson to defend a bishop, even though Westcott was the Christian Social Union president as well.[114] In April of 1895 Marson wrote to the *Church Reformer* giving a complete and breathtaking analysis of "the sick state of the GSM." Summarized, his long arguments stated:

1. Twelve years ago (1883) the Guild was one-third as large and did infinitely more work—a heavy schedule of lectures, meetings, and propaganda. In 1885 it was even known in Australia.

2. The London CSU does excellent work in 1895—most of it by GSM men. Clearly, "the troops are good enough

---

[112] Mackenzie, p. 62.

[113] *Church Reformer*, xiv, No. 10 (October 1895), p. 232.

[114] *Church Reformer*, xiii, No. 2 (February 1894), p. 45. For Headlam's remarks on Westcott, see *Church Reformer*, xiii, No. 1 (January 1894), p. 5. "Rev. Marson makes far too much of our mild notes on Dr. Westcott," he said (*Church Reformer*, xiii, No. 2 [February 1894], p. 28). The "notes" were not "mild," however, although Marson may have exaggerated. In September even the faithful Thomas Hancock protested strongly against the GSM's "open letter" to the bishops (on their voting conduct over the Parish Councils Act). Headlam had failed to circulate all members first (*Church Reformer*, xiii, No. 10 [October 1894], pp. 231-235).

but the handling of those troops [by the GSM] is inefficient, careless and disgraceful."

3. Who is to blame? The warden is not "wholly responsible, though he is to some extent blameworthy." The Council and Guild's Rules are at fault.

4. The Council makes "positive and negative" mistakes:
   (a) Too many "ornamental" members fail to attend, and should be struck off.
   (b) The Council *discourages branches*. "It makes me angry to read of the branch babies . . . stifled in their cradles" (Newcastle, Canada, West Indies, New South Wales, New York, Bloemfontein, Soho, Landport, Sneinton and South London). The Council's alternative is inadequate—" 'Groups' are no good. Local branches are the real power in these societies." (Groups have no voices in the Council and cannot resist its "repressing hand.")
   (c) The Council is *lazy and inefficient*. It holds no more public demonstrations, has allowed "paying visits" and even the Quarterly Services to fall by the way. It offers nothing but "a little warmed-up hash upon Patronage and Temperance." It needs "new blood and new ways." *"Have we no gospel except the London School Board, the Empire Promenade and the Ballet?"*

5. The *country member is ignored;* the GSM is London-dominated. Is there "nothing for the man who lives out of London and prefers all the other arts before that of St. Vitus?"

6. Members should take some interest in elections to the Guild Council. (Their failure to do so is "because no one sets them at it.")

7. *The Rules* need revising. "We are strangled in our own red tape": (a) Past attempts to alter the constitution have been impeded by complex rules (e.g., the attempted alteration of Object 3 in 1884 and 1894). (b) Nominations for Council Elections have to be sent in weeks before

the Annual Meeting, and no one ever remembers (or is reminded of) the closing date.

As a result—"the Council nominates itself in the most oligarchic way in the world."[115]

The attempt to alter Object 3 had been against Headlam's desires, and it was perhaps a reflection of his long regime that the alteration did not become law in spite of winning a majority vote (28 to 7) at the annual meeting of 1894.[116] A convenient rule demanded a certain ratio of members present to members enrolled to make a constitutional change. Since many of the older men, Headlam's supporters, were now in country jobs, the inference was clear. There was justice in Marson's argument that the Guild "is being unnecessarily and gratuitously killed by mismanagement."

It was the valiant henchman Frederick Verinder who answered these charges. Verinder testified that most of the lecturing of years ago was done by two men, Headlam and himself, now grown older and with wider responsibilities.[117] In the eighties Headlam had not been on the School Board, and Verinder was actually out of work for a while. Their colleagues, many of them, had been promoted over the years and dispersed. W. E. Moll was no longer a London curate but a busy Newcastle vicar, and, Verinder added:

[115] *Church Reformer*, XIV, No. 4 (April 1895), pp. 93-94 (italics mine).

[116] The Object was changed from: "To promote the study of social and political questions in the light of the Incarnation" to: "To promote the study *and treatment* . . ." (proposed by H. W. Hill with the unanimous support of C. L. Marson's Bristol branch, Rev. J. Cartmel-Robinson, and Rev. F. L. Donaldson). Other members (R. E. Dell and F. Viney) wanted to insert the words "Socialist" or "Collectivist," on the ground that the GSM had been "studying" for seventeen years now and everyone knew it was socialist; why not say so? T. Hancock, who always supported Headlam, was strongly against this, and the word "treatment" was his reluctant compromise (*Church Reformer*, XIII, No. 10 [October 1894], pp. 232-234).

[117] *Church Reformer*, XIV, No. 5 (May 1895), pp. 117-118. "I am 50% older and more than 50% less certain than I was of my excellence as a lecturer," said Verinder. He hoped that his present work was "more solidly useful than a young man's rush from platform to platform between Newcastle and Plymouth" (*loc.cit.*).

If the Lord Chancellor in his desire to deprive the Council of its most active members should do to Fr. Marson as . . . to Frs. Kennedy, Moll, Donaldson, Garrett and other former members of the Council, and send him to a vicarage in Cornwall or Cumberland, I don't fear that his interest in the Guild . . . will in the least slacken, but he will certainly not lecture in London so often.

With great irony, the same page of the *Church Reformer* announced Marson's appointment to Hambridge Vicarage deep in Somerset, miles away from London.[118]

Verinder's case was well put at this point; but what he said merely supported the general argument that no one man or small group of men could manage the society's affairs efficiently without frequent injections of new blood. His defense over the "stifling of branches" was weaker: many of them had never had but one or two members, and relations with Australia (through the newspaper the *Kapunda Herald*) were broken off largely through an article which Marson himself wrote in the *Church Reformer,* critical of that country. When in Australia, Marson constituted the entire South Australia branch. Verinder defended the ratio rule in constitutional voting on democratic grounds and pointed out that the GSM never, in fact, made any policy statements about ballet or the Empire Promenade. "Perhaps Fr. Marson is a member of the *Church and Stage Guild* and has got things mixed," he suggested. But the man who really confused these issues was Headlam himself, and Verinder's mild words could not hide this confusion.

A correspondent to the *Church Reformer* in July expressed the thought that widespread dissatisfaction with the journal and the warden was resulting in Guild resignations and, therefore, urged members simply to change their warden and publish their annual reports in some other paper. This hurt Headlam, and he replied that the election of a new warden would not do the trick; if his opponents had "the courage of their convictions, they ought to move a *vote*

[118] *Church Reformer*, XIV, No. 5 (May 1895), p. 118.

of censure on the present Warden." Marson, already in Somerset, was shocked, and hurriedly wrote:

> I cannot understand your editorial note. . . . I for one, think that the best thing we can do is to choose a new Warden, chiefly because the private conduct of the Warden has come to be confused with his official conduct. But I should entirely oppose a vote of censure upon the Warden as a thing ungrateful and ridiculous.

Nevertheless, after paying his respects to Headlam's past labors, Marson made clear:

> But there is no inalienable right to the Wardenship. . . . I cannot see how the Warden himself can possibly disagree with this view of the matter. He surely does not want to hold the Guild in his coat pocket?

Most important of all, is the GSM a socialist body or not? asked Marson. He demanded a warden who would answer "a hearty 'yes' in a language understood in regions where our voice has not yet been heard."[119]

Beyond question, what Marson was referring to most pointedly was Headlam's hostility to the ILP and overpartiality to the Liberals. Marson himself was prepared to cooperate more widely with other groups in the labor and socialist field, including the Christian Socialist Society. Both men were devoted Anglo-Catholics, but Marson was thirteen years younger, more radical (with a small "r") , and more of a socialist. In 1914, however (the year of his own death) , he had the grace to dedicate his major work, *God's Cooperative Society,* to: "The bravest of Captains and most skilful of the Swordsmen of the Holy Ghost, Stewart Duckworth Headlam."

The annual meeting of September 1895 at Sion College on the Embankment was bigger than that over the crisis of 1891, and the largest in Guild history. Perhaps in response to Marson's complaints (or Headlam's call) , many country

---

[119] *Church Reformer,* XIV, No. 7 (July 1895), pp. 165f.; XIV, No. 8 (August 1895), p. 190.

members were present. Shuttleworth, leader of the 1891 faction, was no longer a member.

After Headlam's address, Marson moved:

> That Rule 15, so far as it relates to the Warden, be amended by the insertion of the words, "who shall be ineligible for more than one year at a time."[120]

The aim was obviously to unseat Headlam, though Marson carefully paid tribute to the warden's achievements:

> Mr. Headlam had taught them to look for Christian coincidences in movements that do not suspect themselves to be Christian, for example Theatrical Dancing. But any one man is much less broad than the Church at large. . . . They wanted to discover socialist applications in other arts—music, painting and sculpture, as well as in dancing.

As for politics, Headlam "had taught them to look for the gold of Christian socialism in the heaps of quartz and rubble called the Liberal Party." Furthermore, said Marson, and here his moralism came out, in the matter of sexual morality, "They wanted a Warden who would make a strong, immediate and persistent protest on the subject. . .; who would make it very clear that the Guild rejected doctrines subversive of Christian marriage." Above all, the GSM should be independent of Headlam's *private* activities: "It should be made clear that *the members of the Guild are not 'Headlamites' but Christian socialists.*"

The motion was supported by Rev. Dean T. C. Collings who, it will be remembered, had supported his colleague Professor Shuttleworth against Headlam in 1891. (Collings objected to the exclusion of laymen from the wardenship.) The Bristol branch was unanimous for Marson. F. Viney (the lay member from St. Phillip's Mission, Plaistow) asked whether the GSM could afford "to throw away men like James Adderley" who had resigned because of Headlam's

120 This, and the following quotations, are from *Church Reformer*, xiv, No. 10 (October 1895), pp. 219-233 (italics mine).

action, and appealed to members to save the Guild by voting for the Marson motion. A distinguished clerical member, Rev. J. Cartmel-Robinson, disliked Headlam's secular educational doctrines and "did not want the Guild to be made the puppet of Liberal policy."

But once again most members remained loyal to Headlam. He had already been reelected warden. Among Marson's opponents were Rev. T. Hill, and also Rev. C. E. Escreet (Rector of Woolwich), who had disfavored Headlam in 1891 but now felt that the warden "has from time to time done things which have 'made people jump.' They have been justified by history *every time.* The Guild wants a pilot. . . ." The motion was defeated ignominiously and won only seven votes.[121]

The vote on Marson's motion was a personal victory for Stewart Headlam,[122] but an ultimate defeat for the Guild of St. Matthew. As far as deep criticism from the younger generation was concerned, Headlam would sooner scrap both the Guild and the journal than alter his original concepts. Accordingly, pleading financial failure, the *Church Reformer* issued its farewell number in December 1895. "There is a limit to the amount which one individual can be expected to spend on the education of the Church," wrote Headlam. The paper should sell at least two thousand more copies a year to pay, and he had personally spent £1,200 on it over the years—losing about £110 a year. This was doubtless true, but Headlam admitted that circulation had not fallen, and in January had proudly listed at least

---

121 *Ibid.,* p. 232. It is not clear from this statement whether Escreet had now come round to supporting secular education. Marson's defeat was followed by a mild reprimand from Verinder in the form of a motion that no members be nominated for office unless they agreed in writing. He complained that Marson had nominated several candidates who later refused to stand, including Miss Hancock (who was elected to the Council without being consulted). Dearmer seconded the motion and it was carried, Marson being the sole opponent. On his demand for a ballot of the entire Guild, however, he gained wider support.

122 The vote on his reelection was largely a vote of confidence from the Guild after the Oscar Wilde affair (Bettany, p. 91).

ten good causes which the *Reformer* had advanced in the past nine years.[123]

In truth, the journal went down under a hail of critical fire. It suffered two chief failures. The first was journalistic: its inability to attract a working-class readership. The price (2d.) was quite expensive, and there was heavy competition in the field from the "new journalism" of the day—smart, crisp, and secular. "If it went into more than one hundred East End homes I should be surprised," wrote Bettany. In the editor's judgment,

> The large majority of the people for whom we are work-
> ing are completely indifferent to our work one way or the
> other; it may be said that, until their material conditions
> are better . . . we were foolish to expect that they would
> attend us.[124]

The *Reformer*'s second failure was one of political judg-ment. The paper was highly idiosyncratic, and Headlam was a martinet as editor, conflicting with Sarson, Shuttle-worth, Dearmer, and Marson in turn and ignoring to a large extent the demands of a wider readership. Above all, his greatest error was to decry the Independent Labour Party.

In 1903 it was suggested that the GSM should disband. Many of its members had long since defected to the Chris-tian Social Union; the impetus had gone out of the Guild. The prodigal son, J. G. Adderley, however, hastened to lec-ture the members on their past glories and begged them to continue. A representative of the CSU's "radical" wing, he was beginning to feel, as were his closest friends, that the

---

[123] *Church Reformer*, XIV, No. 12 (December 1895); XIV, No. 10 (October 1895), p. 222. The good causes were: a) the idea of "the Church as a real living society, the active body of Christ upon earth"; b) the Church's duty in social and political matters; c) the land question; d) better relations between Church and Stage; e) re-vival of municipal life; f) increased public favor for "Socialism by taxation"; g) teaching of "essentially democratic character of the Church and her Sacraments"; h) abolition of patronage; i) the "decay of Bible-worship"; j) the restoration of the Mass (XII, No. 1 [January 1893], pp. 3-4).
[124] Bettany, p. 120; *Church Reformer, loc.cit.*

CSU was weakening. He looked back to the old radical days of the GSM with pleasure. It was now the turn of the CSU to suffer. Moreover, there had been "a clumsy recrudescence of (I won't call it by so noble a name as secularism) Christian-baiting"; Robert Blatchford's *Clarion* was attacking religion. "Calvinism and Toryism are still confounded with the Catholic faith," said Adderley.[125] This was work for the GSM!

Stewart Headlam, however, was fifty-six years old and fully occupied with educational duties. Shuttleworth (1900), Sarson (1902), and Hancock (1903) were by now all dead. Moll outlived Headlam, but was now totally absorbed by North Country affairs at Newcastle. In brief, there was work for the Guild to do, but no Guild to do it. Marson was in the heart of Somerset; but other young members were extremely restive. Conrad Noel, for instance, possessed a socialism of "a stronger, 'redder' tinge than Headlam's"; Egerton Swann had "modernist tendencies"; "young Cecil Chesterton assumed the position of a critic and made things uncomfortable towards the last."[126] Moll, Marson, Noel, Swann, and Chesterton all joined the rival Church Socialist League (1906) and found themselves in the company of other ex-GSM friends—F. L. Donaldson, P.E.T. Widdrington, Aidan Hancock, G. Algernon West, and Paul Stacy. Two years after the League was founded, the young radical wing of the GSM, led by Swann, tried to impose a pledge on members to support the newer group and work "in close co-operation and consultation" with it. Any "utterance or action of a Guild member inconsistent with the advocacy of such socialism" (that of the League) was to be considered "incompatible with loyalty to the Guild." The impossible pledge was defeated, as was a new attempt to replace Headlam as warden.

The following year (1909), Headlam dissolved the Guild

---

[125] *Commonwealth*, VIII, No. 11 (November 1903), pp. 329-331.
[126] Rev. W.H.C. Malton (Vicar of Thorpe) in Bettany, p. 90; Headlam's own words, *ibid.*, pp. 90-91. The warden told Chesterton: "You may be clever—but you're wrong!"

of St. Matthew to prevent its transformation.[127] Perhaps the surprising thing about his society was not its death but its amazing longevity. It contained a host of independent-minded, vociferous, conflicting men, yet managed to survive under the domination of *one* of them; it stood for widely divergent aims; it ran counter to accepted popular prejudices in matters of religious practice, sex, and personal life; it was hostile to Nonconformity and often narrowly denominational; it stood for the reeducation of the Church of England but disregarded the need to win over general opinion in that church.[128] But in the strikes, demonstrations, and agitations of the socialist revival of the eighties and nineties it had performed yeoman service, and it had pioneered in that essential reinterpretation of Christian dogma to meet the needs of the industrial age without which Victorian religion might not have survived.

Headlam's social theology

When the Guild had long passed its peak and was crumbling away, Headlam published two of his three most important books: *The Meaning of the Mass* (1905) and *The Socialist Church* (1908).[129] One must distinguish between

[127] *Ibid.*, pp. 92-93. "We are doing no work, selling no literature, making hardly any new members. The only thing we do is to talk about the definition of socialism . . . I don't want the name of our Guild to be captured by a few people out of touch with our work—and this might happen at any time at the instigation of a faction. The Church Socialist League will provide a home for these people when the Guild is dead. . . . I am so overwhelmed with L.C.C. work that I can't give the time to petty disputes" (Headlam to G. M. Miller, last Hon. Treasurer of the GSM).

[128] "We have not been able," said Headlam, "to induce the parish churches themselves to regard the work we do as part and parcel of their ordinary Christian duty, neither have we accomplished the justifying of the Catholic religion to the hearts and minds of the people of England" (Binyon, p. 147).

[129] He was also still active on the LCC and in the Fabian Society. In his lecture "Fabianism and Land Values" (delivered to the Society on 23 October 1908) Headlam reminded Fabians of their debt to Henry George. "The first part of our 'Basis' is in fact saturated with the teaching of Henry George," he claimed. To describe the "Actual working of our Society," the "Basis" should read: "The Fabian So-

Headlam and his Guild; his influence as a writer was very much wider than that of the Guild, and many Anglicans who were unable to keep up with all his apparent eccentricities in political and social life found his writing indispensable. These two books, together with a third (perhaps his chief work), *The Laws of Eternal Life* (1887), supplied a satisfying theological basis for Christian social reform.

For Headlam, as for F. D. Maurice, *nothing* was secular. "Secularism" was, therefore, a vast misunderstanding. The Mass sanctifies all human life. Christianity was not merely a religion of social *implications,* but the "sole, sufficient foundation for a true way of life, justifying on Divine authority a claim to penetrate and transform the whole social order."[130] To found all social change on religion was simply a *practical* necessity.

Headlam's "socialism" was sacramental and Christ-centered. First, he thought, the sacraments must be restored to their original position in the Church. "Baptism is the entrance of every human being into the greatest democratic society in the world," said Adderley, explaining "Headlam's gospel," and the Mass is "the weekly meeting of a society of rebels against a Mammon-worshipping world order."[131] "We are a baptized brotherhood of equals," Headlam calmly announced in Westminster Abbey (Maundy Thursday, 1881).[132] The Church's members are admitted "simply on

ciety consists of Bureaucratic Collectivists and admirers of Mr. Bernard Shaw, and concerns itself with almost every social activity except the tackling of the Land Question." (The lecture came at a time of revived Single Tax agitation, which helped to lead toward the Lloyd George budget of 1909.) See Headlam, *Fabianism and Land Values* (London: ELRL, 1908), p. 3; and Jones, Manchester thesis, pp. 240-241. Like most Fabians, Headlam was not a pacifist and supported World War I, though the war brought him great spiritual unrest. See his *Some Old Words About the War* (London, 1915), written to help sustain his old parishioners of Bethnal Green who had relatives on the battle line.

[130] S. C. Carpenter, II, 329; M. B. Reckitt, *Faith and Society* (London, 1932), pp. 83-86.

[131] In *Commonwealth* (December 1926); Reckitt, *Faith and Society*, p. 86.

[132] Bettany, pp. 120-121. In a later address Headlam pointed out that "all these class distinctions which in various ways Liberalism

the grounds of their humanity." They do not have to prove their intellect, family background, property ownership, or spiritual "conversion" before being admitted. The supreme expression of a Christian's faith in the Incarnation was at Holy Communion. Headlam believed in the Real Presence and (in *The Meaning of the Mass*) was willing to accept any title for the supreme sacrament, provided its multiple significance was made clear: one could call it *Holy Communion* ("pledging all who partake of it to be sharers of their wealth, . . . to be Holy Communists"); or the *Holy Eucharist* ("telling us that it is a God of Joy, . . . that human joy is sacred, and religion should be a joyful thing") ; or the *Lord's Supper* ("this name reminds us that this great service took the place of the Jewish Passover Supper. . . . So week by week we keep festival in honor of Christ the Deliverer from all tyrants, the Emancipator of oppressed nations and classes everywhere") ; or simply, the *Mass* (the "international title" for "the same unique Christian service . . . offered in St. Petersburg, Vienna, Rome, Berlin, Paris and London") . In the light of Christ's one great sacrifice, honored in the Mass, Headlam demanded attention for all social evils— land monopoly, sweated industries, lack of education, and so on:

> It becomes impossible for a priest, who knows what the Lord's Supper means, not to take a part to the best of his power in every work of political or social emancipation: impossible for an earnest communicant not to be an earnest politician.

In addition to the sacraments there was also the *personality* of Jesus Christ:

> In the worship of Jesus really present in the Sacrament of the Altar before you, all human hearts can join, and especially secularists, for when you worship Him you are worshipping the Saviour, the social and political Emanci-

---

had to contend against, are condemned . . . by every baptism and Holy Communion, as well as by the teaching of Jesus Christ and His Apostles." This includes "aristocracy of intellect," as of land or family.

pator, the greatest of all secular workers, the founder of the great socialistic society for the promotion of righteousness, the preacher of a revolution, the denouncer of kings, the gentle, tender sympathizer with the rough and the outcast, who could utter scathing, burning words against the rich, the respectable, the religious.[133]

Christ taught by his own actions five principles, said Headlam at the Guild's eleventh annual meeting (September 1888) : the importance of work in *this* world; the need sometimes to be aggressive, even "stern" and "violent" in language;[134] that Christ is King of *all* spheres of human activity; that the Church was intended to be "an organised Brotherhood" for the extension of social justice; and that "the eternal Word of God speaks to many who do not know that it is His voice."[135] Of his anti-Puritanism Headlam said: "Perhaps there is not much of the mystic in me. Perhaps I am too carnal. . . . I have always deprecated other-worldliness, as it is called." Yet, did not Christ himself provide wine for the marriage feast at Cana and institute that service of joy, the Eucharist?

> I am dead against the "other-worldly" folk who promise to the Christian reward in a future life for suffering here, and so virtually encourage apathy in this life towards what is wrong in our social relations.[136]

The Christian should give his loyalty to a Person, not to an infallible Book; and the image of Christ should be in his mind every time he sees social evil:

> The body of Christ, the human race, . . . this in our ignorance we keep crucifying afresh. We don't know whether the very clothes we are wearing are not stained with the lifeblood . . . of our brothers and sisters.[137]

[133] *Loc.cit.*
[134] Headlam himself was once involved in a lawsuit for using "violent language" in Trafalgar Square.
[135] *Church Reformer*, VII, No. 10 (October 1888), pp. 219-221.
[136] Bettany, p. 217.
[137] *The Socialist's Church* (1908) and *Lessons from the Cross* (1886), quoted in Bettany, pp. 214 and 143-144.

The extent of the fusion of theology and economic reform which Headlam achieved is best illustrated by his provocative and caustic statements before the Royal Commission on Ecclesiastical Discipline, to which he was called after an anonymous visitor complained about various "Romanist" practices in his service at All Souls', St. Margaret's-on-Thames in August 1904.

> The reporter is right when he says that I read to myself the "Last Gospel" and genuflected thereat . . . it consists of the first verses of St. John's Gospel—the concentrated statement of the Incarnation of the Eternal Word of God. . . . I "bowed my knee" . . . when I read to myself the words which are the centre of all life and civilisation, which abolish all class distinctions and unbrotherly monopolies, "the Word was made flesh." The most stupendous fact in history! I acknowledge that it brought me to my knees.[138]

Headlam concluded, with great emphasis:

> Ecclesiastical discipline should be directed against the real disorders in the Church; those disorders are social and industrial, and not ritual, and they are terrible.

> Whether I was right in making the sign of the Cross in the air, or in kissing the Altar are matters of infinitesimal importance compared with the fact that in the London diocese and the Canterbury province so many little children have no clean beds to sleep in, . . . so many [men]

---

[138] Bettany, pp. 210ff. Headlam admitted to having a Cross carried before him, kissing the Holy Table and the Gospel Book, genuflecting, holding private devotions during the singing of the Sanctus, and using material from the Roman Missal. He hoped the Archbishop would forgive the man who carried the Cross—"he was not unknown to the Archbishop in his youth, and is now a manager at a well conducted music-hall." The two servers Headlam confessed to were not priests: ". . . one is in a builders' merchant's office, the other, I believe, is a coal merchant," and "the two men, simple laymen as they are had the audacity to ask Almighty God to have mercy upon me, forgive me my sins and bring me to everlasting life." In other words, Headlam insisted that the priest should not "make too much of himself" in the service.

are out of work, so many are overworked, so many are underpaid.

The two chief sacraments of the Kingdom of Heaven on Earth are Equality and Fraternity. In that Kingdom there are no "endless discussions as to how to get the working-classes to Church, how to deal with the lapsed masses, followed by all sorts of dodges and attractions," but instead, a simple recognition that "the people *are* the Church."[139]

[139] *The Socialist's Church*, quoted in Bettany, pp. 143-144.

CHAPTER VI

The Christian Social Union, 1889-1919

The Guild and the Union

STEWART HEADLAM and his disciples were the shock troops of "sacramental socialism." The Christian Social Union was the army of occupation, and its well-to-do academic members enjoyed the privileges thereof. The Union was in many ways the child of the Guild, though the latter was sometimes "not proud of its offspring." The Union grew to a membership of about six thousand, including many bishops. In the years 1889-1913, roughly the period of this study, 16 out of the 53 episcopal appointments made in the Church of England went to CSU men. The CSU rapidly became a highly distinguished and respectable institution.

All this is in ironic contrast with the experiences and character of the luckless GSM. "It passes my imagination to see Gore or even Holland [CSU leaders] at one of Headlam's Sunday night 'at homes,' surrounded by budding poets, painters, writers, actors and ladies of the ballet," said Widdrington some years later. Headlam himself confessed acidly: "I can well understand that it would be perhaps for many reasons a little difficult for some of these distinguished gentlemen to come and join our little society."[1] Nevertheless, the CSU grew directly out of the work already achieved by the more modest Guild and gained many of its first adherents from that source. The London branch of the CSU, for instance, was barely distinguishable from the GSM— including Shuttleworth, Moll, Donaldson, Dearmer, Adderley, Cartmel-Robinson, A. W. Jephson, and others. (This may explain the early split between the London and Oxford CSU branches, London being much more "radical" and Headlamite in spirit.)

[1] C. Noel, *Socialism in Church History*, p. 257; M. B. Reckitt, *Maurice to Temple*, pp. 138-139; *Church Reformer*, VIII, No. 10 (October 1889), p. 219.

Naturally, since in 1889 the Guild was at its height, there was considerable resentment at the foundation of a rival body within the Anglican church. Why not simply swell the ranks of the existing Guild? "No doubt," admitted Shuttleworth, "the members of the GSM do not see quite clearly why these good people, who are now at last interesting themselves in Christian economics, would not come into their ranks and help on the work of which . . . they have been the pioneers." But instead the CSU chose to profit by the previous hard work and preparing of the way by the Guild. The Union thus found a church audience more ready to listen, and robbed the GSM of many potential recruits and former members.[2] Yet Stewart Headlam did his best to be fair and to exclude bitterness, even if he did not always manage to control himself:

> . . . let us, I charge you, have no petty jealousy in this matter. We have laboured and they are welcome to enter into the fruits of our labours. . . . our reward comes not at the end of the day but in the work itself. To have stood socially idle during this last wonderful ten years, not to have been called . . . is their loss.

He was obviously deeply wounded by the establishment of the new group, and tried to take hope in the possibility that the Union might be stillborn:

> But after all, this new and dignified society is not yet founded, and when it is . . . it may not be thorough, uncompromising, definite . . . [therefore] we should increase both the strength and numbers of our Guild.[3]

[2] D. O. Wagner, *The Church of England and Social Reform*, p. 214; W. J. Hocking (ed.), *The Church and New Century Problems* (London, 1901), p. 160 (essay by Dearmer on the CSU).

[3] *Church Reformer*, loc.cit. See also VIII, No. 7 (July 1889), p. 150. Headlam tried to be noble about the CSU, but it is surely too much to suggest, as Gore's biographer does, that he "recognized the wisdom of forming a new organisation into which might be drawn men whose position or convictions made them less reckless of outraging respectability than he was himself." See G. L. Prestige, *Life of Charles Gore* (London, 1935), p. 91.

Headlam's radical suspicions of the probable mild character of the Union were justified. "The leaders of the CSU," said Widdrington, "were unable to free themselves from the accidents of their education. They had been dons, and they were never able to shake off the traditions of the universities." Widdrington partly excluded Canon Scott Holland from this judgment, but Scott Holland himself, though the liveliest of CSU members, dubbed the GSM leaders "Headlong and Shuttlecock." On the other hand, the Union, said Conrad Noel, "glories in its indefiniteness, and seems to consider it a crime to arrive at any particular economic conclusion. . . . An unkind critic has described it as forever learning but never coming to a knowledge of the truth."[4] Despite this vagueness, the CSU was destined to achieve a much greater impact than the Guild on the Church of England in general, and through that church on other religious bodies and the general community. Perhaps the principal difference between the two societies was that the CSU had room for at least three "great men"—Westcott, Gore, and Holland—while in the GSM Headlam would allow only one.

The relationship between the Guild and the Union can be seen on a wider scale, however. It seems natural for any body of church folk to sustain a small "ginger group" of radicals and a larger, milder group of reformists. This is the pattern that actually emerged, at least, in late nineteenth- and early twentieth-century Britain. "Social-Unionism" (as Noel termed the ideology of the reformists) spread from the Church of England to other denominations, just as the settlement movement had spread earlier. The Friends' Social Union was created in 1904, the Wesleyan Methodist Social Union in 1905, the (Roman) Catholic Social Guild in 1909. Among Quakers the radical pressure group corresponding to Headlam's GSM was the Socialist Quaker Society

[4] Reckitt, loc.cit. "So mild was it," quipped Headlam in later life, "that Bishop Westcott could act as its President." See F. G. Bettany, *Stewart Headlam*, p. 90; S. Paget, *H. S. Holland: Memoirs and Letters* (London, 1921), p. 204; Noel, *Socialism in Church History*, p. 257.

(1898) ; among Roman Catholics it was the Catholic Social-ist Society (1906). An "Interdenominational Conference of Social Service Unions," uniting the reformists, was held in 1911; there was, however, no "interdenominational confer-ence" of the more radical Christian socialists.

Origins of the CSU

For the origins of the Christian Social Union other than those shared by the Guild of St. Matthew, one must look, on the one hand, toward a regular private meeting of Anglican priests which called itself, half in fun, the "Holy Party" and a controversial book of theological essays, *Lux Mundi;* and on the other hand, toward a set of economic lectures by W. Richmond and a transitory social discussion group at Oxford called "PESEK." In the background of the year 1889 was, of course, the drama of the great Dock Strike.

The theology of social-unionism flowed out of the Trac-tarian-Maurice-Headlam stream. *Lux Mundi* was a further development of Tractarian theology, combining the "Cath-olic Church" of Pusey with the "Kingdom of Christ" of Maurice, as Headlam did. The members of the "Holy Party," Scott Holland, Illingworth, Talbot, and Gore, first met in 1875. All Oxford men in Holy Orders, their idea was to occupy some small rural parish for a summer month, taking over parish duties (while the incumbent vacationed) and using spare time for discussion and reading. From 1890 right down to 1915 the "parties" were always held at J. R. Illingworth's rectory, Longworth, in Berkshire.[5]

Charles Gore (1855-1932) was younger than the rest of his circle. He came of very aristocratic stock[6] and spent his

---

[5] M. B. Reckitt, *Faith and Society*, p. 88; Prestige, p. 25; Mrs. J. R. Illingworth, *Life and Work of J. R. Illingworth* (London, 1917), pp. 153ff.

[6] Grandson of the second Earl of Arran. Gore's family were Irish peers on both sides, and ultimately of ancient English descent: his grandmother was the great-great-granddaughter of John Pym. Lean, masculine, saintly looking, with a firm nose and a white, pointed beard, Gore looked quite noble—in the El Greco style. See, for instance, the photograph in Prestige, frontispiece. His features were ideal for a man destined to be bishop successively of Worcester, Birmingham, and Oxford.

childhood among the Whig nobility. At Harrow (1866-1871) Gore proved his independence by rejecting the school's evangelical tradition and joining a small High Church group, radical supporters of Gladstone. It was an influence he would never lose, for B. F. Westcott himself was assistant master at Harrow at the time, lecturing the boys on the benefits of monasticism and urging them to attend a weekly Eucharist. Gore had visited that famous ritualist Father A. H. Stanton at St. Alban's, Holborn, while still in his teens. Stanton taught him "to make his confessions, to love the Mass, and to fast on Fridays."[7] At Oxford (Christ Church 1871-1875) in the early seventies, Gore won a First in Greats and a Fellowship at Trinity (1875). He was ordained in 1876. In the Oxford Union the young Gore spoke up for the Liberal government, opposed the cult of athleticism at the university, and publicly supported trade unions. He had been deeply impressed by Joseph Arch's

[7] *Ibid.*, p. 11. Rev. A. H. Stanton (1839-1912). Educated at Rugby and Oxford and for fifty years an unpaid assistant curate, Stanton was always in trouble with the authorities but remained irrepressible and loyal to his church. "I know no liberalism except that I have sucked in from the breasts of the Gospel," he declared, and warned an audience at Stroud, "as the only thing I care much for is socialism, I am a very dangerous lecturer." In truth, he also cared for incense, rich vestments, and the "good life," and fought strongly against Puritanism, teetotalism, and Sabbatarianism. Violently opposed to the Public Worship Regulation Act of 1875 and the mob persecution of St. Alban's which preceded it, Stanton's sermons were wildly misreported in the evangelical press. "What an Act!" he cried, "What a title! As if the House of God was a dairy or a hackney carriage!"; and in 1875 he wrote: "[Rev. E. F.] Russell preached a beautiful testimony last Lord's Day night. He called the Established Church a *dung-hill*, which was 'the word with power,' wasn't it? *I Corinthians*, ii, 4." In May 1877, against official opposition, Stanton organized the post office workers in the St. Martin's League to protect them against long hours, and provide rest-houses and other facilities; in 1879 he joined the Council of Headlam's Church and Stage Guild. Few GSM or CSU members did not owe something to his impressive services. St. Alban's, Kingsway, today gives Stanton only a brief reference in its summary history and is very dilapidated, with no trace of its former ritualistic splendors (1963). See G.W.E. Russell, *A. H. Stanton: A Memoir* (London, 1917), passim; *Crockford's Clerical Directory*, 1894, p. 1254; S. C. Carpenter, *Church and People*, ii, 382; C. Noel, *An Autobiography*, pp. 6-7.

Agricultural Labourers' Union of 1872 and the bitterness of conservative opposition to it; with some other High Churchmen, Gore gave Arch his help.

Like Headlam and Scott Holland, Charles Gore was deeply influenced by T. H. Green; but he added to this interest a searching study of patristics. In Green he found the doctrine of the positive state, and in patristics, religious communalism. (St. Athanasius, in particular, affected Gore's thinking.) During his five years as a Trinity don Gore undertook parish work in run-down areas of industrial Liverpool and lived a very ascetic life. Made vice-principal of the Anglican college at Cuddesdon in 1880, he proved to be a brilliant inspiration to student priests and four years later, at the age of thirty-one, became first principal of the newly established Pusey House at Oxford. Students flocked to him, and he rapidly became the "most potent religious force in Oxford" since Newman. Gore remained at Pusey House from 1884 to 1893.[8]

A childhood friend of Gore at Wimbledon was Henry Scott Holland (1847-1918), another aristocratic youth. Holland's grandfather was a partner of Baring's bank; his uncle, an MP; his father, an independent gentleman of no particular occupation, who enjoyed traveling, hunting, and driving a four-in-hand; his mother, the daughter of Lord Gifford (Master of the Rolls, Chief Justice of Common Pleas, and Deputy Speaker of the Lords). The parents met at a hunt ball; as a matter of course, their son went to Eton and Balliol. At Eton Holland's tutor was the same William Johnson who had taught Stewart Headlam. At Oxford ("Eton over again, on a different stretch of the same river")

[8] Prestige, p. 76. Gore's later career was as follows: established the Society of the Resurrection (1887); founder member of CSU (1889); essayist in *Lux Mundi* (1889); Canon of Westminster (1894-1901); Bishop of Worcester (1901-1905), of Birmingham (1905-1911), and of Oxford (1911-1919). Retired in 1919 but took a small house in London and continued to work for thirteen more years, becoming lecturer at King's College, London, and eventually Dean of Theology there (1924-1928), following in the footsteps of both Maurice and of Shuttleworth (Prestige, passim). See also G. Crosse, *Charles Gore: A Biographical Sketch* (London and Oxford, 1932).

his personal tutor was the great T. H. Green himself. Holland told Green, "You have taught me everything of importance that I have learnt at Oxford."[9] Arnold Toynbee was also a deep influence, and when Holland was elected to a Christ Church studentship (1871-1884), he began to put into practice the ethical precepts of Green and Toynbee. These teachings were strengthened in Holland's mind by a summer session with B. F. Westcott (July 1872). Ordained, Scott Holland ventured out into street preaching in London, and even talked of "organising a connection between Oxford and the socialistic spirit which springs out of the misery of our great cities." He was to spend much of his life in close proximity to this urban misery, for in 1884 he went directly from Christ Church to St. Paul's Cathedral as canon.[10] As far as CSU history is concerned, this appointment opened up the most important part of Scott Holland's life.

The chief host of the Holy Party, Rev. J. R. Illingworth (1848-1915) was different in style from either the charismatic Gore or the witty and popular Canon Holland. Illingworth was deeply intellectual, rather puritanical, and very shy and retiring. Like Gore, he took a First in Greats (1872), followed by a Fellowship at Jesus College and a tutorship at Keble, and finally settled down as Rector of Longworth, a country spot twelve miles from Oxford. His life pattern was now fixed: himself a chaplain's son, he immediately married a country rector's daughter and spent the rest of his life at Longworth, engaged in parish duties, "Holy Parties," and writing. Though he shunned the highways of life, Illingworth was in his quiet way an impressive teacher and a well-known and influential Christian apologist. Molded by

9 Paget, pp. 19, 47, 113.

10 He got the appointment through a family friend—the Prime Minister, Gladstone (*ibid.*, pp. 69-70). Scott Holland worked in London for twenty-six years before returning to Oxford as Regius Professor of Divinity in 1910. He edited the CSU's *Economic Review* for five years (1889-1894), helped to found Adderley's *Goodwill*, and began editing *Commonwealth* in 1896. See H. Martin (ed.), *Christian Social Reformers of the Nineteenth Century* (London, 1927), pp. 207-226 (essay by Adderley).

T. H. Green, John Ruskin, and E. S. Talbot (Warden of Keble and a member of the Holy Party), Illingworth developed a kind of High Church Hegelianism. He was the chief theologian of the group.[11]

When the Holy Party was first conceived in 1875, Illingworth, Scott Holland, and Gore were all Oxford dons, at Jesus, Christ Church, and Trinity respectively. The Holy Party was "the germ of the CSU—of Mirfield, and of *Lux Mundi*," wrote Illingworth in 1912, "rather a prolific fact."[12] Scott Holland was probably the chief inspirer of the idea of a summer "working retreat." The aim of the discussions was to reach some reconciliation between reason (modern science and the higher criticism) and revelation (modern Christian beliefs). Inevitably, the party produced a book of essays. Given the intellectual power and the social distinction of its authors, that work was almost certain to make a stir in late-Victorian Britain.

Lux Mundi: A Series of Studies in the Religion of the Incarnation, edited by Gore and published in 1889, was an uncompromisingly learned volume. Yet within one year it reached its tenth edition. The book was an attempt "to put the Catholic Faith in its right relation to modern intellectual and moral problems." The Faith needed "disencumbering, reinterpreting, explaining" because

> the epoch in which we live is one of profound transformation, intellectual and social, abounding in new needs, new points of view, new questions; and certain therefore to involve great changes in the outlying departments of theology, where it is linked onto the sciences, and to necessitate some general reinstatement of its claim and meaning [so that the Church can reveal] again and again her power of witnessing under changed conditions to the Catholic capacity of her faith and life.[13]

[11] Illingworth wrote six or seven major theological treatises, including *Personality, Human and Divine* (1894), *Divine Immanence* (1898), and *Divine Transcendence* (1911).
[12] Mrs. J. R. Illingworth, p. 168.
[13] *Lux Mundi* (London, 1890), pp. vii-ix.

Twelve essays covered most of the theological questions raised by modern scientific and critical investigations. Holland wrote simply on "Faith," Illingworth on "The Problem of Pain" and "The Incarnation in Relation to Development," and Gore on "The Holy Spirit and Inspiration." For Holland the perplexities of modern life were consistent with continued Christian religious faith, because faith is an elemental, personal act, like love. Faith, he argued, is incapable of analysis, and its object, "Christ, the same yesterday, today and forever," is unchanging.[14] Illingworth emphasized the positive utility of pain in human development; pain is an antidote to sin, a source of sympathy with fellowmen, a secret of union with God through Christ. In his second essay, Illingworth declares the parallelism of theology and science; the first explores the meaning and the second the method of "creative evolution." Christianity is thus compatible with all the verifiable results of scientific teaching.[15]

So far, the essays were a logical and reasonable extension of the earlier *Essays and Reviews* of 1860. The controversy was to rage over the eighth piece—Gore on the Holy Spirit and Inspiration. Christianity, said Gore, is an experienced or manifested life. Its essence is the possession of the Holy Spirit, not belief in any book. Holy Scripture is not a *basis* but merely a necessary article of faith, liable to scientific criticism; such criticism should merely serve to enrich reverence for the "Word of God." While the New Testament was "final and Catholic," the Old was "imperfect, because it represents a gradual process of education by which man was lifted." The Old Testament had a generally truthful air, but contained a heavy admixture of unhistorical elements.

---

[14] *Ibid.*, pp. 1-54. Holland's argument is centered on the personality of Christ, and perfectly illustrates the Christ-centered aspect of Social Gospel theology. Gore's Bampton Lectures of 1891 brought this argument to its fullest development: Christianity means absolute faith in *a person*, Jesus Christ the incarnate God; and all nature is but a progressive revelation of God, culminating in the morally perfect example of Jesus (Prestige, pp. 134ff.).

[15] *Ibid.*, pp. 116-126, 187-188.

Even Christ's own references to Old Testament events did not make them historically true. It was this implication by Gore of limitations to Christ's knowledge which upset many of the orthodox. "Old ladies spoke of Gore," writes his biographer, "as 'that awful Mr. Gore who doesn't believe the Bible.' " Moreover, his emphasis on the Holy Spirit rather than the Word seemed nearer to Quaker beliefs than to Anglican doctrine.[16]

Headlam's *Church Reformer* seized the opportunity in reviewing *Lux Mundi* of claiming its message for the Guild of St. Matthew. The Guild's Oxford branch had "prepared the way" for *Lux Mundi;* the essays tried "to justify God" to the junior members of the University of Oxford. There was nothing "fresh or new" in the book. Gore's essay should not throw doubt on Christ's integrity or knowledge, for "faith in Our Lord's Godhead does not stand or fall with acceptance of the prose accuracy of the story of Jonah and the Whale." The *Church Reformer* hoped that *Lux Mundi,* while greatly inferior to the works of F. D. Maurice, would at least show Oxford students that "there are more important questions to face than the Public Worship Regulation Act, or the Deceased Wife's Sister Bill."[17] Some of the "more important questions" indicated by *Lux Mundi* were, as Headlam would have wished, *social.* Gore insisted on the social character of the work done by the Holy Spirit in the Christian Church: man expresses himself through society; social authority does not restrict but facilitates individual variety, for man cannot realize himself in isolation. Gore's argument directly echoed the idealist principles of T. H. Green and the "positive State," and received theological support from a famous set of Bampton Lectures at Oxford by a Balliol Fellow, W. H. Fremantle, *The World as the Subject of Redemption* (1883). Fremantle (later to become Dean of Ripon), argued forcefully against the evangelical emphasis on piety and individual sin: "The Chris-

---

[16] Prestige, p. 105. As we have seen, the earlier *Essays and Reviews* was also regarded in this light by radical young Quakers.

[17] *Church Reformer,* IX, No. 5 (May 1890), pp. 110-111; IX, No. 6 (June 1890), pp. 126-128.

tian Church," he wrote, "is designed, not to save individuals out of the world, but to save the world itself." The year before the CSU's founding, Fremantle had said that the time had come for Anglicans to take a second, more favorable look at socialism.[18] *Lux Mundi* itself taught that "the accumulation of riches is not in itself a good at all. Neither poverty nor riches make men better in themselves." Property is secondary—a means, not an end. Therefore, if the type of property which exists is *private,* its ownership must be recognized as a *trust,* involving definite social obligations. As for citizenship, the duty of obedience is no stronger than the duty of disobedience for the sake of conscience.

The furor over *Lux Mundi* was a great surprise to its contributors.[19] In the tenth edition (July 1890) Gore tried to set the record straight with a long preface, reviewing criticisms. He complained of the disproportionate attention paid to the book's last twenty pages, and of the failure of critics to grasp the essential purpose of the authors—"to succour a distressed faith" and to "reassure man that his faith in Christ

[18] Fremantle's Bampton Lectures were often used as a source of theological justifications for social action. The American edition, for instance, introduced by a leading US economist and Christian socialist of the Progressive Era, R. T. Ely, called the Lectures "a remarkable presentation of Christian sociology," giving "a religious basis . . . for reform and improvement in every sphere of life" (W. H. Fremantle, *The World as the Subject of Redemption* [New York, 1892]; *The Present Work of the Anglican Communion* [London, 1888], p. 27, quoted also by K. S. Inglis, *Churches and the Working-Classes,* pp. 251-252). Fremantle was a leading spirit in the Charity Organisation Society, which he had helped to found in 1869. (See B. Webb, *My Apprenticeship,* p. 196.) He was still active in the late 1890's: see his plea for a "Welfare State" type of social reform action in "Individualists and Socialists," *Nineteenth Century,* February 1897, pp. 311-324. Here he rejects outright collectivism and state ownership, but rejects Spencerian individualism still more strongly.

[19] See, for instance, Scott Holland to Bishop Copleston (October 1890): "Poor old book! I look at it and wonder. I thought it so dreadfully heavy and dull when I first read it: I never thought we should induce anyone to read it outside the circle of our aunts and mothers . . . and never dreamt of this stormy and excited career. We ourselves seemed to have been saying these things for years: and to have heard everybody else saying them. Now suddenly we find it all spoken of as a bomb, as a new Oxford Movement, &c., &c. We wonder who we are" (Paget, pp. 280-281).

is capable of rational justification."[20] Instead, Gore was criticized for putting science and the social question *before* faith, which he had never intended. This was a standard argument against all radical movements in Christianity and plagued every one of the dozen or so Christian socialist societies that sprang into existence before the First World War.

Meanwhile the "Luxites" had been occupying themselves increasingly with political and social matters. Ten years earlier, in 1879, Scott Holland and Wilfrid Richmond had founded PESEK (standing for "politics, economics, socialism, ethics and Christianity") to discuss social questions. This tiny precursor of the Christian Social Union was confined to private meetings in members' rooms at Oxford. Holland, however, had also helped to establish the Christ Church Mission in Poplar and had lectured to Co-operative Congresses and the like in the 1880's, as had Gore.[21] At the Lambeth Pan-Anglican Conference of 1888 Scott Holland determinedly introduced a discussion of socialism, while the Guild of St. Matthew submitted a long "Appeal" to the conferees, demanding that "every man should work" and that material goods should be divided more fairly by society (St. Paul: "If anyone will not work, neither let him eat"). Scott Holland, Headlam, Shuttleworth, and the labor leader H. H. Champion all addressed the Congress. An encyclical signed by 145 Bishops of the Anglican Faith was eventually issued, deploring "excessive inequality in the distribution of this world's goods, vast accumulation and desperate poverty side by side" and suggesting that "the Christian Church is bound, following the teaching of the Master, to aid every wise endeavour which has for its object the material and moral welfare of the poor."[22] The clergy, said the encyclical even more pointedly, should preach to show "how much of

---

[20] *Lux Mundi*, pp. xi, xiii.

[21] Paget, pp. 100ff., 127; Wagner, pp. 209ff.

[22] *Church Reformer*, VII, No. 8 (August 1888), pp. 180-182. Also see Wagner, *loc.cit.*; and Percy Dearmer, *Socialism and Christianity*, Fabian Tract No. 133 (London, 1907), p. 3. Dearmer points out that this rather surprising encyclical of the bishops was delivered as early as 1888, "when there was no *Clarion* and no Labour Party" (—and in fact, no CSU).

what is good and true in *socialism* is to be found in the precepts of Christ." This was a direct paraphrase of Henry George's aim in *Progress and Poverty*.

More of a direct influence on Holland's little group in that same year was a book by Rev. Wilfrid Richmond, *Christian Economics*. Richmond had been tutor at Keble, Oxford (1876-1881) during Illingworth's tutorship there. A member of the original "Holy Party" of 1875, and a cofounder of PESEK four years later, he joined the CSU the day it was formed.[23]

Christian Economics was a collection of sixteen sermons "to enforce the principle that economic conduct is a matter of duty." Richmond acknowledged a heavy debt to John Ruskin (and also used Marshall's *Economics of Industry*, Arnold Toynbee, Cunningham, and Walker). Rejecting both the classical and the historical approach in themselves, he sought to establish "a Political Economy which shall be a branch of morals." *Justice* was to be the "Law of Exchange," *Love* the "Law of Distribution." Admittedly, economic life is a system of competition as well as cooperation, but " 'the law of saintliness' says at least subordinate competition to co-operation."[24] In the Lent of 1889 Richmond gave four lectures at Sion College on "Economic Morals." The lectures attracted much attention and in 1890 were published as Richmond's second book, with a preface by Scott Holland. While Richmond did not definitely declare himself in favor of full collectivism—the nationalization of the means of pro-

[23] *Crockford's Clerical Directory*, 1886, p. 996; 1894, p. 1119; Mrs. J. R. Illingworth, p. 155; Prestige, pp. 44, 91; Paget, p. 169.

[24] *Christian Economics* (London, 1888), pp. ix-x, 26, and 251. Richmond's book had an impact outside Anglicanism, for in October 1888 at the Congregational Union meeting, Rev. F. H. Stead (brother of W. T. Stead and later founder of the Robert Browning Settlement) delivered a paper on *Christian Economics* which "adopted the same view as that of Rev. W. Richmond." Stead demanded a Christian *science* of economics to replace the unethical orthodox political economy. "Vague exhortations to be just and loving and trustworthy are not enough. . . . We must meet system by system." See *Christian Socialist*, VI, No. 66 (November 1888), pp. 166-167, 169-171; VIII, No. 80 (January 1890), p. 5; and *Brotherhood*, III, No. 2 (September 1888), p. 62.

duction, distribution, and exchange—the lectures did have a socialist bias, and Scott Holland turned them into a movement: the CSU.[25] A provisional committee was established on 14 June 1889, and the name and objects of the Christian Social Union declared at a meeting in St. Paul's Chapterhouse with Canon Scott Holland presiding.

"Social-unionism" in action

The three aims of the Christian Social Union were:

1. To claim for the Christian Law the ultimate authority to rule social practice.
2. To study in common how to apply the moral truths and principles of Christianity to the social and economic difficulties of the present time.
3. To present Christ in practical life as the Living Master and King, the enemy of wrong and selfishness, the power of righteousness and love.

In addition, members were "expected to pray for the well-being of the Union at Holy Communion, more particularly on or about the following days: the Feast of the Epiphany, the Feast of the Ascension, the Feast of St. Michael and All Angels." The similarity of the Union's style with the Guild of St. Matthew is very striking, especially in the latter demand for members' prayers on given dates. Similar, too, was the exclusiveness of the Union. As Holland explained it:

> We did not want to grow indefinitely large: and the difficulty of course is not your excellent Nonconformist, but your fervid socialistic Nothingarian. So we thought it right, without passing a positive exclusive rule, to say that we were men who had a *bond of union in the Sacrament*

[25] Richmond gave the lectures, at Scott Holland's instigation, to relieve what the latter called the "economic blindness of the blackest kind" prevailing in London. "The world seems to have reacted into the mind of 40 years ago," wrote Holland to Richmond late in 1888, "you would think it had never talked democratic language. We are in a mad backwater, eddying furiously" (Paget, p. 169). See also *Economic Review*, I, No. 1 (January 1891), pp. 41-50.

of Christ's Body. Some did not like it: but we passed it and carried it. It is right I think. So there! You see how narrow we are![26]

But despite Scott Holland's willful exclusiveness, the Union was in fact less narrow than the Anglo-Catholic Guild of St. Matthew, and did welcome, at least, all types of Anglicans, High, Broad, and even Low, when it could attract them. "Only Church people," said Gore, "could awaken the Church. Only Church people sharing the same Sacramental system could awaken their fellows to the real social meaning of their baptism, their confirmation and their Holy Communion"; but these church people should also agree on "the need of fundamental social reconstruction . . . whether they refused or accepted the name of Socialist."[27]

CSU members found much of the rhetoric of socialism compatible with their own vocabulary at this stage: "brotherhood"; opposition to "the competitive system"; the demand for "the regeneration of society" to conform to an inner law of altruism. Who could deny the ethical validity of such dreams? "We believe that political problems are rapidly giving place to the industrial problem," declared Scott Holland in the CSU's *The Ground of our Appeal* (1890): "It is the condition of industry which is absorbing all attention, . . . the intolerable situation in which our industrial population now finds itself, that must force upon us a reconsideration of the economic principles and methods which have such disastrous and terrible results."[28] The ultimate solution of the social question could be discovered only in "the person and life of Christ," for "He is 'the Man'; and He must be the solution of all human problems." Not that "sentimental assertion that Christ is all-in-all" is in itself enough—one must go beyond mere acknowledgment to positive social action. Two "deep convictions" should sustain

[26] G. C. Binyon, *The Christian Socialist Movement in England*, p. 158; Paget, pp. 170-171.

[27] Binyon, pp. 242-243.

[28] *Ibid.*, p. 232; Paget, p. 171; W.D.P. Bliss, *The Encyclopaedia of Social Reform* (New York, 1908), p. 261.

the Christian reformer: first, "that the present situation is intolerable"; second, "that its solution must be found in the unfaltering assertion of moral, as supreme over mechanical laws."[29]

In November 1889 a further meeting at St. Paul's elected B. F. Westcott, Gore's former schoolmaster at Harrow, now Canon of Westminster and soon (1890) to become Bishop of Durham, as first president of the CSU.[30] Holland was made chairman of the executive, which included Shuttleworth, Adderley, A. W. Jephson, and other Headlamites from the GSM. Westcott's election certainly set the tone for the new society. Stewart Headlam criticized him harshly for being too mild in social reform matters. Yet Westcott was essentially a scholar, a mystic even, and his later mediation of the tricky coal strike of 1893 was no mean feat for a cleric of his sort. Westcott was a Maurician through and through, as exemplified in his chief social writings, the sermons of 1886, *Social Aspects of Christianity*, the address to the Church Congress of 1890 on "Socialism" (subsequently a CSU and a GSM pamphlet), and his *Christian Aspects of Life* (1897).[31] His "socialism" was of course ill-defined; the word meant

[29] The second "conviction" provoked a bitter attack on Holland and the CSU by a clerical antisocialist, Henson. See J. G. Adderley, *A New Earth* (London, 1903), pp. 47-48.

[30] 1825-1901; leader of the Broad Church school. (Westcott refused even to read *Lux Mundi*, however.) He was a typical member of the CSU elite, and a man on whom many honors were piled; educated at Cambridge (First Class in Classics, 1848); D.D., 1870; Hon. D.C.L. (Oxford), 1881; Hon. D.D. (Edinburgh), 1884; taught at Harrow, 1852-1869; Canon of Peterborough (1869-1883) and Rector of Somersham, Hunts. (1870-1882). These overlapping appointments he held simultaneously with an Hon. Chaplaincy to Queen Victoria and the Regius Chair of Divinity at Cambridge (from 1870). Fellow of King's College, Cambridge, from 1882, and Canon of Westminster 1884-1890 (*Crockford's Clerical Directory*, 1886, p. 1258).

[31] Westcott wrote about twenty books, including a *History of the English Bible* (1869) and an edition of the New Testament in the original Greek (1889). See Reckitt, *Faith and Society*, p. 89n.; A. Westcott, *Life and Letters of B. F. Westcott*, 2 vols. (London, 1903); *William Clarke: Collected Writings*, ed. H. Burrows and J. A. Hobson (London, 1908), pp. 352-356 (review of Westcott); and Wagner, pp. 203ff. For Headlam's criticisms of Westcott, see *Church Reformer*, XIII, No. 1 (January 1894), p. 5, and No. 2 (February 1894), p. 45.

to him (as to Fremantle) a life-theory the opposite of individualism, and which conceives of humanity as an organic whole and adopts cooperation rather than competition as its method of constructing a social system to give every individual the chance to develop his potential.

From the outset there was disagreement among CSU members as to which branch, Oxford or London, had historical precedence. However, at Oxford the branch of the Guild of St. Matthew run by John Carter was dissolved and a Christian Social Union branch established in its place.[32] The Oxford CSU officers were Carter (secretary), Scott Holland (president), Percy Dearmer and others (executive) and a large cluster of distinguished vice-presidents: Gore, Rev. F. J. Chavasse (later Bishop of Liverpool), Rev. W.J.H. Campion (a *Lux Mundi* essayist), Rev. Prof. Sanday, and T. C. Snow. The branch was founded, fittingly, at Pusey House.[33]

In 1892 the CSU tackled Cambridge, from the top. The Master of Trinity (Rev. H. M. Butler) presided at a King's College meeting in November. He reminded the University of its earlier Christian socialist days, and of that famous Trinity student, F. D. Maurice. Westcott urged (by letter from his new bishopric) that all candidates for Holy Orders take CSU lessons in social responsibility. By 1895 there were affiliated societies in the USA, Canada, South Africa, and Australia, and a home membership of over 2,600, grouped into 27 branches. The Oxford and London branches remained the largest, London claiming a membership of about 1,000 in 1895. The CSU was now seven times the size of Headlam's GSM. Its numbers continued to grow, and total membership for the decade 1910-1920 has been estimated

---

32 Bliss, p. 261, claimed precedence for Oxford (16 November 1889) as the first regularly constituted branch. So did John Carter and Scott Holland. Bliss, however, also implies that the CSU was virtually named at the close of Richmond's lectures at Sion College; his facts are not always accurate. Being a prime mover in the American CSU (and the leading American Christian socialist), Bliss probably got his information chiefly from John Carter.

33 P. Dearmer, *The Beginnings of the CSU* (London, 1912), pp. 2-8; Bliss, *loc.cit.*; Prestige, p. 91.

at about 6,000.[34] By 1895 Percy Dearmer had taken over the secretaryship of the London branch. At the annual general meeting that year, Scott Holland gave an aggressive speech, hailing two recent books (the American Christian socialist Professor R. T. Ely's *Socialism* and the progressive English "underconsumptionist" economist J. A. Hobson's *Evolution of Modern Capitalism*) as proof that social evil is inherent in capitalism as an economic system, and that "the great revival of the conception of the Church, and all advances of science and knowledge, conduce to the socialist movement."[35]

The CSU was organized principally to *study* and to *publicize* social and economic problems. It never declared itself for any given platform, as the GSM did in 1884. Its propaganda methods covered public lectures and sermons (especially by the more active London branch), group discussions, the issue of leaflets and studies in considerable quantity, and the use of various journals—the scholarly *Economic Review* (1891-1914) at Oxford, barely distinguishable except for its "ethical" overtones from a normal learned economics journal; J. G. Adderley's more outspoken *Goodwill;* and from 1896 the monthly *Commonwealth,* which survived the Union itself. During its first six or seven years of life, however, the CSU was much taken up with self-education and the conversion of its church to social reform; practical reform suggestions were left to the individual consciences of members. This was a condition that characterized many "Christian socialist" groups.

During the great London Dock Strike of 1889 the London CSU tried to save the popular reputation of the Church of England, such as it was, from too sharp a contrast with the vigorous intervention of Roman Catholicism on the side of the workers in the shape of the redoubtable and aged Cardi-

---

[34] *Economic Review*, III, No. 1 (January 1893), pp. 1-2; Reckitt, *Faith and Society*, p. 92; Prestige, *loc.cit.*; Bliss, *loc.cit. Labour Annual,* 1895, pp. 119-120, estimated a membership somewhat lower, at 2,300 for 1895. There were about 900 members at the opening of 1893 (Carter to Ely, 11 January 1893, R. T. Ely Collection, WSHS).

[35] *Brotherhood*, III, No. 8 (December 1895), p. 102.

nal Manning. Unfortunately for the CSU, the incumbent Bishop of London (Temple) was not at all disposed to cooperate, and only very reluctantly broke off his vacation in Wales to take any action whatsoever on behalf of his troubled working-class flock. After criticizing the dockers, Temple hurriedly returned to Wales and abandoned the problem, leaving it to Manning to resolve.[36] The brand-new Christian Social Union was in a predicament and totally inexperienced. Scott Holland viewed Bishop Temple through rose-colored spectacles, though men like Headlam knew differently. "The noble old chief," said Holland of Temple, "sticks rather hard at certain points, and is rather stiffly economical in the older fashion of economy. But he is so great: and high: and square. And he is now working hard in the cause. . . ." One thing Temple did *not* do was "work hard" in the cause of workingmen. Ben Tillett, the dockers' leader, spoke very highly of Cardinal Manning, of J. G. Adderley, of Canon Barnett and the Toynbee Hall people; but he condemned Temple outright. Tillett watched "the combat of the churches over the bodies of the dockers" with great interest:

> The play of passion and personal interests was centred in the fight the square-jawed, hard-featured Temple put up against the ascetic and spiritual-faced Cardinal Manning; *he would have sacrificed the whole of the dockers to win for his Church.*

Ben Tillett could feel nothing but "contempt" for Temple, who had sent him a "brutal letter" about the struggling dockers. The Roman Catholic Manning, however, "was more humane and subtle, his diplomacy that of the ages and the Church. He chided . . . the pomp of the Lord Mayor, the harshness of Bishop Temple, the pushfulness of [John] Burns." The Church of England gained precious little in the dockers' eyes as a result of the strike of 1889. Til-

---

[36] See J. G. Adderley, "Some Results of the Great Dock Strike," *Economic Review*, II, No. 2 (April 1892), pp. 202-213, for a good CSU analysis of the strike.

lett did have a predilection for Manning, who had given him spiritual counsel at a low ebb in his life; but the dockers' leader was himself a Congregationalist, and his judgment of the role of the various churches in the strike was not unduly biased in favor of the Roman Catholics.[37] The CSU, however, had only very recently been formed and cannot be entirely blamed for this failure. A few years later the Union was prepared to take more of a risk, as, for instance, when Rev. John Carter almost lost his job for inviting Tom Mann to lecture at Exeter College, Oxford (1893),[38] or when the society began to issue its famous consumers' "white lists."

In 1893 the Oxford CSU drew up a list of twenty local firms which had adopted acceptable trade-union wage rates, and it encouraged its members and the public to buy only from such firms. Discriminatory purchasing (a buyers' boycott) was to be the Christian consumer's weapon against the evils of sweated industry. By 1894 the Oxford list included 88 firms and by 1900, 146. Other CSU branches copied the technique. London seemed to be too large a city for this policy to be very practicable; but the Leeds group began with a list of 464 firms in 1898, swelling to 572 by 1900. The idea was not original with the Oxford CSU branch. The Labour Church used the same policy in the Midlands, and the Consumers' League had already been established three years earlier (1890), with Scott Holland as president and a membership including H. C. Shuttleworth, A. W. Jephson, F. C. Baum (London Trades' Council), and Miss Clementina Black (Women's Trade Union Association).[39] "Christian shopping" was of course bitterly opposed by the manufac-

[37] Paget, pp. 170-172; Ben Tillett, *Brief History of the Dockers' Union* (London, 1910), p. 29, and *Memories and Reflections* (London, 1931), p. 137.

[38] Prestige, pp. 150-151. The Bishop of Oxford disapproved of Gore's chairmanship of this meeting, but Gore's presence helped to quell the riotous (and reactionary) Oxford undergraduates of those days, who had no sympathy with Tom Mann.

[39] *Christian Socialist*, VIII, No. 91 (December 1890), pp. 158-159. For Clementina Black's articles on the "ethics of shopping" see *Seedtime*, No. 7 (January 1891), pp. 10-12, and previous issues.

turing and retail trades as "unfair" and "un-English," and one antisocialist spokesman, Canon Henson, damned the policy as hypocrisy: "In time we shall have the advertisement of the 'Christian tailor,'" he sneered. Not all employers were uncooperative, however, and John Carter had the written support of the Masters' Association in Oxford for his "white list."[40]

The CSU also tried to turn its weapon of preferential dealing against the dangerous industry of the potteries. The incidence of lead poisoning was tragically high among the pottery workers, but for various reasons (chiefly alleged cost), the employers were reluctant to adopt the new, completely safe "leadless glaze" technique. The CSU ran a national campaign in favor of buying *only* leadless glaze products, and gradually "the power of the purse" forced Midland industrialists to see the light. The CSU's victory was not single-handed; in fact the Labour Churches of the area were probably the real originators of the leaded glaze campaign.[41] In other trades the Research Committee of the London CSU (and those of Bristol and Birmingham also) made detailed investigations of working conditions. Reports were sent to the Home Secretary, to factory inspectors, to the press, and to MP's, especially on the female trades. The CSU felt strongly about women's employment, though they did not seem to take any strong stand later over women's suffrage. "Because it is the weakest who suffer most from our economic conditions,"[42] and, more to the point, because two prominent women reformers sat on the CSU Research Committee, the Union investigated conditions of women's work. The two women were Constance Smith and Gertrude Tuckwell. Miss Tuckwell, a niece of Lady Dilke and Hon-

[40] J. G. Adderley, *A New Earth*, pp. 52-54. John Carter carried out a survey of business morality (by questionnaires to businessmen) and discovered (a) that larger firms cheated less; and (b) that there was a "more or less general tendency to acquiesce in what Kingsley called the 'cannibalism' of the commercial world." See his article, "Commercial Morality," *Economic Review*, III, No. 3 (July 1893), pp. 318-347.

[41] See the report of the Hanley Labour Church on its campaign, *Labour Prophet*, VI, No. 79 (July 1898), p. 194.

[42] P. Dearmer, *Beginnings of the CSU*, p. 165.

orable Secretary of the Women's Trade Union League (1892-1904), must have resented the paternalism of CSU leaders toward women's movements. Yet her own father, Rev. William Tuckwell, was an outspoken Christian socialist member of the CSU, very radical in language, and fortunate to have New College, Oxford to support him throughout his life. Without this he might never have been gainfully employed, certainly not by his chosen church. "The disease corroding the vitals of English life," he once proclaimed in Birmingham, "is the *monopoly of wealth. . . .* The Landlord, the Employer, the Capitalist . . . are three sworn brothers." As for organized religion, "the Christianity of the Churches is not the Christianity of Christ."[43] (Tuckwell's view of Christian socialism went beyond Henry Georgeism and did not put the capitalist and the worker in the same camp.)

In 1898-1899 a London CSU deputation went to the House of Commons to demand a revision of the factory acts. It was made up of bishops, college heads, and other dignitaries. Their language was not that of a William Tuckwell. But the bill, when it came, was deemed inadequate by the CSU; they criticized it heavily, and it was withdrawn. This was influence of a kind altogether undreamed-of by the tiny Guild of St. Matthew. The Union was becoming, in Dearmer's words, "an informal committee of the English Church upon social questions." Working through its three MP's (H. J. Tennant, J. G. Talbot, and Sir Charles Dilke), the CSU also helped to mold the Factory and Workshops Act of 1901, and the Trade Boards Act of 1909. In 1897 the Cheltenham CSU created a Society for the Improvement of

[43] Rev. William Tuckwell (ca. 1830?-1905), author of *Christian Socialism and Other Lectures* (London, 1891) and *Reminiscences of a Radical Parson* (London, n.d. [1903?]). Despite his Fourth-Class degree of 1852, New College, Oxford gave him a fellowship, made him college chaplain and headmaster of New College School (1857-1864), and continued to protect him in later life. The quotation is from his *Christian Socialism* (Birmingham, 1889), pp. 3-16. See also *Crockford's Clerical Directory*, 1886, p. 1196, and 1894, p. 1345; *Commonwealth*, x, No. 9 (August 1905), p. 255; *Christian Socialist*, ix, No. 95 (April 1891), pp. 46-47; Scott Holland, *Bundle of Memories*, pp. 190-199.

the Housing of the Poor to buy up slum property and act as a model landlord. The London branch meanwhile formed a committee of "experts" ("There is a crying need at the present day," said Dearmer, "for Christian experts") to investigate alcoholism, operating on the avowedly socialist assumption that "you will never destroy drunkenness unless you face the evils of overcrowding and overwork that lie behind it."[44]

Great publicity was gained from the many lecture courses organized by several branches, such as those of Leicester, Manchester, and London. In the City the CSU gave daily sermons to businessmen at Lent, later published as *Lombard Street in Lent* (1894), *A Lent in London* (1895),[45] *The Church and New Century Problems* (1901), and *Churchmanship and Labour* (1906). A lending library was opened, and in the years 1911-1913 Scott Holland edited eight CSU handbooks on "social questions from the Christian viewpoint," which included his own *Our Neighbours*, C.E.B. Russell's interesting and partisan *Social Problems of the North*, and A. J. Carlyle's *The Influence of Christianity upon Social and Political Ideas*. The last book became a minor classic.

In all this activity the CSU method was very Fabian, but in 1905 one of its more radical and imaginative members, Rev. F. L. Donaldson of Leicester, took more direct action. Donaldson led a spectacular mass march of the unemployed from Leicester to London and back again. Leicester, where Donaldson was Vicar of St. Mark's, had suffered severe technological unemployment and a very harsh winter in 1904. Six or seven thousand displaced people were without the means to live, and in April 1905 an "Unemployed Committee" was organized, which met daily and paraded the city streets at noon. Since little or no help was forthcoming from the local authorities, by June the Committee's

---

[44] P. Dearmer, *Beginnings of the CSU*, pp. 161, 169, 173. See also Wagner, p. 268.

[45] This collection of sermons was denounced by orthodox clergy and others. See *Church Reformer*, XIV, No. 9 (September 1895), p. 196, and No. 10 (October 1895), p. 222.

leader, Amos Sheriff, had decided to march a group to London and petition the King. They met in Market Square, and Donaldson was to give them a sermon before they left (5 June). This he did, but was so stirring and so stirred that he became self-appointed chaplain to the march, and helped to lead the men.[46] A crowd of 100,000 came to see them off (out of a city population of 230,000), and they marched out to *Lead Kindly Light*.

"It was the most pathetic sight I have ever seen," said Donaldson, "or ever expect to see"—440 ill-fed, poor, badly clothed, yet undefeated workmen, walking through heavy rain on a two-week journey to London and back. Only two men were "lost" through misconduct. Blasted by the *Times* as "restless, shiftless, simpletons" and as "a class of persons who either cannot or will not work," the displaced men reached the capital only to discover that "Everybody whom they had come to find was *out of town;* except the Archbishop, and he alas! would not see them." It was the Whit Recess.

Donaldson's prayer of June 1905 to the assembled men is worth repeating verbatim:

> Almighty God, we beseech Thee to bless, preserve and keep these Thy sons; consecrate Thou their cause; succour their wives and children in their absence; give them a prosperous journey and a safe return; help them upon their way to lead a Godly, righteous and sober life; set a watch, O Lord, before the doors of their lips and save them from all evil-speaking, bitterness, anger and hardness of heart; grant them the grace of faith and hope and love; faith to persevere, hope to see beyond the present distress and love toward Thee and their fellow men. Grant them Thy peace all the days of their lives, and bring them at last to Thy everlasting Kingdom, through Jesus Christ, Our Lord, to whom with Thee and the

---

[46] This was no sudden conversion for Donaldson, however. He had previously been on the left wing of the GSM's executive committee, and later became chairman of the Church Socialist League. His career is treated more fully below.

Holy Ghost, be all honour and glory, world without end. Amen![47]

F. L. Donaldson believed (going further even than Stewart Headlam would have gone) that *"Christianity is the religion of which socialism is the practice."* He told the men that "a Christian State" must *provide* employment "if the agencies of ordinary commerce fail for lack of discipline." The marchers attended churches along the way and in London went to St. Paul's and Westminster. They returned to Leicester better clothed than when they left, owing to the generosity of people along the route. "I believe that the march of the Leicester unemployed profoundly affected the imagination of the nation," claimed Donaldson. It laid bare the stark reality of the problem, as Annie Besant's matchgirls' strike of 1888 and the Dock Strike of 1889 had revealed the horrors of sweated and casual labor. It proved, he said, that the unemployed, despite the *Times,* were not "riffraff," but "splendid material running to waste and ruin."[48] Not all of Donaldson's CSU colleagues were ready to take such a firm stand, and it would be historically inaccurate to regard the Leicester march as a CSU affair. Even Scott Holland thought the unemployment in Leicester was primarily a *local* matter, writing to Donaldson in June 1905: "I keep thinking of your gallant fellows plodding through that awful rain. It is heroic: even though I doubt whether it is quite war. Leicester is the guilty spot; and Leicester must produce the remedy."[49] In later years the "march" became a common method of appealing to public opinion in aid of a cause; but the men who took that laborious trek to London in 1905 were hungry.

[47] The *Times* condemned the march as "an unconstitutional procedure," which Donaldson regarded as a "foolish" criticism. (This account is based on Donaldson's own description of the march in *Commonwealth*, x, No. 7 [July 1905], pp. 218-220.)

[48] Reckitt, *Maurice to Temple*, pp. 148-149; *Commonwealth, loc.cit.,* Binyon, p. 175 (Binyon mistakenly dates the march in 1904).

[49] Paget, p. 226.

John Carter and an American CSU

By 1900 the Union's original two branches had grown to 35 in number; its original 200 or so members now exceeded 4,000, of whom 1,400 were living in London.[50] The most important foreign branch was that established in the United States under the inspiration of Rev. John Carter and of the Oxford CSU. Unfortunately, its history is too long to describe here, but some of the negotiations that surrounded its emergence illustrate important aspects of CSU history in Britain itself. John Carter was a Canadian, educated in Toronto and in Exeter College, Oxford. He was ordained in 1887 and served a curacy in the depths of Limehouse before becoming the chaplain of Exeter College in 1890. Carter was one of the first four priests to join the monastic order created by Charles Gore, the Society of the Resurrection (whose Yorkshire monastery would later also feature in the history of Anglican socialism), and was attached to Pusey House for many years before his appointment as its bursar. He was treasurer (1885) and vice-president (1886) of the Oxford branch of Headlam's Guild of St. Matthew, and helped to dissolve it in favor of the new CSU.[51] Carter's first contact with the American Christian socialist movement seems to have come about over the question of the CSU's *Economic Review*. Before the *Review* could be launched, correspondents were needed, and since the US already had several economic journals while Britain had none, it was natural for Carter to write to a leading American authority, Professor R. T. Ely. Fortunately, this correspondence has been preserved.[52] On New Year's Day, 1891, Carter wrote to Rev. R. H. Holland, S.T.D., of St. Louis, who had himself been at Oxford:

[50] P. Dearmer, *Beginnings of the CSU*, p. 160.

[51] *Crockford's Clerical Directory*, 1894, p. 225; Prestige, pp. 107, 151, 206; J. Clayton, *Rise and Fall of Socialism in Great Britain* (London, 1926), pp. 50-51. John Carter was elected Mayor of Oxford in 1925.

[52] See Carter to Ely, 28 June 1890, 23 August 1890, and 11 October 1890, Ely Collection, WSHS.

I have great pleasure in delegating authority to you to act on behalf of the Oxford branch of the Christian Social Union with a view to the establishment of branches in America.

The Church in England is trying to realise more and more her obvious responsibility in the face of modern social problems . . . [and] to grapple with the difficulties of our industrial system in the fearless and confident spirit which our Faith should inspire. . . . And in fact there are not wanting signs that some of these perplexing questions may have to be solved first in the New World.[53]

Rapidly the American CSU was established, with the help of that indefatigable socialist, encyclopedist, and organizer, Rev. W.D.P. Bliss,[54] Bishop F. D. Huntington of New York, the distinguished Episcopal preacher Rev. R. Heber Newton, and others. It soon became a substantial organization, considered amalgamating with the earlier American group called CAIL (Church Association for the Advancement of the Interests of Labor),[55] founded by Huntington in May 1887, and demanded complete independence from the Oxford CSU. In April 1891 John Carter had written to Ely: "You know that I am a Canadian, and so a little inclined to find Englishmen slow-moving. Now upon you in America it will depend to make up any deficiency in this respect!"[56] But in that same month Rev. R. Heber Newton

[53] Carter to Holland, 1 January 1891, Ely Collection, wshs.

[54] Bliss founded several socialist societies in his lifetime, including the Society of Christian Socialists (1889, modeled on the British society of 1886), the Brotherhood of the Carpenter (1890), and the American Fabian Society (1895). For the last, see Jean V. Johnson, "The American Fabians, 1895-1900," unpublished M.A. thesis (Smith College, Northampton, Mass., 1961). For Bliss see Arthur Mann, *Yankee Reformers in the Urban Age* (Cambridge, Mass., 1954), in paperback (New York, 1966); and Howard Quint, *The Forging of American Socialism* (Charlestown, S.C., 1953), also in paperback (New York, 1964).

[55] See W. L. Bull to Ely, 25 May 1894, W. H. Van Allen to Ely, 3 October 1892, 30 November 1892, and 6 December 1892, Carter to Ely, 19 September 1894, Ely Collection, wshs.

[56] Carter to Ely, 28 April 1891, Ely Collection, wshs. Percy Dearmer also had high hopes for America—"a country where our faith should make rapid progress since there no sceptre has been laid across the

had already expressed his doubts of too close a cooperation with Britain; he preferred an autonomous American CSU. The American society proved to be faster moving than even Carter had anticipated; it grew to a membership of about one thousand, with members and branches all over the US: Chicago, Minnesota, Philadelphia, Iowa, Boston, New York City—even Omaha, Nebraska.[57] The Union suffered a temporary collapse when the energetic Ely moved from Baltimore to Wisconsin, but recovered in 1894 when its name was changed to the *Church* Social Union and a new constitution gave it a more unified executive, with a working majority in Boston.[58]

The change of name, emphasizing the Episcopal (i.e., Anglican) character of the Union, represented a victory for the British point of view, namely, that the CSU should maintain its exclusively denominational character. Inasmuch as America was and is a plural society, in which Anglicanism played an even smaller part than in Britain, this decision can hardly be regarded as tactically sound. Indeed, the membership of the *Church* Social Union was half that of the former *Christian* Social Union. From the outset there were members who pressed to "Americanize" the CSU, by widening its denominational scope. A Single Taxer, E. P. Wheeler, suggested to Ely that certain sectarian remarks of Dr. Holland be deleted from a CSU report because:

Bible and no Tory prejudice bids Christians to grovel in shivering content or slumber in pot-bellied equanimity. There must be many American Churchmen who have not bowed the knee to the almighty dollar . . ." (*Church Reformer*, x, No. 9 [October 1891], p. 212).

[57] See J. L. Houghteling to Ely, 13 January 1892, Rev. W. White Wilson to Ely, 1 October 1892, Anna C. Watenough to Ely, 7 October and 10 October 1891, L. E. Moultrie to Ely, 20 January 1893, G. Herron to Ely, 16 December 1892, Sidney Lanier to Ely, 27 February 1893, C. P. Mills to Ely, 25 March 1892, J. R. Daly to Ely, 6 October 1892, Ely Collection, WSHS. A *Canadian* branch was established in Toronto in 1892 (Rev. S. Jones to Ely, 8 March 1892, and J. Mockridge to Ely, 30 May 1892, Ely Collection, WSHS).

[58] Bliss, pp. 275-276; James Dombrowski, *The Early Days of Christian Socialism in America* (New York, 1936), p. 99.

There are many of "the sects" to use Dr. Holland's expression, who hold to his idea of the church and society . . . and to whom the idea of "atomism in society" is as abhorrent as it is to him. Every public refusal by our people to co-operate with other Christians, it seems to me, tends to hinder.

A week later, also, Ely was urged by a conservative Lutheran minister to oppose the CSU's selectiveness:

I fail to see why the membership should be restricted to one sect of Christendom. In Economic fellowship, as in Ethical fellowship I can't see where creed subscription or succession from Judas or John is to have place. . . . I say this dear friend, not from pique [but] from an honest conviction that an economy that is dominated by clerics is open to two dangers: 1) The *liberal* application of Christ's economic hints—which would wreck our civilisation in six months, and 2) The spirit of denominational attitudinizing, as it appears in the program of the movement. The Church for the poor is the poor man's Church —not one that patronizes him.[59]

John Carter, however, had no intention of encouraging any such move. "I hope the limitation of the CSU to Churchmen (i.e., Episcopalians) will be maintained," he wrote in May 1891; and nine months later he insisted,

with regard to making the CSU more comprehensive—I do not see how this could be done without seriously departing from the original intention of the Union. Certainly, as you point out, conditions are different in the U.S. But it is also evident that even in the present limitations you will have a very considerable membership. Already you outnumber the English branch. . . .[60]

[59] Wheeler to Ely, 26 April 1891, Rev. E. H. Delk to Ely, 5 May 1891, Ely Collection, WSHS.

[60] Carter to Ely, 14 May 1891, 30 January 1892, Ely Collection, WSHS. In the same letter Carter even rejected Ely's suggestion of a joint transatlantic editorial board for the *Economic Review*. He

The Carter-Ely correspondence illustrates perhaps only too well that British Christian socialism demanded from the economic system something which it was not itself fully prepared to concede in religious affairs—universal brotherhood.

Two prototypes: Scott Holland and Gore

John Carter was no thinker, but an organization and committee man. The economic and social thought of the CSU was virtually that of Gore and Scott Holland, with help from Illingworth. Scott Holland's principal themes were the positive state and the inadequacy of classical economic dogmas. Gore's was the moral failure of the Church and the urgent need for repentance by churchmen before the imminent wrath of God. Illingworth, as we have seen, was essentially a theologian, for whom the prime question was the dualism of spirit and matter. He believed that the material order was merely another aspect of the spiritual order, as did Stewart Headlam. The "material instrument of spiritual communion" was to be found throughout nature, in "the sacraments of storm and calm, and of the sunset and of the star-rise, and in every flash of an eye, a flush of a cheek, or pulse of a hand," as well as in the sacraments of the Church which emanate from the Incarnation. To this thoroughgoing immanentalism, this sense of living in a sacramental universe in which all secular life was holy, Illingworth added, as insistence on God's transcendence: "God would not be immanent in a world which He did not transcend, nor transcend a world in which He was not immanent."[61] The Christian doctrines of the Incarnation and the Trinity emphasize both immanence and transcendence. Illingworth's theology, therefore, provided two of the most common theological arguments for Christian socialism: the sacramental argument and the justification from Divine Immanence.

---

seemed determined to extend the exclusive Oxbridge clubbiness of the English CSU over the Atlantic.

[61] Mrs. J. R. Illingworth, pp. 267-269 (essay by W. Richmond).

Scott Holland and Gore presented contrasting approaches to Christian socialism: Gore, distressed by the sense of the Church's guilt, Holland, witty, buoyant, and full of faith in the future evolution of a Christian welfare state. Gore's prophetic moral passion radiated from everything he wrote. It was not merely that economic selfishness existed in the world, nor even that it dominated Victorian society, but that, he thundered, *"its profound antagonism to the Spirit of Christ is not recognised,* that there is not amongst us anything that can be called an adequate conception of what Christian morality means." The fundamental moral law of God's Kingdom is contained in the Sermon on the Mount, Gore argued, in which we see that the Church was intended to be "a society with a common moral law." Instead, Christian moral opinion is not organized in the modern world at all, especially in such vital areas as commerce, distribution, and the mutual obligations of the social classes. Christ's social principle, *the sonship and brotherhood of man as based on the Fatherhood of God,* must be publicized, especially among church people, whose guilt for social evils is very heavy.[62]

Scott Holland, in contrasting style, emphasized folly rather than guilt, and used the weapon of wit rather than moral fire. Against those conservatives who jeered at welfare legislation and factory acts as "grandmotherly" laws, he used the slogan: *"Every man his own grandmother!"* When similar adversaries told the Church to "keep out of politics," he pointed out that they only meant keep out of liberal or radical politics, for "Conservatism did not count. It was part of the immemorial system of nature. The parson was born a Knight of the Primrose League." We must set aside fallacious and obsolete "economic laws," said Holland, dreamed up *in vacuo* and with no application to real life. We must Christianize the State, which is the major tool of social

[62] Binyon, p. 170; Gore, *The Social Doctrine of the Sermon on the Mount* (London. 1893); *Economic Review,* II, No. 2 (April 1892), pp. 145-160.

change: "We must have all we can get of State order, of State machinery."[63]

Although these recurrent themes can be discerned in the political thought of the CSU leaders, they tended to become more outspoken when "the authorities" were at their worst. In 1887, for instance, a year of labor demonstrations and police restrictions in Trafalgar Square, Scott Holland wrote passionately to Gore:

> Don't believe one word the papers tell you of these unhappy Trafalgar Square meetings. I never read such brazen lies. The crisis has all come about through *outraged* spirit—I never saw a crowd look more innocent of revolution in my life: and there was no disturbance to London—or to the traffic—until the Police smashed their heads. The Government seem *bent* on manufacturing a revolution—I have seldom felt so sad, or so mad at a political wickedness.

And Gore reflected at a Pusey House lunch: "It's a pity they didn't loot the West End!"[64] Five years later, when trade unionism and the "minimum wage" were occupying public thought, Gore and Holland both spoke up for the labor viewpoint. Arbitration was not enough, said Holland, ". . . the crucial question for the men is solely whether the wage is one on which it is possible to live and save. . . . There are no subtleties about it. Wages ought not to drop below it." As for orthodox political economy:

> The market ought to recognize an adequate minimum and to adapt itself to that. What are the dividends at? What are the contracts with the railways? They must yield the necessity of providing the adequate wage. . . . It is human, moral, Christian, to ask for this.

[63] Paget, p. 248; J. G. Adderley in H. Martin, pp. 213ff.; Scott Holland, "The Church of England," *Progressive Review*, IV (January 1897), 319-326; P. Dearmer (ed.), *Sermons on Social Subjects* (London, 1911), pp. 76-90.

[64] Prestige, p. 79.

Gore took much the same stand at a "Living Wage Conference" of 1893 at Holborn Town Hall. The Church of England was still discussing what "attitude" it should "adopt" toward labor and trade unions. At Folkestone in 1892 Holland told the Church Congress bluntly: "We want no attitudes . . . no appropriate pose." The correct attitude should have been struck forty years ago. Trade unions were essential; *isolated labor means enslaved labor:* "Combination . . . can at least moralize the worker, by bringing him into line with his fellows towards whom he is responsible for the wage he accepts."[65] Rev. J. G. Adderley, admittedly on the "left wing" of the CSU, even developed a Christian argument for the "closed shop." He reasoned:

> We believe in Brotherhood, and it is unbrotherly not to recognise your duty to those of your own trade. The non-union man forgets that the liberty he enjoys is very largely due to . . . the Unions. . . . The more complete the organisation of labour, the better for the interests of peace and progress.[66]

The London County Council election manifesto of the CSU for 1892 (issued by Scott Holland as president) was more concrete. It demanded:

1. Wholesome and sanitary dwellings; pure and cheap water; open spaces; public baths.
2. Equalisation of rates.
3. Fairer taxation, especially concerning rent.
4. Municipal licensing power to control the drink trade and gambling.
5. Fair wages and protection of child and female "sweated" labour.
6. Women county councillors.[67]

This was no "revolutionary" program. It was a Radical-

[65] Holland to Bishop Talbot, September 1893, Paget, p. 202; Prestige, p. 165; *Economic Review*, II, No. 4 (October 1892), pp. 441-451.

[66] *A Little Primer of Christian Socialism* (London and Oxford, n.d. [1909?]), pp. 52-53.

[67] *Church Reformer*, XI, No. 3 (March 1892), p. 66.

Liberal-Georgeist platform with humanitarian and mildly feminist clauses. "Social-Unionism" spoke in strong language for labor but fell far short of any genuinely "socialist" economic policy.

A crucial test for the Guild of St. Matthew had been its attitude toward self-organized labor and particularly the ILP. This is where Headlam hesitated and lost. What of Scott Holland and Charles Gore? A "left-wing" group in the CSU was open to the idea of an independent labor party; but the majority were doubtful. J. G. Adderley, for example, was more responsive to the ILP and Labour Church people than was Scott Holland. The latter was shocked by the electoral results of 1895 and the apparently deep conservatism displayed by the British public; he felt that the ILP had helped split the vote and could only ruin itself as a result. Holland and Gore could not help being elitists, believers in middle-class, if progressive, rule. In truth, most Social Unionists were more *anticapitalist* than pro-socialist. They aimed to reestablish the principle of social obligation, inherent in the Church and medieval tradition but, in their view, uprooted by the advance of the industrial machine. The mild Bishop Westcott, although he worked mightily in defense of labor's rights in County Durham, feared that the Union's title suggested Christian socialism, "a most vague phrase." Gore saw eye to eye politically with Canon Barnett, the settlement leader and champion of the Old Age Pension (though of course they were fundamentally opposed in religious practices), and he always supported the Co-operative Movement. ("I am arrayed from head to foot in garments of co-operative production," Gore once told a Co-operative Congress, "these boots I have sent back three times. The wicked shops are best!") [68] But he does not seem to have grasped the significance of the creation of the ILP in Yorkshire in 1893. This link, the direct connection between the industrial worker of the North and

[68] Holland to Adderley, n.d. [1895], Paget, p. 205; Wagner, p. 221. See also Westcott's address in *Economic Review*, v, No. 1 (January 1895), p. 161; A. Westcott, *Life and Letters of B. F. Westcott*, II, 260-261; Prestige, p. 179.

Anglican socialism, was to be forged after 1906 by the Church Socialist League. The CSU's gospel failed to reach the British working class directly.

Imperialism and the Anglican conscience: the Boer War

Charles Gore and Scott Holland felt very strongly about British imperialism. Colonial expansion was the one object of censure common to almost all British Christian socialists during the revival period, from the *Christian Socialist* group to the High Church dissidents. The CSU's president, B. F. Westcott, representing an older generation, was prepared to accept the fact of the British Empire, since it already existed.[69] But Gore, Holland, and others were bitterly ashamed of their country's imperial record. These feelings came to a head with the growth of the imperialist and jingoist popular spirit itself, especially in matters like the Queen's Diamond Jubilee of 1897 and, of course, the South African War of 1899-1902.

The last five years of the old century saw an upsurge of mass feeling over the Empire which bordered on hysteria, and did not recede until after about 1905-1906 (when domestic issues and the growing disquiet in Europe captured public interest). Joseph Chamberlain took over the Colonial Office in 1895 and proceeded to urge an aggressive policy of imperial economic cooperation and federation. The Diamond Jubilee of 1897 was made the occasion for a display of imperial pageantry and jingoism, and certain international events in the following year, including the Fashoda incident in which Britain confronted France in the Sudan and the great scramble for trading concessions in China, sustained the martial spirit. The popular feeling of the late nineties was a culmination of a chain of historical circumstances going back at least to the imperialist visions of Benjamin Disraeli—the purchase of the Suez Canal shares in 1875 and the declaration of Victoria as "Empress of India" in 1877. The movement for strengthening links with the colonies had already achieved the Imperial Federation

[69] See Westcott's essay "The Empire," in Hocking, pp. 17-32.

League (1884), the Colonial and India Exhibition (1886), and a series of Colonial Conferences beginning in 1887 (aiming at "imperial preference" in tariff matters). In the great "Grab for Africa," Britain had taken a lion's share; several British chartered companies had exacted extensive trading concessions—the Royal Niger Company, the Imperial British East Africa Company, the British South Africa Company. Most important, liberal and socialist critics had begun to spin a theory of capitalist economic exploitation to explain the imperialist urge. The Christian socialists more or less accepted this hypothesis of "economic imperialism"; and when war broke out in South Africa in 1899 the conflict rapidly assumed in their eyes the shape of a sinister capitalist plot, engineered by international mining interests.

The economic interpretation of late-Victorian imperialism followed by Christian socialists was laid down, in its classic lines, by the English economist Hobson in 1902. A pacifist and a Radical, John A. Hobson (1858-1940) was the creator of the "underconsumption" or "maldistribution" theory of cyclical unemployment. In later years, buttressed by the similar theories of J. M. Keynes (who in 1936 acknowledged his debt to Hobson), these views had considerable influence on British Labour Party policy. By then Hobson was clearly advocating steeply graduated taxation, the extension of social services, and state nationalization of monopolies. Hobson first brought attention to income inequality as a cause of underconsumption and demand failure in *The Physiology of Industry*, written with A. F. Mummery in 1889. Competitive capitalism, he argued, failed to maintain a correct balance between the production of capital goods and consumer goods; meanwhile, the wealthy minority were guilty of oversaving. In Hobson's *Problem of Poverty* (written for a series edited by the Georgeist J. E. Symes in 1891) and *Problem of the Unemployed* (1896) the argument is developed further, and underconsumption is clearly tied to cyclical failure and mass unemployment.

By 1902 Hobson had extended his maldistribution theory to a full-scale economic interpretation of "imperialism." Industrial capitalism, beset by the fundamental structural flaw of maldistribution, ultimately reaches a stage of economic maturity (at existing income levels) in which the home and normal foreign demand for manufactured goods and investment capital is saturated. Investors seek unusual outlets for idle funds; markets for cotton goods, hardware, and the products of machine industry; fresh fields for railway construction, and so on. The acquisition of colonies provides such outlets. Imperialism thus extends the life of capitalism and enhances existing maldistribution at home. In brief, imperialism is directly attributable to inherent structural weaknesses in the capitalist system. Those who benefit most from it are capitalists with excess investment funds, munitions manufacturers, and industrialists in general. According to Hobson, the "dominant, direct motive" behind the so-called new imperialism of the late nineteenth century was "the demand for markets and for profitable investment by the exporting and financial classes." What gave his economic argument special force was that unlike later determinists Hobson was fully aware of noneconomic factors. In 1901, for instance, he published a study of mass opinion, *The Psychology of Jingoism.*

There is little doubt that Hobson's views were of great intellectual influence on the anti-imperialists of the period, and these views were widely known long before the appearance of his *Imperialism* in 1902 (which served mainly to pull his ideas together on the subject). Though an avowed rationalist, Hobson's approach, which owed much to John Ruskin, was attractive to the Christian dissidents in the CSU and elsewhere, partly because his tone was heavily moral. Also many of his personal friends were religious radicals. He lectured regularly for the Ethical Culture group at South Place, edited the short-lived *Progressive Review* with the Fabian essayist William Clarke and the young Ramsay MacDonald; and with Herbert Burrows (another "ethical" Fabian), Clarke, and the American journalist Henry Demarest Lloyd, he traveled in Europe and the United States.[70]

[70] For J. A. Hobson's letters to H. D. Lloyd (1895-1903), see Lloyd

Hobson's prolific journalism—he wrote a good deal for H. W. Massingham's Liberal-Radical (but strongly pro-Boer) *The Nation*—brought him into contact with C.F.G. Masterman, L. T. Hobhouse, the Webbs, and other opinion-molders. Anglicans like Charles Gore and Scott Holland must have found it more difficult than did Hobson to place in analytical perspective the role of the pulpit in creating mass jingoism, or to criticize freely the role of the missionary in economic imperialism; but they fully shared Hobson's condemnation of the Boer War.

As *Manchester Guardian* correspondent, Hobson traveled extensively in South Africa for some months before the outbreak of hostilities between British and Boer. His book *The War in South Africa: Its Causes and Effects* (1900), supported by a steady stream of articles in the press, dismissed the notion, common among supporters of the war, that British military intervention against the Boer Republics was necessary in order to protect the rights of white non-Boers (many of them British subjects) in the Transvaal. These "Uitlanders," who had flocked to the Witwatersrand area after the rich gold discoveries of 1886 and were now developing the Transvaal's mineral industries, had certainly not been received by the Boer government of the Transvaal with open arms. According to those who supported British intervention, the corrupt, rigid, and rural-minded Boer oligarchy controlling the Transvaal refused to give the newcomers the vote, civil rights, or adequate civil protection; when the distressed Uitlanders petitioned the Queen in April 1899, the London government could not refuse to intercede on their behalf. Hobson, however, on his travels in the region, found little grass-roots discontent among Uitlanders with their treatment by the Boer regime, and no evidence of persecution or intimidation. He painted the Anglo-Boer conflict as a conspiracy of British gold and dia-

Papers, WSHS. Also see J. A. Hobson, *Confessions of an Economic Heretic* (London, 1938). Hobson's debt to Ruskin is especially evident in his later writings on the meaning of work and is seen in his biographical study, *John Ruskin: Social Reformer* (London, 1898), as well as in his edition of Ruskin's *Unto This Last* (London, 1907).

mond miners, anxious to lay their hands on as much as possible of the precious subsoil that lay under the Dutch farms of the Transvaal. For Hobson, in fact, as for the Christian socialists, the Boer War was a classic example of pure economic imperialism.

As early as 1886, the year of the Witwatersrand gold rush, the Anglo-Catholic socialist editor of the *Christian Socialist*, Rev. C. L. Marson, was lambasting English colonial policy without mercy. The whites, said Marson, had no true Christian sense of duty toward the native populations they encountered; the sum total of their work was to "dram, drug and syphilize" the colored populations and to send them missionaries, "Bible in one hand and gun in the other." The language of Scott Holland and Gore was less colorful than this, but equally resolute. In June 1897 Scott Holland bitterly decried the policy followed by the Conservative government led by Lord Salisbury, and the growth of national self-worship and humbug. The Prime Minister, said Holland, made no appeal to national idealism: "The upper classes have ceased to know what such appeals mean. . . . Never was peace more remote, more impossible. . . . Our educated classes, our governing classes, *what belief have they in the inspiration of liberty?* . . . It is a day of small men everywhere." During the South African War itself—in fact, at the very time of the siege of Ladysmith (1900), when popular feelings ran very high—Scott Holland had the moral fortitude and conviction to preach a lacerating anti-war sermon in St. Paul's. He found the "twopenny patriotism of the 'war-party' " beneath contempt, mocked the chauvinists of the music halls and the press. "We at home who risk nothing, who only tingle with the cheap fury of Fleet Street," he declared, "could hardly have believed that we could fall so far from the very memory of Jesus Christ." The British nation had sinned against the Boers. "We should humiliate ourselves for the blundering recklessness with which we entered on the war, and the insolence and arrogance which blinded us so utterly."[71]

[71] *Christian Socialist*, IV, No. 40 (September 1886), p. 36; Wagner,

For Charles Gore the war, with its early British military losses, was a divine chastisement for England's "arrogance and pride." Gore condemned the British filibustering expedition of the winter of 1895-1896 aimed at Johannesburg (the Jameson Raid) as a totally unjust and needless action. He confessed: "I could not say in prayer, 'we believe that our cause is just.'" Imperialism lacked moral content or fiber; it was but "the worship of our unregenerate British selves, without morality or fear of God."[72] But Gore's most caustic invective was reserved for the British "concentration camp" policy. The camps, invented by the British military commanders for handling the white civilian population of the Boer Republic (especially the Boer women and children), received a barrage of Christian criticism. Whatever revisionist historians may say about the camps of concentration, the fact will always remain that about 4,000 Boer women and about 16,000 Boer children (most of them very young) died in these camps through disease and malnutrition. The Dutch farmers at war could not care for their own families adequately; but the British entered upon the policy of concentration without fully understanding its immensity as an administrative problem in time of war.[73] In a letter to the London *Times* which immediately became famous, Gore, Canon of Westminster, excoriated the concentration-camp policy. He was attacked in turn by a violent reply from a Canon of Worcester. How surprised that canon must have been when only two weeks later Lord Salisbury nevertheless promoted Gore to a bishopric—that of Worcester. Opposition to the appointment had been strong from the "Protestant" wing of the Church of England;[74] Salisbury

---

p. 283; Paget, pp. 210-215; W. Stewart, *James Keir Hardie* (London, 1921), p. 156.

[72] Prestige, pp. 224-225.

[73] See, for example, A. C. Martin, *The Concentration Camps, 1900-1902* (Cape Town, 1957).

[74] The crusading Radical journalist W. T. Stead exclaimed in his *Review of Reviews* over the appointment: "Imagine John the Baptist appointed by Pontius Pilate to be Bishop over Galilee when Herod was in his glory . . ." (Prestige, p. 227). Stead himself was a leading

himself, one can imagine, must have suffered severe qualms upon opening the *Times* a fortnight earlier.

The gauntlet now passed again to Scott Holland. The next Christmas (1901), Holland published a devastating onslaught on the John Bull image. He said the traditional figure of John Bull was "ludicrously obsolete" as a national image for late-Victorian Britain in the face of modern imperial problems:

> In the first place, he is fat: and the fat man's day is past and gone. . . . Over the wide horizons of the Empire, the fat men have all disappeared. . . . In their place is the long lean Australian, so curiously American in the type that he runs to. He is tall and compact, bony and muscular. And your African colonist follows suit. . . .[75]

In the competitive industrial world of the 1900's of what use was John Bull? The creature "has no brains. He embodies in his fatuous good humour, in his farmer's suit, in his obvious provincialism, the British horror of ideas." Probably remembering his undergraduate days and the long intellectual struggles with Hegel and T. H. Green, Holland felt particularly strongly the impatience of his fellow nationals with theories. "We revel in our own idea-less stupidity," he said, "at an hour when brains count for more and more . . . and when the sharpest of American wits and the enormous intellectual industry of Germany and the keen subtlety of France are pitted against us." John Bull's worst feature was that he was "without an ounce of imagination." What Britain needed was not this sorry Georgian dummy, argued Holland, but a noble Shakespearean image. Where was the England of the Tudors?

Even Peace Night (June 1902) brought little satisfaction to Scott Holland: "This evil revelry was no illusion of my pro-Boer brain," he wrote to Talbot, describing the street festivities in London. "It was the utter abandonment which

---

opponent of the Boer War and claimed that Britain was pushed or inveigled into it by the aggressive leadership of Milne and Chamberlain.
[75] Paget, pp. 215ff.

was revolting. The faces lose human expression. . . . The ugliness of our joy is so appalling: the fat City men gone mad."[76]

If the word "socialism" traditionally implies anticolonialism and strong opposition to imperialist expansion, then the Christian Social Union as exemplified by its two chief figures, Scott Holland and Gore, was on this score more socialist than the Fabian Society. While the Independent Labour Party was fairly solidly opposed to the Boer War, the Fabians were divided, with the leadership nucleus of the "old guard"—Shaw, Webb, Bland—more or less siding with the Liberal Imperialists. A Fabian "left wing" of younger ILP types (such as S. G. Hobson and Ramsay MacDonald) and a "right wing" of progressive Radicals (like Rev. John Clifford) joined together to oppose the war. Without doubt those Fabians who supported (or refused to oppose) the Boer War had some vision of Empire, of a leadership exerted by "higher" civilizations (Western Europe and America) over "lower" civilizations (Asia and Africa—hedging on the definition of China).[77] Some Anglican socialists, most notably Father Paul Bull of the Church Socialist League, shared this view. But the movement as a whole did not.

Christian socialism and the state education question

In its proposals for reform at home, however, the CSU fell far short of what is traditionally regarded as socialism. The furthest extension of its doctrine toward embracing economic socialism came with Gore's address to the Pan-Anglican Conference of 1908. That year represents also the peak of CSU influence in the Church of England and in British society. Perhaps the Union would have gone further, both in doctrinal evolution and in influence, if it had not been so easily diverted from the main path by side issues, such as the personal need Gore felt to fight the New

[76] *Ibid.*, p. 219.
[77] See, for instance, the analysis in McBriar, pp. 125-126.

Theology movement led by Rev. R. J. Campbell, or to prevent the passage of the Education Bill of 1906.

Gore's diversion to the education question was particularly unfortunate in many ways. Most of the churches, Anglican and Nonconformist, did not emerge from the long battle for control over public education in the 1900's with added public glory. The bitterly sectarian and narrow quality of their struggles, which delayed the progress of education in Britain for decades, gave organized religion a bad name for years to come. One cannot report that the Christian socialists were outstandingly different in this respect. In fact, three principal figures in the movement represented the three principal contesting positions over who should control the education of the British masses. Bishop Gore of the CSU championed the Anglican view; John Clifford, the Baptist leader, of the Fabian Society and the Christian Socialist League, protected the Nonconformist interest; and Stewart Headlam of the GSM, as noted, stood firmly for secular education. Apart from the unusual position taken by Headlam, the Christian socialists split over the education question along strictly sectarian and dogmatic lines.

The "dual system" established by the Forster Education Act of 1870 gave rise to numerous reform suggestions during the last thirty years of the nineteenth century. All state funds spent on elementary education before 1870 went to either one of the two chief religious societies; this system, inaugurated in 1833, allowed public money to be spent to build Anglican and Nonconformist schools managed by religious bodies. The 1870 Act could not destroy this curious semipublic, semiprivate system because, as we have seen, such a large number of elementary schools were built by the churches in the mid-nineteenth century that to set up a *rival* secular system would be ludicrous. The Forster Act therefore had allowed local authorities to establish tax-supported elementary schools in those districts where existing provision by church-managed schools was inadequate or nonexistent. Under the Cowper-Temple clause, already discussed,[78] these new schools, managed by publicly elected local School Boards, were to teach *undenominational* religion, or none at all, as each Board saw fit. The new Board Schools and the old religious schools would continue side by side in a dual system of education. At first the Anglicans anathematized the Forster Act as a Nonconformist victory or, even worse, a victory for irreligion; and the Nonconformists were displeased by the large powers still left to the Anglican church, especially in areas where "adequate" (Anglican) facilities already existed and Dissenting children were thus forced to attend Anglican schools. Over the years, many Nonconformists came around to defending the 1870 Act; the Cowper-Temple clause they now understood to be their real safeguard, rather than a fully secular system of education. Many Nonconformist schools were voluntarily transferred to the Board system, especially in cities. In the countryside, however, where the church schools were usually Anglican (the one-school areas were mainly rural) and very poorly maintained, Dissenters still had a grievance. The "conscience clause" did not function well, because farm laborers' children were too socially intimidated to use it, and sometimes the anomalous situation arose of a Church of England school in a heavily Nonconformist country district (common in Lincolnshire, for example).[79]

Meanwhile the Anglicans, previously suspicious of regular rate aid, were managing very badly and could no longer keep their many schools alive on the basis of haphazard doles from the central government. By 1902, however, when

[78] It is interesting that the W. F. Cowper-Temple (1811-1888) of this much-debated clause was himself a Maurician Christian socialist; an exponent of the "self-supporting villages" of John Minter Morgan, the Anglican cooperationist who had deeply influenced J. M. Ludlow; a pillar of the Society for the Improvement of the Conditions of the Working-Classes (established 1844); and a personal friend of John Ruskin, of whose socialist St. George's Guild in Sheffield he was a trustee. See W.H.G. Armytage, *Heavens Below*, pp. 209, 215, 220, 276-281, 290; and C. E. Raven, *Christian Socialism, 1848-1854*, p. 140.

[79] See M. Cruickshank, *State and Church in English Education*, ch. IV.

the Balfour Education Act was introduced, the Tories were loath to lose the political support they had recently gained from those Nonconformists who had quit the Liberal party and become Tory Unionists over the Irish Home Rule question. The alliance between the Conservative Lord Salisbury and the Liberal-Radical Joseph Chamberlain was uneasy: it was soon to disintegrate when Chamberlain took up the fight for raising tariffs. Nevertheless, Lord Salisbury's nephew A. J. Balfour, who became Conservative Prime Minister in 1902, introduced his new education measure: clerical schools were now to be partly supported out of local rates. All schools, whether "provided" (i.e., wholly state-supported; the former Board Schools) or "nonprovided" (the "voluntary" religious schools that would now receive regular partial aid out of local taxation), would be managed by the newly elected local government structure created under the acts of 1888 and 1894—the county, county-borough, and urban district councils. The local School Boards were abolished. A real attempt was made to placate the Anglicans still further by allowing "voluntary" schools to give religious instruction according to the original stipulations of each school's trust deed and under the supervision of the denominational authorities.

Nonconformists reacted violently. John Clifford organized a widespread campaign for civil disobedience, and won the support of other leaders, such as the Methodist champion Hugh Price Hughes. Among the Anglicans, Stewart Headlam fought the 1902 Act because he liked the old School Boards (especially the London School Board on which he had sat for many years), and feared that the new local government authorities would be too cost-conscious. Also, since Balfour provided that two-thirds of the management of "voluntary" schools could be clerical appointees, Headlam regarded the Act as a step away from his own ideal of a fully secular education system. "The people are to pay," he said, "and the parsons are to manage."[80] He broke sharply

---

[80] *Clarion*, 23 May 1902, quoted in Brian Simon, *Education and the Labour Movement, 1870-1918* (London, 1965), p. 229. It is curious that

with the Webbs and other Fabians on this issue (except, of course, with Rev. John Clifford), damning the Act as the product of "an unholy alliance between the bureaucrats and certain ecclesiastics—between Mr. Webb . . . and the Dean of St. Paul's.[81]

Apart from Headlam, who was, as usual, in a tiny minority, High Churchmen accepted the 1902 Act but wanted more: "facilities" to give *denominational* religious instruction to Anglican children in the fully "provided" schools. This demand met violent opposition from Nonconformists, whose Passive Resistance League, led by Clifford, opposed all rate aid to church schools. The Act was pushed through the Commons during Chamberlain's absence due to a cab accident. Passive resistance continued thereafter for some time, but by 1906 when a new bill was introduced, virtually to repeal certain clauses of the 1902 Act, the Balfour system had become a working reality and was left intact.

The overwhelming Liberal victory of Campbell-Bannerman in the 1906 election apparently gave that party a large mandate on the tariff and education issues. The new president of the Board of Education, Augustine Birrell, lost no time in framing a new Education Bill. This bill, which Charles Gore and the Christian Social Union spent so much

---

Mr. Simon, of all people, tends to exaggerate Stewart Headlam's "radicalism" on this issue and misinterprets Headlam's real views. It is inaccurate to suggest that Headlam "argued forcefully against the elitist scholarship system proposed by Sidney Webb." Webb may well have been an "elitist"; but he at least wanted the scholarship "ladder" to bypass the class system. Headlam's statement, "What we want . . . is not the ladder for a dozen or so a year, but the broad staircase taking up a few thousands *one floor higher* in educational progress *before they begin to earn a living*" (p. 232, italics mine), is certainly no indication that he was more egalitarian than Webb; quite the opposite. Headlam pinned his faith on technical, vocational training, "handicrafts"; his vision of *higher* education for the workers was very limited and commensurate with his low opinion of the workers as potential members of Parliament (already seen in his strong opposition to the ILP).

[81] *Ibid.*, p. 227. For Sidney Webb's pragmatic attitude toward the religious question in education, see his Fabian Tract No. 106, *The Educational Muddle and the Way Out* (London, January 1901); Simon, p. 207; Cruickshank, p. 74.

time and energy in opposing, was cut to ribbons by the House of Lords, in response to Conservative party pressure and the demands of the Anglican hierarchy. Education thus became an issue in the culminating struggle between the two houses of Parliament, that would in 1911 lead to drastic curtailment of the legislative power of the Lords.

Birrell's bill proposed to abolish the dual system and to put all schools under public control. Local education authorities were to be empowered to take over the management of all existing voluntary schools. The religious schools were to be divided into two classes: "moderate" denominational schools (chiefly Anglican), which would provide "ordinary" facilities for denominational religious instruction (two days a week, with Cowper-Temple instruction on other days); and so-called religious atmosphere schools (Catholic, Jewish, and a small number of Church of England schools), which would provide "extended" facilities for doctrinal teaching (every day). In the first category the dogmatic instruction was not to be given by the regular teaching staff; in the second, regular staff could teach daily doctrinal lessons if the local authority permitted. All decisions regarding classification of schools in the "ordinary" or "extended" group remained with the elected local authorities, who were to pay rent for the now transferred voluntary schools. "Ordinary" facilities were to be the norm; "extended" facilities would be granted only in *urban* schools (serving an area of at least five thousand population), after four-fifths of the parents had so requested.[82]

The Liberals felt obliged by their large electoral mandate to abolish any vestiges of religious tests for teachers (hence the decision to relieve teachers in the "moderate" schools from the duty of religious instruction) and to establish popular elective control over all rate-maintained educational institutions. The government of 1906 faced two administratively and politically impossible logical solutions to the religious question: totally secular education, teaching *no* religion at all in state schools; and complete pluralism, teach-

82 See Cruickshank, pp. 93-94.

ing *all* religions in state schools on equal terms. The first solution would have gratified Stewart Headlam and some of his Guild of St. Matthew followers, as well as the Marxist Social Democratic Federation of Hyndman, and a majority of the Independent Labour Party. Its political chances were very low, however, in the society of that day. The second solution was an administrative nightmare to work out, except in areas of very homogeneous population. Instead, Birrell produced a bill somewhere in between these extreme solutions, but one that was undoubtedly harsh on the voluntary schools; and despite his apparent concern to be just to all faiths, a definite subsidiary aim was to smash the Church of England's monopoly of village education.[83]

Siding with the Conservative opposition in Parliament, Bishop Gore derided "Birreligion," opposed the sequestration of church property suggested in the transference of voluntary schools to local councils, and along with other Anglicans pointed out that the bill gave church schools no guarantee of being accepted by the local authorities in either of the two proposed new categories. Gore's *Objections to the Education Bill* became one rallying point in the bitter political fight that ensued. On the Nonconformist side, Rev. John Clifford's National Passive Resistance Committee denounced the giving of tax aid to denominational religious teaching, but Birrell himself told them plainly: "You cannot deal with education in this country unless you adopt boldly the secular course; you can only deal with it in a spirit of compromise." Nonconformists had rejected the secular solution, and this rejection made rate aid necessary. In reaction to Clifford's propaganda, thirty-two trainloads of Anglican clerics from the North hit London during Whit week. Stewart Headlam's pamphlet *Secular Schools, the Only Just and Permanent Solution* was selling widely.[84]

[83] *Ibid.*, ch. v; Simon, pp. 258ff. See also B. Sacks, *The Religious Issue in the State Schools of England and Wales, 1902-1914* (Albuquerque, New Mexico, 1961).

[84] Charles Gore, *Objections to the Education Bill, 1906, in Principle and in Detail* (London, 1906); Cruickshank, *loc.cit.*; Simon, *loc.cit.*; S. D. Headlam, *Secular Schools, the Only Just and Permanent Solution* (London, 1906).

The churches were fully engaged in battle over the body of British public education.

When the Education Bill of 1906 reached the upper house (after a 2:1 government victory in the Commons), their lordships proceeded to hack it about, as in their customary treatment of Liberal measures. Gore and his fellow bishops, many of whom were Christian Social Union members, were active participants in this mutilation. The bill emerged virtually unrecognizable in some clauses. All restrictions were removed from the granting of "extended" facilities, regular staff were permitted to teach religious instruction in all schools, and, still further, the Cowper-Temple clause was relaxed to allow local authorities to provide dogmatic teaching in council schools. The original intention of the bill was subverted: not only were church schools to remain undisturbed, but council schools were to be opened to denominational influence. John Clifford urged the royal creation of enough Radical Nonconformist peers to swamp the Conservative majority in the upper house (a threat adopted again in 1911). The King himself was forced to intervene in the political struggle between the two houses and pressed for direct negotiations between the Liberal Prime Minister and the Archbishop of Canterbury, Randall Davidson; but the Tories and the Lords refused to give way despite the relaxation of the Church of England's attitude, and the government stepped down, allowing the bill to remain a dead letter. In the eyes of some educational historians, the failure of the churches and politicians to compromise and pass the Birrell Bill was one of the great "lost opportunities" of the century.[85]

In following years church schools deteriorated rapidly and were increasingly starved of adequate funds. Religion fell into bad repute with public opinion over this whole issue. Ironically, public education was also perhaps the chief of the many secularizing agents which weakened religious faith in the twentieth century. It is not easy to see what the Christian socialists could have done to *prevent* or

[85] Cruickshank, p. 103.

to ameliorate the jealous rivalry of the denominations over the Education Bills of 1902 and 1906; but they could at least have been a little more "socialist" and ecumenical in spirit themselves. As it was, two of their principal leaders, the Anglican Gore and the Baptist Clifford, became grand contestants in the unedifying and debilitating struggle.

Toward the peak: the Lambeth Conference of 1908

With the popular distraction of the Boer War behind them, those Christian Social Unionists whose energies were not totally sapped by the partisan education battle took up with renewed effort the agitation for social reform. John Carter of the Oxford CSU wrote a Union pamphlet on what he understood to be "Christian Socialism" in 1905, and urged "three great socialistic principles": *ethical*— "each for all and all for each"; *political*—T. H. Green's positive state; and *economic*—the cooperative organization of industry to replace individualistic competition.[86] The following year Bishop Gore informed the Church Congress that the chief test of the vitality of a church of Christ was that it should "represent the wage-earners." We must *return* to social conditions nearer to Christ's intention, "if it may be, without violence or revolution, *but if not, then anyhow to return.*" The year 1906 brought a revival of social reform interest largely due to the labor electoral successes following on the unemployment crisis and march of the Leicester unemployed in the previous year. The new and more radical Church Socialist League was also founded in 1906; younger and more determined members of the CSU were soon syphoned off.

In 1906 Gore began to feel cramped by the CSU. As founder of the Mirfield Community, he was well aware of the existence of the new Church Socialist League in the North. He suggested that perhaps the Union had "done its bit and had better (not dry up) but acquiesce in being academic and leave the socialists to make a fresh start . . .

[86] *Christian Socialism* (Oxford, 1905).

[or] have a more moderate president."[87] The year 1907 saw the sanctioning of the CSU's methods and objects by Convocation: a committee report on "Moral Witness" was adopted, and "Social Service Committees" were projected for each diocese. Perhaps the climax of Social Unionism was reached in 1908, however: in the United States the Federal Council of the Churches of Christ announced its "Social Creed" (a complete assimilation of the Social Gospel), and in Britain the Pan-Anglican Conference met at Lambeth.

The questions at the Lambeth Conference were suffused with socialism. Percy Dearmer gave a paper on the subject, as did T. Summerbell (Labour MP for Sunderland and a collier's son) ; Dr. Sanday (CSU) gave a very critical lecture on St. John, expressing "the unqualified conviction that the Kingdom of God had to be realised on Earth."[88] The Church Socialist League held its own meeting at the Memorial Hall, which was full. At the main conference an inevitable but unedifying split in Christian socialist ranks occurred when the aged J.F.M. Ludlow, the only voice remaining from the 1850's, spoke in favor of Christian charity. True to form, the Guild of St. Matthew, hot in pursuit, submitted a sharp manifesto rejecting charity and demanding socialism. The congress was, nevertheless, in Conrad Noel's words, "a triumph for Christian Social-Unionism."[89] Perhaps what made it so was Charles Gore's impressive paper, *Christianity and Socialism*.[90]

Gore began by defining socialism and rejecting its non-Christian extremes—destruction of marriage and the family, and state control of arts and sciences (which "would hideously dwarf and enslave human life"). Socialism as a

[87] Prestige, p. 274. Gore had held the post since Westcott's death in 1901.

[88] *Church Socialist Quarterly*, IV, No. 1 (January 1909), pp. 56-59.

[89] *Socialism in Church History*, p. 258. In the CSU's *Review* an Archbishop's revolutionary son, Rev. William Temple, declared: "The alternative stands before us—Socialism or Heresy; we are involved in one or the other" (*Economic Review*, XVIII, No. 1 [January 1908], pp. 190ff.).

[90] Published as CSU Pamphlet No. 24 (Oxford, n.d. [1908?]).

theory, however, "is not bound up with hostility to the Christian idea of marriage, or with materialistic narrowness, or the ignoring of the conditions of free personal development." In a few paragraphs Gore demolished, to his own satisfaction, the standard antisocialist case. He went on: ". . . there is nothing in the socialistic idea of the constitution of society which is antagonistic to Christianity and . . . its main idea is closely allied to the Christian idea." Christianity should remain independent of state socialism because religion has other than political work to perform; but in its motives and in its rejection of capitalist society, socialism is at one with enlightened Christianity. "The socialistic movement is based upon a great demand for justice in human life. . . . The indictment of our present social organisation is indeed overwhelming. And with the indictment Christianity ought to have the profoundest sympathy. *It is substantially the indictment of the prophets."* Quoting the New Testament (II Thess. 3: 10; I Tim. 6: 8-10; I Cor. 12: 24-26) , Gore said it was impossible to deny that Christ's sympathy was with the poor and his denunciations were against the rich. The ideals of socialism were positive and ethical; on the whole, therefore, Christianity is with socialism and against individualism. "The mere individual is powerless by himself, or by any merely voluntary association, to alter what is amiss," he declared. Social legislation was the only answer.

Gore's statement so far was forthright but not unusual: it was a standard Christian socialist line. But his central theme was more personal: *penitence.* Running throughout this speech of 1908 was Gore's personal conviction of guilt, a guilt like Arnold Toynbee's. The Victorian Church had failed its people, said Gore, nothing but a "tremendous act of penitence for having failed so long" would assuage that sin: "Now in our present social organisation with all its manifest 'crushing' of weak lives . . . where has been the fire of prophetic indignation in the Church? . . . How vast has been our failure!" Penitence must also lead to *reparation*—"while there is yet time." The apocalyptic note in

Christian socialism appears here: social reform agitation is to be the Church's reparation, "ere the well-merited judgments of God take all weapons of social influence out of our hands."

The CSU thus captured the great 1908 Lambeth meeting and turned it into a "socialist field-day," and its leader Bishop Gore left the minds of his fellow churchmen reverberating with the consciousness of their sin. There was no answer, he said, to the charge that the Church had "failed to champion the cause of the weak and the oppressed." The only atonement was effective repentance and social action: "We must identify ourselves with the great impeachment of our industrial system. We must refuse to acquiesce in it. . . . We must identify ourselves, because we are Christians, with the positive ethical ideal of socialistic thought."

After the peak of 1908 the CSU very rapidly declined in radical potency and in general influence. The very next year rival Christian socialists were complaining of the Union's conservatism, and the more vigorous members, like J. G. Adderley, began to drop out. Competition from the Church Socialist League was too strong. The society was completely reorganized in 1910, and open schism was avoided; but Gore insisted on resigning soon afterward.[91] The First World War struck a severe blow to the CSU and upset its members, as it did Headlam. Scott Holland had totally failed to recognize the war's approach and had raged against armaments and the "German scare" until the very last moment, attending an International Congress of Social Christianity at Basel as late as September 1914. Finally, however, all members of the Union came into line and, unlike some other Christian socialist groups, accepted the war as a necessary evil.[92] Five years later the Christian Social Union merged with the new Industrial Christian Fellowship and lost all separate identity.

[91] *Brotherhood*, No. 16 (August 1909), p. 356; Prestige, pp. 281-282.
[92] Paget, pp. 202-203; Wagner, p. 285. In February 1915 the CSU published a pamphlet (No. 44) on the war, by L. V. Lester-Garland, *Christianity and the War of 1914*, which blamed the conflict on the German invasion of Belgium.

"Socialism" for bishops

By 1908 the CSU had thoroughly permeated the Church of England, especially the hierarchy; it was a form of "socialism" for bishops. Its achievements were partly to be seen in the growing awareness of social problems and sympathy to labor shown by successive annual Church Congresses. The meetings of the 1870's had ignored economic and social matters; those before World War I were dominated by them. Pulling the Church in a Maurician-socialist direction, the CSU helped to stretch its mind.

CSU leaders believed, in Gore's words, that "the wellbeing of society depends upon the exceptional man."[93] They were no more elitist than the secular Fabian socialists, perhaps; but their public school, "Oxbridge," and aristocratic backgrounds shut them off from real contact with the mass of the people. In the Union, commented George Haw, "the spirit is wanting. Workpeople do not belong to the CSU. The Labour Movement knows nothing of it. The union is now largely an appendage of the High Church party whose social zeal workmen welcome, while filled with amazement to see it associated with a form of Church worship . . . to them as far removed . . . as Freemasonry or Mohammedanism." Having in mind the "New Unionism" which opened wide the gates for the unskilled masses and broke the union monopoly of the artisan, Rev. J. E. Watts-Ditchfield (GSM) of Bethnal Green asked: "Are there no men able to do for the Church what Burns, Burt and Crooks have done for the Trade Unions?"[94] There were no such men in the Christian Social Union, and as to relations with the trade unions themselves, the Union "entirely failed to raise up in the ranks of the Church a sufficient body of trade unionists who were also Churchmen to make any effective impression on the Labour movement as a whole."[95]

[93] *Christianity and Socialism* (London and Oxford, n.d. [1908?]), p. 5. See also *The Incarnation of the Son of God*, Bampton Lecture (London, 1891), p. 228.

[94] George Haw (ed.), *Christianity and the Working Classes*, pp. 25-26.

[95] Paget, p. 250. See also J. G. Adderley, *A New Earth*, p. 37, for

Scott Holland, despite his name and fame, did not move in Labour circles. "He had little contact with the masses of the people," said Rev. F. L. Donaldson, a CSU leader who did lead the workers. Holland's name "was not one to conjure with among the people. He could not be described as a Labour man. . . . He met some of the Labour leaders; he was well-informed about their movements. But he was never in and of those movements."[96] The only genuine attempt ever made by the CSU to attract working-class members was undertaken through correspondence in J. G. Adderley's journal *Goodwill* in 1898. A Christian Fellowship League was created under Gore's presidency. The executive, all of them CSU members, included Percy Dearmer and Adderley; the chairman was an ex-Salvation Army officer, H. A. Colville. Some branches were established and some meetings held; but the League seems to have melted away by the end of 1899.[97]

In truth, the Christian Social Union was primarily an Anglican church society, concerned with propaganda among church folk. "What its influence over the rising generation of parsons is going to be," prophesied the *Labour Annual* in 1895, "may be judged by the fact that in Oxford about two-thirds of the undergraduates belong to it—that is, practically all who go in for religion at all." Some years after this judgment, Gore maintained that the Union had *not* succeeded in "stirring up . . . the right spirit in the mass of those who preach in the pulpits or sit in the pews." Perhaps this is not surprising, if true, in view of the enormous lethargy and complacency in the late-Victorian Church. The Union had much to put up with—such as the *Church Times* piously reminding Gore, Scott Holland, Adderley, and oth-

---

a denial that the CSU was deliberately *clerical* in outlook and personnel.

[96] Quoted in H. M. Nevinson, *Changes and Chances* (New York, 1923), p. 44. In the light of this highly informed contemporary view it is hard to accept Wagner's claim (*op.cit.*, p. 215) that Scott Holland "long felt at home among the problems of the working-class."

[97] See Inglis, *Churches and the Working-Classes*, pp. 279-280.

ers in 1894 that their "New Christian Socialism" must take account of the fact that "the spiritual and the material are distinct spheres. . . . Nor is the Church the Church of the poor only, but the rich also." This, forty years or more after the work of the Mauricians. Whatever the impact of the CSU on the hierarchy, thought Gore, the Anglican laity and pastorate in general remained "alien" and "unresponsive" to labor's needs.[98] Even allowing for exaggeration on Gore's part due to disappointment that things had not gone much further, it did seem in the prewar years that a curious situation had arisen in which many of the bishops were radical and the main body of the Church lethargic.

Within the CSU itself there was tension for some years between the Oxford and London branches. Oxford was more academic and cautious, London more active. The two remained autonomous and controlled their own branches, despite the existence of a central executive since 1893. The aggressive John Carter was proud to make clear to the Oxford American branch that the *Economic Review* was the organ, not of the whole CSU, but of the Oxford group alone. "A separate guarantee fund was formed," explained Carter smugly, "to meet expenses; and the London CSU expressly declined to undertake any corporate responsibility for the venture."[99] London radicals accused the Oxford CSU of dilettantism, and even as late as 1908 a deep stir was caused in CSU dovecotes when a London group, led by Dearmer, Adderley, F. L. Donaldson, and C. L. Marson, produced a leaflet manifesto declaring themselves openly for public ownership of the means of production. Their Christian socialism, the group claimed, was "essentially the same Socialism as that which is held by Socialists throughout the world."[100] However, the London CSU itself was not homogeneous. Serious divisions occurred there, too, and Scott Holland as branch president had a difficult task to keep the

[98] *Labour Annual*, 1895, pp. 119-120; *Church Times*, 27 July 1894, p. 801; Paget, p. 250.

[99] J. Carter to R. T. Ely, 28 April 1891, Ely Collection, WSHS.

[100] Leaflet in Pusey House Library, quoted in Inglis, *Churches and the Working-Classes*, p. 279.

livelier men—Adderley, Dearmer, and their friends—under control while trying to wake up what he called the "Respectables."

> The Respectables lie so low: they never show what they think; they will not speak. I do not know who they are or what they expect. I can't get them on the Committee because they are silent and unforward. . . . In a mild sort of way I just serve to mediate; that is all.

The radicals, "partly cracky, partly fervid" in contrast, "always talk":

> They lose their heads nearly always. They shock the "Respectables," yet are not bad enough for me as Chairman to sit upon.[101]

The overall image projected by the Union was a mild one. It seemed to some observers "indeterminate, superficial; halting between two opinions." In Rev. F. L. Donaldson's words, "What was said about it, 'Here's a social evil; let's read a paper on it,' was not so very unfair."[102] This characteristic of the CSU was wittily portrayed by G. K. Chesterton's doggerel:

> The Christian Social Union here
>   Was very much annoyed;
> It seems there is some duty
>   Which we never should avoid,
> And so they sang a lot of hymns
>   To help the Unemployed.
>
> Upon a platform at the end
>   The speakers were displayed
> And Bishop Hoskins stood in front
>   And hit a bell and said
> That Mr. Carter was to pray,
>   And Mr. Carter prayed.

---

[101] Paget, pp. 203-204.
[102] Reckitt, *Faith and Society*, p. 91; Bettany, p. 95.

Then Bishop Gore of Birmingham
  He stood upon one leg
And said he would be happier
  If beggars didn't beg,
And that if they pinched his palace
  It would take him down a peg.

He said that Unemployment
  Was a horror and a blight,
He said that charities produce
  Servility and spite,
And stood upon the other leg
  And said it wasn't right.

And then a man named Chesterton
  Got up and played with water,
He seemed to say that principles
  Were nice and led to slaughter
And how we always compromised
  And how we didn't orter.

Then Canon Holland fired ahead
  Like fifty canons firing,
We tried to find out what he meant
  With infinite enquiring,
But the way he made the windows jump
  We couldn't help admiring.

. . . .

He said the human soul should be
  Ashamed of every sham,
He said a man should constantly
  Ejaculate "I am."
When he had done, I went outside
  And got into a tram.[103]

[103] In Maisie Ward, *G. K. Chesterton* (New York, 1943), pp. 163-164. From *Autobiography* by G. K. Chesterton, copyright 1936, reprinted by permission of Miss D. E. Collins and Sheed & Ward Inc., New York; with proviso that the seventh stanza be omitted.

Scott Holland attempted to inject a little more life into the Union as late as 1911, with his handbook *Our Neighbours* and its clear declaration: "The State must take up our task of neighbourly responsibility or it can never be taken up at all. But this is Socialism, you cry. Exactly. This is the irresistible verity on which Socialism has seized. . . ." But in the following year he complained in *Commonwealth* that "a society which starts in alarm at each fresh enumeration of its own principles can never grow in usefulness and power." In CSU debates, he said,

> No subject may be introduced which "sets class against class." The unfortunate death of Leopold II removed a very safe subject from the list. . . . The City branch may safely discuss rural housing; the rural branches will do well to discuss town planning. . . . This policy is the main cause of our weakness.[104]

The paradox was that because of its nature and size the CSU had become to some extent a microcosm of the Church of England itself, and consequently reflected the illogicalities and conflicting interests of that church; while Stewart Headlam's Guild of St. Matthew, because of its idiosyncrasies and its tiny membership, was able to influence only a minority of Anglicans.

In the course of time Charles Gore came to despair of his church. It had "not succeeded in becoming the Church of the poor as is the Roman Catholic Church in so many parts of Europe, or the Salvation Army, or Primitive Methodism," he lamented. And during World War I, visiting troops in France and seeing the good work of the YMCA, he replied to the man who asked what its alleged equivalent, the Church of England Men's Society, was doing: "I don't know. It's only another failure of the Church of England to seize an opportunity. *I hate the Church of England.*" Strong sentiments, coming from a bishop. Gore added: "You youngish ones must start off the Church of England again.

[104] H. S. Holland, *Our Neighbours* (London, 1911), p. 85; Wagner, pp. 269-270.

We old ones have made a mess of it. The only thing fit for us would be to send us to the trenches to be food for Black Marias."[105]

Social-unionism, however, had made a great difference to Anglicanism. It had been unable to check the decline of religion or to impede that slow process of attrition by which Christianity was becoming a minority faith. This was a task perhaps beyond the power of any church association. But Gore, Holland, and their friends did help to change the *official* attitude of the Established Church to social and economic questions. An aristocratic, privileged, well-traveled, classically educated, academic, and clerical-minded Eton, Harrow, and Oxford elite, the CSU leaders shared that unceasing moral intensity and relentless spirit of intellectual inquiry that characterized their philosophical mentor, T. H. Green. The ideal of Green was a society in which all the citizens were constantly engaged in spirited intellectual debate and pursuits. His committed social philosophy was itself, in Professor Melvin Richter's phrase, a "surrogate faith."[106] Influenced by the Maurician Christian socialists of the 1850's, Green had instilled his pupils with like ideals.

As far as economic socialism was concerned—the Marxian socialism of Hyndman's SDF, the collectivist state socialism of the Fabians, or even the hopes of Conrad Noel and the Church Socialist League—the CSU could be nothing but a disappointment, a promise unfulfilled. "Social-unionism" or "bishops' socialism" usually meant in practice little more than mild consumer action, a friendly nod to Labour from the episcopal palace, and support for some Liberal-Radical measures in the House of Lords. The lethargy of the rank-and-file and lower Anglican clergy was apparently too much to contend with for the reformist bishops. Of all the Christian reform groups of the period, perhaps the CSU exhibited the widest gap between its critical rhetoric and its cautious policy. But though its concrete social and eco-

[105] Prestige, p. 372.
[106] *Politics of Conscience*, p. 19.

nomic achievements were exceedingly small, the CSU, more than any other body, was the mechanism by which the Social Gospel came to Britain. Used as a model, its organization was copied by every other major denomination, as we shall see, and largely because of the great prestige and social and intellectual standing of its members, general church opinion slowly began to change. The Social Gospel of 1908, however vague and mild, was a far cry from the complacent individualism of the 1870's.

CHAPTER VII

Northern Radicalism: The Church Socialist League, 1906-1924

Origins of the League: 1906 and the Labour Party

THE CHURCH SOCIALIST LEAGUE was created at a conference of Anglican clerics held in June 1906 at Morecambe, on the Lancashire coast. The place and the time were no accident. From the beginning the League was dominated by church radicals from the North of England and had more of a "labor" flavor than previous Christian socialist organizations such as the GSM or CSU. And the year 1906 was eventful in the history of the British labor movement, since it saw the official establishment of the Labour Party to replace the Labour Representation Committee of 1900, and a victorious general election which brought to the House of Commons a toal of 53 labor men.

The *socialist* position in 1906 was not as strong as it might appear, however. Of the 53 labor MP's, 24 were "Lib-Labs" and only 29 straight Labour Party men. Among the Labour Party men, 24 were elected in constituencies deliberately unopposed by the Liberals, while 13 independent socialist candidates had all been defeated in three-cornered electoral battles. The point was that the Labour Representation Committee had never declared itself openly for socialism, and since 1903 the Labour parliamentarians had operated politically under a secret alliance with the Liberal Party, drawn up between J. Ramsay MacDonald and the Liberal Chief Whip, Herbert Gladstone, all with Keir Hardie's knowledge and consent. The electoral successes of 1906 were the fruits of this secret alliance.[1] Moreover, Hardie's ILP, whose members had largely controlled the Labour Representation

---

[1] F. Bealey and H. M. Pelling, *Labour and Politics, 1900-1906* (London, 1958), pp. 40-41, 158, 298-289; Ralph Miliband, *Parliamentary Socialism* (London, 1961), p. 19.

Committee, had consistently fought to reject motions to declare the LRC as a socialist organization. It was for this reason that the Marxist Social Democratic Federation had abandoned the LRC in August 1901.

In other words, the Labour Party which emerged in 1906 was not at first a socialist party. As a body it had to be permeated and won over piecemeal to socialism. Thus in 1908 the party resolved in favor of railway nationalization; in 1913, for public ownership of canals and waterways, land and mines, and for a state medical service; in 1914, for a fully socialist program, which was finally written into the party constitution only in 1918.[2] And after the successes of 1906 the Labour Party did not function as a true parliamentary party, but was in practice reduced by the Liberals (who for some time thereafter did not need its votes) to the status of a mere pressure group, an appendage of the Liberal Party, often of less political significance than the bloc of Irish MP's.

In the two general elections of 1910 the Labour Party managed to hold its own, and from that date the Liberal government, owing to its reduced parliamentary majority, did come to depend more on the Labour and Irish votes in the Commons. But Labour did not use this new power well. The party had not made up its mind about the great political issues that agitated public opinion in those days—such as the power of the House of Lords and the female suffrage movement. In the bitter conflicts over the question of reform of the peers and Irish Home Rule, Labour had no distinctive voice. The Liberal alliance was taken with great seriousness, and Labour members tried not to rock the boat. They did not even push as hard as they might have to reverse the Lords' judicial decision in the Osborne case of 1909, which prohibited the use of a trade-union political levy and hit at the heart of their own organization. The Osborne judgment was not overthrown until 1913.[3]

The Victor Grayson incident of 1908 illustrates Labour's

[2] A. M. McBriar, *Fabian Socialism and English Politics*, pp. 317-318.
[3] Miliband, pp. 19-24.

predicament. Grayson was successful as a straight Socialist candidate, in a three-cornered Colne Valley by-election in July 1907. The financial crash of 1907 and the ensuing depression created unemployment and hard times, to which the Labour Party responded by suggesting a Right to Work Bill. This was defeated two to one, and the party took no further real action about unemployment thereafter. When Grayson rose in the House late in 1908 to interrupt the debate on a temperance bill and call attention to the hunger of the unemployed, he was declared out of order and suspended. The vote against him included all but two Labour votes. To socialists it seemed in 1908 as if the Labour Party had failed to put forward its own radical program and helped to punish the one Socialist MP who did try to incite action.[4] Even Keir Hardie, in spite of his continued faith in the trade union-labor alliance, complained: "The Labour Party had ceased to count: the Press ignored it; Cabinet Ministers made concessions to the Tory Party and to the Irish, seemingly oblivious to the fact that there was a Labour Party in the House."[5] And by 1914 Hardie had joined his former critics.

From 1906 to the First World War the Labour Party thus experienced a decline of its influence on the Liberals, accompanied by a decline of socialist influence within the party itself. The history of the Church Socialist League reflects all these problems; and like other socialists who in time became disenchanted with the Labour Party, the ILP, and Fabian collectivism, many League members, as we shall see, turned away from state and parliamentary forms of socialist doctrine toward Guild Socialism. For Christian socialists such an evolution was not unusual; and for the Church Socialist League in particular the evolution was fully explicable, logical, and rooted in the deeper origins of the organization.

[4] See Niles Carpenter, *Guild Socialism* (New York, 1922), pp. 72-73.
[5] *The New Age*, IX, No. 10 (6 July 1911), pp. 222-224; Philip Snowden, *Autobiography* (London, 1943), I, 215; also quoted in Miliband, p. 29. See Keir Hardie's *My Confession of Faith in the Labour Alliance* (London, 1910).

Sacramentalism in Yorkshire: a quarry at Mirfield

The deeper roots of the Church Socialist League were to be found in Charles Gore's monastic Community of the Resurrection—the chief inspiration and source of social sacramentalism among Anglicans in the North of England.[6] From 1898, when the Community first moved to Yorkshire, the brothers began living the communalistic life of the early Christians, devoting themselves entirely to worship and to human service. The "Quarry" at Mirfield had (and still has) a distinctly Northern and industrial character, located in a small working-class village, with a view over rather bleak moorland often shrouded by smog. In this setting Gore's religious Community tried to fulfill the message of Acts 2: 42 and 44: "And they continued steadfastly in the apostles' doctrine and fellowship, and in breaking of bread, and in prayers. . . . And all that believed were together, and had all things common." From the outset the Mirfield brothers were determined not to allow their essential monastic function, the regular and constant worship of God, to overshadow their deep concern for the quality of British social life or to turn them into a purely contemplative order, remote from the needs and necessities of the outside world. Throughout its history CR has revealed an abiding commitment to human liberty and a willingness to become deeply involved in the moral struggles of the everyday world; its tradition now stretches from the British working-class movement of the 1890's to the battle against *apartheid* in South Africa in the 1950's and 1960's, from the Christian socialist Father Paul Bull to the antiracist stalwart Father Trevor Huddleston.[7]

[6] The Community grew out of the earlier Society of the Resurrection established by Gore at Pusey House, Oxford in 1887. Four members of the Society (one of whom was John Carter, later secretary of the Oxford CSU) studied monastic rules with a view to establishing a religious community. "CR" became a reality (with six members) in 1892; six years later they moved to Yorkshire. CR in 1963 had four houses in Britain, four in Africa, and one in Barbados (*C. R.*, *Mirfield* [Mirfield: Mirfield Publications, 1960]; G. L. Prestige, *Life of Charles Gore*, pp. 86-87, 106ff., 138ff.).

[7] The Community's work in South Africa was abruptly terminated

The Quarry was not, of course, a Christian socialist organization, but among its brothers were active socialists and labor sympathizers, and one outstanding member, J. N. Figgis, provided a political philosophy—pluralism—which underlay the basic ideas of the Guild Socialist movement. Moreover, the Church Socialist League grew out of a meeting called at Mirfield. Apart from Father Cyril Bickersteth, a CR member who was also an early secretary of the Christian Social Union, the two leading brothers personally involved in the socialist revival were Samuel Healy and Paul Bull. Healy had been ordained in 1885 and had worked as a curate in two Northern industrial towns, Middlesbrough and Newcastle, before joining CR in 1898. A mild-looking but vigorous socialist campaigner, Healy did not stay long in Yorkshire; he soon became warden of his own "Fraternity of the Imitation of Jesus" at St. Ives.[8] Though Healy played a prominent role in the Church Socialist League and served on its executive committee for the Southeast, Bull was by far the more important of the two CR socialists.

Paul Bertie Bull (1864-1942) joined the fraternity in 1894 before it moved from Oxford.[9] As editor of the homiletic pamphlets, "Manuals for the Million," published at Mirfield from 1906, Bull made the Quarry a propaganda center of

---

by that nation's racist Group Areas Act (1959), which took away CR's native schools. Trevor Huddleston continued to work devotedly for Africa, however, and CR hung on in Southern Rhodesia.

[8] *Church Socialist*, I, No. 8 (August 1912), p. 2 (with photo); II, No. 14 (February 1913), p. 18.

[9] Born in Richmond; son of J. B. Bull, Clerk of Journals in House of Commons; educated at St. John's College, Hurstpierpoint, and Worcester College, Oxford. Taught school for some time; ordained 1889; diocesan missioner in the Southwest, and curate in Guildford before joining CR. (Graveyard cross at Mirfield dates Bull's fraternity vows as 22 September 1896.) Army chaplain in Boer War, winning a medal and five bars. Preached missions in many large English cities and toured India, Canada (1921), and United States (Lecturer in Homiletics, General Theological Seminary, New York, 1924-1927) (*Who's Who*, 1940; P. B. Bull, *The Economics of the Kingdom of God* [London, 1927], Preface by Charles Gore; personal enquiry at Mirfield). I was told at the Quarry in 1963 to visit the Nab Workingmen's Club, opposite the Community House, for authentic information from the older members about Father Bull. It was a genuine Yorkshire source.

Anglo-Catholic socialism. At least forty Manuals were published, of which Bull himself wrote ten.[10]

Father Bull began, like his teacher Charles Gore, of whom he was a faithful disciple, with the assumption that the Church had in many ways failed. For twenty years, Bull pointed out, the number of Anglican confirmations had remained stationary, while the British population had increased by six million. A church inquiry was needed to institute radical reforms. More bishoprics should be created to give younger men greater opportunity and incentive in the Church of England, and priests should be recruited from the working class. It was too difficult for a poor man's son to become an Anglican priest; socialism was needed inside the Church.[11]

Outside the Church, socialism was the only answer to the nation's problems:

> Our present social system wastes life most appallingly. In Leeds, in one miserable little room, an aged mother and an elderly daughter are working 14 hours a day at 1d an hour . . . [to] lay by sufficient money to *bury the one who shall be the first to die!* This is what a false political economy has brought us to!

Socialism derived directly from the Incarnation, the Holy Trinity, the Crucifixion, Resurrection and Ascension, the Lord's Prayer, the sacraments, the church's catechism, and God's immanence. . . . In one pamphlet Bull provides all the major High Church arguments for Christian socialism and some of the Nonconformist ones too. He was no major thinker; but he was a born pamphleteer, and no writer of the period set forth the major tenets of sacramental socialism so clearly, succinctly, and forcibly:

[10] Some of these were concerned with sex and morals rather than with sacramental or socialist problems. A "Moral Instructor" for the Royal Navy for five years, Bull spent much energy in rather simple-minded moralizing to the young. See, for example, his Manual No. 40, *Purity* ("Lectures for Men and Lads only, to be had from the Editor alone").

[11] *Urgent Church Reform*, Manual No. 3 (Mirfield and London, n.d. [1908?]), pp. 1-5.

God has entrusted to His Church the Gospel of Life and Love. Mammon has evolved a system of economics which values money more than Life and profits more than Love. The economics of the last century taught that social life can only be based on self-interest. Christ teaches that it can only be based on self-sacrifice.[12]

Socialism's three principles, said Bull, are: equality of opportunity; common ownership of the means of production, distribution and exchange; and universal cooperation. Belief in the second principle, nationalization, marks off Bull as a fully fledged economic socialist and distinguishes him from many GSM and most CSU members. The Church Socialist League, of which he was an officer, stood as a body for complete nationalization.

Capitalism and war go hand in hand, Bull continued, for: "Competition inevitably involves worldwide war, and keeps ten million men in Christian Europe alone trained to kill one another." The competitive spirit makes the ideal of Christian brotherhood impossible, and is "in direct contradiction to the Cross of Christ." It creates a large "army" of unemployed to depress wages permanently (an argument from Marx); it creates moral as well as material poverty, killing "Joy, Beauty, Worship, all that makes life worth living" (an argument from Ruskin, Morris, and the "aesthetic" tradition); it inflames the gambling urge, tempts the souls of the rich with covetousness, and destroys the family and the home.[13]

Whence comes this competitive spirit? It comes, said Bull, echoing an argument currently being developed by social-

[12] *Socialism and the Church*, Manual No. 4 (Mirfield and London, n.d.), p. 3. I am very grateful to CR's Superior Rev. Fr. Jonathan Graham and to Father Arkell, CR, for conversations about Bull, for access to CR's library, and for truly monastic hospitality at Mirfield in 1963.

[13] In the last argument Bull turned an antisocialist standby into a fresh Christian attack on capitalism. He admitted that some continental socialists had rejected marital and family institutions, but claimed that "there is not one responsible leader of socialism in England who has adopted their teaching" (*ibid.*, pp. 3-9).

reform-minded economic historians, from that historical tragedy, the Protestant Reformation; it comes from "the Nonconformist Religious Bodies, whose Protestant principles have given rise to the present Industrial Individualism. . . ." On the other hand, the "Papal principles" of the Roman Church "can only work out into a highly organized ecclesiastical Despotism." Standing guard between the Roman exaggeration of authority and the Protestant exaggeration of individualism is the English church. "Our Church in England is a true living part of the Catholic Church . . . [which] *deliberately refused* to become a Protestant sect. . . . The Church of England is not Protestant. It is Catholic," Bull insisted. Protestants emphasize the individual, the Bible, and the Church as a human society founded on the will of man; Anglican Catholics emphasize the corporate life, Christ, and the Church as a divine society founded on the will of God. As for the Bible, "When Jesus Christ, the Son of God, became Incarnate and was made man, He did not write a book. He founded a Society, the Holy Catholic Church." Socialism proposes a "rational, orderly, just reorganization of life, based on Goodwill instead of Selfishness, on Public Service instead of Private Gain." The true Christian must support this proposal not merely on the grounds of humanity but because he is a member of the Church, which is "a clearly defined and disciplined body of men, knit together by strong dogmatic creeds and strict Sacramental bonds into a Brotherhood which is stronger than the mere tie of human nature."[14] As a missioner of Mirfield, Bull could believe this very strongly; unfortunately the actual Church of England, as he was well aware, fell very short of the Mirfield ideal. At the Quarry itself it was largely on Bull's insistence that Gore began a college for the training of young men of limited means for the Anglican ministry. Bull returned from the South African War and in 1901-1902 gathered fifteen poor working-class boys in the North who wanted to become priests but had no money.

[14] *Ibid.*, pp. 12-14; *Christian Teaching*, Manual No. 1 (Mirfield and London, n.d.), I, 3-5.

Unitarian, Baptist, and Wesleyan training could be had free, Bull complained, but in the "so-called National Church" it was too expensive and could cost up to £1,000; "we have invented a class priesthood with a money qualification." The college was opened in 1902.[15]

Bull's Christian and sacramental arguments for socialism may be summarized, for convenience, under seven heads.

1. *The Incarnation.* "The right use of Reason justifies us in believing that God is Personal . . . [and] will reveal Himself in *some* way." The "way" was Jesus Christ taking human shape. This action automatically consecrated the human body, consecrated daily life, and blurred the distinction between things material and things spiritual. Bull's argument here follows closely the views of Stewart Headlam, W. E. Moll, and other predecessors in the sacramental socialist movement. The Incarnation demands fullness of life for soul *and body,* gives the "august authority of Christ" to the socialist's protest against "a system which leaves twelve million of our brethren without the means for sufficient life." Daily life is made holy because Jesus, who "was born in a poor stable, lived in a simple cottage, worked in a carpenter's shop," lived it.[16]

2. *The Holy Trinity,* a doctrine which teaches that "Personality can find its perfect realization only in the Corporate Life"—because it posits not one "isolated loveless Individual" but the mystery of Father, Son, and Holy Ghost, in which "the love of One for Another is embodied in a Third."

3. *The Crucifixion, Resurrection, Ascension, and Judgment.* The Cross stands, of course, for supreme *self-sacrifice,* "the direct challenge to the Political Economist who teaches that self-interest is the only reliable instinct," and for *martyrdom,* which in the original Greek means "witness"—the courage to expose evil. Christ was "the People's Champion. He refused to be their King . . . but He exposed the false claims of the ruling classes." Today we need "the courage

[15] Prestige, p. 217.
[16] *Socialism and the Church,* pp. 18-19.

of the Cross" to oppose vested interests and lay bare "the impertinent fraud" of conventional Christianity. Third, the Cross proves *God's sympathy for man*—he suffered with and among us. "Christ is crucified afresh in the lives of all who suffer and all who sin."

The Resurrection and Ascension assure man that sin's triumph is only temporary and that the body "shares the destiny of the soul" and should be reverenced. Judgment is "a *present* process, not a distant possibility"; Jesus "especially assured us that we shall be judged by our Social and Economic life."

4. *The Lord's Prayer,* which is "social in each of its petitions." "Our Father"—not *my* Father; not a blind force either, but a personal god. "Thy Kingdom Come"—"here and now, not some day long hence." "Give us this day our daily bread"—"God gives it but Man takes it away!" "Forgive *us* our trespasses"—not forgive me; society needs mutual forgiveness; every sin is antisocial and "not merely a personal matter between you and God."

5. *The Sacraments.* Bull's argument here is very like Stewart Headlam's: the sacraments preserve and embody the teaching that the whole gamut of life—work, joy, art, science, dance, drama—is consecrated to God.

Holy Baptism, to consecrate the body. ("Each of the 44,000 little hungry children in the London schools whose body is covered with vermin, each one of those bodies is a living Temple of the Holy Spirit.")

Holy Communion, "The Village Carpenter and a few fishermen, breaking bread and drinking wine," continually celebrated, with the Real Presence of the Body and the Blood in the common food of the home, bread and wine, as a constant reminder.

6. *The Catechism* of the Anglican Book of Common Prayer. "Sentence after sentence rises up in condemnation of our present commercial and industrial system." Two sentences have caused misunderstanding, however, said Bull: first, the duty "to order myself lowly and reverently to all my betters": where one should emphasize "betters," not

"richers" nor "granders"; second, "to do my duty in that state of life into which it shall please God to call me": where one should emphasize *shall call,* not (the often misquoted) *has called.* "It is the motto of progress and the sanction of aspiration."

After this careful explanation Father Bull felt justified in claiming: *The Church's catechism is the people's charter of social reform.*

7. *Divine Immanence.* God is *not* like the proverbial "watchmaker" of philosophy. He is "to the Universe as the Soul is to the Body, immanent through and through it, while at the same time He infinitely transcends it." Bull's argument is a simplified form of the CSU theologian Illingworth's. "God is not shut up in a Church. He is in the home and school, the office and workshop, the mine and factory and mill."[17]

To this thoroughgoing and aggressively Anglo-Catholic socialism Father Bull added a belief in a spiritualized imperialism. His attitude to the Empire was very different indeed from Gore's or Scott Holland's, perhaps owing to his own personal experiences as an army chaplain working alongside British Tommies in General French's Cavalry Division in the Boer War. Bull was under fire in many battles and emerged a hero with military decorations. "The distinguishing mark of our age," he declared, "is the revival of a corporate spirit. Imperialism in one direction, socialism in another, is directing attention to the large visions which exceed the bounds of nationality." Like Joseph Chamberlain and others, Bull managed to combine imperialism with social reform, creating a curious "social-imperialism" peculiar to his day and age.[18] In one tale from Africa which Bull used as a homely example to explain the meaning of Baptism, he seems to equate the British Empire with the Kingdom of Heaven. A woman and child flee from a tyrant Afri-

[17] *Ibid.,* pp. 16-17, 19-31.
[18] *Urgent Church Reform,* p. 2 (opening words). For a full treatment of social imperialism in this period see the monograph by Bernard Semmel, *Imperialism and Social Reform* (Cambridge, Mass., 1960).

can king, and cross a stream (Baptism) into British territory, thus passing over "from the Kingdom of Darkness to the Kingdom of Light"—from "cruelty, lust, and hatred" to the British Empire, "where Justice, Righteousness, Liberty and Peace reign supreme . . . under the protection of the British Flag."[19]

Father Bull was more than a visionary imperialist, he was a local patriot, belligerently "Northern"—despite his Surrey birth and Oxford education. He was invited to write for *Commonwealth* in 1906 but complained good-humoredly of the editor's title for his piece, "The *Awakening* of the North":

> When we Northerners want a little rest and sleep, we scamper off to London and the South; with its quaint old-world ways and its dreamy life. Then back again to the North, with its strong, rich, vigorous life, where the destiny of England is being wrought out by strong, thoughtful men, where passions burn and enthusiasms kindle with a splendid glow, and hearts are tender and wills are strong.[20]

Bull's adopted Northernism, his aggressive defense of the Northern working class, tells us more about the sources of his socialism than the many pages of rhetorical propaganda he managed to produce. His chief complaint about British society was its class consciousness, which bordered, in his view, on caste. The worst aspect of class in Britain according to Bull was that people of all ranks simply *took it for granted.* To the deferential society of his homeland Bull contrasted the United States—as did his master Charles Gore. America had problems, such as an "excessive belief in the ballot-box and in legislation"; but her prime strengths were in her ethnic pluralism, produced by immigration,

---

[19] *Christian Teaching*, pp. 19-20.
[20] *Commonwealth*, XI, No. 6 (June 1906), pp. 169-172. Bull also wrote on educational policy and had a division of opinion with Stewart Headlam and the redoubtable C. L. Marson. See *Commonwealth*, XI, No. 10 (October 1906), pp. 290-293; XI, No. 11 (November 1906), pp. 323-325.

and in her universal public education system. In Britain, however, the opposite was the case: there, "the real strength of 'class' mentality is to be found in segregation in education," Bull lamented, as late as 1927.[21]

Paul Bull's Superior at Mirfield in 1906 was Rev. W. H. Frere. During this year a Socialist Conference was called at the Quarry. Frere never claimed to be a "socialist"; but he had served as group secretary for East London of the Christian Social Union and was certainly friendly toward socialist ideals. He had succeeded Gore as Superior of the Community in 1901 and led the brothers until 1923 when he was made Bishop of Truro.[22] The conference of 1906, "to bring about a better understanding between the clergy and socialist organisations in Lancashire and Yorkshire," met in May. W. H. Frere took the chair, and Northern branches of diverse socialist groups were represented, ranging from the secular and Marxian Social Democratic Federation to the gradualist and ethical Independent Labour Party. The conference took this attitude: "We treat socialism as a Theory of Society which anyone may hold, to whatever religion he may belong. But it seems to us a method of organising Society which will make Brotherhood possible."

The following month at Morecambe some sixty Anglican clergymen and a few laymen gathered to establish the Church Socialist League.

The Union, the Guild, and the League

The Conference of June 1906 established a provisional committee, chiefly inspired by Rev. G. Algernon West and including with him Rev. W. E. Moll of Newcastle fame, Rev. F. L. Donaldson of the Leicester unemployed march, Rev. Paul Bull, Rev. H. S. Kennedy (Halifax), Rev. R. S. Greane (Workington), and Rev. J. H. Hastings of Halton

---

[21] Bull's analysis of the American situation was full of insights and revealed a wide reading in American sources. See *The Economics of the Kingdom of God*, pp. 44-51, 122ff. (quotes from pp. 48 and 128).

[22] Nan Dearmer, *Life of Percy Dearmer*, p. 64. See also W. H. Frere's reviews and notes in the CSU's *Economic Review*, e.g., II (April 1892), 256-257 (on profit-sharing).

(Hon. Secretary). West, Moll, and Donaldson, as we have seen, were ex-members of the recalcitrant "left wing" of Headlam's Guild of St. Matthew. The Church Socialist League was more the heir of the GSM than it was of the Christian Social Union. The Guild's affairs were wound up in 1909, while the CSU went on for another decade. Yet the creation of the League in 1906 did also represent a growing dissatisfaction within the Union.

On many occasions open criticism of CSU leadership was voiced from within that organization, as for example in Scott Holland's *Commonwealth* in November 1905, where a certain radical Miss Colville asked: "Is socialism Christian?" Yes, it is, she affirmed, but *Commonwealth*'s policy is merely reformist and placatory—not socialist at all. Holland's reply, a plea for moderation and for the Church's ultimate independence of dogma, was not likely to satisfy Miss Colville, especially since he suggested that "the very fervor of socialism" might lead it to commit political excesses. His tone had changed since 1889. Another anxious correspondent, the Fabian G. Herbert Davis, supported Miss Colville. Davis warned the CSU:

> We, Churchfolk and reformers, *are drawing nigh to a parting of the ways.* . . . We go on studying, preaching, writing. To what end? As a result the reviews fatten, nicknames are bandied, eyebrows raised in Church, or a few belated stragglers join the Oxford branch of the CSU. Little more.[23]

It was a crushing indictment of the achievement of sixteen years of labor by the Union. But by the late 1890's the radical spirit of the CSU was already beginning to wane. Miss Ruth Kenyon said of the Union in 1904: "We stand just as much as all the other reformers now for a mere bread-and-butter, gas-and-water movement; a *socialisme sans doctrines.*"[24] The CSU seemed anemic. Conrad Noel, recalling

[23] *Commonwealth*, x, No. 11 (November 1905), pp. 325-332; x, No. 12 (December 1905), pp. 376-379; xi, No. 6 (June 1906), p. 172.
[24] G. C. Binyon, *The Christian Socialist Movement in England*, p. 189.

the Morecambe discussions of 1906, said: "We poor Southerners . . . soon found . . . that *the North had made its mind up;* the socialist clergy of the North and Midlands were not happy in the CSU or the GSM and were determined on forming a new League."[25]

Noel himself suggested "an extended-type-of GSM" in an attempt to save Stewart Headlam's historic group from oblivion; but the North refused. The Objects of the Guild were "too vague," while its traditions were "too definite." If the GSM had been more definite about socialism and less definite about some other matters, things might have been different. The new League intended to be much less exclusive than the Guild, less rigidly Catholic; it would be open to all schools of Anglican theology, and would not insist on every one of the *seven* sacraments, the worship of the saints, the Real Presence, and membership by communicants only. Also, the League would not "risk the rejection of its socialist propaganda by pronouncing on other points . . . indifferent to socialism and controverted among good socialists" (a fairly obvious personal thrust at Headlam's "outside interests"). Unlike the CSU or the GSM, the League would give little time to "intellectual apologetics," and more to socialist political action.[26] It would "consist solely of people, clerical and lay, who have found what they believe to be *the* remedy . . . *socialism,* as defined in dictionaries and understood by socialist societies." While the CSU could never declare itself in support of Fabian socialism, or of the SDF or ILP, the new Church Socialist League would be able to do so if its members wished. In fact, congratulatory messages reached the conference from Keir Hardie, J. Ramsay MacDonald, and J. Bruce Glasier, among

---

[25] *Commonwealth*, XI, No. 1 (July 1908), p. 222.

[26] The Morecambe Conference would not take up Rev. P.E.T. Widdrington's plea for a "Christian sociology"—the phraseology was strange and alien to the mood of the moment. "Socialism would provide all the 'sociology' necessary, the Conference felt." Widdrington had to wait twenty years—until 1924—to get support for his idea, in the League of the Kingdom of God (M. B. Reckitt, *P.E.T. Widdrington*, pp. 45-47).

others. Speakers at Morecambe included the CR monks from Mirfield, Revs. S. Healy and Paul Bull; Stewart Headlam and his ex-disciples, Widdrington, Stacy, Noel; and Canon M. Ede and Bishop H. Baynes of Nottingham.[27] Headlam accepted his defeat and the creation of a new rival organization in good faith (as he had tried to in 1889 when the CSU emerged), and he gave the League many useful suggestions. But it caused him some pain that not only the "young bloods" were abandoning his Guild of St. Matthew, but even old friends like Rev. W. E. Moll.[28]

The Church Socialist League arose, therefore, out of discontent among Christian socialists with the GSM and CSU. Also, it expressed the general revival of labor enthusiasm as a result of the electoral victories of 1906, previous unemployment demonstrations (like that of Rev. F. L. Donaldson), and the Mirfield Conference. Above all, it stood for the rebellion of Northern church folk,[29] though in London a future League president and Labour Party leader, George Lansbury, had tried to commit the Diocesan Conference to a policy of socialism, and a large branch was soon to emerge there.[30] The League's platform was the most clearly "social-

---

[27] *Commonwealth, loc.cit.*; F. G. Bettany, *Stewart Headlam*, p. 93.

[28] Reckitt, *Widdrington*, p. 47: "Stewart Headlam was magnanimous and said nothing to discourage the new initiative."

[29] The Guild and the CSU "spoke with the accents of the University Common Room to audiences almost wholly unfamiliar with the outlook and the needs of the mass of the people," claimed Maurice Reckitt, the Guild Socialist. "North Country trade unionists were not likely to set much store by the Church and Stage Guild centred in London, or share Headlam's passion for the ballet, which they seldom if ever have any chance to see" (Reckitt, *Widdrington*, p. 43).

[30] In his memoirs Lansbury exaggerated his own role in the formation of the League, and gave a confusing picture of its makeup. In the following quotation he was obviously referring to a later date than 1906; the League was certainly not inimical to the ILP until the conversion to Guild Socialism of some of its members. "I also helped form the Church Socialist League. We were a small and very mixed band of adventurers, who some years ago, gathered in Egerton Swann's rooms at Paddington. We were all rebels against the Capitalist system: this was the one and only thing we agreed about. Some of us, like G. K. Chesterton, were strong individualists. Others were fanatical Guild Socialists, others Syndicalists. The Countess of Warwick, Lewis Donaldson, Conrad Noel, T. C. Gobat, J. West, Percy

ist" of all Christian socialist organizations in the revival years. It declared:

> The Church Socialist League consists of Church people who accept the principles of socialism, viz.: The political, economic and social emancipation of the whole people, men and women, by the establishment of *a democratic commonwealth in which the community shall own the land and capital collectively* and use them for the good of all.

The League's principles were:

1. The Church has a mission to the whole of human life, social and individual, material and spiritual.
2. The Church can best fulfill its social mission by acting in its corporate capacity.
3. To this end the members of the League accept the principle of socialism.
4. *Socialism is the fixed principle* according to which the community should own the land and capital collectively, and use them co-operatively for the good of all.

Membership in the League implied a duty to make oneself "familiar with at least one branch of social reform,"[31] and was open to all baptized persons who did not belong officially to non-Anglican churches. A group of clerical leaders rapidly emerged, however, who were for the most part Anglo-Catholic—including Algernon West, Conrad Noel, P.E.T. Widdrington, F. L. Donaldson, Egerton Swann, and Paul Bull.

Five "Church Socialists"

Unlike the CSU, and more like Headlam's GSM, the League did not attract a homogeneous following, a group

---

Widdrington, and others were Parliamentarians, but very few had any faith in the Labour Party" (George Lansbury, *My Life* [London, 1928], p. 5).

[31] Bull, *Socialism and the Church*, advertisement on back cover; for altered "Principles" of a later date see *Church Socialist*, I, No. 1 (January 1912).

of men from any one particular class, elite, or educational background (apart from their Anglican baptism, of course). League membership was varied, ranging from the remote intellectualism of Widdrington to the simpler political activism of Lansbury, from the aristocratic novels of Adderley to the raw propaganda of Bull. The life and work of five members (West, Noel, Dearmer, Adderley, and Donaldson) will perhaps serve to illustrate this range and diversity, and perhaps also to reveal its limitations.

Rev. G. Algernon West, who chaired the Morecambe Conference, became the League's first president (1906-1909). West was not an English aristocrat; he did not attend a famous public school; he did not even go to Oxford. He entered the Anglican ministry as a Tyneside curate (1891) after one year at a Missionary College in Islington. There was no class condescension in West, no elitism. In politics he favored the Marxist SDF and the working-class ILP; in religion he was a moderate, Broad rather than High: more like Westcott than like Headlam. West joined the Guild of St. Matthew in December 1893 and served it faithfully until he became convinced, along with many other members, of the pressing need for a more effective organization to reach the workers and to preach socialism. He told the Church Congress of 1906: "The League stands for *economic socialism*. It exists to further the socialism of the ILP and SDF among Churchmen."[32] "Society is one organic whole," said West in his presidential address of 1907 to the Church Socialist League's first annual conference (Scarborough).

> This unity is a fact revealed by Christ and confirmed by science and history. . . . We believe that whilst the Divine Spirit has His home in the Church, He is yet the source of all light, truth and knowledge without the Church, and therefore we must be on our guard lest through prejudice, self-interest, intellectual sloth or ignorance, we reject or ignore the truth that is offered to us (from *outside* the Church).

[32] *Crockford's Clerical Directory*, 1894, p. 1141; Binyon, pp. 187, 191-193.

The particular "truth" West had in mind was *socialism:* "the theory of society [that] harmonizes most with the Christian view of the solidarity of the race and the unity of life." Socialism is "divinely inspired" and makes for "fulfillment of the Divine Purpose for the social redemption of man."[33] West's opinion of what was the best method to realize socialism in Britain and his idea of how the League should function were not shared by all his colleagues.

The key policy phrase of the Church Socialist League, as distinct from either of its two Anglican socialist predecessors, the GSM and CSU, was *"economic* socialism." Its principal exponent, apart from Algernon West, was Conrad Noel. "No priest in the country," said Widdrington of Noel, "could claim so wide a knowledge of the Labour movement. His name was familiar in every industrial area and . . . in ILP branches and Labour Churches his lectures and debates created a deep impression and a friendliness which did much to remove the suspicion in Labour circles that the Church was hostile."[34] Conrad le Despenser Roden Noel (1869-1942) was an undeniable "aristocrat," like his companion in the League and in the GSM, Rev. J. G. Adderley. Noel's grandmother was Lady Gainsborough, a lady-in-waiting to Queen Victoria and a strict Calvinist. His mother, Alice de Broe, was the evangelical daughter of a Swiss banker; his father, Roden Noel, was an unusually radical Groom of the Privy Chamber (1867-1871), who wrote the "Red Flag" while living in one of the Queen's "grace and favor" houses at Kew Green. Conrad was born here, under the ample wing of the Sovereign, "by the irony of fate," as he commented later, "for I have never had any love of monarchy, limited or unlimited."[35] Noel also hated the British fashionable public schools, which he regarded as breeding grounds of vice, snobbery, and militarism. Himself "incarcerated" for a time at Wellington and then

[33] Coventry Clarion Fellowship, *Socialism, "A Cancerous Growth": An Open Letter to Rev. George Bainton* (Coventry, 1907), pp. 11-12.
[34] M. B. Reckitt, *Faith and Society*, p. 107.
[35] Conrad Noel, *An Autobiography*, p. 1.

at Cheltenham, he found no "sense of fair play" at either.[36] Fortunately, as a youth Noel had come under the teaching influence of that gentle Fabian and "animals' socialist," H. S. Salt, and of the Joynes brothers at Brighton.

Henry Salt and James Leigh Joynes were brothers-in-law; both were Eton-educated and both became Eton masters. Salt became a socialist after meeting Joynes's American friend, Henry George, and subsequently falling in with a radical crowd: Bernard Shaw, H. H. Champion, Edward Carpenter, William Morris, and others. Like his brother-in-law, Salt graduated from Single Tax to socialism; but he became a Fabian and later founded the Humanitarian League (1891) to protect animals and fight vivisection, while Joynes went in a more Marxist direction, coediting the *Christian Socialist* briefly before joining the SDF executive (1886-1889) and helping the aggressive atheist E. Belfort Bax edit *Today* (1884). This is the same Joynes who traveled in Ireland with Henry George; he was arrested with George and lost his Eton job as a result. Joynes is known to history chiefly as a socialist poet and songster.[37] His brother Herman Joynes, who was the young Conrad Noel's official tutor in classics, was more of an anarchist than a socialist. Dressed in the brown habit of a lay brother, Herman distributed anarchist pamphlets in the streets during the state visit of the Shah of Persia. He was a brilliant scholar and managed to get his pupil into Chichester Theological College (1893). Noel had already been rusticated

[36] Chapter II of Noel's autobiography is entitled, sarcastically, "The Glorious Tradition of Our Public Schools." A slashing attack on private education, it blamed British imperialism, among other things, on the public schools: "Newspapermen and politicians who talk about our glorious empire are identical with those who boast about the glorious traditions of our public schools" (p. 12).

[37] Jones, Manchester thesis, pp. 248-252; H. S. Salt, *Seventy Years Among the Savages* (London, 1924); S. Winsten, *Salt and His Circle* (London, 1951). J. L. Joynes's father, coincidentally, had tutored Stewart Headlam at Eton. Joynes died young (in 1893). Hyndman blamed his death on excessive vegetarianism; Shaw, quite naturally, rejected this and blamed the medical profession. It is said that the anti-medical eccentricities in Shaw's plays can be attributed partly to Joynes's death. Salt, Joynes, and Shaw were all vegetarians and fresh-air fiends.

from Corpus Christi, Cambridge ("Heaven and Hell" as the students called that evangelical college), for heavy drinking and rowdyism, and he never went back. In Chichester he read widely, especially in patristics, discovering ancient support in the "revolutionary writings" of the church fathers—St. Ambrose, St. Gregory the Great, and others—for his own innate radicalism.[38]

Noel worked in the Portsmouth slums with the controversial radical and ritualist Father Dolling until the latter was sacked by his bishop. Noel was then to have become assistant curate to Father Chase (a very High Church priest who later became a Roman Catholic) at All Saints', Plymouth, but Bishop Ryle of Exeter, an extreme Low Churchman, refused to ordain him at the last minute. Ryle accused Noel both of "pantheism" and of extreme Catholicism. So for a while Conrad went to live in a shabby doss-house on the South Lambeth Road in London and made friends with Revs. Percy Dearmer and W. A. Morris.[39]

Rev. W. A. Morris (GSM)—"Brother Bob" to the London gas workers and to the labor demonstrators who carried a banner reproduction of his face—was a New College graduate (1880) who gave up the comfort of Oxford to take up heavy work in the dirtiest back streets of Vauxhall as curate of St. Peter's (1882). There he established a workers' club, "where billiards, entertainments and socialism flourished exceedingly," and lived himself in one corner of the billiards' room, behind a partition. His club became a planning center for labor demonstrations and the headquarters of the great London gas strike, which Morris helped to lead. A radical paper, the *People's Press,* was published there for some time. After ten years as a Vauxhall curate, Morris

[38] Noel, *Autobiography*, pp. 1-28. In 1912 Noel gave as the chief reasons he became a socialist: (1) the Catholic religion; (2) a lecture at Cambridge by Annie Besant; (3) J. L. Joynes's *Socialist Catechism*; (4) the influence of his father, and of Maurice, Headlam, and T. Huxley ("whose *Anarchy or Regimentation* . . . still seems to me to supply the most complete answer to the pseudo-science of the individualists"). See *Church Socialist*, I, No. 2 (February 1912), p. 3.

[39] *Autobiography*, pp. 28-42.

was finally made vicar of nearby St. Ann's by Archbishop Benson.[40] Conrad Noel became his assistant and so learned practical Christian socialism at first hand from a veteran.

The young Noel was ordained in 1894 but, like Stewart Headlam, found it difficult to obtain or to keep curacies. For some years he was out of work; he spent the time in getting married and in moving from lodging to lodging in the industrialized Manchester area, lecturing throughout the North to Labour Churches, socialist clubs, and anybody who would listen to him on Christian socialism. Noel was married by Dearmer, and both bride and groom immediately joined the Guild of St. Matthew.[41] Eventually Charles Gore, as a canon, managed to find Noel a job at St. Phillip's, Salford. Almost instantly the new curate got publicly involved in the free-speech struggle at Boggart Hole Clough, a famous open-air site at which several labor leaders were arrested by the police, including Leonard Hall and Fred Brocklehurst (ILP and Labour Church). During the Boer War, which he naturally opposed, Noel joined Rev. W. E. Moll (GSM) as curate in Newcastle-on-Tyne. There he preached openly against the war—to *munitions workers!* When the men threatened (very aptly) to blow up the church, the stalwart radical Moll merely told Noel: "My dear Noel, by all means let it go on, as it is the truth; and if we lose our church, which is the ugliest structure in Newcastle, we can build a new one with the insurance money." Noel found the rejoicing of Mafeking Night (1900) "an in-

[40] *Ibid.*, p. 42; *Labour Annual*, 1895, pp. 180-183. The Archbishop's motive in promoting Morris was political, as an entry in his diary for 6 March 1891 revealed: "Gave Morris, the instigator of the men in the gas strike, the living of St. Ann's, in the middle of them. . . . It is far better that such a man should work out and help them to work out just solutions than to remove their leader and send someone else who could not sympathize with them. He is a fine, romantic, large-eyed, Chartist-looking fellow, and I think he will make something of his life" (*Commonwealth*, IX, No. 3 [March 1904], p. 79 [obituary by Dearmer]). For the flavor of Morris's appeal see his paper to the GSM meeting of 1889, "The Church and the Unskilled Labourer," *Church Reformer*, VIII, No. 10 (October 1889), pp. 222-225.

[41] *Church Reformer*, XIV, No. 11 (November 1895), p. 259.

decent exhibition of mass hysteria." As for Cecil Rhodes, "the ancestors of such men . . . killed both Jesus Christ and St. Paul."[42]

It is not clear whether Noel or West is to be credited with calling for a new Christian socialist society in 1906. Noel claimed that the initiative came from himself, W. E. Moll, and P.E.T. Widdrington to call the Morecambe Conference; but Algernon West had written to the *Labour Leader* immediately after the electoral victories of 1906 demanding the formation of a new socialist society to propagandize the Church, signing himself "A Durham Priest."[43] Noel was determined to remove the taint of "mildness" or "milk-and-water socialism" from the Christian socialist movement. The new society, he thought, must be *"fully socialist in the ordinary sense understood by the secular socialist bodies";* it must stand clearly for *"economic socialism,* come to by the road of the Christian faith." The vagaries of his career, however, or lack of it, kept Noel out of any large participation in the actual administrative affairs of the League. After 1906 he worked in France, and then as a curate to the "Modernist" Rev. A. L. Lilley, exponent of the latest French Catholic reform ideas at Paddington Green. Noel drifted into the rarefied company of the Cecil and G. K. Chesterton-Alice Meynell-Francis Thompson circle, and in fact prepared Cecil Chesterton for confirmation at St. Mary's, Primrose Hill, with Percy Dearmer in attendance. For five splendid years he lived at "Paycocks," the famous mansion at Coggeshall, Essex, owned by his cousin Noel Buxton (and restored it, ripping away the Georgian plaster to rediscover the original Tudor beneath).[44] At Paycocks Noel wrote his most important book, *Socialism in Church History* (1910), while continuing to preach and lecture on sacramental socialism. In 1910 he took the nearby living of

[42] Noel, *Autobiography*, pp. 50-58; *Labour Prophet*, v, No. 53 (May 1896), pp. 73-74.

[43] *Ibid.*, p. 59; Binyon, p. 193.

[44] Noel, *Autobiography*, p. 60. (The economic historian Eileen Power wrote a book about the mansion Paycocks in 1920.)

Thaxted, offered to him by another aristocratic Church Socialist Leaguer who controlled it, Lady Warwick.[45] For the following thirty years Noel made Thaxted a lively center of High Church socialist propaganda. Gustav Holst trained his choir, and an ex-Benedictine monk and Marxist from the SDF executive, George Chambers, became his first curate.[46]

"For Conrad Noel," wrote William Temple, "the social and individual aspects of Christian life were bound up with one another and quite inseparable. This, I am convinced, is the true view." Noel was very influential and an outstanding figure of the Christian socialist movement, still very active between the two World Wars. From his church at Thaxted, which displayed the Red Flag and the green banner of the Sinn Fein, were emitted reverberations of socialism, anti-Sabbatarianism, anti-imperialism, ritualism, and folk art. In 1918, however, Noel broke with the Church Socialist League and founded his own Catholic Crusade. He did not lose his economic radicalism or his broad and thoroughgoing approach to the problem of social regeneration. Father Dolling, he said, had declared the worst social hindrances to be "the Bishops, the Brewers and the Brothels"; but for Noel in 1912 "our deadliest foes now are the Daily Press, the Liberal Government, the Party System and the Religious Newspapers." Journals like the *Church Times* "call evil good and good evil, and champion a materialism more deadly than that of Marx under the specious cloak of next-worldliness." The chief hope in the future lay in "the

---

[45] Frances Evelyn, Countess of Warwick, an admirer of William Morris, of whom she wrote a biography, was a socialist and a feminist. "I went through the phase of interest in philanthropic work," she explained, "I went about with Bishops and that sort of being, opening bazaars. . . ." But eventually she abandoned this charitable activity and became instead a "whole-hearted socialist," for "how is it possible to build a fine people out of luxury and poverty?" (*Church Socialist*, I, No. 7 [July 1912], pp. 3-4).

[46] Noel was a diabetic for twenty years and totally blind for the last five years of his life. He died of cancer during World War II (1942) and is buried at Thaxted (*Autobiography*, pp. x-xi, 125).

revolt of the people against their 'leaders' as manifest in sympathetic strikes and the general labour unrest." Only the spread of "Catholic Democracy" and "economic socialism" in all camps would finally eradicate the evils of *"Christo-Capitalism."*[47]

A noticeable friendship in the history of radical Anglo-Catholicism was that of Conrad Noel and his one-time vicar, Percy Dearmer (1867-1936). As a young man Dearmer had arrived at Christ Church, Oxford in October 1886, an ardent Conservative and Primrose Leaguer. Within months, influenced by the historian York Powell, he had read William Morris, Ruskin, and the rest. Dearmer became a devoted Maurician, decorated his college rooms with Burne-Jones and Morris tapestries, and dressed outrageously in loud checks and bright suits. He became friendly with Charles Gore at Pusey House and joined the Oxford GSM, becoming its secretary in 1889. In the Guild, as in the later CSU, Dearmer and Noel were young dissidents, bringing consternation to Stewart Headlam and to Scott Holland respectively. A good speaker and writer, Dearmer was a frequent contributor to radical papers, especially the *Church Reformer*, for which he produced verse, criticism, reviews, and articles.

During the London Dock Strike of 1889 Dearmer went as an Oxford student to Poplar to help Rev. J. G. Adderley feed six hundred strikers at Christ Church Mission. "The parsons were fearfully behindhand," he wrote, "but we have worked them up a bit: it is fearful, their ignorance on social matters." As for the strike itself, the movement was "eminently Christian in its two features: 1. unity, 2. self-sacrifice." Christian "unity" of one sort Dearmer displayed himself in 1890 by joining, besides the GSM, the CSU (February), Pusey House (October, as Gore's secretary), and the Fabian Society (December). He was elected secretary of the London CSU in 1891—a post he held until 1912—and be-

[47] *Church Socialist*, I, No. 2 (February 1912), p. 4. See also Noel, *Socialism in Church History*, p. 272.

came curate to "Brother Bob" Morris, working among the Lambeth gas workers for four years (1891-1894).[48]

Fundamentally, however, Percy Dearmer was an artist, not an agitator. His companion, Morris, the treasurer of the Oxford GSM, once wrote: "Socialism for Percy Dearmer meant more than economic change. It meant opening up the Kingdom of art and beauty to all." Dearmer gathered leading artists about him as vicar in Primrose Hill, London (1901-1915) and raised the level of British liturgical art and music through his many distinguished works, now classics: *The Parson's Handbook* (1899; 12th edition in 1931); the *English Hymnal* (1906); *Songs of Praise* (1925, written with the great composer Ralph Vaughan Williams), and the well-known *Oxford Book of Carols* (1926). Dearmer researched the native English tradition in liturgy and ceremonial, and he revolutionized congregational hymn-singing. On the other hand, Conrad Noel complained in later years that his friend was too "mild" in economic matters and that this even affected his musical editions: Dearmer "listened to the clamour of manufacturers who wanted to whitewash the present system," said Noel, and he bowdlerized Blake's *Jerusalem*.[49] The judgment seems a little strained; at any rate, in the 1890's and 1900's Dearmer was regarded by others and by himself as a socialist. The *Labour Annual* of 1895 wrote warmly of him;[50] he contributed to the dissident volume of 1894 edited by A. Reid, *The New Party;* and he produced a Fabian Tract in 1907.

In *The New Party* Dearmer began by attacking denominationalism on the grounds not of a general ecumenicalism but simply because "A divided Church *loses its social char-*

---

[48] Nan Dearmer, pp. 32-37, and 66; Bettany, p. 117; S. Paget, *H. S. Holland*, pp. 203-204; *Crockford's Clerical Directory*, 1894, p. 356; 1897, p. 361.

[49] Noel, *Autobiography*, pp. vii-ix, 57. Dearmer was certainly a very awkward and diffident man: "I christened two babies without strangling them!" he once exclaimed in triumph. See Nan Dearmer, p. 83. He was Professor of Ecclesiastical Art at King's College, London, 1919-1936 and in later life a Canon of Westminster, where he is buried in the Little Cloister.

[50] *Labour Annual*, 1895, pp. 167-168.

acter." Schism is inevitably antisocial, for Nonconformist sects "can never rise above class and national distinctions." The Church must represent the *whole* people:

> Once remove the unity of the Church, and the gentleman, the tradesman, the labourer, the Scotchman, the Welshman, the Englishman, and the Irishman must all have their own particular religions, and class and national divisions are made inconceivably more bitter.

Christian socialism and a divided church did not go together. In the London of 1894, Dearmer argued, quite correctly, "the classes go to Church, the bourgeoisie go to Chapel, and the masses attend a trade union demonstration." If they all worshiped together in one church, ministered by priests drawn from all classes, how long could social inequality survive? "How long would it be possible for the well-to-do . . . to have their clothes washed by laundresses who . . . work 80 hours a week in a temperature of 75°, for two-pence an hour?" The ecumenical movement and socialism are thus one; the "yearning for Church re-union" is "saturated with social enthusiasm." But Dearmer was ahead of his time in his desire for church reunion; certainly most Christian socialists did little to encourage religious unity and squandered their energies in denominational rivalries. Church reunion is a movement now afoot; but it has come *after,* not alongside the acceptance of the Social Gospel. Up to the First World War Christians exhibited in Britain the "unChristian unsocialism" of a divided faith.[51]

Percy Dearmer served on the Fabian Society's executive committee, 1895-1898, and wrote Tract No. 133, *Socialism*

[51] "The Social Work of the Undivided Church," in A. Reid (ed.), *The New Party* (London, 1894), pp. 287-314. In his "Do We Need a Quaker Movement?" Dearmer went so far as to praise the Friends most highly, excuse their rejection of the sacraments, and recommend their doctrine of the "inward light": "They went to God direct, and waited and listened in silence. Modern psychology has entirely justified this method." They are "the salt of the earth" and should be reunited with the Church. See P. Dearmer (ed.), *Sermons on Social Subjects,* pp. 66-75.

and Christianity, in 1907.[52] The Tract owed much to Stewart Headlam, but was the most learned, thorough, and well written of all Fabian writings on religion. Dearmer based his socialist faith on the Incarnation, of course, Christ coming as a worker to proclaim the unity of all mankind. The four forms of His teaching were: (1) *His "signs"* (or miracles) : the struggle against disease, discomfort, and premature death; (2) *His parables:* criticizing money-making and demanding social conscience; (3) *His Sermon on the Mount:* condemning religious individualism, cant, and self-conscious "charity"; (4) *His Prayer:* all ten points of which are social, not individual in character, and teach the essence of socialism—brotherhood and justice.

> By her very existence the Church declares the solidarity of the human race, and its essential unity, free from all distinctions of class, sex, and race, "neither Jew nor Greek, bond nor free, male nor female, for ye are all one man in Christ Jesus," as St. Paul insists in three separate epistles (*Gal.,* iii, 28; *Col.,* iii; I *Cor.,* xii, 13) .

Therefore, Dearmer argued, "Christianity is not Individualism. Neither is it Socialism and water. *It is Socialism and fire.*" The Church has made many mistakes; it is very imperfect. But it has driven home the message of brotherly love which makes socialism at least a possibility in Christian countries: "For the man that loves much is a socialist, and the man that loves most is a saint, and every man that truly loves the brotherhood is in a state of salvation."[53]

Dearmer was distinguished in the world of the arts and music, but as far as literary publicity was concerned, no single writer did as much for Christian socialism in Britain in these years among the general reading public as did the novelist, agitator, and priest Adderley (GSM, CSU, Church Socialist League) . The Hon. and Rev. James G. Adderley was the younger son of the first Baron Norton, the early Victorian penal-law reformer and Gladstonian Liberal. Bar-

---

[52] E. R. Pease, *History of the Fabian Society,* p. 270.
[53] P. Dearmer, *Socialism and Christianity,* pp. 6, 21-23.

on Norton conceived of Heaven as a spiritualized version of Victorian Britain, complete with upper- and lower-class angels. In "the citizenship of Heaven," he believed, there are "many ranks, united in one harmony of love."[54] His son, Father "Jimmy" Adderley, as he was known, had detested the Baron's Victorian preoccupation with social rank. Like Conrad Noel, he also hated public schools as centers of snobbery and caste.[55] Born in 1861, he was educated, as befitted his rank, at Eton and Christ Church, graduating in 1883. Most of his undergraduate time was spent in founding the Oxford Theatre.[56] He became a council member of Headlam's Church and Stage Guild in 1889 and joined the Guild of St. Matthew in 1890. Headlam was a major influence in Adderley's life and thought. What also helped to turn the young aristocrat to socialism was the Congregationalist pamphlet published in his graduation year—*The Bitter Cry of Outcast London*—which he later called "the great turning point in my career." Reviewing the pamphlet in the *Christian Socialist*, Adderley demanded state confiscation of all property in the "fever-den" slum areas, and the complete "overthrow" of *laissez-faire* dogma.[57]

[54] Baron Norton's little book, *Socialism* (London, 1895), was a confused attack on Christian socialism and state intervention, using all the standard arguments—that socialism is "levelling": that laws cannot change "human nature"; that charity is divinely ordained and should be enough; that the "poor ye always have. . . ," etc. Curiously, he praised his son's work *The New Floreat*, perhaps because the book rejects *secular* socialism. Norton declared, "It is part of the scheme of human probation that there should be richer and poorer to serve one another." Laws to regulate hours of labor for women and children, and the income tax, were dangerous invasions of society by the State. "Christian socialists do their cause much harm by tilting at the science of political economy." The true answer to unemployment was emigration to "the Queen's Empire" (pp. 1-35).

[55] See, for example, his "Caste and Public Schools," *Church Socialist*, I, No. 9 (September 1912), pp. 11-15.

[56] See his "The Fight for the Drama at Oxford," *Church Reformer*, VI, No. 9 (September 1887).

[57] *Church Reformer*, IX, No. 10 (October 1890), p. 237. Adderley, as noted, left the GSM over the Wilde affair, but changed his mind after visiting Oscar Wilde in jail. See Bettany, p. 131; *Christian Socialist*,

In 1885 Adderley was made lay head for two years of the newly established Oxford House settlement in Bethnal Green. Once ordained, he led a varied ecclesiastical career in London until 1904 and in Birmingham thereafter.[58] "The nearest approach to persecution that I have suffered was the refusal of the curate of a South London church to sit down at the same table with me," he confessed amusedly in 1894 to the English Church Union. In view of his unflinching Anglo-Catholicism and radical political doctrines, Adderley was fortunate to escape so lightly. He demanded of Christians:

> When you cross yourself, if you are a Ritualist, or when you draw a long face and tell your friends that you are "saved," if you are an Evangelical, just ask yourself this: "Am I prepared to take . . . the Christ's pains to make myself the friend of the suffering poor and to seek the causes of their poverty, not merely get frightened at the results?"[59]

Father Adderley took the pains himself, as his work in three Christian socialist societies, in the London Dock Strike, the settlement movement, the agitation for the ILP, and the fight for a trade-union "closed-shop" policy all illustrate.[60]

No. 6 (November 1883), p. 93; J. G. Adderley, *In Slums and Society* (London, 1916), p. 16.

[58] He was curate in various poor parts of London and Head of Christ Church Mission in Poplar for a while; his first full ministry, ironically, was at Berkeley Chapel in the heart of Mayfair (1897-1901). He was Vicar at Saltley, a crowded industrial ghetto at Birmingham from 1904, with three ILP men as curates, and became Canon of Birmingham Cathedral in 1913 (*Crockford's Clerical Directory*, 1894, p. 7; *Reformer's Yearbook*, 1908, p. 230; *Church Socialist*, I, No. 9 [September 1912], pp. 4-5; *Labour Annual*, 1895, pp. 161-162).

[59] *Looking Upward* (London, 1896), p. 115; *A Little Primer of Christian Socialism*, p. 27.

[60] Ben Tillett, the dockers' leader, praised Adderley's "splendid work" in the strike: "A scholar, a Christian socialist, with unconventional manners and interests . . . we found his influence and his connections invaluable in organizing the work of relief. By his personal efforts he raised over £800 . . ." (Tillett, *Memories and Reflections*, p.

"I never felt very happy in the CSU," Adderley admitted. The teachings of Charles Gore and Scott Holland came to him only "as one already steeped in Headlamism," and even in the GSM he was always a young dissident, like Noel and Dearmer. The Church Socialist League was, therefore, an ideal home for Adderley from the moment of its foundation, and he became a League committee-member for Birmingham.[61] A good deal of his most important writing, however, was done either for the CSU or during the years of his work in that Union. *Stephen Remarx,* published in 1893 after being rejected by twenty publishers, was the most widely read of his socialist novels and reached its twelfth edition in 1904. Of his nonfiction pieces, *Christ and Social Reform* (London, 1893), *The New Floreat: A Letter to an Eton Boy on the Social Question* (London, 1894), *Looking Upward* (London, 1896), and *A New Earth* (London, 1903) date during his CSU phase, and the best known, *Looking Upward,* was dedicated to Scott Holland, his coeditor on the journal *Goodwill.*[62] Scott Holland also wrote the preface to Adderley's popular *Little Primer of Christian Socialism* (n.d. [1909?]).

Stephen Remarx was the heavily autobiographical story of an "Eton boy with a handle to his name who gets ideas at Oxford, and develops them in the East End." These ideas are the reverse of those taught Stephen by his mother,

---

137). Adderley himself claims to have collected only £700 and to have "lost a peer's subscription to the Mission [Poplar] of £50 by doing so." He "went on errands between the Bishop of London and John Burns" and witnessed some of the major negotiations. See Adderley, *In Slums and Society,* pp. 193, 197-198, and "Some Results of the Great Dock Strike," *Economic Review,* II, No. 2 (April 1892), pp. 202-213.

61 *Church Socialist,* I, No. 9 (September 1912), pp. 4-5; Paget, pp. 203-204; F. L. Donaldson, *Socialism and the Christian Faith,* Mirfield Manual No. 12, ed. Paul Bull (London, n.d.), advertisement.

62 *Labour Annual,* 1895, pp. 161-162. See also Adderley's *The Goodwill Catechism* (London, 1894); *Quis Habitabit: Psalm XV: A Meditation for Christian Socialists* (London, 1903); *Prayer-Book Teaching* (London, 1904); *The Legend of the Way of Grief* (London, 1904). In his League period he wrote, among other things, *The Catholicism of the Church of England* (London, 1908), *The Socialist Churchman* (London, 1909), and *The Parson in Socialism* (Leeds, 1910).

namely those of his class "superiority." Cyril Bickersteth (CSU and CR) in reviewing the novel expressed the hope that life in English upper-class country houses was not quite so "vicious" as Adderley painted it. Dearmer found the story "delightful" and full of genuine insight into the mentality of an era. He hoped it would dispel the Tory "snobdom that hides itself in the garments of loyalty, or . . . selfishness that is embroidered with constitutional maxims."[63] In *Christ and Social Reform,* published in the same year, Father Adderley proclaimed his faith that the future of England was in the hands of the working classes and his anxiety to win over the workers to Christianity as a social religion. This could not happen while Christians remained wrapped up in concern for their own individual "salvation." Ideally the Visible Church should offer the most powerful inspiration and the most mature and permanent vehicle for social reform.[64] Nine years later Adderley gathered together various lectures in *A New Earth.* He explained the workers' indifference to organized religion as an expression of their own *higher* ideals of religious life: unlike the bourgeoisie, the workers could not be "content with churchgoing and outward observance" and maintained "an honest fear of hypocrisy or failure to reach a high standard." Like Dearmer, he deplored sectarian divisions in the body of the faith, the most blatant "divorce between practice and precept." The upper-class priest was also to blame:

It is all very well for a comfortable parson, who has had a good night's rest in a clean bed, and has his shaving water deposited at his door by a spruce little parlourmaid or a liveried flunkey, and has walked leisurely across 20

[63] *Economic Review,* III, No. 4 (October 1893), pp. 604-605; *Church Reformer,* XII, No. 6 (June 1893), pp. 139-140.
[64] *Christ and Social Reform: An Appeal to Workingmen* (London: Society for Promoting Christian Knowledge, 1893), passim. The pamphlet was marred by certain condescending phrases ("you workingmen," "we Christian church-people," "your labour leaders," etc.) and an unnecessarily elementary approach, and is a poor example of Adderley's writing skill.

yards of pathway into a well-warmed vestry and thence into the pulpit, to talk in his sermon about "taking no thought for the morrow" and the "sin of worry," and how it is quite as easy, perhaps easier, for a poor man to be good than for a rich man. But one wonders if he could and would talk like that if he had to slave like a tramway or a shop girl.[65]

There was far too much reliance on mere almsgiving on the part of religious apologists, Adderley told the CSU in one Lent sermon: ". . . doles, blankets and soup and so on are not only antiquated but are positively wrong."[66] Christian socialism was the only adequate answer to poverty and unemployment, and in his *Little Primer* of about 1909 Adderley tried to "stir up somebody—not of course to think, but to do something." The primer was terse, biting, amusing, and deliberately antifatalistic. It spoke of Bibles manufactured with cheap sweated labor, poverty in the "richest" and "best-evangelized" country in the world, the Poor Law, the aged poor, and workhouse children; and it defended state interference and the trade-union "closed shop." The contemporary Christian at Judgment Day would be discovered confessing:

> True, Lord, I denied myself nothing for Thee . . . I did not give to the poor; but I paid what I was compelled to the poor rate, of the height of which I complained. I did not take in little children in Thy Name, but they were provided for; they were sent, severed indeed from father and mother, to the poorhouse, to be taught or not about Thee, as might be. *I did not feed Thee when hungry; political economy forbad it:* but I increased the labour market with the manufacture of my luxuries. . . . I did not take Thee in as a stranger; but it was provided that Thou mightest go to the Casual Ward. Had I known that it was Thou! . . .

[65] *A New Earth*, pp. 106-107, 41-42.
[66] P. Dearmer (ed.), *Sermons on Social Subjects*, p. 6. Christians should demand "love not doles, self-giving not money-scattering" (*Little Primer of Christian Socialism*, p. 38).

Taking up the cause of Old Age Pensions, Adderley pointed out: "It would certainly be a conspicuous example of the power of Christianity if the Church would contribute funds to make the scheme possible." But he added wryly that it would take "a revolution among dignitaries." Of course, a "still more Christian" action would be for the Church "to subscribe to the ILP, which aims at abolishing the whole system."[67]

Father Adderley was an eclectic, a defender of the ILP, the Fabians, and even, later on, of the British Socialist Party. The Church Socialist League should concentrate on religion, he thought, but should also encourage its members to take up economic and political work in secular socialist bodies. As for his own taste, he revealed: "I love baiting the Anti-Socialist Union, the Anti-Socialist Sunday School Movement, the religious capitalist, the Catholic landlord, the pious plutocrat, the pharisaic sweater and such-like. . . ."

While Jimmy Adderley wanted "to get at the rich among the Christians," his colleague Donaldson chose to work as leader of the unemployed. It was Rev. Frederick Lewis Donaldson, in later life Canon of Westminster, who gave the Church Socialist League its slogan: *"Christianity is the religion of which socialism is the practice."*[68] Born in 1860 and ordained in 1884, Donaldson was a graduate of Merton College, Oxford (1884) and as an undergraduate helped to establish the Oxford GSM. His wife also joined the Guild as a young girl and was an enthusiastic Christian socialist; they were married by Shuttleworth on New Year's Eve, 1885-1886, at St. Nicholas Cole Abbey, where Donaldson had taken his first job as Shuttleworth's curate.[69] From 1886, the year of demonstrations, to 1895, Donaldson held three further London curacies and engaged in heavy propaganda work for both the CSU and the GSM. Donaldson

---

[67] *Little Primer* . . . , pp. 34-35, 40-41, 36.

[68] *Church Socialist*, I, No. 9 (September 1912), pp. 4-5.

[69] M. B. Reckitt, *Maurice to Temple*, p. 151; *Church Reformer*, v, No. 2 (February 1886), p. 43; *Church Socialist*, I, No. 3 (March 1912), pp. 3-5.

became a Council member of the Guild and a great fan of Stewart Headlam's. His resolution in the GSM annual meeting of 1889 thanking John Burns and company for their fine leadership of the Dock Strike was passed unanimously. Eleven years of socialist and labor agitation in the city came to an end for Donaldson in 1895 when the authorities moved him to Nuneaton; two years later, however, he was moved again to St. Mark's, Leicester, where for many years he established his reputation as champion of the underdog and, of course, as we have observed, as chaplain to the great Leicester-London march of 1905.

Although he was an energetic executive member of the CSU and one of the Union's first members, Donaldson—like his League companions, Noel and Adderley—was always a dissident. Describing his conversion to socialism, Donaldson wrote:

> Liberalism seemed to have outlived its possibilities . . . and was becoming more and more conventional. In the hour of our need the breath of the Spirit came and across Europe swept the philosophy and economic theory of socialism. . . . Many a man like myself found new hope and strength . . . in a new synthesis of life.

He studied Maurice, Kingsley, and Westcott, and became an ardent Headlamite. But it was the Leicester laborers who finally convinced him that "social reform" tinkering was wholly inadequate and too slow to keep up even with the rate of production of social evil by the capitalist system; full socialism was the only remedy.[70] Donaldson was, therefore, a zealot for the League: its emergence paralleled the development of his own socialist thought. He became an executive member, and at the League's conference of 1907 preached a well-known and glowing sermon entitled "The Shout of a King Is Among Them."

[70] *Church Reformer*, VIII, No. 4 (April 1889), p. 92; VIII, No. 10 (October 1889), p. 237; Bettany, pp. 93ff.; *Crockford's Clerical Directory*, 1886, p. 336, and 1897, p. 381; *Christian Socialist*, No. 6 (November 1883), p. 93.

The shout of a King is among them; no longer leaderless, obstinate, headlong, wilful, denying, ignorant, as in the old Chartist days, but drawn up in order and array, looking forward to Him, . . . believing in His call and in their own destiny to build the New Jerusalem upon the earth.[71]

He became chairman of the Leicester Church Socialist League, in 1912 vice-chairman, and in 1913 chairman of the entire League.

A good guide to Donaldson's social theology is his Mirfield Manual *Socialism and the Christian Faith*, written for Father Bull's series. Christian socialism, Donaldson insisted, is not "socialism watered-down or explained away" but *real* socialism, "inspired by the Christian Faith, confirmed by the august authority of Jesus Christ and sustained by the cooperation of His Church." Socialism is a "glorious principle" of organic growth and "development from lower to higher conditions of life and organization." No social system is eternal. Donaldson quoted from widely divergent sources, such as Ramsay MacDonald, the Labour Church Hymn Book, and the great American liberal theologian Rauschenbusch (*Christianity and the Social Crisis*, 1907), to show that the Christian faith rejects "corrupted individualism," indicts the aims and methods and results of capitalism, and demands "social justice, prosperity and happiness" for the people. "Science" now has proved that "mutual aid is a vital fact in evolution. Group organization is as true to Nature as individual struggle." But in real life what do we see? In the name of "individualism" the workers are made to suffer poverty, disease, and the horrors of slum life.

> The "public schools," most of which were founded for the poor, are now appropriated by the rich. The poor may neither hunt nor shoot, nor fish nor even snare a rabbit. The commonlands of the people, like their ancient

[71] Binyon, pp. 213-214.

schools and universities, have been "appropriated," together with wastes and rivers. All, all has been slowly but surely monopolized by the rich. Even their Church has left them. For the historic Church of England is now preeminently the church of the rich and well-to-do classes.

Herod slew the children of Bethlehem; but does this compare with the infant mortality rates in British cities, of 80 per 1,000 in "favoured districts," rising to nearly 500 per 1,000 in slum backstreets? "From the day of the setting up of the Lancashire factory system until now, our industrial system is chargeable before God for the massacre of our innocents."[72]

Church Socialism: policies and problems

The Church Socialist League reached the peak of its activity in about 1912. The year 1909 was a time of troubles which the League managed to survive, and after 1912 its members became increasingly involved in the Guild Socialist movement. Conrad Noel was the League's paid organizing secretary until 1912, and under his energetic leadership in the winter of 1907-1908 alone its members attended 1,000 socialist and labor meetings. By 1909 there were about 1,000 active members and 25 branches in the Church Socialist League. These included branches in traditionally socialist Bristol (where C. L. Marson worked with Cecil Chesterton), Leicester (where F. L. Donaldson and C. Stuart Smith cooperated with the young Rev. Hewlett Johnson—later known as the Communist "Red Dean" of Canterbury), and an experimental federation of branches in Lancashire. By 1911, however, 17 branches were to be found in London alone, and the growing concentration of political organizations and institutions in the capital was forcing the League to concentrate its attention more on that city and less on the provinces and the North.[73]

---

[72] Donaldson, *Socialism and the Christian Faith*, passim.

[73] *Church Socialist*, I, No. 5 (May 1912), pp. 17-18. D. O. Wagner (*The Church of England and Social Reform*, pp. 276-277) says there were 35 branches with 1200 members in 1909, but *Church Socialist*

The League took over as its official organ a journal formerly called *The Optimist,* now renamed the *Church Socialist Quarterly* (1909-1911). The thick first issue under the new regime contained articles by Conrad Noel, A. J. Carlyle, Noel Buxton, G. Algernon West, A. L. Lilley, G. K. Chesterton, Egerton Swann, and others. The *Quarterly* also published some new clauses to the League constitution: the League's "methods" were now to include the deliberate infiltration of church assemblies by socialists ("members shall co-operate as far as possible to secure the consideration of social questions at their various Ruridecanal and Diocesan Conferences, and the election of socialists on these and other representative bodies"). The "due representation of the wage-earning classes" must be secured on "all the official representative bodies of the Church." Moreover, the League should form "Groups" with a secretary for each diocese which would have two representatives each on the League's central executive.

Conrad Noel pleaded for a true *"Church* Socialism," which he distinguished from a milk-and-water *"Christian* Socialism." The "comrades" of *Church* Socialists are "Messrs. Hyndman, Hardie, Blatchford and Shaw" (of these four, three were agnostics and one a Nonconformist); but "their standpoint and their power is the philosophy of the Gospel, the traditions of the Church and the driving force of the Holy Spirit."[74] Noel's plea was met to some extent in 1908 and 1909: the Church Socialist League officially supported the Labour Party candidate in the Taunton by-election and in February of 1909 held a mass meeting of the unemployed in Trafalgar Square, at which a crowd of three thousand were harangued by a variety of speakers—the Baptist Fabian, Rev. John Clifford, Rev. F. L. Donaldson, and others. The League won publicity in such leading

---

Quarterly (IV, No. 3 [July 1909], pp. 182-187) gives the figures quoted above. See also *The New Age,* III, No. 10 (4 July 1908), p. 184.

[74] *Church Socialist Quarterly,* IV, No. 1 (January 1909), inside cover, pp. 80-81, 10-11, 77-79.

papers as the *Times, Morning Post, Daily News, Clarion*—and France's *Le Soir*.[75]

A key annual conference in the history of the League was held at Leicester in May 1909. Noel, Widdrington, Adderley, Smith, Swann, Parker, and others heard Algernon West ask them to support what he called *three historic principles:* "adaptation," "assimilation," and "permeation." By these, the Faith itself had survived over the centuries. Here was a new look in Christian socialist thought, for West had abandoned the patristics argument and cast aside the learned historical "proofs" of Thomas Hancock, C. L. Marson, Stewart Headlam, and the rest. The twentieth century, West argued, was neither the twelfth nor the twenty-fifth. Leaguers should neither seek vain past precedents nor speculate as to future forms: *"We do not want armchair socialism."* The attempt "to consult the spirits of defeated Fathers and Schoolmen brings little or no guidance." Church Socialist propaganda must "be on Christian lines," of course—but only "as far as it is consistent with the needs of our own times." This West called "adaptation." As for "assimilation," this meant taking part in the real world. "We are in danger of isolating ourselves from much that is around us, and yet which contains elements we cannot afford to be without. This principle of assimilation will save us from being bigoted, narrow, intolerant and exclusive—real dangers to which we are liable." "Permeation" meant for West the Fabian political methods he wished the League to adopt. The Kingdom of Heaven is a "leaven, a permeating influence." In no other way could they hope to progress.

In practice Algernon West called upon the League to join an "International Congress of Socialists" abroad ("This will save us from insularity and some other defects of the English race") and the Labour Party at home. The Labour Party, he said, was "the best, if not the only way" of realizing a Church Socialist faith. West would personally have preferred "a purely Socialist Party" but: "as we cannot

[75] *Church Socialist Quarterly,* IV, No. 2 (April 1909), pp. 170ff.

have all we want, let us have what we can. In joining this movement we shall unite ourselves with the vast majority of socialists throughout England and take our place . . . in the people's great movement."[76] West's policy was thus the antithesis of that taken by Stewart Headlam when the ILP first emerged in the 1890's.

Not all League members agreed with the president—especially the influential intellectual, Rev. P.E.T. Widdrington, who was quite at odds with the nontheological tone adopted by the League under West, and wished to develop a "Christian sociology." West's criticism of "armchair socialism" hit Widdrington directly. His desire to shun intellectualism and to identify personally with the labor movement was a reflection of his different social and educational background: West was no Oxford intellectual, as we have seen; even in theology he preferred the undoctrinaire Broad Church position.

What ensued must have seemed to Stewart Headlam to be a vindication of the Guild of St. Matthew, for West's pro-Labour Party and egalitarian policy was not adopted. He resigned promptly from the League's executive and was replaced as president by a man opposed to the idea of "assimilation" with Labour, Rev. A.T.B. Pinchard.[77] Though J. Ramsay MacDonald and George Lansbury attended the League's evening session, though Keir Hardie wrote an article for the *Quarterly* pleading for members to join the Labour Party, and though Lansbury was himself elected vice-president of the League, Pinchard could state in the

[76] *Church Socialist Quarterly*, IV, No. 3 (July 1909), pp. 181-189, 236.

[77] Pinchard (b. 1859) was ordained in 1885 and held urban curacies before going to Latin America for seven years (1888-1895). He returned as Vicar of St. Jude's in industrial Birmingham, and became secretary of the Birmingham Church Socialist League branch in 1896 and League president, 1909-1912. His paper to the Pan-Anglican Conference of 1908 (marking the full tide of CSU influence) was an extremely vague personal definition of socialism. See *Church Socialist*, I, No. 6 (June 1912), p. 2; *Commonwealth*, I, No. 5 (May 1896), p. 200; *Crockford's Clerical Directory*, 1886, p. 936, and 1894, p. 1052; A.T.B. Pinchard, "What Is Christian in Socialism?" in *Pan-Anglican Papers*, S.A. 6[f] (London, 1908).

strongest terms that it would be "suicidal" for the League to identify itself too closely with any wing of the social-reform parties. It was "too premature" for such a political identification, and members "had no right" to express their individual views "in such a manner as to compromise the League."

In 1909, expressed in the rivalry of Pinchard and West, the Church Socialist League faced a classic problem common to the history of most socialist groups: the issue of party political alignment. In rejecting the Independent Labour Party in the 1890's Headlam's Guild had probably made a tactical error. West did not want the League to repeat this error after only three years of existence; but Pinchard was pushing the organization into a nonalignment stance. The issue was clouded, too, by the division between West and Widdrington. The latter wanted to use the League virtually as a seminar of High Church theologians, to devise his so-called Christian sociology.

The League's new president took care to emphasize his concern to work through the executive, to give members that "sense of security" about League policy (which, he hinted, they had missed under his predecessor West). Pinchard said flatly:

> We are a society of Socialists of various shades of Socialist opinion, and our common platform is not that of the ILP or the SDF but that of the Church of God. Our business is to convert Churchmen and make them Socialists, but *the particular tint which may color their Socialism is no concern of the League.*[78]

The League majority followed Pinchard's leadership and rejected a motion to affiliate with the Labour Party together with a second to admit a new class of "associate" membership. Complaints were heard from members that the North had inadequate representation on the executive (this was

[78] *Church Socialist Quarterly*, IV, No. 3 (July 1909), pp. 236-237. Despite Pinchard's stand on this question he was regarded highly by George Lansbury. See Lansbury's *My Life*, p. 90.

remedied immediately by the invitation of three new members from Liverpool, Newcastle, and Lancaster), and that a "triumvirate" regulated the *Quarterly*'s editing. Rev. Samuel Proudfoot resigned as editor, but returned on the promise of the new executive that he would be *sole* editor, with independent responsibility.

Despite these internal dissensions in 1909, the Church Socialist League continued to grow and to proliferate. Branches were formed in Birmingham, Ashton-under-Lyne, Failsworth, Stockport, Glasgow, Elland, Hawarden, Taunton, Derby, St. Leonards, Ramsgate, and elsewhere. Church Socialist League attacks on the CSU and on the general passivity of the Church of England continued throughout 1909. In October, for example, Father Adderley wrote that if all Britain were converted to the Anglican faith overnight the only tangible political result would be the drawing-up of "a white list to tell the clergy where to buy their trousers." All the CSU had achieved was to make the mass of church folk feel uncomfortable, with "the discomfort of those . . . on the edge of a cliff below which surges an awful sea called 'Socialism.' They are standing in their bathing costumes (made without sweating), stripped of much conventional prejudice, wondering whether or not to take a header."[79] This was not enough. The more radical League must "convince the Churchman that Socialism does not consist in buying basins of leadless glaze or voting for Winston Churchill." The pressure for more radical political action by the Church than was possible through the too-distinguished CSU and the defunct GSM was unabated. Labor tensions mounted in the years before World War I, and the parliamentary struggle between the two houses and battles over feminism and the rudimentary welfare-state legislation of 1911 kept the political temperature high. At the height of the struggle between the upper and the lower house the League continued its economic and social propaganda; it was not drawn

[79] *Church Socialist Quarterly*, IV, No. 3 (July 1909), pp. 237-241, 262f.; IV, No. 4 (October 1909), pp. 295-297. See also Conrad Noel's attack on the CSU in *Church Socialist*, I, No. 2 (February 1912), p. 5.

entirely into the dispute over the Lords, as many of its members claimed the Labour Party was.

Abolition of the hereditary upper house featured in the Church Socialist League's manifesto for the first of the two general elections in 1910. But that manifesto contained many other demands. Anglican socialists, said the manifesto, should vote for candidates (*not* for any one particular party) who agreed to support: the elimination "once and for all" of the hereditary principle in the legislature; the complete democratization of the House of Commons (woman suffrage and electoral reforms to "destroy the aggressive power of riches and of the party caucus") ; land taxation (on Georgeist lines); and the abolition of all taxes on food. But "the most vital matter in this and every presentday election," pronounced the League, "is the *poverty of the people.*" Millions of adults were unemployed and hungry—in London alone 100,000 children were destitute.

Pushing aside the House of Lords issue, the League made its central electoral plank the demand for a National Labour Department, to "organize industry" and raise the school-leaving age to sixteen (providing state maintenance at school for children of the needy), establish a 48-hour week at a minimum civilized wage level, regulate casual labor and provide special training and retraining where helpful, and make the right-to-work a reality through state employment on highway projects and extended municipal enterprise in all areas of production and distribution. The old Poor Law should be discarded (as demanded by the Minority Report), and drastic housing reform was needed to prevent "the present destruction of family life" among the workers.[80] The League's platform stood in great contrast to the CSU. In fact, three pro-Marxist articles had appeared in the *Quarterly* in 1909, and in April 1910 H. M. Hyndman himself was a contributor, along with Conrad Noel and Egerton Swann.

The last, Rev. N. E. Egerton Swann, had, it will be remembered, led the younger faction of the GSM which in

[80] *New Age*, VI, No. 10 (6 January 1910), p. 219.

1908 had tried to force Headlam to amalgamate with the Church Socialist League. Swann was, like Rev. A. L. Lilley, a theological "Modernist" and, in his younger days at least, a radical. He was a member of the Fabian Reform Committee of 1912 that demanded total identification of Fabian Society members with the Labour Party to the exclusion of other individual political alignments.

During World War I Swann went much further than other Fabians in supporting the war, and became a super-patriot and hater of Germans; in the 1920's he followed Widdrington in turning his attention to the development of a Christian sociology. Swann criticized Christian socialists in 1914 for conceiving of the Kingdom of God "as merely a human society in which perfect justice rules . . . simply the apotheosis of humanitarianism."[81] *The What and Why of Socialism,* which Swann wrote for the League much earlier, had adopted a different mood. The pamphlet warned readers that Sidney Webb's *Socialism in England* was "to be read with caution" because it was "ultra-evolutionary"; Swann recommended instead Karl Kautsky's *On the Morrow of the Social Revolution.* Swann at this time distrusted the Labour Party, Ramsay MacDonald, and H. G. Wells, and leaned toward a Marxist class-war interpretation. He exclaimed: "There is nothing particularly Christian in crying 'Peace, peace' when there is no peace." One must face the facts; there is "between Capital and Labour a direct antagonism of interest, fundamental, unbridgeable, unending—so long as the system lasts." Swann's socialism, like his modernist Catholic theology, had at this time a heavy continental flavor:

Politics are controlled by the two political parties, both alike thoroughly possessing-class parties, . . . Imperial politics are under the complete control of the rich. . . . In local politics the lower-middle class have a much greater direct share; but the very bitterest anti-Labour

[81] See Swann's *Is There a Catholic Sociology?* (London, 1922); also W. James, *The Christian in Politics,* p. 111; and *New Age,* x, No. 12 (18 January 1912), pp. 271-272 (Fabian Reform Committee).

feeling is nowhere more rife than among these *petits bourgeois.*

His League tract makes no mention at all of religion until the last paragraph, which refers to F. D. Maurice and contrasts production-for-use ("the principle of the Cross") with production-for-gain ("the principle of Judas").

Yet Swann was to become a protagonist of the "Christian sociology" wing, and in 1943 William Temple, the Christian socialist Archbishop of Canterbury, had to placate him with the words: "Of course I completely agree with you that the whole business of applying Christian principles to social questions is secondary to the fundamental truths of the Gospel, and to present the matter in any other way would seem to me to be complete apostasy." Back in April 1910 Swann had asked: "How can it be unChristian to proclaim the class war?"[82] He had very much regretted that modern socialists were so polite to each other, too genteel "to emulate the prophet Amos by addressing a congregation of rich West End ladies as, 'You cows of Belgravia!' "[83]

The radical year: 1912

The *Quarterly* maintained its radical flavor up to 1912, when it reverted to the title *Optimist*. George Lansbury, Swann, the Chesterton brothers, Hewlett Johnson, the young Maurice Reckitt, Adderley, Noel, the Countess of Warwick, all had contributed and kept the *Quarterly* lively to the end. In the Bow and Bromley election of 1910 in which George Lansbury was successful, Lansbury received important help from the League's members, including F. L. Donaldson, whose election pamphlet was sold outside every church in the constituency, Rev. W. H. Paine, Swann, and

---

[82] N.E.E. Swann, *The What and Why of Socialism*, Church Socialist League Tract No. 3 (London, n.d.), passim. On "Modernism" and socialism see Rev. F.A.N. Parker's article in *Church Socialist Quarterly*, IV, No. 2 (April 1909), pp. 117-124; also see William Temple to Swann, March 1943, quoted in F. A. Iremonger, *William Temple* (London, 1948), p. 569.

[83] *Church Socialist Quarterly*, V, No. 2 (April 1910), pp. 179-180.

Father Samuel Healy of the Community of the Resurrection, Mirfield. Noel resigned as organizing secretary of the Church Socialist League and was replaced by Rev. Claude Stuart Smith (1880-1924) in October 1910, an able if dour young radical whose first curacy had been spent (1903) working for Donaldson at St. Mark's, Leicester and who had served on the League's executive since its foundation in 1906.

Smith stood for a genuine *worker's* socialism and thought it "disastrous" of the Labour Party to emulate the middle-class parties and desire their respect. In addition, Smith demanded a "literature of socialist devotion" to integrate socialism fully into daily devotional life. The Church Socialist League would never "find its intellectual footing" in the Church of England, he said, until it produced a book of the stature of *Lux Mundi*.[84] What Smith essentially desired was a complete break with middle-class culture. Even more proletarian-minded than Algernon West, he was later accused of trying to turn the League into "a sort of ecclesiastical racket, run in the interests of the Labour Party." The pendulum of opinion had swung from West to Pinchard and now back again, with a deeper swing, to Smith. "The highest middle-class ideal," he complained, "seems to be that the middle-class should cultivate the simple life and modern ideas in a garden suburb from which the Philistine and the mere workman shall be excluded, while the working-classes shall live in well-inspected municipal model dwellings. *We want a complete breakaway from the civilization of Manchester and Leeds, and not even the Hampstead Garden Suburb is an earthly paradise.*"[85]

The League reached its zenith in 1912. Smith was widening the work of his predecessor, Noel; in London, Egerton Swann was training a large lay group of young men, many

[84] *Church Socialist Quarterly*, VI, No. 1 (January 1911), pp. 1-3; V, No. 4 (October 1910), p. 255; *Church Socialist*, I, No. 21 (December 1912), pp. 2, 5-6.
[85] See M. B. Reckitt, *As It Happened: An Autobiography* (London, 1941), p. 245.

of them trade unionists; George Lansbury became the League's president, and in the coal miners' lockout of that year, he led a League demonstration of five hundred people, with a processional Cross, over Westminster Bridge to Lambeth Place to petition the hierarchy on the Church's failure to aid the unemployed workers.[86] The "militant campaign of protest" included a "Remonstrance" to the Primate:

> We are astounded and dismayed that your Lordships do not frankly espouse their [workers'] cause and in the Name of God Who helpeth them to right that suffer wrong, we submit to your Lordships that no other course is consistent with your own counsel and the tradition of the Catholic Faith.

The wording of the petition worried Father Frere of Mirfield and some other members, but the League's annual conference held in May at Bristol had affirmed:

> That this Conference *welcomes* the "Labour Unrest" as indicating the Revolt of the People against industrial injustice and social wrong and their determination to achieve better conditions of labour and life. . . . it is the duty of the Church to abandon its profession of neutrality and openly to further the revolt.

The conference went on to congratulate the coal miners for their "magnificent and epoch-making achievement" in winning government recognition of the minimum-wage principle.[87]

Earlier in the year the League had petitioned the Upper House of Convocation, with little effect, despite its urgent insistence that "the Labour Unrest is in the last analysis an appeal for *Life*. For this reason it appears to us not only useless but wicked to desire the mere suppression or quieting of the agitation." A Joint Committee of Convocation in

---

[86] Reckitt, *Faith and Society*, pp. 107ff.; *Church Socialist*, I, No. 6 (June 1912), p. 20; I, No. 5 (May 1912), pp. 17-18.

[87] *Brotherhood*, No. 50 (June 1912), p. 250; *Church Socialist*, I, No. 6 (June 1912), pp. 19-20.

1907 had declared that "wages should be the first and not the last charge upon industry," and the League wanted to see this declaration carried out in practice. Instead, the Taff Vale and Osborne Judgements had put the trade-union movement back, and the Church had done nothing. No wonder the League supported the strikers and approved the famous *Don't Shoot* leaflets spread among the troops.

The Bishop of Bristol, among others, could not countenance the League's petitions and demonstrations of 1912, and although the annual meeting was successfully held in that city, the bishop "felt that we were stirring up the forces, of the violence and power of which we were hardly aware, which would inevitably sweep away all barriers of morality. . . ." New branches were announced in five or six English towns and in the USA. The American organizing secretary was E. M. Parker; the branch had been established in 1911 in Chicago by Bishop Spaulding of Utah, Dr. L. P. Edwards, and a High Church Episcopalian cleric, Dr. B. I. Bell, with the support of several prominent reformers such as the Christian Fabian Miss Vida Scudder of Wellesley College. Bishop Spaulding had attended the Pan-Anglican Congress of 1908 and declared himself a Marxist. However, the American branch, like that of the Guild of St. Matthew, "never really got under way."[88]

The Bristol Conference of 1912 also recorded "its emphatic protest" against the government's "attack upon political liberty and freedom of speech, especially in the case of Tom Mann and the leaders of the WSPU [feminists]. . . ." In the election which made Lansbury president, Donaldson became second-in-command, and the eleven-man executive included the young (pre-Soviet) Hewlett Johnson, Widdrington, Father Samuel Healy (CR), Swann, and Noel. Among the League's London members were men whose names were later to be more famous—R. H. Tawney, A. J. Penty, and Maurice B. Reckitt, for example. The resigna-

[88] *Church Socialist,* I, No. 3 (March 1912), pp. 12-14; I, No. 4 (April 1912), pp. 1-2; I, No. 6 (June 1912), pp. 4-6, 19; Reckitt, *Faith and Society,* pp. 197-198.

tion of several bishops was called for, an attack in flavor and style reminiscent of the old Guild of St. Matthew:

> Some of our present Bishops are unequal to the present crisis. The conspiracy of flattery of our Fathers in God should be broken and they should be asked to resign, and this request should be persistently made till their resignation takes place.

This policy of harassing the hierarchy was to be combined with "silent marches," prayers of intercession in leading churches, and street demonstrations. Three Hyde Park meetings were held, for instance, in June, at which Egerton Swann officiated as the new chairman of the London branch.[89] The new journal of the League, which reported these events and filled the gap left by the former *Quarterly,* was the *Church Socialist.* During the year 1912 it emerged as a Guild Socialist paper.

Church Socialism and world war

The last years of the Church Socialist League were troubled by two phenomena: World War I and the Guild Socialist movement. Both brought serious internal disagreement in the League and helped to produce its eventual dissolution.

As the shadow of war moved over the land, the League's seventh annual conference of 1913 (at Coventry) utterly condemned "militarism" as the "foe of democracy." The armaments race and so-called national service on the continental style were only further techniques to subordinate the worker. Peace could best be secured by "the spread of the international socialist movement among the workers of the world." The League's chief pacifists were George Lansbury, Dick Sheppard, and Mary Phelps, a later editor of the *Church Socialist,* who said quite simply, "killing is sinful and war altogether forbidden to Christian people." A Dartmoor Prison branch of the League was founded in May 1917 by members imprisoned for refusing military service;

[89] *Church Socialist,* I, No. 6 (June 1912), pp. 20-23.

one Leaguer was sentenced to death in France. Lansbury was of course the best known of the Anglican socialist pacifists. His influence was felt through his editorship of the *Daily Herald* from 1913 to 1922 (when he was once more elected Labour MP for Bow and Bromley after ten years out of the Commons). Though Lansbury was destined to become leader of the Parliamentary Labour Party in the thirties, he broke with the party on several occasions over the pacifist issue and finally resigned in 1935. At that time Ernest Bevin accused him of carting his conscience round "from body to body, asking to be told what to do with it."[90]

Opposed to the pacifists were moderates, like Conrad Noel, who believed that violence was sometimes necessary to quell evil, and extremists, like Egerton Swann, who "flew off into regions of ecstatic fury" over the evil Germans. Maurice Reckitt took the stand that the war was necessary to preserve the British example of social democracy (a faint echo of the social-imperialist argument of former years). "The English trade unions," Reckitt reasoned, "are the hope of the world. English industrial effort and English democratic aspirations are worth preserving, and who can doubt that they would lose by a victory of Germany and her militarist ideals?"[91] Given these sharp divisions of opinion, the Church Socialist League was incapable of making an agreed public statement about the war. At a stormy annual meeting in 1915 the executive divided on two votes. Lansbury declared that "wars would cease if only a body of men and women could be sent out unarmed to stand between the two fighting lines"; Conrad Noel called this idea a "delusion."[92]

The League's difficulties were but one small illustration of the problem faced by European socialism in general when confronted by the practicalities of a great international war.

[90] *Church Socialist*, I, No. 1 (January 1912), pp. 3-4; K. Hardie, et al., *Labour and Religion* (London, 1910), pp. 68-69; James, pp. 84ff.; G. Lansbury, "Why I Returned to Christianity," in *Religious Doubts of Democracy* (London, 1904), ed. G. Haw, pp. 8-9.

[91] Wagner, pp. 286-287.

[92] Noel, *Autobiography*, p. 107.

In Lansbury's words: "Then came the War, and Church Socialists became as divided as materialist Socialists. Our God of the human race became . . . God of the British."[93]

Pluralism and Guild Socialism: Father J. N. Figgis

While the League was dividing into pacifist and war-supporting wings, it also suffered increasing theological alienation between the more rigid Anglo-Catholics and the rest. Here it was Conrad Noel who numbered among the Catholic faction. He later complained that the League was without a theological foundation; "people joining it could believe anything or nothing, so long as they belonged to the Church of England and were economic socialists."

When he resigned from the League in 1916, Noel took a large number of members with him. Two years later he founded the Catholic Crusade. This split came only after the war was over; except for the war's outbreak it would undoubtedly have come earlier. The Coventry annual meeting of 1913 had been unusually small and quiet: "no one spoke up for 'Webb-ism'. . . , while as for theology, even Mr. Conrad Noel failed to arouse any signs of material disagreement." The members' minds were too heavy with thoughts of world war. But the first definite sign of yet a further split in the League—over economic policy—was given by a *Church Socialist* article of Maurice Reckitt's on "The Future of the Socialist Ideal," in February 1913, with a companion piece in August. A large section of the membership was moving toward the new Guild Socialist movement, whose League leaders were Reckitt and A. J. Penty, Paul Bull, Widdrington, and R. H. Tawney. The Preston annual conference, the League's eighth, debated a formal resolution in favor of Guild Socialism in May 1914.[94]

Guild Socialism brought a different if not an entirely new element into British socialist thought, an element with

---

[93] Lansbury, p. 5.

[94] *Church Socialist*, II, No. 18 (June 1913), pp. 13-15, 18-19; II, No. 14 (February 1913), pp. 13-16; II, No. 20 (August 1913), pp. 8-15 ("Guild Socialism"); III, No. 30 (June 1914), p. 113.

which the Anglo-Catholic mind was in sympathy: *pluralism*—"the idea . . . not of a single, centrally organized corporation, but of a community of communities." It has been called "the last significant attempt in political theory to deny the importance of the State."[95] Historically, Guild Socialism in England developed partly out of a medievalist revival. *Communitas communitatum* was a characteristically Catholic political ideal. The "medievalist" wing of the Guild movement survived into the 1920's. Naturally, Church Socialist Leaguers were at first attracted to this wing; but Christian socialists in general found much to their liking in the Guild Socialist movement, since it revived the Buchez-Ludlow ideal of producers' cooperative associations, and it seemed to offer a road to socialism which bypassed the huge, centralized, bureaucratic secular state. In the movement were to be found the ex-Quaker socialist S. G. Hobson, as well as the Anglican medievalist A. J. Penty.

The roots of Guild Socialism were implanted in English intellectual history. It drew sustenance from many sources: from the "aesthetic" anti-industrial tradition of "Tory Democracy," Carlyle, Arnold, Ruskin, and Morris; from the "Arts and Crafts" movement and the pre-Raphaelites, Burne-Jones, Rossetti, and again Morris; from Robert Owen and the socialists and cooperators of the 1830's and 1840's; from the Chartists; from the Marxians (Labor Theory of Value and surplus value) ; from the Maurician Christian socialists of the 1850's. More than a trace of French syndicalism and American industrial unionism was also evident in Guild Socialism, though the movement was peculiarly English.[96] Other British socialists emphasized the worker's deprivation of the just fruits of his labor, the "expropriation" by the capitalist of the "surplus value" (or, in the case of the Georgeists, the expropriation by the landowners

[95] Ruth Kenyon in N. P. Williams and C. Harris (eds.), *Northern Catholicism*, pp. 392-393; A. B. Ulam, *Philosophical Foundations of English Socialism* (Cambridge, Mass., 1951), p. 81.

[96] The best existing study, written by a member of the movement, is Niles Carpenter's *Guild Socialism*. The subject has been neglected by recent historians and is in need of fresh treatment.

of the "economic rent"). They therefore sought measures to ensure the just distribution of the national product among those who produced it (collective ownership of the means of production or taxation of the economic rent). They emphasized *ownership*. Guild Socialists, however, though they agreed that "surplus value" was stolen from the worker by the capitalist, went beyond the demand for legal ownership by the community to that of *administration* of industry by the producers. And instead of improving or reforming the wage system, as the Fabian collectivists, the ILP state socialists, and the Georgeist Single Taxers were prepared to do, the Guildsmen wanted to wipe away the wage system altogether and create "self-government in industry." On the basis of extended trade unions, a new political structure would be built. All existing parties were discounted, and industrial action was preferred above political action. In the new state, voting would be by occupational groups instead of by arbitrary residential constituencies. The Guild theorists accepted Carlyle's derisive repudiation of the "ballot-box theory" of democracy.

The chief political theorist of the pluralism embodied in Guild Socialism was Father J. N. Figgis, of Gore's monastic Community of the Resurrection at Mirfield. Unlike his socialist brother monks, Healy and Bull, Figgis was essentially a philosopher; he more than any writer spread the idea of political pluralism in these years. We have already seen that his work was derived from Gierke and Maitland. It was necessary to correct the simplistic historical view that Western civilization was the product of a long struggle between the State and the individual, when in truth (according to Figgis), history had witnessed a series of long struggles between the State and various other *groups* in society (the churches, the guilds, and so on). "The real question of freedom in our day," said Figgis, "is the freedom of smaller unions to live within the whole."[97] "Freedom" thus becomes a positive, functional concept, meaning the ability to associate and develop *in groups* of one's own choosing.

[97] *Churches in the Modern State* (London, 1914), p. 36.

Figgis had in mind, quite naturally, the churches and trade unions. Though he apparently never joined the Church Socialist League, he did take some part in its work. For example, as late as August 1914 the Quarry was still being used for socialist conferences, and Figgis debated "The Church's Duty Toward Social Reconstruction" with Rev. F. L. Donaldson, F. W. Jowett, MP, and George Lansbury, MP. His *Churches in the Modern State* (1914) was called by Rev. Paul Stacy "the very spirit of the National Guilds and [their] finest and clearest expression," and there is no doubt that Figgis exercised the greatest influence of any Mirfield member, even including Paul Bull, in the later history of the League.[98]

Figgis was a sacramental democrat. He translated the sentence "there is neither Greek nor Jew, . . . bond nor free; but Christ is all in all" to read:

> In the Catholic Church, entered by baptism, living by faith in a historic Person and nourished by the Eucharist, united by Common Worship, and bound by the one universal tie of love, *there are no barriers of sex or race or age or circumstance.*[99]

But, like Charles Gore, he felt very deeply the gap between ideal and achievement in church history and the guilt of the Church's complacency about the evils of industrialism. "The Church as a corporate society ought to do the deepest penance," he wrote, "for her share in producing the existing relations between the fortunate classes and the disinherited; and also for the widespread opinion, which must have some foundation, that she represents the cause rather of the rich than of the poor."[100] On the other hand Figgis

[98] *Church Socialist*, III, No. 30 (June 1914), p. 122; III, No. 31 (August 1914), p. 163; *Wagner*, p. 279.

[99] M. G. Tucker, *John Neville Figgis: A Study* (London, 1950), p. 54 (italics mine).

[100] *The Fellowship of the Mystery* (London, 1912), p. 101. Figgis explained that he gave up a well-to-do living to join the Mirfield monastery in order to escape the "expensive ecclesiastics who have lived all their life in comfortable and highly-paid posts away from the sin of the world: who throw scorn on any poorer clergy who are

always insisted that Anglicans should "give up playing at being a majority" in Britain. Indeed, Christians in general must not attempt to impose their ideas on non-Christians in a modern, plural society.[101] His insistence on this principle, and on a rigid, monastic concept of the separation of Church and State may to some extent have weakened his argument against the Church's social inactivity and complacency. But an argument for separation of Church and State can mean different things, depending upon which is being "separated" from which. It seems that Figgis wanted to get the State out of the Church rather than to get the Church out of the State. He had in mind such Establishment anomalies as a Baptist prime minister appointing an Anglican bishop.

The earlier Anglican socialists of the revival period (the GSM and the CSU) had leaned heavily on T. H. Green's Hegelian doctrine of the positive state; Figgis and the Guild Socialists in the League regarded the whole theory of state sovereignty as "no more than *a venerable superstition.*" Figgis was influenced by Green's contention that each member of the community can find well-being and positive liberty only in and through that community; but "community" did not mean for him as it did for Green "State." In past history, Figgis argued, individual liberty has never been won except as a by-product of the struggle for the right to exist of some particular group, often religious, which the civil authorities did not want to exist. Moreover, social life does not present itself in fact as a dichotomy between an atomistic individual and an omnipotent state, but as a series of groups (the family, the club, the trade union, the college, the church), "all having some of the qualities of public law, and most of them showing clear signs of a life of their own, inherent and not derived

---

trying to help the cause of the poor, who imply that any effort of the law to improve their lot is a bandits' raid on the well-earned remuneration of company promoters" (p. 104).

[101] Reckitt, *As It Happened*, p. 243; Figgis, *Churches in the Modern State*, p. 130.

from the concession of the State."[102] The CSU, the GSM, the Fabians, and the ILP all envisioned the history of the nineteenth century as the story of ever-advancing liberty, with the central state as its motive-force—an extended political combat between the rearguard of *laissez-faire* individualism and the ever-increasing interventionist welfare state, accruing power and responsibility piecemeal, bill by bill. The eventual outcome was to be democratic collectivism, or "socialism," emergent from the Liberal-Radical reform tradition. Figgis did not swallow this view of British history. He challenged the authority, competence, and legality of that state which T. H. Green and the Christian dissidents like Scott Holland regarded as the true instrument of social democracy.

Guild Socialism was more than a new intellectual and philosophical synthesis of the medievalist revival, pluralism, and associationism. It arose, as did the Church Socialist League a few years previously, in response to a growing dissatisfaction with what was happening to British socialism and the labor movement. Since the creation of the Labour Party in 1906 and the Victor Grayson incident in 1908, in the eyes of some socialists matters appeared to have deteriorated still further. The demands of South Wales miners for a more aggressive union leadership, Tom Mann's return from Australia with a new proletarian gospel, the emergence of syndicalism (1911), and of tough strike activities in Scotland and elsewhere, the growing impatience of the more extreme suffragettes with the ambivalence of the Labour Party toward women's rights, the propaganda of distributivism from 1912, all these developments[103] were manifestations of a general feeling of unease in the economy and society and a disappointment with the apparent impotence of the Labour Party to effect change. The great socialist revival that began in the 1880's seemed to have ground to a halt. A younger generation of socialists were determined to

---

[102] *Ibid.*, p. 224 and J. N. Figgis, *Political Thought from Gerson to Grotius: 1415-1625* (New York, 1960), pp. 233-236.

[103] See Pease, *History of the Fabian Society*, pp. 229-230.

start afresh and incidentally to recapture for British social-ism an essential idea that had somehow been lost on the way between the 1830's and the 1900's: direct worker-control in industry. The new revolt was felt most in the Fabian So-ciety, as we shall see. Among its leaders were prominent Christian socialists.

The League and Guild Socialism

The first writings to appear on guilds were those of the Anglican socialist architect Arthur J. Penty (1875-1937). In true Christian socialist style Penty was a Church Socialist Leaguer and an ILP member as well as a Fabian, and he took a large role as a designer in the Garden City move-ment. His book *The Restoration of the Gild System* was published in 1906. (For some reason Penty and his follow-ers in what was to become the "medievalist" wing of Guild Socialism preferred the spelling "gild" to "guild"). In June 1907 the journalist A. R. Orage (1873-1934) wrote an article in the *Contemporary Review* about the need to restore the guild system and to beware of "dogmatic collectivist So-cialists." But 1906-1907 saw the flood tide of victory for par-liamentary socialism and collectivism: the time was not yet ripe for the guild idea to be taken up.[104]

Arthur Penty was a thoroughgoing medievalist who hated modern industry and wished to go back, quite literally, to an economic system based on small-scale handicraft guilds.

---

[104] See S. G. Hobson, *National Guilds: An Inquiry into the Wage System and the Way Out*, ed. A. R. Orage, 2nd ed. (London, 1917), p. v. A. R. Orage himself described the condition of British socialism in 1907 and his own relation to it in the following way: "Socialism was a cult, with affiliations in directions now quite disowned. With theosophy, arts and crafts, vegetarianism, 'the simple life.' Morris had shed a medie-val glamour over it with his stained-glass *News from Nowhere*. Ed-ward Carpenter had put it into sandals. . . . Cunninghame-Graham had mounted it upon an Arab steed to which he was always saying a ro-mantic farewell. Keir Hardie had clothed it in a cloth cap and red tie. And GBS, on behalf of the Fabian Society, had hung it out with in-numerable jingling, epigrammatic bells and cap. My brand of Socialism was therefore a blend, or let us say an anthology, of all these" (A. Fremantle, *This Little Band of Prophets*, p. 168). The description is misleading and seems to refer to an earlier period.

Modern technology was to be abandoned, and society was to revert deliberately to a relatively low level of division of labor. According to Penty, "the whole issue between Medievalism and Modernism, between a Christian sociology and Socialist economics, will be found to turn on the attitude we adopt towards the division of labour. If out of timidity we acquiesce in it, then I contend that disaster will overtake any efforts we may make to establish a new social order. . . ." Christian socialists should demand the abolition of the division of labor "because of its contempt of personality." Once such a break is made with twentieth-century productive methods and the wage system, "there is no stopping, until we get back to the Middle Ages. . . ."

Like John Ruskin before him, but in a more simpleminded fashion, Penty had for professional reasons studied the glories of Gothic architecture, and had been led on to a consideration of the economic and social conditions which had made that marvelous human achievement possible.[105] Hopelessly idealizing the Middle Ages, he had fastened upon its guild system, which he misunderstood, and had built a wildly unrealistic plan for a world without division of labor. Clearly, Penty was an economic crank. But his passion as an artist for economic reform was conditioned entirely by the desire to create a kind of society in which good architecture could flourish. One can only regret his

[105] A. J. Penty, *Towards a Christian Sociology* (London, 1923), p. 189. Penty's disenchantment with the Fabian Society arose partly over their philistinism with regard to the architecture for the new London School of Economics buildings in Clare Market in 1902. E. R. Pease calmly informed Penty that the Society chose its architect by "the statistical method," inviting three men to submit plans and choosing the one with the most classroom floor space. "I did not reply," wrote Penty, "I was speechless. The gulf between me and the Fabian mind was apparent. It was the turning-point in my thought. . . ." He felt unable to complete a pamphlet he was writing for the City ILP on "Socialism and Architecture" because he now realized that collectivist socialism "could only mean the death of architecture" at the hands of municipal and state "Architectural Departments." Moreover, "from discovering the incompatibility between collectivism and architecture I began to see the incompatibility between collectivism and the needs of society." Three years or so later, Penty consulted with Orage in Leeds and then wrote *The Restoration of the Gild System* (Niles Carpenter, pp. 82-84).

failure and the crushing of his hopes by the onrushing forces of collectivism and the emergent welfare state, forces which refused to be "delayed" by "artistic" considerations.

The "medievalist" reaction dated back to the romantic revival and politically, of course, to William Cobbett, whose *History of the Protestant Reformation in England and Ireland* (serialized in 1823-1824) contrasted the glories of medieval civilization with the poverty and degradation of the masses, caused, he claimed, by the Reformation. Cobbett's more famous *Rural Rides* (1830) also expressed regret for the decay of feudal relationships between lord and peasant and bemoaned the passing of a sturdy free peasantry. According to Penty, William Cobbett was among "the first to expose . . . the conspiracy against things medieval."[106] There was nothing new in Penty's vilification of the Reformation and his linking it causally to the rise of capitalism. Stewart Headlam, Thomas Hancock, and other High Church socialists had already done this in the early 1880's, and the idea became a theme for economic historians such as Max Weber and R. H. Tawney, whose views about medieval society were infinitely more sophisticated than Penty's but not entirely unfavorable, nevertheless. Meanwhile a famous literary group, composed of the Chesterton brothers (who have already entered this story in connection with the latter days of Headlam's Guild of St. Matthew) and the Roman Catholic Hilaire Belloc, took up arms in the fight to reinstate the Middle Ages. In 1922 G. K. Chesterton was also converted to Rome, thus making the picture complete. (Father Figgis of Mirfield has been compared in appearance to Chesterton's most famous fictional hero, the detective Father Brown.) [107]

Penty's ideals, like those of William Morris, were soon passed over in favor of a form of Guild Socialism which would allow its proponents to have their cake and eat it too: after Penty the movement took account of modern

106 A. J. Penty, *A Gildsman's Interpretation of History* (London, 1920), p. 102; Niles Carpenter, p. 40.
107 Reckitt, *As It Happened*, p. 244.

industrial technology and tried to solve the problems of industrialism while simultaneously preserving the material benefits and advances that modern factory production brings. The figure chiefly responsible for altering Penty's medieval craft concept into a modern *industrial* guild system was yet another Christian socialist, the one-time Quaker S. G. Hobson.

For some time Hobson labored hard as a Fabian socialist and in the ILP before he grew tired of and frustrated by collectivism, and began to develop fears that the worker would end up being no more free under middle-class bureaucratic socialism of the Fabian type than under capitalism. As for Penty's ideas, Hobson had gained experience in the United States that convinced him there was no going back, no reversal of the Industrial Revolution. To achieve worker control in modern society, Hobson proposed to enlarge the powers and functions of existing trade unions, outside the sphere of the State. The State would simply *charter* the unions, changing them legally into industrial guilds which would thenceforward be free of central government control. S. G. Hobson spread the gospel of National Guilds in speech and writing, cooperating closely with A. R. Orage on the *New Age*. This journal, together with the League's *Church Socialist*, introduced Guild Socialism to the British public.

The phrase "Guild Socialism" was apparently first adopted by the *New Age* in October 1912;[108] but long before this, the terms "Guild," "Gild," and "Gild System" had been used, as we have seen, by people who also called themselves socialists. The idea existed long before the actual juxtaposition of the words "Guild" and "Socialist" took place. Five months or so before the title was coined, the *New Age* had produced a series of articles attacking the wage system, rejecting "meliorist politics" (as followed by the Liberals,

[108] Beginning with 10 October 1912 and in succeeding issues, *New Age* printed eight articles describing what it called "Guild Socialism," and a ninth, "Miscellaneous Notes," *New Age*, XI, Nos. 24-27, and XII, Nos. 1-5 (10 October through 5 December 1912), pp. 558-559, 583-585, 606-607, 630-632, and pp. 6-7, 24-31, 54-56, 77-78, and 101-103.

Fabians, Labour Party, and ILP) , and equating state socialism with state capitalism. "[T]here can be no emancipation
save only from the wage-system. *The way out is to smash
wages.*" The old Marxist SDF was preferable to Fabian and
Labour Party collectivism because Hyndman and his group
had at least struck out at wages as a system.[109]

The articles of 1912 through which Guild Socialism made
its formal debut were the logical extension of ideas that had
been built up gradually since at least 1907, when the almost-
defunct *New Age* was purchased from Joseph Clayton by
A. R. Orage and Holbrook Jackson, two young provincial
radicals newly arrived in London from Leeds and anxious
to stir things up in the capital. With help from the generous-
minded Bernard Shaw to the tune of £500, Orage and Jackson set out to make the paper into a kind of socialist *Spec-
tator.*[110] It attracted writers of the highest caliber, such as
the Chestertons, Belloc, Shaw, and H. G. Wells. In its pages
appeared the most famous literary battle of wits fought by
G. K. Chesterton and Hilaire Belloc with Bernard Shaw
and Wells, during the winter and spring of 1907-1908.[111]
Apart from its verbal pyrotechnics, this four-sided debate
illustrates an early manifestation of deep-seated dissatisfaction, at least among some intellectuals, with the existing
collectivist brand of socialism.

Anticollectivist writings of men of the stature of G. K.
Chesterton (1874-1936) and Belloc (1870-1953) , who had
themselves been, as we have seen, on the fringes of the
Christian socialist movement, had considerable public im-

[109] "Emancipation and the Wage System," *New Age*, x, No. 26 (25
April 1912), pp. 606-607; "The Horror of Wage Slavery," *New Age*, xi,
No. 1 (2 May 1912), p. 15; "State Socialism and the Wage System,"
New Age, xi, No. 3 (16 May 1912), pp. 53-55 (see also the editorial on
the Guild System).

[110] S. G. Hobson, *Pilgrim to the Left*, pp. 1-44; A. Fremantle, *This
Little Band of Prophets*, pp. 168-169.

[111] See *New Age*, ii, October 1907 to April 1908. The debate's main
theme was socialism in modern thought; but it became the vehicle for
a highly personal and idiosyncratic verbal match, as willfully eccentric
as, for instance, Chesterton and Belloc's entry into the Savoy Hotel on
donkeys (A. Fremantle, *This Little Band of Prophets*, p. 169).

pact. Belloc's many pieces were gathered together in an important book of 1912, *The Servile State*,[112] in which he took the view that, contrary to the confident statements by Fabians and others, Britain was not in fact evolving toward true socialism at all, but toward a social order where the capitalist class would be as strongly entrenched in power as ever and the workers would be reduced to a castelike subservience by a heavy mass of legislation—all under the guise of social reform. For this so-called *socialism,* Belloc said, one should read "the putting of the means of production into the hands of the *politicians* to hold in trust for the community."[113] His solution, *distributivism,* was in effect some form of peasant proprietorship. But the Church Socialists who shared his fears of collectivist bureaucracy did not follow Belloc into a rural arcadia. And, A. J. Penty aside, the Church Socialist Leaguers who became Guildsmen tended to take the S. G. Hobson model of *industrial* guilds. Divisions among Guildsmen were so frequent that the movement has been likened to "a gasoline engine" moving by "a series of internal explosions."[114] The leader of the Hobson type of Guild Socialism within the League was Maurice Reckitt, and he naturally became Penty's chief opponent.

The *New Age* gradually constructed an increasingly stronger case against the Labour Party, the Fabians, and their Liberal allies. "As the months fly past, the Labour Party grows more moderate and reactionary," wrote Hobson in July 1908. The ILP should recover itself, infiltrate the

[112] For earlier pieces on the same theme in addition to the Shaw-Chesterton-Wells debate, see Belloc's "The Three Issues," *New Age,* III, No. 1 (2 May 1908), pp. 8-10; and "The Servile State," *New Age,* VII, No. 4 (26 May 1910), pp. 77-79. See also the Belloc pamphlet (S. W. London ILP), *Socialism and the Servile State* (London, 1911).

[113] Hilaire Belloc, *The Servile State,* 1st American ed. (New York, 1946), p. xxi. According to R. H. Tawney, "The social theory of Luther, who hated commerce and capitalism, has its nearest modern analogy in the Distributive State of Mr. Belloc and Mr. Chesterton," an observation which must surely have amused both those Roman Catholic gentlemen. See Tawney, *Religion and the Rise of Capitalism,* Penguin ed. (London, 1938), p. 80.

[114] Wagner, p. 279.

larger party, and turn it into a truly socialist organization. A few months later, about a week before his controversial suspension by the House of Commons, the independent Socialist MP for Colne Valley, Victor Grayson, was appointed coeditor of the *New Age* with Orage, the aim being to guarantee "fearless and independent" journalism. Naturally, when his suspension came and was supported (as noted) by Labour votes, the *New Age* made a great issue out of it.[115]

By November 1908 demands were being made to replace the Labour Party altogether. "We sent the Labour Party to Parliament to make war on Toryism and Liberalism, not to make terms with them," thundered *New Age*. "The Labour Party is dead." Plans were formulated to create, on the model of the Labour Representation Committee of 1900-1906, a Socialist Representation Committee to produce a genuine Socialist Party. The idea was mainly S. G. Hobson's, and it was Hobson who pushed the proposal hard inside the Fabian Society (there being as yet no organized Guild Socialist movement). The *New Age* had already taken great exception to Fabian policy over the threatened railroad strike of 1907, a strike which was settled by Lloyd George for the government by evading what Hobson and Orage regarded as the real issue—trade union recognition. The Fabian executive had commended George because it felt the national transportation system was too vital to be subject to strike activity. The *New Age* took this to be an implicit denial by the Fabians of the right to strike. In later years Orage called the railway settlement of 1907 "infamous." However, shortly after the Grayson incident Hobson took the opportunity of forcing a motion on the Fabian Society (8 January 1909) to demand its disaffiliation from the Labour Party and its aid in creating a rival Socialist Representation Committee. The motion was heavily de-

[115] *New Age*, III, No. 10 (4 July 1908), p. 188, and No. 11 (11 July 1908), pp. 209-210. For the Grayson appointment and parliamentary incident see *New Age*, III, No. 25 (17 October 1908), p. 482, and No. 26 (24 October 1908), p. 504 (as described by Grayson himself).

feated, and Bernard Shaw moved that the Labour Party affiliation be confirmed. "It is the Fabian debacle," said the *New Age*, both sadly and hopefully.[116] Hobson resigned from the Fabian Society.

The proposed SRC came to nothing; but opposition to the existing Labour Party on the part of Guild Socialists did not wane. In May, June, July, and August of 1911, Cecil Chesterton produced a steady stream of articles, eight all told, depicting "The Decline and Fall of the Labour Party," from the socialist revival of the 1880's, through the Grayson incident of 1908, to the "final surrender" of 1909-1911 (when the party subordinated everything to the bogus issue of reform of the Lords). If only Chesterton had known what we now know about the secret entente of 1903 between the Liberal Chief Whip, Herbert Gladstone, and J. Ramsay MacDonald, he could have made out an even stronger indictment. The knowledge would have given added weight to Chesterton's claim that "the doctrine of the Class War is the very foundation of trade unionism. The Labour Party had abandoned that doctrine. . . ." It would also have helped him to understand Labour acquiescence in the National Insurance Bill of 1911, with its workers' contributions, a measure he retitled "A Bill for the Reduction of the Working-Classes of Great Britain to a Condition of Chattel Slavery." His only hope about this melioristic welfare measure was that opposition to it might create a real Social Democratic Party. "Mr. Lloyd George had a good deal to do with the undermining of the old Labour Party. He may yet

---

[116] *New Age*, IV, No. 2 (5 November 1908), pp. 23-24; X, No. 12 (18 January 1912); IV, No. 11 (7 January 1909) and No. 12 (14 January 1909), pp. 235-236. The journal described the Fabian rejection of Hobson's motion in a vituperative and personal way, which was to characterize all its dealings with other socialist groups: "The most deplorable aspect of the discussion was . . . Mrs. Snowden's sentimental slosh and Mr. Will Crooks's vulgar tosh. . . . Everything now depends upon the acuteness of Mr. Bernard Shaw's last headache or the weaving of the latest political Webb. . . . When next the Fabian 'old gang' have to make a political pronouncement, who will believe in their sincerity?" See also Niles Carpenter, pp. 86-88.

have something to do with the creation of a new one."[117] By January 1912 the *New Age* was printing a series of articles by A. J. Penty on the "perils" of large organizations,[118] and the scene was set for its formulation of "Guild Socialism" in the following fall.

The movement of ideas away from the Labour Party and collectivism and toward Guild Socialism traceable in the pages of the *New Age* from 1907 to 1912 can be seen equally well in the history of the Church Socialist League and in the pages of its two successive journals. A growing radicalism has already been discerned, leading up to the "radical year" of 1912. By February 1913, only three months later than the arrival of the *New Age* at the same conclusion, Maurice Reckitt was seriously reconsidering "The Future of the Socialist Ideal" in the *Church Socialist* and coming out in favor of "Guild Socialism"; by May 1914 the League's annual conference at Preston was voting the issue.[119] Reckitt, Widdrington, and other Leaguers feared the expansion of bureaucracy and "State Capitalism" under Fabian and collectivist auspices as much as did the secular Guild Socialists. They also wished to resist the collectivist trend which had captured the British socialist revival in its early stages and had controlled it ever since. Said P.E.T. Widdrington, putting it another way:

> I date the movement within the League away from party politics towards an endeavour to rediscover a Christian Sociology, to the time when Guild Socialism began to be discussed in the *Church Socialist* and in our branches. It

[117] *New Age*, IX, No. 16 (17 August 1911), pp. 365-366. For the previous seven articles see *New Age*, IX, Nos. 2, 4, 6, 8, 10, 12, and 14 (from 11 May to 3 August 1911). For a separate attack on the National Insurance Bill as a sellout to the employers, see *New Age*, IX, No. 3 (18 May 1911), pp. 49-50.

[118] *New Age*, X, Nos. 11-13 (11 January to 25 January 1912), pp. 247-249, 272-274 and 296-297.

[119] *Church Socialist*, II, No. 14 (February 1913), pp. 13-16, and No. 20 (August 1913), pp. 8-15 ("Guild Socialism"); and III, No. 30 (June 1914), p. 113.

made us reconsider many ideas which we had too readily accepted, and turned our minds back to the social tradition of the Church.[120]

Obviously, Widdrington approved the "movement away from party politics"; perhaps he had already forgotten his heroic first wife, Enid Stacy, and her unflagging labors for the ILP, the Labour Churches, and the Fabian Society. Or perhaps he had never agreed with her in the first place.[121]

Be that as it may, Guild Socialism had a lot to offer the Anglican socialists that collectivism did not. Its debt to the Mauricians and to Buchez and French producers' associations is clear. Christian socialists could find in the Guild movement a system which they hoped would preserve individual choices and freedoms, guard against the secular excesses of centralized administration, and give to the workers and producers a genuine and direct voice in running the national economy. For Maurice Reckitt, Guild Socialism would provide for

> the craftsmen's challenge and the blazing democracy of William Morris; the warning of Mr. Belloc against the huge shadow of the servile state, and perhaps, something

[120] Reckitt, *Faith and Society*, pp. 108-109.

[121] Enid Stacy (1868-1903) was the sister of the GSM and Church Socialist League stalwart, Rev. Paul Stacy, and an outstanding socialist and feminist agitator who died tragically early (of what the doctors of her day diagnosed as "thrombosis"). Enid overshadowed her husband; she was well known by socialist leaders like Blatchford, Hardie, John Trevor, Webb, and Bernard Shaw. Ramsay MacDonald was in love with her; Shaw kept up a correspondence with her. She sat on the National Administrative Council of the ILP and was one of the first lecturers for the London School of Economics. She spoke up to three times a day for weeks on end, traveled all over the country, and toured the USA twice for the Fabians. She dropped dead, instantaneously, while laying the tea table one day in 1903. See *Labour Annual*, 1895, p. 188; "Minutes," *Second Annual Conference, ILP*, Manchester (Glasgow, 1894), p. 1; *Labour Prophet*, v, No. 53 (May 1896), p. 72, and vi, No. 74 (February 1898), p. 159; Pease, p. 125; Reckitt, *Widdrington*, pp. 31 and 37, and *Maurice to Temple*, pp. 147-148; *Commonwealth*, viii, No. 10 (October 1903), pp. 306-307. See also, for her articles and other references, *Labour Prophet*, ii, No. 15 (March 1893), pp. 20-21 and 24, and No. 20 (August 1893), p. 71; iii, No. 26 (February 1894), pp. 18-19; and vi, No. 81 (September 1898), p. 215.

also of his claim of the individual's control over property; the insistence of Mr. Penty on the evils of industrialism and its large-scale organization. . . . [S]omething of French syndicalism, with its championship of the producer, something of American industrial unionism, with its clear vision of the need of industrial organization; and something of Marxian socialism, with its unsparing analysis of the wage-system by which capitalism exalts itself and enslaves the mass of men.[122]

In its pluralism, Guild Socialism offered protection for the churches in a secular world and seemed to vindicate the decentralized society of the medieval ideal, naturally attractive to the Anglican religious mind. A general study of Christian political movements in modern European history reveals in fact a consistent pattern of Christian support for pluralism (rather than collectivism) and for personalism (rather than individualism or communism). The pluralism supported by Christians until very recent history has, no doubt, been horizontal rather than vertical pluralism[123]—a free plurality of social groups outside the State rather than a free plurality of religions and denominations, Catholics, Protestants, and Jews all living together. (Continental "Christian Socialist" parties in the nineteenth century were often merely anti-Semitic parties under a new label; true "cultural pluralism" was an unknown concept.) But the general pattern certainly applies to the Church Socialist League in its sympathy for Guild Socialism.

The history of the Guild movement after the First World War is of much less concern to us here, not only because of the necessary time limitations of this study of the Christian socialist revival, but because Guild Socialism shed its medieval and Anglican carapace in the 1920's and was taken over largely by G.D.H. Cole, the renegade Fabian intellectual. It is true that the young Douglas Cole was at Oxford a

---

122 M. B. Reckitt and C. E. Bechhofer, *The Meaning of National Guilds* (New York, 1919), pp. xiii-xiv.
123 For these distinctions see M. P. Fogarty, *Christian Democracy in Western Europe, 1820-1953* (Notre Dame, Indiana, 1957).

disciple of William Morris's ideas, and a student of Maitland (and later of Figgis). He also became a pluralist. As a brilliant Fellow of Magdalen, Cole read a paper to the Aristotelian Society in 1919 making a definite break with Jean-Jacques Rousseau (whose *étatiste* doctrines he had previously admired) because he wanted to substitute for an "omnipotent political democracy" a "functional democracy."[124]

Cole's main driving interests at this time were syndicalism and the labor movement. Under his leadership Guild Socialism lost its stained-glass character. Yet R. H. Tawney (1880-1962), one of the two greatest Christian socialists of the twentieth century (the other was Archbishop William Temple), remained important in Guild Socialism after the war. One of his best-remembered books, *The Acquisitive Society* (1920), was virtually a Guild Socialist tract, taking the "functional principle" of Guild philosophy and applying it to an indictment of the sickness of capitalist society. Social rights are objective, he argued, not subjective or "Natural," and are conditional upon the performance of some useful social function by an individual or a group. "Private property" is an invalid theory because to be morally justified all property ownership should be functional and "active." Therefore, control should pass out of the hands of functionless owners into the hands of workers and producers. Tawney seemed to think that medieval society was more functional and therefore more moral and just than industrial society under private-enterprise capitalism. Unfortunately, his work, like that of William Temple, does not enter under the rubric of this study.

Between 1918 and 1921 at least two major divisions of opinion occurred within the Guild Socialist movement. First, S. G. Hobson and G.D.H. Cole disagreed about the consumer aspect of the movement and the role of the State; Hobson accepted the notion of state sovereignty and would have the State allocate but not perform functions (more or less following Figgis), while Cole, younger and brasher, com-

[124] See Niles Carpenter, p. 89.

pletely denied any role for the State whatsoever and wanted to replace it by a vague "commune" or grouping of functional bodies.[125] Cole had virtually captured the leadership of the Guild movement in May 1915, when, as a brand-new executive committee member of the Fabian Society, he had immediately begun a radical campaign to transform the Society into a trade-union research group oriented fundamentally toward industrial action. His revolt failed, of course, and he told the "Old Gang" (the Webbs, Shaw, and the rest) that they were fools. Then, having second thoughts, he said: "I withdraw that statement. You are bloody fools. I resign from the Executive and from the Society."[126] This angry young man of 1915 was nevertheless president of the Fabian Society for many years in later life. The National Guilds League had been formed a month before the Fabian split, and Guildsmen were no longer dependent solely on the use of outside bodies like the Fabian Society to advertise their opinions.

The second division within Guild Socialism came when some of its adherents were lured by the Social Credit movement of Major Clifford H. Douglas (1879-1952). Douglas had in fact worked out his underconsumptionist theory of depressions with A. R. Orage. Obviously, he was heavily in debt to the work of John A. Hobson too. Believing, as did J. A. Hobson, that lack of purchasing power was a vital factor in economic depressions, Major Douglas proposed to *redistribute* purchasing power by issuing dividends to every citizen. (Since the US federal government in its "War on Poverty" in the 1960's is considering the technique of the "reverse income-tax," schemes like Social Credit may appear less incredible; a Social Credit political party was represented in the Canadian legislature from 1935 down to 1958.) S. G. Hobson severed his connection with the *New*

[125] For the Cole-Hobson split see S. G. Hobson, *National Guilds and the State* (London, 1920), especially ch. 11.

[126] Niles Carpenter, pp. 94-95; Pease, pp. 229-232; A. Fremantle, *This Little Band of Prophets*, p. 210; Margaret Cole, *Growing Up Into Revolution* (London, 1949), p. 64.

Age in 1920 because of his rooted opposition to the Douglas scheme.[127]

Bernard Shaw maintained from the start that Guild Socialism was a contradiction in terms; it was either all Guild and no Socialism, or vice versa. If Guild production meant that self-controlled industries must somehow "pool their products," then some central agency was implied to receive, check, and distribute these products, a central agency representing in some just and equitable manner the citizens not as producers but as consumers—which simply "reintroduces the whole machinery of collectivism." For Shaw, therefore, the Guild Socialist critical barrage against the collectivist state was foolish and unreasonable.

The Webbs were very inimical to Guild Socialism too, and rejected the hope that producers' cooperative associations would ever work: the failure of such experiments in the past, said Beatrice, had been "complete and catastrophic."[128] Yet many ex-Fabians (Penty, Hobson, Cole) moved into the Guild movement because it appealed, at a time of great labor unrest, to those who were tempted by syndicalism but felt unable to go that far. On the other hand, as intellectuals and Christian socialists they were repelled by the compromises of political life and felt unable to fall back on the ILP or Labour Party path to socialism. S. G. Hobson, the one-time Quaker, wrote of the ILP: "Not an idea of the slightest vitality has sprung from it, its literature is the most appalling nonsense, its members live on Dead Sea fruit. . . . It is the happy hunting-ground of cheap and nasty party hacks and organizers," while its leader, the simple soul Keir Hardie, "apparently does not yet realize that he is dead."[129] The tone is middle class, self-consciously "brilliant" and intellectual.

Stewart Headlam had opposed the ILP because he

---

[127] S. G. Hobson, *National Guilds and the State*, ch. ii.

[128] Pease, p. 266 (Appendix ii, by Bernard Shaw); S. and B. Webb, *The Consumers' Cooperative Movement* (London, 1921), pp. 448-462; B. Webb, *My Apprenticeship*, pp. 379 n. 1, 451.

[129] S. G. Hobson, *National Guilds: An Inquiry*, pp. 19-20, and 23. (Keir Hardie died in 1915.)

thought that a workers' party would be too class-conscious to govern fairly and the workingmen were incapable of holding high public office. The Guild Socialists, on the other hand, despised the ILP and Labour Party for the conservatism and empiricism of its members, the flight of the average Englishman from ideas. Though the ultimate aim of Guild Socialism was *true* socialism, not mere government ownership but workers' control, the movement itself failed to win a working-class following. The Church Socialist Leaguers who went with Penty and Reckitt into the Guild movement thus ironically cut themselves off from the workers as much as did Headlam's Guild of St. Matthew. Tactically, this move was unsound. As R. H. Tawney said much later (1952) of the labor alliance: "The trade union basis has been criticized, but its advantages, in my judgement, outweigh its drawbacks. It has ensured that Socialism in this country rests on broad popular foundations; has averted the deadly disease of dogmatic petrification which afflicted the pre-1914 German Social Democrats; and has saved British Socialism from *the sterility which condemns to impotence a party, like the French, severed from working-class roots.*"[130] As Stewart Headlam had discovered somewhat earlier, the politically active workers and trade unionists chose to stick with the Labour Party. Keir Hardie was not as dead as Hobson thought.

Latter days of the League: "Christian sociology"

By 1923 Church Socialist League membership had dropped to one-quarter of its earlier strength, and branch interest had flagged. A final appeal was made in that year by the persistent Rev. Claude Stuart Smith to persuade the League to affiliate with the Labour Party, but the appeal only served to exacerbate still further the League's inner tensions, not only between Guild Socialists and Labour Party supporters but between zealous High Churchmen and those of a more relaxed theological attitude. Smith asked, *à propos* of this theological split: "What of those who can-

[130] *The Radical Tradition* (London, 1964), p. 169 (italics mine).

not toe the Anglo-Catholic line? To confine the society to Anglo-Catholics is to narrow its scope most seriously and to invite the repetition of the GSM."[131] But "the repetition of the GSM" was something not unacceptable to certain League members, who by the early 1920's had begun to look back with fond memories on that uncompromisingly Anglo-Catholic organization.

At the Birmingham annual conference of May 1923 negotiations to reform the Church Socialist League broke down completely. The Catholic faction was already organized separately in Conrad Noel's Catholic Crusade of 1918. The Guild Socialist and "Christian-sociology" rump, who were by no means homogeneous or agreed, published a volume of essays in 1922, *The Return of Christendom*, to which Penty, Reckitt, Niles Carpenter, Father Paul Bull, and A. J. Carlyle contributed, Charles Gore wrote an introduction, and G. K. Chesterton an epilogue. The group abandoned the Church Socialist League and created a new society, the League of the Kingdom of God, with Reckitt as its chairman. In 1924, the year of Stewart Headlam's death, the old League was finally dissolved.

The League of the Kingdom of God was less active than Conrad Noel's Crusade, but it was also less dogmatically Anglo-Catholic. Its main effort was directed toward indoctrinating in socialism the Anglican church rather than the laity. The new League sought to recapture for the Church its lost and forgotten traditional social beliefs, while Noel's group was equally interested in changing the world itself. At Keble College, Oxford each summer the League held what it called Summer Schools of Sociology (using the term "sociology" very loosely). Widdrington was usually the dominant mind of these affairs; but other members included Reckitt, Tawney, and the old-timers from the GSM and Church Socialist League days, W. E. Moll and Algernon West.[132] Moll in particular must have looked back in those

131 Wagner, p. 301.
132 Williams and Harris, p. 393; Noel, *Autobiography*, pp. 107ff.; J.

summer meetings to the pioneer days of the 1880's and Headlam's Guild. As Headlam's biographer points out, the League of the Kingdom of God "abandons the position, disputes about which led to the disappearance of the GSM, and reverts to the very thing that Mr. Headlam contended for"—a policy combining socialism with sacramentalism, not identified with the Labour Party or any other party.[133]

For those Anglican socialists who followed Stuart Smith in his fear of the "repetition of the GSM" and his demand for affiliation with the Labour Party, a haven was to be found in the newly established Society of Socialist Christians. This Society was also created in 1924, out of the old core of the defunct Socialist Quaker Society and other fragmentary groups (including labor-minded adherents of the Catholic Crusade).

The men who now mourned the old Guild of St. Matthew were Paul Stacy and P.E.T. Widdrington. The policy disagreement between Widdrington and Stuart Smith was a clear parallel to the division within the Church Socialist League between Algernon West and Pinchard in 1909. Widdrington and Stacy had been related by marriage, albeit only for about six years, since, as we have seen, Enid Stacy died in 1903. Rev. Paul Stacy had been brought up, like his sister, "in an atmosphere of Catholic Socialism" in Bristol by their father, H. E. Stacy, a radical artist; Enid became an agnostic, while Paul became a High Church Anglican parson. He joined the Guild of St. Matthew in 1890 and became secretary of its Bristol branch, active in the coal miners' lockout of 1893. Stacy was a prominent orator at socialist and labor meetings of all types from the 1890's on. He seems to have had some connection with the Mirfield monastery, and he joined the Church Socialist League in 1906. As Stacy had been a solid supporter of the opposition to Stewart

Lewis, K. Polanyi and D. K. Kitchin (eds.,) *Christianity and the Social Revolution*, pp. 197ff.

[133] Bettany, pp. 92-93.

Headlam, led within the GSM by Rev. C. L. Marson,[134] he had more cause than most to mourn the Guild in the early 1920's when League affairs were not going well.

The principal thinker in the League of the Kingdom of God, and perhaps the leading theologian of the sacramental socialist movement in the 1920's, was P.E.T. Widdrington (1873-1959). As a Christian socialist he did not rank in influence and importance with William Temple or R. H. Tawney; he was too diffident and scholarly to influence a broad public with his theology. One could not imagine Widdrington, for example, taking the large role in the Workers' Educational Association that both Tawney and Temple were temperamentally able to take. Though volatile and eager to change society, Widdrington found it a great "pain and grief" even to commit himself to paper in scholarly writing. He seemed to suffer from chronic indecision, and married Enid Stacy in 1897 only after considerable bickering. He never completed his autobiography, projected as "Canon off the Red." After "three years penal servitude" in the City (forced upon him by his patrician but anxious parents), Widdrington was finally allowed to go to Oxford in 1893, where he immediately joined the Oxford GSM and became its secretary a year later at the age of twenty. Constant political agitation and neglect of his academic work brought rustication for two terms. He studied hard with Rev. C. L. Marson at Cambridge for five months in the winter of 1895-1896 and managed to scrape a Third at Oxford in 1896. For four years Widdrington worked as a curate in industrial Tyneside for Rev. W. E. Moll; then followed four years in Lancashire, where he came under the influence of two other Christian socialists, Rev. Harold Hastings of Halton (first general secretary of the Church Socialist League) and a veteran campaigner, Rev. J. Llewelyn Davis of Kirkby Lonsdale. In 1904 Hastings and Widdrington established the Halton Fellowship, which became increasingly socialistic. Both men helped to form the Church So-

134 *Church Reformer*, XII, No. 11 (November 1893), pp. 256-257; *Labour Prophet*, II, No. 17 (May 1893), p. 37; Bettany, pp. 93, 220.

cialist League in 1906. At St. Mark's, Coventry, where he was made vicar in February 1906, Widdrington built up his urban working-class parish into a center of socialist and High Church propaganda. He was aided by a series of eager young curates, two of whom were CR men, trained at Mirfield. In later life Widdrington was Rector of Great Easton and a canon.[135]

In 1900 the two brothers-in-law, Stacy and Widdrington, had a deep disagreement with their vicar, W. E. Moll, at Newcastle, which even Headlam could not resolve. Moll was a colleague of Enid Stacy's on the National Administrative Council of the ILP, and, as we have seen, a respected and veteran Christian socialist and labor champion. But he was too much of a Catholic "rigourist" for his young curates. For obvious reasons, Conrad Noel, his previous assistant, had found the post very congenial. In 1901, however, Stacy and Widdrington found new jobs.[136] With this history, it is understandable that they also followed the League of the Kingdom of God group in 1924 rather than Noel's Catholic Crusade. At the zenith of Church Socialist League history, 1912, Widdrington publicly expressed his disquiet about the organization: "I have been a socialist for more than 20 years and my impression is that the movement has lost much of its enthusiasm and power of vision. We have become tacticians and polite persons." Labour MP's and trade-union leaders, he said, were drifting away from true socialism, while the League had become too "diffuse." Stuart Smith's notion of close affiliation with the Labour Party was very dangerous for the League, the main function of which should be to concentrate on converting *the Church* to socialism. All else would then follow.

Widdrington not only reacted against the dominant wave of collectivism within the British socialist movement; he also sought to construct a "valid theological basis for social

[135] *Church Reformer*, XII, No. 5 (May 1893), p. 90, and XIII, No. 1 (January 1894), pp. 18-19; Bettany, p. 93; *Church Socialist*, I, No. 11 (November 1912), pp. 2-5; Reckitt, *Widdrington*, passim.
[136] Reckitt, *Widdrington*, pp. 31ff.

action," a "Christian sociology."[137] It is not easy to determine exactly what Widdrington meant by "Christian sociology"—certainly not what is meant by current social scientists when they talk of the subdiscipline, "sociology of religion." Apparently participants in the Keble College summer schools mentioned earlier occupied themselves a good deal in trying to define "Christian sociology." Was its function to proselytize British society, which was so increasingly and obviously non-Christian in theory and in practice? Or was it to redefine for the faithful minority still within the Church the modern meaning of "the Christian life"? To make traditional dogma more consonant with contemporary social needs?[138] Widdrington suffered from the same difficulties as Thomas Hancock, the theologian of the Guild of St. Matthew, and in addition he lacked Hancock's power of brilliant and mordant writing. His influence was mainly wielded over his own colleagues, especially over Reckitt, and he left for posterity little tangible evidence of his intellectual power and achievements.

Meanwhile Conrad Noel, despite his deep interest in the National Guild idea, turned his energies mainly toward fighting the Nonconformists. His Catholic Crusade strove:

> To create the demand for the Catholic Faith, the whole Catholic Faith, and nothing but the Catholic Faith. To encourage the rising of the people in the might of the Risen Christ and the Saints, mingling Heaven and earth that we may shatter this greedy world to bits. . . . To demand that portion of common with personal ownership as shall encourage our self-expression as free people in fellowship. *To fight the soul-saving gang and their glory-for-me religion.*[139]

Obviously anti-Nonconformity was as strong a motivation of the Catholic Crusade as socialism, perhaps stronger. Con-

---

[137] *Church Socialist*, I, No. 11 (November 1912), pp. 2-5; Reckitt, *Widdrington*, p. 54; Reckitt, *As It Happened*, pp. 249ff.
[138] See Binyon in Lewis, Polanyi, and Kitchin, pp. 197ff.
[139] Wagner, p. 301.

rad Noel had reintroduced a divisive note into Christian socialism. Such bitterness of sectarian feelings reads very strangely in the history of the Britain of the 1920's. The vision of ultimate ecumenical Christian unity held by Noel's friend Percy Dearmer seemed further from reality than ever. To this degree, though men like Noel (who always claimed to be a full "economic socialist") and Headlam before him were more energetic and radical than Dearmer as social and political agitators, they appear more alien to the Christian spirit of the 1920's pervading such bodies as the Mirfield Community.

Noel, like Hancock, Headlam, and others, failed to see the ambiguity of a self-professed broad socialist faith combined with a narrow sectarian theology. For Noel "Nonconformity" and "Christo-Capitalism" were synonymous terms of abuse. Christian socialism he regarded as the monopoly of Anglo-Catholics. Nevertheless, his Catholic Crusade, with its religious limitations, was "radical": it claimed to champion for society at large "a classless, co-operative world of free men and free nations."[140]

Neither the Catholic Crusade nor the League of the Kingdom of God appears to have had the influence or impact of earlier Christian socialist groups like Headlam's Guild or the Church Socialist League—certainly they had nothing like the significance or membership of the CSU. We are still in need of a study of Christian socialism and allied movements of the 1920's and since, and of the emergence of those two great figures, R. H. Tawney and Archbishop William Temple. Perhaps if that study is made, we will be better able to assess the work of the small splinter-groups that formed in the 1920's from the League and took sustenance from other sources.

---

[140] The Crusade's own monthly journal was *The Catholic Crusader—A Challenge to Capitalism*. Its supporters included Robert Woodifield, Harold Mason, and John Marshall (a director of the department store Marshall and Snelgrove, killed in World War I). The journal's first battle was against the Duke of Argyll for his bad treatment of Scots crofters. A Crusade meeting at Essex Hall in 1917 welcomed the Soviet Revolution. See Noel, *Autobiography*, pp. 107-108.

The Church Socialist League was born in what promised to become a grass-roots radical awakening of the Northern working class. It died out in a backlash of sectarianism and intellectualism. Yet the League, through its Guild Socialist activities, brought back to the Christian socialist tradition (and to British socialism generally) the forgotten ideal of worker participation, the producers' cooperative association-ism of the ardent J. M. Ludlow of the 1850's and of Buchez. Those members of the Church Socialist League who founded the League of the Kingdom of God shared F. D. Maurice's concern to find a theological justification and foundation for social life. Those who seceded with Noel seemed to reaffirm the sacramentalism of the Guild of St. Matthew and of the Oxford Movement.

Part Three

The Socialism of Nonconformity

CHAPTER VIII

Organized Protestant Socialism

THE ESTABLISHED CHURCH, which of all religious denominations suffered the greatest relative decline in late-Victorian Britain, produced many Christian socialist clergymen, writers, and speakers, and three leading propaganda societies: the Guild of St. Matthew, the Christian Social Union, and the Church Socialist League. Yet from outside the Anglican fold, the world of labor could look very different, and our rather deep absorption in Anglican socialist affairs in the previous three chapters should not persuade us to forget that, however influential the sacramental socialists were in the general movement of Christian socialism, Anglicanism was a minority faith among the people.

If we were to concentrate our attention not on the history of organized Christian socialist societies but on the impact of religion in general on the labor movement, groups other than the Anglo-Catholics would loom large. Among Protestants it was the Congregationalists who produced the largest number of socialist agitators, though they usually worked as individuals and not within formal political propaganda societies. On the other hand, it has often been said that the Primitive Methodists were closer to the workers, and were a true church *of* the people, not simply a middle-class church *for* the people. Recent revisionist historical writing has thrown some doubt on this accepted characterization of the Primitive Methodists; their importance was apparently local (for instance, among miners in the Northeast) and was often (as in Sheffield) mainly confined to the better-off skilled artisans, "the most respectable of the working-class," with even an admixture in their congregations of upwardly mobile wealthier tradesmen who had made money but were still loyal to their old associations.[1] The numbers of Primitive Methodists, too, remained small.

[1] E. R. Wickham, *Church and People in an Industrial City*, p. 134.

305

By far the biggest Methodist faction were the Wesleyans, three times the size of the Primitives in 1850, when the latter still numbered only 100,000 or so.[2] This does not alter the fact, however, that wherever Primitive Methodism existed in strength, and this was normally in the smaller industrial and mining hamlets of the North rather than in the big cities, it offered to its members a free training in the mechanics of public affairs, a place in which to make maiden speeches, to organize group activities, to deliberate minor policy decisions. In the words of the prominent Durham labor pioneer, Jack Lawson:

> The Chapel gave them their first music, their first literature and philosophy to meet the harsh life and cruel impact of the crude materialistic age. Here men first found the language and art to express their antagonism to grim conditions and injustice. Their hymns and sermons may have been of another world, but the first fighters and speakers for unions, cooperative societies, political freedom, and improved conditions, were Methodist preachers.[3]

The detailed studies by R. F. Wearmouth, however, despite their exaggeration of the working-class character of Methodism, provide us with a more than adequate factual coverage of this field.[4]

Nonconformist *socialism*, on the other hand, is elusive and harder to define than the sacramental variety. Even though the doctrine of Divine Immanence runs through its theology, there is no clear or well-defined dogmatic core,

---

[2] K. S. Inglis, *Churches and the Working-Classes*, p. 12.

[3] Jack Lawson, *A Man's Life*, new ed. (London, 1949), pp. 69-70; also quoted in Donald Read, *The English Provinces*, pp. 198-199.

[4] R. F. Wearmouth: *Methodism and the Working-Class Movements of England, 1800-1850* (London, 1937); *Some Working-Class Movements of the 19th Century* (London, 1948); *Methodism and the Struggle of the Working-Classes, 1850-1900* (Leicester, 1954); *Social and Political Influence of Methodism in the 20th Century* (London, 1957); *Methodism and the Trade Unions* (London, 1959).

and its adherents were often as deliberately antitheological in outlook as some British socialists were deliberately anti-ideological. Keir Hardie provides in himself the model for both. In the twentieth century, Rev. R. J. Campbell's New Theology movement of 1907, linking immanentalism with the labor movement, was in part an attempt to fabricate somehow an intellectually respectable dogmatic foundation for the socialism of Nonconformity.

By its very nature, immanentalism (as opposed to sacramentalism) imparts a diffuseness and a vagueness to Nonconformist thinking in this period. A good example is the widely read Independent Labour Party tract of 1905 by Philip Snowden, *The Christ That Is to Be*. Snowden begins with a strong immanental bias, goes on to reduce Christ to human stature, and ends up praising the good that is to be found in all the world's religions. The train of thought is common enough. "In degree but not in kind does Christ differ from all great teachers," said Snowden, ". . . these truths are not the laws of Christ, any more than gravitation is the law of Sir Isaac Newton, or evolution the law of Darwin. . . . This law of sacrifice, this law of love, of association, of cooperation, is not only the foundation of Christian teaching, but it is the basis of all the great ethical religions of the world, and of all schools of morality."[5]

Given the formless and vague nature of Nonconformist social doctrine, we shall first review the activities of such propaganda groups as did exist in these years, and then treat in a subsequent chapter the achievements of the major denominations. Nonconformist socialist organizations were hardly less sectarian than the Anglican groups. The major body, the Christian Socialist Society, tried to open its doors and its membership to all Christians, but died in the attempt.

[5] Philip Snowden, *The Christ That Is to Be*, 3rd ed. (London: ILP, 1905). I am very grateful to Mr. Fenner Brockway, MP (now Lord Brockway), for an illuminating conversation in 1963 which drew my attention to the importance of this pamphlet.

The Christian Socialist Society, 1886-1892

The undenominational Christian Socialist Society was founded in London in April 1886 after a long debate in the columns of the *Christian Socialist*. One of its chief creators, a Christian layman and Fabian socialist, Alfred Howard, began the correspondence in October 1885. Howard received letters of support for the idea, and with H. H. Gore (the Bristol Christian socialist and GSM member) he planned a Christian socialist organization that would admit to membership any sympathetic person, irrespective of religious creed. In the December issue Howard explained why Headlam's Guild of St. Matthew was inadequate to the needs of the day and why a new group was called for, open to "non-sacerdotal Christians," a society "to which *any and every* Christian Socialist may point and say that in its creed may be found the truths underlying *every system* of Socialism."[6] The December appeal brought still further support, including a letter from the American Christian socialist, Rev. H. C. Vrooman of Kansas. (The leader of the American movement, Rev. W.D.P. Bliss, founded his own Society of Christian Socialists three years later in Boston.) More encouraging still was an editorial by Stewart Headlam's opponent in the GSM, Rev. C. L. Marson, in March 1886 on "The Need for a Christian Socialist Society."

Marson, displaying his greater tolerance of the unbaptized than Headlam, had been editor of the *Christian Socialist* since 1884 and became a founder-member of the new society. He cast off any narrow loyalties to the Guild of St. Matthew or Headlam, and wrote: "All the present socialist societies are missionary agencies but none of them are striving to convert those to the common faith who are non-sacerdotal Christians."[7] Surveying existing socialist

6 *Christian Socialist*, III, No. 29 (October 1885), p. 75. Howard said very much the same at a Fabian meeting at Dr. Williams' Library, November of the same year (*Christian Socialist*, III, No. 30 [November 1885], pp. 91-92).

7 *Christian Socialist*, III, No. 31 (December 1885), p. 102; No. 33 (February 1886), pp. 139-140; No. 34 (March 1886), pp. 146-147.

groups, Marson found that in Hyndman's SDF there was "too much talk of guns and armies"; Morris's Socialist League had "repelled" the attempts of Christians to show interest in its work; and the Fabians were too bourgeois and respectable. "The middle-class has had Moses and the prophets. We wish the Fabian Society more success!" the *Christian Socialist* had declared two years earlier.[8] As for the Guild of St. Matthew, it was "doing good work among those who see behind the drapery of the ecclesiastical letter and find comfort in symbolic teaching; but many followers of Jesus do neither."[9]

Under Marson's editorship the *Christian Socialist* became increasingly radical in language and began denouncing, in addition to the capitalist system, such things as the Irish Union ("the union of thumb and thumbscrew"), the Pall Mall clubmen who incited the labor demonstrators of 1886 by jeering from West End windows ("low-minded and over-pampered scoundrels"), the "booby police," Sunday observance, Anglican bishops ("Rt. Rev. Creepy Crawleys," "a flock of aged sheep," "the old ladies of Convocation"), and the Established Church ("an interesting piece of archaeology" condemned alike by "political sanitation and moral health"). Besides providing this useful cathartic outlet, Marson's editorship led the journal to the creation of the Christian Socialist Society.

The new society published its manifesto in May 1886:

> The ideal of Christian Socialism is found in Jesus Christ, and all its operations will be based on the spirit of His life. . . . The Society then, is *independent of all theological views,* and welcomes as members all who desire to make self-sacrifice for men the rule of their lives, and to work as brothers one of another, who are bound to subordinate their private advantage to the good of the commonwealth and of mankind.

[8] *Christian Socialist*, II, No. 19 (December 1884), p. 99.
[9] *Christian Socialist*, III, No. 34 (March 1886), pp. 146-147. The reference to "guns and armies" in the SDF was probably a thrust at the *Christian Socialist*'s previous editor, the ex-army officer, H. H. Champion, who was in the habit of drilling the unemployed marchers.

Here indeed was a simple, Christ-centered socialism. Even Marson was not that broadminded: "It does not breathe altogether the Catholic spirit, and needs a little re-wording," he suggested hopefully.[10] The aims of the new group as of May 1886 were:

1. The union of men in a real universal brotherhood free from all artificial distinctions founded merely upon class.

2. Education, liberal, free, compulsory, industrial, for all.

3. Substitution of a system of production for use for the present system of production for profit.

4. The organization of society on a basis of industry and manual worth, rather than of wealth, privilege and monopoly as at present; industry being understood to comprise both mental and manual work.

5. Public control of land, capital and all means of production, distribution and exchange, involving the abolition of all interest.

6. The ennobling of domestic, public and national life; the development of free and independent nationalities; the union of labor; and the promotion of peace and goodwill all over the world.[11]

Fittingly, Alfred Howard, the Fabian socialist whose letter to the *Christian Socialist* had initiated the plans to form the group, was made secretary of the Christian Socialist Society. Miss Emily Guest, its treasurer *pro tempore*, answered C. L. Marson's criticism of the manifesto—that "God the Father" was not mentioned and that the manifesto was politically vague—by subsuming God's Fatherhood under the brotherhood concept of the first aim, and by admitting that many of the Society's members as yet had "no defined goal of politics." But the manifesto did, in its fifth aim, call for total nationalization: evidently some of its adherents could

10 *Christian Socialist*, III, No. 36 (May 1886), p. 190; III, No. 37 (June 1886), pp. 194, 201-202; IX, No. 103 (December 1891), pp. 129-130.
11 *Christian Socialist*, III, No. 36 (May 1886), p. 190.

not be satisfied with Miss Guest's delightfully airy faith, that "as we live towards a 'real universal brotherhood' the ideal policy and the ideal form of State will, under the majestic law of evolution, shape themselves before us." Almost caricaturing Christian socialist sentimentalism and idealism, she waxed forth: ". . . and we shall behold as in a glass the glory of the Lord's Humanity, and be changed into the same image from glory to glory, till the eternal Idea is fulfilled in us."[12]

The Christian Socialist Society held its first public meeting on 21 June 1886, and papers were delivered by Miss Guest and by Rev. C. L. Marson. In the following month the Society's future leader, W.H.P. Campbell, took the chair at an executive meeting in Bedford Chapel Vestry and a campaign was planned for summer outdoor meetings on Peckham Rye. Already a branch society had been created in Bristol—the Clifton and Bristol Christian Socialists—with Marson's blessing, Hugh Holmes Gore (GSM) as secretary, and E. D. Girdlestone as treasurer. The Bristol group excited considerable local attention; Gore was elected to the Bristol School Board and later (in a sharply contested struggle) to the Town Council.

At Leicester in January 1891 another branch was established and Miss Annie W. Vice was its first secretary. This group, the Leicester Christian Socialist Society (1891-ca. 1895?), outlived the parent organization and was still operating as late as September 1895. Charles Wynne was its secretary from 1893, and as a member of the Society of Friends he also joined the Socialist Quaker Society upon its foundation in 1898. A Glasgow branch of the Christian Socialist Society was formed in January 1887 by Rev. John Glasse, who was regarded by Sidney Webb as one of the two "most influential Scotch Socialists"; it was still functioning in 1892. A Liverpool branch emerged in 1887.[13] These

---

[12] *Christian Socialist*, III, No. 37 (June 1886), pp. 205-206.

[13] *Christian Socialist*, IV, No. 38 (July 1886), p. 7; IV, No. 39 (August 1886), p. 27; IV, No. 40 (September 1886), p. 44; V, No. 46 (March 1887), p. 43; VI, No. 58 (March 1888), p. 43; IX, No. 93 (February 1891), p.

branch societies did not on the whole produce significant figures in the history of British Christian socialism, but Girdlestone deserves an aside.

E. D. Girdlestone[14] was an Anglican layman and a member of A. R. Wallace's Land Nationalisation Society before he became a very disputatious member of the Bristol Christian Socialist Society branch. In 1890 he became founder-member of the Birmingham Fabian Society, and during the 1890's he was a frequent contributor to *Seedtime,* the organ of the ethical New Fellowship that was the parent of the Fabian Society. Three lively little tracts made Girdlestone's name familiar to socialists; one of these, *The What and Why of Christian Socialism,* was serialized in the *Christian Socialist* during 1889-1890.[15]

The leading figure in the Christian Socialist Society, however, next to C. L. Marson, was W. Howard Paul Campbell, B.D. (1855-?), a Canadian, son of a New Brunswick Scots minister and a socialist mother, who left Canada at the age of fourteen and made his life in England in various

---

24; IX, No. 96 (May 1891), p. 56. See also *Brotherhood,* VI, No. 7 (February 1892), p. iii, and No. 8 (March 1892), p. 192; New Ser., I, No. 5 (September 1893), p. 74; III, No. 5 (September 1895), p. 66; and Sidney Webb, *Socialism in England,* pp. 42, 61.

14 Not to be confused (e.g., in D. O. Wagner, *The Church of England and Social Reform,* p. 151) with Canon E. Girdlestone, also of Bristol, the champion of the rural laborers, who died in 1884. The two men were very probably related; but research in Bristol reveals little or no information about E. D. Girdlestone.

15 The other two were: *Society Classified* (Weston-super-Mare, 1876), of which a third edition was published by the Clifton and Bristol Christian Socialists in 1886 and a fifth in London in 1896; and *Christian Socialism versus Present Day Unsocialism* (Limavady, Ireland, 1888), published by J. Bruce Wallace. Girdlestone also wrote polemics against vivisection (1884) and capital punishment (1904). See *Christian Socialist,* No. 3 (August 1883), p. 38; No. 7 (December 1883), pp. 106-108; V, No. 50 (July 1887), p. 107, and No. 51 (August 1887), pp. 113-115; VII, No. 71 (April 1889), pp. 60-61; VII, No. 74 (July 1889), p. 109; VIII, No. 89 (October 1890), p. 135 (Fabian Society report); IX, No. 109 (July 1891), pp. 13-14. Also see *Church Reformer,* VIII, No. 12 (December 1889), p. 287; *Seedtime,* No. 4 (April 1890), p. 16; No. 5 (July 1890), pp. 3-6; No. 6 (October 1890), pp. 14-15; No. 8 (April 1891), pp. 3-7; and *Brotherhood* (articles by Girdlestone every week from the first issue [April 1887] on).

occupations. Campbell joined the Marxist SDF in 1884 and became an early writer for its outspoken journal, *Justice*. His well-known tract *The Robbery of the Poor* was, in fact, an SDF publication of 1884. Campbell led the Christian Socialist Society with Alfred Howard and edited the *Christian Socialist* as the group's official journal from 1887 to 1890. Nevertheless, his career with the Christian radicals was but a brief flirtation. When the Society disbanded in 1892, Campbell turned to Fabianism. He also helped to found the London Labour Church (with P. H. Wicksteed, J. Bruce Wallace, and others); but by 1895 he had reverted to his former secular position and "disclaimed the prefix 'Christian,'" although he "retained sympathy" for the religious socialist movement. Campbell was later treasurer of the London ILP. He had come to socialism via Carlyle and Ruskin and was never at any time a "theological" socialist.[16]

The Robbery of the Poor was a leisurely tract of 54 pages, originally a paper read to the Carlyle Society. It tried to define socialism "within the limits of the 8th Commandment," and its arguments were very Christ-centered, except for a novel attempt to list the historical social reform successes of Christianity (abolition of infanticide, "gladiatorial shows," slavery; provision of hospitals, just treatment of criminals). Campbell spoke much of individual regeneration and used the "old-time religion" (revivalism) to push socialism. "As a people we have forgotten God," he declared. That is why religion had been able to commit the worst sins of the modern world—"selfishness and indifference to the welfare of the masses." Henry Georgeism and the taxation of land values was not enough; both land and capital must be confiscated, without compensation if need be. Like other Protestants, Campbell borrowed from the famous Congregationalist pamphlet *The Bitter Cry of Out-*

[16] *Labour Annual*, 1895, p. 167; *Labour Prophet*, I, No. 3 (April 1892), p. 27; *Christian Socialist*, No. 10 (March 1884), pp. 147-148, and No. 12 (May 1884), pp. 182-183; *Brotherhood*, VI, No. 10 (May 1892), p. 223.

cast London; so did the Christian Socialist Society in its Tract No. 1.[17]

The thinking of the Christian Socialist Society could be characterized as a sort of "Christian theism," more socialist than Christian. At times its Christianity seemed very thin. Campbell, as we have seen, joined the non-Christian and vaguely pantheistic Labour Church. Another member, better known in the Christian socialist movement than Campbell but playing less of an executive role in the Society, was Rev. J. C. Kenworthy, a Tolstoyan who became pastor of the Croydon Brotherhood Church established in June 1894.[18] The "Christian theism" aspect of the Christian Socialist Society is well illustrated by Kenworthy, and also by the membership in the group of that famous preacher, Rev. Alexander Webster (1840-1918), the leader of Unitarianism in Scotland. Webster was from the outset a steadfast Henry Georgeist, a deep personal friend of Michael Davitt, Richard McGhee (the Single Tax MP), and other Irish nationalists and supporters of land reform, and an active member of Henry George's first British propaganda committee. Webster was a prolific pamphleteer and orator; he never missed a weekly sermon for forty years; and he never once stopped struggling to make sense of life. During the early 1890's he was president of the Independent Labour Party in Kilmarnock.[19]

17 W.H.P. Campbell, *The Robbery of the Poor* (London, SDF, 1884), passim; *Christian Socialist*, No. 2 (May 1884), pp. 182-183; *Social Reformation on Christian Principles*, Christian Socialist Society Tract No. 1 (London, n.d.), p. 16.

18 *Labour Prophet*, III, No. 31 (July 1894), p. 90.

19 Webster was self-educated and had to support his family from the age of eleven, when his father died. He was a Unitarian minister in various parts of Scotland from 1872 to 1901. His personal religious experiences and evolution formed the basis of a spiritual autobiography, *My Pilgrimage from Calvinism to Unitarianism* (1889, 5th ed., 1904). Chapter II describes Webster's experimentation "with Arminianism, Atheism, Swedenborgianism and Broad Churchism" before he found "Rational Religion." See *In Memoriam: Rev. A. Webster, Pioneer and Reformer, Aberdeen Appreciations* (Glasgow, 1919), passim; *Labour Annual*, 1895, p. 192; *Christian Socialist*, VII, No. 68 (January 1889), pp. 1-3; VIII, No. 71 (April 1889), pp. 57-59; *Brotherhood*, VI, No. 14 (September 1892), p. 321; and A. Webster, *Memories of Ministry* (Glasgow, 1913).

Rev. John C. Kenworthy (1863-19—?) was a Liverpool man who worked in business for some years before settling down to a career of full-time experimentation in communitarian social reform. The failure of the Liverpool Ruskin Society (of which he was a member) to establish an "industrial colony" in 1881 put Kenworthy on the path of a long search for the essential something that was lacking. He found most of his answers in Tolstoy's demand for a complete break with the centralized state and the construction of a new "organic" Christian order—small, cooperative, federated communities of free men, close to nature and the soil, and animated by a new practical religion, a Christianity purged of its dogmas and mysticisms. Leo Tolstoy translated some of Kenworthy's writings into Russian, and he exerted the greatest influence on Kenworthy's thinking. For a brief time Kenworthy was affected by the very different ideas of the American industrial socialist Edward Bellamy, author of a best-selling utopian novel, *Looking Backward, 2000-1887,* and founder of a middle-class socialist movement called "Nationalism" in the United States. Kenworthy had toured the States before he finally settled down in London in 1892, and he became vice-president of the Nationalisation of Labour Society, an organization of English Bellamyites led by Rev. J. Bruce Wallace and the Swedenborgian socialist Rev. A. Potter, to be discussed later. But his flirtation with Bellamy's ideas was superficial; he remained at heart a Tolstoyan.[20]

After the death of the Christian Socialist Society, whose ephemeral Liverpool branch he organized in 1887, Kenworthy worked for its successor, Rev. John Clifford's Christian Socialist League, and as an executive committee member of the ethical New Fellowship (from 1894). Most of his energies, however, went into his voluminous writing and into the communitarian movement. *The Anatomy of Misery* (1893), his most popular book, put Kenworthy immediately into the limelight. He lived for a time at Mansfield House

[20] See Kenworthy to H. D. Lloyd, 3 June 1896, Jane Addams to Lloyd, 21 June 1896, Lloyd Papers, WSHS.

Settlement in London and became intimately acquainted with reformers of his day—William Clarke, Herbert Burrows, the economist J. A. Hobson, the gas workers' leader Will Thorne, Keir Hardie, Percy Alden, and others. Active in the English Land Colonization Society, whose initial aim was to form a residential farm colony near London to help middle- and lower-middle-class people to escape from the conditions of city life, Kenworthy hoped to recreate a genuine "yeoman" class based on cooperative landholding and farming in so-called Home Colonies. A group settled at Purleigh in February 1897 and seemed to prosper at first. Kenworthy built himself a house there. But internal dissensions and Kenworthy's own personal eccentricities caused the little colony to break up acrimoniously in the summer of 1899. Kenworthy then went to Russia to visit his master Tolstoy once more and upon his return to London occupied himself in producing two books on Tolstoy (1901 and 1902). He ended up, like several of his unfortunate comrades from the Purleigh colony, in a mental institution.[21]

Kenworthy's economics owed nothing to Karl Marx, and he repudiated the collectivism of the Fabians. Like the Guildsmen of ten or twenty years later, Kenworthy did not want to "mend" the capitalist system but to "cease taking part" in it altogether. The agrarian type of associationism he attempted at Purleigh was closer to the ideas of the entirely utopian and medievalist A. J. Penty than it was to those of the industrial Guild Socialists, S. G. Hobson and company, though Kenworthy held no strange ideas about eliminating division of labor from human society. In *Seedtime* in 1894 he attacked the "evolutionary socialists," saying their views on the inevitability of socialism provided a comforting rationalization for rich people not to give up their "mansions, carpets, cigars, pianos and fashions" (of

[21] This account depends heavily on W.H.G. Armytage, *Heavens Below*, pp. 302-303, 336-354. But see also *Labour Annual*, 1895, p. 177; *Labour Prophet*, III, No. 31 (July 1894), p. 90; *The Prophet* (single issue only, March 1894) pp. 15-16; *Christian Socialist*, v, No. 52 (September 1887), p. 141; *Brotherhood*, New Ser., II, No. 1 (May 1894), p. 15; III, No. 3 (July 1895), p. 40; *Seedtime*, No. 22 (October 1894), p. 15.

which he seemed to disapprove). The present capitalist system was "dishonest, corrupting to the soul and murderous to the body." Decent socialists should "opt out" and organize their own industries on cooperative lines, which could link up with J. Bruce Wallace's distributive Brotherhood Trust (to be described later) and with the "London Amalgamated Cooperative Builders." "Neighborhoods" should be organized, twenty-five or so families uniting; if they spent cooperatively £2,500 a year they could save up to £750 through not paying unnecessary profits, and could use the money to create self-supporting industrial communities. "In economics," wrote Kenworthy, "we are socialists; in our ideal we are communists; in politics we are, some of us, anarchists of peace, which is to say we have no politics."[22] It is difficult to "have no politics" or to "opt out" of modern industrial society; Kenworthy and his associates cut themselves off from the mainstream of British socialism in the 1890's by attempting to do so.

Informality and the absence of religious dogmatism were both the strength and weakness of the Christian Socialist Society. Kenworthy, strangely enough, was determined to resist the tendency to "de-Christianize" ethical socialism, and though he strongly supported the Labour Church and often spoke for it, he came into conflict with its creator, John Trevor, on matters of theology. The Labour Church's attitude to Christianity, expressed in Trevor's statement at a Socialist Congress in August 1896 that it was anachronistic to apply Christ's sayings to modern problems, kept potential Christian supporters out of the movement, thought Kenworthy. He agreed that "the name of Christ is still a fetish in Religion"; but the message of the Labour Churches—the Fatherhood of God and brotherhood of man—formed "the very foundations of the teaching of Jesus," if not of his teaching alone. "Hundreds of millions of people acknowledge . . . the authority, the worth, of Jesus as a teacher. Then, why not make it our effort to hold people to the

[22] "A Gospel of Reconstruction," *Seedtime*, No. 22 (October 1894), pp. 1-3. See also No. 24 (April 1895), pp. 14-15.

guide. . . ?" The question of Christ's divinity could be shelved; his life and message were all that mattered. To begin by telling would-be converts to socialism that they must give up Jesus was "to throw out of our hands the most powerful weapon which the wisdom of the past and social tradition has put into them." It is noticeable, however, that Kenworthy's argument for the retention of Jesus was purely expedient and pragmatic, and a far call from the mystical Trinitarian faith of the Anglican sacramentalists. R. A. Beckett (assistant editor of the *Labour Prophet*) and other Labour Church men nevertheless rejected Kenworthy's demands. They accused Jesus Christ of recommending "indiscriminate almsgiving" and of making no "contribution to sociology"! Christ was, they said, "pre-eminently not a thinker." Furthermore, organized Christianity was only "another one of those commercial productions which must go, along with sweating, slumdom and physical poverty." As for the popularity poll, the Labour Church's exclusion of Christ-worship would keep out of its membership only those who were basically inimical to socialism anyway, for "The great number of people who prefer Christianity in order to be respectable, will naturally prefer the interpretation of it promulgated by Respectability." No one chose to answer directly Kenworthy's question: "Has the Labour Movement a gospel different from, better than, the gospel of Jesus Christ, not according to the churches, but according to Himself?"[23] Perhaps, after all, it takes a religion to destroy a religion.

Three other active members of the Christian Socialist Society were even more anxious than Kenworthy to preserve Christianity along with socialism, for all three were Anglicans: Rev. C. L. Marson, E. D. Girdlestone, and Rev. Philip Peach. Marson's contribution probably diminished very rapidly once the Society was established, and it vanished altogether when he gave up the editorship of the *Christian Socialist* in 1887 to W.H.P. Campbell. E. D. Girdlestone summarized his own position in *The What and Why of Chris-*

[23] *Labour Prophet*, v, No. 57 (September 1896), pp. 156-157, 162.

tian Socialism, which called for the nationalization of land and capital, equality of opportunity, and the "utter abolition" of all class distinctions. He wished to "socialize both men and institutions." As for the competitive principle, "The Christian Socialist indeed, is not blind to the moral value of a 'struggle'; but he thinks the struggle should be of united men against the infirmities of their common nature and the difficulties of their common environment." A truly *Christian* socialism, argued Girdlestone, should aim to socialize *the individual* "from the nursery upwards" by socializing *the educational system.*[24]

In one important area Girdlestone was deeply at odds with his Christian socialist colleagues. As we have seen, except for Father Paul Bull, almost all Christian socialists, even the aristocratic elite of the CSU, were bitterly opposed to "imperialism," and many of them were strong Republicans too. Under the three years of Marson's editorship the *Christian Socialist* had lambasted the missionaries and treated the monarchy and nobility with contempt. In 1886 it fumed: "To supply blacks with soda water and blue pills is not the end of our duties towards them. Our efforts to cheat, rob, murder and enslave them require as much denunciation as the fact that we dram, drug and syphilize them."[25]

W.H.P. Campbell, as editor, continued this anticolonial policy. Girdlestone, however, would have none of it. He wrote with irritation in 1887 disavowing the journal's radical attitude on the Irish question and objecting to its hostility toward the Queen. Not all socialists supported the Irish Nationalists, he claimed; personal attacks on men like Gladstone and Bright should be avoided. He "knew not how it might be with Nonconformists," but Anglicans at least prayed for the Queen each Sunday. "Because we owe stronger sympathy to others, are we to give none at all to

24 *Christian Socialist,* VII, No. 76 (September 1889), pp. 133-135; No. 78 (November 1889), p. 161; VIII, No. 80 (January 1890), pp. 9-11; No. 81 (February 1890), p. 29.
25 *Christian Socialist,* IV, No. 40 (September 1886), p. 36.

her?" he asked. Girdlestone resented the implication that a monarchist was by definition a "snob," a "flunkey," and a "heathen." Campbell, however, defended the policy of the paper in angry terms: "I can listen with patience to a good many things . . . but I confess when Mr. Girdlestone remarks that he has been rejoicing with the Queen . . . because 'she has enjoyed so large a measure of prosperity as Queen,' it is almost more than I can stand." As for Victoria, "any great and distinguishing qualities" were "markedly absent from her character." Campbell also refused to treat Gladstone and the Liberals with kid gloves.[26] Two years later, in 1889, a prominent Christian socialist member, Rev. T. Travers Sherlock (1853-1915), published an article on jingoism which criticized Lord Wolseley, and Girdlestone again sprang to the defense. A bewildered Sherlock replied: "I quite admit a socialist may be a Jingo or a Unionist, but I submit the case is rare."[27] There was no doubt about Girdlestone's socialism at home, as his work for the New Fellowship and the Fabian Society witness. He continued to agitate in the 1890's when he had moved to Birmingham, and constantly opposed charity schemes, the Single Tax, and other measures short of the "unlimited socialism" which alone, in his view, was "ever likely to get rid of Pauperism."[28]

[26] Christian Socialist, v, No. 50 (July 1887), p. 107; No. 51 (August 1887), pp. 118-119.

[27] Christian Socialist, vii, No. 74 (July 1889), p. 109. Rev. T. T. Sherlock was a Congregational socialist, a graduate of London University, and minister in Smethwick for thirty-two years (1883-1915). Chairman of Staffordshire Congregational Union; elected unopposed to the first County Council there; served on the local School Board for nine years. His main interests were land reform and trade unionism, and he wrote a widely read tract, God and the Land (n.p., n.d.). See Congregational Yearbook, 1916, pp. 188-189; Index of Congregational Ministers, Dr. Williams' Library, London (quoted in future as DWL Index).

[28] Christian Socialist, vii, No. 76 (September 1889), pp. 140-141. Girdlestone denounced Charles Booth, H. V. Mills ("Home Colonization"), and Henry George. He had a genius for upsetting people and was involved in long correspondences and debates in every journal for which he wrote. In a series for Brotherhood Girdlestone attacked the evangelical conservatives under the heading "Bibliolatry and Social-

Like the Nonconformist J. C. Kenworthy, Rev. Philip Peach, Anglican vicar of Pawlett, took up the cry against the erosion of the Christian Socialist Society's Christianity. Peach objected to an article by John Glasse (August 1887) advocating Lamennais's dictum that men should labor for themselves and not for others; and Peach finally deepened his objections into an attack on the new policy of the *Christian Socialist* since Marson had given up the editorship. "The spirit of the paper seems so entirely to have altered," complained Peach, that he felt he must resign from the Society altogether. Peach would not accept what he called "the Gospel according to Mr. Howard." The editors were too apologetic about religion, he said, and truckled to the Marxist SDF and the Socialist League. The editors "make haste to effusively apologize to Messrs. Hyndman and Morris, and to assure them that the epithet Christian means nothing at all. Now I maintain it means a very great deal. . . . Christian socialism is something very different from Mr. Morris's socialism." Moreover, the journal's theological policy was impossible. "It is supremely ridiculous to say that a man can be a Christian and yet be supremely indifferent to all theological opinion." Alfred Howard claimed to have no theological position, but then admitted he was in disagreement with Calvinism and with the doctrine of baptismal regeneration. However, "he is kind enough," added Peach, "to allow the socialists a belief in a future life."[29]

There was justification for Peach's complaints; the editorial reply he received was extremely vague, made some mention of God and Emerson but little of Christian doctrine, and was truculent to the point of discourtesy. Peach's position can be inferred from his work in the Guild of St.

---

ism." The most dead and stubborn opposition to socialism came from Bible-worshipers, he said. Reliance on the Bible alone produces ignorance, lack of "reasonableness," and arrogance. He recommended a "Society for the Promotion of Christian Knowledge *Among the Clergy*" (*Brotherhood*, II, No. 1 [6 January 1888] to II, No. 6 [10 February 1888]).

[29] *Christian Socialist*, v, No. 52 (September 1887), pp. 139-140; No. 53 (October 1887), pp. 138-139, 149-150.

Matthew. He was no Anglican apologist, but a moderate, a Broad Churchman. Only the year before (1886) he had "uttered a most distinct protest" against the theological narrowness of Headlam's Guild. "I can conceive of nothing more mischievous, especially at the present crisis, than the continued unfounded assertion that the Church of England in fact only consists of the baptized persons in England. Nothing could be more offensive or more likely to alienate the religious Nonconformist. What a travesty on Christianity this is. . . ." Clearly, he shared C. L. Marson's interest in cooperating with non-Anglican bodies in the cause of socialism. The GSM wasted too much time, said Peach, "trying to justify *Baptism* to the people"; Christ would not exclude the unbaptized.[30] Peach was not an unreasonable man, and in the light of his criticisms of the *Christian Socialist* editors, it is not easy to justify their continued use of the title *Christian* Socialist Society. "I do not look upon Christianity as merely an additional shovelful of coals in the engine-furnace of socialism," he testified.[31]

Six months after the formation of the Christian Socialist Society, Rev. C. L. Marson could rejoice that it had become "a greater success even than we dared to hope. The untiring energy of its officers both in the London and Clifton branches has produced an important society in a very few months, and that out of the most diverse and scattered materials."[32] In the autumn of 1886 the Society began holding weekly meetings in the Industrial Hall, Bloomsbury, addressed by men like Marson, Campbell, Stewart Headlam, and the Fabian ethicalist Percival Chubb. A Special Propaganda Fund was created and four leaflets issued.[33] In Jan-

[30] *Church Reformer*, v, No. 2 (February 1886), p. 44; *Christian Socialist*, III, No. 36 (May 1886), pp. 179-180. See also *Church Reformer*, VIII, No. 10 (October 1889), pp. 236-237. Naturally, Peach became involved in a bitter dispute with Rev. Thomas Hancock on baptism. But he remained a GSM member (*Church Reformer*, v, No. 7 [July 1886], p. 165).

[31] *Christian Socialist*, v, No. 53 (October 1887), pp. 149-150.

[32] *Christian Socialist*, IV, No. 41 (October 1886), p. 58.

[33] The leaflets were: "The Manifesto; Is It Just?"; "The Christian's

uary 1887 the Society took over the *Christian Socialist* as its official organ, confidently expecting to make that paper self-supporting and to widen its circulation.[34] The new editors, Howard and Campbell, continued the more aggressive propaganda policy which had been inaugurated the previous autumn and gave space to the American socialist Laurence Gronlund for a series of articles on economic socialism.

Gronlund was a revisionist socialist, known in Britain even before his public disagreement with Henry George and his forceful rejection of the Single Tax had brought him into the news.[35] His widely quoted *Cooperative Commonwealth,* published in New York in 1884, presented an American interpretation of Marxism, omitting the "class war." Gronlund was an "ethical idealist," and some of his ideas were incorporated in Edward Bellamy's *Looking Backward* three years later; in fact Gronlund deliberately halted the sales of his own book in 1887 to speed the circulation of Bellamy's socialist novel. A few years later in *Our Destiny: The Influence of Socialism on Morals and Religion* (which was published in London in 1890 and sold 1,000 in the first month of British sales), Gronlund moved still further away from "scientific" socialism of the Marxian type toward religion: "I more and more have become convinced that Karl Marx's doctrine, that the bread-and-butter question is the motive force of progress, is not tenable, but that

---

Duty in relation to Society"; and "What Is Christian Socialism?" (*Christian Socialist,* IV, No. 42 [November 1886], pp. 74-75).

[34] *Christian Socialist,* IV, No. 43 (December 1886), pp. 85-86, 93.

[35] Laurence Gronlund, 1848-1899. Danish-American, emigrated to USA in 1867; teacher, barrister. Became a socialist, surprisingly, after reading Pascal. Despite his wide influence in the US and Britain, Gronlund's life was in many ways a failure. Constantly penniless and out of work, he turned to drugs and died in obscurity and want. See F. W. Tomkins to H. D. Lloyd, 26 July 1893, Gronlund to Lloyd, 10 December 1894 and 20 October 1898, Lloyd to Gronlund, 22 October 1898, W. M. Salter to Lloyd, 26 October 1898, Lloyd Papers, WSHS. See also *Labour Annual,* 1900, p. 81; *Dictionary of American Biography,* VIII; W.D.P. Bliss, *Encyclopaedia of Social Reform,* p. 674; Howard Quint, *The Forging of American Socialism* (Charleston, S.C., 1953), pp. 28-30. A reissue of Gronlund's major work, *The Cooperative Commonwealth* of 1884, was recently edited by Stow Persons (Cambridge, Mass., 1965).

we must grasp the very highest moral and religious truths." Gronlund felt by 1890 that the working masses were "naturally religious at bottom" and only needed leaders "from among our profoundly religious minds."[36] Such a flattering idea could hardly fail to win approval from self-styled Christian socialists; the phrase "cooperative commonwealth" recurs in their rhetoric throughout the 1890's and 1900's.

Gronlund lived in Europe during the years 1885 to 1887. He worked for a while in William Morris's Socialist League, and seemed to cast a spell over the editors of the *Christian Socialist*—hence Rev. Philip Peach's complaint about SDF and Socialist League influence in the Christian Socialist Society. Gronlund's break with Henry George in July 1887 and the publication of his two anti-Single Tax polemics, *The Insufficiency of Henry George's Theory* and *Socialism versus Tax Reform,* in that year helped to destroy the uneasy alliance that George had maintained both in the United States and in Britain with the economic socialists.[37] The *Christian Socialist* had, of course, repudiated its own Georgeist origins and rejected the Single Tax as early as January 1884. Perhaps the new competition from the SDF's paper, *Justice* (founded in that same month), which certainly cut into the circulation figures of the *Christian Socialist,* spurred the editorship in this increasingly socialist direction. From 1887 E. D. Girdlestone became a very vocal Gronlund disciple; he explained Gronlund's theories in a series of long and detailed articles in *Brotherhood* during 1887-1888. The *Christian Socialist* carried the American socialist's own articles in 1887, and Gronlund also lectured to the Christian Socialist Society in February and March.[38]

36 Bliss, *loc.cit.*; *Economic Review*, I, No. 3 (July 1890), p. 453.

37 For Gronlund's reception in Britain by Christian socialists see *Church Reformer*, IV, No. 6 (15 June 1885), pp. 128-129, and V, No. 2 (February 1886), p. 32; *Christian Socialist*, III, No. 25 (June 1885), p. 7; III, No. 37 (June 1886), pp. 195-199; V, No. 50 (July 1887), p. 98. The break with Henry George is covered in Jones, Manchester thesis; see also E. P. Lawrence, *Henry George in the British Isles* (East Lansing, Michigan, 1957), ch. VII.

38 *Christian Socialist*, V, No. 45 (February 1887), p. 28. The first of his articles appeared on pp. 17-19. For the rest see Vol. V, No. 46

Gronlund's articles and lectures could hardly be called "Christian" in emphasis, despite his open dissatisfaction with secular socialism and his "ethical" overtones. Peach must have been as much offended by them as by Rev. John Glasse's stated preference for the plain title "socialist"— dropping the adjective "Christian" because it sounded too "sectarian." At any rate the Society's journal became increasingly economic in tone in 1887 owing to Gronlund's influence and the undoubted impact of outside events such as the unemployment and labor demonstrations of 1886-1887. "Let there be no mistake about it," the *Christian Socialist* asserted. "We believe that Rent is robbery and that Profit is plunder. To prevent this . . . we would vest the ownership of land and capital in the people. . . . This is plain, straightforward Socialism, is it not?"[39] It was in fact plain, straightforward collectivism, and some members, including J. C. Kenworthy, would take exception to the policy later.

The annual meeting of May 1887 still failed to agree on a clear *political* program. Travers Sherlock, who chaired the meeting, declared himself "strenuously opposed" to any such consensus being established: Christian socialists had no single religious creed and should therefore have no single political platform. There was wide division of opinion, Sherlock said, on questions like Ireland and public education. After only nine months as the Society's organ, the *Christian Socialist* had to be voted back to independence at a special meeting in September 1887, owing to lack of funds. The high hopes of January were shattered, and W.H.P. Campbell actually moved to *dissolve* the Christian Socialist Society itself, "owing to the refusal of members to give it support, financial or otherwise" (the move was seconded by H. H. Gore of Bristol). The Society survived the year 1887 only against strong pressure from the Bristol

---

(March 1887), pp. 33-34, and No. 47 (April 1887), pp. 49-51. He concluded: "Karl Marx certainly did not say the last word."

[39] *Christian Socialist*, v, No. 45 (February 1887), pp. 25-26; No. 48 (May 1887), p. 69.

group to disband, and by the single deciding vote cast by the meeting's chairman, Rev. A. H. Smith.[40] It still had five years of life to spend.

From 1887 the *Christian Socialist* joined the fight for independent labor representation in Parliament—for a "Socialistic Labour Party"—and began to identify itself closely with Labour. The group thus went in the opposite direction from the GSM. R. A. Beckett (Labour Church) wrote condemning the Trade Union Congress for its orthodoxy and respectability, and in December good coverage was given to the London demonstrations of the unemployed and the brutal police action against the columns. Middle-class reconciliatory and melioristic agencies like Toynbee Hall were dismissed as (borrowing William Clarke's phrase) "rose-water for the plague."[41] Alfred Howard resigned as coeditor in March 1889, and in that year George Cuttle became Hon. Secretary of the Society. In July he announced a new manifesto:

> Christian socialism aims at embodying the principles contained in the life and teaching of Jesus Christ in the industrial organization of Society. . . . The Society is independent of special theological views and welcomes as members those who desire to subordinate their private advantage to the good of the commonwealth and of mankind and to strive for the knowledge and the power of doing it in the best and highest manner possible.[42]

The great event of 1889 was, of course, the Dock Strike, for which the executive committee of the Christian Socialist Society passed a resolution of sympathy and managed to scrape together the sum of £3.6s.3d. The churches were reproached for their lack of interest in the dockers' plight, and Bishop Temple of London as well as the Nonconformists came in for criticism. January 1890 brought renewed

[40] *Christian Socialist*, v, No. 49 (June 1887), pp. 91-92; No. 53 (October 1887), pp. 156-157.
[41] *Ibid.*, v (October 1887), pp. 148, 153-155; No. 55 (December 1887), pp. 177-178, 187; also see Vol. vi, No. 57 (February 1888), pp. 25-26.
[42] *Christian Socialist*, vii, No. 74 (July 1889), p. 109.

hopes of future growth for the Christian Socialist Society. There had been some slight improvement in the paper's circulation and in membership and in May the Society held a large conference at Westminster Chapel under the title "Social Christianity: Is It Possible?"[43]

This conference of 1890 is a high-water mark in the history of the Christian Socialist Society. George Cuttle acted as conference secretary, Rev. T. Travers Sherlock was in the chair, and two other well-known radical Congregational ministers took the platform with W.H.P. Campbell. They were the ex-missionary to Fiji (and ex-Wesleyan) Rev. William Whittley, who had just become a socialist in the previous year,[44] and Rev. Charles Fleming Williams, the London County Council alderman who was for forty years Congregational minister in Stoke Newington and was active in the Christian Socialist League in the late 1890's.[45] C. F. Williams claimed that socialism was "growing at a terrific rate" in 1890; "God alone knew what the next year would see. . . ." After all, "Christ was King, and Christian Socialism was His cause." The meeting, however, was not all froth: Campbell carried a unanimous resolution urging all Christians to use their political power in favor of socialism. Presumably, this was meant to be a directive of some kind.

Throughout 1890 the *Christian Socialist* cooperated with socialist movements of all types. Its pages contained excellent reports of Fabian meetings; it welcomed the new Christian Social Union and hailed its *Economic Review* as the "academic organ of Christian socialism"; it kept Christian socialists in touch with the speeches of Headlam as much as with those of Bernard Shaw. *Lux Mundi,* it affirmed,

[43] *Christian Socialist,* VII, No. 77 (October 1889), p. 148; VIII, No. 80 (January 1890), p. 8; No. 85 (June 1890), pp. 85-87.

[44] Rev. William Whittley, 1836-1902. Wesleyan missionary in the Pacific, 1859-1863; Congregational minister in Britain from 1863 (DWL Index; *Congregational Yearbook,* 1903, p. 206).

[45] Rev. C. F. Williams, 1849-1937. Alderman on London County Council from 1889; Congregational minister in various parts of London from 1874, ending up in Stoke Newington (1885-1925) (DWL Index; *Congregational Yearbook,* 1938, p. 674).

stood for brotherhood and corporate life. Yet the journal once again hit rock bottom financially, threatened to cease publication at the year's end, and was reprieved by friends only at the eleventh hour.[46] Ideally, a paper and a socialist society open to *all* Christians was greatly to be desired; in practice, supporting funds flowed through predetermined channels that were strictly denominational.

In December 1890 W.H.P. Campbell resigned as editor, though he still remained on the executive of the Society.[47] The year 1891 was the last for the *Christian Socialist*. George W. Johnson of Balham edited the paper and depended very heavily for contributions on Rev. T. A. Leonard, Christian socialist and Congregational minister at Colne. Leonard was a frequent lecturer at Labour Churches and other meetings in the 1890's; he gave the short-lived Leicester Christian Socialist Society's first public lecture in April 1891.[48] G. W. Johnson's editorship was more "literary" than Campbell's had been and less politically oriented. Johnson rejected at the outset all dealing with bodies like William Morris's Socialist League. He accused secular socialists of spending too much energy "attacking the great beliefs and institutions of mankind" rather than busying themselves with the necessary work of socialism. Johnson repudiated what he called the attempt of secular socialists to "tie the living body of socialism to the corpse of materialistic Atheism." He abruptly changed previous editorial policy by making the journal aggressively "religious," or, more accurately, antisecular. "Against this anti-religious, anti-moral, or non-moral socialism we shall raise a perpetual protest; for we hold with Laurence Gronlund in his recent

[46] *Christian Socialist*, VIII, No. 89 (October 1890), pp. 126, 130, 135-136; No. 90 (November 1890), pp. 141-142.

[47] *Christian Socialist*, VIII, No. 91 (December 1890), p. 154.

[48] Rev. T. A. Leonard also founded the Cooperative Holiday Association. After 1899 he became a Quaker. He was apparently still alive as late as 1944 when his daughter married the Headmaster of Bootham School, York (DWL Index). For his lecture at Leicester in 1891 ("Is Christianity Practicable?") see *Christian Socialist*, IX, No. 96 (May 1891), p. 56.

book, *Our Destiny* . . . that 'Socialism is eminently religious.' "[49] Attacks on the Socialist League or on H. M. Hyndman and other nonreligious British socialists of the day were not likely to swell the circulation figures of the *Christian Socialist,* and since financial aid was not forthcoming from religious sources, the journal died. Johnson's "perpetual protest" lasted exactly twelve months.

By October it was clear that no amount of fresh blood in management could keep the paper going in a denominationalized market. Circulation had been virtually stationary for too long. No further help was elicited, and the *Christian Socialist* quietly succumbed in December 1891 "for want of insufficient [sic] subscribers." The editor rather complacently assumed from this fact that the journal had "reached the limit of its usefulness." There was no longer any point in "preaching to the converted."[50]

Meanwhile the Christian Socialist Society itself had experienced a further slight growth in 1890-1891. Seventeen new members were added, making a total of 116 (not including the Glasgow branch, which continued to thrive). A further public conference was held in May 1891 on "Social Progress in London," at which Rev. T. A. Leonard took the chair and Percy Alden of Mansfield House Settlement gave a typical speech on behalf of the worker as a man and his right to trade-union organization. In October 1891 the Society organized its own conference in the midst of the Congregational Union meetings. Leonard was again in the chair, and the speakers included Rev. C. F. Williams, John Trevor of the Labour Church, J. Bruce Wallace, and Rev. T. T. Sherlock.[51] Once the *Christian Socialist* had died, J. Bruce Wallace's *Brotherhood* carried the Society's own column for a short time. The Glasgow and Leicester branches still held regular meetings; W.H.P. Campbell had by now become a Fabian. The London society was being absorbed

---

[49] *Christian Socialist,* IX, No. 92 (January 1891), pp. 6-7, 11.

[50] *Christian Socialist,* IX, No. 103 (December 1891), pp. 129-130.

[51] *Christian Socialist,* IX, No. 96 (May 1891), p. 56; No. 97 (June 1891), pp. 63-65; No. 102 (November 1891), pp. 122-123.

into the radical wing of the Congregational Church, though some of its members later found a place in the Baptist Rev. John Clifford's Christian Socialist League.

Finally, in June 1892 the London branch formally dissolved. The reasons given by its secretary, Cuttle, were:

1. Discontinuance of the *Christian Socialist,* which made it difficult to unite scattered members, many of whom were busy in several other organizations.
2. The movement was tending to crystallize around the various religious bodies, as a branch of their general activities at their local centers.

Cuttle recommended members not to cease their propaganda work for socialism in their own neighborhoods, and to continue supporting *Brotherhood.*[52] But it was clear that by 1892 the only significant and organized attempt in the history of the British Christian socialist revival to create a society for Christian socialists of *all* denominations had failed. The Christian Socialist Society had foundered and come apart on the unyielding rocks of two kinds of sectarianism—religious and socialist.

John Clifford and the Christian Socialist League, 1894-1898

Four later attempts, mainly Protestant, to organize Christian socialist opinion in Britain were represented by: the Christian Socialist League (1894-1898) ; its direct successor, the Christian Social Brotherhood (1898-1903?); the English branch of the American group, the Christian Socialist Fellowship (1909-?) ; and the more sectarian Free Church Socialist League (1909-?) .

The president of the Christian Socialist League was Rev. John Clifford, an active Fabian socialist and the most distinguished Baptist of his day. Its vice-president was Rev. J. Bruce Wallace, and its secretary Rev. John H. Belcher. Council members included Percy Alden, Will Reason, Rev.

---

[52] *Brotherhood,* VI, No. 7 (February 1892), p. iii; No. 8 (March 1892), p. 192; No. 10 (May 1892), p. 223; and No. 11 (June 1892), p. 263.

C. F. Williams, and the sacramentalists from the GSM and CSU, Revs. C. L. Marson and H. C. Shuttleworth. The League originated in a "Ministers' Union" begun by John Clifford, which declared that "this country cannot accurately be called Christian so long as people in their collective capacity, by their social, industrial and commercial arrangements, practically deny the Fatherhood of God and the brotherhood of man." The teaching of Christ, said the Union, is "directly applicable to all questions of sociology and economics." The Ministers' Union was socialist in fact but not in name for some time. Finally, in 1894, by a nearly unanimous vote, it adopted the title Christian Socialist League. The League idealistically "recognized no denominational distinctions," and its officers cut across sectarian lines.

According to W.H.P. Campbell, the League carried on the work of his own defunct Christian Socialist Society; but Bruce Wallace thought of the organization rather as a broader, unsectarian version of the Christian Social Union.[53] Certainly the League, like the former Society, had the widest-based membership of any Christian socialist body; it was truly interdenominational. In 1894 twenty-six members joined the new group; a year later the "central organization" consisted of eighty members, all of them radical clergymen or active socialist laymen.

John Clifford's League did much the same sort of work as the Society had done: its main function seems to have been to hold interdenominational socialist demonstrations and conferences. Unlike the Society, the League did not venture to establish a journal. Its members issued a lecture-list, showing the repertoire of willing members, and lost no time in holding their first public meeting (8 May 1894) at Essex Hall. Meanwhile two Leaguers canvassed the Congrega-

---

[53] *Brotherhood*, New Ser., I, No. 12 (April 1894), p. 174; *Labour Annual*, 1895, p. 111. See also H. M. Pelling, *Origins of the Labour Party*, p. 135 n. 3. Mr. Pelling correctly distinguishes between Clifford's League and the sacramental *Church* Socialist League (though the name of the latter is wrongly printed in his footnote).

tional Union annual meeting and handed out League hand-
bills at the doors of the City Temple and the Memorial
Hall. The first Essex Hall debate had a small audience, despite a striking address by C. L. Marson and the chairmanship of the very popular preacher Clifford.[54]

As the League got under way, however, it began to spread
its influence into the provinces, often following the movements of the Nonconformist annual meetings in various
cities. At Liverpool in October 1894, for instance, during the
autumn assembly of the Congregational Union, a League
meeting was held at Pembroke Chapel, chaired by the president of the Liverpool Fabians, J. Edwards, and supported
by the oratory of Bruce Wallace, J. H. Belcher, and a
recognized Congregationalist authority and ILP member,
Rev. Dr. Charles Leach. An ex-Methodist (trained at Ran-
moor College, Sheffield), Leach held very successful ministries in Birmingham, London, and Manchester, and he
claimed that large congregations of working people (up to
3,000 at Birmingham) flocked to hear his sermons, which
were highly orthodox and conservative but sensationally
publicized. However, after a Congregational Union meeting of 1892 in which Leach had a verbal fight with Keir
Hardie, the preacher was converted to social reform. He
joined Hardie's Independent Labour Party on its creation
in 1893 and began to advocate public ownership and nationalization of the railways, land, and public utilities.
Leach became Liberal MP for Colne Valley in 1910, de-
feating Victor Grayson.[55] The Church Socialist League was
the ideal organization for men like Leach.

By the fall of 1894 the League was able to hold regular

---

[54] *Brotherhood*, II, No. 10 (February 1895), pp. 156-157; No. 1
(May 1894); No. 2 (June 1894), pp. 28-29.

[55] Charles Leach, 1847-1919. A prolific writer, journalist, and preacher
who visited the Holy Land nine times, Leach received a D.D. from
Ohio University after touring the United States (DWL Index; *Congregational Yearbook*, 1920, p. 1106). *Labour Prophet*, I, No. 11 (November 1892), pp. 85-86, gives a full account of the Hardie-Leach inter-
lude at Bradford. See also K. S. Inglis, *Churches and the Working-
Classes*, pp. 296-297.

weekly meetings in London, to publish a propaganda pamphlet on *Interest* by Bruce Wallace, and to campaign hard for the Fabian-Progressives in the London School Board election. Two Christian socialist missions (described as "very successful" by the organizers) were carried out in Newport, Monmouthshire by Bruce Wallace and the Congregationalist-turned-Unitarian Rev. J. H. Belcher, the League's secretary and a strong Labour Church supporter.[56] The London organization began to sprout metropolitan branches. At Forest Gate (established in March 1894), Rev. James Wright led a group of 25 League members who met twice on Sundays as well as during the week to agitate against suburban slums and to canvass in local municipal elections. Three years later, led by E. W. Wooley, the Forest Gate Christian Socialist League was to be found planning a communitarian land-settlement scheme in Essex. A Walthamstow branch of 31 Leaguers (established in July 1894) was also active, and a Glasgow branch (50 members) grew to be second in size to the London group.[57]

The League headquarters encouraged the formation of branches (unlike Headlam's Guild of St. Matthew) to "assist in the reconstruction of society upon the principles of Jesus Christ." It recommended to branch societies the use of lectures and sermons, publications, and "civil, personal and other efforts" to propagandize the doctrines of Christian socialism. With the return of spring in 1895, Bruce Wallace and Belcher began to hold open-air meetings at London Fields. But despite these suggestions and efforts, at all times the numbers of the League and of its branches remained small—smaller even than the GSM. Indeed, by 1898 the Christian Socialist League was already "in a state of suspended animation."

[56] *Brotherhood*, ii, No. 7 (November 1894), p. 107; No. 8 (December 1894), p. 112. For Rev. John Henry Belcher, see DWL Index.

[57] *Brotherhood*, ii, No. 10 (February 1895), pp. 156-157; Armytage, *Heavens Below*, p. 349. By the end of 1895 the Glasgow branch had 58 members and was holding regular monthly public lectures (*Brotherhood*, iii, No. 7 [November 1895], p. 88).

As usual, the trouble was a lack of new recruits to take the increasing burden off the founding members. Bruce Wallace was becoming deeply involved with his cooperative schemes, the Brotherhood Church movement, and publishing ventures. John Clifford had heavy responsibilities in the Baptist ministry and was an energetic Fabian. In the 1900's Clifford devoted all his energies to the passive-resistance campaign he organized against the Education Bills of 1902 and 1906, as we have observed. The two or three provincial branches and the one remaining active London suburban branch deserved better support than this.[58] The League attracted to its membership able individuals, but they were not "organisation men," and none of them was prepared to give up other pet schemes or crusades in order to devote his attention full-time to the League. The society thus never passed beyond the initial enthusiasm of its first stage into self-sustaining, organized growth. The impetus of the first days was soon lost. This was a problem common to most Christian socialist propaganda societies—unless they had a Frederick Verinder (Guild of St. Matthew) or a John Carter (Christian Social Union).

The outside interests of the better-known Anglican executive members of the League such as C. L. Marson, Shuttleworth, and Percy Dearmer[59] have already been described. Rev. Will Reason was, among other things, secretary of the Mansfield House Settlement, which as a Congregationalist he had helped to found. His major interests were economics and public education; but he always urged that only full economic socialism could defeat capitalism.[60] Percy Alden,

[58] *Brotherhood*, II, No. 11 (March 1895), p. 170; III, No. 1 (May 1895), p. 10; V, No. 11 (March 1898), p. 127.

[59] C. T. Bateman, *John Clifford* (London, 1904), p. 198.

[60] Rev. Will Reason, 1864-1926. Graduate of London University, 1886; subsequently M.A., London, 1890 and a First Class in Theology, B.A., at Mansfield College, Oxford, 1891. Mansfield House Settlement, 1893-1898; Friern Barnet, Middlesex, 1898-1910; Hon. Secretary of the Christian Socialist Fellowship, 1909; secretary of the Social Service Committee of the Congregational Union, 1910-1920; pastor of Soresby St. Chapel, Chesterfield, 1916-1920; corresponding secretary of the *Christian Social Crusade* (1920-1926; merged with the Christian Con-

later Sir Percy Alden, MP, has already been discussed as an expert on church problems and an enthusiast for the "institutional church" idea. He was active in many socialist organizations, including the Christian Socialist League, the Christian Social Brotherhood, and the Socialist Quaker Society. Educated at Balliol and Mansfield College, Oxford, Alden was deeply influenced by Jowett and by T. H. Green. He entered Congregational social service as the first warden of Mansfield House Settlement (1891-1901) but seceded to the Quakers after 1901, taking over as organizing secretary of the Friends' Social Union (1903-1911). Alden was very eclectic in his views and activities: he served on the Fabian executive for four years (1903-1907), as a borough councillor (1892-1901) and later Deputy Mayor (1898) of West Ham, and on the London School Board (1903). One of three Fabians elected to Parliament in the victorious Labour year of 1906, Alden worked as an MP for many years thereafter. He was a prolific propagandist, wrote several books on housing and unemployment, and traveled extensively in the United States, Australasia, and the Far East.[61] Clearly, Alden had little real time to spare for the Christian Socialist League. A born organizer, he tended to take over the administration of almost every movement with which he became connected. In the late 1890's, however, Alden was more than fully occupied with settlement work and local government duties.

The vice-president of the Christian Socialist League, Rev. J. Bruce Wallace (1853-1939), was also an extremely active man, a vegetarian, an "internationalist" and Christian pacifist, a Garden City protagonist, a Congregationalist, and a socialist. In Ireland, where he was educated (M.A., Dublin,

---

ference on Politics, Economics and Citizenship, known as COPEC). See *Labour Annual*, 1897, p. 234; DWL Index; *Congregational Yearbook*, 1927, p. 150; *Brotherhood*, AU Ser., No. 29 (September 1910), pp. 387-392.

61 Percy Alden, 1865-1944. He represented Tottenham as a Radical, 1906-1918, and South Tottenham as a Liberal, 1923-1924. Killed in a German air raid on London in June 1944. See DWL Index; *Labour Annual*, 1897, pp. 219-220; *Reformers' Yearbook*, 1909, pp. 151-216; E. R. Pease, *History of the Fabian Society*, p. 270.

1874), Bruce Wallace held a Congregational ministry at Clifton Park, Belfast (1880-1885). Here he came under the direct influence of the American Henry George and spent five years preaching the Single Tax before converting to full economic socialism in 1885, at which stage he left the ministry. His conversion was caused by another American, Laurence Gronlund. From Limavady in County Derry, Wallace began in 1887 to publish the influential Christian socialist paper *Brotherhood*, which lasted until 1931. He also edited the socialist Belfast *Evening Star* (1889) and visited cooperative colonies in the United States in 1890. Two years later he founded the movement for which he is most remembered: within, but independent of the Congregational Union, Wallace began the first Brotherhood Church (1892-1902). This was followed by his creation of a much wider organization, the Brotherhood Trust, in 1894.[62]

Wallace's Brotherhood Trust was a complex cooperative structure, invented to carry on trade and industry, and paying good trade-union wage rates to all its workers, together with old-age pensions, sickness and accident benefits, and so on, all out of profits. The Trust hoped to build a complete cooperative colony with its own farms, factories, stores, and homes. Its two original "trustees" were Bruce Wallace and (naturally) Rev. J. C. Kenworthy, who took over one of the first three Brotherhood Churches (Croydon); but the two men later drifted apart.[63] Two cooperative shops were opened (Croydon and Kingsland) in the London area in

[62] J. Bruce Wallace was born in India, son of a Presbyterian missionary. He succeeded Percy Alden as warden of the Mansfield House Settlement in London (1903-1905) and retired to Limavady in 1905, but continued to labor in pastoral service and socialist journalism for a further thirty-four years, dying at the age of eighty-six. See DWL Index; *Labour Annual*, 1895, p. 191; *Labour Prophet*, VI, No. 69 (September 1897), p. 114; *Congregational Yearbook*, 1940, p. 684.

[63] In 1900 Bruce Wallace wrote of Kenworthy, for some reason minimizing his formative role in Wallace's movement, as a man "who was associated with us in the early days of the first Brotherhood Trust in its early tentative form, and is probably well-known to many of our readers . . ." (a considerable understatement). See *Brotherhood*, VIII, No. 4 (August 1900), p. 62.

1894-1895. For a time the Trust flourished and had a reverse influence in America (where Wallace had first conceived the idea) : an "Industrial Brotherhood" was created in the USA with N. W. Lermond as treasurer-secretary, and an advisory committee of well-known American reformers, including Professor Frank Parsons, Rev. B. Fay Mills and T. W. Higginson. An *international union* of trusts was contemplated.[64]

Bruce Wallace's dreams seemed too good to come true. To organize a million members into one great "cooperative commonwealth" (on the lines of Laurence Gronlund's book) and thus to shame the capitalist system into surrender— this was his ultimate vision. Meanwhile the Trust also established the Brotherhood Publishing Company. When Kenworthy visited Leo Tolstoy in Russia in 1895-1896, Tolstoy gave him the full legal rights over all English versions of his works, all the English royalties to go to the Brotherhood Company. Kenworthy devoted many months to his Tolstoy studies, but the royalty promise did not seem to work out, and the Brotherhood Publishing Company was "captured" by another friend of Tolstoy, the Dukhobor leader Tchertkoff, together with the publisher A. C. Fifield and was reorganized as the Free Age Press, the prime function of which was to print Tolstoy editions to smuggle *into* Russia.[65]

Another dream of Bruce Wallace's became more of a reality, though the reality itself was somewhat prosaic: the Garden City movement. In 1903 Wallace left Croydon and took up residence at Letchworth Garden City, along with his close associate, a prominent member of the ethical Fellowship of the New Life, W. J. Jupp; in 1911 Wallace married a Letchworth girl, Mary T. Pole.[66] The new town be-

---

[64] Lermond to Lloyd, 21 July 1899, Lloyd Papers, WSHS. See also J. Bruce Wallace, *Towards Fraternal Organisation* (London, 1895), passim. Like Percy Alden and the institutional church idea, Wallace was always strongly affected by American influences. See, for instance, *Christian Socialist*, IX, No. 95 (April 1891), p. 39.

[65] See Armytage, pp. 344-346, 357.

[66] *Ibid.*, p. 341; *Congregational Yearbook*, 1940, p. 684.

came the headquarters of the Brotherhood Trust. Bruce Wallace had worked as secretary to Ebenezer Howard, the father of the Garden City movement, whose famous book *Tomorrow: A Peaceful Plan to Real Reform* (1898) had projected the planning, in rural settings, of ideal small cities of 30,000 people each. Howard was heavily under the influence of Henry George and Edward Bellamy, and he put Bruce Wallace in charge of answering the many questions he received about his book. In June 1899 the Garden City Association was established under the presidency of the soft-drink manufacturer T.W.H. Idris. With the already existing towns of Bournville and Port Sunlight to guide them, the Association chose Letchworth for their site and had built there sufficiently to declare the city publicly open by 9 October 1903. Georgeists, land nationalizers, Ruskinians, communitarians, and Christian socialists of all sorts claimed a hand in its success and went to settle there in the early days. (Even Lenin was there for a visit in 1907.[67]) Bruce Wallace and, through him, other Christian Socialist Leaguers were thus intimately and deeply involved in the Garden City movement.

Meanwhile the Brotherhood Churches continued to play an interesting minor role in socialist history. They never became as widespread or as influential as John Trevor's Labour Churches were in the North and Midlands. But at least one of them, the original "tin tabernacle" just off Southgate Road, Islington, taken over in 1892 by Bruce Wallace himself, became the scene of a strange international political drama in 1907: the meeting in exile of the fifth congress of the Russian Social Democratic Labour Party. The humble Southgate Road church of the British Christian socialists so despised by Lenin and the Marxists became for three weeks the headquarters of some three hundred Russian revolutionaries. Lenin, Trotsky, Gorki, Plekhanov, Martov, Stalin, Rosa Luxembourg—it was a program of all-stars throughout the month of May. The future of the entire

[67] Armytage, pp. 370-384.

Russian socialist movement was at stake; and the bill was paid for by the American soap-manufacturer and ardent Henry Georgeist, Joseph Fels. The Russians were welcomed by J. Ramsay MacDonald, H. M. Hyndman, H. N. Brailsford, T. Fisher Unwin, R. B. Cunninghame-Graham, Constance Garnett, a galaxy of British names. (During the First World War the old tabernacle shielded yet another famous radical, Bertrand Russell, from an antipacifist mob; the building was finally demolished in 1924.) The longest-surviving Brotherhood Church, lasting through the 1930's, was that of Pontefract in Yorkshire, which was experimenting as late as 1921 with a cooperative colony based on knitting and beekeeping.[68] The Brotherhood Trust itself was assimilated into the London Cooperative Society in 1920.

J. Bruce Wallace was a figure well known to such people in the British socialist and labor movement as Keir Hardie, Ramsay MacDonald, R. J. Campbell, and the Fabians. He took part in Fabian Society activities,[69] as well as those of the Christian Socialist League, the Christian Social Brotherhood, and other groups. Like other executive members of the League, Wallace was too busy to give that society much of his attention and time despite the fact that he was its vice-president. In any case, the League and Wallace's Brotherhood Trust were created in the same year, and Wallace also was interested in the Labour Church movement and was a founder-member of the London Labour Church.[70]

There was nothing especially original in Bruce Wallace's social theology: it was simply and straightforwardly Christ-centered. His pamphlet *Why and in What Sense Christians*

[68] *Ibid.*, pp. 358, 376-377, and A. P. Dudden and T. H. von Laue, "The R.S.D.L.P. and Joseph Fels: A Study in Intercultural Contact," *American Historical Review*, LXI, No. 1 (October 1955), pp. 21-47, See also Bertrand Russell, *Portraits from Memory* (London, 1956), pp. 31-32.

[69] See, for example, *Christian Socialist*, IV, No. 38 (July 1886), pp. 14-16.

[70] *Labour Prophet*, I, No. 4 (April 1892), pp. 26-27; for examples of his frequent Labour Church lectures see *Labour Prophet*, III, No. 36 (December 1894), p. 167; and v, No. 51 (March 1896), p. 45.

Ought to Be Socialists was an unqualified plea of the Sidney Webb kind for "the use of the vote, and of all rights of citizenship, all powers of legislation and administrative reform, . . . the use of steam, gas, electricity . . . , the use of the power to coordinate and organise labour" for socialist ends. For "so long as there is human need in the world, the coping with it claims all that a Christian has."[71] Lack of an original social theology was naturally to be expected in both the Christian Socialist Society and the League, considering that many members of both these nondenominational organizations were barely Christians and felt more at home in the vaguely pantheistic Labour Church. But the League's president, Rev. John Clifford, was a notable exception. Moreover, as virtual leader of English Baptists, his influence was wide. At Westbourne Park Chapel, which he made into a famous preaching center, Clifford attracted regular weekly audiences of well over two thousand people, year in and year out.

John Clifford (1836-1923) was a brilliant working-class intellectual. At the age of eleven he labored a sixteen-hour day in a lace factory; at thirteen he learned to read Emerson while tending the machines. He was both a boy Chartist and a boy religious convert (age fifteen). He owed his education to the Baptist college in Leicester (1855-1858), though he later graduated in three faculties of London University (Arts, Science, and Law), studying while engaged in full-time preaching (1861-1866). Clifford spent all his preaching life in Paddington and eventually built Westbourne Park Chapel there as his own creation.[72] The great

[71] Originally published in *Brotherhood* in January 1896 and revised for Vol. VI, No. 1 (May 1898), pp. 3-5. It was published as a separate pamphlet later.

[72] See Bateman, *John Clifford*, passim; Sir James Marchant, *Dr. John Clifford, C.H., Life, Letters and Reminiscences* (London, 1924), passim. Unfortunately, there is no definitive (or even good) life of Clifford. In later life he became president of the Baptist World Alliance (1905-1911) and deputy-president (1911-1923); president of the Baptist Union (Britain), 1888 and 1899, of the National Council of Free Churches (1898-1899), and of the World Brotherhood Federation (1919-1923). Author of a hundred books and pamphlets and a prolific

moral issues of his life were the Baptist faith, socialism, secular public education, and pacifism. He fought desperately hard and with considerable courage for all four causes. In religious matters he was quite sectarian—not a whit less rigid than were the Anglo-Catholics. Scott Holland, Stewart Headlam, and the rest strongly resented Clifford's attacks on Anglicanism.[73] But the old fire-and-brimstone school of Baptist theology was not for him. When that great traditionalist preacher C. H. Spurgeon quit the Baptist Union in 1887 because he objected to its liberalized theology, Clifford was its vice-president and had led the fight to cast off Spurgeon's fixed credo. Nevertheless, Clifford never lost his ardent Protestant evangelicalism, his antiritualism and dislike for Establishment in religion. The foundation of his theology was essentially the *personal* experience of redemption in Christ; in other words, Clifford, unlike the great majority of Christian socialists, remained a theological individualist despite his repudiation of the political individualism traditionally associated with such a religious stand.

Clifford was an energetic Fabian and author of two Fabian Tracts.[74] Slow at first to support the dockers in the great strike of 1889 he eventually took part in a public conference of Nonconformist clergy which expressed sympathy for the men and against the employers.[75] In February 1891 he preached in Leeds on the "Latest Phases of the Social Gospel," asking for "recognition that moral and spiritual

---

editor and correspondent. However, his voluminous letters have apparently been lost without trace. This is a blow to scholars, as the existing biographies are lacking in analytical content and omit all reference to his socialist activities.

[73] See, for example, G. L. Prestige, *Life of Charles Gore*, pp. 163-165; *Church Reformer*, xiv, No. 10 (October 1895), p. 245.

[74] No. 78, *Socialism and the Teaching of Christ* (London, 1897), and No. 139, *Socialism and the Churches* (London, 1908).

[75] *The Christian Socialist* (vii, No. 77 [October 1889], p. 148) was suspicious of Clifford's excuse for delay in intervening: publishing the opinion that "the Nonconformist ministers had every confidence in 'the splendid generalship of John Burns' and did not wish to interfere with him in his work." This paper was, for some reason, often hostile to Clifford (e.g., vi, No. 66 [November 1888], p. 171).

progress was largely dependent upon our environments."
And a few weeks later he regretted being unable to attend
a Christian Socialist Society meeting with the words:

> I gladly . . . express my sympathy with the efforts of your
> Society. I regard the adoption of your "Aim" as incum-
> bent upon every disciple of Jesus . . . and though I can-
> not see my way to the . . . public control of capital, I
> think . . . the laws as to land should be reformed in the
> direction your manifesto expresses.

Clifford's socialism was gradually evolving beyond land reform toward the philosophy he finally reached in his Fabian Tracts. In November of 1891 he addressed the Baptist
Union at Manchester on "The Christian Conception of Society" and created a profound impression by demanding
that the churches should deliberately train their young in
social-reform subjects. In the previous month Rev. C. Fleming Williams (Christian Socialist Society) had said the same
thing to the Congregationalists at Southport. Clifford was
carrying out his own suggestion in London at the training
institute he created in 1885; young men studied "loaded"
questions such as:

1. Can the excesses of competition be adequately re-
   strained by Government interference? . . .
2. Criticize the statement: "It is futile to attempt to raise
   wages by artificial means."
3. Can co-operation be regarded as a permanent cure for
   the evils of competition? . . .
4. Must there always be a large class of society dependent
   for maintenance on the more common forms of physical labour and constituting what we know as a "labouring class"?[76]

Two years after the Manchester conference of Baptists,
Clifford wrote a pamphlet for the Christian Socialist Society

[76] *Christian Socialist*, IX, No. 94 (March 1891), p. 27; IX, No. 97
(June 1891), p. 67; IX, No. 102 (November 1891), p. 127; Marchant,
pp. 62-63.

of his home town, Leicester: *The Effect of Socialism on Personal Character* (Leicester, 1893). His approach was obvious from the title, and one to be expected from an evangelical leader. He supported the miners' strike of 1893 and was active in the London County Council and School Board elections of 1894.[77]

By 1894 Clifford's socialism was sufficiently matured for him to come out openly as leader of the newly created Christian Socialist League. All the League's annual general meetings were held at his famous chapel. His father had been a Leicester Chartist, and Clifford's evolution seemed fitting. Looking back, he explained:

> I began life in a factory and I have never forgotten the cruel impressions I received there . . . Ebenezer Elliott's prayer was on our lips daily—"When Wilt Thou save the people?"

> So I came to have sympathy with the working classes of which I was one . . . and I have never lost it after 80 years and I feel it stronger today than ever. . . .

> I was brought up to admire Will Lovett and the advocates of enlightening Christian education as the best way of reform, and to detest Feargus O'Connor as a wild demagogue.

O'Connor had led the "physical force" Chartists, Lovett the moderate parliamentary wing. Another great Chartist leader of the 1840's, Thomas Cooper, was a personal friend of Clifford's family.[78] Clifford's career seems almost to have been predetermined. How could he have ended up as anything else but a Baptist Fabian?

Socialism and the Teaching of Christ (Fabian Tract No. 78, 1897) rejects the notion that Christianity is somehow

[77] See *Labour Prophet*, ii, No. 21 (September 1893), p. 84 (advertisement); *Labour Annual*, 1897, p. 224.

[78] Marchant, pp. 1, 3. His biographer, Marchant, however, either ignored or deliberately suppressed the story of Clifford's Fabianism and made no mention at all of his Tracts. See also J. W. Grant, *Free Churchmanship in England, 1870-1940* (London, n.d.) pp. 172ff.

"above" material matters, as a "pagan" idea; collectivism can provide a better environment for Christ's work and will "lift competition on to a higher level," creating leisure time for the cultivation of personal character. The Tract implies some reservations on Clifford's part about "full collectivism." The next great question that Clifford confronted, however, was not capitalism but war. An avowed pacifist, he was as bitterly against the Boer War as were the Anglican socialists. He cooperated with W. T. Stead on the "Peace Committee"; he denounced (as did Scott Holland and Gore) the concentration camps again and again, and was forced to defend his besieged church for three nights against an angry mob of chauvinists.

Clifford's pamphlet *Brotherhood and the War in South Africa* (January 1900) gave a mordant analysis of the changing excuses given by Britain for entering the war. Since the outbreak of hostilities, he wrote, there had been "a steadfast growth of the idea that we are fighting for the emancipation of the natives from Boer tyranny. It is not for gold. It is not for the Empire. It is not to give the Outlander the vote . . . no! It is 'to proclaim the acceptable year of the Lord' to the South African natives. . . . Of course, everyone knows that not a syllable was said of the 'native' till we were far on in the quarrel and had been beaten again and again." In Clifford's mind the Boer War was clearly imperialistic. "Forty millions of people are at war with a people who number less than the whole of the population of the city of Liverpool," he commented. "Beware a false Imperialism—the Imperialism of pride and conceit, of infinite brag and senseless vaunting of mere bigness." A Stop-the-War Committee had no difficulty in recruiting the distinguished preacher as chairman of its council. In 1901 Clifford managed to persuade Free Church ministers to confer and negotiate a unified war policy:

1. Immediate surrender of all arms.
2. Unlimited amnesty.
3. A federation of South African states, with autonomy for each guaranteed.

4. *Equality for all races.*
5. Protection of African natives and their rights as workingmen to be secured.[79]

Throughout the Boer War, which roused intense mass passions, John Clifford showed deep moral fortitude and courage. His position, of course, was quite at odds with that of most of his socialist colleagues in the Fabian Society.

Clifford's political stand over the Lloyd George budget issue of 1909 and the fight to curb the power of the House of Lords was never in doubt. His great oratorical powers had already been called into play to help defeat the Tories in the 1906 general election, and a Tory House of Lords received short shrift from him in 1909: "This is a great Christian budget," he cried to a crowd in Hyde Park estimated at 250,000 strong; "Britons *will* be slaves, as long as the veto of the Lords is allowed to exist. Therefore it is the duty of the friends of freedom to abolish that veto." And to R. Mudie-Smith, the editor of the 1903 census and an ex-pupil, Clifford wrote: "I go to Southampton today to speak at a meeting for the abolition of the veto of the Lords. The counter-revolution must be started. The Lords have started this revolution, now it is our turn. We will not submit. We must not have any compromise."[80]

At this stage Clifford was already seventy-three years old. He had recently told the Forest Hill Baptist Church that "Socialism, in the soul of it, is Divine. It is of God." His second Fabian Tract (No. 139, 1908), based on the Forest Hill sermon, defined socialism as "a pushing forward of the inner soul of humanity towards its predestined goal." Socialism is universal, for all classes and creeds: "It knows no separating class arrangements. It is the foe of caste. Mammon-worship is swept utterly away by the flowing waters of the Church's generosity. Race antipathy is alien to its

[79] John Clifford, *Brotherhood and the War In South Africa* (London, 1900), pp. 2-3, 24; *Brotherhood*, VII, No. 11 (March 1900), p. 163; Marchant, p. 152.

[80] Marchant, pp. 130-131.

spirit."[81] No plainer speaking seems possible. For John Clifford, socialism was simply "the plan of God."

Owing to the Christian Socialist League's "suspended animation" in 1898 a conference was called in February of that year by Percy Alden at Mansfield House Settlement. Clifford, full of new vigor after a voyage around the world, was elected president of what was in essence the League's successor body, the Christian Social Brotherhood. Members included transfers from the League such as Rev. C. Fleming Williams and Will Reason (secretary), Rev. Richard Westrope (treasurer), and Rev. C. S. Horne.[82] Richard Westrope became a Quaker in 1907 and moved into the Socialist Quaker Society in 1908 along with his close friend Percy Alden. He was an unhappy Congregationalist, having been forced out of a Leeds pastorate in 1896 because leading laymen thought he was too radical in politics.[83] Silvester Horne, on the other hand, was a friend of Rev. R. J. Campbell of the New Theology movement, a strong supporter of Percy Alden's "institutional church" concept, and a considerable socialist influence on many young men later to gain political prominence, including Mr. Fenner Brockway. Horne was elected to Parliament in 1910 as a Liberal; he was at that time chairman of the Congregational Union. As a Christian socialist Horne believed especially in the Free Churches, which were, he said, "predestined in the power of God" to achieve a social reformation.[84]

[81] E. A. Payne, *The Baptist Union: A Short History* (London, 1959), p. 174 n. 18; John Clifford, *Socialism and the Churches* (a version of this Fabian Tract appeared in Welsh as No. 141).

[82] *Brotherhood*, v, No. 11 (March 1898), p. 127.

[83] *Labour Prophet*, v, No. 52 (April 1896), p. 58; also mentioned in Inglis, *Churches and the Working-Classes*, p. 300. From Leeds (Belgrave Chapel, 1890-1896) Westrope moved to Westminster Chapel, London (1896-1902). He died in 1941. See DWL Index; *Congregational Yearbook*, 1907, p. 471; Dictionary of Quaker Biography (a card index being prepared by E. H. Milligan of Friends' House Library, London; quoted in future as DQB).

[84] Personal conversation of the author with Lord Brockway in 1963; see also F. Brockway, *Inside the Left* (London, 1942), pp. 12-15; and *Brotherhood*, AU Ser., No. 12 (April 1909), pp. 161-162. Horne was born in 1865 and died early, aged fifty-four, on a steamer crossing Lake

The aim of the new Brotherhood, as announced in February 1898, was indistinguishable from that of Clifford's League—"to bring the teaching of Christ to bear directly" on social problems. But the Brotherhood emphasized in particular the need to make that teaching "operative in the Churches," and to this end adopted the word "social" rather than "socialist" in its title in the hope of attracting the cautious. Three months later a more precisely formulated body of Objects was declared:

1. To secure a better understanding of the idea of the Kingdom of God on earth.
2. To re-establish this idea in the thought and life of the Church.
3. To assist in its practical realization in all the relations and activities of human society.[85]

Members had to pledge in writing their consent to the Objects and to various suggested "methods of operation," namely, use of the pulpit, the lectern, the press, and the pamphlet for agitation, and maintaining close contact with "the people," infusing social movements with "the religious spirit," and giving each other public support in defense of truth and freedom of speech. The Brotherhood's first annual general meeting was held at Bishopsgate Chapel in February 1899, when existing officers were reelected. The report noted growing social awareness among younger ministers and student pastors. In November 1899 Bruce Wallace's *Brotherhood* was adopted as the group's official organ. Little more is heard of the Christian Social Brotherhood, though it was still functioning in February 1903.[86]

Ontario (1919). Son of a minister, educated at Glasgow University and Mansfield College, Oxford; married the daughter of Lord Cozens-Hardy (1892); pastor in Kensington (1889-1903) and at Whitefield's Tabernacle, Tottenham Court Road (1903-1914). See DWL Index; *Congregational Yearbook*, 1915, p. 154. The *Life* by W. B. Selbie (London, 1920) is, unfortunately, very poor.

[85] *Brotherhood*, v, No. 11 (March 1898), p. 127; vi, No. 1 (May 1898), p. 16; vi, No. 3 (July 1898), p. 39; vii, No. 8 (December 1899), p. 119.

[86] *Brotherhood*, vi, No. 11 (March 1899), p. 166; vii, No. 7 (Novem-

In 1909 two further Protestant socialist groups emerged, the Free Church Socialist League and the Christian Socialist Fellowship. The Fellowship was a British section of an American socialist organization; its motto was "the Golden Rule v. the Rule of Gold" and its principles stated:

1. That the principle of Brotherhood as taught by Jesus Christ cannot be adequately wrought out in life within the present system of industrial and commercial competition and industrial ownership. . . .

2. That the faithful and commonsense application of this principle of Brotherhood must result in *the socialisation of natural resources.* . . .

3. That this spiritual principle and this economic embodiment are *necessary to each other,* alike for the amplest production of material wealth and for its fullest use in ministering to human life.

Will Reason, as before, was secretary, and British support for the group came again from Mansfield House Settlement. Rev. H. Cubbon, Warden of the House in 1909, was president of the British section of the Christian Socialist Fellowship. There is apparently no longer any trace of its monthly, the *Christian Socialist,* of which at least one issue is reported to have appeared in May 1909.[87]

The Free Church Socialist League and Philip Snowden

Unlike the Christian Socialist Society or John Clifford's Christian Socialist League, the Free Church Socialist League did not attempt to represent all denominations. Instead, it tried to do for Free Church folk what the *Church* Socialist League did for Anglicans. It was, like the Christian Socialist

ber 1899), p. 112; x, No. 10 (February 1903), p. iv. At a meeting in Bishopsgate 27 November 1899 the Brotherhood expressed sympathy with the leading American Christian socialist, Rev. G. D. Herron (1862-1925) at his forced resignation from Iowa College (Grinnell). Evidently Clifford kept the group in touch with outside events (*Brotherhood*, vii, No. 9 [January 1900], p. 136).

[87] The Fellowship's corresponding secretary was Joseph Reeves of S.E. London (*Brotherhood*, au Ser., No. 14 [June 1909], pp. 256-258).

Fellowship, an ephemeral body, and politically it came to little. Its president, Rev. Herbert Dunnico, was a Baptist, like John Clifford. His supporters in the League included Philip Snowden, Rev. W. Younger, and Rev. J. E. Rattenbury, all three Methodists. The League was created by the unanimous vote of sixty delegates to the Swansea conference of the Free Church Council in March 1909, who met separately for the purpose.[88]

Rev. William Younger (1865-1956) was typical of his sect, the Primitive Methodists: hard-working, tough, an ex-miner from a poverty-stricken Northumbrian colliery village, endowed with a fine physique and a natural poetic oratory or "gift of the gab."[89] His supreme passion was to preach. Sixty-two years a minister, he died at the age of ninety-one, having preached in America, Canada, and Europe. His chief written testament was *The International Value of Christian Ethics*, published in London in 1924. Rev. J. E. Rattenbury (d. 1962), on the other hand, rose to great distinction in the Wesleyan Church. Rattenbury began to call himself a Christian socialist at least as early as 1907, when he first took over the Great Queen Street Chapel, London. He lectured for Rev. C. Silvester Horne at Whitefield's Tabernacle on "Socialism and the Kingdom of God" and was welcomed by the socialist press as "a new fighting recruit to the forces of Progress" in the capital.[90]

[88] Not in 1905, as reported by Ramsay MacDonald, *The Socialist Movement* (London, 1911), p. 81. See *Brotherhood*, AU Ser., No. 12 (April 1909), p. 164.

[89] By sheer moral fiber and hard labor, Younger got himself out of the pit and into Hartley College (1892-1894). He subsequently worked in five northern circuits, ending up at Anlaby Road, Hull (1930-1939). Younger presided at the terminal Primitive Methodist Conference and was a signer of the Act of Methodist Union. See *Methodist Recorder*, LXXV, No. 3999 (19 July 1934), p. 19; *Methodist Annual Conference: Minutes*, 1956, p. 193 (I found this last and other Methodist biographical material in the newly organized [1963] Methodist Archives and Research Center at Epworth House, London, E.C.I. My thanks are due to the archivist, Rev. J. C. Bowmer).

[90] *Christian Commonwealth*, Vol. 28, No. 1357 (16 October 1907), p. 43. "Were he not a Christian he would be a cynic," said the reporter of Rattenbury. "Had he been born a Romanist he would

The president of the Free Church Socialist League, Rev. Herbert Dunnico (1876-1953), was a leading Liverpool socialist and at various times president of Liverpool's Fabian Society, its Labour Party, and its Free Church Council. The eldest of nine children of a North Wales miner, Dunnico worked in a cotton mill at the age of ten, graduating to a coal mine at twelve. In the grocery trade he rose to be a manager, and eight years later, by spare-time study alone, won a scholarship to University College, Nottingham. After theological training, Dunnico became a Baptist minister in 1902. He was Labour MP for Consett (Durham), 1922-1931 and Deputy Speaker of the Commons, 1929-1931. Dunnico rose from penury to great distinction in British public life and received many honors, including a knighthood in 1938.[91]

The League grew out of the Free Church Council, a body created in 1896 to stimulate the idea of unity among the so-called Free Churches. Its past presidents had included radical figures such as John Clifford (1898-1899) and the Quaker reformer J. Rendel Harris (1907-1908). Before the League emerged, the Council already had a "Social Questions Committee" in operation (since 1906), led by the controversial communitarian, J. B. Paton, whose English Land Colonization Society (1892) had taken over the well-known Starnthwaite socialist colony in 1900. The radical

---

probably have become a Jesuit. If he were not a preacher he would inevitably be an actor. Every inch an ecclesiastic, he is yet a man of the people." Rattenbury's socialism was "refreshing" (*Christian Commonwealth*, Vol. 28, No. 1355 [2 October 1907], p. 6).

[91] Dunnico also became chief magistrate for Ilford; secretary of the International Peace Society of London (1916-1953) and Hon. Director of the Bureau International de la Paix of Geneva; Hon. Warden of Browning Settlement (1932-1953); vice-president of the Corporation of Certified Secretaries, of the Billiards Control Board, and, during World War II, of ENSA (an organization for entertaining troops); president of the Football Association; Hon. Chaplain to the Air Training Corps; president of the Ilford Girls Choir, and a director of Radio Luxembourg. See *Who Was Who*, v (1951-1960), 329-330; newspaper clippings, Liverpool Record Office. (I am grateful to Mr. N. Carnick of the Record Office and to Mr. G. Chandler, Liverpool City Librarian.)

economist J. A. Hobson prepared the Land Colonization Society's report of 1895, *Cooperative Labour Upon the Land*; and Rev. J. C. Kenworthy, of course, was also involved in Paton's group.[92] Moreover, the Free Church Council was addressed in 1908 at Southport by the Labour Party chairman, Arthur Henderson, while the young J. E. Rattenbury delivered a "magnificent defence of socialism" and argued pragmatically: "Socialism needs Christianity, and Christianity can use Socialism."[93] With all this previous preparation of the way, the birth of the Free Church Socialist League in the following year seemed logical.

"The primary object of the Free Church Socialist League," said Herbert Dunnico in his "fraternal greeting" to the Anglo-Catholic Church Socialist League, "is to take some part in the destruction of the present commercial and industrial system which is based upon greed, lust and unholy rivalry, and the creation of a better system based upon equality, brotherhood and co-operation." But the League, he added, was mainly "an ethical and educational rather than a political organisation."[94]

J. Bruce Wallace, and no doubt other Christian socialists too, wondered if it was wise to add to the list yet another society which openly proclaimed its sectarian quality. It was clear why High Church socialists should need a separate organization of their own, in order "to leaven the Church of England." But, asked Wallace, did Nonconformists require an exclusively Free Church league? "Nonconformists may not be eligible to the Church Socialist League; but that is no reason why they should not make churchmen of all types welcome." Bruce Wallace, therefore, expressed his preference for the broader-based American-created Christian

[92] Rev. Dr. J. B. Paton (1830-1911). See Armytage, pp. 325, 337; J. A. Hobson (ed.), *Cooperative Labour Upon the Land* (London, 1895); E.K.H. Jordan, *Free Church Unity: A History of the Free Church Council Movement, 1896-1941* (London, 1941), pp. 153-155, 247. (Jordan makes no mention of Dunnico or the Free Church Socialist League.)

[93] *Brotherhood*, AU Ser., No. 12 (April 1909), p. 164.

[94] *Church Socialist Quarterly*, IV, No. 3 (July 1909), pp. 221-226.

Socialist Fellowship.[95] The Free Church league, in fact, seems to have made no prominent mark on the historical record after 1909. The main contribution of Free Church members to the rich tradition of British socialism was not to be made through organized propaganda societies.

The most famous Free Church Socialist League member was Philip Snowden (1864-1937), the Methodist weaver's son who became Chancellor of the Exchequer in 1924 and 1929-1931, Lord Privy Seal, and a Viscount. Snowden joined Keir Hardie's Independent Labour Party in 1895, coming to it via the Social Gospel, direct experience of working-class life, and Henry Georgeism. The Single Tax appealed to Snowden, and his budget of 1931, later reversed, contained Georgeist land-tax clauses.[96] Snowden's work is well known. His style was more that of the Labour Church orator than of a speaker for "Christian socialism." Though in a very popular and influential pamphlet produced for the ILP in 1905 Snowden emphasized the figure of Jesus throughout, he reduced the Christ-figure to the dimensions of a human genius, as did Labour Church doctrine. This tract, *The Christ That Is to Be*, was a highly effective piece of writing, directed more to convert Christians to socialism than to convert socialists to Christianity.

"The life of Christ," said Snowden, "is the great example of human perfection." Despite the materialism, sycophancy, and paganism of the churches, "there still remains the great and potent fact that Christ has been the greatest influence in the world's history." Christ's law of sacrifice, love, and cooperation is the foundation of "all the great ethical religions of the world," not merely of Christianity alone.

> The religion of the future will recognise . . . the complete organic unity of the whole human race. And *this religion will be a political religion* . . . which will seek to realise its ideal in our industrial and social affairs by the application and use of political methods.

[95] *Brotherhood*, AU Ser., No. 14 (June 1909), p. 256.
[96] See Jones, Manchester thesis, pp. 281-284; also P. Snowden, *Autobiography*, 2 vols. (London, 1934), I, 48.

Snowden concluded that "the only way to gain the earthly paradise is by the old hard road to Calvary—through persecution, through poverty, through temptation, by the agony and bloody sweat, by the crown of thorns, by the agonizing death. And then the resurrection to the New Humanity— purified by suffering, triumphant through sacrifice." Lecturing to the Labour Churches in the late 1890's, Snowden had emphasized the obsolescence of the old theological individualism. "Salvation from Hell for Original Sin is getting out of date," he said. "With another generation of School Board education it will disappear altogether." In a happy phrase Snowden said, "Personal Salvation and Social Salvation are like two palm trees which bear no fruit unless they grow side by side."[97] Labour leaders could always count on Philip Snowden to "put a bit of 'Come to Jesus' in."[98] If any one document may be taken to illustrate the framework of mind of the Free Church Socialist League, and of Nonconformist socialism in general, it is Snowden's *The Christ That Is to Be.*

Swedenborgian socialism

It may seem a far call from Philip Snowden, Herbert Dunnico, and John Clifford to the Swedish scientist, philosopher, and mystic, Emmanuel Swedenborg (1688-1772), but the distance is actually not so great. Swedenborg did not himself found a church. He lived for much of his life in England and died in London, and a Swedenborgian Church, or "New Church signified by the New Jerusalem in the Revela-

[97] *The Christ That Is to Be*, passim; *Labour Prophet*, VI, No. 76 (April 1898), pp. 169-170.
[98] A working-class socialist from Wibsey (near Bradford), chairman of a labor meeting in the 1890's, instructed his speaker (Fred Bramley, later secretary of the TUC): "Now look here Fred. Tha' knaws they're an ignorant lot at Wibsey, so don't be trying any of that scientific socialism. We want no Karl Marx and surplus values and that sort of stuff. Make it plain and simple. Tha' can put in a long word now and then so as to make them think tha' knaws a lot, but keep it simple, and then when tha'rt coming to t'finishing up, tha' mun put a bit of 'Come to Jesus' in, *like Philip does"* (Snowden, *Autobiography*, I, 82 [italics mine]).

tion," was formed in 1787 by Robert Hindmarsh (1759-1825), a Clerkenwell printer. From the start Swedenborgians divided into separatists and nonseparatists, and many remained within the Church of England—including, for example, Rev. John Clowes (1759-1831), Rector of St. John's, Manchester.[99]

Swedenborgian religion was and is a kind of Christian Unitarianism, if there can be such a thing. "The crucifixion of Jesus Christ was not to appease an angry Father," said the Swedenborgians. "There was no angry Father." Jesus was God; there is no orthodox doctrine of the Trinity. The Bible, or rather selected parts of it,[100] contains God's words. These words have a hidden "Spiritual and Divine sense," which it was given to Swedenborg (instructed by God and by the spirit world) to interpret correctly. The inner meaning of the Bible is revealed according to the "science of correspondences," i.e., Biblical truth is essentially parabolical. Salvation is deliverance from sinning itself, not from its consequences. Atonement is the reconciliation of man to God, not of God to man, and is attained by exercising God-given free choice in life, according to acknowledged criteria of goodness and truth. Everyone is created for Heaven; those who go to Hell *choose* to do so.[101] Judgment is the disclosing of character; life after death is continuous and is spent in Heaven by those who try to do right and serve God and their neighbor. All religion has relation to life, and the life of religion is to do good.[102]

Obviously this humane, relaxed theology has more affinity

[99] Lancashire today has by far the heaviest concentration of Swedenborgian churches—25; there are also five each in London, Yorkshire, and the Midlands and two in Scotland (*The New-Church in Britain* [London, n.d. (1963?)], brochure).

[100] Namely, the Pentateuch; Joshua, Judges 1 and 2, Samuel; I and II Kings; Psalms and Prophets; the four Gospels and Revelation. See *One Hundred Points of New-Church Doctrine* (London, n.d. [1963?]), pamphlet.

[101] There are three New-Church heavens and three hells; but such refinement does not concern us here.

[102] *Loc.cit.* See also C. A. Hall, *True Christian Doctrine Given to the World Through E. Swedenborg* (London, n.d.).

with the "New Theology" of twentieth century Nonconformity, as espoused by Rev. R. J. Campbell and others,
than with the orthodox evangelical dogma of the Victorians.
Some kind of social theology was bound to emerge out of
New-Church beliefs in the period of the Christian socialist
revival. In fact, long before the 1880's Swedenborgians had
been associated with radical political and economic ideas.
In the United States, for example, the "New-Church" was
one of several religious sects which prepared the way for
communitarian socialism in the 1820's. Robert Owen's New
Harmony experiment received strong support from Swedenborgians in Indiana, and a Cincinnati minister was a leading Owenite socialist.

The New-Church Socialist Society was established in
1895 "to study and promulgate the teachings and practice
of our Lord Jesus Christ as applied to every human duty."
And a journal of Swedenborgian socialism, *Uses,* was published by the Society from 1896 to 1901.[103] New-Church socialism was not sacramental, of course, though the sect does
recognize two sacraments, Baptism and the Holy Supper.
(The bread and wine in the Lord's Supper signify for
Swedenborgians not the Body and Blood, but Love and
Wisdom.)

The establishment of the society was first publicly announced in December 1895 with Rev. S. J. Cunnington
Goldsack of Keighley, Yorkshire as its secretary. On joining,
members signed a declaration which acknowledged "that
the Lord's Kingdom is based upon the principles of the Fatherhood of God and the Brotherhood of Man"—a system
denied by existing capitalist institutions.[104] The title *Uses*

---

[103] For Owenite Swedenborgians see Arthur E. Bestor, *Backwoods
Utopias* (Philadelphia, 1950), p. 210, and M. B. Block, *The New
Church in the New World* (New York, 1932), passim. For the creation
of the NCSS, see *Brotherhood*, v, No. 58 (October 1896), p. 161; *Uses*,
I, No. 1 (March 1896), p. 8. My thanks are due to the Swedenborg So-
ciety, London, for permission to use its library facilities; and to
Rev. C. H. Presland, secretary of the New-Church General Conference,
for admission to the Swedenborgian archives.

[104] *Brotherhood*, III, No. 8 (December 1895), p. 99.

("a monthly New-Church Journal of Evolutionary Reform") represented Swedenborg's slogan: "All life is the life of Use." Dissatisfied with Victorian industrial society and the "restriction of the number of good Uses into which the glorious truths of the New Dispensation were being ultimated [sic] and brought out practically," the journal took as its own object:

> To deduce and develop the true science and order of society on earth from the order of society in heaven revealed to man through the instrumentality of Emmanuel Swedenborg.[105]

That "order of society" was socialistic. Previously Swedenborgians had "studiously avoided" applying their "truths" to the political and economic side of life. Now at last a "forward movement" was being led by Goldsack. The point was put, very gently:

> . . . it is hoped that, however some of us may be opposed to that designation, we will admit that there is such a thing as Christian Socialism, recognize the vote of the majority and loyally try to prove what such Christian and New-Church Socialism is.

The whole range of political ideas were to be welcomed, even anarchism.[106]

Apart from Goldsack, the officers consisted of T. D. Benson (treasurer, and editor of *Uses*), Rev. Thomas Child (vice-president), and L. P. Ford (president). Of Ford little is known;[107] Child was much more active in the society, as

---

[105] *Uses*, I, No. 1 (March 1896), p. 1; *Brotherhood*, IV, No. 6 (October 1896), p. 72.

[106] *Uses*, I, No. 1 (March 1896), pp. 1-2.

[107] L. P. Ford lived in Shortlands, Kent and was the author of a pamphlet, *On the Reorganisation of the New Church*, rewritten by Rev. J. Presland (Shortlands, 1897). One would guess that he was a "moderate," drawn into the society as a figurehead. There was some trepidation as to the reaction of nonsocialist New-Church folk to the society: "All New-Church people believe in gradual evolution and development," said *Uses* hopefully, "and none will therefore, we trust, try to stop this progressive step" (*Uses*, I, No. 1 [March 1896], p. 2).

were several nonexecutive members, such as G. Trobridge, Rev. A. Potter and Charles Hill. Rev. Thomas Child (1839-1906) was an ex-Congregational minister of humble social origin, who had resigned in 1872 to become a New-Church man. For twenty years he was New-Church minister at Palace Gardens Terrace, Kensington (1886-1906), where his most significant work was done. A constant contributor to *Uses,* Child's major book was *Root Principles in Rational and Spiritual Things* (London, 1905). He enjoyed a considerable vogue for some years and was known in other faiths. He lectured for the Christian Social Brotherhood, for example, and made a deep impression on John Clifford as a man of "genial spirit, large sympathies and marked abilities." Child's many books were pushed by Sir Isaac Pitman (1813-1897), the publisher and inventor of shorthand, who had been a Swedenborgian since 1837.[108] Thomas Child was certainly the most distinguished and the best generally known Swedenborgian writer of his day. He lectured all over the nation and was as much at home in Glasgow workingmen's clubs as in Kensington parlors. At his funeral service in 1906, attended by John Clifford and other admirers, Rev. W. A. Presland said of Child's socialism:

> In the present state of the world, New Church people may too easily acquiesce in the things that are. Mr. Child's whole nature turned spontaneously to those that might be, with a great desire for an all around improvement of outward conditions as well as of inward states.[109]

Child was the theologian of Swedenborgian socialism and its chief apologist. "Socialism becomes, in our conception," he stated, "the inevitable form and embodiment in public life of the principles exhibited in the Writings" (of Swedenborg) —"inevitable" because in Swedenborgian doctrine all

---

108 *Dictionary of National Biography,* 2nd suppl. I (1912), 359; DWL Index; *Congregational Yearbook,* 1873, p. 226; T. Child, *The Glorification of the Lord's Humanity* (London, 1906), pp. 9ff. (biographical sketch by Rev. W. A. Presland); *New-Church Magazine,* xxv (May 1906), 234-235.

109 *New-Church Magazine, loc.cit.*

things are Providential and "there is no such thing as Chance."[110] This was a doctrine which could be made to fit in fairly readily with Marxian determinism; hence the possibility of a Swedenborgian SDF man, like T. D. Benson. At the outset Child faced the objections to socialism within the Swedenborgian community: that the New-Church Socialist Society was a mere appendage, a creature, of the Marxist Social Democratic Federation; that socialism was alien to Swedenborgian doctrine and not mentioned at all in the Writings; that it was a worldly and materialist movement. Child countered that socialism was the best economic and political *means* to achieve New-Church *ends;* that many things besides socialism received no mention in Swedenborg's Writings, including the New-Church itself; and that the NCSS was not schismatic, but simply a society within the Swedenborgian Church: "To me the very title 'New-Church Socialism' is tautological, since there can be no other socialism than that which the Word and the Writings plainly contain." Child concluded that socialism was "the developed relation of New-Church principles to social life."[111]

Goldsack, the society's organizer, promulgated four agreed principles in October 1896:

1. That the present system and conduct of life, being disorderly and un-Christian, hamper the spiritual, moral and material welfare of the people.

[110] *Uses*, I, No. 1 (March 1896), pp. 2-4; *What the New-Church Is* (London, n.d. [1963?]), brochure. See also Goldsack on Swedenborg's dictum: "The Divine Providence of the Lord extends to the most minute particulars of the life of man." Goldsack calls this "one of the basal theorems of Christian Socialism" (*Uses*, I, No. 3 [May 1896], pp. 27-29).

[111] *Uses*, I, No. 1 (March 1896), pp. 2-4. Swedenborg's key word, said Child, was *unity*. "Dissociation is unthinkable. . . . In human affairs too, *union,*—fellowship, society—is there presented as the law of being." Individualism and the Writings are incompatible because "every individual in true Social Order derives his goods and means of subsistence, directly from the Community or Common Good" (*Uses*, I, No. 6 [August 1896], pp. 64-65). "Individuals are related to the Common Good or Community through Uses done primarily for it as the end" (*Uses*, I, No. 9 [November 1896], pp. 89-109). Hence the title *Uses* for the socialist journal.

2. That the true economy is to be found in the words and life of the Lord Jesus Christ, as interpreted by the New-Church; and that this is known at the present time[112] as Socialism.

3. That this can only be established by the gradual moral and spiritual advancement of the people; but that no advancement can be made without some progress towards the ideal upon the ultimate plane.

4. Therefore that the Church should be the first to proclaim the true economy and *the first to practise it,* leaving individuals free to follow that course which seems to them to be truest and best.[113]

S.J.C. Goldsack became in later life a governing figure in his church: he was three times president of its Conference, and an executive council member from 1911 to 1946; Goldsack held New-Church ministries all over Britain for over fifty years.[114] But in the 1890's the young socialist was regarded with some hostility by older members of the sect. The general body of Swedenborgian economic and political opinion at that time was solidly bourgeois, orthodox, and *laissez-faire.* Goldsack complained of "hot" opposition, "fostered by journalistic sensationalism and cruel perversion" of the truth of the socialist message. "Socialism is a good thing. It is heaven-born as are all good things. It is idealistic

---

112 "At the present time" here signifies that at some time in the future the answer may *not* be socialism; truth evolves and unfolds. Cf. Child: ". . . the Writings were never *intended* to apply to life universally, seeing that its facts could never even be named in their very language" (*Uses,* I, No. 1 [March 1896], pp. 2-4).

113 *Uses,* I, No. 9 (November 1896), p. 118.

114 Rev. Stephen James Cunnington Goldsack, 1868-1957. Son of a New-Church family. Worked as a post-office telegraphist, 1883-1889; joined Kensington Swedenborgian Society in 1889 and studied at New-Church College, Islington (1889-1893). Ordained by Rev. John Presland, and took his first pastorate at Keighley (1893-1897). Served in India in World War I. Secretary of New-Church Conference (1919-1929). One son (Sydney, 1897-1959) was director of Collins publishing house; one grandson is at present a nuclear physicist (*New-Church Herald,* 38, No. 1490 [4 May 1957], pp. 70-71; *General Conference of the New-Church, Yearbook,* 1957-1958, pp. 100-101; personal conversations with Rev. C. H. Presland [1963]).

as are all good things," he insisted. "The study of socialism is itself a highly moral education." Appealing directly to the religious sentiment, Goldsack wrote:

> New-Church Socialists believe, first of all, in *internal regeneration,* and that a company of men and women struggling to regenerate themselves will find infinite sources of solace, help and encouragement in mutual improvements and consociation, in mutual love unlimited.[115]

Goldsack had no particular distinction outside the charmed circle of the tiny Swedenborgian church. Thomas Child exerted a wider influence, mainly through his philosophical writings. Other Swedenborgian socialists took a still greater role in the world outside the New-Church. The artist G. Trobridge, A.R.C.A. (1851-1909), for example, was a water-colorist, a biographer of Swedenborg, and a prolific writer of fiction, criticism, and religious works. For twenty-one years from 1880 Trobridge was Headmaster of the Belfast School of Art. He never seemed to have become a full economic socialist, but his contributions to *Uses* were frequent, and he was an influential sympathizer with the Goldsack group.[116]

Among London radicals Rev. Arthur Potter was well known as a Swedenborgian minister whose Walworth New Jerusalem Church was a Labour headquarters and scene of frequent socialist lectures and debates. H. M. Hyndman spoke out for the SDF there in 1893 and demanded "no compromise" with trade unionists, reformists, and the like. Nothing short of full national and international socialism should satisfy the worker, Hyndman said. A few months

---

[115] *Uses,* I, No. 1 (March 1896), pp. 4-5.

[116] *New-Church Magazine,* 28, No. 329 (May 1909), pp. 218-220. Trobridge preferred the title "Brotherhood of Use" for the Society but deplored popular prejudice against the word "socialism." In a leading article of June 1896 he declared: "The most powerful instruments for the creation of wealth are used not for the producers but against them" and quoted from Marx and Hyndman to support his view (*Uses,* I, No. 3 [May 1896], pp. 31-32; I, No. 4 [June 1896], pp. 33-35).

earlier Keir Hardie had lectured the New Jerusalem congregation in a typical address (Consider the lilies . . .") on the iniquities of wasting parliamentary time debating congratulations to Royalty on family events while the nation starved and suffered. On the spot the assembly passed a resolution about the issue and sent it to Gladstone. Rev. Potter himself "dealt very extensively with the evils arising from our social system." Other speakers included the ubiquitous Rev. J. C. Kenworthy of the Christian Socialist League, who made a collection for Hull dockers on strike, and the famous socialist pamphleteer J. Morrison Davidson.[117]

Such meetings at Potter's church were virtually Labour Church affairs, and indeed some were so described.[118] Potter, in fact, drifted away from Swedenborgianism and was no longer officially listed as a minister after 1894, though he remained a conference member until 1897. Much of his time was absorbed in working with Bruce Wallace and J. C. Kenworthy in the short-lived Bellamyite Nationalisation of Labour Society, of which he was president. Its aim was "to propagate the principles of Universal Brotherhood and Industrial Co-operation," and for a time it was responsible for the publication of Bruce Wallace's *Brotherhood*.[119]

[117] *Brotherhood*, I, No. 5 (September 1893), p. 73; I, No. 4 (August 1893), pp. 50-51; I, No. 2 (June 1893), p. 23.

[118] The wording is interesting, for example "a Labour Church was held" (at the New Jerusalem Church, Walworth). See *Brotherhood*, *loc.cit.*, and previous citation.

[119] *Brotherhood*, I, No. 1 (May 1893), pp. 11, 13, 17. Other Swedenborgian socialists included Rev. W. Rees, New-Church minister at Ynysmeudwy, who preached in Welsh to the men of the Swansea valley and translated Swedenborg's major tomes into Welsh. He was an ex-Congregationalist minister, like Child, and wrote in *Uses* (I, No. 7 [September 1896]) on "The Infinite Socialist": "When Jesus Christ appeared, the day of love and sympathy dawned on the wretched state of the "poor" (pp. 77-78). Rev. W. Heald (1858?-1936), of Skipton, Yorks. and later of Dundee, another New-Church socialist, was in later life disowned by his church and achieved notoriety by prophesying World War I and the King's illness and death, using a "raygraph." He wrote *A First Study in Practical Colour Psychology*, published in London in 1928 (*Sunday Mail*, 26 January 1936, p. 9 [clipping in New-Church archives]).

Like the *Church Socialist, Brotherhood,* the *Christian Socialist,* and the *Church Reformer,* the journal of the Swedenborgian socialists was deeply anti-imperialist. The Spanish-American War of 1898 over Cuba was painted as "a struggle between the American Sugar Trust supporting the insurgents, and Paris bankers [supporting] the Spanish government," while the earlier Venezuela Boundary dispute of 1895-1896 between the USA and Britain was a sordid "financial squabble" between rival British and American syndicates to grasp the rich resources of the Orinoco valley. When the US annexed Hawaii, this was seen simply as a coup by the Sugar Trust. "The only hope of combating the money power lies in Socialism"—but, fortunately, trusts must inevitably lead to socialization. As for the British adventurers in Africa—"the Rhodes gang"—Liberals and Tories alike were trying to whitewash their activities, reported *Uses.* Meanwhile, the Africans suffered at the hands of the unscrupulous white capitalists.[120] The Boer War was the "greatest crime of the generation," according to Swedenborgian socialists. It came about because the Boers were "driven to desperation by the massing of Imperial troops in South Africa." The Transvaal was "goaded into war for the sake of its gold mines, and to enrich the Jewish financiers who control them." (With superbly ironic muddle-headedness, *Uses* went on to call the Transvaal "England's Dreyfus Affair"—after having blamed the Dreyfus affair itself on the "anti-Semitic power of French Jesuits."[121]) New-Church socialists used Thoreau's *Civil Disobedience* to justify their hostile attitude during the Boer War. They found other churches "only too willing to throw in their lot with

120 *Uses,* I, No. 1 (March 1896), pp. 6-7; II, No. 17 (August 1897), p. 77; II, No. 18 (September 1897), p. 94; II, No. 20 (November 1897), p. 124; II, No. 24 (March 1898), p. 189.

121 *Uses,* IV, No. 43 (October 1899), p. 109; IV, No. 44 (November 1899), p. 126. The curious anti-Semitic note is also to be observed in 1896, when *Uses* wrote without disfavor of the anti-Semitic party in the Vienna City Council and, with extraordinary simple-mindedness, characterized European anti-Semitism as a revolt against "usury" (Vol. I, No. 1 [March 1896], p. 6). Anti-Semitism was not entirely absent from the CSU's strong opposition to the Boer War either.

ignorant Jingoes." The Wesleyans, claimed *Uses*, "want Chamberlain's money, and *he* needs their support." The national press had adopted a "conspiracy of silence." The whole affair brought "moral humiliation" to Britain.[122]

More divisive issues inside the New-Church Socialist Society were feminism and the Single Tax. *Uses* generally supported the women's movement, and a contributor to the journal was the feminist Miss E. Sawers, whose writing brought her into conflict with Trobridge.[123] The Single Tax was strongly championed by a Georgeist Swedenborgian, Henry Horner, in September 1896, and in July 1897 Goldsack himself wrote that "Land Nationalisation appears to me to be a sound, a necessary, a certain reform. One of the first with which the nation must deal." But a later contributor, C. H. Spencer, denounced the Single Tax and land reform as fallacious, on the socialist grounds that such techniques did not go far enough.[124] In the long correspondence ensuing, little was settled. In other Christian socialist societies the majority had usually moved on beyond George to a fuller program of socialism.

The major problem the Society faced was not internal disagreement but external apathy. The New-Church Socialist Society existed almost solely for the purpose of socialist evangelizing among Swedenborgians. From 1898 on the pressure group came increasingly into conflict with the sect authorities, especially the more conservative official journals, *Morning Light* and the *New-Church Magazine*. Thomas Child in particular fought a running battle with the last from September 1898 to July 1899.[125] New-Church socialists

122 *Uses*, IV, No. 47 (February 1900), p. 174; IV, No. 48 (March 1900), pp. 189-190; V, No. 50 (May 1900).
123 *Uses*, I, No. 4 (June 1896), pp. 35-37; I, No. 6 (August 1896), pp. 72-73.
124 *Uses*, I, No. 7 (September 1896), pp. 84-86; II, No. 16 (July 1897), p. 54; II, No. 23 (February 1898), pp. 167-170. See also Vol. V, No. 60 (March 1901), pp. 165-169.
125 *Uses*, III, No. 30 (September 1898), pp. 89-92; III, No. 32 (November 1898), p. 124; III, No. 34 (January 1899), pp. 145-148; III, No. 36 (March 1899), p. 179; IV, No. 39 (June 1899), pp. 43-44; IV, No. 40 (July 1899), p. 61.

compared their church unfavorably with the Church of England and wrote glowingly of the radical stand taken by ritualists.[126] They found their own church general conferences (as at Blackpool, 1898 and Manchester, 1899) to be sterile and frustrating, and gradually they turned for satisfaction to other movements.[127] Thomas Child became (like Bruce Wallace) a Garden City devotee, for example, and in the last issue of *Uses* (March 1901) C. H. Spencer, who had rejected the Single Tax as too moderate three years earlier, wrote of Indian mysticism and spiritualism as advances in human thought, which were clearing away materialism.[128]

Swedenborgian socialism was largely exemplified by Child, Goldsack, and T. D. Benson, who remained with the Society throughout its short life. All three claimed to be socialists. Child insisted that the only way to realize the socialism implicit in Swedenborg's writings was through collectivism— "Communal Production and Distribution effectual through the State." Goldsack declared: "We are told by Swedenborg that God can only aid man through the agency of man." Therefore, his Society was "thoroughly socialistic and absolutely Christian." He had no time for either of the two main parties and wished the Liberals out of the way so that socialists could fight the Tory enemy properly.[129]

T. D. Benson, of course, as an ILP man, agreed with this policy for the NCSS. "Socialism," said Benson, "is a policy founded on and deduced from the prevailing economic conditions, the validity and righteousness of which deductions are confirmed by the revelations of Swedenborg."[130] He had been converted to the idea of independent parliamentary representation for labor by a close reading of Robert

---

[126] *Uses*, III, No. 32 (November 1898), p. 124; IV, No. 38 (May 1899), pp. 17-19.

[127] *Uses*, II, No. 29 (August 1898), p. 69; IV, No. 40 (July 1899), p. 61.

[128] Annie Besant had taken much the same path in the 1880's. *Uses*, IV, No. 41 (August 1899), pp. 76-77; V, No. 60 (March 1901), p. 176.

[129] *Uses*, II, No. 26 (May 1898), p. 21; II, No. 13 (March-April 1897), p. 10.

[130] *Uses*, II, No. 14 (May 1897), p. 19. The 1896-1897 issues of *Uses* contain letters which explore the doctrinal connections between Swedenborgian thought and socialism in academic detail.

Blatchford's *Clarion* in 1893 (when forced to spend eighteen months in Switzerland owing to bad health and had as a result read "every socialist book he could get"). On returning to England in 1894 Benson immediately contacted Keir Hardie, joined his brand-new ILP, and subsequently became assistant treasurer (1895) and then treasurer (1900) of its election fund. Benson was a radical economic socialist and at the same time a member of Hyndman's SDF, and in 1898 he was elected to the Clitheroe Board of Guardians with no less than three other SDF men. He left the Marxist SDF in 1901, when ill-health forced him also to give up writing for *Uses*.[131]

The Swedenborgian socialist journal had given Benson an outlet for his ideas; but a much wider market was found for his ILP tract *Socialism and Service*, no less Swedenborgian in rhetoric as a result of its ILP sponsorship. In fact, the pamphlet formed the chief written contribution of New-Church socialism to the socialist movement in general. It was thoroughly in line with standard Swedenborgian socialist doctrine.

The main theme of *Socialism and Service* was "the principle of use or service," and Benson quoted from Darwin, Haeckel, and Marx and Engels, but for some reason did not mention Swedenborg by name: "The principle of Use is, according to Darwin, the progressive principle of natural selection. . . . One species is superior to another by the greater number of uses secured to it in the course of its evolution. It therefore follows that the principle of Use is the basis of every form of life throughout all nature." As Jesus said: "He who would be the greatest in the Kingdom of Heaven must be the servant of all." Industrial capitalism, in contrast to this principle, was based on "an *alien principle,* existing nowhere else in nature": production for profit, instead of for use. Socialism, however, is at one with nature

[131] *Reformers' Yearbook,* 1907, p. 236. Benson's son, Sir George Benson, at present (1963) MP for Chesterfield and a former pacifist and prison reformer, also became treasurer for the ILP (conversation with Lord Fenner Brockway).

and with the underlying principle of use. Inevitably, according to the scientific laws of evolution to which all things are subject, socialism must come.

> To attempt to resist this infinite and eternal energy which gradually created the earths in the Universe, developed the human form from the dust of the earth, and has gone already far in the reorganisation of society, is as futile as to bemoan our birth and resist our death.

In a thoroughly Swedenborgian amalgam of science and philosophy, T. D. Benson inferred the rules of human society from those of human physiology and concluded that service for the common good was no less than "a biological principle."[132]

Nothing further is heard of the New-Church Socialist Society after the death of *Uses* in 1901, "owing to insufficient support." Goldsack gave his subscription list to Bruce Wallace to use for *Brotherhood,* and T. D. Benson began to write for that journal instead. The circulation of *Uses* had never exceeded one thousand. Its impact outside Swedenborgian circles was probably almost nil.

After five years of socialist propaganda by the paper, Goldsack found little change among Swedenborgians in general. The New-Church was still too narrow and inward-looking, controlled by a small directing clique. Its official journals were still closed to free discussion of controversial political matters. The sect needed radical governmental and structural reform.[133] The New-Church Socialist Society, on the other hand, had provided a useful outlet of energies for radical Swedenborgians and directed the most determined of them to other movements more suited to their needs— theosophy, the Garden City movement, the Labour Church,

---

[132] *Socialism and Service*, ILP Tract for the Times No. 11 (London, n.d.), pp. 1-7. See also Benson's Tract No. 7, *The Workers' Hell and the Way Out* (London, n.d.), and his article "The Churches and the Working Class," *Uses*, v, No. 52 (July 1900), pp. 33-36.

[133] *Brotherhood*, IX, No. 1 (May 1901), p. 7; *Uses*, II, No. 13 (March-April 1897), p. 10; v, No. 60 (March 1901), p. 170. See also Vol. II, No. 25 (April 1898), pp. 10-12.

the ILP. Its activities form a rather unusual minor chapter in the history of British socialist thought.

Quaker socialism

The Socialist Quaker Society was established in 1898, and its affairs were wound up by its last secretary, Mr. Stephen James Thorne,[134] in 1924. On 2 April 1898 Mary O'Brien, Joseph Theodore Harris, Thomas Dent, H. G. Dalton, and five other members of the Society of Friends met at 27, Yonge Park, London, N., and founded the Socialist Quaker Society, in order to make clear to the Society of Friends:

1. The meaning of Socialism;
2. Their responsibilities towards Socialism as a solution of the problems of today;
3. Their unique position for the spread of Socialism.[135]

From the outset the aim was clearly to convert Quakers to socialism, not to convert socialists to Christianity or even to spread socialism among non-Quakers.

There were many good reasons why Quakers should be socialists. The three historic Quaker beliefs—the priesthood of all believers, the sacredness of every personality, and the "Inner Light"—were essentially democratic and egalitarian. George Fox (1624-1691) would have been repelled by Victorian "churchianity." In the eyes of some Quakers the historic faith of the Friends had been subverted, however. As the democratic sect became an established church, its members shed their radicalism. They succeeded brilliantly, as debarred minorities without civil rights are wont to do, by specializing at the trades and professions left open to them

[134] I am grateful to Mr. Thorne for an enlightening conversation about the SQS and related matters. He is at present the recording clerk of the Society of Friends. The history of the SQS can be traced through two manuscript Minute Books (1898-1909; 1910-1913), the journal *Ploughshare* (1912-1919), and the Society's Tracts (1898-1901) (Friends' House Library, London).

[135] SQS Minute Book I, 2 April 1898. The longhand minute books are unpaginated. Quotations will be made by date of entry, and quoted hereafter as Minute Book I or Minute Book II.

by society, which in the case of the Friends were banking and the iron industry. In the eighteenth century they became respectable, some of them even rich, and consequently quietist and socially conservative. The evangelical revival of the early nineteenth century, which affected all churches, produced a crop of ethical reformers and humanitarians among Quakers, people like Joseph Sturge and J. G. Whittier (the abolitionists), Elizabeth Fry, Joseph Lancaster, John Bright, and J. J. Gurney. Quakers led the Anglo-American movements for abolition of the slave trade, penal reform, care of the insane, abolition of capital punishment, pacifism, universal education, temperance, women's rights, and religious toleration. But the evangelical Quakers were emphatically individualistic, bourgeois, and charity-prone. J. J. Gurney, for example, a younger brother of Elizabeth Fry, though full of moral passion was extremely evangelical; he preached in America and England a terrifying gospel of original sin and innate moral depravity. His group dominated the London Yearly Meeting and imposed on the faith a Bible-worshiping, morally and social stultifying creed which almost choked out of existence the central tenet of seventeenth-century Quakers—the "Inner Light." By the mid-Victorian era, Gurney's "fire and vision" had died away, leaving behind what one Quaker scholar has called a "harsh and rigid scoria of credal thought which none must be allowed to question."[136]

Roughly, the "left wing" and "right wing" of Victorian Quakerism were represented by belief in the Inner Light and worship of the Bible respectively. After an attempt was made by conservatives to abandon altogether the Inner Light doctrine at the Yearly Meeting of 1861, a radical movement of young Quakers came into prominence at Manchester, led, as we have seen, by David Duncan. By the eighties and nineties the more advanced Quakers were ready to liberalize their theology and to revert to long-

[136] R. C. Scott, *Journal of the Friends' Historical Society*, Vol. 49, No. 2 (Spring 1960), p. 75.

obscured Quaker traditions. J. W. Graham (1859-1932) [137] of Dalton Hall, Manchester, E. Vipont Brown (1863-1955), and J. W. Rowntree (1868-1905) between them hammered out a modern Quaker faith. "We stopped thinking in the 17th century," said Rowntree. "The thought-stuff of Fox, Penington and Barclay was never properly worked-out. We never understood the Inward Light. . . . The solution lies in a deeper interpretation of the person and message of Jesus Christ." This rediscovery of *"the indwelling God"* in every human was accompanied, said Rowntree, by "a notable stirring of the social conscience. Poverty in its hideous shape is regarded not as a fixed institution but as a social disease, an evil too great to be borne. That the many should suffer a stunted life while a few enjoy the freedom of wealth and leisure is a contradiction of brotherhood." [138]

When the Richmond (Indiana) "Declaration of Faith" was announced in the USA in 1887—a conservative declaration full of evangelistic promises of eternal punishment (or bliss), and centered on Bible worship—the huge London Yearly Meeting of the following year refused to accept it. The meeting was divided because Edward Grubb had led a young faction to oppose the Declaration, therefore no official comment was made on the document at all. [139] Brit-

[137] A biography of J. W. Graham is being prepared by his son, Michael Graham, of Eccles, Lanes (personal knowledge).

[138] J. W. Rowntree, *Essays and Addresses* (London, 1905), pp. 242-244.

[139] J. Dudley, *Edward Grubb* (London, 1940), p. 57. The 1888 Meeting was a contrast with that of five years before, at which the traditional *Book of Christian Discipline* was revised and the following inserted: "Let the poor of this world remember that it is Our Heavenly Father's will that all his children should be rich *in faith*. . . . Do your utmost to maintain yourselves and your families in an honourable independence and by prudent care in time of health to provide for sickness and old age. . . ." Here spoke the Quaker employer. In 1870, however, a classic statement of the upper-class position was made by Robert Barclay, objecting to the admission of "the lower orders" to membership in the Society of Friends: "They *have* the benefit of attending our Meetings and Mission Halls. . . . Do you wish to invite chimney-sweepers, costermongers, or even blacksmiths, to dinner on First-day? Do you intend to give their sons and daughters a boarding-school education? . . . There is the crossing-sweeper! He is a Christian.

ish Quakerism was starting on a different and more socially conscious road than its US counterpart.[140] Stewart Headlam's *Church Reformer* spoke very highly of British Quakers in 1889 for their opposition to "Bible-religion" and their notion of the Holy Spirit.[141] But the great turning point in Quaker history was the Manchester Conference of 1895.

The Yearly Meeting called in November 1895 an extraordinary conference to consider, for the first time, the place of Quakerism in modern society and thought. About 500 delegates and up to 800 visitors met, with men and women treated equally.[142] The chairman, Dr. R. Spruce Watson,[143] pleaded for a "careful, anxious, open-minded" consideration of all social ideas, including socialism. Watson's distinction between Christian and state socialism, disparaging to the latter, did not please H. C. Rowe of the Labour Church;[144] but Watson emphasized that "if the religious view is good for anything, it is good for everything." Mrs.

. . . But is that any reason . . . [to] invite him to dinner and encourage your daughter to associate with him in her civil and social capacity?" (R. E. Stogg, "Friends' Queries and General Advices, 1860-1928," *Journal of the Friends' Historical Society*, Vol. 49, No. 5 [Autumn 1961], p. 260; the *Friend*, New Ser., Vol. 23 [1883], p. 148; the *Monthly Record*, I, No. 9 [15 January 1870]. For the last quotation I am grateful to Mr. E. H. Milligan, Librarian of the Society.)

140 See Rufus M. Jones, *The Later Period of Quakerism*, 2 vols. (London, 1921), II, 942, 951-958. Jones ascribed a good deal to the Adult Education Movement, begun by Joseph Sturge: "It has gradually carried almost the entire body of Friends in Great Britain into a solid and serious consideration of the basic questions of economics, politics and social order, and it has changed them from the most exclusive religious denomination—a peculiar people—into a body as deeply concerned as any in the world for the reformation and reconstruction of the social and economic conditions." He made no mention of the Socialist Quaker Society.

141 *Church Reformer*, VIII, No. 12 (December 1889), pp. 281-282.

142 *Labour Prophet*, IV, No. 48 (December 1895), pp. 179-180.

143 1837-1911. Born in Gateshead; son of an Anti-Corn Law leader; educated at University College, London. President of the National Liberal Club, Fellow of the Royal Geographical Society, Toynbee Trustee, etc. (DQB), "Poet, prose-writer, traveller, lawyer and orator" (E. N. Armitage, *The Quaker Poets of Great Britain and Ireland* [London, 1896], p. 283).

144 *Labour Prophet*, loc.cit.

Frances Thompson spoke of evolution much as Thomas Child or Cunnington Goldsack did: "Darwin's dictum, that those communities which included the greatest number of the most sympathetic minds would flourish best, is a scientific fact." Liberal Social Darwinism, linking evolution and progress, should be "peculiarly congenial to a Church which holds as its cardinal belief the guiding Inward Light, or the immediate inspiration of every soul without the intervention of priest or ritual. We, of all people, should hail with joy the thought that knowledge of all kinds is progressive." Mrs. Thompson was strongly supported in her optimistic reform Darwinism by J. W. Graham. Henry Priestman of Leeds said that the writings of socialism revealed a passionate Christian demand for justice and brotherhood. Another Priestman—Walter—attacked urban slums:

> In Birmingham you find places of gross darkness, where the little children play and if you ask the ratepayers to light them, they say if you light the courts and alleys the rates will go up. Are the little children to die in the darkness because it is a question between the landlord and the public rate?

S. G. Hobson, future leader of Guild Socialism, and at this time Keir Hardie's secretary, told his fellow Quakers not to miss the great opportunity for Christian social reform which capitalism had created. The momentous conference concluded by condemning the "startling contrasts between great luxury and extreme poverty."[145]

The Quakers, commented the *Labour Prophet,* had "more influence and more wealth" than any other religious body of a similar size. "It will be a great day for Socialism when the Society of Friends adds Industrial Freedom to the long list of causes for which it has toiled, suffered, and shed both its blood and its gold." Two years later the Fabian Society thought fit to republish an eighteenth-century Quaker pamphlet, John Woolman's *A Word of Remembrance and Cau-*

---

[145] *Manchester Conference of the Society of Friends, 1895* (London, 1896), pp. 138-146, 157-158, 167-168, 197-199, 202.

tion to the Rich, as its Tract No. 79.[146] Such were some of the deep-rooted and the immediate origins of the Socialist Quaker Society.

The constitution of the SQS was modeled on that of the Society of Friends. Its only "office," that of "clerk," was held by J. T. Harris for nine years, 1898-1907. Anyone desiring membership in SQS was "understood to have unity with its principles" and admitted usually after interview. At the first meeting fifteen likely Friends not present were circulated by printed draft and many of them subsequently joined, including C. H. Wynne of Leicester and Arthur Priestman.[147] The latter, a socialist Town Councillor of Bradford, was a local cloth manufacturer who had faced the social question at first hand in Adult School and as an employer. He had long searched for an "intermediate resting-place in some form of Liberalism or Radicalism," but had ended up a socialist. On the Bradford Council he worked steadily for municipalization, and would extend it from trams, gas, water, and electricity to milk, bread, alcohol, and other spheres. He sat on Keir Hardie's election fund committee in 1900, and wrote SQS Tract No. 3, *The Gambling Spirit* (1904).[148]

Arthur Priestman was responsible for inviting the famous American socialist and evangelist Rev. J. Stitt Wilson to Bradford. Stitt Wilson (who will be discussed later) com-

---

[146] *Labour Prophet, loc.cit.* See also *Brotherhood,* III, No. 8 (December 1895), p. 99; *A Word of Remembrance and Caution to the Rich,* Fabian Tract No. 79 (London, 1897). At one time or another the executive committee of the Fabian Society included the Quaker Socialists Mary O'Brien and S. G. Hobson. Percy Alden (Friends' Social Union) was also an executive member. E. R. Pease was, of course, of a distinguished Quaker family, though not an active Friend. He lectured for the SQS on 28 January 1901.

[147] Minute Book I, 2 April 1898. Wynne was secretary of the Leicester branch of the Christian Socialist Society (see the section on the Society above). He was an active member of SQS (admitted 23 April 1898) in Leicester, and his lecture at the Yearly Meeting of 1902 on "Competition" was demanded as an SQS tract (Minute Book II, 25 May 1900, 25 February 1902, 25 March 1902, 29 April and 29 May 1902).

[148] Minute Book I, 25 January 1900, 26 April 1904, 31 May 1904. See also *Friends' Quarterly Examiner,* October 1904, pp. 16ff.; and W. Stewart, *Keir Hardie* (London, 1921), p. 173. Priestman was not formally admitted to the SQS until 1909 (Minute Book I, 28 October 1909).

pared Priestman to the Christian socialist Mayor "Golden Rule" Jones of Toledo, Ohio: "He seeks social righteousness. As an individual he is a man of royal character. . . . His break from the capitalist class to which he naturally belongs has caused them dismay and has not been without cost to him." Stitt Wilson held a dozen socialist meetings for Quakers in Bradford, York, and elsewhere. Wilson claimed that his own emphasis on Divine Immanence was a twentieth-century statement of the Quaker Inward Light doctrine— God is in every man. Both Arthur Priestman and his wife (Board of Guardians), were elected to local office on a Socialist ticket in Bradford.[149]

Another Bradford Priestman—Alfred Tuke Priestman— was admitted to the SQS in June 1901, after giving "a strong, clear paper" at that year's Yearly Meeting, "Socialism, an Essentially Christian Movement," subsequently published as SQS Tract No. 2. "The last generation," he said, "placed political power in the hands of the people; the political problem of this generation is how to teach the people to use that power." Furthermore, "the past generation learned how to produce material wealth in practically unlimited quantity; this generation has yet to learn how to distribute it." A. T. Priestman felt that "events were moving very fast . . . in all human probability it largely depends upon us who are here tonight whether the Society of Friends takes its right place in making the social changes of the twentieth century a truly religious reformation." Have Christians the faith in the vital truths they profess to hold? Socialism, at the least, is "an experiment, on the hypothesis that Christ's teaching is true."[150]

Joseph Theodore Harris (1870-1958), SQS secretary, had been educated at Bootham and Owen's College (Manchester University) as a Dalton Hall resident. In Manchester,

[149] *Brotherhood*, VII, No. 12 (April 1900), pp. 182-183.

[150] Minute Book I, 28 March, 25 April, 14 May, 25 June, 30 June, 30 July 1901. *Friends' Quarterly Examiner* (July 1901) also published A. T. Priestman's talk (*Socialism, an Essentially Christian Movement*, SQS Tract No. 2 [London, 1901], pp. 1-16).

Harris had already helped with John Trevor's Labour Church movement, and he was also involved in Bruce Wallace's Brotherhood Trust. As a Quaker radical he was naturally a member (along with the Baptist John Clifford) of the No-Conscription Fellowship in World War I and the National Peace Committee.[151] Harris's wife, the former Dr. Mary O'Brien, was an extremely energetic SQS member and author of its Tract No. 1 (1898). She served on the Fabian Society's executive committee for three years (1898-1901) and worked for the Fabian Women's Group in later years.[152] They were married in 1901, after three years of running the SQS together. Mary O'Brien pointed out to fellow Quakers at a Stoke Newington address in the winter of 1899: "While we as Friends had been willing to accept Christ's teaching as regards oaths and war, we had not ventured to apply His almost equally explicit teaching as regards wealth and possessions." All this was now past, and, added her husband-to-be, Friends were "specially fitted by organization, by education and by tradition" for the work of socialism. Individual workers, said J. T. Harris, must "renounce the self-life" and work collectively "for the uplift of Humanity, which is enslaved by the collective action of Society." Otherwise Quakers would be bypassed by history, and "their candlestick . . . removed out of its place."[153]

The first action taken by the couple in the new socialist society was to call a separate conference within the Yearly Meeting of 1898 to discuss "the best methods for spreading

---

[151] "A Hebrew prophet—his bearded and unkempt visage, with clear and burning voice reminded many of Elijah." In later life (he died at eighty-eight) Harris dominated Yearly Meetings, taking usually a conservative stand on issues of personal morality. It is hard to imagine what he would make of the recent (1963) "Quaker Report" on sex (conversation with Mr. E. H. Milligan; DQB).

[152] For some reason she opposed (as did E. R. Pease) the H. G. Wells Committee suggestion that a feminist clause be inserted in the Fabian Society's "Basis," but Beatrice Webb and Mrs. Pember Reeves pushed the motion through on 11 January 1907 (Pease, pp. 177, 271, 282).

[153] Minute Book I, 25 January 1900. Mary O'Brien Harris's Tract, *The Oneness of Religious and Secular Life*, a reprint from the *Friends' Quarterly Examiner*, was printed for SQS by the Brotherhood Press in 1898 (Minute Book I, 30 June 1898, 29 September 1898).

socialism amongst the Society of Friends." About eighty people attended and "admitted that Friends might be influenced towards Socialism." If their "sense of honesty" was appealed to, "they might easily be led to see that every man should have the opportunity of work." (This was perhaps a wise approach to a church so dominated by successful employers.) A monthly letter would be placed in the *Friend;* the secretary was to keep in regular touch with the growing country membership of the SQS; the Society must itself hold regular monthly meetings.[154]

Joseph and Mary Harris recommended Bruce Wallace's Brotherhood Trust as a good movement for their fellow Quakers to join. Their own interest in this and other cooperative and communitarian ventures became especially strong immediately after the First World War. J. T. Harris was also involved in a Ruskinian Production-for-Use League. His wife, at a postwar London Yearly Meeting, called for a "new ethic" to meet the needs of British society; the special investigating committee which was appointed to look into this question reported in favor of communitarian experimentation (with the support of Percy Alden). In February 1918 the Friends established the Pioneer Trust, with Mary O'Brien Harris as a director, and (in cooperation with Bruce Wallace's organization) moved into the Garden City movement.

Still, in the main, the Harrises' advice to Quakers in 1898 was that "each Friend should be encouraged to faithfully follow the Light within, by thinking out these questions for himself." Socialist Quakers should lay bare the individual's responsibility as a producer (to produce *useful* things), and as a consumer (not to make present conditions worse). "It is necessary to give back to the community as much as is received."[155]

At the Friends' Yearly Meeting of 1899 over 150 people met separately to hear papers by Arthur Priestman, J. T. Harris, and Percy Wallis on socialism, unemployment, and

[154] Minute Book I, 23 April, 16 May, 2 June 1898.
[155] Minute Book I, 30 June 1898. See also Armytage, pp. 357, 403-404.

municipalization at the SQS's own meeting. At a smaller session the time was not yet judged ripe for a Quaker socialist journal. Branches were flourishing, however, in Bradford, Leicester, and in Birmingham (with which group closer cooperation was demanded).[156] The SQS grew slowly and sedately as its work—mainly consisting of public lectures, propaganda at Yearly Meetings, and tracts—prospered.[157] In 1900 the big moral issue was naturally the Boer War, and the SQS attracted an audience of about 150 Friends to a debate on "War and Economics."[158] In 1901 the group considered giving political support to certain candidates in London County Council elections, but did not take this momentous step—at least not as a society. Much time was taken up, as among Swedenborgians and others, with consideration of what was meant by "socialism." Quakers sought a practical and detailed definition; Wynne's paper at the 1902 Yearly Meeting provoked a "somewhat unsettled" discussion, mainly of the difficulties of *implementing* socialism.[159]

Gradually the original *élan* of the SQS seemed to be receding, despite the Society's choice of the left-wing socialist S. G. Hobson to talk at the Yearly Meeting of 1903. Discussion was poor among the 175 present, and numbers fell off after 1903. Only 70 attended the SQS lecture at the Yearly Meeting of 1905, 55 in 1906, and members stopped attending the monthly meetings of SQS itself. During 1906 business was sometimes conducted with only two or three present. J. T. Harris retired as clerk in 1907, and some resignations of members occurred.[160]

156 Minute Book I, 26 June 1899, 27 September 1899.

157 Any paper to be delivered on behalf of the SQS at a Yearly Meeting was first read privately to the group itself for friendly criticism and emendations.

158 Minute Book I, 28 June 1900. C. H. Wynne reported that "the South African War overshadows everything in Leicester" (25 May 1900).

159 Minute Book I, 28 February 1901, 30 August 1901, 29 May 1902.

160 Minute Book I, 31 March, 30 June 1903, 27 June 1905, 13 March, 10 July 1906, 29 October 1907, 28 January 1908. Harris was replaced by Charles Fowler (1907-1910), a recent new member (5 November 1906). H. G. Dalton and M. Dalton resigned in January 1908.

The major source of trouble for the SQS was the creation of a more moderate and respectable rival body, the Friends' Social Union, in 1904; its members included powerful figures such as B. Seebohm Rowntree and George Cadbury, J. W. Graham, and Edward Grubb. The FSU damaged the Socialist Quaker Society in the same way that the CSU had damaged the Guild of St. Matthew. In and after 1908, however, the SQS had a considerable resurgence.

A major disadvantage of the SQS (like that of the Swedenborgians) was the hostility of Quaker authorities. For almost two years the Society fought for the right to use official Devonshire House rooms for its meetings. The Friends' "Premises Committee" consistently refused permission until 1900.[161] Official Quaker journals were reluctant to print SQS material or reports of SQS meetings and resolutions; in 1899 the group had to send a special letter to the editors of the *Friend* and the *British Friend* explaining that they were not "anarchists":

> The SQS is under a living concern to know the Divine Will in respect to the pressing economic problems. . . . The fact that the Churches have been slow to obey the teaching of their Master . . . is a special call to us who lay so much stress on Spiritual Truth. . . . The SQS is inspired by the Spiritual Realities of Quakerism and desires to manifest these in social life.[162]

Things improved a little after 1901, when the liberal-minded Edward Grubb became editor of the *British Friend,* but its companion journal remained recalcitrant. The *Friends' Quarterly Examiner,* on the other hand, was quite cooperative in printing articles by SQS members and allowing many offprints for the group's use.[163]

It was difficult to devise a socialist Quaker propaganda

---

[161] Minute Book I, 27 April 1899, 22 February, 27 September 1900.

[162] Minute Book I, 30 November 1899. SQS had been accused of having connections with an Anarchist Colony in Gloucestershire, where certain "excesses" had occurred. (Some other Quakers, in fact, had been involved.)

[163] Minute Book I, 9 November 1900, 30 July 1901, 29 October 1901.

which would appeal to "intellectual Friends on the one hand and 'evangelical' Friends on the other." Should the SQS appeal to the heart or to the head? The evangelicals spoke "a different theological language"; their "intense individuality" was a barrier to reception of the socialist message. But, one meeting reported, "there is a spiritual force working through Evangelicalism which we should recognize and if possible work along with," in spite of the fact that "ignorance and fear largely keep Evangelicals from seeing further than their creed." Looking back from the vantage point of 1963, Mr. Stephen James Thorne sees the inner dynamic of Quaker socialism to be a status conflict between a group of young, unestablished, intellectual radicals of modest means and the great, sturdy Quaker business families, deep-rooted, socially conservative, pious, and rich.[164] This "sociological" interpretation does not alter the fact, however, as Mr. Thorne himself would be quick to point out, that the SQS was fighting to reaffirm what it regarded as a genuine historic Quaker social faith too long forgotten.

In 1908 SQS affairs began to prosper once more: a hundred and twenty Friends were attracted to a successful conference on the "Socialist Attitude to Poverty," chaired by E. V. Brown at the Yearly Meeting. Two hundred heard Ralph Crowley's paper on "Socialism and Philanthropy" in 1909, and the group was encouraged by the new growth to plan bigger meetings. Four of its monthly conferences were thrown open to the Quaker public (October 1909-February 1910).[165] J. T. Harris undertook a heavy lecturing program all over the country, ranging from Manchester to Maidstone, in 1910-1911. All was still not well between the SQS and the Society at large, however. The Yearly Meeting's "Committee on Social Questions" published in 1910 a pamphlet-report, *The Stewardship of Wealth*, which socialist

[164] Minute Book I, 26 June 1899, 26 July 1900; personal conversation with Mr. Thorne.
[165] Minute Book I, 30 June, 28 July 1908, 29 June 1909. Mary E. Thorne replaced Fowler as "clerk" of SQS in 1910. She and her husband (A. B. Thorne) had both been admitted on 30 November 1909.

Quakers found very unsatisfactory. The report recommended "Social-Unionism" of the Anglican CSU kind, "Christian shopping," and pleas to employers not to take advantage of their workers. "It seems little short of mockery," said the SQS, "to suggest the purchase of articles 'truly useful, well-made and produced under righteous conditions,' when we know that however good the conditions in one stage of production may be, there are conditions . . . on which we have no check." Only socialism could provide all the necessary checks; the Committee's suggestions were "a blank wall of impracticability." Moreover, the stewardship dogma could be used to satisfy "current feelings of social compunction" and "divert effort from the more radical changes necessary." Quaker employers and property owners "should only consider themselves Stewards *until* the community is ready to take over the means of production." Community stewardship was better than individual stewardship.[166]

Disappointing SQS meetings were held at Peckham and at Hampstead (where L. H. Wedmore spoke on "Some Economic Aspects of the Kingdom of God") in 1911, and the Society concluded it was useless trying to attract to special conferences Friends who were not already socially conscious. ("Until we can get Friends to think impersonally it is impossible to make much progress.") Socialists must work from within normal Yearly and Monthly Meetings.[167] All the same, the SQS circulated in September 1911 a handsomely designed and printed Letter to fellow Quakers urging their support for the "direct social mode of *production for use*" as against the "indirect individual mode of *production for profit*." The echoes of John Ruskin and of the ideals of Bruce Wallace's Brotherhood Trust were loud and clear in this Letter. About 9,000 copies were distributed. The Letter defined socialism (a word from which "many

---

[166] Minute Book II, 26 July 1910. The *Friend* refused to publish this criticism (Minute Book II, 25 October 1910); but it was placed as a letter in the *British Friend* in November 1910 (Minute Book II, 29 November 1910).

[167] Minute Book II, 28 March and 18 June 1911.

Friends shrink") in three ways: as "the recognition of a long and hastening evolution" ("trustified" capitalism), and as "a series of propositions made in the sphere of politics tending to facilitate the transference of industry from its individualist "business" mode of production . . . to its true social mode." Industrial capitalism has obscured the primary function of industry, and "streams of evil continuously flow from a system that asks no questions as to the ultimate *utility* of its processes, so long as a *profit* be found." Foreign policy was also subjected to economic analysis, in terms now traditional in Christian socialism:

> Preparation for war and war itself has of late years become a logical extension of the competitive struggle for markets and spheres of commercial influence. Modern war must be recognized as an adjunct to the nation's business and is entered upon solely in the interests of the capitalist class.

This line of argument could not be better calculated to appeal to pacifist Friends: "the highest aim of Socialism is to render war—industrial, commercial and military—no longer necessary."[168]

Quaker reaction to the Letter of 1911, which soon became a *cause célèbre,* revealed hidden depths of conservatism among many Friends. One correspondent "abhorred" socialism, which he thought was "ruining the Nation, body and soul" in 1911:

> If, instead of preaching Socialism you endeavoured to make all contented with their allotted sphere of life and to seek to glorify God in the place where he has put them, great good might be done. . . . It is only a wild chimera to suppose we are all going to be equal, we were never intended to be, and never shall be. *The more money the rich have the better it is for the poor.*

[168] "A Letter from the SQS to Their Fellow Members of the Society of Friends" (February 1911); Minute Book II, 30 April 1912. The Letter was also reprinted in the *Friend,* New Ser., 51, No. 44 (November 1911), p. 715.

What England lacked, he said, was religion. A similar writer found the very term Quaker socialist "quite as objectionable as Quaker Whiskey, and that was stopped." Socialism was "the greatest curse of the present time—setting class against class." And this correspondent added tartly: "May I ask if our Yearly Meeting has sanctioned the absurd doctrines propounded in your letter?" Yet another conservative claimed that "black and white do not differ more than the Spiritual life aimed at by the Friends of old and the material life which appears to be the paradise of the Socialist." One extraordinary objection for a Quaker to make was that "the Roman Church has spoken very clearly to Christians in reference to Socialism. . . . Until Pius X or his successors are guided to an expression of a more favourable opinion, I do not think that any Sect should step in where the Church cannot tread."[169] Many letters of approval were also received, and nine new members joined the SQS, including Katherine Parker, who was directly influenced by the Letter.

Perhaps it was the reaction to the Letter of 1911 that caused some Quaker socialists to think it would be politic to retract a little at the 1912 Yearly Meeting. It was suggested that "great care should be exercised not to antagonize Friends by introducing Socialist economics. . . . The first point to be aimed at is to help Friends to *feel a conviction of sin* for the present system of industry."[170] Nevertheless, telegrams of fraternal greeting were exchanged with the ILP Conference at Merthyr Tydfil. At an open meeting of the SQS six months later L. H. Wedmore examined "Why the Society of Friends Does Not Want Socialism." Quakers, said Wedmore, generally fell into five classes:

1. *The feeble-minded:* which statistics show form a larger proportion pro rata than of any other religious body in England.

169 Report of the SQS Committee that drafted the Letter, Minute Book II, 30 April 1912 (names of correspondents are not given).
170 Minute Book II, 4 June 1912.

2. *The Nominal Quaker:* who forms so effective a padding to our books of membership today.
3. *The Evangelical or Conservative* element.
4. *The Higher Criticism or Radical* element.
5. A small remnant of *Independent thinkers.*

The only hope for Quaker socialism lay in groups 4 and 5. Group 1, Wedmore explained, had grown up through the constant intermarriage of rich Quaker families over the years in order to avoid the breaking-up of large fortunes![171]

November 1912 saw the first issue of the SQS quarterly: *Ploughshare.* Its title was the invention of Dr. Mary O'Brien Harris;[172] its editor was William Loftus Hare (1868-1943), pioneer photoengraver and color printer, town planning enthusiast, Tolstoyan, expert on comparative religion, and theosophical lecturer. Hare was at one time a church elder and was an original member of the Friends' War and Social Order Committee. In *Ploughshare* he "gave the best of his theological and philosophical knowledge, and preached with that deep earnestness that was his, the gospel of a new and more Christian social order."[173] Until the end of World War I, Hare was aided by Hugh William Peet (1886-1951).[174]

Ploughshare was created to proselytize more successfully among Quakers as well as to give greater unity to existing socialists within the Society of Friends. In addition, the

171 Minute Book II, 28 January 1913.
172 Minute Book II, 27 August 1912.
173 A Derby man; admitted to SQS on 16 February 1911. Executive member of the Garden Cities and Town Planning Association and editor of *Town and Country Planning* for four years. Founder-member of the Society for Promoting the Study of Religions, and editor of its journal, *Religion* (1930-1935). Author of several works on comparative religion, meditation, and mysticism (the *Friend,* CI [5 March 1943], 171-172).
174 Born in Dulwich; a journalist on *The Byestander* (1903) and later assistant editor of the *Daily News.* Moved to the Society of Friends out of Congregationalism around 1910. Secretary of the Friends' Central Literary Council (about 1920). Jailed for pacifism during World War I. Peet edited the *Friend* from 1932 to 1949, doubling its circulation (DQB).

journal looked outward to the day when it could "take part in establishing the principles which will transform capitalism into socialism" in the world at large. "The promoters . . . aspire therefore to the generation of a spiritual force which shall direct and control the activities of those who engage in that social reconstruction." After fourteen years' existence the SQS needed its own journal to obviate being refused space elsewhere. The facts had to be published: that the rich in England were "81 times as rich as the poor"; that one-tenth of the population owned nine-tenths of the wealth; that civilization faced the three alternatives —continuation of the present injustice, violent revolution, or the "middle way" of democratic socialism. "The loss of spiritual life of which our empty meeting-houses and churches and our feverish self-examination and anxious search for remedies are but symptoms," wrote Mrs. Harris, "cannot be repaired till material conditions for rich and poor . . . are ruled by the laws of righteousness."[175] Accordingly, *Ploughshare* began criticizing the mild reformism of the Friends' Social Union, and agitated for improved public education, municipal socialism, and socialized medicine.

The medical expert of the SQS was Dr. C. A. Parker (F.R.C.S., Edinburgh), a well-to-do Upper Wimpole Street surgeon who denounced the British Medical Association as Britain's "most ruthless trade union." His wife, Katherine Parker,[176] held SQS meetings at their London home and

[175] *Ploughshare*, No. 1 (November 1912), pp. 1-3; No. 2 (February 1913), p. 19.

[176] Katherine Eleanor Borradaile Parker, 1866-1949. Brought up in the Church of England, but disliked its ritual. Attracted by a Quaker annual gathering at Jordan's (ca. 1890); began to attend regularly at the Westminster Meeting and later at Hampstead (ca. 1900). Studied Quaker literature very deeply during her absence from London. Admitted to the Society of Friends as a full member on 13 July 1911 (and to SQS on 27 February 1912). The delay was caused by her difficulties over accepting pacifism. Left London in 1914 and remained a staunch Quaker; an elder in High Wycombe (1914-1941); moved to Bath (1941-1948) and died in Cheltenham, aged eighty-three (the *Friend*, LII, No. 48 [15 November 1912]; Minute Book II, 27 August and 29 October 1912; "Westminster & Longford Monthly Meeting: Minutes," Vol. 27, No. 269 [1911]; information traced by Mr. E. H. Milligan, Friends' House Library).

was a critic of "Social-Unionism." (Edward Grubb refused to publish her socialist criticisms of his own articles on "Christianity and Business" in the *British Friend*.) Her husband gave "Some Reasons for a Complete State Medical Service" in *Ploughshare* (February 1913), while Katherine took up an earlier theme of A. T. Priestman, "Socialism, an Essentially Christian Movement," at the Yearly Meeting in the summer. She cited the communism of the early Church and contrasted it with more recent statistics of inequality. Jesus, she said, set about "the democratization of religion, which for the first time in history ceased to be the privilege of a class set apart." Socialism, in spite of its emphasis on political and economic matters, was in its origins "essentially spiritual," and not until justice had been won in material life could "the spiritual uplifting of the human race as a whole" make a beginning. The Society of Friends "in its very form is a Socialist organisation." Quakers should, therefore, fight for socialism, so that "true Individualism [which] is only possible in a State where wealth, health and opportunity are common to all," can be realized as soon as possible.[177] Dr. Parker's stand for socialized medicine was not unusually advanced for his day. The idea had been around in socialist circles for some years. The *New Age* had publicized propaganda for such a proposal in 1908 (M. D. Eder), and a Socialist Medical League had been created in 1909. Sidney and Beatrice Webb in *The State and the Doctor* (1910) had suggested a plan for a State Medical Service administered through Local Health Authorities and Medical Officers of Health. In 1913 the Labour Party included a proposal for a state medical service among its resolutions for the nationalization of canals, railways, land, and coal.[178]

[177] Minute Book II, 30 April, 4 June 1912, 10 June 1912. See also *Ploughshare*, No. 4 (August 1913), pp. 41-43, No. 2 (February 1913), pp. 20-23; Katherine Parker, *Socialism: An Essentially Christian Movement* (Cambridge, 1913), passim.

[178] Apart from the relevant volumes of the *New Age* and the Webbs' work, see A. M. McBriar, *Fabian Socialism and English Politics*, pp. 276, 318.

Like the Anglican socialists of the Church Socialist League, the Quakers were deeply disturbed by two phenomena in the late 1900's: the approach of World War I and the emergence of Guild Socialism. For obvious reasons the coming of the war helped to double the membership of the SQS between 1909 and 1913, and in the winter of 1913 the society began to cooperate fully with ILP pacifists in the "No-Conscription" battle. An SQS member, J. T. Walton Newbold, wrote pacifist articles in the *Labour Leader,* and an SQS leaflet declared:

> The organised forces of the aristocratic hierarchy of Army and Navy, and of the financial interests of banks, bondholders, shareholders in the armament ring, and profitmongers of all descriptions—will be difficult to meet. . . . Friends of peace in the Labour world will need all the help that can be got from other lovers of peace throughout the country. . . . The spirit shown at the time of the Boer War is readily evoked in the ignorant and unbalanced section of the public.

The Friends' Social Union was belabored for its failure to rise to greatness and for its "highly philosophic" piety about economic problems. "Behind the Defence Acts of the Colonies stands 'business'; behind the Balkan Wars, new and old, in the end will be found 'business,'" said *Ploughshare,* and the Yearly Meeting's "Committee on Business Difficulties," it claimed, had failed to penetrate to the roots of the problem.[179] In the ILP a prominent Quaker artist, Joseph Edward Southall (1861-1944), played an important role as a pacifist leader.[180]

Meanwhile, Guild Socialism came to the SQS through the direct medium of one of its principal exponents, S. G.

[179] Minute Book II, 25 May 1913; *Ploughshare,* No. 4 (August 1913), pp. 37-40.

[180] Southall attended regular Monthly Meetings only after he was forty years old. As a young artist he had become a disciple of William Morris, Ruskin, and Carpaccio. He served the Friends' Peace Committee for forty years (*A Testimony to the Life of J. E. Southall* [London, 1946], passim).

Hobson (1864-1940). Samuel Hobson, whose work in the Guild movement has already been described above in this chapter, joined the Socialist Quaker Society on 27 April 1899. Politically he was without doubt the most radical Quaker of his day. A founder-member of the ILP and an active Fabian socialist for over twenty years (1887-1909), Hobson served on the Fabian executive from 1900, and wrote Tract No. 119 in 1905, *Public Control of Electric Power and Transit.* As we have seen, he was a dissident, always at odds with the "old gang," Bernard Shaw and the Webbs, and it was Hobson whose defiant motion of 1909, soon after the Victor Grayson affair, split the Fabian Society. Hobson came to the Quaker socialist movement in 1899 via the Bristol socialists and a Welsh Fabian group in Cardiff, of which the Irish chemist H. C. Rowe (later editor of the *Labour Prophet*) was a dominant member. Hobson was rapidly drawn into the Labour Church movement and was elected to its executive council, where his main function seems to have been to mediate between its two warring leaders, John Trevor and Fred Brocklehurst. Another Cardiff Fabian, Richard Thomas, was a great influence in Hobson's evolution. Together they studied "one of the germinal books of history," *Fabian Essays,* in 1890. In 1894 Hobson became Keir Hardie's private secretary and grew deeply involved in the infant ILP, becoming also a contributor to Hardie's *Labour Leader.* At the crucial Manchester Conference of the Society of Friends in 1895, as noted, Hobson spoke up strongly for socialism. He chastised Quakers for driving out of the faith the young radicals. Having urged socialism in orations on street-corners for seven years, he felt qualified to "speak with an intimate knowledge of what is going on in the advanced labour movement," and he warned his fellow Quakers that "The Labour movement of today is essentially a non-dogmatic religious movement. It only needs the guidance of Friends of leisure and culture to give it that religious enthusiasm which can alone secure a great future for social progress." Defections from the Quaker faith by young people were heavy, he claimed. A "great corporate pronouncement" by the Conference in favor of socialism was the only answer.

Hobson worked hard for the ILP and the Fabians. It was his idea to set up a "Labour Members Guarantee Fund" (originally his resolution at a Fabian meeting). In 1901 he was the official Fabian spokesman for this scheme at the Labour Representation Committee Conference, and a year later the "Parliamentary Fund" to pay Labour MP's salaries became a reality. But as early as the Fabian Conference of 1892 Hobson was already a member of the provincial "ginger group" who seemed restive under the thumb of the London Society. In 1899 he struggled with Bernard Shaw, the executive's spokesman, against Fabian policy on the Boer War. His demand that the Society "dissociate itself from the Imperialism of Capitalism and vainglorious Nationalism" by a formal vote of censure on government policy and a repudiation of the war was refused. Hobson stayed with the Fabians all the same for another ten years and finally resigned from the executive after his failure of 1909 to convince the Society's leaders that they should disavow the Labour Party and create a rival Socialist Representation Committee. From that point on he drifted increasingly into the *New Age* orbit and toward Guild Socialism. Looking back on many years of activity and experience in the British socialist movement, the essence of Hobson's reaction was that "A democracy is futile if it depends upon its aristocrats. For twenty years the British socialist movement suffered from that defect." Fabian elitism and Labour Party bureaucracy alike could not give the British worker real industrial democracy.[181]

Through S. G. Hobson, his lifelong friend A. B. Thorne (whose wife, Mary Doeg, later became SQS secretary), and others, the Guild Socialist influence infiltrated into the Socialist Quaker Society from 1913 onward, as it had infil-

---

[181] S. G. Hobson, *Pilgrim to the Left*, pp. 1-44, 118-119, 138-139; Minute Book I, 27 April 1899, 31 March 1903, and 27 September 1906; *Manchester Conference of the Society of Friends*, 1895, pp. 197-199; Pease, pp. 105, 130, 134, 271.

trated the Anglican Church Socialist League through Reckitt and Penty. *Ploughshare* began to redefine its socialism in
this direction from November 1913. The dissatisfaction of
post office workers, it argued, showed that collectivism could
not guarantee the workers' rights. There was no evidence
that socialized industries would treat workers any better
than large corporations had. "Webbism" was inadequate.
Socialism was "more than mere State employment." A genuine worker-controlled socialism was needed, "an industrial
movement of the workers themselves, to resist the downward pressure of Capitalism upon their class, so as to gain
complete emancipation from employment as mere wage-
earners, either by private capitalists or the State." Quaker
socialists should therefore strive to make the Labour movement more "intelligently self-conscious." To found true socialism, a new socialist political party was required, with its
own press organs. The partial incursion of the State into the
ranks of the employers (through collectivist nationalization)
would only *strengthen* capitalism, *Ploughshare* argued, in
a prescient and shrewd passage.[182] The argument was entirely Hobsonian and Guild Socialist.

After November 1915 *Ploughshare* became a monthly. Its
later history and that of the SQS down to 1924, unfortunately, do not form part of this particular study. Rev.
Percy Dearmer argued in 1911 in favor of the Quakers, on
the grounds that they were "at the heart of all that is best,
most strenuous, most serviceable, most Christian in the life
of the nation." The essential thing they had grasped, Dearmer said, was "the doctrine of Enthusiasm . . . of the indwelling Spirit of God in every man." They were a Society
of the Holy Ghost and "adopted a view of Holy Scripture
which has enabled them to ride easily on to the waters of
modern science and criticism." Quakers were "instinctively
at the head" of all social movements from antislavery to
Garden Cities.[183] Dearmer clearly understated the conserva-

[182] *Ploughshare*, No. 5 (November 1913), pp. 51-56; No. 6 (February
1914), p. 66.
[183] "Do We Need a Quaker Movement?" in Dearmer's *Sermons on
Social Subjects*, pp. 66-75.

tive aspects of Victorian Quakerism. Yet Quaker socialism was based solidly, as the thought and activities of the Socialist Quaker Society show, on age-old Quaker traits: love of simplicity in life, honesty, intellectual inquiry and freedom from dogma, equality between the sexes, and rejection of war and needless competitive strife.

The Quaker socialists, like the Swedenborgians, did not suffer especially in their organizational structure from lack of devoted administrative talent. The Harrises were to the SQS what Goldsack was to the New-Church Socialist Society, and what Verinder was to the Guild of St. Matthew, and John Carter to the Christian Social Union. The SQS did not, of course, enjoy the abundance of administrative genius to be found in the secular Fabian Society, where in addition to the Webbs and their companion bureaucrats, E. R. Pease was willing to become the constant workhorse. The Quakers certainly lacked the financial resources and political connections of the much larger and more influential Christian Social Union, with its bishops and deans and friendly Cabinet ministers. But no other Christian socialist society could wield the power of the CSU—despite the leadership in individual cases of such national religious figures as Rev. John Clifford. The minor Protestant (or would-be interdenominational) societies such as Clifford's League, suffered from the absence of a permanent, trained secretariat. They remained stillborn largely because no one was prepared to canalize his activities into one organization. The Quakers and Swedenborgians, on the other hand, never gained national significance or influence because from the outset they deliberately chose to limit themselves to the policy of *internal* conversion. They had strong "in-group" feelings and aimed their socialist propaganda activities at the members of their own minority faiths, thus neglecting the wider goal of reshaping the outside world nearer to their desire.

CHAPTER IX

Socialism and the Sects

THE EXTENT of the contribution of Nonconformist radicals to the Christian socialist revival is difficult to measure for a number of reasons, not the least of which is the radicals' lack of distinct intellectual identity. One could compile an exhaustive list of late-Victorian socialists and labor leaders and check off those with known religious affiliations. But the task would prove to be tedious in the extreme and not especially rewarding, for it would tell us little about the real relationship between their socialism and their religious beliefs, if indeed such a relationship existed.

Sacramental socialists shared a fairly distinctive and recognizable theological foundation despite their many differences; Nonconformist socialists, however, lacking an ideological or dogmatic core of beliefs, were often indistinguishable in their writings and speeches from the generality of British socialists, who happened to adopt, chameleon-like, the residual religiosity of rhetoric and expression common to the late-Victorian age. Thus the statement has often been made that British socialism owed more to Methodism than to Marxism. But how profoundly is such a statement to be taken? It is easier to establish historically the British disdain for Marxist ideology than it is to demonstrate any essentially "radical" intellectual or political content in British Methodism. Were these reformers socialist *because* of their Nonconformist faith? Or were they merely socialists who happened to go to some kind of Nonconformist chapel on Sundays? If they were actually ministers, how far had their "socialism" been acquired from their theology? The vague "immanentalism" which, as we have noticed, they all shared added little that was distinctive to their socialist creed. From this point of view, the theological weakness of an extreme immanentalism was that, pushed to its limits, the doctrine led to a diffuse pantheism and in some notable

cases to theosophy and mysticism. If, as the Anglican socialist critic G. C. Binyon suggested, it means "All is God,"
then, finding God everywhere, it would probably end up
in finding him nowhere: *atheism*. If, on the other hand, it
means "God is All," then, finding no real existence in anything, it would probably end up in denial of the material
world altogether: *acosmism*. From this same viewpoint, the
practical weakness of Nonconformist immanentalism was
that, lacking dogma, it was a flimsy faith which faded easily.
As Binyon put it, too great a dependence on a vague feeling
of "brotherhood" and comradely spirit may be satisfactory
in hard times, but "when a boom in capitalist industry has
brought prosperity to the workers, or when election has
brought promotion, this religion is liable to fade."[1]

The problem was compounded because, unlike the Anglicans, Nonconformist socialists maintained only the most
casual affiliations (or none at all) with formally organized
Christian socialist propaganda societies. The Christian Socialist Society and League, the Free Church Socialist League,
and the even more ephemeral groups represented only
a fraction of the active number of Nonconformist socialists.
Countless Christian radicals pressed in the North and elsewhere for the great municipal reforms which helped eventually to civilize the urban jungles of such cities as Glasgow, Liverpool, Manchester, Leeds, and Sheffield. But their
stories are lost, embedded deep in antiquarian local his-
tories and in the files of long-forgotten city newspapers. Rev.
D. B. Foster, for example, became Lord Mayor of Leeds in
1928 after a lifetime of work as a Wesleyan socialist and
Labour Church official, while Rev. Peter Forsyth's contribution to Congregational socialism was made through his individual writings and the headship of Hackney College.
Others labored simply as ministers; they won little space
even in local or denominational records, but they expended their lives in preaching socialism, brotherhood, and
solidarity to the members of their own class and to the

[1] See Binyon's essay in J. Lewis, K. Polanyi, and D. K. Kitchin (eds.),
Christianity and the Social Revolution, p. 184.

workers (sometimes the two were the same group). Non-doctrinal Nonconformist socialists operated through secular organizations like the ILP, local Fabian groups, city councils and workingmen's clubs, and through their own denominational channels and committees. We conclude, therefore, with a brief survey of four major denominations: the Baptists, Unitarians, Methodists, and Congregationalists.

Baptists

The denominational statistics of Chapter III showed that the Baptist faith managed to hold its own in the late-Victorian period despite the general decline in church attendance and religious enthusiasm. Yet Baptists remained among the most socially and politically conservative of all Nonconformists. It was at the Baptist Church House that the Nonconformist Anti-Socialist Union was founded in 1909 to "exterminate socialism from Church and State" and to "discountenance politics in the pulpit."[2] Prominent in this Baptist right-wing pressure group was Rev. J. G. Greenhough, who, as president of the Baptist Union in 1895, had delivered a violent denunciation of all socialism.[3] Previous Baptist presidents had been little more sympathetic to the movement: Rev. James Owen in 1890 told Baptists their main aim was not to help the poor but to "save" individual souls. But Owen did admit the influence of environment on character, and with the passage of time even the Baptist Union could not stay entirely impervious to social forces. President R. H. Roberts addressed the fall assembly of 1892 on "The Kingdom of Heaven on Earth" and quoted Isaiah on the land question, denouncing monopolists who, in the prophet's words, "join house to house, lay field to field, till there be no room and ye be made alone to dwell in the midst of the land." Two-thirds of all England and Wales, said Rev. Roberts, belonged to a mere 10,207 indi-

[2] *Brotherhood*, AU Ser., No. 12 (June 1909), p. 258. Its members included Rev. G. Freeman (sec.), Rev. A. Mursell, Rev. J. G. Greenhough, and Rev. D. T. Young.
[3] *Church Reformer*, XIV, No. 5 (May 1895), p. 101.

viduals, while "a dozen men claim a quarter of Scotland [and] 744 persons own half Ireland." At the following spring meeting Rev. J. G. Carlile spurned "a religion that allowed men to be thieves and swindlers," and a Baptist socialist from Lincoln declared himself openly for radical political and economic reform.[4]

Victorian Baptists made a special effort to maintain orthodoxy of doctrine (as compared with the more relaxed Congregationalists, for instance). Their dogmatic teaching was very rigid and based solely on the Bible. As a result, such factions as did appear were based on minute differences of theology; these ranged from the least orthodox and almost Unitarian "General Baptists" to the "Particular Baptists," who believed that Christ had died for a *definite number* of persons, even for designated individuals, thus limiting salvation very strictly to the "elect." "Particular Baptists" could hardly become socialists. Most of the flock, however, were "Open Baptists" and less exclusive: salvation for them depended on the individual's own acceptance of Christ. The large and successful tabernacles in the lower-middle- and upper-working-class areas were of this variety. Sin and the fires of Hell dominated the theology of almost all Baptists. Perhaps the lower orders could accept these horrors because, as Charles Booth suggested, "Among the awful personal realities of such views of life, 'class' sinks to nothingness, while differences of religious discipline and faith spring into prominence." Baptists were, therefore, usually nonpolitical: a man may be rich or aristocratic, but he still may not be "saved." Perhaps this was a leveling thought and a consolation to the luckless Baptists, instructed by their great preacher C. H. Spurgeon to "serve the Lord Christ by *quiet acquiescence* in the arrangement of Providence."[5]

It was most exceptional that a Baptist of John Clifford's stature and distinction should become a socialist leader too.

---

[4] *Christian Socialist*, VIII, No. 85 (June 1890), p. 79; *Brotherhood*, VI, No. 16 (November 1892), p. 375; New Ser., I, No. 2 (June 1893), p. 18.

[5] Booth, *Life and Labour*, 3rd Ser., Vol. 16, pp. 121-123; *Brotherhood*, VI, No. 8 (March 1892), p. 178.

No other Baptist, except Rev. Herbert Dunnico of the Free Church Socialist League, managed to achieve both prominence and socialism. *Brotherhood* called Clifford "the strongest of all Christian socialists," and undoubtedly as an individual he wielded considerable popular influence. In 1900 at the Baptist autumn meetings in Leicester he persuaded his colleagues to accept "the strongest and clearest resolutions that have yet been adopted by any ecclesiastical assembly." The resolutions condemned war and "racial animosity," and demanded land reform, housing and educational legislation, care of the aged poor, and licensing reform.[6] But there were limits to the changes that any single man, however great a preacher or faithful a socialist, could bring about.

Unitarians

Baptist fundamentalism and Unitarian rationalism may seem far apart theologically, but by the late-Victorian period the two denominations were socially not so distinct. From the death of Servetus at Calvin's hands in 1553 down through the seventeenth-century leadership of John Biddle (1616-1662; "father" of English Unitarianism) and the Victorian preaching of James Martineau (1805-1900), Unitarians have stood out as a more rational minority against the religious dogmas of eternal punishment, inherited guilt, vicarious atonement, the Trinity, and hell-fire. No official statement of Unitarian belief was ever issued. But Anglo-American Unitarianism had Harvard as its theological headquarters, the writings of Emerson as its transcendentalist philosophical creed, and a host of illustrious radical intellectuals and scientists to lead it, including Rev. Joseph Priestley, F.R.S., Rev. Richard Price, F.R.S., Josiah Wedgwood I, F.R.S., Major John Cartwright, Mary Wollstonecraft, John Fielden, Mrs. Gaskell, Ebenezer Elliott, Flor-

[6] *Brotherhood*, New Ser., I, No. 2 (June 1893), p. 18; VIII, No. 7 (November 1900), p. 108. For general Baptist history see R. G. Torbet, *History of the Baptists* (Philadelphia, 1950), and W. T. Whitley, *History of British Baptists* (London, 1932).

ence Nightingale, Walter Bagehot, W. S. Jevons, Joseph Chamberlain, and Charles Booth. Thus its democratic tenor was obvious enough. The Duke of Wellington called the Reform Act of 1832 a victory for Unitarians, and Unitarians led in feminism, public education, and local government reform.[7] On one issue, however, they sharply divided in the nineteenth century—working hours for adults.

Like the Quaker minority, Unitarians had succeeded in business, and had evolved from an ebullient sect into a somewhat staid, rich, middle-class church. Among their number were families who dominated the cotton, chemical, railway, and engineering industries—Strutt, Greg, Ashton, Brunner, Rathbone, Oldknow, and Potter. The economist Ricardo was Unitarian, and as an employer class the Unitarians swallowed whole orthodox economics with its convenient "Iron Law of Wages," the "law" attacked by Henry George in *Progress and Poverty*. In Northern industrial cities Unitarian capitalists wielded great political and social influence. As humanitarian individualists, they stood for a freedom that was negative rather than positive. They were not easily convinced of the need for socialism, despite their emphasis on "the dignity and divine possibilities of man" and the present life. Very few trade-union leaders were Unitarians, and ILP men and Labour MP's tended to come not from their ranks, but from orthodox Nonconformity. Thomas Burt, MP (1837-1922), the Northumberland miners' leader was the one exception, and even he is also claimed by the Methodists.[8]

[7] Unitarians were attracted to liberal journalism; the *Manchester Guardian* was owned and edited by Unitarians (C. P. Scott, for example) down to the 20th century. They played a chief role in the founding of provincial universities at Manchester, Liverpool, Birmingham, Leeds, and Sheffield and in urging the establishment of public libraries and galleries (Sir Henry Tate was a Unitarian). They created the *first* Mechanics' Institute in 1789. Under the Act of 1835 the first Mayors of Manchester, Liverpool, Bolton, Derby, and Leicester were all Unitarians. Rev. H. S. Solly, founder of the "Workingmen's Club and Institute Union" in the mid-19th century was also a Unitarian. See R. V. Holt, *The Unitarian Contribution to Social Progress in England* (London, 1938).

[8] Holt, pp. 23-26. Professor George Unwin, a pioneer economic his-

Stewart Headlam's *Church Reformer* was quick to expose Unitarian desires for respectability. Unitarians no longer opposed the Blasphemy Laws, "now that they are not likely to be used against Unitarians," said the paper, and at Unitarian conferences, workingmen were "as rare as nightingales in Piccadilly." Unitarians only began to denounce sweating when it became "almost fashionable" to do so, and they said nothing of land monopoly. "We might have expected this," said Headlam. "Only the Incarnation and the Sacraments can make men see the intimate connection of the bodily and the spiritual."[9] Despite his criticism, there were a few socialists among the Unitarians, though they revealed themselves mainly in work through Labour Church and ILP movements, not being specifically "Christians." John Trevor himself was succored by Unitarians, trained by them in America, and employed as a minister by them in England before he founded the Labour Church.[10] H. B. Holding, a member of the Fabian executive (1894-1896) and chairman of the special Fabian meetings about the H. G. Wells episode of 1906-1907, was a Unitarian lay preacher who gained prominence in the Labour Church and tried to urge the Unitarian Lay Preachers' Association to ally itself fully with the growing demands of the labor movement and to support the London Labour Church.[11] Rev. Harold Rylett, socialist-radical journalist (one-time editor of the *New Age*) and an ardent Georgeist Single Taxer, read the lesson at the first Labour Church meeting in Manchester (4 October 1891). Rylett, like S. G. Hobson,

---

torian who began writing the history of these families (a biography of Oldknow), was himself Unitarian. See *Religion in American Life*, ed. J. W. Smith and A. L. Jamison, 4 vols. (Princeton, N.J., 1961), IV, 696; R. F. Wearmouth, *Methodism and the Struggle of the Working Classes, 1850-1900*, pp. 185f.; T. Burt, *Pitman and Privy Councillor* (London, 1924), p. 85; and Holt, p. 205.

[9] *Church Reformer*, v, No. 7 (July 1886), pp. 151-153; x, No. 5 (May 1891), p. 104.

[10] John Trevor, *My Quest for God* (London, 1897). See pp. 129-131 for Trevor's comment on Unitarianism.

[11] E. R. Pease, *History of the Fabian Society*, p. 271; *Labour Prophet*, II, No. 18 (June 1893), p. 49.

H. C. Rowe, and J. Bruce Wallace, was an Irish Nonconformist radical. As candidate in the Tyrone by-election of 1881, Rylett was fully supported by H. M. Hyndman's newly created Democratic Federation. He joined the George-Headlam-Verinder group, the English Land Restoration League, and was elected to its committee in October 1884, remaining thereafter a Single Tax advocate. Like the Anglican Headlam but unlike the Unitarian H. B. Holding, Rylett opposed the idea of an independent political party for labor and was unsympathetic toward Hardie's ILP.[12]

Other Unitarians active in the Labour Church movement included Rev. Stopford Brooke, Rev. H. V. Mills, the communitarian, and Rev. P. H. Wicksteed, the economist. It is certain too that the Scots Unitarian leader and ILP man Rev. A. Webster of the Christian Socialist Society supported Labour Church meetings. Stopford A. Brooke, like Rylett, Hobson, and the others, was also an Irish radical. His defection from the Church of England created a public commotion in 1880: the Victorian press played it up because Brooke came from a fashionable circle and was a well-known author and one of Queen Victoria's own chaplains. Brooke found his way, via William Morris and the pre-Raphaelites, from Broad Church Anglicanism to left-wing Unitarianism. At a London Unitarian ministers' meeting in 1893 Brooke demanded of his colleagues "fearless preaching" on contemporary topics. Mankind's future was in the labor movement, he said, therefore "the whole future of the Unitarian Body" lay in "taking the side of the people as opposed to the privileged classes." He became a Fabian socialist, since he favored the collectivist approach to social problems.[13] Rev. Herbert V. Mills (b. 1856) preferred the

[12] *Labour Prophet*, I, No. 2 (February 1892), p. 13; I, No. 3 (March 1892), pp. 18-19; I, No. 5 (May 1892), p. 40. See also *Christian Socialist*, II, No. 18 (November 1884), p. 95; and S. G. Hobson, *Pilgrim to the Left*, pp. 138-139.

[13] William Clarke, *Writings*, ed. H. Burrows and J. A. Hobson, pp. 242-258; see also Clarke's essay, "The Fabian Society and Its Work," in *Fabian Essays*; *Labour Prophet*, IV, No. 37 (January 1895), p. 15; "London Unitarian Ministers' Meeting: Minutes," 4 vols., handwritten notebooks, I, 20 November 1893, Dr. Williams' Library, London.

communitarian answer. A Northerner, Mills held Unitarian ministries in Liverpool and in Kendal, where in the 1890's he was a Labour county councillor for Westmorland. It was at Liverpool that he first established the Home Colonization Society, already mentioned, in 1887. This group opened a colony under Mills's leadership in 1892 at Starnthwaite. It failed mainly because Mills turned out to be too authoritarian a director; he was heavily criticized by many Christian socialists.[14]

Another Unitarian, Rev. Philip H. Wicksteed (1844-1928), played a large part in the evolution of Fabian economic theory, chiefly through his direct personal influence over Bernard Shaw. In that period of confusion during the early 1880's when Fabians, Marxists, Radical-Liberals, Anarchists, and so on had not yet sorted themselves out, when the SDF was emerging out of the "Democratic Federation" and the Fabians were still feeling their way toward collectivism (with the inevitability of gradualness, no doubt), Christian socialists and Single Taxers were difficult to tell apart, as we have seen. Wicksteed, who was Unitarian minister at Dukinfield, near Manchester, was at this time undergoing direct experience of Northern industrial life. The son of a Unitarian minister and educational reformer (Charles Wicksteed) and the brother of a land nationalizer and one-time president of the Kettering Liberal Association (Charles Wicksteed, Jr.[15]), P. H. Wicksteed came of a radical family tradition. He became a disciple of Henry George in 1880, and two years or so later, on reading W. S. Jevons for the first time, he was converted to marginal utility economic theory. *Progress and Poverty,* Wicksteed wrote in a letter to Henry George of 1882, "has given me the light I vainly

---

[14] See, for example, *Christian Socialist*, VII, No. 78 (November 1889), pp. 164-165; *Brotherhood*, VI, No. 10 (May 1892), pp. 227-228; *Church Reformer*, XII, No. 10 (October 1893), pp. 224-226. For a favorable view of Mills see *Seedtime*, No. 16 (April 1893), pp. 8-11, and for his career see *Labour Annual*, 1895, p. 104.

[15] Author of *The Land for the People* (London: 2nd ed., 1894) and *Our Mother Earth* (London, 1891). See *Christian Socialist*, III, No. 34 (March 1886), pp. 154-155.

sought for myself; . . . has made 'a new Heaven and a new earth.' " And later: "I felt a kind of necessity to put myself into communication with you, as I was in a state little short of delirium." The two men became friends on George's subsequent visit to England, and Wicksteed took an executive role in Single Tax organizations, speaking and presiding at land reform meetings. At the inauguration of the Georgeist Land Reform Union (5 June 1883) Wicksteed said of the American reformer that he had "drawn to a focus the scattered rays of converging thoughts which, when once revealed by him, were to be found everywhere in economic writings."[16] Wicksteed was the most remarkable product of late-Victorian Unitarianism. A great Dante scholar, and, of course, a leading (yet virtually self-taught) economist of the new marginal analysis school, his text *The Commonsense of Political Economy* (still in print today after many editions) provided for many decades the most comprehensive exposition of marginalist theory. Henry George first brought Wicksteed's mind to bear on economic analysis, and *Progress and Poverty* was a major influence in his evolution from the status of a broad-minded clergyman-scholar into that of a great economist of the new school with distinctly socialist leanings.

Wicksteed's development beyond George to Jevons and marginal analysis was soon to affect the theory of the Fabians. At a lecture on Karl Marx, Wicksteed brought Bernard Shaw "to a standstill" by criticizing Marxist economics, and especially the Labor Theory of Value, in marginalist terms. "This was the first appearance in socialist controversy of the value-theory of Jevons," wrote Shaw. George Bernard Shaw consented to rebuff Wicksteed in *Today,* and

16 Hunter's Autobiographical Notices, MS, Dr. Williams' Library, London; J. W. Connell's typescript notes on P. H. Wicksteed's life (1929), among the Hibbert Trust Papers, Dr. Williams' Library; Wicksteed to Henry George, 26 October 1882 and 4 February 1883, HGC; *Christian Socialist,* No. 2 (July 1883), suppl., pp. ii-iii. See also T. W. Hutchison, *Review of Economic Doctrines,* p. 98. It was at Wicksteed's request that Arnold Toynbee gave the lectures on "Progress and Poverty" which proved to be the last work of his brief life.

later commented characteristically on his own attempt: "My reply, which was not bad for a fake, . . . elicited only a brief rejoinder; but the upshot was that I put myself in Mr. Wicksteed's hands and became a convinced Jevonian. . . . Accordingly, the abstract economics of the *Fabian Essays* are, as regards Value, the economics of Jevons."[17] Since Shaw had been first "converted" by Henry George, his evolution paralleled that of Wicksteed.[18]

In 1874 Wicksteed had replaced the great Unitarian leader Martineau as minister of the Little Portland Street Chapel in London (where he remained until he left the ministry in 1897).[19] His sermons were full of social criticisms, and three were published in 1885 as *Our Prayers and Politics*. Here Wicksteed maintained: "All agree that an era of socialistic legislation is upon us . . . and that society, by its corporate and collective action, must, and can in large measure, make the crooked straight." He was moving toward a mild Christian socialism. "I am sometimes supposed to be a Socialist by my friends who are not Socialists," Wicksteed wrote, "and I am generally not considered one by my friends who are." Meanwhile, his influence was spreading through extension lectures on such topics as "Ethical and Theological Aspects of Sociology," "The Social Organism," and so on, the theme of which was that "Man only becomes human in society" and that the highest goal of the individual is realized only "when the reaction between him and his environment is exalted into Communion."[20] It was presumably at such a lecture that Wicksteed so affected Bernard Shaw. He also influenced his pu-

[17] Pease, Appendix I, pp. 260-261. Wicksteed had also deeply influenced Bernard Shaw's view of Ibsen through his university extension lectures on that playwright. (Wicksteed had taken the pains to learn Norwegian, as well as Italian and Dutch.)

[18] See Jones, Manchester thesis, pp. 70-72, 211-215.

[19] Hutchison, pp. 96-97; Rev. H. S. Perris, *Little Portland Street Chapel* (London, 1900); P. H. Wicksteed, *Our Prayers and Politics* (London, 1885), p. 10.

[20] Various lecture syllabi, 1889-1890, in the Wicksteed Papers, British Library of Political and Economic Science, London School of Economics.

pil G. K. Chesterton (on Dante) [21] and many lesser folk; he was a very popular lecturer and teacher.

In 1888 Wicksteed's assistant minister at Little Portland Street was John Trevor, who stayed with him two years. From Wicksteed, Trevor picked up many of the notions he later embodied in the Labour Church movement, and from 1891 Wicksteed was a vigorous coworker with him among the Labour Churches. "From the first he understood what I meant by the Labour Church," attested Trevor. "Long before anyone else understood, . . . his sympathy . . . sustained me through many a dark hour. . . . He knew more of the meaning of my work than I myself did." Wicksteed wrote frequent pieces for Trevor's *Labour Prophet* and gave it financial help too. For example, his article "Is the Labour Church a Class Church?" (subsequently reprinted as a Labour Church Tract) tried to answer the standard arguments leveled by opponents against the movement. Wicksteed reasoned that the Labour Church should be a "warning to all classes that they have no right to exist except so far as they serve the masses and make their life fuller and greater." Later, in the *Manchester Guardian,* he wrote: "The Labour Church is frankly, even passionately, democratic." Naturally, Wicksteed was a founder-member of the London Labour Church of 1892. He spoke all over the country for the movement, as did his brother Charles and his own son, J. H. Wicksteed.[22]

The Labour Church story is part of the history of the British labor movement but not, strictly speaking, of "Christian socialism." Wicksteed's deep and long association with it (he was still campaigning at Labour Churches in 1899[23])

[21] Wicksteed found G. K. Chesterton a keen student, very helpful in classes. They were linked through a family friendship of Chesterton's fiancée. See Wicksteed's letters to Rev. J. M. Connell (e.g., 9 January 1924) among the Hibbert Trust Papers, Dr. Williams' Library.

[22] Trevor, *My Quest for God,* p. 219. See also *Labour Prophet,* I, No. 1 (January 1892), p. 1; I, No. 2 (February 1892), p. 10; I, No. 12 (December 1892), p. 93; II, No. 19 (July 1893), p. 58; III, No. 35 (November 1894), pp. 156ff. But for Wicksteed's monetary aid, the *Labour Prophet* would have collapsed in 1898 (see Vol. VI, No. 78 [June 1898], p. 188).

[23] *Labour Church Record,* No. 1 (January 1899), pp. 3-4.

was a result of his Unitarian faith and his profound personal distaste for snobbery and caste. The driving force of Wicksteed's radicalism was no doctrinal or dogmatic truth, no sacramental faith but a simple, untheological, and not especially "Christian" egalitarianism. Wicksteed's hatred of class segregation extended even to intellect and scholarship, where he was himself so outstanding. He could not bear "insufferable pedantry and priggishness" in the learned; scholars should keep "in touch with the life of their brethren." Social democracy, he insisted, is not leveling. Contrary to the fears of many intellectual snobs, democracy will not destroy any culture that is worth keeping. He extended this egalitarianism to peoples of different races. In 1896 Wicksteed persuaded his Unitarian colleagues to vote unanimously at one meeting to express "shame and sorrow" at Britain's treatment of native populations. "The human race is *not* born for the few," he declared. "The history of race oppression has been still more horrible than the history of class oppression." The two issues, class and race, were linked because "the struggle that puts the British workman in command of his own destinies also puts him in command of the destinies of hundreds of millions of the 'subject-races'. . . ."[24]

Wicksteed's nearest approach to anything that could be called a specifically "Christian" socialism was a sermon on "Christianity and the Personal Life" in which he dismissed the pacifist notion that Christians should never use force ("Christianized" and "socialized" force) in society as a means to achieve the ultimate end, about which "Christianity is clear and emphatic." In other words, Wicksteed argued, despite "endless difficulties," Christianity is a "practicable proposition," provided people are realistic in their appraisal of social needs and means. Truly, Wicksteed was a genuine, thoroughgoing egalitarian democrat. He was also an outstanding example of the strenuous Victorian scholar-reformer. "I would cry aloud that the man . . . who

24 A. Reid (ed.), *The New Party*, pp. 337, 340-341, 350-351; "London Unitarian Ministers' Meeting: Minutes," 1 (27 May 1896); *Labour Prophet*, III, No. 33 (September 1894), pp. 118-119.

has not grappled with the intellectual problems of our industrial and social life till the sweat bursts from his brow, . . . already sleeps the sleep of death."[25]

The *intellectual* problems of industrial and social life: that was the way Wicksteed, the radical Unitarian, conceived of the "Social Question" of the late Victorians—as a challenge to his intellect to find a rational and humane solution. But official Unitarian opinion remained untouched by Wicksteed's intellectual passion. The *Christian Life and Unitarian Herald,* for example, called the Labour Church for which he worked so hard "a sectarian society of the worst kind, the aggregating of a class of men (and on a Sunday too!) in the name of religion, chiefly to foster spite and to denounce the employers of the great mass of mankind." The Labour Church, it said, was "permeated with the poison" of socialism, and was "a travesty and a contradiction of the Divine Idea." Like John Clifford among the Baptists, Wicksteed was one among a few isolated examples in his church. In 1906 he did manage to found (and became the first president of) a kind of Unitarian CSU, the Unitarian and Free Christian Union for Social Service, which with other social-union religious organizations, ultimately resulted in COPEC (Christian Conference on Politics, Economics and Citizenship, est. 1924).[26]

Methodists

Considering its size, the Methodist Church produced few Christian socialists. In addition Methodists rarely featured in socialist societies. The Fabian Society's executive, for instance, contained at one time or another people of Quaker, Congregationalist, Baptist, Unitarian, Anglican, and agnos-

[25] P. H. Wicksteed, "Christianity and the Personal Life" (sermon at Little Portland St. Chapel, London, 1888), Wicksteed Papers, British Library of Political and Economic Science, London School of Economics, passim; Holt, p. 28. See also, among the Wicksteed Papers, "The Churches and the Industrial Unrest" (clipping from *The Enquirer,* 7 September 1912) and "Manchester College, Oxford: Conference 1909," Item 11.
[26] *Labour Prophet,* v, No. 46 (January 1896), pp. 14-15.

tic belief, but no Methodists. Congregationalists dominated most Protestant socialist societies; only in the ephemeral Free Church Socialist League of 1909 did Methodists take much part. There Revs. W. Younger and J. E. Rattenbury served, along with Philip Snowden, as we have seen. Yet it appears that Methodism and trade unionism (at least of the skilled artisans) were parallel movements, appealing and ministering to much the same people. Many a trade unionist received his training in the arts of public life as a lay preacher; the mass of evidence presented by R. F. Wearmouth lists eighty or more full-time trade-union leaders who owed their career, position, and influence to their Methodist experience and training.

Twentieth-century Methodism saw its years of greatest expansion between 1906 and 1908[27]—years of political excitement which also witnessed the emergence of Anglican, Wesleyan, Roman Catholic, Unitarian, and Congregationalist social-union types of reform organizations, a Labour electoral victory, and the appearance of a more radical spirit among socialists both secular and Christian.

Of all the Methodist branches—Wesleyan, New Connexion, United Methodist, Bible Christians, and Primitive Methodist—the last produced twice as many labor leaders as all the rest put together.[28] Drawing together conclusions from Wearmouth's studies, we can summarize the position of the various Methodist sects regarding "social work," trade unionism, and political action as shown in Table 6.

The Primitive Methodist journals supported such schemes as profit-sharing and Booth's old-age pension plan. In 1890 the *Primitive Methodist Magazine,* however, went further than this and rejoiced: "Demos is coming to know his power and the right he has to better conditions of life. . . . *Socialism in one form or another is steadily working its way among the masses* and the injustices of their condition will have to be remedied." In party-political affiliation most

27 R. F. Wearmouth, *Social and Political Influence of Methodism in the 20th Century,* pp. 46ff.
28 R. F. Wearmouth, *Methodism and the Trade Unions,* p. 38.

TABLE 6[29]

POSITIONS OF METHODISTS ON
LATE-NINETEENTH-CENTURY SOCIAL ISSUES

	WESLEYAN	NEW CONNEXION	UNITED METHODIST FREE CHURCHES	PRIMITIVE
Social Work	Established the most missions	Established the fewest missions	Moderately interested in legislative action instead	Demanded positive social legislation instead of charity
Trade Unions	Indifferent to unions	Made no contribution	Fairly sympathetic to unions	Active unionists
Political Action	Tory until 1890's; Gladstonian later (while claiming at all times to be "non-political")	Liberal	Liberal	Radical (Labor)

Primitive Methodists were Radical and voted for Liberal party candidates until the coming of the ILP, and for "Lib-Lab" and Labour men thereafter.[30] Despite the great number of trade-union leaders the sect provided, it furnished few actual socialist propagandists.[31] For these one must look to the other end of the theological spectrum within Methodism, to the "High Church" element, the Wesleyans. S. E.

[29] Table 6 is based mainly on pp. 141-232 of Wearmouth's *Methodism and the Struggle of the Working Classes, 1850-1900*.

[30] *Ibid.*, p. 159.

[31] There were, however, two land nationalizers: Rev. Hugh Gilmore (?-1891) and Rev. Robert Bryant (1842-1905). See *Primitive Methodist Connexion: General Minutes*, 1892, pp. 23-25; *Primitive Methodist Church: Annual Conference: Minutes*, 1906, pp. 7-10. The Scots Primitive Methodist leader, Rev. Joseph Ritson (1851-1932), a leading advocate of Methodist unification who died at the age of eighty-one before he was able to vote for the Union, was in his younger days a bitter critic of social conditions, especially the control exerted by landlords over rural workers (see *Methodist Annual Conference: Minutes*, 1933, pp. 239-240).

Keeble, Peter Thompson, and D. B. Foster were all Wesleyan Methodists, and in that branch of the church there flourished a Methodist member of the Marxist SDF, Rev. E.J.B. Kirtlan of Northampton, author of a widely distributed left-wing socialist sermon, *Socialism for Christians* (1907), which forthrightly demanded total collective ownership of all national resources.[32]

The leader of the "Forward Movement" that reinvigorated Methodism in the 1880's and 1890's, and the chief Methodist of his day, was Rev. Hugh Price Hughes (1847-1902).[33] He established the *Methodist Times* in 1885 as a "journal of religious and social movement," written "by young Methodists for young Methodists." As editor, Hughes wrote deliberately for working-class and female tastes, and he became the prophet of a kind of Radical-Liberal-Socialism inside Wesleyanism. Hughes told delegates at a denominational conference in 1884 that the salvation of individual souls was no longer enough: "the great need of our time is for Christian Socialism." Five years later his *Social Christianity* (St. James's Hall sermons) was published and passed through several editions. The sermons were a scathing attack on Victorian industrial life: "The masses of the people

---

[32] Kirtlan's sermon was delivered in 1905 and published as Pioneer Pamphlet No. 1 at Northampton in 1907. "Well now, without any bunkum, I stand before you as a Socialist," Kirtlan began aggressively. ". . . There are persons who are Socialists without being Christians. I can conceive of Buddhist Socialists and of Mahometan Socialists. . . . The Socialist theory is the only theory which, applied to common life, will ensure absolute and perfect justice to all citizens."

[33] Born in Carmarthen, son of a Welsh doctor and a Jewish mother. (He was mourned by London Jews in 1902.) Grandson of a famous Welsh Methodist, Rev. Hugh Hughes; "converted" at age thirteen; local preacher at age fourteen (Swansea Circuit). Entered Richmond College (1866); minister in Dover, Brighton, Stoke Newington, Oxford, Brixton. First superintendent of West London Mission (1887) with headquarters at St. James's Hall; president of Methodist Conference, 1898, which established "The 20th Century Fund." Founder-member of National Free Church Council and its president in 1896. See D. P. Hughes, *Life of H. P. Hughes* (London, 1907); *Wesleyan Methodist Church, Annual Conference: Minutes*, 1903, pp. 131-134. For comments on the "Forward Movement" see *Christian Socialist*, VII, No. 78 (November 1889), p. 168.

even in London are harassed and neglected. They are harassed by the dogs of Hell, who take advantage of their helplessness. Oh, the anguish of the starving poor! It seems as though every man's hand was against them. . . . *How do you expect virtue and morality from people living in one room?*"[34]

Hughes's social theology was simple and Christ-centered. "Jesus Christ was essentially a man of the People—a working man," he wrote; "the laws and policies of States must be subjected to the teaching of Jesus Christ." Christ's love extended to *everyone,* whatever his class or condition: "a harlot is dying in a back slum. . . . That harlot is as dear to Christ as the Queen of England herself. . . . Let us once realize the sacredness of every human being, however poor, however ignorant, however degraded, and tyranny becomes impossible, lust becomes impossible, war becomes impossible. This is the new idea which Jesus Christ introduced into human society." Christ's message to mankind was clear: "Inasmuch as ye did it unto one of the homeless poor in Trafalgar Square, or unto one of the downtrodden harlots in Piccadilly, ye did it unto Me."[35]

The tenor of Hugh Price Hughes's message was social egalitarianism: he wanted to remove the middle-class, employer-class taint from Methodism. He complained in the *Methodist Times* (20 October 1892) :

Middle-class, well-dressed and well-fed Dissenters are in great danger of assuming an attitude of more or less conscious antagonism to the New Democracy. . . . Very rarely indeed are the arrangements of Methodist churches adapted to the tastes and preferences of the working-classes. Office and authority are almost everywhere in the hands of tradesmen and professional men. It is the rarest thing to find a genuine representative workingman on any of the governing bodies of our Church.

[34] *Social Christianity* (London, 1889), pp. 8, 14. The last question is reminiscent of Keir Hardie's *Can a Man Be a Christian on a Pound a Week?* (London and Glasgow, n.d. [1905]).

[35] H. P. Hughes, pp. 3, 49, 61-62.

This complaint would be truer of the Wesleyan than of the Primitive or Bible Christian branches; but the Wesleyans were by far the biggest group.

Methodists of a more radical outlook than Hughes often complained of his mildness. S. E. Keeble said that Hughes "had reactionary tendencies which came out with fearful force at times." Keeble affirmed, however, that "on the whole" Hughes was the leader of whatever progressive forces were to be found in Methodism.[36] The truth is that Hugh Price Hughes was the Clifford of Methodism; but, unlike Clifford, he was no Fabian socialist. He did not involve himself with secular or religious socialist organizations. Instead, he used the vocabulary of the socialist and the policy of the social-mission worker.

A Methodist reformer who was more prepared to cooperate with secular groups and with trade unions was Rev. Peter Thompson (1847-1909), who combined years of devoted labor among London's submerged poor with active aid for strikers. Thompson concentrated on the worst trades, and was a founder-member of the Anti-Sweating League. He only reluctantly accepted his East London Mission in 1885 but soon became a zealot in the work and an acknowledged expert on slum life. He demanded of his fellow Methodists that they "denounce the competition which means a curse, denounce the sweating which means the degradation of the poor." Sympathizing with the poorest of the poor, Thompson said: "I want Methodism to write over the forehead of every harlot, to put right across the face of every poor docker, right in front of every man and woman, 'My brother,' 'My sister.' "[37] He was elected to the Mansion House Committee in 1892.

[36] M. Edwards, *S. E. Keeble* (London, 1949), p. 57.

[37] *Christian Socialist*, IX, No. 95 (April 1891), p. 38. Thompson's chief practical achievement was to establish Central Hall, Stepney as the headquarters for East End mission work. In 1887-1888 he took over two notorious gin bars (Paddy's Goose and the Old Mahogany Bar), and dockers and strikers used them as labor centers for meetings, food, and social services. See R. B. Thompson, *Peter Thompson* (London, 1910), passim; R. G. Burnett, *These My Brethren: The Story of the London East End Mission* (London, 1946), pp. 46-57.

More of a socialist still was D. B. Foster (1858-1948), who became Labour Lord Mayor of Leeds in 1928. Foster had worked his way up from nothing to a comfortable level of success in the drapery business in Yorkshire. Then in 1897 at the age of thirty-nine he gave it all up, at great pain to his family, and decided "to live on the worker's economic level." Foster had already seen plenty of poverty at first hand on the Holbeck Board of Guardians (1891-1892) and elsewhere; he had been a founder of the Holbeck ILP and Social Reform Union and advocated total nationalization at an early stage. In 1902 he was made secretary of the Leeds Labour Representation Committee and in 1912-1916 of the Leeds Labour Party; he had been beaten in seven consecutive elections before he finally got onto the Leeds Council as Labour member for Hunslet in 1911. At all times D. B. Foster supported the collectivist view and the Labour Alliance; he never strayed from the party line in his socialism, though he lived to the ripe age of ninety and wrote countless pamphlets.

Foster was a local Wesleyan preacher at the age of seventeen, joined the Labour Church in 1895, and was its leader for a while (president of the Labour Church Union, 1902-1903). Finding the organization too non-Christian, Foster tried to start his own "socialist Christian Church" in Bradford. He also worked closely in Leeds with Rev. J. C. Kenworthy to build up the Leeds Brotherhood Church (1897-1898) as part of J. Bruce Wallace's organization. In short, Foster was very much the true Christian socialist rather than a mere Labour-minded preacher. He complained, however, that Wesleyan officials refused to use his services because he was such an outspoken socialist and Labour Party man, and this forced him to adopt a Christian socialist stand that was independent of both the ecclesiastical tendencies of many Wesleyans and the ILP-dominated character of the Labour Churches. To the end of his long life Foster believed that "Socialism and the Christ are one, as body and soul are one."[38]

[38] D. B. Foster, *Socialism and the Christ: My Two Great Discoveries*

The most thoroughgoing socialist among the Wesleyan Methodists was Rev. Samuel E. Keeble (1853-1946). An ex-Anglican and ex-City businessman, Keeble worked as a Wesleyan minister for over forty years and in fourteen circuits between 1879 and 1921. He was especially influential as a preacher in Sheffield, Manchester, and Bristol; but Keeble is mainly remembered for his heavy literary output, among which his *Industrial Daydreams* of 1889 was well known. Keeble was undoubtedly the most politically advanced Methodist of his era. He was responsible for helping to convert Philip Snowden to socialism; he bitterly opposed purely "social-work" organizations like the Charity Organization Society; he split with Rev. Peter Thompson after criticizing the East End Mission as being insufficiently radical; he split with Hugh Price Hughes for similar reasons, stopped writing for Hughes's *Methodist Times,* and began his own more outspoken *Methodist Weekly.* The *Weekly* (1900-1903) died as a result of Keeble's strong anti-Boer War propaganda, for he was as uncompromising a pacifist as he was a socialist. Keeble founded the Wesleyan Methodist Union for Social Service, modeled on the CSU, in 1905. But he refused to be absorbed by "Social-Unionism" or Liberalism, and in politics he "never allowed himself to be known as anything but a Christian Socialist." S. E. Keeble reached the height of his influence within Methodism and within the socialist movement in about 1921, when his Fernley Lecture at the Wesleyan Conference was delivered: "Christian Responsibility for the Social Order." He was by then no longer a voice in the wilderness.[39]

---

in a Long and Painful Search for Truth (Leeds, 1921), p. 63. Foster's other works include: *Leeds Slumdom* (Leeds, 1897) ; *The Logic of the Alliance, or the Labour Party Analyzed and Justified* (Leeds, 1911); *The Kingdom of God: What It Is and How It Is Coming* (Leeds, 1935); *Godly or Godless? Life's Supreme Question* (Leeds, 1939). See *Brotherhood,* vi, No. 3 (July 1898), p. 46; *Yorkshire Post,* 12 July 1948 (obit.). I am grateful to Mr. A. B. Gaver, Acting City Librarian of Leeds (1963) for his help in locating information about D. B. Foster.

[39] Edwards, *S. E. Keeble,* pp. 90-91; *Methodist Annual Conference: Minutes,* 1947, p. 128; Wearmouth, *Methodism . . . 20th Century,* pp.

In Keeble's *Industrial Daydreams,* which went through several editions, he admitted that many secular socialists thought Christian socialism was "a wolf in sheep's clothing," caring not for the people but for "making religious capital" out of the social struggle: "The Christian Socialist has to bear all this meekly, knowing that the Christian Church has given only too much ground for this hostility and suspicion." But "a purified socialism is simply an industrially applied Christianity." *The Social Teaching of the Bible,* a book of collected essays, sold five thousand copies soon after its display at the 1909 Methodist Conference and was demanded in the USA and Europe; a Hungarian translation was made as late as 1928. The two great commandments of the Bible, said Keeble in his Introduction, were Love of God and Love of Neighbors. "If the world but knew it, the Bible is the charter of its freedom." Keeble's greatest work on Christian responsibility confessed "the guilt of the Christian Church in her shortsightedness and indifference to social evils in the past." The Christian's social duty was based on his "law-book" (the Bible) and was "grounded in Reason and the nature of things." Yet the Churches had permitted two evils: "the hardening of law" and "the heathenizing of theory."[40]

Unlike many other Nonconformist socialists, Keeble was a considerable scholar of social and economic history and socialist thought; his work was studded with references to

190-191, 216, 245. Keeble earned the distinction of being considered important enough for mention in an Anglican history of Christian social reform: see M. B. Reckitt, *Faith and Society,* p. 97. Keeble's other writings included: *The Social Teaching of the Bible* (1909); *Christianity and Socialism* and *Christianity and the Wages Question* (both pamphlets, 1907); *An Annotated Bibliography on Social Questions* (1907); *A Legal Minimum Wage* (1912); *Towards a New Era* (1916); and *The Ethics of Public Ownership* (1920).

[40] Keeble, *Industrial Daydreams: Studies in Industrial Ethics and Economics* (London, n.d. [1916?]), pp. 91, 152; Edwards, *S. E. Keeble,* p. xvii; S. E. Keeble (ed.), *Social Teaching of the Bible* (London, 1909), pp. 5-6; S. E. Keeble, *Christian Responsibility for the Social Order* (London, 1922), pp. 7, 19, 29, 109ff.

recent and past thinkers, American, British, and European. His own socialist aims and ideals were summarized in a sermon on the theme of Joel 2:28, "your young men shall see visions." He wanted them to "see" universal education, the elimination of needless competition, public control of both capital and labor, full social and economic justice for women, the eradication of economic insecurity and unemployment, the "moralization" of production and distribution, planned adjustments between economic supply and demand.[41] Active in COPEC from its foundation in 1924, Keeble was a solid Labour Party man, and no admirer of Ramsey MacDonald or party-political "alliances." He was happy to live to witness the victory of 1945, but died (aged ninety-three) before the welfare state got under way.

S. E. Keeble, Peter Thompson, D. B. Foster, even Hugh Price Hughes, and certainly E.J.B. Kirtlan were exceptional among Methodists in being so articulate in their Christian socialism. Yet Methodists infiltrated and inspired the labor movement, whether or not they made much contribution to Christian socialism proper. In the words of Sidney Webb on County Durham:

> The Methodist, whatever his shortcomings, became a man of earnestness, sobriety, industry and regularity of conduct. Family after family became thus transformed, to serve in its turn as a centre of helpful influence. . . . It is the men who are Methodists . . . whom we find taking the lead and filling the posts of influence [in working-class movements]. From their ranks have come an astonishing large proportion of the trade union leaders. . . . They swarm on Co-operative and Friendly Society committees. They furnish today . . . most of the working class J.P.'s and members of the House of Commons.[42]

[41] Edwards, *S. E. Keeble*, p. 21. For other references to Keeble's work see *Brotherhood*, AU Ser., No. 17 (September 1909), pp. 366-368; No. 19 (November 1909), p. 479.
[42] *Story of the Durham Miners* (London, 1921), pp. 22-24.

Congregationalists

The Congregationalist contribution to the Christian socialist revival begins at the opening of the period of this study with *The Bitter Cry of Outcast London* (1883) and continues throughout, reaching its climax in the social agitation of R. J. Campbell. In contrast with the direct participation of some Methodists in the British labor movement, Congregational socialists took more of a Fabian role. Congregationalism, after all, was "more than any other, the Church of the middle classes." Its memberships ranged only between upper-middle- and lower-middle-class origins. "Where those classes prevail," wrote Charles Booth, "Congregationalists are to be found in force; where not, churches lead a struggling existence." Congregational socialism, therefore, was a socialism for the workers but not necessarily of the workers. In other words, it both followed and set the pattern of Christian socialism in general—perhaps of British socialism as a whole, both secular and religious.[43]

The Congregationalist faith was in some ways more amenable to Social Gospel influences than, for instance, was the Baptist. By the late-Victorian period the general tendency in Congregational theology was a drift toward unorthodoxy. Rather than adhering to a strict belief in Christ as divine and in the Crucifixion as "the great sacrifice of a Risen Saviour," Congregationalism was becoming somewhat hard to distinguish from Christian humanitarianism—at least to the theologically unsophisticated. It was becoming ethical rather than sacramental, "an ideal affecting human life and human relationships" rather than a body of theological dogma.[44] Congregationalists did not find it especially difficult to become Quakers or Unitarians, as we have seen in the cases of men like Rev. Percy Alden and Rev. Richard Westrope (Christian Social Brotherhood and SQS). It was within Congregational theology, too, that "immanentalism"

---

[43] Booth, *Life and Labour*, 3rd Ser., Vol. 16, p. 112.
[44] *Ibid.*, pp. 119-121.

was most developed, and it became linked with socialism in Rev. R. J. Campbell's "New Theology."

The Bitter Cry of Outcast London was written for the London Congregational Union by Rev. W. C. Preston, using material gathered under the supervision of the Union's secretary, Rev. Andrew Mearns, in a survey of East London poverty.[45] No single revelation or piece of writing had as great an impact on Christian thinking. Men and women of all churches were deeply shaken by the brutal facts it exposed. A wave of activity creating settlement houses, philanthropic missions, and social investigations followed, and the government was moved to establish a Royal Commission which resulted in 1885 in a report on the Housing of the Poor.[46] *The Bitter Cry* was packed with authentic accounts of crowded and leaky cellar-dwellings, child prostitution, incest, and disease. Using this explosive journalistic material (some of it borrowed from a previous pamphlet of the

[45] There is great confusion about the pamphlet's authorship. It was published anonymously, the only name mentioned being that of Mearns (as secretary of the Congregational Union). The docker's leader Ben Tillett ascribed it to Arnold White; S. C. Carpenter, to G. R. Sims (in *Church and People*); other authorities, to various writers, including Mearns, W. T. Stead, "James Clark" (untraceable). R. F. Wearmouth, the Methodist historian, and Francis Williams of the Labour Party, both of whom make many errors of fact in their writing about the period, even ascribe this famous Congregational pamphlet to the Anglo-Catholic "Stewart Headlam group." Very recently (since the original writing of this book) K. S. Inglis threw some light on the matter by quoting Mearns's own statement in the *Contemporary Review* of December 1883 that the pamphlet was prepared under his direction by Rev. James Munro of Limerick and was actually *written* by W. C. Preston. Since the power of the piece is in its title and writing, I regard W. C. Preston as the true author.

See W. J. Rowland, "Some Free Church Pioneers of Social Reform," *Congregational Quarterly*, Vol. 39, No. 2 (April 1957), pp. 134-145; B. Tillett, *Memories and Reflections*, p. 92; S. C. Carpenter, II, 329; *Primitive Methodist Magazine* (1883), p. 763; *Economic Review*, I, No. 1 (January 1891), p. 144; Wearmouth, *Methodism . . . 20th Century*, p. 235; Francis Williams, *Fifty Years March* (London, 1949), p. 48; K. S. Inglis, *Churches and the Working-Classes*, p. 67.

[46] *Church Reformer*, VIII, No. 11 (November 1889), p. 257; D. P. Hughes, pp. 190, 193; S. E. Keeble, *Christian Responsibility for the Social Order* p. 182; R. T. Jones, *Congregationalism in England* (London, 1962), pp. 343f.

same year by G. R. Sims, *How the Poor Live*[47]), W. C. Preston produced a skillful and telling exposé. Preston, who had direct experience of urban poverty in Lancashire and elsewhere (especially during the cotton-famine days of the American Civil War), was also an outstanding journalist. He had edited local newspapers and was the author of numerous stories and pamphlets, besides being an effective orator (he filled the Alhambra Music Hall regularly during his Hull ministry of 1872-1880).[48] Turning his literary powers and popular experience to the facts collected by others, Preston created a minor classic in the literature of exposure. The arresting title was probably inspired by Elizabeth Barrett Browning's *Bitter Cry of the Children* (1843); it was followed, in 1906 by the American John Spargo's *Bitter Cry of the Children*.

"In a Christian land," wrote Preston," where it is criminal to ill-treat a horse or an ass," the case had occurred of a poverty-stricken family losing its second child, "and this dead baby was cut open in the one room where its parents and brothers and sisters lived, ate and slept, because the parish had no mortuary and no room in which post-mortems could be performed." Despite revelations such as this, the pamphlet was, if anything, carefully toned down. The very worst horrors were not revealed. State intervention was demanded, and much blame was put on the churches. A "terrible flood of sin and misery" was gaining on the nation, said

[47] Inglis, *Churches and the Working-Classes*, p. 69.

[48] Rev. William Carnall Preston (1837-1902). Born in Wakefield, educated at Owen's College (Manchester University); forty-three years a Congregational minister. Ordained 1859; pastor in Liverpool and Wigan to 1867; left ministry to become a newspaper editor (1867-1870); reentered ministry (1870) at Spalding. Moved to London from Hull (1880) and wrote *The Bitter Cry of Outcast London* (1883). See DWL Index; *Congregational Yearbook*, 1903, pp. 193-194.

Rev. Andrew Mearns (1837-1925), born in Glasgow and educated at Glasgow University (1857-1860) and United Presbyterian Theological Hall, Edinburgh (1860-1864). Minister at Great Marlow (1864-1866), Chelsea (1866-1879); Secretary of Congregational Union, 1876-1906. Editor of *Congregational Magazine*. Died, aged eighty-eight, at Burnham-on-Sea (DWL Index; *Congregational Yearbook*, 1926, p. 170; 1903, p. 453).

Preston; the churches, with all their agencies, were doing but one-thousandth part of the social work needed. The pamphlet was a direct plea for cheap-housing legislation and for the awakening of the churches to the needs of the poor and underprivileged.[49]

Annual Congregational conference reports of the 1880's show a generally increasing involvement with social and economic questions; but frequent relapses would occur, and speakers would break out with an attack on Keir Hardie and the ILP or on the Labour Churches or the trade unions. Congregational ministers were still occasionally expelled by the Union for their political radicalism. An extraordinary nadir was plumbed in 1886, the year of constant labor demonstrations, street disturbances in London, and massive unemployment. The Congregational Union met in the fall of that tragic year and declared calmly:

> No great public question in which the interests of the Churches or of national morality were involved, has during the year called for the judgment of the Committee. Political issues of first-rate importance have been before the nation, but these . . . had no direct bearing on the position and work of the Churches, or on the interests which the Union is set to protect.

The chairman (Mr. E. White) chose for his inaugural address an eminently church-worthy subject: "Free Church Federations: or the application of the Apostolic Distinction between Law and Grace to the theology, ethics and politics of modern Independency"! In 1889, however, Rev. W. Whittley (Christian Socialist Society) preached a sermon later published as a pamphlet, in which he cried angrily: "What is the use of preaching patience to toiling and suffering ones? It is unnatural! It is brutal! Tell them to have patience only when you are busy trying to strike off the fetters." Christian socialism, he said later, was "one of the greatest [movements] ever started in the history of the

---

[49] *The Bitter Cry of Outcast London* (London, 1883), pp. 12-13 and passim.

world";[50] and in 1892 the Congregational Union was addressed by Keir Hardie.

The impact of the *Bitter Cry of Outcast London* was not, of course, confined to Congregational circles. In fact, its influence was greater outside those circles, and the confusion over the pamphlet's authorship is one illustration of this— few readers may have known even of its religious origin. Perhaps the chief single reason for its wide success was that the energetic reform journalist, W. T. Stead (who was the author of a popular attack on American urban problems in 1894, *If Christ Came to Chicago*), took up the Congregational Union's tract and popularized it in his *Pall Mall Gazette*. The *Bitter Cry* inspired a conference in London between the principal Protestant denominations (Wesleyan, Baptist, Presbyterian, Congregationalist) on the spiritual and social condition of the poor; its influence spread rapidly throughout the churches. As far as general public opinion was concerned, however, the *Bitter Cry* stood for housing reform.[51]

Only two years after the publication of the Mearns-Preston pamphlet, the Congregational Union issued a sequel, *Light and Shade: Pictures of London Life* (1885), which proudly recorded the flow of aid to the unfortunate London poor from charitable organizations since 1883 and seemed to view with some complacency the results of the

---

[50] *Congregational Yearbook*, 1887, pp. 2, 25f.; see also 1881, pp. 40, 194ff.; 1884, pp. 75-106; *Brotherhood*, VI, No. 11 (June 1892), p. 258; VI, No. 16, pp. 370-371; New Style, II, No. 2 (June 1894), pp. 17-18; II, No. 6 (October 1894), p. 81; III, No. 2 (June 1895), p. 19; III, No. 7 (November 1895), p. 80; *Labour Prophet*, V, No. 52 (April 1896), p. 58; V, No. 59 (November 1896), p. 175; *Christian Socialist*, VIII, No. 85 (June 1890), pp. 85ff.; VIII, No. 90 (November 1890), pp. 142-145.

[51] The American revivalists Moody and Sankey visited England in 1884, a year after the publication of the *Bitter Cry of Outcast London*, and they agreed that bad housing was the most immediate social fact to be seen in Britain at that time. "The great thing you need in London is *homes*," they said. "Homes! there, that is your great lack. The great mass of your population is homeless. . . . There is no sense of permanence of ownership such as we have in America. . . . Keep hammering away at the 'dwellings of the poor' question" (*Church Reformer*, III, No. 8 [15 August 1884], p. 179).

intervening months of work. Nine Mission Halls had been opened, 30,000 garments distributed (in 1884), 10,000 free breakfasts to children, and so on. The author of the sequel accepted this as a victory over the problem. Obviously, the Congregational Union as an official body was easily pleased; its policy had not yet gone beyond the charitable "social-work" phase.[52]

As individuals, some Congregational ministers took an active part in the work of organized socialist groups. They tended to dominate the Christian Socialist Society, as we have seen, and the British branch of the Christian Socialist Fellowship was organized by the Congregationalist Rev. H. Cubbon (1864-1933).[53] To a lesser extent Congregationalists featured in the Labour Church. Rev. B. J. Harker (1843-1916) of Bolton, for example, turned his Congregational church into a Labour Church in 1892, the year in which was published his tract *Christianity and the New Social Demands*. Harker claimed that "it is the Capitalist Church which necessitates the Labour Church. . . . Socialism demands no more than its right to the spring of God's bounty —the privilege of all and not the few to drink what is needful of the water of life."[54]

Congregationalist radicals, like others, were attracted for a time by Henry George's Single Tax doctrines, and one lay president of the Congregational Union (1893), Albert Spicer, MP, of Hull, was a confirmed Georgeist.[55] Also, several prominent Labour Party men were Congregationalists, including Ben Tillett (1860-1943) and Keir Hardie (1856-

[52] *Light and Shade: Pictures of London Life: A Sequel to "The Bitter Cry of Outcast London"* (London, 1885), p. 163 and passim.

[53] See above, Chapter VIII, for the work of the Congregational ministers Revs. T. A. Leonard, C. Fleming Williams, W. Whittley, T. Travers Sherlock, H. Cubbon, and J. H. Belcher (Christian Socialist League).

[54] Harker was an ex-Methodist minister. He held Congregational posts in Wales, Yorkshire, and the Midlands before moving to Bolton (1882-1902). See *Labour Prophet*, I, No. 10 (October 1892), p. 80; DWL Index; *Congregational Yearbook*, 1917, pp. 183f.; B. J. Harker, *Christianity and the New Social Demands* (Manchester, 1892), passim.

[55] *Brotherhood*, III, No. 6 (January 1889), p. 182; New Ser., I, No. 2 (June 1893), pp. 18-19.

1915).[56] Hardie, however, was Arminian rather than Calvinist in religious outlook, and therefore readier to accept the nondoctrinal faith of John Trevor's Labour Church. Hardie began his reform career in the temperance movement and evolved into a socialist. According to Fenner Brockway, the Hardie family, parents and child, were alienated from the Church by bitter experiences, and the young Hardie's reading and natural idealism led him slowly, as he grew up, "to appreciate anew the beauty and truths of the teachings of Christianity." He rejected "the doctrinal accretions" but "identified himself with what seemed to him to be the simplest organized expression of Christianity, the Evangelical Union." Keir Hardie was a true international socialist, a man of broad sympathies, a feminist, a campaigner for animals (pit-ponies) as well as miners, an antiracist, a pacifist in both the Boer War and World War I. "Socialism is a great moral movement," said Hardie. "I am a Socialist because Socialism means Fraternity founded on Justice, and the fact that in order to secure this, certain economic changes are necessary is a mere incident in our great human crusade. *My protest is against economics being considered the whole of Socialism or even the vital part of it.*" Lord Brockway has written of the creator of the ILP, "He was always conscious of a Divine Purpose, and he revered above all the life and teachings of Christ, who lived it so completely. Toward the end of his life he said that were he to live it again he would devote it to the advocacy of the Gospel of Christ."[57]

For Keir Hardie, "the things that wound most deeply are not the material things." Two other Congregationalists,

[56] For Tillett see his *Memories and Reflections*. For Hardie's religious life see his "The Christianity of Christ," *Labour Prophet*, I, No. 11 (November 1892), pp. 85-86; Fenner Brockway's essay in H. Martin (ed.), *Christian Social Reformers of the 19th Century*, pp. 229-242; Keir Hardie, *From Serfdom to Socialism*, ch. IV; and R. J. Campbell, *The New Theology and the Socialist Movement* (Stockport, 1908), pp. 5-6.

[57] Fenner Brockway, in H. Martin (ed.), *Christian Social Reformers*, pp. 233, 237-238, 242.

Revs. F. H. Stead and P. T. Forsyth, were in agreement with this position. Rev. F. H. Stead (1857-1928), the brother of the journalist W. T. Stead, developed a line of Christian socialist argument taken mainly from the Anglican lectures on "Christian Economics" of Rev. W. Richmond of 1888 (CSU). Apart from assisting his brother on the *Review of Reviews* (1894-1912), founding the "League to Abolish War," editing the *Independent and Nonconformist* (1890-1892) and managing the Browning Settlement, Walworth (1894-1921) more or less as a labor center, Stead worked with Charles Booth in the Old-Age Pension movement and was a prolific author.[58] Rev. Dr. Peter Taylor Forsyth (1848-1921) was much more of a theologian and less of a socialist than Stead; but the Congregational authorities thought him too heterodox for his name to be admitted into the denomination's Yearbook until 1884. Forsyth became principal of Hackney College in 1901, and for twenty years thereafter the influence of his social theology was felt by Congregational students. Among his works perhaps the two best known were *Socialism, the Church and the Poor* (1908) and *A Holy Church the Moral Guide of Society* (1905). The latter, based on a speech of 1905 to the Congregational Union, later published by the denomination's paper, *The Examiner*, has been called "a powerful theological exposition of the proper social concern of the Gospel." In it Forsyth rejected charity, however "magnificent," as the cure for the ills of capitalist society. "Philanthropy can deal with symptoms and effects," he said, "and we ought to get at causes. . . ." The social theory of capitalism, *laissez-faire* individualism, was inadequate and immoral, thought Forsyth, "a mere mosaic of free egoisms." Under this atomistic theory,

[58] See F. H. Stead, *How Old Age Pensions Began to Be* (London, n.d. [1915?]); *Congregational Yearbook*, 1929, pp. 231-233; *Brotherhood*, III, No. 2 (September 1888), p. 62; New Ser., III, No. 7 (November 1895), p. 89; DWL Index; *Christian Socialist*, VI, No. 66 (November 1888), pp. 169ff.; Keir Hardie et al., *Labour and Religion* (London, 1910), passim; R. T. Jones, p. 345.
Original source material for W. T. Stead (who needs a good biographer) is to be found in the H. D. Lloyd Papers, WSHS.

society "becomes a field of hostilities, desolated by a war of classes and even nations. The sight of huge capital alongside huge misery, of overproduction on the one side and starvation on the other, has its slow moral effect on the public, and many, like Bishop Gore, are driven into sympathy with Labour." Some critics of socialism are suspicious of legislation as a channel of reform; but, said Forsyth in 1908, "Laws have a moral and educative effect. They can be agents of grace as they may flow from the action of grace."[59] P. T. Forsyth thus "theologized" T. H. Green's doctrine of the positive state and the efficacy of legislative action. He was clearly much affected by the Anglican CSU and the example of Charles Gore.

The climax of the Congregational social movement came in 1907 with Rev. R. J. Campbell's "New Theology" propaganda and the creation of his Progressive League. England's top preacher, Campbell could draw crowds of over seven thousand at a time when rival congregations steadily dwindled. His advent in 1903 to the City Temple marked, in Rev. J. G. Adderley's words, "an epoch in London Christianity."[60] The young preacher of thirty-seven was already the subject of a biography and had recently returned triumphant from an American lecture tour. Campbell had not yet been converted to socialism and had not yet developed his "New Theology"; his ideas, in fact, seemed highly orthodox and respectable at this stage.

[59] E. R. Wickham, *Church and People in an Industrial City*, pp. 200-203; P. T. Forsyth, *A Holy Church the Moral Guide of Society* (London, 1905), passim, and *Socialism, the Church and the Poor* (London, 1908), passim; DWL Index; *Congregational Yearbook*, 1922, pp. 104f.; G. O. Griffith, *The Theology of P. T. Forsyth* (London, 1948). The Keir Hardie quotation that opens the paragraph is in R. J. Campbell, *The New Theology and the Socialist Movement* (London, 1908), pp. 5-6.

[60] J. G. Adderley, *In Slums and Society*, pp. 124-125. Campbell was of Ulster Nonconformist clerical stock. Educated at University College, Nottingham and Christ Church, Oxford (B.A., 1895, D.D. 1919). After a brief period as an Anglican at Oxford, Campbell became a Congregational minister at Brighton (1895-1903) and then for twelve years at the City Temple (1903-1915). See C. T. Bateman, *R. J. Campbell* (London, 1903), pp. 1-25; DWL Index.

In 1904 Campbell, a great popular preacher with enormous personality and influence, began to turn toward socialism. He described this transition in a volume three years later. In 1904 he attacked the British workers in a *National Review* article for their nonobservance of Sunday. An outbreak of labor protests ensued, and he was asked to repeat his charges face-to-face at a trade-union mass meeting. Campbell had the courage to agree, and soon discovered how ignorant he was of the labor point of view. "Ever since that memorable meeting I have been more or less closely in touch with some of the more prominent leaders of the Labour movement in this country," he wrote. He began to abandon his other-worldly sermons, came under Keir Hardie's spell, and spoke for Labour Churches, trade unions, ILP meetings, and Fabian debates; he was even elected to the Fabian executive in 1908-1909.[61] Campbell's formal, public declaration of his new-found socialist faith came in a sermon on "Christianity and Collectivism" in the City Temple during the autumn of 1906. The effect was immediate: "Forthwith all the Labour platforms were thrown open to me," he wrote. "When the New Theology controversy broke out in January [1907] . . . these were almost the only platforms I had left."

This "New Theology" of Campbell's was nothing more nor less than the Social Gospel, with an almost exclusive emphasis on the Divine Immanence argument. The controversy actually opened in September 1906 with an address by Campbell to the London Board of Congregational Ministers. His orthodoxy had long been suspect, and in January 1907 the publication of his lively sermons as *The New Theology* touched off an outbreak of violent denunciations against "City Temple-ism." The congregation of that great church remained loyal to its minister throughout the attacks, but he was excluded by other churches and carefully

---

[61] However, he was too busy ever to attend a single Fabian Committee meeting. See Pease, p. 187; *Reformers' Yearbook*, 1909, p. 218; R. J. Campbell, *Christianity and the Social Order* (London, 1907), p. x.

isolated by the Congregational old guard. "All my Free Church Council engagements were cancelled by the churches themselves, as were most of my preaching appointments with other ecclesiastical organizations," said Campbell. He was "quietly excluded from an active share in every Nonconformist organization . . . with the exception of the City Temple itself." The New Theology, Campbell explained, "is an untrammelled return to the Christian sources in the light of modern thought. Its starting point is a re-emphasis of the Christian belief in the Divine Immanence in the Universe and in Mankind." According to this theory, every man is "a potential Christ, or rather a manifestation of the Eternal Christ." The dangerous doctrine of Transcendence, said Campbell, pushed too far, creates an unwanted *dualism* which leads men "to think of God as above and apart from His world instead of expressing Himself through His world."[62] This too-typical "theologizing" implies crudely that God is "quite distinct from His creation." In contrast: "The New Theology holds that we know nothing and can know nothing of the Infinite Cause whence all things proceed, except as we read Him in His universe and in our own Souls. It is the immanent God with whom we have to do." Campbell's emphasis was thus on *man's* divinity, not on the gulf between man and God.[63]

The New Theology was "the religion of science," and its God was defined by Campbell as "the uncaused Cause of all existence, the unitary principle implied in all multiplicity." To disbelieve in God was therefore to disbelieve in one's own existence.

> The God of the ordinary churchgoer . . . is an antiquated theologian who made His universe so badly that it went wrong in spite of Him. . . . Why He should ever have

[62] A similar idea was developed much later in the Bishop of Woolwich's *Honest to God* (London, 1963).

[63] *The New Theology*, Popular ed. (London, 1909), pp. v-vi, ix-x, 3-4; E. A. Payne, *The Baptist Union*, p. 174. For parallels with Woolwich's *Honest to God*, see especially pp. 16-17.

created it is not clear. Why He should be the injured party in all the miseries that have ensued is still less clear.

Do not sweated laborers have "some sort of claim upon God, apart from being miserable sinners who must account themselves fortunate to be forgiven for Christ's sake"? Campbell concludes: "Faugh! It is all so unreal and so stupid. This kind of God is no God at all . . . He is spiteful and silly." In opposition to this kind of thinking, the New Theology was "the religious articulation of the social movement." It was the theology of the Labour Movement, "whether the Movement knows it or not." The universe and human society were "one instrument or vehicle of the self-expression of God. God is all; He is the Universe, and infinitely more. . . ." He is, therefore, in every "moral movement," every social revelation and advance. In brief: *"The New Theology is spiritual Socialism."*[64]

For Campbell in his radical heyday of 1907-1910, socialism was "simply the revival of Christianity in the form best suited to the modern mind." To remove the "supernaturalism" from Christianity was not to destroy it, for the faith had a practical job of social reconstruction to do—"the demolition of all barriers of privilege between nation and nation or man and man."[65] A summer school was begun at Penmaenmawr in 1907 for "linking the movement more closely with social reform." The following year it met at Aberystwyth, and meanwhile Campbell had written to the *Christian World* and his own organ, the *Christian Commonwealth,* complaining of "repression" by church authorities of his New Theology disciples and demanding the establishment of a "League of Progressive Thought and Social Service" to unite, encourage, and protect them. The Progressive League was founded forthwith. Its first organizing secretary was an ardent ILP man, Rev. F. R. Swan (1868-1938),

[64] *The New Theology*, pp. 12ff., 22, 255; R. T. Jones, p. 344.
[65] R. J. Campbell, *Christianity and the Social Order*, pp. 149-150. See also *Brotherhood*, AU Ser., No. 6 (15 April 1908), pp. 259-64.

a Congregational minister who campaigned for Campbell for four years (1906-1910) and then took over J. Bruce Wallace's own Southgate Road Brotherhood Church (1910-1938). Swan was also a *Daily Herald* staff member (1912-1938) and a strong pacifist. He wrote *The Immanence of Christ* in 1907.[66]

R. J. Campbell, of course, became president of the new Progressive League, and Rev. T. Rhondda Williams and J. A. Seddon, MP, vice-presidents. The League's principles were:

1. That the spiritual unity of mankind, expressed in the words: "We are members one of another," should be embodied in all social and industrial life.
2. That all material things and conditions should be used and valued for the highest well-being of society and of the individual.

The League proposed "to work for a social reconstruction which shall give economic emancipation to all workers, with fullest opportunities and the most favorable surroundings for individual development; and establish a new social order based upon co-operation for life instead of competition for existence."[67] More specifically, Campbell stood squarely for collectivist socialism, for national ownership of all natural resources (to be taken over gradually and with compensation for former owners), and socialization of capital. He did not stop at Henry Georgeism or land reform, but demanded public ownership of railroads and all basic industries. Campbell rejected half-measures and melioristic reforms such as profit-sharing, emigration schemes to solve unemployment, cooperatives, and peasant proprietorship.

[66] See R. J. Campbell's review of Swan's piece in *Christian Commonwealth*, 28, No. 1355 (2 October 1907), p. 9. See also DWL Index; *Congregational Yearbook*, 1939, p. 713.

[67] R. J. Campbell, *Primitive Christianity and Modern Socialism*, Progressive League Series No. 1 (London, n.d.), p. 2 (advertisement); see also *Brotherhood*, AU Ser., No. 6 (15 April 1908), pp. 253-256; No. 8 (15 October 1908), pp. 339ff. See also *New Age*, III, No. 26 (24 October 1908), p. 519.

He also urged freedom for women; ". . . man," he said quite correctly, "is woman's capitalist."[68]

The Progressive League thrived from 1908 until 1911, when the New Theology was finally welcomed into the Congregational fold and Campbell's long theological dispute (with Rev. P. T. Forsyth, among others) came to an end.[69] The League had held many rallies and demonstrations and engaged in extensive Social Gospel mission campaigns in various cities. In Wales Campbell preached in English and T. Rhondda Williams in his native Welsh. In London Campbell, Williams, Hall Caine, and Bernard Shaw harangued a large demonstration in October 1909.[70] Rhondda Williams (1860-1945), Campbell's closest friend and disciple, was a Welsh demagogue, who pushed the New Theology to such an extreme that it was barely "Christian" at all.[71] He was an ILP stalwart, full of Welsh "soul" —a dramatic, if unoriginal, orator.[72]

A preacher of wider fame and eloquence in the fold of Campbell's League was the American socialist-evangelist Rev. J. Stitt Wilson. According to Fenner Brockway, Stitt Wilson was much more radical than either Campbell or Williams and had a much better grasp of socialist economics. He was a disciple of the leading American Congregational Socialist, Rev. Professor G. D. Herron (1862-1925), and founder of a Herronite socialist propaganda organization in the USA in the nineties: The Social Crusade. Stitt Wilson's group supported the left-wing socialist American Social

[68] R. J. Campbell, *Christianity and the Social Order*, passim.

[69] At the autumnal assembly of Congregational Union in Nottingham, 1911. See *Brotherhood*, No. 43 (November 1911), pp. 454-455.

[70] *Brotherhood*, No. 9 (January 1909), p. 36; No. 18 (October 1909), pp. 443-444.

[71] Conversation with Fenner Brockway, MP (1963).

[72] Born in Glamorgan; son of a Calvinistic Methodist minister. Congregational minister at Dowlais, Neath, Bradford (1888-1901) and Union Church, Brighton (1909-1931). Chairman of the Congregational Union, 1929-1930 (DWL Index; *Congregational Yearbook*, 1946, p. 456). His books include *The Social Gospel* (London, 1902) and the autobiographical *How I Found My Faith* (London, 1938). For his address of 1908 in Aberystwyth, see *Brotherhood*, No. 8 (15 October 1908), pp. 340-344.

Democratic Party, and Wilson openly declared his vote in 1900 for E. V. Debs—"the natural nominee of the workers of America." He organized an SDF local in Cedar Rapids, Iowa and campaigned for "scientific socialism" in Chicago.

Stitt Wilson's English campaigns of 1900 and 1907-1908 concentrated on Bradford and South Wales. (An earlier visit to London (1899) was cut short by family illness.) In January 1900 he made the Brownroyd Congregational Church, Bradford his campaign headquarters and stayed there for several months, drawing huge crowds. His preaching was magnificent, and all his lectures were known by heart and "acted out." He made four trips to England as a socialist missionary[73] and in 1910 was nominated Socialist candidate for the governorship of California, polling 50,000 votes. The following year, in a whirlwind and messianic campaign, Stitt Wilson became Socialist mayor of Berkeley, California.[74] The subject matter of his British orations included: "Moses —the greatest of labour leaders," "The Messiah Cometh, riding upon the Ass of Economics," "The Message of Socialism to the Church," and so on, and many of these lectures were published as separate pamphlets in England. One com-

[73] *Brotherhood*, VI, No. 8 (December 1898), p. 124; VI, No. 11 (March 1899), p. 167; VII, No. 1 (May 1899), p. 16; VII, No. 2 (June 1899), pp. 19-20.

[74] In San Francisco, Stitt Wilson kept a large hall for several years, in which he lectured every week to capacity crowds on the Single Tax, women's rights, temperance, prison reform, the abolition of capital punishment, international peace, and socialism. Born in Canada, 1868, and educated at Northwestern and Chicago universities, Wilson gave up a Methodist ministry in Chicago to devote himself to full-time socialist agitation, moving to California about 1901. He wrote a good deal, including: *The Impending Social Revolution* (1902); *The Human Prophets and the Social Revolution* (1907); *The Harlots and the Pharisees* (1913). See *Who's Who in Berkeley* (1917); J. E. Baker (ed.), *The Past and Present of Alameda County, Cal.* (Chicago, 1914), II, 275-277; *Berkeley Gazette*, 29 August 1942. I am most grateful to Florence M. Marr of the Berkeley Public Library for facilitating research in California on Stitt Wilson. For English comments on Wilson's election battles, see *Brotherhood*, No. 31 (November 1910), p. 472; No. 32 (December 1910), pp. 536-538. See also T. J. Morgan to H. D. Lloyd, 15 October 1900, H. D. Lloyd Papers, WSHS; and H. Quint, *The Forging of American Socialism*, p. 138 n. 121.

mentator (Binyon) called Stitt Wilson "the most powerful figure that has ever appeared" in English Christian socialism. Wilson lectured to Labour Churches, Quaker meetings, and ILP audiences, climaxing his 1900 campaign by speaking every night for three weeks and holding at the conclusion two mass meetings of 4,000 people each in St. George's Hall, Bradford. After a week's "mission" to Tunbridge Wells, Wilson sailed for the USA in March 1900.[75]

In 1907-1908 Wilson once more descended on Bradford, and to support his personal evangelism this time he published a Bradford version of his Herronite Chicago journal, the *Social Crusade*—"a blazing half-penny propaganda sheet." From August 1907 well into 1908 Stitt Wilson held meetings night after night, pulling together all the socialists of the area for "the greatest mission for social righteousness ever held in any city of the Kingdom." His cospeakers included F. W. Jowett, MP, the socialist Quaker Arthur Priestman, the socialist Methodist D. B. Foster, Rev. F. W. Swan, Bruce Wallace, and the Anglo-Catholic Rev. W. B. Graham (described by the *Clarion* as "six feet of socialist and five inches of parson"). "We wish to avoid any merely theological or ecclesiastical issues," said Stitt Wilson. "But we do propose to arouse the social energies of the people and their new ethical zeal . . . and place that power as a dynamic behind the Socialist programme." There was no doubt as to the intent of Wilson's revivalistic Social Gospel: "This campaign is intended to be *a straight attack upon the capitalistic system,* as unChristian, unjust and cruel, and responsible for the perpetuation of poverty in the midst of superabundance."[76]

After Bradford came Glasgow, Halifax, Leeds, South

[75] *Brotherhood*, VII, No. 9 (January 1900), p. 144; VII, No. 10 (February 1900), p. 159; VII, No. 11 (March 1900), pp. 169-170; VII, No. 12 (April 1900), pp. 182-183. See also *Church Record*, April 1900, p. 4; G. C. Binyon, *The Christian Socialist Movement in England*, p. 184.

[76] *Brotherhood*, AU Ser., No. 4 (15 October 1907), pp. 147-152; No. 5 (15 January 1908), pp. 220-222. The last contains a selection from the *Social Crusade*; a small sample of its language will illustrate the tone: "Old age, uncheered, sits in penury in tens of thousands of homes, chilled and faint for lack of blood sucked away by Capitalism. . . .

Wales. *Halifax Labour News* was astonished by the rapid success of Stitt Wilson's telling combination of revivalism and socialism. After the first fifty really new converts (always the most difficult to win) came a landslide and massive crowds.

> The people had been chained down. . . . Stitt Wilson had bid them "Come Out!" He had led them up to see the promised land. . . . He claimed for them the Bible, as their property, with its great store of hope and record of the world's struggle for humanity towards a higher life.

His Halifax campaign ended with the largest socialist procession (half-a-mile long) ever seen in the city, "led by the *Clarion* cyclists, followed by the Trades Council with their huge banner." The audience was said to number 10,000. Soon afterward the Welsh campaign opened in Cardiff, with afternoon crowds of 3,000 and evening crowds of 7,000.

Stitt Wilson's manner was deeply messianic, like that of the earlier American who proselytized in Britain, Henry George. Wilson discounted all past movements and all theological niceties: "The Messianic age does not come primarily with a New Theology or a new code of ethics, but with a new social vision . . . ," he declared. This was perhaps further than the more disciplined and less radical R. J. Campbell was prepared to go. Stitt Wilson's campaigns of 1907-1908 and Campbell's Progressive League agitation of the same years were complementary; but the League gradually became less socialist and more liberal. Its name was changed in 1910 to the *Liberal Christian League* and on its roster of speakers for that year was Lloyd George.[77]

The chief weakness of Stitt Wilson (as of his great hero, George Herron) was his liking of hero worship. This was

---

While Mammon . . . goes forth intoxicated with pride and power crying for more 'Profits! Profits! Profits!'—fleecing the sheep—and leaving them to die by the roadside! . . . the cry comes to our ears of a despoiled, exploited, and outraged humanity—bruised, beaten, baffled—calling for help!"

[77] *Brotherhood*, AU Ser., No. 7 (15 July 1908), pp. 297-298; No. 8 (15 October 1908), pp. 338, 361-362; No. 26 (June 1910), p. 270; No. 31 (November 1910), pp. 465-472.

even more marked in R. J. Campbell. The "Campbell cult" sickened some of his more socialist young followers like Fenner Brockway. Campbell was publicized as if he were a modern film star, with huge photographs in journals, a large sale of autographed portraits, a personal journal (*Christian Commonwealth*)—even an *R. J. Campbell Birthday Book.* Some followers were attracted by the humane New Theology and the Christian socialism of Campbell more than by the preacher himself. Brockway was nauseated by the crowd of "rich, adoring young women" who surrounded the preacher; his personal experience in Campbell's campaign (as a journalist on the staff of the *Christian Commonwealth,* about 1907-1910) made Brockway, if anything, *less* "Christian" and *more* "socialist" in his emphasis.[78] After World War I, R. J. Campbell actually repudiated his former faith, *withdrew* his book *The New Theology,* and rejoined the Church of England, into which his old opponent Charles Gore welcomed him, of course, with open arms. Campbell then rose to considerable distinction in the Anglican faith and died Canon Emeritus of Chichester Cathedral![79]

The R. J. Campbell, New Theology crusade marked the crest of prewar Congregational social-reform enthusiasm. With the coming of World War I, Congregationalism settled down once more, albeit further to the political left. The Congregational Union created its own Social Service Committee in 1910, and thus made social-unionism and the Social Gospel the established pattern in Congregational Christianity, as it was in Anglicanism, Methodism, Unitarianism, Quakerism, and the other denominations.

[78] R. W. Sorensen, MP (1963), was also a Campbell man in his youth (F. Brockway, *Inside the Left,* pp. 15ff.; personal conversation with Lord Brockway).

[79] Campbell's later career in the Anglican Church was as follows: Curate of St. Philip's, Birmingham (1916-1917); Vicar of Christ Church, Westminster (1917-1922); licensed preacher in London, 1922-1924; Vicar of Holy Trinity, Brighton, 1924-1929; Canon of Chichester Cathedral, 1930-1934; Chaplain of Bishop Otter College, Chichester, 1933-1936; Chancellor of Chichester Cathedral, 1930-1946; Canon Emeritus, 1946-1956 (DWL Index; *Who Was Who,* 1951-1960, p. 178; J. W. Grant, *Free Churchmanship in England, 1870-1940* [London, 1955], pp. 131-142; J. G. Adderley, *In Slums and Society,* pp. 124-125).

CHAPTER X

Conclusion: The Enigma of Christian Socialism

"Christian Socialism," said Marx in the *Communist Manifesto*, "is but the holy-water with which the priest consecrates the heart-burnings of the aristocrat." His British disciple Ernest Belfort Bax added that "the establishment of society on a Socialist basis would imply the definitive abandonment of all theological cults, since the notion of a transcendent God or semi-divine prophet is but the counterpart and analogue of the transcendent governing-class."[1]

For Bax, socialism was humanism, and religion was a great irrelevancy. Many British late-Victorian socialists did not feel this way, and we have tried to discover why and to describe and explain the revival of active Christian socialism between the late 1870's and the First World War. The men and women studied here called themselves "Christian socialists" and we have accepted their self-description, whether or not on any objective definition use of the word "socialist" is justified in any particular case. Stewart Headlam, for example, clearly regarded his Guild of St. Matthew as a socialist organization. He also wrote a book called *The Socialist's Church* in 1907 and a Fabian Society Tract, *Christian Socialism,* in 1892. It is true that in his own politics he advanced little beyond the land-taxation ideas of his American friend Henry George, and that like some other Fabians he tended to vote Liberal and had no sympathy with the Independent Labour Party. Yet on these grounds are we to exclude Headlam from a history of the Christian socialist revival? It would be a strange history indeed if Headlam did not figure in it largely.

Among the dozen or so organized Christian socialist societies with which we have dealt, those which openly sup-

[1] E. B. Bax, *The Religion of Socialism*, p. 81.

ported some definition of socialism as understood by secular socialists—whether collectivist or pluralist—included the Church Socialist League (Anglican), the Christian Socialist Society (interdenominational, but at times barely "Christian"), the ephemeral Christian Socialist Fellowship (mainly supported by Congregationalists), and the New-Church Socialist Society (Swedenborgian). The Socialist Quaker Society, though it made no open declaration in favor of total nationalization, is clearly to be included in this group, and it was eventually absorbed into Guild Socialism, along with the Church Socialist League. The Guild of St. Matthew, the even milder Christian Social Union, John Clifford's Christian Socialist League and Social Brotherhood, and the Free Church Socialist League did not demand, as organized pressure groups, either full collectivization or guild-type worker control. The GSM was, of course, Georgeist, the CSU to all intents and purposes Liberal (with welfare-state additives), the Clifford groups were mildly Fabian on a Georgeist base (with a strong working-class flavor), and the Free Church movement was a short-lived adjunct of the Labour Party, again with a Georgeist base. These classifications do not cover the countless individual reformers all over the nation who worked in municipalities, ILP offices, local Fabian headquarters, and trade-union halls, and who thought of themselves as Christian socialists but did not join any formal organization. Moreover, within each society was a variety of individual opinions. The communitarianism of J. C. Kenworthy and the cooperativism of J. Bruce Wallace owed much to Laurence Gronlund's *Co-operative Commonwealth* and to the experiments and writing of John Ruskin and Leo Tolstoy. The Christian Guild Socialists owed much to the pluralism of Father J. N. Figgis and the original producers' cooperative associations of Buchez and Ludlow.

One could attempt to impose a more ambitious, if somewhat confusing, distinction between "Christian socialists" and "socialist Christians." Some felt themselves to be socialists because they were Christians; others were simply Christians who happened also to be socialists or socialists who happened also to be Christians. Using this division, under the rubric "Christian socialists" would go many of the sacramentalists, Headlam and his GSM confederates (Moll, Hancock, Sarson, and so on), Scott Holland and Gore in the milder CSU, and some members of the Church Socialist League, notably Bull, Donaldson, West, Adderley, and Noel. The League, however, because it was closer to the Northern working class, the ILP, and the trade unions, also attracted to its fold many socialist Christians. Rev. G. Algernon West was undoubtedly a socialist because he was a Christian, and could argue theologically for socialism. But as League president, as we have seen, he was responsible for a policy of discouraging the traditional Christian socialist arguments for socialism ("armchair socialism," as he called it), in favor of a nontheological and straightforward attachment to the Labour Party. West's call for a Church Socialist League propaganda policy "on Christian lines" but only "as far as it is consistent with the needs of our own times" sounds much more socialist Christian than Christian socialist.

The undogmatic and nontheological Christian Socialist Society can be seen as a debating ground between socialist Christians and Christian socialists. W.H.P. Campbell, who, as noted, later became a Fabian and an ILP local treasurer and dropped the prefix "Christian" altogether, was at the time of his leadership of the Christian Socialist Society a socialist Christian rather than a Christian socialist. His struggle inside the Society with Rev. J. C. Kenworthy illustrates the distinction quite well. Kenworthy's thought was highly eclectic; Edward Bellamy, Ruskin, Tolstoy, and Gronlund loomed in his writings, along with traditional Christianity. But Kenworthy clearly thought of himself as the champion of the Christian element in a "Christian socialism," the foundations of which were to be found embedded in religion. He was not, however, as profoundly Christian socialist as men like Father Paul Bull, and he was prepared to admit that the name of Jesus had become a "fetish" among Christian reformers. Other Christian Socialist Society members, following the lead of Campbell and the Labour Churchman R. A. Beckett, rejected Kenworthy's arguments. Their line of reasoning went so far that they can hardly be termed even "socialist Christians," and they fall outside *both* classifications; they wished to exclude "Christworship" altogether.

In the remaining ephemeral groups the Baptist leader Rev. John Clifford can be fairly termed a Christian socialist, though he learned his Fabian socialism only very gradually, and one might logically have expected him to discover the "socialist" message implicit in Christianity much earlier. His denomination, on the other hand, was extremely conservative in political and social matters, and Clifford had much to contend with, quite apart from the fact that his own theology remained throughout his life surprisingly individualistic and evangelical. The Swedenborgian and Quaker socialists developed their sectarian arguments in favor of social radicalism. Thomas Child and S.J.C. Goldsack in the New-Church seem to have been socialists out of Swedenborgian conviction. The ILP's treasurer, T. D. Benson, though he adopted thoroughly Swedenborgian arguments in his ILP pamphlet *Socialism and Service,* would in all probability have become a socialist without any religious influences. The members of the SQS, Joseph Theodore Harris and his wife, Mary O'Brien, the editor W. L. Hare, and their colleagues, were chiefly concerned with converting the members of the Society of Friends to socialism. They were not simply socialists who happened to be Christians, but Quakers seeking to return to what they deemed to be the original social message of their faith.

There is little point in trying to apply the distinction between socialist Christians and Christian socialists to the minor figures in other societies. The distinction is by no means watertight and if applied too closely, becomes patently absurd, for it involves judgments of the depth and sincerity of the religious convictions of individuals. On the other hand, the difficulty in applying this distinction throws light on the inherent contradictions of Christian socialism as an idea.

This narrative has attempted simply to distinguish between more "radical" and less "radical" Christian socialists, and between sacramentalists and immanentalists, Anglicans and Nonconformists, and to fix their work and ideas in the wider setting of the history of British socialism in the nineteenth and twentieth centuries.

The original Christian socialists of the 1850's followed the Frenchmen Buchez and Lamennais in economic matters and found that Maurician theology, with its rejection of the supernatural, its search for a rational, reasonable faith, its humanity, its optimistic faith in human progress assured by a benevolent God, its social emphasis, and its determination to take rational account in its arguments of the latest scientific and social trends of the day, provided a suitable foundation for a "social gospel." The Mauricians and their French predecessors emphasized the Fatherhood of God and the subsequent brotherhood of man. What political and economic embodiment of this theme could be more suitable than that which both of these groups proclaimed— *associationism?* The Mauricians, like the voluntarist Buchez, eschewed worship of, or dependence on, the all-powerful central state. They demanded, as one would expect of Christian socialists, a political doctrine that could guarantee the freedom of the individual Christian conscience and that could make full use of the concept of Christian duties. Workers' cooperatives, organized outside the aegis of the State (though afforded its ultimate protection), met these demands ideally.

The Christian socialists of the revival period had much less unity of belief as far as political methods were concerned. The range of ideas and personalities among them was considerable, from the bohemian Stewart Headlam to the abstemious Methodist mayor D. B. Foster; from the imperial-minded monk, Father Paul Bull, to the Guild Socialist S. G. Hobson. Their greater range of methods reflected the more advanced state of evolution of British socialism and the labor movement in the late-Victorian era as compared with the 1850's and the greater complexity of the social and economic problems posed by structural historical changes.

Sacramental socialists, members of the GSM, the Church Socialist League, and, to a lesser degree the CSU based their theological arguments for "socialism" on the symbolic message of the sacraments. The doctrinal argument was for them of prime importance. Their theology was ultimately derived from Maurice, who had taught some of their leaders; but they laid greater emphasis on the sacraments as such than he would ever have done. The sacramental argument is to be seen at its clearest in Headlam, Bull, and Moll. The ceremony of Baptism, they argued, regularly carried out by the Church, reasserts the doctrine of Christian brotherhood and fundamental human equality before God every time the priest performs it. The Mass, or the Lord's Supper, performed weekly, is the supreme expression of a Christian's faith in the Incarnation and in Christ's supreme sacrifice for all mankind. Christ took human shape, said Bull, and thereby consecrated forever the human body and the daily life of man and blurred the distinction between the material and the spiritual. The claim of theological individualists that religion is concerned with "spiritual" matters and socialism with "material" matters and that never the twain shall meet is therefore untenable. Christians are as much responsible for the material life of their fellows as for their spiritual needs. Christ's miracles, moreover, were secular works of mercy. The Crucifixion stands for supreme self-sacrifice and for God's sympathy and love for mankind, Bull asserted. Since we are all brothers under God's Fatherhood, "Christ is crucified afresh" every time one of our fellowmen is sinned against.

Rev. W. E. Moll, the champion of Tyneside labor, declared (following Maurice), that the Church was the Kingdom of God on earth and its mission was "to realize the unity of mankind revealed by the Incarnation." The Church should give its members guidance in social problems, and since (echoing T. H. Green) the State is a "sacred organism," Christians must fight for state laws in favor of socialism and righteousness. At this point Moll goes beyond the men of 1850 (and beyond many Christian socialists of his own day). But his confidence that socialism is righteousness and that poverty is evil is founded ultimately on the same base as the optimism of Buchez or Maurice—the benevolence of God. It is blasphemous to blame poverty on the Divine Will, said Moll, and he decried the false political economy which "teaches men to say that there are those for whom God has placed no plate at the banquet of life." The sacramentalists made use of all the arguments, summarized for convenience in Chapter III above, which concentrated on the social character of the sacraments themselves and the Book of Common Prayer, and on the arguments based on a study of patristics, which revealed (to their satisfaction) that the church fathers had supported "socialistic" views.

There were no *economic* elements common to the thought of all sacramentalists which one could use to distinguish their "socialism" from that of the Methodists, Quakers, or other groups. The Anglo-Catholic GSM, for example, was Henry Georgeist; but so was the Free Church Socialist League. The Church Socialist League, on the other hand, stood for full collectivization (before the onslaught of Guild Socialism), but the CSU went only as far as consumer action and mild protective legislation; yet both were sacramental.

The Guild of St. Matthew contained many discordant voices. Its general economic and social policy was nonetheless fairly clear. Headlam managed to take a voting majority with him in support of the Single Tax on land values, secular education, the eight-hour day, and in opposition to the idea of independent labor representation. Sarson, Symes, Shuttleworth, and Moll were all Single Taxers and had all known George personally. Though Marson, Dearmer, and Moll disagreed with Headlam's political policy and favored the ILP (Moll later joining its Council, as we have observed), it would be fair to characterize the economic thought of the Guild as a whole as Georgeist and Radical-Liberal rather than collectivist. It was this residual loyalty to the Liberal party which impeded the development of Headlam's economic thought and prevented him from moving, as others such as Bernard Shaw did, from Georgeist taxation of rent to a more strictly "socialist" socialization of capital. Perhaps there were deeper reasons, for it is evident from his remarks that Headlam shared some of the doubts and fears of his master, F. D. Maurice, on the subject of democracy.

The Christian Social Union chose a theological course that was sacramental but nonritualist—Broad rather than High Church, in contrast with the GSM. Its sacramental statements were less blatant and obvious than those of Headlam or Bull; but equally, its social policy was very much milder than that of either the GSM or the League. In fact, we have chosen here to describe its thought as "social-unionism" (a term used slightly pejoratively by Noel) rather than "Christian socialism." One CSU activist, Rev. John Carter, thought of the Union in different terms, for he called his CSU tract of 1905 *Christian Socialism*. Scott Holland followed his former teacher T. H. Green in justifying the positive welfare state, though in practice few suggestions were made by the CSU for advanced welfare legislation—nothing at all to compare, for example, with the Socialist Quaker Society's plea for socialized medicine.

On the subject of imperialism, colonial policy, and war, both Gore and Scott Holland spoke and wrote in terms as critical of government policy as did any secular socialist. In home affairs, on the other hand, the limitations of "Christian shopping" must have been only too apparent to the Union's more radical colleagues. In any case, the technique of consumer action against the market economy was not new, and the Labour Church, as we have noted, did at least as much as the CSU in promoting such action against the leaded-glaze industry of the potteries.

A small section of the CSU (led by Father "Jimmy" Adderley) offered support to the ILP, and Gore favored the cooperative movement; the Union as a whole encouraged trade unions and advocated legislation in the fields of sanitation, fair wages, progressive taxation, and women's rights. Gore and Holland, however, were elitists (Holland opposed the ILP). Their Union was a middle-class and upper-middle-class affair, held together by Oxford, public school, and clerical ties. The men of the CSU were born into the Establishment; it made them, and they served it well. The major reason behind the curious state of affairs in the Anglican church in the early twentieth century, in which the bishops and upper clergy appeared more "radical" in political and social matters than the rank and file of the church, was that, given their breeding, social status, education, independent means, and ecclesiastical preferment, the leaders of the CSU could wield great influence with the ruling class of which they were a part. Bearing this in mind, the paucity of their achievement is rather astonishing. Social-unionism petered out eventually into that even milder form of activity known as "social service," which is, after all, not far from the mere charity which "Christian socialists" originally arose to decry in the early eighties.

The Church Socialist League, in contrast with the CSU, represented sacramental socialism of the most radical and economic variety. Father Bull, CR, sounded the note echoed throughout the League's history in his Mirfield Manual No. 4, which claimed socialism as the sole answer to the nation's problems outside the Church, and claimed the three principles of socialism to be equality of opportunity, common ownership of the means of production, and "universal cooperation." The last was particularly important, Bull thought, because, in his words, "competition inevitably involves worldwide war." Although he found capitalism and war to be two sides of the same coin, Father Bull did not share the unreserved suspicion of imperialism expressed by Gore, Scott Holland, and other Christian reformers of the period. For Bull, as we have noted, imperialism was another aspect of the growing "corporate spirit" of which socialism was itself an example. Naturally, his "imperialism" is one of "large visions"; perhaps he thought that if socialism were to be achieved at home, the Empire would enable it to spread beyond those "bounds of nationality" which he found rather restrictive. Other Christian socialists were less hopeful as to the probable results of the exploits of the "Rhodes gang," though E. D. Girdlestone of the Christian Socialist Society was one exception.

The socialism of the League was distinctly more "advanced" politically than any Christian socialism which had gone before in nineteenth-century Britain, because its central tenet was the common ownership of the means of production, distribution, and exchange. Closely linked with the ILP in the North of England, the League stood for state socialism in its early days and put its faith in independent labor political action. After 1912, however, the League came round increasingly to a point of view more in line with the traditional Christian socialist approach as exemplified by Ludlow or Buchez, now embodied in Guild Socialism: "associationism" in a new form.

Even before the League had become drawn into the Guild Socialist movement, its members were not agreed as to the general course of action the organization had been pursuing —i.e., favoring the ILP and state socialism. We have observed that Algernon West led the League in a "socialist Christian" direction, shunning intellectualism and theology, and supporting the ILP. He would have preferred, as he said, "a purely Socialist Party," but was willing to "make do" with the ILP because he realized that the party was the true indication of the future historical course that British socialism was likely to take. By 1906 the party itself was a much more likely prospect than it had been in 1893, when Headlam and Scott Holland opposed it. West's policy was rejected by Widdrington, an intellectual, as we have seen, with totally different aims for the League. Widdrington stood for social theology *par excellence,* and wished to develop a so-called Christian sociology. Pinchard, who replaced West, sided with the opposition and tried to turn the League away from its ILP alliance toward a kind of socialist neutralism.

Pinchard argued that the true purpose of the Church Socialist League was not to follow the ILP-LRC-Labour Party line or the SDF, but "to convert churchmen and make them socialists." The question he raised was an important one, which bedeviled the history of several Christian socialist organizations. The question did not come to much in the League, however. The League, in fact, remained activist, and only a year later (1910) Egerton Swann was demanding a rejection of Fabian gradualism in favor of a more strenuous policy. It will be remembered that he asked: "How can it be unChristian to proclaim the class-war?" In that same year Rev. C. S. Smith became the new organizing secretary and began to campaign for a genuine workers' socialism; far from leaving the ILP-Labour Party in order to concentrate his efforts on Anglican churchmen alone (as Pinchard recommended), Smith was trying to push the League *beyond* the Labour Party (which he thought was itself becoming too middle class) toward a more genuinely *socialist* platform—i.e., one that stood for worker participation and control. These were among the early hints of Guild Socialism. More important were the articles by Reckitt on the subject in the *Church Socialist* in 1913. The League, as we have already seen, formally accepted Guild Socialist doctrines by a resolution of May 1914. Sacramentalism had thus ended up in associationism.

The keynote of the theology of Nonconformist socialism was not the Incarnation but the doctrine of Divine Immanence. This doctrine reached its limits in the New Theology of R. J. Campbell and Rhondda Williams. According to the New Theology, man himself was divine because he was the "manifestation of the Eternal Christ." God was immanent everywhere and was not "distinct from His creation." The New Theology, said Campbell, is "the religious articulation of the social movement."

In point of fact, however, many Nonconformist reformers chose to avoid theology altogether. The Christian Socialist Society, initially established to provide an organization for nonsacerdotal Christians, soon became open to influences which were not even Christian at all, and the society's title seemed a misnomer. Having begun with a vague theology of which the only theme was the personality of Christ, it ended in utter theological doubt and confusion. The economic philosophy of the Christian Socialist Society was at first Georgeist, but rapidly broadened to include total nationalization. The Danish-American revisionist Laurence Gronlund was the major influence in the later economic thought of this group.

Milder and of less significance were John Clifford's groups and the Free Church Socialist League. They had no distinctive or original social theology. Clifford himself never lost an opportunity to attack the Church of England, though his League was not especially sectarian. After careful consideration, Clifford eventually became a Fabian socialist. He was the author of two Fabian tracts on Christian socialism. The campaigns of John Clifford's somewhat scatterbrained but very active and hardworking Christian socialist colleague J. Bruce Wallace included vegetarianism, internationalism and pacifism, the Labour Church, the Garden City movement and, above all, producers' cooperatives. Wallace's Brotherhood Trust organization and Brotherhood Churches provide us with the chief example of the persistence of the associationist-cooperative ideal in Christian socialist thought between the Mauricians and the emergence of Guild Socialism, though its roots do not stem from the Mauricians in the cases of Wallace and Kenworthy.

The theology of the SQS and the New-Church Socialist Society offer little material from which general statements can usefully be made. Each of the two groups was concerned with its own kind and had an internal theological history, apart (to a great extent) from the general currents outside. There were elements of theology in both schools, as we have shown in their respective chapters above, which made them conducive to socialist interpretations. Politically, both were willing to work with the ILP. Several Swedenborgians, including Rev. Arthur Potter, the cooperative agitator, drifted into the Labour Church, and T. D. Benson was treasurer of the ILP. From the Quakers, the artist J. E. Southall joined the ILP and became a pacifist leader within the party. The SQS and the NCSS both advocated complete socialization, though the Quakers made no common policy statement on the subject. Naturally, the SQS took a strong stand on all matters involving personal freedoms, women's rights, and war. Quaker socialism was more distinctive in its type than the Swedenborgian variety. The socialism of the SQS was a kind of ethical Fabianism. Quaker socialists believed, with Webb, that socialism was already developing out of capitalism, via countless legislative and administrative changes, via radical liberalism and municipal reform, and via all the other "collectivist" pressures of the times, not least of which was the industrial trend toward "trustification." Capitalism was thus preparing itself for socialism, and Quakers should recognize this "long and hastening evolution" and help to accelerate the process. The SQS regarded democratic socialism as the only viable way, the "middle way" between revolution and social stagnation. Among the chief aims of the society, before it was won over to Guild Socialism by S. G. Hobson and others, were municipal socialism and the institution of a National Health Service.

As we look back over the aims, activities, and ideas of the various Christian socialist groups in these years, what general statements can we make about the movement as a whole? What ideas did they have in common? What problems did they share? How does their achievement compare with that of earlier Christian socialists?

First, Christian socialists shared a common fund of religious ideas, and it would be safe to generalize that they all were agreed upon two points: first, that "applied Christianity" was a possibility; second, that the essential message of Christianity was the brotherhood of man. The idea that Christianity *could* be applied to human society was voiced more often by the more religious and clerical Christian socialists, of course. But trade unionists like Ben Tillett or labor leaders like Keir Hardie or Philip Snowden from time to time would also describe their socialist aims as the mere application of Christian beliefs. The conviction that Christianity is a "working hypothesis" is an optimistic one. The Christian socialists of the revival years were united in the Maurician assurance that social progress through the application of basic Christian principles was guaranteed by God himself. For the sacramentalists, God's love was embodied in the Incarnation and Crucifixion; for others, God was immanent and part of the universe itself. For them all, as for Buchez and Maurice, God was essentially benevolent. In the rhetoric of some affable, relaxed, popular churchmen (Shuttleworth, for instance), this doctrine is not without its absurd aspects; God appears to take on some of the attributes of an easy-going Anglican Santa Claus.

This idea of benevolence and progress is linked with the second belief common to all Christian socialists, the brotherhood of man under God. As a religious theme, the brotherhood of man was reiterated constantly by the French Christians Lamennais and Buchez. For Lamennais, man's brotherhood meant that nothing but complete egalitarian political democracy, the establishment of a society of equals before the law, could ever be the legitimate form of human society under God. Kings and aristocrats must be swept away. Moreover, any attempt by philosophers to base the doctrine of human equality on other, nonreligious grounds was doomed to failure. The concept of "Nature" was no guide; the Fatherhood of God was the only sure and unequivocal foundation for egalitarianism. With all this the Christian socialists of the late nineteenth century were in agreement, though some of them might not have been completely satisfied with the latter part.

In Maurice and Ludlow the idea of brotherhood was also dominant, and in practice it took the shape of their cooperative associations (as for Buchez it took the form of his aid to Louis Blanc's *ateliers sociaux*). Wherever we look among the late Victorians we find the idea of the Fatherhood of God and the brotherhood of man—in Headlam ("We are a baptized brotherhood of equals") ; in Gore and the CSU; and throughout Nonconformity. While the Christian socialists of the later period were in accord on the principle of Christian brotherhood, however, they did not agree as to the political or economic means of implementing that ideal in human society. The cooperative method of Buchez and Ludlow was not at all widely accepted as the best means of achieving socialist brotherhood. Rev. H. V. Mills's cooperative colony at Starnthwaite came in for bitter criticism from some Christian socialists; Bruce Wallace's Brotherhood organizations were more successful, but they did not win the adherence of any major Christian socialist propaganda society. The truth was that the attention of Christian socialists in the eighties and nineties was diverted from such direct modes of brotherly activity as cooperation by the growth of Fabian collectivism, state socialism, and, after the Bradford Conference of 1893, by the ILP. It was not until a large enough number of Christian socialists had become disenchanted with collectivism and the Labour Party that the cooperative ideal again became dominant—in the new form of Guild Socialism.

Still another religious theme, apart from the brotherhood of man, which was common to the reformers of the eighties, if not to those of the fifties as well, was the great emphasis laid upon the personality of Jesus Christ—Christ the man, who lived a life of purity, social service, and supreme self-sacrifice and gave the world a philosophy of brotherly love, a selfless ethic, and a social ideal for all time . . . Christ, the lowly carpenter, who healed the sick and helped the poor and cast the money-changers out of the temple. The reasons for this "personal" and human emphasis are not hard to find. The religious faith of the late nineteenth century was sorely tried, as we have already pointed out, by the Darwinian evolutionary theory and by the growth of scientific Biblical criticism and comparative religion. Doubts were cast on the validity of the miracle stories and (by *Lux Mundi,* among other works) upon the omniscience of the incarnate Christ. When Trinitarians like the Luxites seemed to question Christ's supreme powers, what were Nonconformists and Unitarians to believe? It was clearly safer for Christian apologists to concentrate on Christ's personality and works and leave aside the tricky question of his divinity. Moreover, the homely image of the carpenter was suited for the working-class audiences which Christian preachers, whether "socialist" or not, hoped to attract. The "theology," such as it was, of the churches which were closest to the mass of the people (apart from the Labour Church) was therefore pragmatically "Christ-centered."

What economic ideas were held in common by Christian socialists? Our previous survey of their attitudes and activities reveals that the Quakers, the Swedenborgians, the Christian Socialist Society members, and the Anglo-Catholic sacramentalists of the North who were organized into the Church Socialist League all favored complete nationalization of the means of production, distribution, and exchange. Meanwhile, the Headlamites, the social-unionists, and the members of other minor groups were wary of committing themselves to full public ownership. At one time or another, however, almost all Christian socialists (in common, as I have shown elsewhere, with countless trade-unionists, Fabians, ILP-men, and even SDF and Socialist League members) had been Henry Georgeists. With Christian socialists the Georgeist influence very often did not easily rub off.

George's *Progress and Poverty,* combining, as it did, a plausible economic argument with powerful emotional and even religious appeal, was particularly attractive to many Christians who were unhappy with the social conditions of late-Victorian Britain yet uncertain as to the causes of unemployment and distress. In George many of them found a ready answer, and his best-selling book was reinforced by the lecture tours he gave in the 1880's. Sweeping away the fatalistic Wages Fund Theory and Malthusianism, and reiterating his sturdy faith in a benevolent Creator for whom "divine miscalculation" of the Malthusian sort was unthinkable, Henry George provided *economic* arguments to buttress the optimistic theology of the Mauricians. Like Moll, Headlam, and others, George could not bring himself to blame God for misdeeds that were essentially man's. He could not "reconcile the idea of human immortality with the idea that nature wastes men by constantly bringing them into being where there is no room for them." On the basis of Ricardian rent-theory, as we have seen, George built his justification for one great Single Tax to take away the unearned, socially created increment of land value at present being absorbed by the rent-receiving class. His technique was legal, nonrevolutionary, parliamentary. It involved no massive collectivist state, no complex guild structure. Men like Headlam learned their economics from *Progress and Poverty* without discovering the more sophisticated economic analysis of Jevons and Wicksteed. Other Christian socialists went on to full economic socialism; they followed Buchez (and Marx) rather than Saint-Simon (and George) in placing the capitalists in the exploiter class along with the landlords.

Nevertheless, George's *technique* for bringing about social change remained. The Single Tax, a steadily increasing toll on the increment of land values, raised eventually to the point of virtual confiscation, was a simple administrative device. No revolution or class struggle was involved; no violent take-over of political power; no *coup d'état*. Existing democratic machinery (which George was willing to improve by experimentation with new voting systems and so on) could be used to wipe out the major social evil of the day—land monopoly—and all else would follow. Georgeism, like Fabianism, was an extension of the Liberal-Radical adoption of the power of the positive state.

The Fabians too, as we have seen, took the Ricardian and Georgeist concept of "economic rent" as their major analytical tool rather than Karl Marx's idea of "surplus value." Bernard Shaw, stimulated by Henry George to think his first economic thoughts, moved on to socialism, fit-

447

tingly, via yet another of George's converts, the Unitarian economist P. H. Wicksteed. Thus, through the medium of Henry George and Wicksteed the Fabian Society became Jevonian in its economic theory. Here is at least one direct theoretical contribution of the Georgeist wing to the evolution of British socialist thought. The essentially "Christian" element in the contribution, however, is not especially noticeable.

In addition to the Headlamites in the GSM, other societies which came under the Single Tax spell were the Christian Socialist Society and the Swedenborgians. Some CSU members also felt the pull of Henry George, particularly when George lectured at Oxford and was given publicity in the posthumous publication of Arnold Toynbee's lectures. Rev. John Clifford was also a Single Taxer. In all these cases, however (except the GSM), the Single Tax influence was a passing phase in the development of Christian socialist ideas and policies. A host of lay "Christian socialists" (like Albert Spicer, the Hull MP and one-time lay president of the Congregational Union) were ardent Georgeists. But the Christian Socialist Society very soon overthrew its own Single Tax origins, began to publish attacks on George's ideas, and eventually moved over from *Progress and Poverty* to Gronlund's *Cooperative Commonwealth*— led by E. D. Girdlestone, the principal Gronlund disciple in the Society.

The majority of Christian socialists, who were not consistently Georgeists, tended to borrow whatever economic ideas and techniques seemed appropriate from the secular movements around them: from the Fabians, the ILP, the cooperative movement, the municipal reformers, the Garden City protagonists, and so forth. This condition continued down to the full emergence of Guild Socialism in 1912 out of the medievalist "Gild Restoration" movement led by A. J. Penty in the Church Socialist League. After the first excitement about *Progress and Poverty* had died away, the economic and political proposals of the Christian socialists lacked a particular unifying principle. Christian socialists were vague and sentimental (like Miss E. Sawers of the Christian Socialist Society) or highly abstruse, remote, and academic (like Thomas Hancock or P.E.T. Widdrington), or in contrast they were so anxious to avoid theological refinement and to come to grips with the real labor movement that their thought became indistinguishable in character and tone from that of the vaguely pantheistic Labour Church (for example, W.H.P. Campbell). In sum, their "socialism" was an intellectual ragbag, and most of them never faced up to the dominant question: What is specifically "Christian" about Christian socialism? After 1912 some attempt was made by Widdrington and his followers to define a "Christian sociology," but this was a rarefied and philosophical investigation by a donnish and clerical circle.

As for the remoteness of many Christian socialists from the labor movement, the Church Socialist League, the SQS and the New-Church Socialist Society had some advantages over other groups because of their direct contacts through the ILP. The League, in particular, tapped the deep fount of Northern working-class radicalism, at least for a time. In sharp contrast, Headlam's Guild and the CSU cut themselves off almost willfully from such popular wellsprings. They thus remained essentially upper-middle-class and exclusively Anglican organizations, and for this reason the mainstream of British labor history (which meant essentially the ILP-LRC-Labour Party current) passed them by.

Next to the ILP, the Fabian Society was the socialist group that received most aid and encouragement from Christian socialists and with which they had the deepest relationship. Christian socialists disagreed violently with the Fabians in the late 1890's and ultimately split with the Society over Guild Socialism; they could not stomach Fabian policy over the Boer War, and they came to suspect Fabian collectivism. Nevertheless, for a long time the Fabians' evolutionary gradualism and insistence on nonviolent social change, and Webb's useful historical hypothesis that "socialism" was merely the continuing transformation of the Victorian Liberal-Radical democratic state, suited Chris-

449

tian socialists admirably. Some were happy to call themselves "Christian Fabians." Even the mild Christian Social Union occasionally thought of itself in such terms. The Fabian executive, as we have already noticed, contained at various times three Quaker socialists (Mary O'Brien Harris, Percy Alden, and S. G. Hobson), one Baptist socialist (John Clifford), one Congregationalist socialist (R. J. Campbell), one Anglo-Catholic socialist (Stewart Headlam), and one Unitarian socialist (H. B. Holding). Many nonexecutive members were also Christian socialists, including the Broad Church Anglican Percy Dearmer and the High Churchman Sidney Dark. Provincial Fabians were less ready to countenance the permeation policy of the London leadership and did not care to work so closely with the Liberals, especially in the North, where the ILP and Labour Church became entrenched. Local Fabian groups did not persist for very long (except for Liverpool) and were rapidly absorbed into the ILP after 1893; but where they existed, they received much support and aid from local Christian socialists.

The London Fabians, like Headlam, were reluctant to recognize Keir Hardie's party when it first appeared because in the capital and on the London County Council and London School Board, Fabians had formed a useful working alliance with Radicals and Liberals. Stewart Headlam worked hard on the Board and on the Council in the cause of secular education, pursuing the same aims as other "Progressives," i.e., Fabian-Radicals. His loyalty to the Liberals and shortsightedness about the possible future of the Independent Labour Party idea were shared at least by many Fabian socialists of the same period.

With the winning over of the Church Socialist League and the Socialist Quaker Society to Guild Socialism from about 1912, the British Christian socialist movement came full circle, from the producers' cooperative associationism of J. M. Ludlow through Henry Georgeism and a variety of social reform ideas, including in some cases full collectivist socialism, back to associationism. We have observed that Guild Socialism was initially set in motion by the Christian socialist architect and medievalist A. J. Penty, whose book *The Restoration of the Gild System* first appeared in 1906. Penty wanted to return to his idealized, small-scale handicraft system, abandoning modern division of labor and specialized technology. His model was William Morris's *News from Nowhere* rather than Edward Bellamy's industrial *Looking Backward*. Some Christian socialists followed Bellamy and Gronlund rather than Morris—J. Bruce Wallace and J. C. Kenworthy, for example (Kenworthy being the more agrarian-minded of these two). Penty's medievalism and agrarianism was soon passed by in favor of an *industrial* guild philosophy as expounded principally by the Fabian SQS member S. G. Hobson. Genuine workers' control of modern industrial plant management was Hobson's ultimate aim, and the construction of a politically decentralized, functional social order. The central state would charter the industrial guilds but leave them as essentially autonomous bodies. Working with A. R. Orage (and later with the brilliant and brash young G.D.H. Cole, with whom he disagreed on many points of principle), Hobson brought back to political life and debate the associationism of Buchez, Blanc, and Ludlow. Underlying the whole Guild movement, of course, was the philosophical pluralism of Father J. N. Figgis of Gore's Community of the Resurrection at Mirfield. It is very noticeable that the Owenite tradition is ignored in Christian socialist literature; no references are made to Robert Owen's plans of the 1830's for a Grand National Consolidated Trades Union, which would supplant the function of Parliament; no references to the Owenite churches (nor to the Chartist Churches); and few references to Robert Owen's work at all.

The Church Socialist League became increasingly disenchanted with the Fabian, permeative style of socialism and with the collectivism of the ILP and LRC. After the anticlimax following the electoral victories of 1906, the "Liberalization" of Labour MP's, the Grayson incident, and the introduction of rudimentary welfare-state legislation by the Liberals (which seemed to satisfy the general public for the time being) Christian socialists of varying tempers and types turned away from the mainstream of labor political history in disgust. Against this setting came the appearance of syndicalism, distributivism, and Guild Socialism. The last seemed to be a movement halfway between the now-discredited collectivism and the projected violence and class war of syndicalism. Anticollectivist writings by religious intellectuals such as Hilaire Belloc and G. K. Chesterton, who had been on the fringes of the Christian socialist movement for some time, combined with the pluralism and medieval organicism of Father Figgis, pushed the League toward Guild Socialism. Church Socialist Leaguers discovered in the Guild movement a system to give the workers and producers a genuine say in the management and organization of the national economy without necessitating a gigantic centralized state and an oppressive middle-class bureaucracy. Yet it would be a distortion to assume that most British Christian socialists became fully enamored of the Guild system or fully disenchanted with the collectivist and parliamentary mainstream. Guild Socialism appealed most to intellectuals, to philosophers, to Anglo-Catholic dogmatists, and medievalists. Few, if any, actual working trade-unionists joined the movement. The bulk of British Christian socialists ("socialist Christians," using our earlier distinction) were undogmatic, untheological, and not aggressively intellectual. Their political and economic philosophy was vague and unconscious, like their immanentalist theology. One would guess that the modal type of Christian socialist was D. B. Foster or Keir Hardie rather than S. G. Hobson or P.E.T. Widdrington.

How does the record of the Christian socialist revival appear when placed in the historical balance with the achievements of the Mauricians? The late Victorians had, of course, a much greater range of ideas and took part in a greater variety of reform movements because socialism itself was more developed in their day. They did not create or synthesize a more sophisticated or integrated corpus of Christian socialist thought—and one could perhaps have expected this—over the decades since Lamennais, Buchez, Maurice, and Ludlow. The best that the Christian socialists of the 1900's could do in the area of socialist thought was to adapt the Guild idea to their own theoretical needs. Conrad Noel claimed that the Church Socialist League was far in advance of the "socialism" of Maurice, Ludlow, and Kingsley. This is true; but the "socialism" even of the League was for the most part derivative and unoriginal, excluding perhaps Penty's initial contribution to the Guild movement. The pioneer work of associating Christianity in Britain with the word and the idea of socialism was undertaken by the Mauricians, and though many later Christian socialists seemed to owe little or nothing in their philosophy to the men of the 1850's, it is hard to surmise what shape or form Christian socialism might have taken (if any) if Maurice had never existed.

The very idea of "Christian socialism," as this book amply illustrates, is difficult and ambiguous. Christian socialism is an enigma. The two elements of its makeup have been in a constant state of tension throughout the movement's history. Christian socialists have complained either that their particular organization was too doctrinal or that it was too secular. Those who became heavily involved in reform politics often ended up with the least theology (if they did not begin that way) : the ILP-Labour Church syndrome. Those who shunned active politics became too remote and too exclusively concerned with theology; many sacramental types suffered from this condition. According to G. C. Binyon, the Christian socialist movement split into two parts: (1) the "warning voices," pleading for redemption but doing little, and (2) the doers. "The whole movement has shown a wavering," he wrote, "between generalities and an adoption of the Labour programme of the moment."[2] Such a division is built in, inherent in the concept of Christian socialism itself. Genuine Christian socialists, however, were always fewer in number in the late-Victorian period

[2] G. C. Binyon in J. Lewis, K. Polanyi, and D. K. Kitchin (eds.), *Christianity and the Social Revolution*, p. 193.

than the larger mass of unthinking, or at least less articulate, "socialist Christians." The majority group were not disturbed by the inner contradictions and tensions of Christian socialist philosophy. They were Congregationalists, or Methodists, or Unitarians who were also Single Taxers, municipal reformers, supporters of the ILP, and members of trade unions, and their credo rarely became explicit. The connections between the two halves of their lives seemed too obvious to require any elaborate dialectical justification. Naturally, their contribution to the evolution of British socialist *thought* was therefore minimal.

The contribution of Christian socialism to *Christian* thought has been perhaps a little greater. The function of Christian socialism in history has been to modify or to temper the secular socialist movement on the one hand and the inherently conservative nature of institutionalized Christianity on the other. As an independent school of thought, however, Christian socialism has always had to face the enormous difficulty of distinguishing the precise content or contribution of its adjective "Christian." In the words of T. S. Eliot, "Many of the changes which [Christian economic reformers] advocate, while deducible from Christian principles, can recommend themselves to any intelligent and disinterested person, and do not require a Christian society to carry them into effect, or Christian belief to render them acceptable." But if the Christian element in the socialism is not of prime necessity, the socialist element in the Christianity would certainly, Eliot thought, "make it more possible for the individual Christian to live out his Christianity."[3] On these grounds, the challenge thus seems to be not to create a Christian society out of which socialism will and must emerge, but to create a social order in which the Christian life will become a real possibility. In such a case the entire emphasis of Christian socialist policy in past history would seem to be tactically incorrect. Active Christian socialists on the whole have not, in fact, been concerned with creating a new social order *as a priority*. They have

[3] T. S. Eliot, *The Idea of a Christian Society* (London, 1939) , p. 10.

tried to Christianize society first, or at least they have limited their efforts to political proselytizing within their own denominations.

On the other hand, at least in British history, the Christian socialists did make considerable contributions, outside the realm of social theory, to the growth of the socialist and labor movements. The work of countless individual Christian socialists and of the various formal groups added to the general socialist momentum of the late-Victorian era. There is no doubt that many "waverers," who might never have joined the ranks of socialism because of its association in the popular mind with atheism, were swayed by seeing such a large number of reverends, doctors of divinity, and church dignitaries attach themselves to labor organizations and adopt the title "socialist." British Christian socialism could have achieved much more than this but for certain serious internal weaknesses.

First, the Christian socialists were divided by sectarianism. Much of their energy was wasted away in interdenominational rivalries and struggles over niceties of theology. One cannot, of course, argue that theological differences *should* have been unimportant; that would be to presume too much upon the ground of religious convictions. Nevertheless, it is objectively true that a smaller number of Christian socialist societies, accompanied by greater cooperation between Christian socialists, would have produced appreciably better effects in propaganda and social agitation. The unedifying squabble between the churches for control of British public education, a squabble in which some of the very figureheads, Clifford, Gore, Headlam, and others were self-confessed "Christian socialists," did little to commend organized religion to the general public. Ben Tillett's vision of the churches fighting over the dockers in the great strike of 1889 did little to commend those churches to the workers.

Second, the emergence of social-unionism took the wind out of the sails of the Christian socialist bodies and stole many of their members. The historical pattern in most churches was that a small, radical "ginger group" would emerge first of all, preaching a social gospel—sometimes outright socialism (SQS) —and demanding greater social action and support for social reform and labor groups on behalf of church members. Then, a few years later, a milder, more generally acceptable and better-supported group would appear, on a larger scale, a social-union group rather than a Christian socialist group. This would quickly establish social inquiry committees and local social-service branches. Leading members of the congregation would support it and man its committees. The smaller group would gradually decline, and a social-union ("social gospel") climate would overtake the entire church. Socialism would by then be effectually bypassed in the church, as by the Liberal welfare legislation in the political arena after 1906. The exemplars of this social process are, of course, the GSM and CSU; the SQS and Friends' Social Union; the Christian Socialist Society and League; and the Free Church Socialist League and the Wesleyan, Congregational, and interdenominational social unions which sprang up in the 1900's.

Third, the Christian socialists were weakened by their persistent inward-looking attitude. The SQS and the NCSS were established primarily to spread socialism among members of the Society of Friends and the Swedenborgian faith respectively. An attempt was made to turn the Church Socialist League into a similar type of inward-looking organization concerned with its own church. As we have seen, this attempt came to nothing.

F. D. Maurice's declared aim had been to Christianize socialism.[4] It is an aim which typifies his middle-class approach to the social problem. Socialists who did not wish to be "Christianized" (like the Chartists who were harangued by Maurice after their failure in 1848) might argue that in a world full of social evil and distress it is surely a poor use

---

[4] *Tracts on Christian Socialism*, No. 1 (London, 1850), pp. 2f., quoted in H. M. Pelling (ed.), *The Challenge of Socialism* (London, 1954), pp. 88-92.

of human resources to spend the time of sincere and well-meaning men in trying to spiritualize those reformers who are already at work in society. To Christianize socialism, on the one hand, and to spread socialism in one's own church, on the other, are two possible functions of a "Christian socialism." But was not the third the more significant function, namely, to socialize the world?

It seems curious to the outside observer that so few Christian socialists took as their principal and overriding object the spreading of socialism in the nation at large in order (reiterating T. S. Eliot's phrase) to "make it more possible for the individual Christian to live out his Christianity." The Church Socialist League chose this wider aim; so did the smaller Christian Socialist Society. The GSM, however, in spite of all its work for the Single Tax and public education, had its hands full in "justifying God to the people." The CSU looked outward to the social problem but was content with writing studious articles about it. Even in the SQS, it has been suggested, dissidence was to some degree an expression of revolt *within* the Society of Friends against the dominance of the traditional great Quaker families. The less privileged and younger Quakers were forced into national politics, and into the support of central state action, in reaction to the control already exerted by richer Friends over local government and local outlets for social work.[5] This may help to explain why Quaker socialists were so fully concerned with convincing *Friends* (rather than the general public) of the need for socialism.

The revival of Christian socialism in late-Victorian England helped to advance the interests of the socialist and labor movements in general by breaking down prejudices, especially on the part of religious people, against the idea of socialism. The Christian socialists helped to make socialism more respectable. One cannot estimate to what extent specific social changes or legislative reforms were influenced by Christian socialist activities. One can say, on the other

[5] Personal conversation with Mr. Stephen James Thorne.

457

hand, that such activities made substantial contributions to the development of the Fabian Society and the Independent Labour Party, and that innumerable Christian socialist individuals labored in the provinces and in the capital to gain municipal reforms, to improve public education and public health, to oppose war and imperialism, and generally to support "collectivist" (in the sense of A. V. Dicey, Sidney Webb, or Joseph Chamberlain) measures.

The weakness of most Christian socialists was one they shared with other types of socialist: their middle-classness. They did not suffer from this limitation as badly as the Mauricians; Charles Kingsley's chief desire, it could be said with some justice, was to wash the British workers bright and clean with good middle-class soap and water, like his *Water Babies*. The late-Victorian Christian socialists, whether sacramental or Nonconformist, were somewhat less patronizing and less concerned with the personal morality and cleanliness of the working class. Yet they also failed in the end to break through the class barrier and to make sustained and successful communication with the urban masses.

The Labour Churches achieved a near-success in the 1890's but were not essentially Christian. Could the churches, with the aid of Christian socialism, have captured (or "recaptured," as they wrongly conceived the situation) the working-class movement and thus have brought about a deep religious revival? They surely had, as the American Social Gospel leader Walter Rauschenbusch put it, "a tremendous stake in the social crisis." Neutrality was an impossibility for the churches. If they remained entirely quiescent, they would by default be supporting the existing Victorian capitalist social order. If they came out in support of the privileged classes (as they did in the mid-Victorian era), they would simply condemn themselves to "a slow and comfortable death." The Protestant churches had built their power on an alliance with the rising bourgeoisie of intelligence and wealth created by industrialization. If the workers were to be the dominant class of the future, organized religion could only hope to survive in modern society by espousing the dreams and desires of that class. It was the parable of the Wise and Foolish Virgins.[6]

But the facts and figures of the working-class alienation from institutionalized Christianity (as suggested in Chapter III) offer but meager hope of any such "capture" of the labor movement. By the 1880's it was already too late; Victorian religion was already lost to the urban masses. Perhaps the "capture" would have faced fewer problems in the 1850's, but the Mauricians were far too class-conscious ever to have accomplished such a social revolution. By the twentieth century the British working class had built up a strongly positive pattern of class life, a sturdy and independent subculture to which organized religion was an irrelevancy. The spiritual vacuum was filled by the labor movement itself, if by anything.

As for the Christian churches, the Social Gospel, leading them to abandon Victorian theological individualism and the automatic political and social conservatism that accompanied it, was spread through the "social-union" organizations of which the Church of England's Christian Social Union was the first example. The previous existence of the more radical Christian socialist societies and their influence in causing the denominations to create, in reaction, as it were, social-union institutions validate the judgment that the Christian socialist revival accelerated the acceptance of the Social Gospel in twentieth-century Britain. In turn, the new social emphasis helped to prevent the total and final alienation of Church and people in Britain, although it could not prevent the continuing erosion of the Christian faith.

[6] Walter Rauschenbusch, *Christianity and the Social Crisis*, ed. Robert D. Cross, Harper Torchbook ed. (New York, 1964), p. 331.

Guide to Source Materials

MANUSCRIPT ARCHIVES

Archives, Community of the Resurrection, Mirfield, Yorkshire

British Library of Political and Economic Science, London School of Economics: P. H. Wicksteed Papers (1844-1928)

Dr. Williams' Library, London, Manuscript Collections: Index of Congregational Ministers (DWL Index) ; Hibbert Trust Papers; Hunter's Autobiographical Notices; "London Unitarian Ministers' Meeting: Minutes" (4 vols., handwritten, 1893-1894)

Friends' House Library, London: Dictionary of Quaker Biography (DQB—ongoing card index compiled by E. H. Milligan) ; Socialist Quaker Society, Minutes

New York Public Library: Henry George Collection (HGC)

Wisconsin State Historical Society, Madison (WSHS) : R. T. Ely Collection; Henry Demarest Lloyd Papers

NEWSPAPERS AND PERIODICALS OF THE PERIOD

All serials were published in London unless otherwise indicated.

Atlantic Monthly (Boston, Mass.)
The British Friend
Brotherhood (Limavady, Ireland)
Christian Commonwealth
Christian Socialist
Church Reformer
Church Times
Church Socialist
Church Socialist Quarterly (1909-1911; begun as *The Optimist*, 1906-1908 and continued under that title, 1912-1916)
Commonweal
Commonwealth
Economic Review (Oxford)
Fabian News

The Friend
Friends' Quarterly Examiner
Goodwill
Justice
Labour Annual
Labour Church Record
Labour Prophet (Manchester)
Methodist Recorder
Monthly Record (Friends)
The New Age
New-Church Herald
New-Church Magazine
Ploughshare
Primitive Methodist Magazine
Progressive Review
Seedtime
The Times
Uses

WRITINGS OF THE PERIOD

Abraham, W. H. *Studies of a Socialist Parson.* Hull, 1892.
Adams, Maurice. *Ethics of Social Reform.* London: New Fellowship, 1887.
Adderley, C. B. (Baron Norton). *Socialism.* London, 1895.
Adderley, J. G. *Stephen Remarx.* London, 1893.
———. *Christ and Social Reform.* London: Society for Promoting Christian Knowledge, 1893.
———. *The New Floreat.* London, 1894.
———. *Looking Upward.* London, 1896.
———. *A New Earth.* London, 1903.
———. *Quis Habitabit—Psalm XV: A Meditation for Christian Socialists.* London, 1903.
———. *Prayer-Book Teaching.* London, 1904.
———. *The Catholicism of the Church of England.* London, 1908.
———. *A Little Primer of Christian Socialism.* London and Oxford, n.d. [1909?].
———. *The Parson in Socialism.* Leeds, 1910.

———. *In Slums and Society*. London, 1916.

Alden, Percy. *Democracy in England*. New York, 1912.

Anti-Socialist Union. *Speakers' Handbook*. London, 1911.

———. *Socialism Exposed*. London, 1914.

———. *Christianity and Socialism* [n.p., n.d.].

Arch, Joseph. *The Story of His Life, Told by Himself*. London, 1898.

Armour, S. C. *Christianity and Socialism*. Liverpool, 1887.

Ball, Sidney. *Moral Aspects of Socialism*. London, 1896. (Fabian Tract No. 72.)

Bax, E. B. *The Religion of Socialism*. Third edition, London, 1891. [First edition, 1885.]

———. *Essays in Socialism*. London, 1887.

Belloc, Hilaire. *Socialism and the Servile State*. S.W. London: ILP, 1911.

———. *The Servile State*. First edition, London, 1912; first American edition, New York, 1946.

Benson, T. D. *Socialism and Service*. London, n.d. [1906?]. (ILP Tracts for the Times, No. 11.)

———. *The Workers' Hell and the Way Out*. London n.d. (ILP Tracts for the Times, No. 7.)

Best, K. D. *Why No Good Catholic Can Be a Socialist*. London, 1890.

The Bitter Cry of Outcast London. London: Congregational Union, 1883.

Blatchford, R. *Merrie England*. London, 1895.

———. *Socialism: A Reply to the Pope's Encyclical*. London, 1895. (Clarion Pamphlet No. 1.)

———. *Real Socialism; What It Is and What It Is Not*. London, 1907. (Clarion Pamphlet No. 3.)

Bliss, W.D.P. *The Encyclopaedia of Social Reform*. New York, 1908.

Blissard, W. *The Socialism of Christianity*. London, 1891.

———. *The Ethics of Usury and Interest*. London, 1892.

Blount, G. *The Blood of the Poor: An Introduction to Christian Social Economics*. London, 1911.

Booth, Charles. *Pauperism and the Endowment of Old Age*. London, 1892.

Booth, Charles. *Life and Labour of the People in London,* Third Series, Vol. 16: *Religious Influence.* London, 1902.

Booth, William. *In Darkest England and the Way Out.* London, 1890.

Boyd, H. J. *Christianity and Socialism.* London, 1910. (Anti-Socialist Union, No. 79.)

Bradlaugh, C. *The Land, the People and the Coming Struggle.* London, 1882.

Brocklehurst, Fred. *A Socialist's Programme.* London, 1899.

Bull, Paul B. *Economics of the Kingdom of God.* London, 1897.

———. *Christian Teaching.* London and Oxford, n.d. (Mirfield Manuals for the Million, No. 1.)

———. *Urgent Church Reforms.* London and Oxford, n.d. (Mirfield Manuals for the Million, No. 3.)

———. *Socialism and the Church.* London and Oxford, n.d. (Mirfield Manuals for the Million, No. 4.)

Butler, Samuel. *Erewhon.* First edition, London, 1872; New American Library paperback edition, New York, 1961.

Campbell, R. J. *The New Theology.* First edition, London, 1907; Popular edition, 1909.

———. *Christianity and the Social Order.* London, 1907.

———. *The New Theology and the Social Movement.* London: ILP, 1907.

———. *The New Theology and the Socialist Movement.* Stockport, 1908. (People's Penny Pamphlets, No. 1.)

———. *Primitive Christianity and Modern Socialism.* London, n.d. (Progressive League Series, No. 1.)

Campbell, W.H.P. *The Robbery of the Poor.* London, 1884.

Carter, John. *Preferential Dealing.* Oxford: CSU, 1900.

———. *Christian Socialism.* Oxford: CSU, 1905.

Carwithen, W. H. *Is Ritualism Popular Among the Masses?* London, 1894.

Child, Thomas. *The Glorification of the Lord's Humanity.* London, 1906.

———. *Root Principles in Rational and Spiritual Things.* London, 1906.

Christian Social Union. *Lombard Street in Lent.* London, 1894.

————. *Lent in London*. London, 1895.

Christian Socialist League. *Rules*. Glasgow, ca. 1900.

Christian Socialist Society. *Manifesto*. London, ca. 1886.

————. *Social Reformation on Christian Principles*. London, n.d. (Tract No. 1.)

Church Reform League. *Church Reform Handybook*. London, 1901.

Clarke, William. *A Collection of His Writings.*, ed. H. Burrows and J. A. Hobson. London, 1908.

Clifford, John. *The Inspiration and Authority of the Bible*. London, 1895.

————. *Jesus Christ and the State Churches*. London, 1897.

————. *Socialism and the Teaching of Christ*. London, 1897. (Fabian Tract No. 78.)

————. *Brotherhood and the War in South Africa*. London, 1900.

————. *The Housing of the Poor*. London, 1902.

————. *Socialism and the Churches*. London, 1908. (Fabian Tract No. 139.)

Congregational Yearbook. London: various years, as quoted.

Congreve, Rev. Father. *The Church and the Child Races*. London and Oxford, n.d. (Mirfield Manuals for the Million, No. 13.)

Connolly, J. *Labour, Nationality and Religion*. Dublin, 1910.

Conway, K. St. J. (Mrs. Bruce Glasier). *The Religion of Socialism*. Manchester, 1890.

Cunningham, W. *Socialism and Christianity*. London, 1909.

————. *Christianity and Economic Science*. London, 1914.

Davidson, Thomas. *The Education of the Wage-Earners*. New York, 1904.

Davis, J. *Labour Speaks for Itself on Religion*. New York, 1929.

Dearmer, Percy. *Socialism and Christianity*. London, 1907. (Fabian Tract No. 133.)

————. *Reform of the Poor Law*. London, 1908. (CSU No. 16.)

————. *The Church and Social Questions*. London, 1910.

465

Dearmer, Percy. *Sermons on Social Subjects*. London, 1911.

———. *The Beginnings of the CSU*. London, 1912.

———. *Christianity and the Crisis*. London, 1933.

Dell, R. E. *The Catholic Church and the Social Question*. London, 1899.

Dolling, R. *Ten Years in a Portsmouth Slum*. London, 1896.

Donaldson, F. L. *Socialism and the Christian Faith*. London and Oxford, n.d. (Mirfield Manuals for the Million, No. 12.)

Ede, W. M. *Socialism from the Christian Point of View: A Sermon*. Newcastle, 1887.

———. *The Attitude of the Church to Some of the Social Problems of Town Life*. Cambridge, 1896.

Ellis, Havelock. *Can the Capitalist System Be Managed?* London, 1896.

Fabian Essays. Edited by G. Bernard Shaw, with an American introduction by Edward Bellamy and an additional essay by William Clarke, "The Fabian Society and Its Work." Boston, 1894.

Figgis, J. M. *Political Thought from Gerson to Grotius, 1414-1625*. First edition, London, 1907; Harper Torchbook edition, New York, 1960.

———. *Religion and English Society*. London, 1910.

———. *The Fellowship of the Mystery*. London, 1912.

———. *Churches in the Modern State*. London, 1914.

Ford, L. P. *On the Reorganisation of the New-Church*. Shortlands, Kent, 1897.

Forsyth, P. T. *A Holy Church the Moral Guide to Society*. London, 1905.

———. *Socialism, the Church and the Poor*. London, 1908.

Foster, D. B. *Leeds Slumdom*. Leeds, 1897.

———. *The Logic of the Alliance; or The Labour Party Analysed and Justified*. Leeds, 1911.

———. *Socialism and the Christ: My Two Great Discoveries in a Long and Painful Search for Truth*. Leeds, 1921.

———. *The Kingdom of God: What It Is and How It Is Coming*. Leeds, 1935.

———. *Godly or Godless? Life's Supreme Question.* Leeds, 1939.

Fremantle, Canon W. H. *The World as the Subject of Redemption* (Bampton Lectures). Oxford, 1883; American edition [introduction by R. T. Ely], New York, 1892.

———. *The Present Work of the Anglican Communion.* London, 1888.

Frere, W. H. *God and Caesar: or the Laws of Church and State.* London and Oxford, n.d. (Mirfield Manuals for the Million.)

Fry, T. C. *A Social Policy for the Church.* London, 1893.

George, Henry. *Progress and Poverty.* First edition, New York, 1879; second edition, London, 1919.

———. *Social Problems.* London, 1884.

———. *The Condition of Labor: An Open Letter to Pope Leo XIII.* London, 1934. [First edition, 1891.]

Girdlestone, E. D. *Thirty-Nine Articles as the Profession of Christian Socialists.* Bristol, 1886.

———. *Christian Socialism versus Unsocialism.* Limavady, 1887.

Glasier, J. B. *Labour: Its Politics and Ideals.* London, 1903.

Gore, Charles, ed. *Lux Mundi.* First edition, London, 1889; second edition, London, 1890.

———. *The Incarnation of the Son of God* (Bampton Lecture). London, 1891.

———. *The Social Doctrine of the Sermon on the Mount.* London: CSU, 1893.

———. *Objections to the Education Bill, 1906, in Principle and in Detail.* London, 1906.

———. *Christianity and Socialism.* London and Oxford, n.d. [1908?]. (CSU, No. 24.)

———. *Christ and Society.* London, 1928.

Gosman, A. *Socialism, in the Light of Right Conduct and Religion.* Melbourne, 1891.

Gronlund, Laurence. *The Cooperative Commonwealth,* ed. Stow Persons. Cambridge, Mass., 1965. [First edition, 1884.]

Gronlund, Laurence. *Our Destiny: The Influence of Socialism on Morals and Religion*. London, 1890.

Grubb, Edward. *Social Aspects of the Quaker Faith*. London, 1899.

Hancock, Thomas. *The Peculium*. London, 1860.

——. *Christ and the People*. London, 1875.

——. *The Pulpit and the Press*. London, 1884.

Hardie, J. Keir. *Can a Man Be a Christian on a Pound a Week?* London [1905?].

——. *From Serfdom to Socialism*. London, 1907.

——, ed. *Labour and Religion*. London, 1910.

——. *My Confession of Faith in the Labour Alliance*. London, 1910.

——. *After 20 Years: All about the ILP*. London, 1913.

——. *Socialism and Christianity*. London: ILP, n.d.

——. *Speeches and Writings, 1888-1915*, ed. Emrys Hughes. Glasgow, n.d.

Harker, B. J. *Christianity and the New Social Demands*. Manchester, 1892.

Haw, C., ed. *The Religious Doubts of Democracy*. London, 1904.

——, ed. *Christianity and the Working Classes*. London, 1906.

Headlam, S. D. *Priestcraft and Progress*. London, 1882.

——. *The Laws of Eternal Life*. London, 1887.

——. *Christian Socialism*. London, 1892. (Fabian Tract No. 42.)

——. *Secular Schools: The Only Just and Permanent Solution*. London, 1906.

——. *The Secular Work of Jesus*. London: GSM, 1906.

——. *The Socialist Church*. London, 1907.

——. *Fabianism and Land Values*. London, 1908.

——. *The Meaning of the Mass*. London, 1908.

——. *Maurice and Kingsley*. London, 1909.

——. *Some Old Words About the War*. London, 1915.

Hill, T. *The Church, Capitalism, Labour and Land*. Louth, 1908.

Hird, Dennis. *Jesus, the Socialist.* London, 1896. (Clarion Pamphlet No. 46.)

Hobson, J. A. *The Problem of Poverty.* London, 1891.

——, ed. *Cooperative Labour Upon the Land.* London, 1895.

——. *The Problem of the Unemployed.* London, 1896.

——. *John Ruskin: Social Reformer.* London, 1898.

——. *The Economics of Distribution.* New York, 1900.

——. *The War in South Africa: Its Causes and Effects.* London, 1900.

——. *The Psychology of Jingoism.* London, 1901.

——. *Imperialism.* London, 1902.

——. *Confessions of an Economic Heretic.* London, 1938.

Hobson, J. A., with A. F. Mummery. *The Physiology of Industry.* London, 1889.

Hobson, S. G. *Public Control of Electric Power and Transit.* London, 1905. (Fabian Tract No. 119.)

——. *National Guilds: An Inquiry into the Wage System and the Way Out,* ed. A. R. Orage. London, 1917.

——. *National Guilds and the State.* London, 1920.

Hocking, W. J., ed. *The Church and New Century Problems.* London: CSU, 1901.

Holland, H. Scott. *The Labour Movement.* London, 1897.

——. *Our Neighbors.* London, 1911.

——. *A Bundle of Memories.* London, n.d.

Howard, Ebenezer. *Tomorrow: A Peaceful Plan to Real Reform.* London, 1891.

Hughes, H. P. *Social Christianity.* London, 1889.

Hunter, Robert. *Poverty.* First edition, New York, 1904; Harper Torchbook edition, ed. Peter d'A. Jones, New York, 1965.

Hyndman, H. M. *The Historical Basis of Socialism in England.* London, 1883.

——. *Record of an Adventurous Life.* London, 1911.

——. *Further Reminiscences.* London, 1912.

Independent Labour Party. *First General Conference Report, 1893.* Glasgow, 1893.

Independent Labour Party. *Second Annual Conference: Minutes, 1894.* Glasgow, 1894.

Ingram, E. M. *How to Recover the Lapsed Masses to the Church.* London, 1885.

Joynes, J. L. *The Right to the Use of the Earth.* London, n.d. [1880?]. (Land Reform Union Pamphlet No. 2.)

——. *Adventures of a Tourist in Ireland.* London, 1882.

——. *The Socialist Catechism.* London, 1884.

——. *Socialist Rhymes.* London, 1885.

Kaufmann, M. *Utopias: or Schemes of Social Improvement.* London, 1879.

——. *Socialism and Communism.* London, 1883.

——. *Christian Socialism.* London, 1888.

——. *Socialism and Modern Thought.* London, 1895.

——. *Social Development under Christian Influence.* Dublin, 1900.

Keeble, S. E. *Industrial Daydreams.* London, 1907. [First edition, 1889.]

——. *Citizens of Tomorrow.* London, 1906.

——. *Annotated Bibliography on Social Questions.* London, 1907.

——. *Christianity and Socialism.* London, 1907.

——. *Christianity and the Wages Question.* London, 1907.

——. *The Social Teaching of the Bible.* London, 1909.

——. *Towards a Legal Minimum Wage.* London, 1912.

——. *Towards a New Era.* London, 1912.

——. *The Ethics of Public Ownership.* London, 1920.

——. *Christian Responsibility for the Social Order.* London, 1922.

Kenyon, Ruth. *A History of Socialism.* London and Oxford, n.d. (Mirfield Manuals for the Million, No. 14.)

Kingsley, Charles. *Yeast.* Fourth edition, London, 1859. [First edition, 1851.]

——. *Life and Letters.* 2 vols. London, 1884.

——. *Works,* Vol. III: *Cheap Clothes and Nasty.* London, 1887.

————. *Works,* Vol. IV: *Yeast.* De Luxe edition, Philadelphia, 1899.

Kirtlan, E.J.B. *Socialism for Christians.* Northampton, 1907. (Pioneer Pamphlets No. 1.)

Labour Annual, 1895-1909, ed. Joseph Edwards. London.

Labour Church. *Form of Prayer, Confession and Supplication.* Manchester, 1891.

Labour Church Union. *Labour Church Hymn Book.* Bradford, 1906.

Land Nationalization Society: Report for 1881-83. London, 1883.

Leach, Charles. *How I Reached the Masses.* London, 1887.

Leatham, James. *Was Jesus a Socialist?* Aberdeen, 1891.

Lester-Garland, L. V. *Christianity and the War of 1914.* London, 1915. (CSU No. 44.)

Light and Shade: Pictures of London Life: A Sequel to "The Bitter Cry of Outcast London." London: Congregational Union, 1885.

Ludlow, J. M. "Some Words on the Ethics of Cooperative Production," *Atlantic Monthly,* LXXV (March 1895), 383-388.

————. "The Christian Socialist Movement of the Middle of the Century," *Atlantic Monthly,* LXXVII (January 1896), 109-118.

Lux Mundi. See Gore, Charles, ed.

M'Candlish, J. M. *A Study of Christian Socialism.* Edinburgh and London, 1898.

MacDonald, J. Ramsay. *The Socialist Movement.* London, 1911.

Manchester Conference of the Society of Friends, 1895. London, 1896.

Mann, Tom. *A Socialist's View of Religion and the Churches.* London, 1896. (Clarion Pamphlet No. 10.)

————. *From Single Tax to Syndicalism.* London, 1913.

Manning, Cardinal. *The Rights and Dignity of Labour.* London, 1887.

Marson, C. L. *God's Co-operative Society.* London, 1914.

Marx, K. and F. Engels. *Letters to Americans, 1848-1895: A Selection*. New York, 1953.

———. *On Religion*, ed. R. Niebuhr. New York, 1964. (An English edition was first published in Moscow in 1957.)

Methodist Annual Conference: Minutes. London, 1933; 1947; 1956; and others.

Mill, J. S. *Autobiography*. London, 1873; American Dolphin edition, New York, n.d. [1960?].

———. *Socialism*. Chicago, 1879.

Molesworth, Sir G. *The Sham of "Christian Socialism."* London, 1911.

———. *The Dangers of "Christian" Socialism*. London, 1913.

Muddock, J.E.P. *Socialism Antagonistic to Christianity*. London, 1909. (Anti-Socialist Union No. 32.)

Mudie-Smith, R., ed. *The Religious Life of London*. London, 1904. (*Daily News* Census.)

Noel, Conrad. *The Labour Party: What It Is and What It Wants*. London, 1906.

———. *Socialism in Church History*. London, 1910.

———. *An Autobiography*, ed. with foreword by Sidney Dark. London, 1945.

Orage, A. R. *An Alphabet of Economics*. London, 1917.

Orage, A. R. and C. H. Douglas. *Credit-Power and Democracy*. London, 1920.

Pan-Anglican Congress, 1908. *Pan-Anglican Papers*. London, 1908.

Parker, Katherine. *Socialism, an Essentially Christian Movement*. Cambridge, 1913.

Penty, A. J. *The Restoration of the Gild System*. London, 1906.

———. *Old Worlds for New*. London, 1919.

———. *Gilds and the Social Crisis*. London, 1920.

———. *A Gildsman's Interpretation of History*. London, 1920.

———. *Gilds, Trade and Agriculture*. London, 1921.

———. *Post-Industrialism*. London, 1922.

————. *Towards a Christian Sociology.* London, 1923.

Preston, W. C. *The Bitter Cry of Outcast London.* London, 1883.

Primitive Methodist Church: Annual Conference: Minutes. London, 1906.

Primitive Methodist Connexion: General Minutes. London, 1892.

Reason, Will. *Social Problems for Christian Citizens.* London, 1912.

Reckitt, M. B. *As It Happened: An Autobiography.* London, 1941.

Reckitt, M. B., and C. E. Bechhofer. *The Meaning of National Guilds.* London, 1918.

Rees, T. *The Church and Dissent.* London and Oxford, n.d. (Mirfield Manuals for the Million, No. 18.)

Reid, A., ed. *The New Party: Described by Some of Its Members.* London, 1894.

————. *Vox Clamantium: The Voice of the People.* London, 1894.

Richards, T. B. *Socialism and the Catholic Church.* Birmingham, 1901.

Richmond, W. *Christian Economics.* London, 1888.

————. *Economic Morals.* London, 1890.

Rickaby, J., S.J. *Socialism: A Reply to Laurence Gronlund.* London: Catholic Truth Society, 1886. [First edition, 1885.]

————. *Three Socialist Fallacies.* London, 1898.

————. *The Creed of Socialism.* London: Anti-Socialist Union, 1910.

Rogers, R. R. *The Story of My Life.* Leeds, 1921.

Rowntree, J. W. *Essays and Addresses.* London, 1905.

Russell, C.E.B. *Social Problems of the North.* London, 1913. (CSU Handbook.)

Sanday, W. *Some Weak Points in Christian Socialism.* London, 1912.

Shaw, G. Bernard. *Plays Pleasant.* First edition, 1898; Penguin edition, London, 1946.

Shaw, G. Bernard. *Intelligent Woman's Guide to Socialism.* London, 1928.

——. *Sixteen Self-Sketches.* London, 1949.

Shuttleworth, H. C. *The Christian Church and the Problem of Poverty.* London, 1894.

Snow, T. B. *Christian Aspects of the Labour Question.* London, 1894.

——. *The Church and Labour.* London, 1895.

Snowden, Philip. *The Christ That Is to Be.* Third edition, London, 1905. (ILP Pamphlet.)

——. *The Socialist's Budget.* London, 1907.

——. *A Few Hints to Lloyd George.* London, 1909.

——. *Autobiography.* 2 vols. London, 1934.

Social Democratic Federation. *John E. Williams and the Early History of the SDF.* London, 1886.

Socialist Almanac. New York, 1898.

Socialist Annual. London: SDF, 1906-1908, 1913.

Socialist Party of Great Britain. *Socialism and Religion.* London: Library No. 6, 1910.

Socialist Quaker Society. *Tracts.* 2 vols. London, 1898-1901.

——. "Minute Books." 2 vols., handwritten. 1898-1909, 1910-1913.

——. *A Letter from the S.Q.S. to Their Fellow-Members of the Society of Friends.* London, 1911.

A Socialist Ritual. London: SDF, 1893.

Soltau, G. W. *A Letter to the Working-Classes on Ritualism.* London, 1883.

[Southall, J. E.] *Testimony to the Life of J. E. Southall.* London, 1946.

Soutter, F. W. *Reflections of a Labour Pioneer.* London, 1923.

Stead, F. H. *The English Church of the Future.* London, 1892.

——. *How Old Age Pensions Began to Be.* London, n.d.

Stubbs, C. W. *Socialism and Social Reform.* Cambridge, 1881.

——. *Christ and Economics.* London, 1893.

——. *The Church in the Villages.* London: CSU, 1893.

———. *Christianity and Democracy.* London, 1894.

———. *A Creed for Christian Socialists.* London, 1897.

Tillett, Ben. *Brief History of the Dockers' Union.* London, 1910.

———. *Memories and Reflections.* London, 1931.

Toye, Charles. *The Blight of Socialism.* London, 1910.

Trevor, John. *An ILP.* Manchester, 1892.

———. *Man's Cry for God.* London, ca. 1895.

———. *My Quest for God.* London, 1897.

———. *Theology and the Slums.* London and Manchester, n.d. (*Labour Prophet* Tract No. 1.)

———. *From Ethics to Religion.* London, n.d. (*Labour Prophet* Tract No. 2.)

———. *The Labour Church in England.* London, n.d. (*Labour Prophet* Tract No. 4.)

———. *Our First Principle.* London, n.d.

Trobridge, George. *Swedenborg and Modern Thought.* London, 1899.

Tuckwell, W. *Christian Socialism.* Birmingham, 1889.

———. *Christian Socialism and Other Lectures.* London, 1891.

———. *Reminiscences of a Radical Parson.* London, n.d. [1903?].

Wallace, J. Bruce. *Towards Fraternal Organisation.* Fourth edition, London, 1895.

Ward, Mrs. Humphrey. *Robert Elsmere.* London, 1888.

Webster, A. *My Pilgrimage from Calvinism to Unitarianism.* Aberdeen, 1889.

———. *In Memoriam: Pioneer and Reformer.* Aberdeen, 1919.

Webb, Beatrice. *My Apprenticeship.* London, 1926.

———. *Our Partnership.* London, 1948.

Webb, Beatrice and Sidney. *The State and the Doctor.* London, 1910.

———. *The Consumer Cooperative Movement.* London, 1921.

Webb, Sidney. *Socialism in England.* London, 1890.

475

Webb, Sidney. *The Education Muddle and the Way Out.* London, 1901.

——. *Story of the Durham Miners.* London, 1921.

Wells, H. G., et al. *Socialism and the Great State.* New York, 1912.

——. *Experiment in Autobiography.* New York, 1934.

Wesleyan Methodist Church: Conference: Minutes, 1903. London, 1903.

Westcott, B. F. *Social Aspects of Christianity.* London, 1887.

——. *Socialism.* London, 1890.

——. *The CSU.* London, 1895.

Westminster and Longford Monthly Meeting, Society of Friends: Minutes, Vol. 27, No. 269 (1911).

Wicksteed, Charles, Jr. *Our Mother Earth.* London, 1891.

——. *The Land for the People.* Second edition, London, 1894.

Wicksteed, P. H. *Our Prayers and Politics.* London, 1885.

——. *Christianity and the Personal Life.* London, 1888.

——. *The Religion of Time and the Religion of Eternity.* London, 1899.

——. *The Kingdom of God.* Glasgow, n.d.

——. *What Does the Labour Church Stand for?* London, n.d. (*Labour Prophet* Tract, 2nd Ser., No. 1.)

Woodman, John. *A Word of Remembrance and Caution to the Rich.* London, 1897. (Fabian Tract No. 79.)

Younger, W. *The International Value of Christian Ethics.* London, 1924.

LATER WRITINGS AND SECONDARY WORKS

ARTICLES AND THESES

Aldcroft, D. H. "The Entrepreneur and the British Economy, 1870-1914," *Economic History Review,* 2nd Ser., XVII, No. 1 (August 1964), pp. 113-134.

Beales, H. L. "The Great Depression in Industry and Trade," *Economic History Review,* V, No. 1 (October 1934), pp. 65-75.

Coppock, D. J. "British Industrial Growth during the 'Great Depression' (1873-96) : A Pessimist's View," *Economic History Review*, 2nd Ser., xvii, No. 2 (December 1964), pp. 389-396.

Davies, Wallace E. "Religious Issues in Late-19th Century American Novels," *Bulletin of the John Rylands Library*, 41, No. 2 (March 1959), pp. 328-359.

Dudden, A. P. and T. H. Von Lave. "The R.S.D.L.P. and Joseph Fels: A Study in Intercultural Contact," *American Historical Review*, lxi, No. 1 (October 1955), pp. 21-47.

Duffy, A.E.P. "New Unionism in Britain, 1889-1890: A Reappraisal," *Economic History Review*, 2nd Ser., xiv, No. 2 (December 1961), pp. 306-319.

Fletcher, T. W. "The Great Depression of English Agriculture, 1873-96," *Economic History Review*, 2nd Ser., xiii, No. 3 (April 1961), pp. 417-432.

Inglis, K. S. "Patterns of Religious Worship in 1851," *Journal of Ecclesiastical History*, xi, No. 1 (April 1960), pp. 74-86.

Jones, Peter d'A. "Henry George and British Socialism, 1879-1931." Unpublished thesis, Manchester University, 1953.

————. "Christian Socialism in England, 1880-1914." Unpublished thesis, London University (London School of Economics and Political Science), 1963.

Mayor, S. H. "Some Congregational Relations with the Labour Movement," *Congregational Historical Society Transactions*, xviii (August 1956), 23-25.

Musson, A. E. "British Industrial Growth during the 'Great Depression' (1873-96) : Some Comments," *Economic History Review*, 2nd Ser., xv, No. 3 (April 1963), pp. 529-533.

————. "British Industrial Growth, 1873-96: A Balanced View," *Economic History Review*, 2nd Ser., xvii, No. 2 (December 1964), pp. 397-403.

Rowland, W. J. "Some Free Church Pioneers of Social Reform," *Congregational Quarterly*, xxxv, No. 2 (April 1957).

Saville, John, ed. "Studies in the British Economy, 1870-1914," Special Number, *Yorkshire Bulletin of Economic and Social Research*, 17, No. 1 (May 1965).

Scott, R. C. "Authority or Experience: J. W. Rowntree and the Dilemma of 19th Century British Quakerism," *Journal of Friends' Historical Society*, 49, No. 2 (Spring 1960).

Summers, D. F. "The Labour Church." Unpublished thesis, Edinburgh University, 1958.

Wilson, Charles. "Economy and Society in Late-Victorian Britain," *Economic History Review*, 2nd Ser., XVIII, No. 1 (August 1965), pp. 183-198.

BOOKS

Abell, A. I. *The Urban Impact on American Protestantism, 1865-1900*. Cambridge, Mass., 1943.

Allchin, A. M. *The Silent Rebellion: Anglican Religious Communities, 1845-1900*. London, 1958.

Argyle, Michael. *Religious Behaviour*. London, 1958.

Armitage, E. N. *The Quaker Poets of Great Britain and Ireland*. London, 1896.

Armytage, W.H.G. *Heavens Below: Utopian Experiments in England, 1560-1960*. London, 1961.

Ashley, A. *W. J. Ashley*. London, 1932.

Ashworth, W. *An Economic History of England, 1870-1939*. London, 1960.

Ausubel, Herman. *The Late Victorians*. New York, 1955.

———. *In Hard Times*. New York, 1960.

Ausubel, H., J. B. Brebner, and E. M. Hunt. *Some Modern Historians of Britain*. New York, 1951.

Barker, Sir E. *Political Thought in England, 1848-1914*. London, 1947.

Barnett, Mrs. H. O. *Life of Samuel Barnett*. 2 vols. London, 1914.

Bateman, C. T. *R. J. Campbell*. London, 1903.

———. *John Clifford*. London, 1904.

Bealey, F. and H. M. Pelling. *Labour and Politics, 1900-1906: A History of the Labour Representation Committee*. London, 1958.

Beck, G. A., ed. *The English Catholics, 1850-1950*. London, 1950.

Beer, Max. *History of British Socialism*. 2 vols. London, 1929.

Bell, H. E. *Maitland: A Critical Examination and Assessment*. London, 1965.

Bestor, Arthur E. *Backwoods Utopias*. Philadelphia, 1950.

Bettany, F. G. *Stewart Headlam: A Biography*. London, 1926.

Binyon, G. C. *The Christian Socialist Movement in England*. London, 1931.

Bosanquet, Helen. *Social Work in London, 1869-1912: A History of the Charity Organisation Society*. London, 1914.

Boutard, C. *Lamennais: sa vie et ses doctrines*. 3 vols. Paris, 1913.

Briggs, Asa. *Seebohm Rowntree, 1871-1954*. London, 1961.

Briggs, Asa, and J. Saville, eds. *Essays in Labour History*. London, 1960.

Broadhurst, H. *Story of His Life*. London, 1901.

Brockway, Fenner. *Inside the Left*. London, 1942.

―――. *Socialism over Sixty Years*. London, 1946.

Burnett, R. G. *These My Brethren: The Story of the London East End Mission*. London, 1946.

Burt, T. *Pitman and Privy Councillor*. London, 1924.

Carpenter, Niles. *Guild Socialism*. New York, 1922.

Carpenter, S. C. *Church and People, 1789-1889*. 3 vols. London, 1959. [First edition, 1933.]

Casson, E. R. *Postscript: H. N. Casson*. London, 1952.

Chorley, E. C. *Men and Movements in the American Episcopal Church*. New York, 1948.

Christensen, T. *Origins and History of Christian Socialism, 1848-54*. Aarhus, 1962.

Clark, G. Kitson. *The Making of Victorian England*. London, 1962.

Clayton, J. *The Rise and Decline of Socialism in Great Britain, 1884-1924*. London, 1926.

479

Clegg, H. A., A. Fox, and A. F. Thompson. *History of British Trade Unions since 1889*, Vol. 1: *1889-1910*. London, 1964.

Cole, G.D.H. *The World of Labour*. London, 1913.

———. *Guild Socialism Restated*. London, 1920.

———. *British Working-Class Politics, 1832-1914*. London, 1941.

———. *History of Socialist Thought*, Vols. I, II, and III (Part I). London, 1954-1960.

Cole, Margaret. *Growing up into Revolution*. London, 1949.

Community of the Resurrection. CR, *Mirfield*. Mirfield, 1963.

Court, W.H.B. *Concise Economic History of England, from 1750 to Recent Times*. Cambridge, England, 1964. [First edition, 1954.]

Craig, Robert. *Social Concern in the Thought of William Temple*. London, 1963.

Cripps, Stafford. *Towards Christian Democracy*. London, 1945.

Crockford's Clerical Directory. London, 1886, et seq.

Crosse, G. *Charles Gore*. London and Oxford, 1932.

Cruickshank, Marjorie. *Church and State in English Education, 1870 to the Present Day*. London, 1963.

Cuvillier, Armand. *P.-J.-B. Buchez et les Origines du Socialisme Chrétien*. Paris, 1948.

Dangerfield, George. *The Strange Death of Liberal England*. New York, 1935.

[Davidson, Thomas] *Memorials of Thomas Davidson,* ed. W. A. Knight. London, 1907.

Davies, Horton. *Worship and Theology in England*, Vols. III, IV, and V. Princeton, 1961-1965.

Dearmer, Nan. *Life of Percy Dearmer*. London, 1940.

Demant, V. A. *Religion and the Decline of Capitalism*. London, 1952.

De Vries, Peter. *The Mackerel Plaza*. New York, 1958; London, 1963.

Dolléans, E. *Le Caractère Religieux de Socialisme*. Paris, 1906.

Dolléans, E., and M. Crozier. *Mouvements: Ouvrier et Socialiste: Chronologie et Bibliographie, 1750-1918*. Paris, 1950.

Dombrowski, James. *The Early Days of Christian Socialism in America*. New York, 1936.

Dorfman, J. *The Economic Mind in American Civilization*, Vol. III. New York, 1949.

Dorré, Jean-René. *Lamennais: ses amis et le mouvement des idées à l'époque Romantique, 1824-34*. Paris, 1962.

Dudley, J. *Edward Grubb*. London, 1946.

Durkheim, E. *Elementary Forms of the Religious Life*. London, 1912.

Duroselle, J.-B. *Les Débuts du Catholicisme Social en France, 1822-1870*. Paris, 1951.

Edwards, Maldwyn. *Methodism and England, 1850-1932*. London, 1943.

———. *S. E. Keeble*. London, 1949.

Egbert, D. D. and S. Persons. *Socialism and American Life*. 2 vols. Princeton, 1952.

Eliot, T. S. *The Idea of a Christian Society*. London, 1939.

Elliott-Binns, C. E. *Religion in the Victorian Era*. London, 1946. [First edition, 1936.]

Ensor, R.C.K. *England, 1870-1914*. First edition, London, 1936; second edition, London, 1949.

Faber, G. *Oxford Apostles*. London, 1936.

Fogarty, M. P. *Christian Democracy in Western Europe, 1820-1953*. Notre Dame, Indiana, 1957.

Foxwell, H. S. *Archdeacon Cunningham*. London, 1919.

Fremantle, Anne. *This Little Band of Prophets: The British Fabians*. London, 1959.

———. *The Papal Encyclicals*. New York, 1956.

Garvin, J. L. *Life of Joseph Chamberlain*. 3 vols. London, 1931-1934. [A fourth volume, by L. S. Amery, was published in London, 1951.]

George, Henry, Jr. *Life of Henry George*. New York, 1900.

Glasier, J. Bruce. *Keir Hardie: The Man and His Message*. London: ILP, 1919.

481

Gloyn, C. K. *The Church in the Social Order*. Forest Grove, Oregon, 1942.

Grant, J. W. *Free Churchmanship in England, 1870-1940*. London, n.d.

Gray, Sir Alexander. *The Socialist Tradition: Moses to Lenin*. London, 1946.

Griffith, G. O. *The Theology of P. T. Forsyth*. London, 1948.

Gulley, E. E. *Joseph Chamberlain and English Social Politics*. New York, 1926.

Guttsman, W. L. *The British Political Elite*. London, 1963.

Halévy, E. *Histoire du Socialisme Européen*. Paris, 1948.

Hall, C. A. *True Christian Doctrine Given to the World through E. Swedenborg*. London, n.d.

Hamilton, M. A. *Arthur Henderson*. London, 1938.

Hearnshaw, F.J.C. *A Survey of Socialism*. London, 1928.

Herford, C. H. *P. H. Wicksteed*. London, 1931.

Hobsbawm, E. J. *Primitive Rebels*. New York, 1965. [First edition, 1959.]

Hobson, S. G. *Pilgrim to the Left*. London, 1938.

Hofstadter, R. *The Age of Reform*. New York, 1955.

Holt, R. V. *The Unitarian Contribution to Social Progress in England*. London, 1938.

Hopkins, C. H. *Rise of the Social Gospel in American Protestantism, 1865-1915*. New Haven, 1940.

Hsiao, Kung Chuan. *Political Pluralism*. London, 1927.

Hughes, D. P. *Life of H. P. Hughes*. London, 1907.

Hunter, Robert. *Socialists at Work*. New York, 1908.

Hutchison, T. W. *Review of Economic Doctrines, 1870-1929*. London, 1953.

Illingworth, Mrs. J. R. *Life and Work of J. R. Illingworth*. London, 1917.

Inglis, K. S. *Churches and the Working-Classes in Victorian England*. London, 1963.

Iremonger, F. A. *William Temple*. London, 1948.

Isambert, F.-A. *Christianisme et Classe Ouvrière*. Paris, 1961.

James, W. *The Christian in Politics*. London, 1962.

Johnson, L. G. *Social Evolution of Industrial Britain.* Liverpool, 1959.

Jones, Peter d'A. *The Consumer Society: A History of American Capitalism.* London, 1965.

——. (ed.) *Robert Hunter's "Poverty": Social Conscience in the Progressive Era.* New York, 1965.

Jones, R. M. *The Later Period of Quakerism.* 2 vols. London, 1921.

Jones, R. T. *Congregationalism in England, 1662-1962.* London, 1962.

Jordan, E.K.H. *Free Church Unity: A History of the Free Church Council Movement, 1896-1941.* London, 1941.

Lansbury, George. *My Life.* London, 1928.

Lawson, Jack. *A Man's Life.* New edition, London, 1949.

Lawrence, E. P. *Henry George in the British Isles.* East Lansing, Michigan, 1957.

Lenski, G. *The Religious Factor.* Garden City, New York, 1961.

LeRoy, Maxime, ed. *Les Précurseurs Français du Socialisme.* Paris, 1948.

Leslie, S. *Cardinal Manning.* Dublin, 1953.

Lewis, J., K. Polanyi, and D. K. Kitchin, eds. *Christianity and the Social Revolution.* London, 1935.

Loubere, L. A. *Louis Blanc.* Chicago, 1961.

Lowndes, G.A.M. *The Silent Social Revolution: Public Education in England and Wales, 1895-1935.* London, 1937.

Lubac, Henri de. *The UnMarxian Socialist: A Study of Proudhon.* London, 1948.

Lynd, H. M. *England in the 1880's.* London, 1945.

McBriar, A. M. *Fabian Socialism and English Politics, 1884-1918.* London, 1962.

McEntee, G. P. *Social Catholic Movement in Great Britain.* New York, 1927.

Mackenzie, Sir Compton. *Certain Aspects of Moral Courage.* New York, 1962.

McLachlan, G. *The Methodist Unitarian Movement.* Manchester, 1919.

483

Mann, Arthur. *Yankee Reformers in the Urban Age.* Cambridge, Mass., 1954; paperback edition, New York, 1966.

Mann, Tom. *Memoirs.* London, 1923.

Marchant, Sir J. *Dr. John Clifford.* London, 1924.

Martin, A. C. *The Concentration Camps, 1900-1902.* Cape Town, 1957.

Martin, H., ed. *Christian Social Reformers of the 19th Century.* London, 1927.

Masterman, N. C. J. M. *Ludlow: Builder of Christian Socialism.* Cambridge, England, 1963.

Mathew, D. *Catholicism in England.* London, 1954.

Maurice, F., ed. *Life of Frederick Denison Maurice, Chiefly Told in His Own Letters.* 2 vols. London, 1884.

May, H. F. *Protestant Churches and Industrial America.* New York, 1949.

Métin, A. *Le Socialisme en Angleterre.* Paris, 1897.

Miliband, R. *Parliamentary Socialism.* London, 1961.

Mitchell, B. R., with Phyllis Deane. *Abstract of British Historical Statistics.* Cambridge, England, 1962.

Montague, F. C. *Arnold Toynbee.* Baltimore, 1889.

Moody, J. N., et al. *Church and Society: Catholic Social and Political Thought and Movements 1789-1950.* New York, 1953.

Morris, May. *William Morris: Artist, Writer, Socialist.* 2 vols. Oxford, 1936.

Neill, S. *Anglicanism.* London, 1958.

Nethercot, A. H. *The First Five Lives of Annie Besant.* Chicago, 1960.

Nevinson, H. M. *Changes and Chances.* New York, 1923.

New-Church, London. *Yearbook, General Conference.* London, 1957-1958.

————. *The New-Church in Britain.* London, n.d. [ca. 1963].

————. *100 Points of New-Church Doctrine.* London, n.d. [ca. 1963].

Niebuhr, H. Richard. *The Social Sources of Denominationalism.* New York, 1957. [First edition, 1929.]

Paget, S. H. S. Holland: Memoirs and Letters. London, 1921.

Patterson, W. M. Northern Primitive Methodism. London, 1909.

Payne, E. A. The Baptist Union: A Short History. London, 1959.

Pease, E. R. History of the Fabian Society. London, 1916.

Peck, W. G. Social Implications of the Oxford Movement. London, 1933.

Peel, A. The Congregational Two Hundred. London, 1948.

──────. These Hundred Years, 1831-1931. London, 1931.

Pelling, H. M. The Challenge of Socialism. London, 1954.

──────. Origins of the Labour Party, 1880-1900. London, 1954.

──────. America and the British Left. New York, 1957.

──────. History of British Trade Unionism. London, 1963.

Perris, H. S. Little Portland Street Chapel, London. London, 1900.

Petri, Barbara P. The Historical Thought of P.-J.-B. Buchez. Washington, D.C., 1958.

Pope, Liston. Millhands and Preachers. New Haven, 1942.

Prestige, G. L. Life of Charles Gore. London, 1935.

Quint, Howard. The Forging of American Socialism. Charleston, S.C., 1953; paperback edition, New York, 1964.

Ramsey, A. M. F. D. Maurice and the Conflict of Modern Theology. London, 1951.

Rauschenbusch, Walter. Christianity and the Social Crisis. First edition, New York, 1907; Harper Torchbook edition, ed. Robert D. Cross, New York, 1964.

Raven, C. E. Christian Socialism, 1848-54. London, 1920.

Read, Donald. The English Provinces, 1760-1960. New York, 1964.

Reckitt, Maurice B. Faith and Society. London, 1932.

──────. Maurice to Temple. London, 1947.

──────. P.E.T. Widdrington. London, 1961.

Richter, Melvin. The Politics of Conscience: T. H. Green and His Age. Cambridge, Mass., 1964.

Russell, Bertrand. *Portraits from Memory*. London, 1956.

Russell, G.W.E. *H. C. Shuttleworth: A Memoir*. London, 1903.

———. *Arthur Stanton: A Memoir*. London, 1917.

Sacks, B. *The Religious Issue in the State Schools of England and Wales, 1902-14*. Albuquerque, N.M., 1961.

Saint-Simon. *Selected Political Writings*, ed. F.M.H. Markham. Oxford, 1952.

Selbie, W. B. *Life of C. S. Horne*. London, 1920.

Semmel, B. *Imperialism and Social Reform*. Cambridge, Mass., 1960.

Simon, Brian. *Education and the Labour Movement, 1870-1918*. London, 1965.

Smith, J. W. and A. L. Jamison, eds. *Religion in American Life*. 4 vols. Princeton, 1961.

Snowden, Philip. *Autobiography*. 2 vols. London, 1934.

Speek, P. A. *The Single Tax and the Labour Movement*. Madison, Wisconsin, 1917.

Spencer, P. H. *Politics and Belief in 19th Century France*. London, 1954.

Stewart, H. L. *A Century of Anglo-Catholicism*. New York, 1929.

Stewart, W. *J. Keir Hardie*. London: ILP, 1921.

Sykes, J. *The Quakers*. London, 1958.

Tawney, R. H. *The Agrarian Problem in the 16th Century*. London, 1912.

———. *The Acquisitive Society*. London, 1921.

———. *The British Labour Movement*. New Haven, 1925.

———. *Religion and the Rise of Capitalism*. First edition, 1926; Penguin edition, London, 1938.

———. *Equality*. London, 1931.

———. *The Attack and Other Papers*. London, 1953.

———. *The Radical Tradition*. London, 1964.

Temple, William. *Christianity and the Social Order*. London, 1942.

———. *The Hope of a New World*. New York, 1943.

———. *Social Witness and Evangelism*. London, 1943.

Thompson, R. B. *Peter Thompson*. London, 1910.

Tiltman, H. H. *J. R. MacDonald*. London, 1929.

Toch, Hans. *Social Psychology of Social Movements*. Indianapolis, 1965.

Torbet, R. G. *History of the Baptists*. Philadelphia, 1950.

Tracey, H., ed. *The Book of the Labour Party*. London, 1925.

Traill, H. D. and J. S. Mann, eds. *Social England*. New York, 1909.

Troeltsch, E. *Social Teaching of the Christian Churches*. 2 vols. New York, 1960. [First edition, 1911.]

Tsuzuki, C. *H. M. Hyndman and British Socialism*. Oxford, 1961.

Tucker, M. G. *J. N. Figgis: A Study*. London, 1950.

Ulam, A. B. *Philosophical Foundations of English Socialism*. Cambridge, Mass., 1951.

Underwood, A. C. *History of the English Baptists*. London, 1947.

Verhaegen, P. *Socialistes Anglais*. Gand, 1898.

Vidler, A. R. *Prophecy and Papacy: A Study of Lamennais, the Church and the Revolution*. London, 1954.

Villiers, B. *The Socialist Movement in England*. London, 1908.

Vipont, E. *The Story of Quakerism, 1652-1952*. London, 1954.

Wagner, D. O. *The Church of England and Social Reform since 1850*. New York, 1930.

Walker, Eric A. *Cambridge History of the British Empire*, Vol. VIII: *South Africa*. Cambridge, England, 1963.

Ward, C. K. *Priest and People: A Study in the Sociology of Religion*. Liverpool, 1961.

Ward, Maisie. *G. K. Chesterton*. New York, 1943.

Wearmouth, R. F. *Methodism and the Working Class Movements of England, 1800-1850*. London, 1937.

———. *Some Working Class Movements of the 19th Century*. London, 1948.

———. *Methodism and the Struggle of the Working Classes, 1850-1900*. Leicester, 1954.

4 8 7

Wearmouth, R. F. *Social and Political Influence of Methodism in the 20th Century.* London, 1957.

———. *Methodism and the Trade Unions.* London, 1959.

Weber, Max. *The Sociology of Religion.* Boston, Mass., 1964. [First edition, 1922.]

Westcott, A. *Life and Letters of B. F. Westcott.* 2 vols. London, 1903.

Whiteley, W. *J. B. Glasier—A Memorial.* London, 1920.

Whiteley, W. T. *History of the British Baptists.* London, 1932.

Wickham, E. R. *Church and People in an Industrial City.* London, 1957.

Williams, Francis. *Fifty Years' March.* London, 1949.

Williams, N. P. and C. Harris. *Northern Catholicism.* London, 1933.

Wilson, J. *Memoirs of a Labour Leader.* London, 1910.

Wood, H. G. *F. D. Maurice.* Cambridge, England, 1950.

Woodward, E. L. *Three Studies in European Conservatism.* London, 1962. [First edition, 1929.]

Woodworth, A. V. *Christian Socialism in England.* London, 1903.

Yinger, J. M. *Religion, Society and the Individual.* New York, 1957.

Young, A. F., and E. T. Ashton. *British Social Work in the Nineteenth Century.* London, 1956.

INDEX